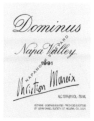

# EXPLORING
## *Wine*

# EXPLORING *Wine*

## The Culinary Institute of America's Complete Guide to Wines of the World

Steven Kolpan

Brian H. Smith

Michael A. Weiss

## JOHN WILEY & SONS, INC.

New York   Chichester   Weinheim   Brisbane   Singapore   Toronto

*Maps and Charts:* TCA Graphics, Inc., Tom Cardamone, Ann Cardamone

**The Culinary Institute of America Staff:**

*Project Director:* Tim Ryan

*Studio Photographer:* Lorna Smith

This text is printed on acid-free paper. ⊖

3   4   5   6   7   8   9   10   01   00   99   98

**Library of Congress Cataloging-in-Publication Data**

Exploring wine : the Culinary Institute of America's complete guide to wines of the world.
    p.   cm.
    Includes bibliographical references and index.
    ISBN 0-471-28626-5 (hardcover)
    1. Wine and wine making.   I. Culinary Institute of America.
TP548.E96      1996
641.2'2—dc20                                                    95-35579
                                                                      CIP

Printed in the United States of America

*Dedicated to our Families, Loved Ones,*
*Colleagues, and Students*

# Contents

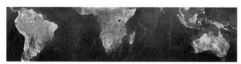

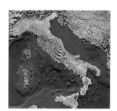

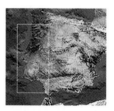

# Foreword

$\mathscr{I}$ am happy to be able to write this foreword to *Exploring Wine,* a comprehensive text about my favorite subject. Steven Kolpan, Brian Smith, and Michael Weiss have written a work that includes an extensive survey of the wines of the Old and New Worlds; I would expect nothing less from three distinguished wine educators. However, the authors have gone much deeper into the subject of wine, creating a valuable reference that is unlike any other.

*Exploring Wine* is not an encyclopedia, but it is encyclopedic in its depth and breadth. The book is not a dictionary, but its glossary of wine terms will serve that purpose well. It is not a wine atlas, but its full-color maps are easy to read and up-to-date. *Exploring Wine* is the definitive wine textbook, yet it will bring hours of pleasure to the novice reader.

*Exploring Wine* delves into the history, theory, and practice of viticulture—the growing of grapes—and viniculture—the making of wine. Wine tasting is presented in a way that makes the experience educational, but without pretense or dogma. The book takes a common-sense approach to the difficult subject of food and wine pairing, yet manages to break some new ground in the explanation of taste. I am particularly pleased that an entire chapter of *Exploring Wine* is dedicated to a discussion of wine and health, including the latest thinking of the scientific and medical communities.

Perhaps what sets this book apart is that it not only presents wine as a practical and intellectual subject, but also examines the issues of wine as a vital profession. Chapters on wine lists, purchasing and storage, and wine service go a long way to addressing the needs and questions of service professionals and wine customers alike. There is no other book that simultaneously serves both the public and the profession—*Exploring Wine* makes that leap with grace and style.

As wine instructors at The Culinary Institute of America, where they teach in the state-of-the-art Wine Spectator Classroom, authors Kolpan, Smith, and Weiss have had the opportunity to impart a thorough appreciation of wines to more than 12,000 students. *Exploring Wine* is the distillation of that collective teaching experience placed between the covers of one book; but it is more than that.

Many of the photographs in *Exploring Wine* were taken by the authors on their trips to the classic wine-growing regions of the world. The sidebar features on wine makers from around  the world contained in the book come from first-hand knowledge and respect for the traditions and innovations put in place by contemporary wine makers. Kolpan, Smith, and Weiss write in a friendly but authoritative style, because they know and love the places and the faces that make up the wine world. These authors want to pass along their excitement and enthusiasm not only for the subject of wine, but for the people who inhabit its global village.

Join me as I raise my glass to toast the arrival of *Exploring Wine,* an essential and significant addition to wine literature. I welcome it and recommend it to you.

Marvin R. Shanken
*Editor and Publisher*
*Wine Spectator*

# Foreword

The Culinary Institute of America has been America's center for culinary education since 1946, and is the only college totally dedicated to the culinary, baking, and pastry arts. Now in its fiftieth year, the Institute has become more than the preeminent school for motivated students to learn the basics of good cooking. We teach history and culture, health and nutrition, sanitation, basic skills, product identification, ethnic and regional cuisines, restaurant service and management, facilities and menu design, and of course, the appreciation of wines as part of a fine meal.

The wine program at the Institute is an integral part of our Associate's degree curriculum. Students must successfully complete a rigorous six-week course in the wines of the world as a requirement for graduation from the Institute.

Likewise, the serious study of wine is a cornerstone of our new Bachelor's degree program. Its curriculum includes the intellectual, historical, cultural, agricultural, and financial issues surrounding the wide-ranging subject. In fact, all of our Bachelor's degree students are required to take a six-week wine and food seminar in which four of those weeks are spent at Greystone, our new West Coast campus in the Napa Valley. During the four weeks, students explore the North Coast wine country—experiencing the agriculture and viticulture of the area.

The development of our basic wines course, where our students learn about wines on a theoretical and practical level, as well as the food and wine seminar that is built into the Bachelor's degree program, ensure that wine maintains its meaningful place in a complete culinary education.

Steven Kolpan, Brian Smith, and Michael Weiss, wine educators and faculty members at The Culinary Institute of America, have played pivotal roles in the development of the Institute's multi-level wine programs. They have helped to engender a serious and abiding interest in wine in more than 30,000 graduates, some of whom pursue professional careers in the wine industry and wine service. Two years ago, they began a project to codify what they teach and to expand the professional discourse. The outcome of that project is this book, *Exploring Wine*.

I am pleased to see such a comprehensive text of the most current information on wines of the Old and New worlds, with up-to-date maps and photographs. In addition, I am happy to note that the authors have included discussions on the basics of grape varieties, wine making, wine tasting, and wine lists. They have also focused their energies on demystifying food and wine pairings, as well as addressing the increasingly important topic of wine and health.

*Exploring Wine* is a unique volume—a book that can be used, not only as an introduction to wine for the novice, but also as a reference for the serious student or wine professional.

The Culinary Institute of America is proud to have provided the academic setting for the authors to nurture their ideas. We have encouraged their travels to the classic wine regions of the world and welcomed wine makers from all over the world who have visited our Hyde Park campus (and now, Greystone) to share their knowledge with our students, faculty, and staff.

Ferdinand E. Metz
*President*
*The Culinary Institute of America*

# Acknowledgments

## FROM STEVEN KOLPAN

I would like to thank, first and foremost, my colleagues and co-authors, Brian Smith and Michael Weiss, for their energies, abilities, and knowledge, and to Melissa Rosati, Jackie Martin, Louise Kurtz, and Mike Suh of Van Nostrand Reinhold for their unstinting work and devotion to this project.

For providing the stimulating academic environment in which to write, thanks to Ferdinand Metz, President of The Culinary Institute of America, and to Tim Ryan, Senior Vice-President of Education, who encouraged the authors to write this book in the first place.

Colleagues at The Culinary Institute of America who have helped me and supported this work include Henry Woods, Charles Rascoll, Gary Allen, Markus Färbinger, Roger Riccardi, Greg Drescher, Jonathan Zearfoss, Len and Karen Allison, Eve Felder, Joseba Encabo, Reuben Katz, Ramiro Santos, Catherine Brandel, Bill Reynolds, Ezra Eichelberger, Kim Jordan, and Fred Mayo.

For exposing me to the world of wine I must thank John Novi, Kevin Zraly, Lidia Bastianich, Aldo Vacca, Angelo Gaja, Bruno Ceretto, Raffaella Bologna, Massimo Martinelli, Philip di Belardino, Roberto Stucchi-Prinetti, Katrin Naelapaa, Ana Fabiano, Anita Mizner, Robin Kelley O'Connor, Pat Iocca, João Portugal-Ramos, Loch Jones, Peter Lehmann, Brian Croser, Rocky O'Callaghan, Jane Mitchell, Peter Sichel, Helmut Jung, and Cindy Krebs. Also, the Italian Trade Commission, Wines from Spain, the Portuguese Trade Commission, Food and Wines from France, the Bordeaux Wine Bureau, the German Wine Information Bureau, the Swiss Trade Commission, the South Australian Tourist Board, and Oldways Preservation & Exchange Trust.

Finally, I want to thank for his friendship, encouragement, and welcome counsel, Bob Schuler; for their love and patience, my family; and, of course, thanks for anything and everything to Suzanne Hamlin, my life partner.

## FROM BRIAN H. SMITH

Firstly, my thanks go to my colleagues and co-authors, Steven Kolpan and Michael Weiss, for their strength and perseverance in seeing this project through, and for encouraging me along the way. Similarly, I offer my thanks and appreciation to Ferdinand Metz and Tim Ryan of The Culinary Institute of America for providing the opportunity to produce this work.

Those who have given me direct and invaluable assistance with information for the text include Michael Jones of Domaine Chandon, Bob Betz of Stimson Lane, Larry Fuller-Perrine of Gristina Cellars, Cindy Krebs of the German Wine Information Bureau, Mary Crane of the White House, Eliza Uchida of The Culinary Institute of America at Greystone, Amy Albert of Food and Wines from France, Katie Yeo of the Napa Valley Vintners Association, Jane Davies of the British Columbia Wine Institute, Wendell Lee of the Wine Institute, Bryan del Bondio of Markham Vineyards, Ed Weber of the University of California Extension Office Napa County, Dave Whitmer of the Napa County Agricultural Commission, and Niki Singer of Marvin Shanken Communications Inc.

As always, my love and appreciation go to Andrea, Lauren, and Drew for their support and understanding.

## FROM MICHAEL A. WEISS

I thank first and most of all my parents Sabina and Jack (Csoki) who exposed me to the importance of good food, wine, and conversation and my brother Richard Weiss for his wit.

I wish to thank President Ferdinand Metz and Senior Vice-President Tim Ryan who gave me the opportunity to work on this book. I thank my co-authors Steven Kolpan and Brian Smith, for the sharing of facts, opinions, and humor when needed.

I would like to thank the faculty and staff of The Culinary Institute of America, whose influence and support have allowed me to develop and explore my knowledge and feelings about wine and food. Thanks to my personal friends and to those in the trade with whom I look forward to breaking bread again: Coussaie Agha, Suzanne and Dan Anber, Amelia Barad, Jessica Bard, Bob Bath, Eric Gordon Bell, Franco Biondi-Santi, Christian Bizot, Sandro Boscaini, Susi and Kenny Brault, Kim and Bob Brewster, Michael Broadbent M.W., Jack Cakebread, Rory Callahan, John Campbell, Archie Casbarian, Juan Cusine, Roger Dagorn, Steven Diab, Lou Fiore, Carol and Steve Ford, Josh Greene, Paola Gloder, Chef Todd Humphries, Julie Hill, Pasquale Iocca, Gérard Jaboulet, Reuben Katz, Barbara Kelly, Chef Gray Kunz, Harriet Lembeck, Robert Lipinski, Carol Lyman, Professor Guy Millisor, Anita Mizner, Sharron McCarthy, Lesley and Roger Myers, Siobhan and Sean Murphy, Barry Ogden, Steve Olsen, Paul Nichols, Nina and Earl Raven, Roger Riccardi, Sally and John Smuglovsky, Audrey, Joy, Lawrence, and Barry Sterling, Emmanuela and Roberto Stucchi-Prinetti, Chef Karl Ronaszeki, Peter Sichel, Jonathan Smiga, Lucio Sorré, Forrest Tancer, Barbara and Art Watson, Lisa Weiss, Helen Wong, and Chefs Pam and Jonathan Zearfoss.

I also wish to thank the following organizations: Portuguese Trade Commission, Italian Trade Commission, Wines of Spain, Foods and Wines of France, Bordeaux Wine Bureau, Champagne Information Bureau, Swiss Wine Information Bureau, German Wine Information Bureau, Fundacion de Chile, Seagram's Chateau and Estates Wine Co., Dreyfus Ashby, Kobrand, and F. Wildman.

And in memory of Chef Oszyasz (Oscar) Zimet, my grandfather, whose strength, love, and chicken soup inspired me to pursue a career in food and wine.

# EXPLORING
## Wine

# Fundamentals: Wine Making and Wine Tasting

Wine is ancient, and yet the beverage we enjoy today is thoroughly modern. For eight thousand years, through the great civilizations of Mesopotamia, Greece, and Egypt, to the Roman Empire and on into medieval Europe and the boundless opportunities of the New World, wine has been enjoyed by millions. Despite this ancient history, the student of wine today is likely to see more changes and more developments in viticulture and vinification than at any other time in wine's existence. As in many other areas of activity, technology has allowed grape growers and wine makers to know the unknown, to control the uncontrollable, and even to improve the greatest and the least of all wines.

The first part of this book is dedicated to exploring what wine is and how grapes become wine, starting with the simplest definitions, and expanding into seemingly innumerable alternatives. The notion that wine comes from grapes is at once exact and misleading, since there are thousands of different grape varieties with countless variations in chemical and flavor composition. Chapters 1 and 2 investigate the basics of wine making and list and describe the major grape varieties used by today's wine makers. Chapter 3 explores what it means to taste wine and lays the foundations for developing your own method of tasting wines for years to come.

The modern, technological era of wine is very recent, no more than a miniblip in the life pulse of wine's history. For thousands of years, farmers and merchants have relied on the favor and the mercy of the gods to bless them with a pleasing wine. And sometimes they got what they prayed for, without ever knowing why. All they saw were healthy, vigorous vine plants, laden with heavy, sweet succulent bunches of grapes, languishing in the warm sun, full of ripe, juicy flavors. And when the grapes were heaped into a large vat, the juices would run and the liquid would churn about as heady fumes and aromas escaped into the air, leaving behind the richly colored, strongly scented and flavored liquid, probably sweet and certainly intoxicating. In other years they were not quite so blessed. The summers were cool, the grapes did not swell and take on rich vibrant hues, and the liquid in the vats would only hiccup sporadically as fall turned to winter, producing a thin, sour liquid with no obvious relationship to the glorious nectar which came from the same plants the year before.

Thus wine can and does make itself. The fruit sugars in the ripe grapes, if brought into contact with the yeast cells that naturally collect on the grape skins, will be transformed into alcohol and carbon dioxide gas. This process is called *fermentation*. Placed in its simplest context, wine is nothing more than alcoholic grape juice. For thousands of years, it was undoubtedly used only in that context. As evidence of a bountiful harvest, and as the magical liquid which had gone through a mysterious transformation, it was used in dedications to deities of all kinds in all religions. It remains as a symbol in the principal celebrations of Christianity and Judaism. As mild intoxicant, it has been ministered to the sick and ailing, and still finds a place in some hospital diets when the benefits of induced relaxation are believed to help the body heal itself. Most importantly, once it was known that a beverage containing alcohol is more likely to be relatively sterile and free of infection, wine became the daily beverage of all classes of people in countries where it could be made, in preference to the local water source, which was likely to be infected with all kinds of disease and pestilence.

In addition to such practical uses of wine, there are numerous accounts throughout ancient and medieval history of reverence paid to a particular wine, though these are most often mere signals of the blessings of a favorable growing season. But if modern wine drinkers had access to even the best of these ancient wines, we would most likely be unimpressed by their style and character. For wine has changed, dramatically. In some parts of the world, even as recently as the middle of the twentieth century, the notion of what constituted good wine was very different from today's standards. One has only to try the current homemade versions of old-style Italian household wines to recognize that their daily beverage used to be fuller, richer, and headier than today's commercial versions from the same region.

What has not changed though is the romance associated with wine. It may well be that the historic accounts and anecdotes of great and memorable wines have more to do with the event at which the wine was served than with the wine itself. Nevertheless, it remains true that a fine bottle of wine makes a grand meal even grander, and many a simple picnic has become an unforgettable meal in the company of even the simplest wine. It seems that nothing will change the fact that good wine can magnify the pleasure we find in good food and good company. This seemingly commonplace piece of knowledge appears to have been at least readily accepted if not understood by our forebears.

Part 1 of this book will help you to strip away the mystical aura which too often surrounds wine, and prepare you to explore the worlds of wine and discover its romance and pleasure. For all the changes which the modern era of technology will bring to wine, we hope that wine will continue to bring pleasure to the lives of those who drink it wisely.

# How Wine Is Made

## Introduction

One of the most fascinating things about wine, for both the novice and the experienced wine consumer, is the broad array of wine styles available around the world and even within any single geographic area. Wines come in all shades of colors, generally categorized within the broad ranges of white, blush (rosé), and red. Wines come with bubbles **(sparkling),** and without bubbles **(still).** Some wines are intended for aging, others are much more enjoyable within months of being bottled. Many wines seem light in body and flavor, others appear fuller and richer, with more complex flavors present. There are sweet wines and not-sweet wines, high-alcohol wines and low-alcohol wines. There are even wines that have had alcohol added to them **(fortified),** and some that have had flavorings added **(aromatized).**

This chapter will introduce the reader to the many choices faced by wine makers in producing the style of wine which they believe will please the consumer. We will also consider the major influences which sometimes dictate how a wine will turn out, and at other times can be employed by the wine maker to achieve the desired result. Having learned the basics of wine making, or **vinification,** you will then be ready to study the characteristics of the major grape varieties in the world, and the resulting wine styles in the major wine-producing countries.

Reduced to the simplest terms, there are four major influences on the final characteristics of a wine. These are:

• The grape variety used to make the wine

• The climate in the vineyard, including weather conditions during the growing season

• The soil in the vineyard

• The wine maker who makes choices and decisions all through the grape-growing and wine-making process.

We will look at the first influence—the grape variety in Chapter 2. The importance of the second and third influences—soil and climate—will be discussed throughout the regional chapters. This chapter will concentrate on the fourth influence—the activity of the wine maker.

In the past decade, the dominant trend has been toward decreased production of jug, or table wines, and increased concentration on high-quality wines. In the Old World European wine-making countries (especially France, Italy, Spain, Portugal, and Germany) this means that more wines are being produced within strict government regulatory systems, often referred to as **appellation** (or naming) systems. In the New World countries, where appellation systems are not so meticulously detailed, the move to higher-quality wines means a greater concentration on wines made from single-grape varieties, or from blends of certain varieties which are known to complement each other. In all cases, higher quality means that more wines are produced for retail in bottle and magnum (two-bottle) sizes, with a cork or synthetic material closure, with decreased marketing of gallon jugs or three-liter boxes.

The statement that more wine makers are concentrating on high-quality wines begs the question: what constitutes high quality in a wine? From the producer's pont of view, we would suggest that these are the major considerations:

• The wine should offer distinct taste and flavor characteristics which are typical of the grape variety or varieties used to make the wine.

• The wine's style, taste, and flavors should reflect the place of origin of the grapes.

• There should be no unpleasant or "off" aromas or flavors.

• Last, but by no means least, within the other considerations listed above, the wine should please the customer.

# Ancient Peoples Discover Wine and the Influence of Color

Wine and wine making can be both mind-bogglingly simple and excruciatingly complex. At its most basic, wine is nothing more than the fermented juice of a fruit, usually grapes. Grape juice becomes wine when its sugar content is converted into alcohol by the action of yeasts.

The vast majority of all wine in the world is produced from grapes of many different varieties. Grapes have the optimum proportions of sugar content to liquid, and more than any other fruit, grapes at harvest time develop a microscopic covering of dust on the outside of the skin. This dust, or **bloom,** is, in fact, made up of millions of microorganisms, many of which are yeast cells, but not just any old yeast cells. The "wild" or "natural" yeast cells on a grape skin include a high proportion of *Saccharomyces ellipsoidium,* which, in its various forms, is considered the best yeast strain for converting grape sugars to alcohol.

Modern wine making is a complex process that is controlled by detailed knowledge of organic chemistry and microbiology, as well as by the wine maker's skill, artistry, and judgment. But wine is a natural substance that people have been making since ancient times. All the ancients needed to do was to put grapes into a large container and lightly crush the fruit, in order to break the skin of the grapes. This allowed the liquid sugar inside the grapes to come into contact with the yeast cells on the skin of the grapes, which, in turn, would convert the sugar to alcohol. Carbon dioxide would be released into the atmosphere in the process.

One of the primary considerations of wine consumers and of wine makers is the color of a wine. As well as discovering that grapes, left to their own devices, produce an alcoholic liquid, the ancients also discovered that red- or black-skinned grapes produced a dark red wine, while white or yellow grapes produced a yellow/green or straw-colored wine. At some point wine makers realized that, in the great majority of cases, red grapes have the same color juice as white grapes; the juice is almost clear, with just the slightest yellow tint, no matter the color of the skins. Historically, this is where wine making begins to show some complexity, and it is important for today's consumer and wine lover to comprehend that the color of the grape variety sometimes plays an important role in determining the style of a wine, especially if the grape skins are allowed any contact with the grape juice during the wine making process.

**Figure 1.1** A Champagne Label.

**Figure 1.2** A California Blanc de Noirs Label.

A Bottle of Sutter Home White Zinfandel.

True French Champagne (see Figure 1.1) is produced using one white grape variety (Chardonnay), and two red grape varieties (Pinot Noir and Pinot Meunier). Without the inclusion of the clear juice from the two red grape varieties, the wine would be a less-complex, lighter style of wine.

Blanc de Noirs sparkling wine from California and other areas in the United States is produced from red grapes, often Pinot Noir and Pinot Meunier (see Figure 1.2). Some Blanc de Noirs sparkling wines are slightly pink or salmon colored; others are much closer to a white-wine color. Again, sparkling wines made using only white grapes are generally lighter and more delicate in style.

White Zinfandel from California is made from the red Zinfandel grape. Some White Zinfandel wines are slightly pink in color; others are white. The same applies to wines labeled White Merlot, or Cabernet Blanc, or Blanc de Pinot Noir: some may indeed be white, but they are all made from red grapes, giving them a noticeable red fruit flavor characteristic.

Once ancient wine makers identified that the color of grape juice is neutral, it was an easy jump for them to control the exact color of the wine. By using a press to squeeze the juice from white grapes they found that it is possible to produce a very-light-colored white wine. Perhaps more significant was the fact that the same result could be achieved by gently pressing red grapes and extracting the clear juice to make a white wine with some of the fruit flavor characteristics of red wine. During pressing, the juice absorbs yeast cells from the grape skins, and fermentation proceeds as usual, but without the grape skins as part of the process. To make a red wine, the dark-colored grape skins—which can span the color spectrum from the lightest violet to the deepest purple—need to be left in contact with the grape juice during fermentation, so that the color pigments that make the wine look red can be dissolved from the skins, with the alcohol produced during fermentation acting as a solvent.

## The Modern Approach

Modern wine making all around the world is based on the very simple principles outlined above of yeasts converting sugar to alcohol and the recognition that different grape varieties contribute various characteristics, including color, to wine. As already stated, a wine's character is strongly influenced by the choice of grape variety and the vineyard site. Once the grapes are harvested, modern wine makers employ several different processes to achieve distinct styles of wine. The most important of these, in likely chronological order, are

- Pressing or crushing the grapes (almost all wines)

- Controlled fermentation (almost all wines)

- Malolactic fermentation (some wines)

- Aging (some wines)

- Clarification (almost all wines)

These processes will be described as they apply to the production of white, red, and rosé wines. We will then look at the special considerations given to the production of sweet wines, fortified wines, aromatized wines, and sparkling wines. Before that however, we need to make note of how grapes are harvested, and why and how wine makers estimate the level and usability of the sugars in the grapes and yeasts on the grape skins.

# Harvesting

## The Vintage

In English-speaking countries around the world, the harvesting of grapes is called the **vintage,** from the French word *vendange* which means harvest. When people refer to wine as being from the 1994 vintage, they are indicating that the grapes that were used to make the wine were harvested in 1994 (see Figure 1.3). Similarly, the phrase "a good vintage" is sometimes used to describe a wine, indicating that the climatic conditions that prevailed that year were such that the grapes were harvested in excellent condition and the

A General Harvest Scene.

**Figure 1.3** The Vintage Date on a Label.

resulting wine should be very good. If the wine is produced from grapes of a single year's harvest, the vintage date usually appears somewhere on the label.

Not all wines are made from one single vintage. Those wines which do not have a vintage date on the label are called **nonvintage** wines, and are usually blends of several wines from different vintages. The intent behind a nonvintage wine is to provide the consumer with a product which will be exactly the same every time. The philosophy behind a vintage-dated wine is to take the grapes from one single harvest and to make the best wine possible given the growing conditions in that vineyard that year. In other words, a vintage-dated wine is the wine maker's bottled expression of the combination of climate and grape variety from a single year.

## Deciding When to Harvest

The wine maker and grape grower decide the optimum time to harvest the grapes based on both a chemical and taste analysis of the grapes. By sampling grapes from many different areas of the vineyard, it is possible to get an accurate picture of the state of maturity of the entire vineyard. The chemical analysis reveals the relative sugar level and acidity level in the grapes, as well as the **pH** level. For the wine maker these are important readings as the sugar level will dictate the alcohol level and/or the sweetness level of the finished wine, and the acidity level is an important component for balance in the final flavor profile of the wine (see Chapter 3 on Wine Tasting). The pH level is an indicator of the potency of the hydrogen ions in a solution; solutions with more hydrogen ions have a stronger acid content. Since pH measurements are based on negative exponent numbers, lower pH measurements indicate high acid levels. The pH level also indicates how well the grape juice and wine will resist bacterial spoilage, given that wines with lower levels of pH are more resistant to bacterial infection.

As grapes ripen on the vine, the sugar levels rise in the presence of increased heat and light—in a word, sunshine—during the growing season. At the same time, the heat and humidity levels affect the acidity levels in grapes. In general, hot, dry conditions drive the acid levels down. So, the cooler the climate, the higher the acid levels; the warmer the climate, the higher the sugar levels. The relationship between sugar and acidity in the grapes at harvest will be reflected in the resulting taste components in the wine (see Chapter 3 on Wine Tasting). Most importantly, the sugar content of the grapes at harvest will determine the maximum level of alcohol produced during fermentation.

## Measuring Sugar Levels

All wine makers are interested in the sugar content of the grapes or grape juice. The sugar content of grape juice is measured by a hydrometer which compares the specific density of the juice to that of water. The hydrometer (see Figure 1.4) is a calibrated instrument which is dropped into the grape juice: the

Scene from Hot Rhône Valley Vineyard Where Grapes Reach High Sugar Levels.

**Figure 1.4** A Hydrometer.

**Figure 1.5**  A Wine Label Showing a Reference to Brix.

higher the hydrometer floats, the greater the concentration of sugar in the juice. Higher specific density readings for grape juice indicate higher levels of sugar dissolved in the juice. The scale used to calibrate the hydrometer varies from country to country. Since wine labels sometimes refer to sugar levels, it will be useful here to review the different scales used to measure sugar.

In North America, the Brix (also called Balling) scale is a measurement of the density of sugar in the grape juice solution, expressing the sugar content as a percent of the total weight of the solution (see Figure 1.5). When wine makers know the Brix measurement of the grape juice, they can estimate the total amount of alcohol which the sugar content of the juice will produce, and make a decision as to how much sugar could be left unfermented in the wine as a sweet taste.

In France, the Baumé scale has been and is still used as the measurement of sugar in the juice. The hydrometer has been scaled to equal the amount of alcohol which the sugar content of the juice could produce if all of the sugars are fermented to alcohol.

In Germany, the Öeschle scale, measured in degrees, represents the number of grams by which the weight of one liter of grape juice exceeds the weight of one liter of water, again giving an indication of how much alcohol could be produced from the sugar content or how much of the sugar could be left in the wine as a sweet taste.

It is also very important for the grape grower and/or wine maker to taste the grapes to determine that they show the appropriate level of flavors and character associated with the specific grape variety being harvested. Generally, wine makers know ahead of time the kind of wine they want to produce. So, they specify to the growers what acidity and sugar levels they are looking for, and what degree of ripe flavors they want in the grapes.

## Picking

When the grapes are ready to be harvested, they may be picked by hand or harvested by mechanical harvester. Both methods have their advocates, who

Hand-picking.

cite various advantages and disadvantages. Those who prefer handpicking claim that their grapes are more carefully handled, because good pickers carefully select only the fully ripe bunches as they progress through the vineyard. Certainly for those grape growers with vineyards on steep hillsides, handpicking is almost mandatory since machines cannot work the steep hillsides. Those who use mechanical harvesters suggest that their grapes exhibit more uniform quality characteristics, since they have been harvested rapidly and within a short time period. It is also possible to harvest by night using a mechanical harvester. This can be an advantage in a hot growing area, where cooler grape temperatures at night mean less extraction of bitter components from the skins. Cooler grape temperatures also reduce the likelihood of spontaneous, uncontrolled fermentation. Once harvested, the grapes proceed to the pressing or crushing stage, depending on whether they are being made into white or red wine.

## Chaptalization

In many parts of the wine-making world, cool weather patterns in some years result in lower sugar levels than desired or needed. If the wine maker wants the wine to reach a certain alcohol level, it is permissible in some of these regions to add regular beet or cane sugar to the juice *before* fermentation starts or during fermentation. In other words, the practice of adding sugar, referred to as **chaptalization,** is intended for the purpose of achieving a higher level of alcohol in the wine. It is not intended as a method for producing sweet wines.

Chaptalization originated in France and is widely practiced there. The practice is forbidden by national, state, or local law in Italy, Spain, Australia, and California. It should be remembered that some of the areas that forbid chaptalization have warm or even hot growing conditions anyway. Also, these areas have several other legal methods, such as **governo** (see Chianti in Chapter 7) to ensure that there is enough sugar to reach the desired alcohol level.

## Yeast Selection

There has been much debate among wine makers in recent years about the use of "natural" yeasts, those occurring naturally on the grape skin at harvest time, as opposed to specifically selected pure yeast strains, which are purchased and added to the grapes or grape juice to begin fermentation. There are proponents for both, and while this debate is too complex to detail here, the issue highlights the fact that different strains of yeast will result in different characteristics in the finished wine.

If there is a problem using "natural" yeasts, it is that the bloom on the grape skins contains many other microorganisms in addition to the *Saccharomyces ellipsoidium,* or wine yeasts. Several kinds of bacteria or undesirable yeast strains may be present on the grape skins, and, in large-enough quantity, they can spoil the fermentation process from its beginnings, leaving the wine maker with something closer to vinegar than wine.

However, some of the world's most-respected and highly prized wines continue to be made using natural yeasts without any problems. There is also a trend toward wine makers developing their own yeast strains, broadly based on the wild yeasts. These proprietary yeasts combine the best of both worlds: a yeast close to nature that can be controlled by the wine maker. Other wine makers prefer to inoculate their grapes or juice with a pure, certified, bacteria-free yeast strain whose characteristics and influence on the final wine are known ahead of time. For example, some of these pure yeast strains produce wines with lower levels of acidity, and some are more capable of achieving high levels of alcohol. Both of these conditions would greatly affect the final taste and flavor balance of the wine (see Chapter 3 on Wine Tasting).

# White Wine Production
## *Pressing*

White wines can be made from white or red grapes as the color of the juice in red and white grapes is the same: light yellow. In either case, the general process requires rapid processing of the grapes to extract the juice as quickly as possible and place the juice (sometimes referred to as **must**) in a closed container. Throughout the whole wine-making process (see Figure 1.6), the wine maker needs to carefully control the amount of oxygen that is allowed to come into contact with the juice or wine. Although small amounts of oxygen might be encouraged, to stimulate yeast activity or to develop flavors during fermentation and aging, it is generally considered that air is the enemy of wine, and contact between the two needs to be carefully controlled. Just as rusting is an **oxidation** process—oxygen in the air attacks paint and metal—oxygen can attack wine during fermentation, prematurely aging and changing its character.

At the winery building, the grapes are most often channeled mechanically through a destemming machine, which separates the grapes from the stems. This machine may also crush the grapes, though the term "crush" may be too harsh. What the machine really does is break the skin of the grapes, making juice extraction quicker and easier.

The romantic notion of vineyard workers stripping off their shoes and clothes and jumping into a large wooden tank filled with grapes in order to "tread" them is woefully inaccurate these days. Even the use of wooden-slatted presses similar to apple or cider presses has decreased dramatically, giving way to mechanical pneumatic presses that can apply very gentle pressure to the grapes. The press pictured here (see Figure 1.7) is the most common type in use. Inside the horizontal steel drum is a rubber membrane which can be inflated to gently press the grapes against the inside surface of the closed cylinder. In addition the steel drum is rotated on its horizontal axis.

**Figure 1.6** White Wine Flow Chart.

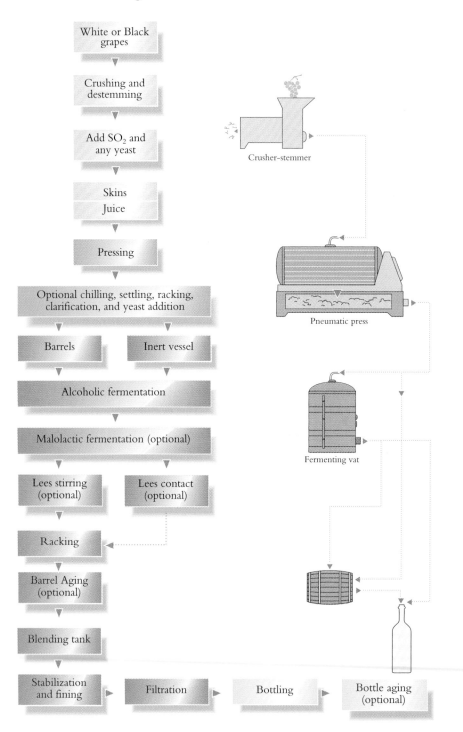

**Figure 1.7** Horizontal Pneumatic Press.

The efficiency of this type of pneumatic press is based on a very simple principle: *the more gently the grapes are pressed, the better the* quality *of the juice.* This is because the best juice, with the purest varietal flavors and the best ratio of sugar to acidity, comes from the band of pulp between the grape seeds and the skin. The harder the grapes are pressed the more likely it is that unwanted harsh and bitter flavors will be extracted from the pulp areas nearest the seeds and close to the skin.

However, this principle has a necessary corollary: *the more gently the grapes are pressed, the lower the* quantity *of juice extracted.* This inverse relationship of quality to quantity runs all the way through the grape-growing and wine-making process. A wine maker who wants to produce the best wine possible will not be able to produce huge quantities. This obviously means that availability is limited on certain wines, and this relative rarity allows some wine makers to charge more for their wine. That is why some wines, such as Château Petrus, Château Lafite-Rothschild, and Dom Perignon, are so expensive. Alternatively, if a wine maker wants to increase production without growing or buying more grapes, quality will suffer.

After pressing for white wine production, most wine makers allow the must to sit overnight, sometimes in a refrigerated tank, to encourage any solid particles of pulp or skin to settle out. Some wine companies, especially very large ones, centrifuge the must to render it absolutely clear of solid matter. Ironically, recent research has prompted many wine makers to allow their juice to fully oxidize at this stage (see comments on oxygen contact in this chapter, page 13). Apparently, if some of the juice components are allowed to oxidize at this stage, they will not be there to oxidize during the rest of the wine making process, thereby reducing the need to add chemicals, such as sulfur dioxide, to prevent oxidation. However, there is some evidence that allowing oxidation in the juice form will result in a less fruity wine.

## Controlled Fermentation for White Wine Production

Some wine makers who want a fuller-bodied and more strongly flavored white wine allow the juice of white grapes to sit in contact with white grape skins for a short period of time. This skin contact time extracts more flavor components and more yellow pigments from the skins.

***Containers.*** When the wine maker is ready to let fermentation begin, the juice is pumped into the container of choice, which may be any of the following:

- An Open-top Cement Tank.

- A Closed, Glass-lined Cement Tank.

- A Large, Refrigerated Stainless Steel Tank (see Figure 1.8).

- A Cured Fiberglass Tank.

- A Large Wooden Upright Vat.

- A Large Wooden Barrel (see Figure 1.9).

- A Small Wooden Barrel.

The choice of container is often driven by economics. However, even if money is no object, the choice of container depends largely on the style of wine that the wine maker wants to make. Modern commercial wine makers frequently choose either stainless steel or wooden barrels (most often made from oak) for fermentation. While there are exceptions to these generaliza-

### TABLE 1.1  STAINLESS STEEL VS. WOOD

| *Stainless Steel* | *Small Wooden Barrel* |
| --- | --- |
| light- to medium-weight wine | usually fuller, richer style |
| crisp, clean style | more rounded, softer |
| simple, aromatic fruit flavors | more complex, multidimensional |

tions, Table 1.1 highlights the differences between a wine fermented in stainless steel, and the same wine fermented in a small wooden barrel. Although slightly different techniques are used to make wine in stainless steel as opposed to wooden barrels, it would be true to say that, even if every step of the process was exactly the same, the wine from each container would be noticeably different. Principally, this is true because wood does not provide a neutral container: a wooden barrel imparts some of its characteristics to the wine. Most obviously, the aroma and taste of wood infuses the wine; secondly, the wine may extract varying levels of **tannins** and **vanillin** from the wood, especially if it is an oak barrel, and both of these elements will affect the taste and flavor of the final wine. The tannins from wood, along with any tannins from grape skins, may initially taste bitter and harsh, but they provide some structure to the wine (i.e., they give a sense of firmness and even a feeling of height on the palate), and are usually balanced by softer elements in the wine. Vanillin may be one of those softer elements, smelling and tasting soft and sweet like vanilla essence. (For more information on tannin and taste see the sidebar on tannin in this chapter, page 19, and Chapter 3 on Wine Tasting. For more information on the effects of wood, see the section on aging in this chapter, pages 24 to 26.)

***Requirements of Fermentation.*** Once the juice is in the container, fermentation begins, either in the presence of natural yeasts or the yeasts added to the juice. For the yeasts to be active, the temperature of the fermenting juice needs to be controlled carefully. If the temperature rises above 90°F (32°C) or falls below 38°F (3°C), fermentation is likely to stop, as the yeasts cannot function at these extreme temperatures. The temperature during fermentation will also have an effect on the eventual style and flavor of the wine. Generally, cool fermentations proceed at a very slow, gentle pace, producing wines with noticeably clean, crisp, aromatic characteristics, such as Riesling from the Mosel Valley in Germany. Hotter fermentations are much quicker and more vigorous, producing fuller-flavored and more complex, heavier wines, such as the red Châteauneuf-du-Pape of the Rhône Valley in France.

**Figure 1.8** Large, Refrigerated Stainless Steel Tanks.

**Figure 1.9** Large Wooden Barrels.

**Figure 1.10**  An Eiswein Label.

**Figure 1.11**  A Côte du Rhone Label.

**Figure 1.12**  A Sauternes Label.

The increasing use of stainless steel tanks makes it easier to maintain cool, even temperatures, most often by pumping a coolant through a refrigerated jacket on the outside of the tank. Obviously, it is much less practical to try to cool a wooden barrel.

The fermentation of any wine proceeds until one of three things happens:

• All of the sugar is converted to alcohol, resulting in what is called a **dry** wine, meaning a wine which is not perceptibly sweet because it has little or no grape sugars left in it.

• The alcohol level gets so high that the yeast cells can no longer function; this usually occurs at around 14.5 to 15 percent alcohol by volume. At this point, all the natural grape sugars may have been converted to alcohol, creating a dry, high-alcohol wine, or sugars may remain unconverted, creating a sweet, high-alcohol wine.

• The wine maker intervenes and stops the fermentation before all of the grape sugars have been converted to alcohol, leaving a small amount of **residual sugar** in the wine which will result in a slightly sweet taste in the final wine. This is most often achieved commercially by stopping the fermentation via rapid chilling of the fermenting wine, and then removing the yeast cells from the wine using a centrifuge or a sterile filtration system.

When the fermentation has stopped, the wine is made. The next steps are to ensure that the wine is bright, clean, and clear (see the section on clarification in this chapter, pages 26 to 28). For some white wines, there will be the additional process of aging the wine (see the section on aging in this chapter, pages 24 to 26).

---

### ALCOHOL LEVEL IN WINE

Across the entire range of wines, alcohol levels vary dramatically, from as low as 6 percent alcohol by volume in some German Eiswein (see figure 1.10), to as much as 13.5 percent in some Côtes du Rhône reds (see figure 1.11), to 14.5 percent in a sweet white Sauternes (see Figure 1.12) from Bordeaux, to 21 percent in a sherry that has been fortified by the addition of brandy.

The average alcohol level of wine is 12 percent, with many producers making light-style wines at around 11 percent alcohol by volume.

---

# Red Wine Production

## *Pressing*

The most obvious differences between white and red wine production are that to make red wine the grapes have to be red and the skins have to be part of the process (see Figure 1.13), since the skins provide the pigments

## T A N N I N

Tannin is present in grape skins, as well as in tea leaves and coffee beans. Different grape varieties contain different concentrations of tannin in the skin, and red grape varieties contain more tannin than white varieties.

Tannin has a noticeably bitter taste, and a rough, astringent feel, causing the mouth to dry out. It's a bit like chewing an aspirin. So why would wine makers want to have tannin in the wine if it tastes so awful?

Tannin is useful to the wine maker for two main reasons:

1. It is a natural preservative. Therefore, if a wine maker has made a wine (probably red) that is supposed to develop and improve with age, the presence of tannin in the wine increases the likelihood that the wine will remain sound through the aging process.

2. It is a substance with a natural affinity for protein. Tannin acts as a catalyst with any protein-containing **fining agent** added to the wine, so that the tannin molecules are attracted to the fining agent. This attraction causes a mass of colloidal matter to collect and sink down through the wine, pulling other particles with it as it sinks. (For more information on fining agents and colloids, see the section on clarification in this chapter, pages 26 to 28.)

---

that make the wine appear red. The pigments are usually extracted just before or during fermentation. This means that red grapes are crushed (the skins are broken), but they are *not* pressed before fermentation; they will however be pressed later during the process, usually after the fermentation has been completed, or after the wine maker is satisfied that the skins have provided enough color to the wine. The wine maker can increase the amount of pigment and flavor extraction by agitating the red grape skins during fermentation. It is important to note that color is not the only thing which is extracted from red grape skins. They also contain varying levels of a naturally occurring substance called tannin, depending on the specific grape variety, and wine makers work hard to ensure that their red wines contain a level of tannin appropriate to the type of wine.

## Controlled Fermentation for Red Wine Production

The same considerations of which container to use apply to red wine as to white wine, but the process of making the wine is not the same (see Figure 1.14). To start the fermentation, the red grapes are processed through the destemming machine, and the grape skins are broken to allow the juice to come into contact with the yeast cells. Again, the wine maker may choose to use natural yeasts or to introduce a specific strain of pure yeast to start the

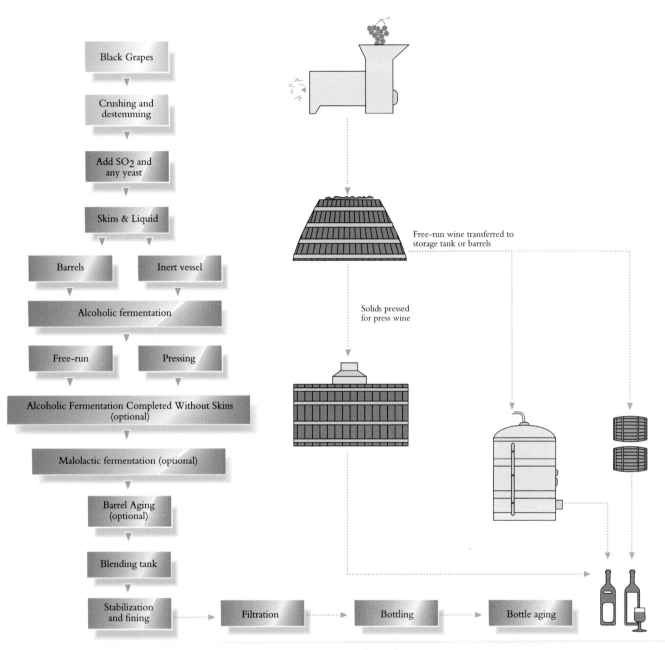

**Figure 1.13** Red Wine Flow Chart.

fermentation. As with white wine production, modern technology allows wine makers to monitor the fermentation closely, allowing them the option of removing the red grape skins as soon as they feel that enough pigments, tannins, and flavor components have been extracted from the skins. This may occur before the fermentation ends. The fermentation will proceed until one of the conditions mentioned in the white wine production section (in this chapter, page 18) is met. Most red wines are fermented to complete dryness, with little or no residual sugar remaining.

Whether the red grape skins are removed during fermentation or left in until the fermentation is complete, the skins will at some point be retrieved in order to press them and extract what will be reserved as **press wine.** The press wine is more concentrated in flavors, tannins, color, and body, and lower in acidity: it may be used later by the wine maker to blend back into the rest of the wine to achieve the desired style and flavor. The skins can be used as fertilizing material in the vineyard.

*Carbonic Maceration.* For centuries, the wine producers of Beaujolais (see Chapter 6 on France) have employed an alternative method of red wine fermentation, called carbonic maceration. Because this method results in a lighter, easy-drinking style of wine, it has recently been adopted by many wine makers in other parts of the world.

Carbonic maceration occurs when whole, unbroken red grapes are placed in a closed container which has been previously saturated with carbon dioxide gas. Generally, the weight of the grapes in the container causes the bottom 10 to 15 percent of the grapes to be crushed. The sugar solution in those grapes is then transformed, by the natural yeasts on the grape skins, into alcohol and carbon dioxide (maintaining the carbon dioxide level in the container).

Each individual uncrushed grape in the upper part of the closed container undergoes its own minifermentation *inside* the grape. In fact, what happens is that, since each grape is deprived of oxygen, the metabolism of the grape changes to provide energy from the intercellular fermentation of the grape's sugar reserves. One of the by-products of this intercellular fermentation is alcohol, which helps to dissolve the skin so that the skin is eroded, and alcoholic grape juice—wine—is expelled from the grape.

Carbonic maceration (see Figure 1.14) does not involve any physical movement of the grapes to extract extra color or tannin from the skins. The result is a light-colored red wine that is low in tannins. Wines produced this way, such as Beaujolais from France and Gamay Beaujolais from California, are enjoyed particularly for their fresh fruit flavors.

# Rosé Wine Production

Good-quality rosé wines are produced by allowing red grape skins to remain in limited contact with the grape juice before fermentation starts, thereby creating a pink-tinted juice. The skins are then extracted, and the pink juice is treated in the same manner as white juice.

**Figure 1.14** Carbonic Maceration.

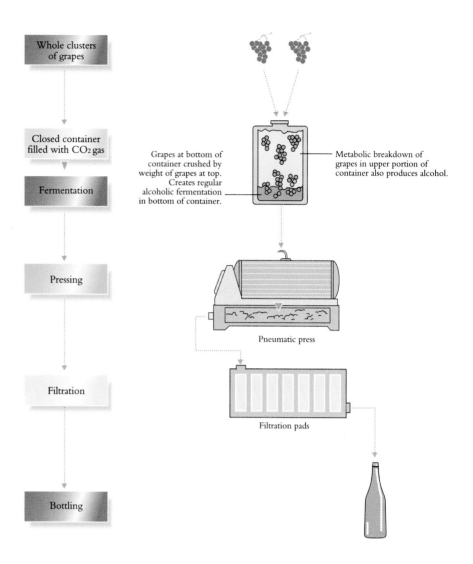

It is legal in most countries to produce a pink wine by blending a small amount of red wine with a large amount of white wine. In the United States it would not be legal, however, to produce a White Zinfandel this way, as the inclusion of the name Zinfandel on the label indicates that at least 75 percent of the wine was produced using the Zinfandel grape (see the United States Wine Laws in Chapter 4).

To all intents and purposes, the terms pink, rosé, and blush mean the same thing. All refer to pink-tinted wines.

# Malolactic Fermentation

The style of any wine can be controlled to a large extent by the wine maker. Some style parameters might be that grapes must be harvested at certain acidity and sugar levels, or that a certain kind of container must be used for fermentation. In addition to these and other stylistic choices, the wine maker may choose to put the wine through an additional step, the process known as **malolactic fermentation.** This process can take place simultaneously with the basic alcoholic fermentation, or it may follow the alcoholic fermentation. It can occur naturally, without any intervention from the wine maker, or it can be induced by the wine maker.

The agents which cause malolactic fermentation are bacteria, usually *leuconostoc* which are in the *Lactobacillus* family, familiar to people who enjoy yogurt. These bacteria may naturally be present in and around the winery, in which case malolactic fermentation occurs without any action from the wine maker.

Alternatively, the bacteria can be purchased and added to the wine. Once the bacteria are introduced to the wine, they act upon the **malic acid** component of the wine, converting it to **lactic acid.** The overall effects are as follows:

- The sharp, harsh malic acid is converted to softer, smoother lactic acid (the acid in milk), changing the taste and flavor profile of the wine.

- A small amount of carbon dioxide gas is created and released into the atmosphere.

- The total measurable acidity of the wine is reduced.

Most red wines, and some white wines (particularly Chardonnay wines from cooler climates) go through malolactic fermentation, making them generally smoother and softer on the palate.

## GRAPE ACIDS

Three major acids are found in grapes, though the actual content of each acid varies from variety to variety and from climate to climate. The three acids are:

Tartaric acid, found primarily in grapes

Malic acid, as in green apples (Granny Smith, for example)

Citric acid, as in lemons, grapefruit, etc.

These three acids all have a sharp, piercing taste, and all cause the mouth to salivate. (For more information on the effect of acids on taste, see Chapter 3 on Wine Tasting.)

# Aging

A Barrel-aging Warehouse.

A Barrel Being Made—Placing the Rings at One End of the Barrel.

Once the wine is made, it is either prepared for bottling or stored at the winery and allowed to **age,** or **mature.** The decision of whether to age a wine at the winery depends mainly on the style of the wine, although wine makers sometimes bottle wines before they are ready, either because there is a high demand for the product or the company needs to generate sales.

Ideally, of course, the decision to age is driven purely by the style considerations of the wine. It is a common belief that all wines improve with age. This is not true. Only a small percentage of the world's wines derive any benefit from aging and, even then, aging a wine is very much a gamble.

The vast majority of all wines produced are made in a style that makes them most enjoyable when young. These wines are best consumed within two to three years after production. They are enjoyable for their attractive, fresh, clean fruit flavors and aromas which will only diminish as time goes on. Wine makers all around the world produce huge quantities of this type of wine, and most consumers buy it and enjoy it. Only a very small percentage of wine consumers have the money, the facility, and the time to buy wine with the intention of aging it. In fact, better than 90 percent of the world's wine is consumed within two years of its vintage date.

Most wines, then, do not go through any aging process. When a winery decides to age a wine before releasing it to the public, it is because the wine maker feels that the wine will somehow improve by holding the wine back and keeping it in a suitable container. A red wine aged at the winery will lose some of its harsh, youthful abrasiveness (often derived from the combination of tannins and intense, just-ripe fruit flavors), and offer the consumer a red wine which is softer, more developed in its flavors, and generally more appealing. A very small percentage of white wines are aged to develop more complexity and a smoother texture.

After Bending the Staves in, Rings are Fitted to the Opposite End.

Firing, or Toasting the Inside of the Barrel.

The Head, Ready For Placement on the End of the Barrel.

When deciding on the type of container in which to age or ferment wine, the first consideration is: What kind of material? For many wine makers, the natural choice, especially for aging complex wines, is wood. So, what kind of wood?

Traditional wisdom says that oak is the best wood to use, though wine makers around the globe have used and continue to use chestnut or (in California) redwood.

So, where to get the oak from? Again, traditional wisdom suggests that French is best, but some wine makers prefer American, Italian, or Slavonian oak.

Where exactly in France? Five main forests in France supply most of the oak for wine containers: Nevers, Limousin, Vosges, Tronçais, and Allier. As to which is better, you will find a different opinion for every wine maker and French barrel maker you speak to.

All right, so you go with a French forest. Now, what size container?

The size which is becoming increasingly popular around the world is the **barrique,** which is approximately 60 gallons, or 225 liters. There are many other sizes and shapes available. The main consideration is: How much surface area contact do you want the wine to have with the wood? Since the smaller barrels contain a smaller quantity of wine, the overall effect of the oak on the wine is greater.

Great, who do you buy from?

Well there are many **coopers,** or barrel makers, all with their own special trade secrets which make their barrels better than anyone else's. Among the various considerations are how the wood is split or sawn, how the wood is dried, how long it is seasoned, how thick the staves are, how the staves are bent, and so forth.

O.K., so you select a cooper. How do you place the order?

First, you need to specify whether you want the barrels **toasted** (fired) on the inside. The options are light, medium, and dark toast. If the barrel is dark-toasted, the influence of the oak will not be so harsh, but the wine will pick up toasty aromas and flavors.

Now you've got the barrels *chez vous.* Do you just put the wine in them?

You really have to decide whether you want *all* of the wine to have oak treatment, or just a half of the wine, or maybe a third, or . . . Then you need to figure out whether the wine (all, or half, or a third, . . .) goes into all new barrels, or does some go in new barrels (if so how much?), and some go in used barrels, and should the used barrels be one, two, or three years old, or should it be a combination of one, two, and three?! Obviously, the oak influence is very strong in a brand new barrel and decreases with every year the barrel is used. Some wine makers have gotten some oak influence out of seven-year-old barrels, but very, very little. After that, the barrel will still be usable as a storage container, as long as it is kept in good condition.

Now, when you've gotten all the oak influence you want from the barrel, do you just throw it away?

You could, but you could also sell it to another wine maker who wants less oak influence, or you could get somebody to shave one-quarter to one-eighth of an inch from the inside of the barrel (see Figure 1.15), revealing virgin wood on the inside, and effectively giving you a brand new barrel, which, of course, you may decide to retoast.

By the way, how much will this fancy French barrel cost?

In 1995, a single good, new, French-oak barrique cost around $600. American oak barrels cost about half that amount.

If a wine is to be aged, the wine maker must first decide what kind of container to store it in. Should the wine be left in the container in which it fermented, possibly in contact with the yeast sediment from the fermentation process? Or should the wine be moved into a clean container and, if so, what kind? The container options for storing wine during aging are basically the same as the options for fermenting the wine. However, it may also

**Figure 1.15** Shaving a Barrel.

be desirable to age the wine in bottles at the winery, or a combination of containers may be used, simultaneously or successively.

If the principal objective is to soften the texture of a white wine, this can be achieved by leaving the wine in contact with its yeast cells in the original container, occasionally stirring up the yeast sediment into the wine. The presence of nutrients in the yeast sediments is a source of energy for the bacteria which produce the malolactic fermentation. This is easier in a small container, such as a wooden barrel, but it can also be done in a stainless steel tank.

If the objective is to give a white wine more complexity, this is more often achieved in small wooden barrels. The barrel will impart wood aromas and flavors, and possibly a darker yellow color, to the wine; the wine will extract vanillin from oak barrels (if that is what is being used); and it is commonly assumed that the small barrel will allow a small exchange of oxygen into and out of the wine (though this notion has been contested), causing oxidation and development of the wine's aromas and flavors. Wines left in contact with yeast sediment will also take on yeast aromas and flavors. Aging of red wines is almost always done in small oak barrels to allow some oxidation, to extract vanillin from the oak, to develop oak aromas and flavors, and to give the wine time so that the original grape variety flavors and aromas can develop and emerge. After aging in the barrel, the wine may be aged in the bottle before release, to enhance the wine's character, and to minimize what is called bottle shock—the transfer of the wine from barrels to the bottle seems to numb the wine, temporarily masking its positive characteristics.

# Clarification

Consumers around the world expect wine to be clear and free of any particles or haze, so most commercially produced wines go through some kind of clarification process. Some clarification methods are considered to leave the wine with more of its character intact than other methods: these are usually slow, laborious, and time-consuming. As such, they are more suitable for smaller quantities of wine. Other methods allow large quantities of wine to be processed in a short period of time, though it is often suggested that these methods strip the wine of some of its character.

The principal clarification methods used today are (from slowest to quickest):

- Time and gravity, or **racking** (moving from one container to another)

- **Fining** (adding a catalytic agent to precipitate solids), followed by racking

- Refrigeration or cold stabilization, followed by racking

- Filtration

- Centrifuge (a machine which spins solids out of the wine)

## Racking

Wine makers who are not rushed (by their sales department or loan officers) may simply leave the wine to sit so that gravity will slowly pull any solid matter to the bottom of the container. The wine can then be gently racked, or siphoned, separating it from the sediment which collects on the bottom of the container. However, there are some dangers in this method: leaving the wine to sit increases the risk of contact with air; the wine may begin to lose its fresh flavor; the sediment may begin to decompose and spoil the wine if sediment and wine remain in contact for too long. It is also possible that some solid matter will remain in a hazy suspension in the wine, and will never drop out.

## Fining

The racking process can be accelerated by adding a fining agent to the wine which will cause any solid particles or haze to mass together and fall to the bottom of the container. This happens for a variety of reasons. Some fining agents used are high in protein and the solids in wine, particularly any tannins, have a natural affinity for proteins.

Alternatively, the fining agent may have the opposite electrical charge from that of the suspended solids and, since opposites attract, the solids are attracted to the fining agent. Lastly, some fining agents neutralize the charges which are keeping like charges repelled. Many natural fining agents are still used, such as egg whites, gelatin, isinglass (a gelatinous, gluey substance obtained from fish bladders), and Bentonite (a clay mined in many parts of the world, including Wyoming in the United States). Bentonite works particularly well since it attracts any protein in the wine, and the protein matter attracts any tannins in the wine. After fining, the wine is racked off the sediment before decomposition occurrs. Egg whites have particular limitations, and are more suited for use in small containers of wine, such as barriques.

## Refrigeration

With the correct equipment, wine makers can refrigerate large quantities of wine, which encourages much of the solid material to precipitate to the bottom of the container. Again, following precipitation of all solids, the wine is racked off the sediment.

## Filtration

A more rapid and more certain method of clearing the wine of all foreign matter is to pump it through a series of cellulose pads. Since even a single

**Figure 1.16** An Australian Riesling Label.

**Figure 1.17** U.S. Chenin Blanc Label.

**Figure 1.18** A Mosel Riesling Label.

microscopic cell can spoil an entire batch of wine, many wine makers appreciate the reassurance afforded by using at least one filtration process on their wine. Critics of filtration charge that it can rob the wine of some of its color and flavor components. Those who believe this sometimes label their wines as "unfiltered."

## Centrifuge

A centrifuge provides a rapid and surefire way of clearing the wine of all solid particles as it spins the wine at high speed and any solids are literally flung out of the wine. This method is very efficient at clarifying large quantities of wine but, like filtration, it has been criticized for removing color and flavor components.

# Sweet Wines

A sweet wine is one that contains residual (i.e. unfermented) sugar. In all the famous sweet wines of the world, such as the great Sauternes wines from the Bordeaux region of France or the Beerenauslese wines of Germany, the sugar in the wine *must,* by law, be derived from natural grape sugars which were present in the grape at harvest. While this is true in any sweet wine made to high-quality standards anywhere in the world, there are many bulk, inexpensive sweet wines whose sugar content has been increased by adding a sweetening agent after fermentation.

Our concern is with those sweet wines whose sugar content is from natural grape sugars. Some of these wines are only slightly sweet, others are very rich, luscious, and extremely sweet.

For slightly sweet wines (see Figure 1.16, 1.17, and 1.18), the most likely way for these wines to achieve their sweetness is for the wine maker to halt the fermentation before all of the naturally present grape sugars have been converted to alcohol. Good examples of such wines are many of the Riesling, Gewürztraminer, or Chenin Blanc wines from various parts of the United States or Australia. The residual sugar in most of these wines is around 1.5 to 2 grams per liter, giving a noticeable but only light impression of sweetness on the palate.

An interesting alternative to this method is the use of what German wine makers call *süssreserve* (literally "sweet reserve," or sweet grape juice which has not fermented). After the grapes have been pressed, but before fermentation, some wine makers put aside a portion of the juice and sterilize it so that it will not ferment. The rest of the juice is allowed to ferment, possibly to complete dryness, and then the süssreserve juice is added to the wine to enhance its sweetness and fruitiness. In this instance, the added süssreserve juice is considered to be a natural source of grape sugars, not the addition of a sweetening agent.

A similar practice has been used in parts of Italy for centuries, though it is much less common today than in years past. What the Italians refer to as the **governo** system involves separating a portion of the grapes at harvest and allowing those grapes to dry or dehydrate. This will result in higher grape sugar concentrations in those grapes. The remainder of the grapes are used to make wine in the regular manner, and the "governed" grapes or their juice can be added during or after the fermentation (see the section on Chianti in Chapter 7). The addition of grapes or juice with higher concentrations of grape sugars often, though by no means always, results in a sweeter wine.

## Botrytis Cinerea

The most unusual, intriguing, risky, and complex method of producing a sweet wine relies on a naturally occurring mold, *Botrytis cinerea*. *Botrytis* is one of a family of molds likely to attack the grapes in a vineyard. All of these molds are simply looking for somewhere to live and something to eat, and a ripening or ripe bunch of grapes is an ideal location. Of all the molds in this family, *botrytis* is the only one which is considered beneficial: all of the other molds have to be prevented or removed or they will completely ruin the affected grapes.

If a wine maker wants *botrytis* to affect the grapes, there are certain climatic conditions which favor its development: cool, moist, even misty mornings, followed by warm, dry afternoons. These conditions should be prevalent over a period of days or weeks if the majority of a vineyard is to be affected.

There are certain grape-growing areas where such conditions can almost be relied on to occur every growing season. Such areas usually include a fairly large body of water and some steeply sloping land. As the night air cools and rolls down the slope to the water, a mist is formed, and the mist will enshroud any nearby vineyards, keeping the grapes cool and damp and allowing the *botrytis* mold to grow and spread from grape to grape, from bunch to bunch, and from vine to vine. As the air warms up, the mist will be burned off by the sun, and the vineyards will have a chance to dry out. The most famous areas that enjoy these conditions include:

- Sauternes, Barsac, and adjacent areas in Bordeaux (see Figure 1.19)

- Napa Valley, pulling fog from the San Francisco and San Pablo bay (see Figure 1.20)

- Mosel and Rhine vineyards in Germany (see Figure 1.21)

- Finger Lakes District in New York (see Figure 1.22)

Once the *botrytis* mold has settled on a bunch of grapes, it needs nutrients to prosper, and it finds most of these in the form of sugars inside the grapes. To reach the sugars, the mold pierces the skin of the grape with its

The mold responsible for some of the best sweet wines in the world goes by different names in different countries. Its botanical, Latin name is *Botrytis cinerea,* or "gray mold."

| Country | Mold Name |
| --- | --- |
| Most English-speaking Countries | Botrytis, noble rot |
| France | Pourriture noble |
| Germany | Edelfaule |
| Italy | Muffa noble |

The gray mold is related to many other molds that attack grapes that, unlike *botrytis*, have no beneficial effect at all on the grapes or the wine.

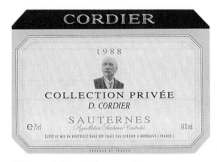

**Figure 1.19** A Regional Sauternes Label.

**Figure 1.20** A *Botrytis* Sauvignon Blanc Napa Label.

**Figure 1.21** A Rhine Auslese Label.

tiny filaments and draws out minute quantities of sugar solution. During the warmer, drier periods, the water content of the grape evaporates through the infinitesimal holes made in the grape skin, and the grape dehydrates on the vine. The net result is a very messy-looking rust-colored grape, but one which contains an extremely high concentration of sugars, acids, and flavors in a much-reduced quantity of liquid.

The wine which is made from these grapes is extremely rich, viscous, and sweet. It is also, for obvious reasons, produced in very limited quantities. Château d'Yquem (see Figure 1.23), the most famous estate in Sauternes, produces approximately one bottle of wine from eight vines, as opposed to the standard yield for a regular dry wine of three to four bottles of wine per vine. Such figures make for very high prices. For example, a bottle of the Château d'Yquem from the 1966 vintage is valued at $500, while a bottle of 1976 Beerenauslese wine from the Schloss Vollrads estate in Germany (see Figure 1.24) is valued at $600. (For more information on these wines, see the section on Sauternes in Chapter 6, and on quality wines in Chapter 10 on Germany.)

It is important to note that, if the climatic conditions are right for *botrytis,* the mold is completely indiscriminate in terms of which grapes it attacks. It will attack grapes at any stage of maturation, but for the mold to be beneficial to the wine maker, it must attack only fully ripe grapes with fully developed flavor characteristics. In addition, the mold will attack *any* grape variety, red or white. With very few exceptions, fine *botrytis* wines are made only from white grapes, but even within the white grape types, certain varieties are considered to be much more suitable for producing *botrytis*-affected wines.

The best white grapes for making *botrytis* wines are

- Riesling, especially in Germany, Australia, and the United States

- Sémillon, especially in Sauternes and Australia

- Sauvignon Blanc, especially in Sauternes, Australia, and the United States

- Chenin Blanc, especially in the Loire Valley

**Figure 1.22** A Label from the Finger Lakes Region.

**Figure 1.23** A Château d'Yquem Label.

**Figure 1.24** A Schloss Vollrads Beerenauslese Label.

**Figure 1.25** A Vintage Porto Label.

**Figure 1.26** A Fino Sherry Label.

- Vidal and Vignoles (hybrid varieties), especially in the eastern United States

# Fortified Wines

Some famous wines are classified as fortified wines because their alcohol content has been strengthened, or fortified, by adding a high alcohol **spirit** to the wine. The most illustrious examples of such wines are Porto, or Port, from Portugal, and Jerez, or Sherry, from southern Spain.

It has often been claimed that the original reason for fortifying wines was to stabilize and preserve the wines, since alcohol is both a preservative and stabilizer. There is some truth in this claim, evidenced by the fact that both Porto and Sherry (see Figure 1.25 and 1.26) were largely developed by British merchants, who shipped the wine fairly long distances, as they built the British wine trade. It is also true that in Andalucia (Andalusia), where Sherry is produced, the local inhabitants and winery workers drink a lower alcohol version of Sherry than that which is exported. Perhaps the most important factor in discussing fortified wines, however, is that it is generally agreed that the table wines from these fortified wine areas are not particularly good.

Whatever the reason, fortification of a wine means simply that a high alcohol spirit, usually a locally made **brandy** or *eau de vie,* is added to the wine during or after fermentation. The difference between adding the spirit during or after fermentation is the difference between a dry and a sweet fortified wine.

If the spirit is added during fermentation, as is the case in Porto, the addition of the spirit will raise the alcohol level of the fermenting wine to a level at which fermentation will stop—beyond 14.5 percent alcohol. However, not all of the original grape sugars will have been converted to alcohol, leaving residual sugar in the now-sweet fortified wine.

If the spirit is added after fermentation, as is the case in Sherry production, the original grape sugars in the grape juice are all converted to alcohol, producing a dry wine. When the spirit is added to this wine, it becomes a dry fortified wine. (In the case of Sherry, producers have the option of sweetening the Sherry at a later stage; see the section on Sherry in Chapter 8 on Spain.)

## Aromatized Wines

Perhaps lending credence to the notion that, at least historically, fortified wines come from areas where the regular wines are of poor quality, some fortified wine producers choose to add flavorings to their fortified wines. The flavorings usually come in the form of herbs and spices, as well as barks, roots, and flowers. Many of these wines fit into the group known as **vermouths,** with most of the base wines coming from southern France or southern Italy, both areas of notoriously large productions of mediocre bulk wines. Red and white aromatized wines come in both sweet and dry versions.

# Sparkling Wines

As grape juice ferments to become wine, carbon dioxide gas is formed as a by-product and released into the atmosphere. The end result is a still, or nonsparkling wine. If the wine maker, at some stage of the process, prevents the carbon dioxide gas from escaping, the end result is a sparkling wine (see Figure 1.27).

The most famous sparkling wine in the world is **Champagne.** For most wine-consuming countries, the use of the word "Champagne" indicates a specific sparkling wine made from specific grape varieties grown on

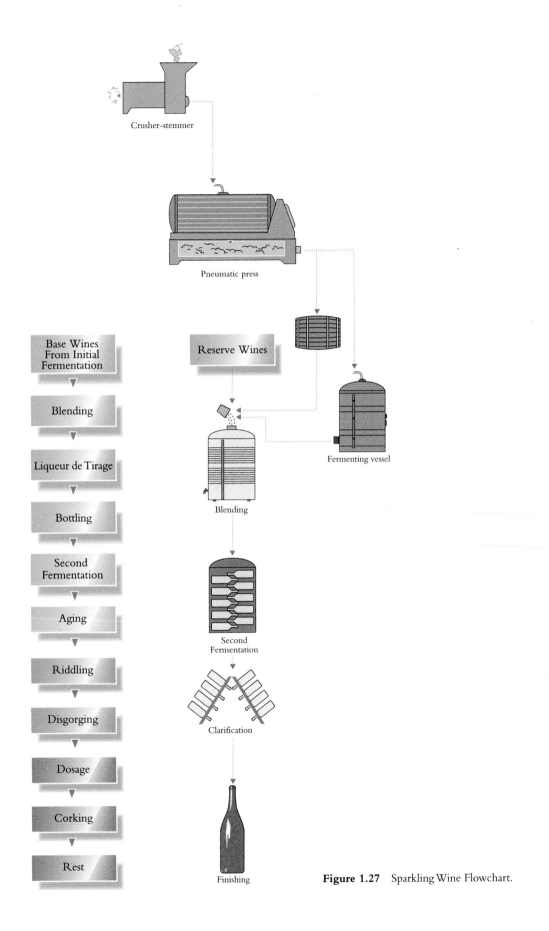

**Base Wines From Initial Fermentation**

↓

**Blending**

↓

**Liqueur de Tirage**

↓

**Bottling**

↓

**Second Fermentation**

↓

**Aging**

↓

**Riddling**

↓

**Disgorging**

↓

**Dosage**

↓

**Corking**

↓

**Rest**

Crusher-stemmer

Pneumatic press

Reserve Wines

Fermenting vessel

Blending

Second Fermentation

Clarification

Finishing

**Figure 1.27** Sparkling Wine Flowchart.

specific soil types in specific microclimates in the namesake region of northern France. Some other countries, the United States in particular, still use the generic term "champagne" to indicate any wine with bubbles in it.

The fame and respect earned by the sparkling wine producers of the Champagne region in France are reflected in the fact that many producers of sparkling wine around the world have adopted the methods of production developed there centuries ago. Three major methods are employed in making sparkling wine today:

- *Méthode Champenoise* (the traditional method of second fermentation in the bottle)

- **Transfer method** (a modified version of Champenoise)

- *Charmat* **(tank) method** (carbon dioxide gas is trapped in the tank)

*Méthode Champenoise.*   The word *"Champenoise"* refers to something that or somebody who comes from or belongs to the region of Champagne. True French Champagne producers are very protective about their heritage and about the use of terms and words which they believe are uniquely theirs. Thus, they have gone to great lengths in recent years to prevent non-Champagne producers from using the words *"Champagne"* or *"méthode Champenoise"* in the labeling or marketing of any non-Champagne product. The fervor with which today's French Champagne producers apply their protective efforts derives from a singular history which has inarguably provided immeasurable pleasure to millions of people (see the section on Champagne in Chapter 6 on France).

It is important to understand that from the second fermentation through the aging, release for sale, and service of the wine, true méthode champenoise sparkling wines stay in the same bottle. This entire process can last anywhere from 18 to 40 months, with some exceptional wines spending even longer in the aging stage (see late-disgorged Champagne in Chapter 6 on France). The pillars of the Champagne method are time and quality. It is a long, protracted, labor-intensive method, and usually reserved for higher-quality grape varieties.

*Initial Fermentation.*   Since almost all sparkling wine is white, we will restrict our commentary to the production of white sparkling wines. Sparkling wine starts its life the same as any other wine: white or red grapes are pressed, rapidly and gently, to provide a clear grape juice which is then put through the fermentation process, creating a dry white wine of 10.5 to 11 percent alcohol by volume. As with other still wines, the choice of container for the initial fermentation process will have an effect on the eventual flavor characteristics of the sparkling wine. Most base wines that later become sparkling wines are fermented in stainless steel.

*Blending.*   The majority of all Champagnes and other sparkling wines are nonvintage wines, blended together from wines from several years' harvests.

Blending Base Wines.

After a new batch of wine has been made from the most recent harvest, it is used as the primary base wine to which several other wines from previous years will be added with the intention of creating a still base wine which will eventually become a sparkling wine. The resulting wine offers the same characteristics and flavors as previous nonvintage bottlings from that producer. The intention is to offer a completely consistent product from bottling to bottling. The task of blending is enormously complex and challenging, and requires exceptional skill to marry together numerous wines into a final base wine whose character will change as it becomes sparkling wine, but will continue to reflect the consistent style of the individual producer.

***Bottling.*** The next stage in the méthode Champenoise is for the wine to be bottled. During the bottling process, a small quantity of a liquid yeast and sugar mixture, called the ***liqueur de tirage,*** is injected into each bottle of wine, and the bottle is capped with a "crown" cap, very much like a beer bottle cap. A few sparkling wine producers continue to use a cork, secured with an ***agraffe*** (metal clasp) to close the bottle at this stage.

The bottles are then stored on their sides, preferably in a cool, constant-temperature environment, like an undeground *cave* or cellar. During this time, the liqueur de tirage will work to cause a second fermentation in the bottle. The carbon dioxide gas created by the second fermentation remains trapped in the bottle. This second fermentation will take only three to four weeks to complete. All of the additional sugar will be converted to alcohol, resulting in a completely dry wine, with an *additional* 1 to 1.5 percent alcohol by volume, bringing the total alcohol by volume to approximately 12 to 12.5 percent.

A Sparkling Wine Bottle in Storage.

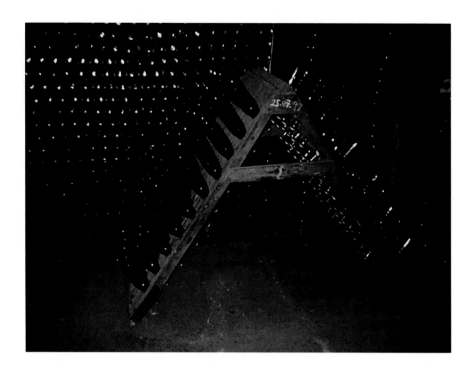

LA PROPRIETE DE L'
ÉT & CHAN

**DOM PÉRIGNON**
**1639 - 1715**

Dom Perignon.

The bottles remain in storage, on their side, for many more months. Producers of high-quality sparkling wines try to leave the bottles untouched for at least 12 months. In the case of some very fine Champagnes (from France), this time period may be as long as three years. During this time, the spent yeast cells from the second fermentation will lie as sediment along the lower side of the bottle, in contact with the wine in the bottle. The yeast cells are slowly destroyed by their own enzymes, a process referred to as **autolysis.** The slow breakdown of the yeast cells provides new opportunities for flavor development in the wine. This yeast contact time is of major importance in determining the style and character of the final sparkling wine. With a longer contact time, the wine develops more yeast characteristics, which will be noticeable in the aroma and flavor of the wine when it is opened. The most common descriptions of a wine with long yeast contact are that the wine has a "toasty," "biscuit," or "mealy" (as in freshly milled grains) aroma and flavor.

There is another important aspect to the length of time that the bottle remains in storage at this stage, following the second fermentation. A by-product of the second fermentation is carbon dioxide gas. In the second fermentation in the bottle, the gas cannot escape and is trapped in the bottle. There appears to be a correlation between the length of time in storage after the second fermentation and the size, consistency, and persistence of the bubbles that form when the bottle is opened. The longer the wine remains undisturbed, the more the carbon dioxide gas becomes incorporated into the wine, and the more slowly it will be released from the wine in the glass, assuming that the bottle has been opened, and the wine has been poured, in an appropriate manner (see the section on Champagne service in Chapter 15).

This stage of sparkling wine production underscores an extremely important point, not only with respect to sparkling wines, but to all wine production. There are some steps in wine production which most wine makers would agree are preferable because they result in a "better" wine. Some of these preferable steps, such as storage, take time—lots of time. And time, as the saying goes, is money. It requires a huge outlay on the part of any producer to harvest grapes in September, for example, make the wine, bottle it in January of the following year, and then leave the wine untouched until January or February of the next year—and even then the wine is not ready for distribution or sale. During all this time the wine has not earned one penny, but production costs continue to mount.

After Dom Perignon (see the section on Champagne in Chapter 6), those who followed in his footsteps worked on refining and developing the méthode Champenoise.

By the nineteenth century, the first commercial producers of Champagne deliberately put extra yeast cells and sugar into bottles of wine, and left them there, because they wanted the wine to develop the characteristics of yeasty aromas and flavors and small, fine bubbles. Yet they knew, as do modern sparkling wine producers, that this process presents an unenviable problem—a bottle of potentially fine sparkling wine, but marred by the presence of yeast sediment inside the bottle. There is some evidence, such as frosted Champagne glasses from previous centuries, to suggest that it was once accepted that yeast sediment in the bottle, even in the glass, was the price to pay for such a fine wine. The frosting on the glass would hide from sight any sediment which made its way from the bottle into the glass. It was not until the mid-nineteenth century that an indomitable and famous widow, Veuve Clicquot-Ponsardin, perfected the methods of working the sediment to the mouth of the bottle and then removing it without an ap-

Veuve Clicquot-Ponsardin.

Hand-riddling.

preciable loss in gas pressure (which would rid the wine of its precious bubbles).

The two steps in the process attributed to Veuve Clicquot are:

- *Rémuage* (riddling) to work the sediment to the mouth of the bottle

- *Dégorgement* (disgorging) to remove the sediment from the bottle

*Rémuage (Riddling).* When Veuve Clicquot first developed the riddling system, every step was done by hand, meaning that the complete process would take anywhere from six to eight weeks for a batch of about 5000 bottles. Some producers still use this hands-on method. After the second fermentation in the bottle, and after the aging period on the yeast sediment in the bottle, the bottles are taken from their resting place and inserted into large A-frame wooden racks, called *pupitres,* with the neck of the bottles pointing slightly downward. The yeast sediment at this stage appears as a strip, with many of the yeast cells adhering to the side of the bottle. The objective is for the *remueur,* or **riddler,** to maneuver the sediment into one manageable lump inside the bottle, and then to work the sediment down the inside of the bottle, into the bottle neck, and onto the stopper in the mouth of the bottle.

In order to do this, the following steps are performed repeatedly on each bottle:

- manually grasp the bottom end of each bottle

- shake the bottle slightly to dislodge any stuck yeast cells

- turn the bottle approximately one-eighth of a turn

- raise the bottom end of the bottle slightly

**Figure 1.28** Automated Riddling Machines.

• drop the bottle back into the hole in the rack

Gradually, this handling of the bottle coerces all of the sediment into the neck of the bottle, at which point the bottle is almost completely inverted in the rack.

Most large producers of méthode Champenoise sparkling wine use modern automated methods to riddle the wine (see Figure 1.28). In these systems, the bottles are placed upside down in large metal crates which are mounted on two large mechanical arms. In seven to ten days, through a series of rocking motions, these machines can riddle as many bottles as the remueur would take six to eight weeks to complete. There are also "semiautomatic" devices called gyro-palettes, where a hexagonal metal basket with an inverted cone-shaped base is filled with inverted bottles and occasionally rotated from side to side.

***Dégorgement (Disgorging).*** Again, when Veuve Clicquot first developed her methods, all disgorging was done by hand, bottle by bottle. The bottles were taken from their inverted position on the riddling rack and, using a pair of pliers, the stopper was removed from each bottle, allowing just a very small amount of wine to escape. When done properly, all of the sediment was carried away as well. Obviously, this method was haphazard at best. A major refinement came when Madame Clicquot realized that the whole bottle of wine should be as cold as possible, thereby reducing the carbon dioxide pressure in the bottle, and also reducing the tendency of the gas to escape when opening the bottle. (This is a very useful point to remember when opening any bottle of sparkling wine—always make sure it is well chilled.)

A modern refinement of this method is to freeze a small amount of wine in the inverted neck of each bottle (see Figure 1.29). When the stopper is removed, the gas pressure in the bottle is enough to propel the ice pellet (and all of the yeast sediment which is trapped in the pellet) from the bottle. In large modern facilities, all of these steps are now automated with large machines, which perform all of these functions within a very short space of time.

***Final Dosage or Liqueur d'Expédition.*** While the stopper is off the bottle, most producers of sparkling wine add a small amount of wine and liquid

**Figure 1.29** Yeast Sediment in the Neck of the Bottle.

Freezing the Yeast Sediment.

Adding the Final Dosage.

## TABLE 1.2
### SWEETNESS STYLES

| Category | Sweetness Level |
|---|---|
| Extra-Brut | Bone-dry, no dosage, or minimal dosage added |
| Brut | Dry, small dosage added |
| Extra-Dry | Medium-dry, noticeable sweetness |
| Sec | Medium-sweet |
| Demi-sec | Sweet |
| Doux | Very-sweet |

**Figure 1.30**  Champagne Corks.

sugar—the final **dosage**—to the bottle before inserting the cork (see Figure 1.30).

The amount of sugar added determines the style of the sparkling wine (see Table 1.2). The terms listed in Table 1.2 are the official sweetness designations for Champagne from France. Many of these terms, especially Brut, have been adopted by other sparkling wine-producing regions, with approximately the same meaning. After the final dosage, the bottles of wine are allowed to rest for three to six months before being released for sale.

## Transfer Method

Another method of making sparkling wine, the transfer method is similar to the méthode Champenoise, up to and including the second fermentation in the bottle. However, the transfer process differs radically from the méthode Champenoise after the fermentation in the bottle is complete. In an effort to save time, money, and labor, the sparkling wine is transferred to a special machine, where, under pressure, it is filtered in order to get rid of the sediment, dosage is added, and the wine is rebottled. This process does away with both rémuage and dégorgement, and produces a less-expensive, and some would say lower-quality, sparkling wine. Wines made by the transfer method, especially in North America, have labels which are permitted, by law, to state "fermented in the bottle," whereas sparklers made by the méthode Champenoise are permitted to use the phrase "fermented in *this* bottle" on the label.

## Charmat (Bulk) Method

A far cry from either the méthode Champenoise or the less-expensive transfer process, this method is simple, direct, and inexpensive. Still wine is placed in a closed, pressurized tank, and sugar and yeast are added to it to create a sparkling wine. The wine is filtered and clarified in bulk, and then bottled. In North America, if a sparkling wine is produced by this method (and many inexpensive sparklers that bear the generic label "champagne" are) the wine must be labeled as either "Bulk Method" or "Charmat Method." (If you were producing cheap sparkling wine, with bubbles the size of marbles, which label term would you choose: the endearing "bulk," or the oh-so-French "Charmat"?)

# Summary

Wine making is truly an art and a science. Pure scientific knowledge is applied in different humanistic, artistic ways to the same basic raw materials to achieve a broad and fascinating array of wine styles. The true art of the wine maker lies in the intuitive knowledge of what to do in different circumstances to achieve the desired result. At harvest time each year, the wine maker is presented with a completely different set of circumstances for each grape type, given that the growing conditions in any two years will probably never be identical. For every vintage, wine makers set out to make the best wine they can from the raw materials which come from the vineyards, and to do this they make a series of choices which determine how the wine will be made. They make judgments about pressing, about skin contact time, and about acidity and sugar levels. They decide whether a wine should age, how long it should age, and what kinds of containers should be used.

In Chapter 2 you will learn about the different grape varieties, their characteristics, and their principal areas of production. In the subsequent regionally themed chapters you will bring together the wine making practices and the grape varieties to learn about the prominent styles of wine from the major producing areas in the Old World and the New World.

### Chapter Two

# Wine Grapes

## Introduction

"That which we call a rose by any other name would smell as sweet" opines Juliet in Shakespeare's *Romeo and Juliet*. Those words were written in the latter half of the sixteenth century, when the world known to Europeans consisted mostly of Europe and North Africa, with the Mediterranean Sea at the center, and when the notion that the earth revolved around the sun was still looked on as heresy. Among the myriad changes which have occurred since those times, a rose is no longer simply a rose, it is a "Peace," or a "Sally Cousins," or any other of tens of thousands of different varieties.

The same rapid expansion of varieties within major groups has occurred in the world of fruits, so that the discerning apple consumer now asks for Empire, Mutsu, or Red Star King, and any grape grower in the world is faced with a dizzying array of choices, from the ubiquitous Chardonnay to the relatively obscure Madeleine Angevine.

This chapter surveys the evolution of grapes for wine making into two distinct groups: The *Vitis vinifera* species from Asia and Europe, and the very large group of native North American species. We will see how these two eventually came together, allowing for the continued survival of "wine as we know it."

Within the dominant *vinifera* family (more accurately referred to botanically as a species), we will describe the major grape varieties and some of the characteristics of wines made from each one. Lastly, this chapter will provide some basic information on grape growing, or **viticulture,** and outline the typical annual vine cycle and the principal systems used to train the vines as they grow each year. Our intention is to provide readers with enough information to associate the different grape varieties with some major growing areas, and to understand the stylistic variations of the major grape types.

# History
## *Eastern Origins*

Although there is archeologoical evidence of grapes and vine leaves from before the great Ice Age, most historians of wine agree that the modern grape used for wine production probably evolved as the family *Vitis vinifera* in what is now Iran around 2000 B.C. *Vitis* is the genus for many vine plants: *vinifera* comes from two Latin words meaning "to bear, or carry wine." In other words, these grapes are prized for use in making wine. Recognized as a plant which could be easily transplanted and as an economically stable crop, grape vines were commonly introduced by successive waves of invading tribes into newly dominated territory. In this way, the vine made its way out of the Middle East into the eastern Mediterranean; from there, around 500 B.C., the Greeks introduced grapevines into North Africa and southern Italy, and the Romans took the vines along in their occupation of western Europe as early as the first century B.C.

As the vine was transplanted into different climates, different "varieties" developed through mutations and sexual crossings. Subsequently, growers began to categorize the varieties and even "cloned" new varieties by vegetative propagation, using cuttings or buds taken from a "mother" vine. With time, some ancient varieties have been lost, and new varieties have emerged.

The spread of the vinifera grape varieties continued with the European colonization of new continents, and today hundreds of different varieties of vinifera grapes are grown throughout the world. In terms of consumer recognition, the major wine grape varieties grown across the globe are as follows:

| *White* | *Red* |
| --- | --- |
| Chardonnay | Cabernet Sauvignon |
| Sauvignon Blanc | Merlot |
| Riesling | Pinot Noir |
| Chenin Blanc | Cabernet Franc |

*(table continued on facing page)*

| White | Red |
|---|---|
| Gewürztraminer | Sangiovese |
| Pinot Blanc | Tempranillo |
| Pinot Gris | Syrah |
| Trebbiano | Grenache |
| Muscat | Zinfandel |
| Sémillon | Gamay |
| Müller-Thurgau | Nebbiolo |
| Seyval (a hybrid variety, limited mostly to the Eastern United States) | |

## The Western Parallel

Throughout all this period of time, vines were probably also growing on the North American continent. Certainly in the twelfth century, the Norwegian explorer Lief Erickson saw enough evidence of vines on the coastal stretches of North America to name the region "Vinland." But these vines were, and remain, a completely different family from the vinifera species, with very different characteristics of aroma, flavor, and balance of fruit to acid. In fact, the North American continent is home to several different non-vinifera species, with many varieties within each family. The principal species in North America are *Vitis labrusca, Vitis riparia, Vitis aestivalis,* and *Vitis rotundifolia.*

All of these native American species grow wild to the east of the Rocky Mountain range, but there were no vinifera varieties growing in America until they were imported from Europe.

It is reasonable to assume that Native American Indians used these grapes as food, and perhaps even made a beverage from them. There is certainly ample evidence to suggest that early European settlers made wines from these grapes, though they quickly realized how different they are from the vinifera grape varieties they had known in Europe. Early attempts by European settlers to grow vinifera vines in the eastern United States were thwarted by cold temperatures and diseases which killed the relatively delicate vinifera vines.

It was not until the mid-nineteenth century that the two distinct groupings of European vinifera grapes and the North American grape families came together as the solution to the pest *Phylloxera vastatrix* which had decimated most of France's vineyards, starting in the 1860s, and continuing on through the end of the century (see Chapter 6 on France).

## Phylloxera

The mid-1800s was an age of tremendous discovery, including the realization that science could be put to the service of humans. In the rush to learn

**Figure 2.1** *Phylloxera Vastatrix.*

*Phylloxera* continues to be a major pest in vineyards around the world.

*Phylloxera* Feeds on the Roots of Grapevines.

and explore, American vines were shipped to Europe as part of a general program of plant material exchange. It was not realized at the time that various plant diseases and microscopic insects were shipped along with the plant material. Having evolved with the diseases and insects, the American vines had developed immunity to them.

Thus, when the American vines were shipped to Europe, either an adult live form or the larva form of some insects went along with the vine, and among those insects was the *Phylloxera vastratix* (see Figure 2.1), hitherto unknown in Europe. As the American vines were planted in French soil, the *phylloxera* rapidly multiplied and spread onto existing vinifera vines.

The *phylloxera* bug has a very complex life cycle, the many stages of which live on different parts of the vine. In its "adolescent " aphid stage, *phylloxera* is a louse which lives on the root system of the vine, sustaining itself by sucking sap from the roots. The bug copes with its waste by injecting it back into the vine's roots. To the misfortune of all vinifera vines, the *phylloxera's* waste is poisonous to the vinifera family, and any vinifera vine infected by *phylloxera* will die within a couple of years.

*Grafting.* Although American vines are immune to the effects of *phylloxera,* European grape growers and wine makers did not want to plant American vines in their vineyards, because they could not accept the very different flavor profile of wine made from American vines. The solution was to graft the desirable fruit character of vinifera onto the sturdy, *phylloxera*-resistant American root system (see Figure 2.2). This is done by cutting a healthy fruit cane from the desired vinifera variety in such a way that it will fit into an accommodating cut made in the selected American root type.

Just as grape varieties differ in flavor, vine root types also exhibit different characteristics, and the prospective grape grower must select the correct root type for whatever grape variety is to be grown and for the soil type and climate.

The development of this solution and the perfection of grafting techniques took several years, by which time the *phylloxera* bug had spread throughout the vineyards of France and into the surrounding countries of Germany and Italy. With the solution of grafting, French grape growers could begin to reestablish their vineyards, but that was not the end of *phylloxera,* which went on to "conquer" almost every vineyard area in the world. There are areas which have remained *phylloxera*-free, either because of soil types which the *phylloxera* does not thrive in (e.g. Chile), or because of strict laws which govern the movement of machinery, people, and certified-disease-free cuttings (e.g. South Australia).

Still today, wherever anybody wants to grow vinifera grapes the only practical solution to *phylloxera* is to graft the vinifera grape varieties onto American rootstock. Even then, the grape grower may not be safe, as many Californian grape growers recently discovered. Though they had followed recommendations from the University of California at Davis to use a rootstock called AxR1, many vineyards in Napa Valley have now been infected with *phylloxera,* and the vines are dying. And it seems that the *phylloxera* has mutated into what is referred to as "bio-type B," to which some AxR1 root-

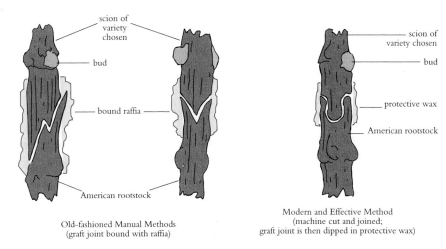

scion of variety chosen

bud

bound raffia

American rootstock

Old-fashioned Manual Methods
(graft joint bound with raffia)

scion of variety chosen

bud

protective wax

American rootstock

Modern and Effective Method
(machine cut and joined;
graft joint is then dipped in protective wax)

**Figure 2.2**   Newly Grafted Stock.

stocks are not resistant. The only solution, for now, is to replant the vineyards, this time using a more-resistant rootstock, and to hope that the *phylloxera* bug will not mutate for many human generations. For more information, see the section on *phylloxera* in Chapter 4.

## A New Family Grouping

The physical combination of an American rootstock onto the vinifera budding stock was only the beginning. Even in the late 1800s scientists, particularly in France, had begun experimenting on the biological cross-pollenization of different vine varieties and families. Botanists theorized, quite rightly, that it should be possible to create a *phylloxera*-resistant vine by crossing a vinifera plant with a North American plant.

From these crossings emerged a third group of grape vines called **direct producers**, or French-American **hybrids**. At one time, hybrid vines accounted for several millions of acres of vineyards in various parts of France. Today that acreage is drastically reduced, though there are still pockets of hybrid vineyards to be found. These vines have, to varying degrees of success, combined the winter hardiness and *phylloxera*-resistance of American vines with the fruit and flavor characteristics of the vinifera family. New hybrid grape varieties are still being developed in North America, most notably at the Cornell Viticultural Research Station in Geneva, in the Finger Lakes region of New York State.

Some of the more favored hybrid grapes grown for wine production are:

| White | Red |
|---|---|
| Seyval | de Chaunac |
| Vidal | Baco Noir |
| Vignoles | Maréchal Foch |

In North America, hybrid varieties are found mostly in cool growing regions, especially in the eastern United States and eastern Canada. A few areas in South America, particularly Brazil, also grow hybrid varieties. With one exception, hybrid grapes are not used to produce any *"vins de qualité"* in France, the exception being the white grape Baco 22A, which is widely used in the production of the base wine which is subsequently distilled into Armagnac brandy.

The science of cross-pollinating to create new grape varieties is not restricted to the creation of hybrids by crossbreeding between two vine families. The practice has been very successfully applied *within* the vinifera species to create new varieties which are still considered vinifera. This is especially true of the work done at Geisenheim in Germany, where new grape varieties are being developed to better cope with the cool climate and growing season of some of Germany's vineyard areas (see the section on grape types in Chapter 10 on Germany).

## Clones

As we have already stated, vines often adapt to new surroundings and climates, taking on slightly different characteristics from the parent plant. The differences are visible on the vine in terms of leaf formation or bud position and, occasionally, minor variations in the finished wine become apparent. These slight variations have resulted in what grape growers refer to as different "clones" of the same grape variety. To take a classic example, whereas it is correct to say that Chardonnay is the grape used to make white wine in the region of Burgundy in France, it is not true that exactly the same type of Chardonnay is being grown throughout Burgundy. As only a few examples, there is the Beurot clone, the Auxerrois clone, and the Musqué clone. Though they all taste of Chardonnay, there are differences in the way the vines grow, and there may be slightly different emphases in the flavor profile of each one. The same pattern is repeated with Pinot Noir within Burgundy, and with all grape varieties wherever they are grown.

# Major White Grape Varieties
## Chardonnay

Chardonnay is the grape for white French Burgundy wine, including the classic wines of Chablis and the Côte de Beaune (see Figure 2.3). This grape became the darling of the worldwide wine industry in the late 1980s when consumers felt comfortable requesting wines by specific grape type. For some reason, Chardonnay caught on in a big way, and more and more grape growers planted it so that more and more wine makers could produce it. To some extent, we are now seeing the backlash of such extreme popularity as

**Figure 2.3** Chardonnay Grapes.

consumers are faced with an ocean of fairly mediocre wines labeled as expensive Chardonnay.

Nevertheless, Chardonnay does deserve its prominent place in the wine world since, at its best, it is responsible for the wonderful white wines of Burgundy, and can produce extremely good wines in the United States, Australia, and South Africa. When grown in a conducive, cool climate, Chardonnay will retain enough acidity to keep the wine tasting fresh and to balance the ripe apple flavors which are the benchmark of this grape. The very best examples of cool-climate Chardonnay wines can develop a depth and length of flavor which will make for truly memorable experiences.

What perhaps makes the Chardonnay grape so attractive to grape growers and wine makers is that it responds well to many different growing conditions and wine making techniques. It grows well both in the coolest regions of northern France and the warmer regions of California. Many wine makers have successfully used stainless steel throughout the production process; others prefer to use oak barrels from beginning to end (see the section on containers in Chapter 1 on How Wine Is Made).

Most importantly perhaps, consumers have shown various preferences, from the completely dry, acidic, steely, true Chablis, to the fruity, forward, squeaky-clean California-style Chardonnay, to the big, ripe, oaky, buttery style of Australia. Because of the plethora of styles, it is difficult to offer a general description of Chardonnay, except that it is usually made in a medium-to full-bodied style, with medium to full intensity of apple fruit aroma and flavor. Its concentrated, complex character becomes even more noticeable if the grapes are from a warmer climate, or if the wine was made or aged in oak barrels.

| Classic growing areas: | Burgundy and Champagne in France. |
| | Northeastern Italy |
| New growing areas: | Just about everywhere wants to grow Chardonnay, but the areas doing a good job include: |
| | California, Oregon, Washington State, and New York in the United States |
| | Western Australia, South Australia, and Hunter Valley in Australia |
| | Stellenbosch in South Africa |
| | Marlborough in New Zealand |
| | Toscana in Italy |

## Sauvignon Blanc

**Figure 2.4** Sauvignon Blanc Grapes.

Sauvignon Blanc is the principal grape of many of the great white wines of Bordeaux, and the only grape in some of the Loire Valley's fine white wines (see Figure 2.4). If there is any chance that Chardonnay will one day lose its prominent position, Sauvignon Blanc is the main pretender to the crown. In the past, some wines made from Sauvignon Blanc have been criticized for having too much of a grassy, haylike character. At its worst, Sauvignon Blanc does seem to develop an aroma of cat urine. However, the days of such wines seem to be in the past. Wine makers all over the world are now sensitive to the demands of Sauvignon Blanc, and realize that it needs careful nurturing as a grape and as a wine.

What we generally find now are fresh, clean, fruity wines which are medium bodied with medium-flavor intensity. In the coolness of the Loire Valley in France, or the Marlborough region of New Zealand, Sauvignon Blanc shows the character of only-just-ripe green fruit such as gooseberry or green plums, with very high, piercing acidity. In the warmer areas of California or Bordeaux, the fruit quality may be closer to that of apricots.

In the Loire Valley, the local grape growers refer to Sauvignon Blanc as the "Blanc Fumé," and other grape growers around the world have adopted that name or "Fumé Blanc" to label their wines.

| Classic growing areas: | Bordeaux and Loire in France |
| | Northeastern Italy |
| New growing areas: | Marlborough in New Zealand |
| | Washington State and California in the United States |
| | Stellenbosch in South Africa |
| | Maipo Valley in Chile |
| | Toscana in Italy |

**Figure 2.5** Riesling Grapes.

# Riesling

Riesling is the prized grape of Germany's noble wines from the Mosel and Rhine areas (see Figure 2.5). For some reason, the Riesling grape seems to have lost favor among consumers, though it was once highly sought after, and may again enjoy a prominent position in the future. Wines made from Riesling are usually of a light to medium body, with a floral, very fruity character and an implicit, if not obvious, sweetness.

Perhaps Riesling's current lack of popularity stems from the perception that Riesling wines are always sweet; such is not the case. There are some excellent dry Riesling wines made in Alsace, and some producers in California, New York, and Australia make very good dry Rieslings. Despite its reputation for sweet wines, Germany also produces some fine dry Rieslings (see Chapter 10, on Germany).

When made as sweet wine, Riesling can be outstanding, mostly because of the ability of the Riesling grape to retain fresh balancing acidity even with high sugar. New World sweet Rieslings are usually identified as "Late Harvest" or *"Botrytis."* Though prized as a noble grape variety, Riesling can be difficult to grow, as it really needs a long, cool growing season to come to perfect ripeness, leaving it at the mercy of both spring and fall frosts.

Classic growing areas:   Mosel-Saar-Ruwer, Rheingau, Rheinhessen, and Pfalz in Germany

Alsace in France

Northeastern Italy (where it is labeled "Rhine Riesling" or "Riesling Renano")

**Figure 2.6** Gewürztraminer Grapes.

| New growing areas: | New York, California, and Washington State in the United States (where it is labeled "Johannisberg Riesling" or "White Riesling") |
| | South Australia in Australia (where it is labeled "Rhine Riesling") |

## Gewürztraminer

Along with the Riesling variety, Gewürztraminer has been one of the jewels in the crown of Alsace for many years (see Figure 2.6). This grape produces very attractive wines, offering everything that Riesling does, but with more emphatic fruit character, and an unmistakable touch of cinnamon spice. Some people say that it smells just like lychee nuts.

| Classic growing areas: | Alsace in France |
| | Trentino in Italy |
| New growing areas: | New York, Washington State, and California in the United States |

## Chenin Blanc

For many wine lovers, Chenin Blanc finds its best expression in the Loire Valley of France where the cool climate seems to provide perfect growing conditions (see Figure 2.7). Wines made from Chenin Blanc are usually light in body and flavor intensity, with delicate flavors and just a hint of implicit sweetness; they may exhibit aromas of melons or honey with a nutty over-tone, and some smell a bit like beeswax. The tendency of the grape to main-

**Figure 2.7** Chenin Blanc Grapes.

**Figure 2.8** Pinot Blanc Grapes.

tain high acid levels keeps the wines fresh and clean, when made semi-sweet to sweet as they sometimes are in the Loire Valley in France.

Classic growing areas:      Loire in France

New growing areas:          California in the United States

South Africa (where it is often called "Steen")

## Pinot Blanc

Wines made from Pinot Blanc often come across as light- to medium-bodied, with similar characteristics to Chardonnay, but they are much less obvious in flavor and somehow more simple and less elegant (see Figure 2.8).

| Classic growing areas: | Alsace in France |
| --- | --- |
| | Trentino in Italy (where it is called "Pinot Bianco") |
| | Baden and Württemburg in Germany (where it is called "Weisburgunder") |
| New growing areas: | California in the United States (where it is often used as one of the grapes in the blend used to make sparkling wines, contributing ripe fruit and spice aromas as well as a fullness of texture) |

## Pinot Gris

A slightly nutty overtone in aroma and flavor adds a complexity or layered effect to wines made from the Pinot Gris (see Figure 2.9). Depending on their origin, the wines can be light-bodied and refreshing, as in Italy, or medium-to full-bodied with more emphatic flavor, as in Alsace.

| Classic growing areas: | Alsace in France (where the label may read "Tokay d'Alsace Pinot Gris") |
| --- | --- |
| | Northeastern Italy (where it is called "Pinot Grigio") |
| | Baden in Germany (where it is called "Grauburgunder" or "Rülander") |
| New growing areas: | Oregon in the United States |
| | Toscana in Italy |

**Figure 2.9** Pinot Gris Grapes Showing Signs of *botrytis* Mold.

## Trebbiano

In terms of acreage, this is a very important grape, inside and outside of Italy, although, on its own, it does not produce any great wines. The straight Trebbiano wines of central Italy are simple, light, and honest. Sometimes compared to a "weed" because it is so prolific, Trebbiano has the honor, however, of adding to the fruitiness of such Italian greats as Chianti and Soave. It is also thought to be the same grape as the Ugni Blanc, which is widely planted in Cognac and Armagnac where it is used to make brandy.

| Classic growing areas: | Throughout Italy |
| --- | --- |
| New growing areas: | California in the U.S. |

## Muscat

There are many clones of the Muscat grape, and most of them are associated with sweet wines. While Muscat is made as a great sweet wine in places around the Mediterranean basin, dry versions of the Muscat can be found in Alsace. It is also the grape used to make Asti (formerly Asti Spumante), a very fruity, light, sparkling wine in northern Italy. In all cases, the fruity character of the Muscat grape shines through with full, luscious flavors. The sweeter wines usually display a greater richness in the glass and on the palate.

| | |
|---|---|
| Classic growing areas: | Alsace, Southern Rhône, and Midi in France |
| | Southern Portugal |
| | Most of Italy |
| | Greece |
| | Crete |
| New growing areas: | Victoria in Australia |
| | California in the United States |

## Sémillon

Sémillon is a much-overlooked grape which produces some truly outstanding wines on its own (see Figure 2.10). It is grown throughout the Graves region in Bordeaux, France where it is blended with Sauvignon Blanc to make dry white wines. In Sauternes and Barsac it is often affected by *botrytis* and is a major component in the sweet white wines of those areas (see Figure 2.11).

**Figure 2.10**  Sémillon Grapes.

**Figure 2.11**  Sémillon Grapes with *botrytis.*

Depending on the vintage, it is sometimes the only grape used to make the glorious sweet Sauternes wine, Château d'Yquem. It has been produced for decades as a dry wine in parts of Australia, resulting in a wine of great depth and exceptional aging ability. It is also made as a sweet wine in Australia.

As a dry wine, it has medium to full body and flavor intensity, with an aroma of lanolin and peaches or ripe apricots. The sweet versions are more viscous and more concentrated in their fruit character.

Classic growing areas:    Bordeaux in France

New growing areas:    California and Washington State in the United States

Hunter Valley in Australia

## Müller-Thurgau

Developed by Professor Müller at the Geisenheim research station in Germany from a cross between Riesling and Silvaner, the Müller-Thurgau grape provides growers with an early ripening, very fruity variety. It is a grape variety which offers many of the attractive, delicate aromas and flavors of the Riesling variety, but within a shorter growing season, making it a more dependable ripener in cooler climates. Because of these attributes it is now the most widely planted grape throughout Germany. It produces wines with atttractive fruitiness, a hint of sweetness, but without the depth and breed of the Riesling grape.

Classic growing areas:    Most of Germany

Trentino-Alto Adige in Italy

New growing areas:    England

New Zealand

## Seyval

To date, this seems to be the one hybrid grape variety which has won unconditional acceptance from grape growers, wine makers, and (most importantly) consumers, at least in the eastern United States. It has the adaptability of Chardonnay, offering a light, clean, fruity wine when cold-fermented in stainless steel, or a heavier, richer, more-intense and complex wine when given oak barrel treatment.

Classic growing areas:    None

New growing areas:    Eastern United States

## Secondary White Grape Varieties

(in alphabetical order)

*Albariño/Alvarinho.*   Planted mostly in Spain and Portugal for light, refreshing wines.

*Aligoté.*   Used in Burgundy in France for lesser-quality wines.

*Colombard.*   Fairly neutral in flavor, but a high-acid grape, grown in Western France mostly for brandy production. Very large acreage in California for bulk wine production and for inexpensive sparkling wines.

*Cortese.*   Grown in Northern Italy to make light, refreshing wines.

*Garganega.*   The major grape in Soave from Northern Italy.

*Macabeo.*   One of the grapes used in most blends to make Spanish sparkling wines.

*Marsanne.*   Associated mostly with Rhône Valley in France, but increasing acreage in Australia and California. Produces fruity, medium-bodied wines.

*Melon de Bourgogne.*   Planted widely in the western section of the Loire Valley in France to make light, refreshing Muscadet wines.

*Parellada.*   Used in Spain, usually in blends for still and sparkling wine production.

*Rkatsiteli.*   Planted widely in Russia to produce fragrant, light wines with a hint of sweetness. Small acreage in New York.

*Thompson Seedless.*   Widely planted in California and Australia, producing neutral base wines for blending in jug wine production. Also used for raisin production.

*Viognier.*   Grown in the Rhône Valley in France to make medium-bodied, fairly complex white wines. Increasing acreage in California.

*Xarel-lo.*   One of the grapes used in most blends to make Spanish sparkling wines.

# Major Red Grape Varieties
## Cabernet Sauvignon

Cabernet Sauvignon is the major grape responsible for the great Bordeaux wines of Château Lafite-Rothschild, Château Mouton-Rothschild, Château

**Figure 2.12** Cabernet Sauvignon Grapes.

Margaux, and Château Latour (see Figure 2.12). In recent years, what Chardonnay has been for white wines, Cabernet Sauvignon has been for red wines. Why this is so is hard to understand since Cabernet Sauvignon is definitely not everybody's favorite red wine. Its apparent popularity may be due to its reputation as the major grape used to produce the fine Bordeaux château wines. But this apparent popularity does not necessarily translate into case sales when Cabernet Sauvignon is produced as a single-variety wine, as is the case in the United States and other New World areas.

As a grape, Cabernet Sauvignon is very small, with one of the highest ratios of skin to juice. It is a grape with medium to high acidity, with intense blackcurrant aromas and flavors which can be masked by high levels of tannin.

Produced as a single-variety red wine, Cabernet Sauvignon can be everything that white wine drinkers hate about red wine. At its worst, it may appear to be harsh and astringent (from the tannin), sour (from the acidity), very dry and drying, and strongly flavored (if you could get behind the tannins to taste anything). That is why more and more producers in the New World are following the Bordeaux model of blending Cabernet Sauvignon grapes with softer, less-aggressive varieties, such as Merlot, in California or Shiraz, in Australia, thus producing a more approachable wine with fewer hard edges and a softer, smoother character. Nevertheless, it should be noted that there are some fine examples of 100 percent Cabernet Sauvignon wines to be found and enjoyed.

Classic growing areas:    Bordeaux in France especially Médoc and Graves

Northeastern Italy

New growing areas:     California, Washington State, Texas, and New York in the United States

Western Australia, South Australia, and Victoria in Australia

Toscana in Italy

Penedés and Ribera del Duero in Spain

Maipo Valley in Chile

Mendoza in Argentina

## Merlot

Merlot is the primary grape of the Pomerol district of Bordeaux in France, contributing up to 95 percent of the blend in the great wine of Château Petrus (see Figure 2.13). Having learned the hard way with Cabernet Sauvignon on its own, many consumers have recently turned to Merlot as their preferred single-variety red wine. The Merlot grape is bigger than Cabernet Sauvignon, with a lot more juice as compared to skin area. It is a thinner-skinned grape, with lower tannin levels and lower acid levels. Measure for measure, Merlot always produces a softer, smoother, fruitier, more-accessible wine than Cabernet Sauvignon, though many would argue that in the long haul, Cabernet Sauvignon will always retain the crown of champions as the main ingredient in some of the world's finest red wines.

Classic growing areas:     Bordeaux in France, especially Pomerol and St-Emilion

Northeastern Italy

**Figure 2.13**   Merlot Grapes.

New growing areas:        California, Washington State, and New York in the United States

## *Pinot Noir*

Pinot Noir seems to be in its element when grown in Burgundy in France where it produces some of the world's finest red wines (see Figure 2.14). Outside of Burgundy, the thin-skinned, lightly-pigmented Pinot Noir produces some of the lightest, least-tannic red wines. But it is a difficult grape to grow, requiring a long, cool growing season, and it is a difficult grape to turn into good wine. There are many in the wine world who would agree that when Pinot Noir is good, it is exceptional, but when it is bad it is atrocious. For this reason, its success has been limited, in terms of both where it is grown and how well the consumer has accepted it.

At its finest, Pinot Noir will produce a wine of medium intensity of fruitiness, just enough tannin to give it structure, high acidity for delicacy and freshness, a floral, herbal aroma, red berry or cherry flavors, and a silky seductive texture which is truly beguiling. At its worst, the floral aroma will decay into the euphemistically named "barnyard" aroma (an unattractive animal, feral smell), the wine's delicacy becomes lightness, fruitiness just is not there, and the acidity only provides a sour taste.

Perhaps more than any other wine, Pinot Noir is the model for *caveat emptor* ("let the buyer beware") when it comes to wine. Consumers must rigorously seek out and demand quality, and stick with a quality producer when they find one; even then, there will sometimes be surprises.

Classic growing areas:     Burgundy and Champagne in France

New growing areas:       California, Oregon, and New York in the United States
Marlborough in New Zealand
Toscana and Alto-Adige in Italy

**Figure 2.14**  Pinot Noir Grapes.

## Cabernet Franc

Related to the Cabernet Sauvignon, Cabernet Franc is also a small grape with high acidity, but it has a less-intense flavor profile and a distinctive mineral, ash-like aroma (see Figure 2.15). With the exception of the Loire Valley in France, where for decades it has been produced as a single variety wine, Cabernet Franc is most often used to blend with Cabernet Sauvignon and Merlot, as in Bordeaux.

As a blending grape, it is prized for its acidity, distinctive aroma, and strawberry-like fruit qualities. As a single-variety wine, it is usually light to medium-bodied, with fresh acidity and medium intensity of flavor.

Classic growing areas:     Bordeaux and Loire in France

                           Northeastern Italy

New growing areas:         Limited quantities in California, Washington State, and
                           New York in the United States, usually for blending

**Figure 2.15**   Cabernet Franc Grapes.

## Sangiovese

For many years, this grape remained relatively obscure, since its main notoriety was as the majority grape in the blend used to make Chianti (see Figure 2.16). It is now recognized as capable of producing very fine wines on its own, both within Italy and elsewhere. It is prized for its distinctive floral and herbal aromas and its sour cherry flavors. The most famous examples of 100 percent Sangiovese wines are labeled Brunello di Montalcino. As with all grape varieties, there are sub-varieties and clones. In the most simplistic terms, Sangiovese can be subdivided into the Sangiovese Grosso sub-variety

**Figure 2.16**   Sangiovese Grapes.

(Brunello, Prugnolo Gentile, and Morellino clones), and the Sangiovese Picolo sub-variety.

| | |
|---|---|
| Classic growing areas: | Toscana in Italy |
| New growing areas: | California in the United States |

## Tempranillo

Again, this grape has only recently received the recognition it deserves as the key to some of the finest wines produced in northern Spain, where it provides the wine with sturdiness, a backbone of acidity and tannin, and a depth of fruit flavor.

| | |
|---|---|
| Classic growing regions: | Rioja, Ribera del Duero, and Cataluña in Spain. |
| New growing regions: | Small acreage in California in the United States |

## Syrah

To wine lovers all around the world, Syrah means the Rhône Valley in France, particularly the northern section where it is used to produce the great wines of Hermitage and Côte Rotie. This very full-flavored grape is renowned for producing strong, sturdy wines of deep purple color, capable of aging for many years. It seems to thrive in warmer climates, providing a lot of tannins, but retaining enough acidity to keep the wines tasting fresh.

| | |
|---|---|
| Classic growing areas: | Rhône Valley in France |
| New growing areas: | South Australia, Victoria, and Hunter Valley in Australia (where it is called "Shiraz") |
| | California in the United States (where it is sometimes spelled "Sirah"—the grape called the "Petite Sirah" in California has been identified as the "Durif," also grown in southern France) |
| | Toscana in Italy |

## Grenache

In the southern section of the Rhône Valley, the Grenache is the dominant grape, being the primary grape in the blend for such great wines as Châteauneuf-du-Pape (see Figure 2.17). Another grape which thrives in warmer climates, Grenache produces soft, smooth, round wines with mouthfuls of ripe, sweet, red plum flavors. Like Syrah, with which it is often blended in the Rhône Valley, it can attain high sugar levels when ripe, providing the wines with alcohol levels in the 13, 14, even 15 percent range. Its

**Figure 2.17** Grenache Grapes.

major disadvantage is that it is prone to oxidation, as a grape, as juice, and as wine, which often means that the wines turn out with a distinct orange-brown note in the color. The advantage of wines which oxidize quickly is that they are usually softer and more accessible when young.

| | |
|---|---|
| Classic growing areas: | Rhône Valley in France |
| | Sardegna (Sardinia) in Italy where it is called "Cannonau" |
| | Rioja and Cataluña in Spain (where it is called "Garnacha") |
| New growing areas: | California and Washington State in the United States |

## Zinfandel

This grape is often thought of as *the* California grape (see Figure 2.18), though researchers have identified it as being the same as the Primitivo grape of southern Italy. It is an adaptable grape for wine making. Decades ago, Zinfandel was already a mainstay of many blended wines produced in California since it was recognized as providing huge amounts of ripe berry flavors, and lots of sugar for sweetness and alcohol. Its main use now is in the production of the light "blush" or pink wines called White Zinfandel which are fruity, simple-but-honest wines. Zinfandel grapes can also be used to produce classic, full-bodied red wines, particularly from the Sierra Foothills and North Coast areas of California.

**Figure 2.18** Zinfandel Grapes.

# SUTTER HOME'S WHITE ZINFANDEL

According to the president of Sutter Home Winery, Louis "Bob" Trinchero (see Figure 2.19), the story goes something like this: The Trinchero family had owned the Sutter Home Winery on the main highway in Napa Valley since 1947, and Bob learned wine making from the ground up, taking over all wine-making duties when his uncle retired in 1958.

The preferred style of wine for Americans at that time was strongly flavored, high-alcohol, even sweet red wines, and Bob was able to meet the demand for that style of wine easily by buying various grapes from growers around the valley. Bob unabashedly accepts that it was a jug wine business. That's to say, people would bring a large jug to the winery, and Bob would fill it up for a dollar!

A man named Darrel Corti owned, with his brother, an upscale grocery store business in Sacramento. In 1968, during one of his visits with Bob Trinchero, Corti asked Bob to taste a homemade Zinfandel wine made from grapes grown in the Sierra Foothills of Amador County. Bob was so impressed by the full-flavored intensity of the wine that he arranged to buy Zinfandel grapes from the same grower that fall, and Bob made the first of many highly acclaimed Amador County Zinfandels.

For the 1972 vintage, Bob thought he would try to make the Zinfandel even fuller by extracting some of the clear juice from the red grapes before fermentation. This had the effect of reducing the amount of juice in relation to the quantity of pulp and skins which provide the color and flavor. The result was indeed a bigger, sturdier, fuller-flavored Zinfandel.

Not wanting to waste anything, Bob had also made the clear juice from the Zinfandel grapes into a dry, barrel-aged white wine, thus creating the first White Zinfandel which became very popular with some of the locals and winery workers. Three years later, the batch of White Zinfandel did not ferment to complete dryness, leaving a small amount of residual sugar in the wine, a style which the tasting room regulars enjoyed even more and which has become the standard for Sutter Home White Zinfandel ever since.

Of all the wines sold by single-grape variety label in the United States, White Zinfandel held the number one position for many years, and of all White Zinfandel sold, Sutter Home sells more than any other label. In 1994, this number one sales position was taken over by Chardonnay.

**Figure 2.19** Louis "Bob" Trinchero, Chairman of the Board and Chief Executive Officer of Sutter Home Winery.

Classic growing areas:     California in the United States

New growing areas:     Brazil

South Africa

## *Nebbiolo*

The grape responsible for producing Barolo, the wine referred to as "the king of wines, and the wine of kings" (see Chapter 7 on Italy) is obviously something to be reckoned with. Nebbiolo is capable of producing big, full-bodied wines, with high tannin levels when young, but capable of evolving into elegant, velvety-smooth wines with flavors of ripe fruit, overtones of tea, and a distinct aroma of tar and leather. Some Nebbiolo wines have more noticeable wood character if they are aged in small oak barrels as opposed to the more traditional large oak casks.

Classic growing areas:     Piemonte in Italy

New growing areas:     Very limited quantities in California in the United States

# Gamay

In the wine lexicon, the Gamay grape and wine from the Beaujolais region of France are almost synonymous (see Figure 2.20). The more lowly but no-less-dignified Gamay is at the opposite end of the spectrum from the revered and powerful Cabernet Sauvignon. Once vilified by Philip the Bold as "that filthy grape" and banished by him from the northern stretches of Burgundy forever, the Gamay now thrives in Southern Burgundy and other parts of France, and has found a home in the New World. The wines made from Gamay vary in intensity, but the majority are light, fresh, and fruity. Were it not for the fresh, bright red color, they would be more in the style of many white wines than red, making them the perfect red wine for outdoor barbecues, picnics, and summertime drinking.

Classic growing areas:    Beaujolais in France

New growing areas:    California in the United States (though the grape called the "Gamay Beaujolais" in California is in fact a clone of Pinot Noir).

**Figure 2.20**   Gamay Grapes.

# Secondary Red Grape Varieties

(in alphabetical order)

***Alicante Bouchet.***   Widely grown in Spain for lesser-quality wine production. Once widely grown in California for the same purpose, but has decreased in acreage. Some renewed interest in California for producing Rhône-style wines.

***Barbera.***   Grown in Northern Italy for medium- to full-bodied wines with dark ruby color and high acidity. Also once occupied large acreage in California for jug wine production and is found in Argentina.

***Carignane.***   A grape which thrives in warmer climates such as California or Southern France.

***Cinsaut (sometimes spelled Cinsault, especially in the United States).***   One of the grapes used in blends in the Southern Rhône Valley in France. Increasing acreage in California. Widely planted in South Africa.

***Corvina.***   One of the grapes used in the blend to make Valpolicella and Bardolino in Northern Italy.

***Molinara.***   One of the grapes used in the blend to make Valpolicella and Bardolino in Northern Italy.

***Mourvèdre.***   One of the grapes used in blends in the Southern Rhône Val-

**Figure 2.21** Pinot Meunier Grapes.

ley in France; widely planted in South Australia as **Mataro**. Increasing acreage in California.

***Petit Verdot.*** One of the grapes authorized for use in the blends of red Bordeaux wines. Also being planted in California and Australia for the same purpose of blending.

***Pinot Meunier.*** The other red grape permitted in the blend to make Champagne in France (see Figure 2.21). Also increasingly used by New-World sparkling wine producers.

***Rondinella.*** One of the grapes used in the blend to make Valpolicella and Bardolino in Northern Italy.

# Viticulture

## *The Vine Cycle*

The following description is necessarily general, and the months mentioned apply only to vineyards in the Northern Hemisphere. Add six months for the Southern Hemisphere; for example, March becomes September. Since grape growing is a never-ending cycle, it is difficult to choose a starting point. We will start at the point immediately following harvest, as the plant goes into dormancy, and then follow the vine's developments through the following year's harvest.

In many of the classic grape-growing regions of Europe, such as Bordeaux or Piemonte, the harvest is completed by the end of September or beginning of October, and once the fruit has been picked the plant goes into a dormant stage as the leaves turn color and drop. (Figure 2.22 shows the parts of a vine plant.) At the same time, as the sap falls back toward the trunk and the root system, where it is protected from cold temperatures in the months to come, the canes (branches) that bore fruit during the summer become more brittle.

There are two major tasks to be accomplished in the vineyard during the winter months. The first is to protect the vine from severe cold, and the second is to prune the vine in readiness for fruit production the following spring and summer. If cold weather is a factor, some vineyard managers mound earth around the base of each vine to provide an extra layer of insulation for the trunk and root system. In even colder climates, grape growers have been known to untie the vines from the wire support system, lay them on the ground, and cover the entire plant with earth.

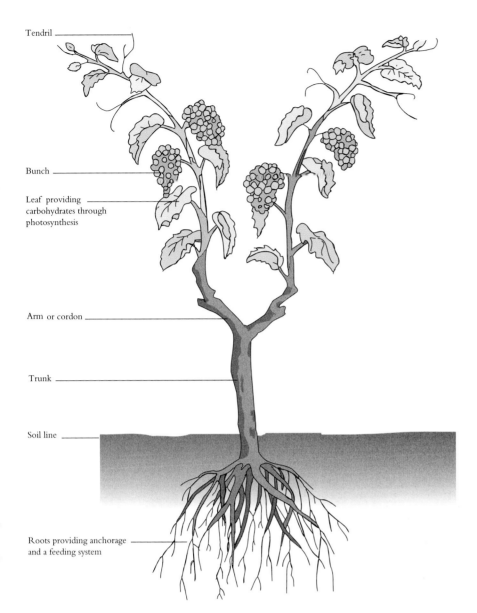

Tendril

Bunch

Leaf providing
carbohydrates through
photosynthesis

Arm or cordon

Trunk

Soil line

Roots providing anchorage
and a feeding system

**Figure 2.22** Diagram of Vine Plant
Showing Parts.

## Pruning

In most grape-growing areas, pruning is done during the two to three
months following harvest. Again, in climates where cold weather sets in very
quickly, the pruning is delayed until late winter or early spring. This helps to
delay the bursting of the buds in spring so that they will not be affected by
frost. It is the buds at the end of the cane which burst first. If the canes are
left unpruned in cold climates, it is the buds at the very tip of the previous
year's long canes which will develop first and be hit by any damaging frost.
The buds left after pruning will remain undamaged.

Pruning is really a controlling process, since it dictates how many buds
will bloom next spring, and therefore how many flowers and grapes will de-

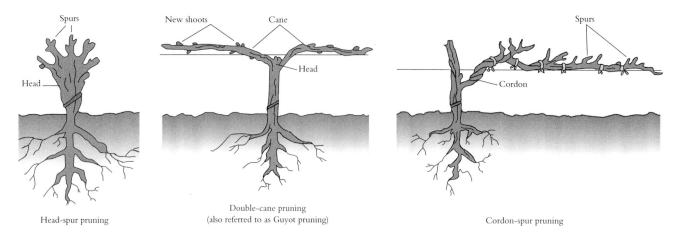

Figure 2.23   Three Main Types of Pruning.

velop. Left to its own devices, a vine will produce an abundance of foliage and fruit, but the grape grower tends to follow the old axiom that "lower quantity brings higher quality." So, pruning is a balancing act between producing a small number of high-quality bunches, and producing enough grapes to be profitable.

As the vine is pruned, the vine canes are trained to grow in a certain manner. The three main types of pruning are:

- Head-spur pruning

- Cane pruning

- Cordon-spur pruning

The **head-spur** system (see Figure 2.23), which leaves the vine in a small bush shape, has traditionally been used in places such as Beaujolais and the Rhône Valley in France. This system is particularly favored by grape growers who want to keep the grape bunches close to the ground where they can benefit from heat reflected from the soil during the day, and from radiated heat given off in the evening as the air temperature cools. The disadvantage of such a system is that grapes developing close to the ground can be more easily hit by late spring frosts, so it is generally not used in cool climates.

The **cane pruning** system has many variations, but essentially one, two, or four canes will be left after pruning (see Figure 2.23). Each cane will have a predetermined number of buds left on it, as decided by the grape grower; each bud will produce new shoots. Throughout the world, the most common type of pruning has been the two-cane system.

The third system, **cordon-spur,** is a combination of the other two, with established canes extended along the support system (see Figure 2.23). The vine is then pruned to short spurs, usually having two buds each, along the cordon. The cordon-spur system is particularly suited to mechanical pruning and harvesting and is therefore becoming increasingly popular.

## Spring Growth and Flowering

After pruning, a vineyard looks its tidiest, with the neatly trimmed vines standing in orderly array against the stark winter earth. With the warm temperatures of spring, the sap rises, and the buds left by the pruners break open to produce leaves and new cane growth. This generally happens in April, depending on the climate, and by the beginning of June the vine's flowers are visible. The months of March, April, and May can be hazardous for grape growers anywhere, as the vines are often subjected to sudden late frosts, battering winds, or even hailstorms. Assuming that the vine escapes these hazards and produces flowers, tradition holds that the fruit will be harvested 100 days after flowering.

## Fruit Development

After the flower petals drop the grape berries are visible, though at this stage the grapes look like tiny, green ball bearings.

Regardless of whether the vine is a red or white grape type, the grapes stay green until they have reached full size, around the middle of August. At this point, the grapes go through **veraison,** or color change, so that the grower begins to see the more familiar yellow-green of so-called white grapes, or the deep purple of so-called red grapes.

Though harvest is not far off, the grapes still taste very sour since they contain high levels of tartaric and malic acids, and a small amount of citric acid, as well as energy in the form of carbohydrates. As the carbohydrates are converted to sugars, the grapes take on more and more sweetness and develop their own varietal flavor characteristics.

## Harvest

To predict a harvest date, the grape grower begins taking readings of sugar levels and acidity levels (see additional information on sugar readings in Chapter 1 on How Wine Is Made). It is important to monitor these levels regularly, as they change rapidly depending on the weather. In good years, the weather will stay warm into September, allowing the sugars to build and acidity levels to drop. Any rain at this point may be drawn up from the soil by the vine and distributed to the grapes, resulting in a diluted sugar level. Any cold temperatures close to harvest will keep acidity levels high and sugar levels low. However, high temperatures at this time can be just as damaging, resulting in either low acid levels in the grapes (which translate into a flat, dull character in the wine) or elevated sugar levels (which will give the wine too much alcohol or too much sweetness). Prolonged hot temperaures also tend to "bake out" or weaken some of the flavor components, leaving a less complex flavor and aroma.

The harvest of any agricultural product is a joyous time for all involved as another season's work comes to a close and the fruits of one's labor can be seen, touched, and tasted. In the case of wine, as the grape harvest moves into the winery to be transformed into juice and then wine, work in the vineyard continues as the vines move into the dormancy stage ready for pruning again.

## Trellising Systems

If a vine is left untrained, it will grow in an abundant but very random manner. The practice of training the vines on a trellis provides a support for the weight of the leaves and fruit and makes it easier for the vines to be tended throughout the year. It also allows the grape grower to control the amount of growth of leaves and fruit, and to place the leaves and grape bunches in specific locations to gain optimum sun exposure or shade. The science of trellising, which includes this element of **canopy management,** is now so far advanced that, for any given grape type, grape growers know how many leaves are needed for each bunch of grapes to be provided with the right amount of carbohydrates through photosynthesis.

Different trellising systems are favored in different regions. Most are variations on three main systems:

- Vertical Trellis system

- Geneva Double Curtain system

- Lyre system

Depending on the vine type, the rootstock type, the climate, and the soil, the grape grower selects the trellising system and pruning method that will provide exposure to the sun, shading from the sun, air circulation, and optimal growth of foliage. In all of the trellising systems, the vines are trained to grow onto a network of wires which are supported by posts along the vine rows. Very often the wires are movable so that they can be raised as the vine's shoots get longer.

The **Vertical Trellis system** is used on a very widespread basis in many wine countries around the world (see Figure 2.24). Stationary wires near the top of the vine trunk act as the support to train cordons or canes horizontally away from the trunk, and movable wires are strung in pairs along the vine rows at different heights. The new shoots are trained upwards within the wires, creating a hedge-like effect.

The **Geneva Double Curtain system** is a straightforward vertical set of wires on which the new shoots are trained to grow downwards from the highest support wire (see Figure 2.25). This allows the foliage to cascade down from the top wire of the trellis in a curtain effect or on both sides of the trellis.

The **Lyre system** is really a double vertical trellis (see Figure 2.26). The vine is trained from the trunk onto two separate, small trellis systems with the new shoots growing upwards, again allowing for full air movement through the vine's foliage. The movement of air helps to reduce moisture

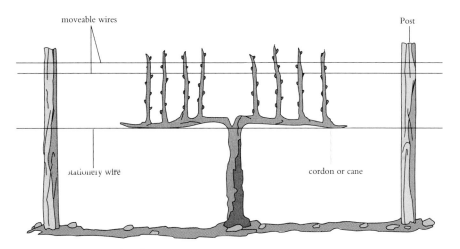

**Figure 2.24** Vertical Trellis System.

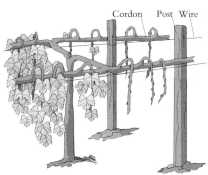

**Figure 2.25** Vertical Trellising System.

buildup among the leaves and grape bunches, and thereby reduces the chances of various molds developing on the grapes.

No single trellising or pruning system is right for any one place or any one grape type, and grape growers must experiment with many different systems before they find the best combination for any particular site.

## Summary

Grapes come in many different varieties, far too numerous for us to list all of them in this book. We have chosen to list and describe the grape varieties which have received the most attention from grape growers, wine makers, and consumers around the world for the production of quality-level wines. Grape varieties are chosen by growers for their suitability to the local growing conditions, for the flavors they offer, and for the marketability of the wines they produce. As with most plants, grape vines need to be tended, and growers will select the most appropriate pruning and trellising system to obtain optimum flavor and yield.

From this preliminary discussion of grape types, you are now ready to move on to tasting wines, and then to exploring the famous wines of the major wine-producing countries in the world.

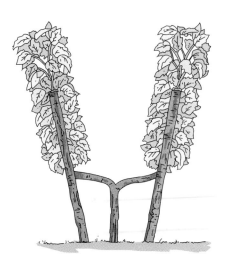

Cross section of **lyre**-trained vines during the growing season.

Vine training to the **lyre** system showing spur pruning (cane pruning can also be used)

**Figure 2.26** Lyre Trellising System.

# How to Taste Wine

## Introduction

Unlike a painting, a bottle of wine is not all that inspiring, although the wine inside the bottle is, to some, a work of art. And while some people look upon wine—as they do with art—as an investment to be coveted, the true artistry, the true aesthetic experience, lies *within* the bottle. No matter how visually appealing the bottle, label, and name, it's what's inside and how it tastes that's important. Wine tasting has a reputation of being complicated and unapproachable to a majority of wine drinkers. That's not necessarily true. *Tasting* is really a catchall phrase for using all the senses to understand and capture many of the properties and dimensions of the wine.

The basic purpose of wine tasting is, of course, to determine whether the taster enjoys a wine and also the reasons why or why not. The reasons we enjoy certain wines more than others springs from an **organoleptic** response to the wine, which refers to all the major senses. Sight, smell, touch, taste, and even sound are involved when participating in a wine tasting. Tasting is *aural,* starting with the "popping" of the cork; tasting is *visual,* as the color hints at the depth, power, and/or style of the wine; tasting is *olfactory,* as the associative memory attaches significance and/or emotions to the smells that are beyond simple grapes; tasting is *tactile,* as the mouth reacts to the interplay of tannins, acids, sugar, alcohol, and/or bubbles. Depending on the surroundings, the company, the mind set and emotions of the taster, and, of course, the wine, tasting may even be inspirational.

With some experience and using a predetermined set of criteria and terminology the wine taster's response can be quantified and shared.

Tasting is identifying what is perceived by the senses and applying objective terms to subjective impressions. These points of judgment and jargon can also be useful when applied judiciously and honestly. Tasting wine is, at best, an inexact science, since it is based largely on personal preference, but tasting is also what constitutes the true pleasure of wine. The terms used can be fanciful such as "violet" or "banana-scented," "silky-textured," or "voluptuous body." A beginning wine taster should not be intimidated by the vast range of descriptive terms available, but should taste at a personal comfort level. The morning seems to be the best time for most tasters to be able to discern the character of wines. Allow at least an hour before tasting after using toothpaste, strong mouthwash, or having a hearty breakfast as the palate could be negatively affected. Some find the evening is the best time to taste and there is no universal rule about when to taste. For the first few wine tastings "light" or "dark" red may suffice for "color," and if no smells are immediately identifiable, the taster has no cause for worry. The flavor and intensity of the wine can still be recorded, and these fundamental question answered: Is the wine enjoyable? Refer to Parts 2 and 3, Wines of the New World and Wines of the Old World, to understand the major characteristics to look for in wines from the various regions around the world. Keep in mind: Nobody is perfect the first time (or first few times) they try anything.

A novice enjoying a vacation in an area that makes wine may venture into a tasting room, have a quick taste, and decide "this stuff is OK" and buy a couple of bottles as a souvenir of the experience. This is the least formal kind of tasting and perhaps the most pleasurable. It is a judgment based on individual taste (including aroma) and the taster never thinks of it as a formal, tasting.

In a formal professional tasting, whose purpose is to market expensive wines to restaurants and wine sellers, a wine importer or sommelier may be risking a large amount of money on decisions made in a few minutes.

Naturally many other circumstances between the two extremes—the vacation tasting on the run, and the formal professional tasting—could be illustrated, but it is clear that wine is tasted in different ways for different reasons, and on different occasions.

# A Formal Wine Tasting: Setting and Procedure

The following are the ideal conditions for a formal tasting. Obviously it is impossible to meet all these criteria on all occasions:

- The tasting room should be a comfortable temperature, well ventilated, and free of any distracting smells;

# TYPES OF TASTINGS

**General tasting:**   Wines of different styles are tasted.  A good starting point is to taste a light-bodied dry white and then a fuller-bodied white wine. Or try a bone-dry white, then a semidry wine, and finally a sweet wine. Light purple, translucent reds could be compared to darker red wines and to an older wine displaying shades of reddish brown.

*A general tasting example.* A dry, light-bodied Muscadet from the Loire region of France, followed by a dry medium-bodied Albariño from Galicia Spain; next a dry, full-bodied barrel-fermented Chardonnay from California; next a semidry Riesling from New York or Washington; then end with a sweet Recioto di Soave white from Veneto, Italy. This general tasting is a good way to develop confidence about perceiving the weight or body of a wine and the difference between dry, semidry, and sweet.

**Vertical tasting:**   The same wine or similar wines are tasted through a series of vintages. The general rule in a vertical tasting is to start with the youngest, most powerful wines and proceed chronologically to the older vintages. These tastings allow participants to focus on the distinct style of the producer or wine region. When the soil types and grape varietals are constant, the dynamics of the growing conditions of the vintage and the aging process can be isolated.

*A vertical tasting example.*   Vintage Porto 1991, 1990, 1985, 1977, 1963, 1955, and 1945. A further control could be to use wines from one producer to avoid stylistic differences between firms. Porto is known to age well but there are many other age-worthy wines that could be used such as those made from the Cabernet Sauvignon grape. In these vertical tastings, notes will usually contain information that points to the red wines becoming less harsh and the flavors being more integrated or harmonious over time. Experts are making educated guesses when they try to project how much longer an old wine will be enjoyable before its demise.

**Horizontal tasting:**   The quality of a specific vintage is assessed by concentrating on one region or grape type and focusing on the styles produced.

*A horizontal tasting example.*   Try Cabernet Sauvignon of the 1987 vintage from the Stags Leap, Rutherford, Howell Mountain, and Mount Veeder zones of Napa along with two examples from the Alexander Valley in Sonoma County, one from Monterey and an example from Paso Robles, California.

**Blind tasting:**   The taster attempts to discern what the wine is by tasting, and using information and experience obtained from years of studying the major grape types and regions of the world and how they interact. A knowledge of producers and vintages is also required for this difficult task. The advantage of tasting blind is that it is good training for the palate and mind, as the taster cannot presuppose the nature or quality of a wine. It causes the taster to rely on natural senses and any lessons learned thus far.

**Semi-blind tasting:**   The tasters have a limited amount of information, such as the country or grape type, and taste the wines without knowing such vital information as vintage, producer, or product. The advantage of this kind of tasting is that judgments are not prejudiced, and the most appealing wines will show well. A good example of this type of tasting is when restaurants and hotels often form tasting circles which meet on a regular basis to taste wines in silence to avoid one taster unduly affecting another's opinions. Participants then declare their top three choices in each flight. A *flight* is the term used for a set of wines that will be followed by another, such as California Chardonnays between $5 and $10 tasted together, and then a separate flight for those over $10. Professional tasters trying 80 wines might break them down into ten flights of eight wines at a time.

**Comparative tasting:**   Similar styles of wines, such as powerful reds, are tasted together and compared to each other.

*A comparative tasting example.*   A tasting of powerful reds could include a Barolo from Italy, a Châteauneuf du Pape from France, a Ribera del Duero from Spain, a Bairrada from Portugal, and a Syrah from Argentina or Australia.

Tasting Glass

Champagne

All Purpose
White Wine
Glass

All Purpose
Red Wine
Glass

Red Bordeaux

Red Burgundy

Port

Sherry

**Figure 3.1** Examples of Glassware.

- To judge the true color of the wine, judging by natural daylight in a room surrounded by windows is best. If artificial light is used, incandescent is preferable to fluorescent. A white tablecloth, place mat, or tasting sheet provide a neutral background. This is important in judging the color of the wine and the attendant properties of color (see the section on color in this chapter);

- Glassware should be clear, unadorned, and free of any soapy residue. It should be polished with a lint-free cloth, hand rinsed, or run through an extra rinsing cycle without detergent. The best glasses to "nose" a wine tend to have a wide bowl and a tapered top. Standard "tasters" are just

fine for most tastings. It is always instructive fun to be able to taste wines in glasses made especially for a particular style of wine or grape type or region (see Figure 3.1). The concentration of odors and the ability to perceive them really does differ by glass.

- Spittoons should be provided; they could be simply large paper cups or larger buckets. The palate tires over time, and if much wine is consumed during a formal tasting, the taster cannot stay sharp and the senses are numbed somewhat by the numerous wines. Spitting takes a bit of practice and some getting used to, but does not interfere with the appreciation of the nose and flavor elements of the wine. In fact, spitting is necessary to allow true appreciation of the wine.

- A pitcher of water and water glass should also be provided for clearing the palate between wines. Local tap water may be used or a still mineral water as long as neither have strong chlorinated or mineral flavors.

- Service staff should be briefed about each of the wines to be poured and they should be equipped with corkscrews and white cloth napkins. The person in charge of service should keep a running inventory of the number of bottles of each wine poured.

- Decanted wines (see Chapter 15 on Wine Service) should be organized with a bottle of the wine in front of the decanter, so that the label is prominent (unless this is a blind tasting). A small sticker with the wine's number or name could also be affixed to each decanter to avoid the problem of having the wrong wine poured. It is best to have one person coordinate the issuing of the wines so servers do not confuse types.

- A paper mat with a numbered circle indicating where each glass is to be placed.

- Tasting sheets should be provided so comments on the wines may be recorded and the identity of the glass numbered on the mat is indicated.

Food and Wine Tasting at the CIA.

- Promotional materials may be placed at the table, along with a pencil and maybe a notepad for preliminary notes. The promotional materials often answer the most asked questions about the wines being tasted. Historical, geographic, and technical data on the vineyards and wine-making process assist the taster to understand the conditions that created the wine in front of them.

- If bread of crackers are provided they are for the purpose of neutralizing the palate, and should therefore be as neutral as possible. Salty or sweet bread or crackers should be avoided.

- A reception desk is used at events to collect invitations or business cards, check identification to ensure participants are of legal drinking age, and to assign seat or table numbers at very large tastings.

## Tasting Procedure

The pouring of wines at a formal tasting is coordinated by one person whose concerns are the order in which the wines are served, when to open them, at what temperature they are served, and the amount poured.

# TASTING SHEETS

Unless it is a blind tasting, in which case the names of the wines are never revealed in advance, tasting sheets with the name of the product, producer, area, and vintage should be provided (see Figure 3.2 a–h). Each wine should be numbered on the sheet, with the corresponding number on the decanter and/or bottle of wine, so that the sequence of tasting is clear. The sheet may be informal, with some room to make general comments, or it may be quite specific, with labeled categories, such as **color, nose, taste, body, finish,** and boxes for personal comments and a numerical rating. Other tasting sheets may list descriptors of nose and taste, with a box to check off each relevant descriptor. This method serves as a guide for the tasters, giving them choices instead of asking for evaluations and relative numerical ratings.

**Figure 3.2** Tasting Sheets.

(a)

| | TOTAL SCORE 20 | | | |
|---|---|---|---|---|
| | 18 – 20 | EXCELLENT | 7 – 8 | FAIR |
| | 15 – 17 | VERY GOOD | 4 – 6 | POOR |
| | 12 – 14 | GOOD | 1 – 3 | EXTREMELY POOR |
| | 9 – 11 | AVERAGE | | |

NAME

WINE

DATE

| SAMPLE NO. | APPEARANCE | | | | BOUQUET AND AROMA | | TASTE | | OVERALL IMPRESSION | | TOTAL SCORE | PREF. (RANK) |
|---|---|---|---|---|---|---|---|---|---|---|---|---|
| | COLOR | 2 | CLARITY | 2 | | 6 | | 8 | | 2 | | |
| CONTROL | | 1 | | 1 | | 3 | | 4 | | 1 | 10 | |
| | | | | | | | | | | | | |
| | | | | | | | | | | | | |
| | | | | | | | | | | | | |
| | | | | | | | | | | | | |
| | | | | | | | | | | | | |
| | | | | | | | | | | | | |
| | | | | | | | | | | | | |

**(b)** A Detailed Tasting Sheet by A. Castell for Institut Nations al Appellations Origine (INAO) Differs the Terminology for the Taster.

| Wine Type (White/Rosé/Red) | | | Appellation: |
|---|---|---|---|
| | | | Type: |

| Laboratory Observations and Conclusion | | | Date of Analysis |
|---|---|---|---|
| Specific Gravity | | | Total Acidity |
| Alcohol | | | Fixed Acidity |
| Residual Sugar | | | Volatile Acidity |
| Potential Alcohol | | | (corrected for sulphuric acid) |
| Total $SO_2$ | | | |
| Free $SO_2$ | pH | | |
| | color index P/x | | |
| | Index of permanganate | | |

**Method of Vinification**

| Visual Examination | Surface of the Liquid | | Brilliant – dull<br><br>Clean – iridescent – oily |
|---|---|---|---|
| | Color | White Wine | Pale with green or yellow tints – pale yellow – straw yellow – canary yellow – gold – amber |
| | | Rosé Wine | Pale with violet or rose tints – grey – light rose – deep rose – partridge eye – onion skin |
| | | Red Wine | Red with crimson or violet tints – cherry red – ruby – garnet red – red brown – tile red – mahogany – tawny |
| | | Color Hue | Frank – oxidized – cloudy |
| | Aspect | | Crystalline – brilliant – limpid – hazy – cloudy – turgid – lead – grey/white – opaque, with or without deposit |
| | Legs/Tears | | Quick or slow to form – non-existent – slight – heavy |

| Temperature of the Wine | | | Any factor hindering the tasting |
|---|---|---|---|

| Olfactory Examination | First Impression | | Pleasant – ordinary – unpleasant |
|---|---|---|---|
| | Aroma | Intensity | Powerful – adequate – feeble – non-existent |
| | | Quality | Very fine – racy – distinguished – fine – ordinary – common – not very pleasant – unpleasant |
| | | Character | Primary – secondary – tertiary – floral – fruity – vegetal – spicy – animal – oxidized |
| | | Length | Long – average – short |
| | Abnormal odors | | $CO_2$ – $SO_2$ – $H_2S$ – mercaptan – strongly oxidized – woody – lactic acid acescence – phenolic – corky<br><br>Flaw { temporary – permanent / slight – serious |
| | Details | | |

**Any factor hindering or stopping the continuation of the tasting**

| Gustatory Examination | First Impression | | | |
|---|---|---|---|---|
| | Flavors and Sensations | Sweetness | Sugar | Heavy – very sweet – sweet – dry – brut |
| | | | Glycerine and alcohol | Soft – unctuous – velvety – smooth – rough – dried out |
| | | Acidity | Excessive | Acid – green – tart – nervy – acidulous |
| | | | Balanced | Fresh – lively – supple – smooth |
| | | | Insufficient | Flat – flabby |
| | | Body | Alcoholic strength | Light – sufficient – generous – heady – hot |
| | | | Flesh | Fat – round – full – thin – meager |
| | | | Tannin | Rich – balanced – insufficient – astringent – bitter |
| | | Aromas in the mouth | Intensity | Powerful – average – weak – long – short |
| | | | Quality | Very fine – elegant – pleasant – common – faded |
| | | | Nature | Floral – fruity – vegetable – spicy – wood – chemical – animal – other<br>young – developed – complex |
| | Inherent or Abnormal Flavours | 'Terroir' | | Marked – noticeable – faint – nonexistent |
| | | Sickness | | Grease – turned – aldehydes – sweet – sour – rancid – acetic acid – lactic acid |
| | | Accident | | Stagnant – mould – lees – woody – cork – metallic – $H_2S$ – herbaceous – acrid |
| | Final Impression | Balance | | Harmonious – bold – correct – unbalanced<br>Xs acid, Xs sugar, Xs tannin, Xs alcohol |
| | | Aftertaste | | Straightforward – unpleasant |
| | | Resistance of taste and aroma | | > 8 sec    5–7 sec    4–5 sec    < 3 sec<br>Very long    long     medium    short |
| Conclusions | Conformity to appellation or type | | | |
| | Score out of 20 | | | |
| | Summary of tasting (character of wine – future, readiness for drinking) | | | |

**(c)** Official Tasting Sheet of German Amtliche Prüfungsnummer (Quality Control) Board.

**1.**

| Vintage | |
|---|---|
| Grape variety/varieties | |
| Quality status | |
| Wine growing region | |
| Style: dry, semi dry... | |
| Shipper/Producer | |

**2.** Preconditional Examination          Your assessment

| | | | |
|---|---|---|---|
| Vintage | yes | no | |
| Grape variety(ies) | yes | no | |
| Quality status | yes | no | |
| Wine growing region | yes | no | |
| Color | yes | no | |
| Clarity | yes | no | |

**3.** Examination of Sensory Characteristics

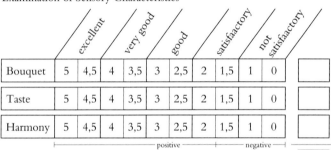

| | excellent | | very good | | good | | satisfactory | | not satisfactory | | |
|---|---|---|---|---|---|---|---|---|---|---|---|
| Bouquet | 5 | 4,5 | 4 | 3,5 | 3 | 2,5 | 2 | 1,5 | 1 | 0 | |
| Taste | 5 | 4,5 | 4 | 3,5 | 3 | 2,5 | 2 | 1,5 | 1 | 0 | |
| Harmony | 5 | 4,5 | 4 | 3,5 | 3 | 2,5 | 2 | 1,5 | 1 | 0 | |

├─────────── positive ───────────┼─── negative ───┤

Total: ☐ : 3 = ◯ ─·─

additional or overall characteristic/
your personal impression                                                 passed/not passed

_____

_____

_____

**(d)**

## CM/CV — SUGGESTED TASTING SHEET FOR SPARKLING WINES

(modeled after the work of Georges Hardy, Station Enotechnique de Champagne, Epernay)

Vintage: _____        Producer: _____

Appellation: _____        Style: _____

| VISUAL EVALUATION: | |
|---|---|
| Foam | |
| Bubbles | |
| Color | |
| EVALUATION BY NOSE: | |
| Aromas | |
| Overall quality | |
| EVALUATION BY PALATE: | |
| Sugar/acid balance | |
| Body | |
| Development of flavors | |
| Overall quality | |
| GENERAL CONCLUSIONS | |

| SUMMARY | | | | | |
|---|---|---|---|---|---|
| (Give a mark between 1 and 20 for each category) | | | | | |
| Visual | Olfactory | Taste | Quality of Vinification | Overall Appeal | TOTAL |
| | | | | | |

**(e)** The Vedel Tasting Sheet is Used for Competitions.

Commission No:            Sample No:
Taster's No:               Category:
                               Vintage:

| | | Excellent Extremely strong | Very good Very strong | Good, strong | Adequate Acceptable | Eliminated | Comments | For official use only | Coefficient | Personal comments |
|---|---|---|---|---|---|---|---|---|---|---|
| Appearance | Color | | | | | | | | 1 | |
| | Limpidity | | | | | | | | 1 | |
| Nose | Intensity | | | | | | | | 1 | |
| | Quality | | | | | | | | 2 | |
| Palate | Intensity | | | | | | | | 2 | |
| | Quality | | | | | | | | 3 | |
| Harmony | | | | | | | | | 2 | |
| Length: | | | | | | | Total Medal Class | | | |

**(f)** The Tasting of the Bordeaux Institute of Oenology Allows Tasters to Use Their Own Terminology.

Descriptive tasting sheet             Date . . . . . . . . . . . . . . . . . .

Taster's name . . . . . . . . . . . . . . . . . . . . . . . . . . . . . . . . . . . . . . . . . . . . . . .
Wine . . . . . . . . . . . . . . . . . . . . . . . . . . . . . . . . . . . . . . . . . . . . . . . . . . . . . . . .

**Appearance**
Color (intensity, hue). . . . . . . . . . . . . . . . . . . . . . . . . . . . . . . . . . . . . . . . . . . .
Limpidity. . . . . . . . . . . . . . . . . . . . . . . . . . . . . . . . . . . . . . . . . . . . . . . . . . . . . .
Other observations . . . . . . . . . . . . . . . . . . . . . . . . . . . . . . . . . . . . . . . . . . . . . . .

**Nose**
Cleanness. . . . . . . . . . . . . . . . . . . . . . . . . . . . . . . . . . . . . . . . . . . . . . . . . . . . . . .
Intensity . . . . . . . . . . . . . . . . . . . . . . . . . . . . . . . . . . . . . . . . . . . . . . . . . . . . . . .
Description . . . . . . . . . . . . . . . . . . . . . . . . . . . . . . . . . . . . . . . . . . . . . . . . . . . . .
Quality . . . . . . . . . . . . . . . . . . . . . . . . . . . . . . . . . . . . . . . . . . . . . . . . . . . . . . . .
Defects, if any. . . . . . . . . . . . . . . . . . . . . . . . . . . . . . . . . . . . . . . . . . . . . . . . . . .

**Taste**
Description      Attack . . . . . . . . . . . . . . . . . . . . . . . . . . . . . . . . . . . . . . . . . .
                   Evolution . . . . . . . . . . . . . . . . . . . . . . . . . . . . . . . . . . . . . . . . .
                   Finish. . . . . . . . . . . . . . . . . . . . . . . . . . . . . . . . . . . . . . . . . . . .
Balance and overall structure . . . . . . . . . . . . . . . . . . . . . . . . . . . . . . . . . . . . . . .
. . . . . . . . . . . . . . . . . . . . . . . . . . . . . . . . . . . . . . . . . . . . . . . . . . . . . . . . . . . . .
Aroma in the mouth (intensity and quality) . . . . . . . . . . . . . . . . . . . . . . . . . . . . .
Aromatic persistence . . . . . . . . . . . . . . . . . . . . . . . . . . . . . . . . . . . . . . . . . . . . . .
Other observations . . . . . . . . . . . . . . . . . . . . . . . . . . . . . . . . . . . . . . . . . . . . . . .

**Judgment**
**Conclusions** . . . . . . . . . . . . . . . . . . . . . . . . . . . . . . . . . . . . . . . . . . . . . . . . . . .
. . . . . . . . . . . . . . . . . . . . . . . . . . . . . . . . . . . . . . . . . . . . . . . . . . . . . . . . . . . . .
. . . . . . . . . . . . . . . . . . . . . . . . . . . . . . . . . . . . . . . . . . . . . . . . . . . . . . . . . . . . .
Assessment. . . . . . . . . . . . . . . . . . . . . . . . . . . . . . . . . . . . . . . . . . . . . . . . . . . . .
Corresponding score (out of 5 − out of 10 − out of 20)[1]

[1]Delete accordingly

# THE CULINARY INSTITUTE OF AMERICA
## WINE APPRECIATION — TASTING SHEET

TASTING: _____          DATE: _____

| | WINES | COLOR | NOSE | BODY | TASTE | FINISH |
|---|---|---|---|---|---|---|
| 1 | | | | | | |
| 2 | | | | | | |
| 3 | | | | | | |
| 4 | | | | | | |
| 5 | | | | | | |
| 6 | | | | | | |
| 7 | | | | | | |
| 8 | | | | | | |
| | | Depth of Color<br>Hue of Color<br>Clarity | Aromas<br>Bouquet | In Glass<br>In Mouth<br>Due to Sugar<br>and Alcohol | Components | Duration of<br>Taste<br>New Flavors |

**(h)** The Culinary Institute of America's Wine Sensory Data Record.

# THE CULINARY INSTITUTE OF AMERICA      WINE SENSORY DATA RECORD

TASTING _____ DATE _____ EVALUATOR _____

WINE # _____      RANK _____ OF _____      BLIND      yes      no

_____  _____  _____  _____
　　COUNTRY　　　　　　REGION　　　　　PRODUCER/SHIPPER　　　VINTAGE

OTHER INFO. _____ CURRENT COST _____

Mark with an X the descriptors that apply. Check or write in at least one per column, more than one may be checked.

COLOR　　　　　　　NOSE/SMELL　　　← may be crossover →　TASTE　　　BODY / FINISH

| COLOR | NOSE/SMELL | | | TASTE | BODY / FINISH |
|---|---|---|---|---|---|
| **Red Wine** | **PLEASANT** | | **UNPLEASANT** | | **BODY** |
| ❏ Purple | ❏ Wood | ❏ Caramel | ❏ Alcohol | ❏ Acid | ❏ Thin |
| ❏ Blue | ❏ Cedar | ❏ Butterscotch | ❏ Chemical | ❏ Sweet | ❏ Medium |
| ❏ Garnet | ❏ Oak | ❏ Butter | ❏ Moldy | ❏ Bitter | ❏ Full-bodied |
| ❏ Red | ❏ Grass | ❏ Banana | ❏ Detergent | ❏ Salt | ❏ |
| ❏ Orange | ❏ Bamboo | ❏ Flint | ❏ Vegetative | ❏ Astringency | ❏ |
| ❏ Brown | ❏ Chocolate | ❏ Grapefruit | ❏ Burned | ❏ Cleansing | ❏ |
| ❏ Pink | ❏ Floral | ❏ Lemon | ❏ Sweaty | | |
| ❏ Brick | ❏ Rose | ❏ Lime | ❏ Artificial Fruit | ❏ Hot | **FINISH** |
| ❏ | ❏ Violet | ❏ Gooseberry | ❏ Plastic | ❏ Dry | ❏ Lingering |
| ❏ | ❏ Spicy | ❏ Wet Fur | ❏ Rubber | | ❏ Pleasant |
| | ❏ Clove | ❏ | ❏ Kerosene | ❏ Warm | ❏ Short |
| **White Wine** | ❏ Pepper | ❏ | ❏ Sherry | ❏ Rounded | ❏ Unpleasant |
| ❏ Pale | ❏ Mint | ❏ | ❏ Corky | ❏ Balanced | ❏ Watery |
| ❏ Straw | ❏ Citrus | ❏ | ❏ Sulfur | ❏ Unbalanced | ❏ Crisp |
| ❏ Green | ❏ Berry | ❏ | ❏ Rotten | ❏ Tannic | ❏ Muddy |
| ❏ Gold | ❏ Blackberry | ❏ | ❏ Dirty | ❏ Sour | ❏ |
| ❏ Yellow | ❏ Raspberry | ❏ | ❏ Oxidized | ❏ Chalky | ❏ |
| ❏ Amber | ❏ Strawberry | ❏ | ❏ | ❏ Gritty | ❏ |
| ❏ Browning | ❏ Black Currant | ❏ | ❏ | ❏ | ❏ |
| ❏ | ❏ Fruity | | | ❏ | |
| ❏ | ❏ Cherry | | | ❏ | |
| | ❏ Grape | | | ❏ | **Finish Flavor** |
| **Clarity** | ❏ Jam | | | ❏ | ❏ |
| ❏ Dull | ❏ Peach | | | | |
| ❏ Bright | ❏ Pear | | | | |
| ❏ Clear | ❏ Apple | | | | |
| ❏ Opaque | ❏ Raisin | | COMMENTS: | | |
| ❏ | ❏ Prune | | | | |
| ❏ | ❏ Fig | | | | |
| | ❏ Vegetable | | | | |
| **Sediment** | ❏ Stemmy | | | | |
| ❏ Yes | ❏ Green Pepper | | | | |
| ❏ No | ❏ Eucalyptus | | | | |
| | ❏ Asparagus | | | | |
| | ❏ Olive | | | | |
| | ❏ Earthy | | | | |
| | ❏ Mushroom | | | | |
| | ❏ Soil | | | | |
| | ❏ Tar | | | | |
| | ❏ Yeast | | | | |
| | ❏ Smoke | | | | |
| | ❏ | | | | |

COMMENTS:

_____

_____

_____

_____

## AGING POTENTIAL

VINTAGE GUESS _____

Place an X on the gray bar indicating what stage the wine is at currently.

X ⟶ 

| SHOT | DRINK NOW | 5 YEARS | 10 YEARS | 10 YEARS + |

## FOOD PAIRING    Place an X on the gray bar indicating what food and wine pairing may work.

MILD ⟶ INTENSE

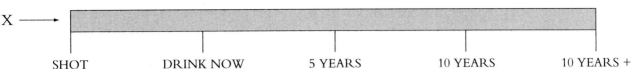

X ⟶

| Drink Alone<br>As Cocktail | Mild Fish<br>Meat With<br>Mild Cooking Methods | Chicken Or Pork<br>No Strong Sauces<br>Or Flavors<br>Could Be Fish With<br>Stronger Flavors | Cream     Game<br>Beef<br>Strong Flavors<br>Roast, Spicy |

### FOODS THAT MAY WORK
- ❏ Oysters
- ❏ Clams
- ❏ Shrimp
- ❏
- ❏

- ❏ Pasta
- ❏ Pasta/Cream
- ❏ Pasta/Tomato
- ❏
- ❏

- ❏ Lemon
- ❏ Asparagus
- ❏
- ❏
- ❏

- ❏ Cheese
- ❏ Goat Cheese
- ❏ Swiss
- ❏ Morbier
- ❏ Brie
- ❏ Blue Cheese

COMMENTS: _____

_____

_____

## OVERALL QUALITY    Place an X on the gray bar indicating what you feel is the overall quality of the wine.

X ⟶

| 0 | 2 | 3 | 4 | 5 |
| TERRIBLE<br>Would not serve | BELOW AVERAGE | AVERAGE<br>OK. But not for a<br>special occasion. | ABOVE AVERAGE | EXCELLENT<br>One of the best wines<br>I've ever had. |

COMMENTS: _____

_____

_____

The usual procedure is to arrange and serve the less-powerful dry whites and sparkling wines before the more "tannic" reds. Rosés may be served in between whites and reds with the sweet and fortified wines served at the end of the sequence of wines to be tasted. This is done so the taster is not overwhelmed by the initial wines and may still appreciate those at the end of the exercise.

Sparkling wines should be opened as close to the time of the actual tasting as possible in order to preserve the lively action of the bubbles. Still wines should be opened at no more than a half hour in advance so any change in nose and taste is minimized. Fine wines poured for a large group may also be "nosed" before pouring for a large group. A knowledgeable wine steward or other trained staff person can smell the wine to make sure there are no unpleasant or off odors. The nose is very sensitive and will react quickly to off odors.

The correct temperature for serving the wines is indicated in the section on Temperature in Chapter 16. The sparkling and white wines are usually chilled so they should not be prepoured too far in advance so they do not get too warm. Reds are usually served at room temperature and may be poured in advance. A speaker conducting a tasting may request that no wines be poured in advance. The speaker may instruct the staff to coordinate the serving of wines to specified times in the seminar or may just give the word when a wine is to be poured.

A tasting portion (a "pour") is generally about one to one and a half ounces, so a bottle should easily provide 16 to 25 tasting portions. If a few wines are to be tasted *with food,* tasting portions may be larger.

The servers should pour the wines at the location where the tasters are seated; they should not bring glasses, already filled with the wine, from another location. The person in charge should give a demonstration of how the bottles are to be held, the amount of the pour, and how to use a napkin to wipe the lip of the bottle so that no wine splashes onto the tasting mat.

# The Three Basic Steps to Tasting Wine

## *Appearance*

A wine's color is the first clue to the wine's taste. It should be inviting and true to its varietal, geographic, or stylistic type. When we talk about the *color* of a wine, we mean its overall appearance. Descriptions of color may be as general as "red" or "white" or as specific as "pale garnet with pinkish-blue highlights" or "pale yellow with a green tinge and watery rim." In any case, color is the first indicator we look for when we taste wine. Even before smelling and actually tasting the wine, color clues can speak volumes about the wine's character.

To determine a wine's true color, hold the tasting glass by its stem, against a white background. Tilt the glass to about a 45° angle so the wine may be

## WALK-AROUND TASTINGS

Another type of tasting situation is when there is a large room and the tasting is done standing up. Wine festivals and trade tastings usually have these tastings. Participants would go to different tables or booths and sample a wine or two from each location. The taster is provided with one glass as he or she enters and each table has a water pitcher for them to rinse out their glass and perhaps have some water to cleanse their palate as well. Spit buckets are always provided at each table as tasters may have a hundred or more wines to sample.

It is best to have a strategy when attending large walk-around tastings. A catalog and floor plan are usually provided and one may plan in advance which wineries' products are a priority to taste.

An estimated time schedule can also be useful. An example would be to break down a 2½-hour tasting to taste the lighter and drier wines before those that are heavy or sweet so the palate is not overwhelmed in the early stages of the tasting. Tasting a sweet wine just before a dry or semidry wine would strongly affect how those wines are perceived. The hint of sweetness in a semidry wine would not be easily detected after tasting one much sweeter. Devote the first hour for white wines and dry sparkling wines, the next hour for dry reds, and the remaining time for sweet and fortified wines.

The Wine Experience is the largest event in the United States and it combines daytime seminars and tastings with evening walk-around tastings. It alternates each year between New York and San Franciso, and is run by The Wine Spectator Scholarship Foundation. The top European events are VinItaly which is held annually in Verona, and VinExpo held every other year in Bordeaux, France.

viewed on its side. On first glance, notice the general color category of the wine. Is it a white, rosé, or red wine? Within these three broad categories a second glance will help to define the hue and shading of the wine's color.

A good rule of thumb is that most of the paler white wines, such as Galestro from Tuscany (see Chapter 7 on Italy), are the lightest in flavor intensity. A pale color could also be the result of a farmer taking too high a yield for the vine, which reduces not only the color but the flavor as well. A pale color with green highlights usually indicates a wine from a cooler growing area, often promising a good vein of acidity in its flavor. Wines with a "buttercup-yellow" shade will show more powerful flavors, aged characteristics, or sweet tastes. White wines gain color with age and, depending on that age, can be a deep golden hue. The oldest white wines can be even amber or tawny. Most simple white wines are not meant to age more than two or three years. Assuming that they are consumed within that time period, they will never develop the richer yellow shades of color. More complex whites, like certain oak-aged Chardonnay-based wines, can improve with age, and a rich golden color is much appreciated. White wines that have a deep yellow hue may come from warmer climes, be oak-aged, or come from a grape variety that exhibits more color, such as Gewürztraminer (see Chapters 1 on How Wine Is Made and 2 on Wine Grapes). "Straw yellow" is a common in-between color indicator, usually belonging to a wine of moderate flavor intensity and appropriate age. Holding the wine glass at an angle, notice how a deeper gold may be exhibited throughout the wine.

Red wines may range from purple, garnet, black cherry, or ruby in young wines, to the mahogany, orange-red, and brownish colors, in older wines. Young red wines usually show a uniformity of color shading throughout the wine, whereas an older red wine will show gradations of shading, often with a medium ruby color at the heart of the wine, and paler orange hues towards the outer edge. Red wines get their color from contact with the grape skins; the darker the skins and longer the contact with the grape must, the deeper the color. Moderate to warmer climates tend to produce darker-hued red wines. In the aging process of red wines, color pigments and tannins fall out of suspension in the wine and create a sediment in the bottle. Because of this process, and because of the browning caused by slow oxidation, red wines lose their vibrant red and purple hues as they age. Each varietal has the potential to give different shades of red from its youth to its maturity. The vineyard and winery methods as well as climate also have a dramatic effect on the colors of whites, reds, or rosé wines. Rosé (blush) wines may range from a salmon to light pink to bubble-gum pink or pink/pale red. Since rosé wines are actually "red wines," their color depends on the grape types used and the length of skin contact during the winemaking process.

**What does Color Indicate?**   Depth of color is often an indication of a wine's "power." Opaque, dark-red wines are heavier on the palate than translucent, lighter reds. Paler wines are usually from cooler growing areas, or vintages beset by wet and cool conditions close to harvest. Grapes grown and harvested under rainy conditions will result in a less-concentrated wine with a shorter lifespan. See Figures 3.3–3.11 for color styles of various wine types.

Whites, rosés, and reds all start to brown first at the edge of their surfaces—the rim of the glass. When the browning extends towards the center bowl of the glass the wine is usually past its prime and may be referred to as **oxidized**. The wine has aged beyond its prime (oxygen being the agent of aging), and has a smell and taste akin to that of the fortified wine Madeira. Some wine lovers enjoy *slightly* madeirized wines, but in general the degree of oxidation interferes with the true smell and taste characteristics of the wine. (Of course, fortified wines as well as very old sweet wines may exhibit a "tawny" shade of brown, but this hue is appropriate to those wines.) The **meniscus** (edge or rim ) of the wine gives an indication of age and style. Beaujolais (see Chapter 6 on France) will demonstrate a light purple hue with pinkish-blue highlights and translucence in its youth. It is not meant to be drunk more than a few years beyond its vintage, and any significant signs of browning in the wine is a sign of trouble. On the other hand a young

Cabernet Sauvignon from Napa Valley (see Chapter 4 on North America), harsh and tannic in its youth, will be a deep black-cherry color, totally opaque, with just a bit of browning on its rim. As it ages, losing tannins and throwing sediment, a lighter color, and a decidedly brown rim will be noticeable. An experienced taster can sometimes analyze the age of a wine by the gradations of color in the glass, with the lightest shades on the rim giving way to darker hues toward the center of the glass.

**Clarity** of the wine is also viewed as a quality factor associated with color. The wine should be bright and clean. Radiant, or star bright clarity is preferred to lackluster cloudiness. In white or red wines small crystal deposits, **tartrates,** sometimes accumulate on the cork. These deposits are sometimes in the bottle of wine as well, and by pouring slowly the server avoids stirring them up so most do not wind up in the glass. The effect on flavor of the wine would not differ, but for some the appearance is less attractive with these pottasium bitartrate crystals while others may refer to them as "wine diamonds" that are more commonly found in German wines. A hazy color is the first warning sign that the wine contains particles other than tartrates or sediment. A dull, hazy appearance is an early warning sign of poor wine making, improper storage, or too much age on the wine. However, it is important to remember that older wines may have quite a bit of sediment, and may need decanting to bring out their true clarity.

Most wine is filtered to achieve clarity and stability (see Chapter 1 on How Wine Is Made). Some wine makers believe that this process strips the wine of some of its character. As a point of pride many of these producers

**Figure 3.3**  Color Styles—Chardonnay from Chassagne Montrachet, Burgundy, 1990 and 1966. Older White Wines Gain Color.

**Figure 3.4**  Color Styles—Sauvignon Blanc from California 1992 and 1986 and Half-bottle 1981 *Botrytis.* Notice How Older White Wines Are Deeper in Color.

**Figure 3.5** Color Styles—Riesling from the Mosel and Rhine Regions of Germany. The Younger Mosel Wine Is Lighter in Color with a Green Tinge. The Bottles Reflect the Style Difference, with Mosel Wines Traditionally in Green Bottles and the Rhine Wines in Brown Bottles.

**Figure 3.6** Color Styles—Rosé Wines Will Vary by Length of Time of Skin Contact. From Left to Right, an American White Zinfandel, a Portuguese Example from Bairrada, and a Bandol Wine from Provence, France.

**Figure 3.7** Color Styles—American Reds. From Left to Right a Pinot Noir, a Syrah, and a Gamay Beaujolais. The Color Difference is Due to the Varietal with the Most Tannic Syrah Having the Darkest and Most Opaque Hue.

**Figure 3.8** Color Styles—A Sangiovese-based Tuscan Red from Italy and a Tempranillo-based Ribera del Duero from Spain. The Brunello Italian Clone is Deeper in Color Than Many Other Sangiovese Wines and the Tinta Aragones Clone Also Gives a Darker Color Than Many Other Tempranillo-based Wines of Spain.

**Figure 3.9** Fortified Wines—Sherry Styles. From Left to Right, Fino, Amontillado, and Oloroso.

**Figure 3.10** Fortified Wines—Porto and Madeira Styles. From Left to Right, Ruby, Tawny, Vintage Porto, and a Five-Year-Old Malmsey from Madeira.

print the word "unfiltered" on the bottle label. Unfiltered wines sometimes meet with customer resistance, since consumers want their wines to be bright and clear. While unfiltered wines are gaining in popularity, proponents of filtering believe that the process has no adverse effects.

**"Legs"** or **"tears"** may be seen running down the side of the glass after the glass is swirled. Using thumb and forefinger on the stem, slowly swirl the wine in the glass. The rivulets that are formed on the side of the glass, hint at the degree of the wine's power, and result from higher levels of alcohol, glycerol, or sugar in the wine. Richer and later-harvest wines form more distinct "legs" which take longer to fall in the glass.

As with smell or taste, the task is to use color reference words that are easy to understand. The Davis Color Wheel (see Figure 3.12) uses terms such as garnet, tile red, mahogany, tea rose, poppy, crimson, and vermillion to describe red wine. Each term allows the audience to visualize the color of the wine described. You may choose to use terms that are easily recognized by the audience. For instance, when speaking to culinary students, the terms cranberry juice, sun-dried tomato, or ancho chili may be more familiar than references to gemstones or tiles. Describing colors in wines is subjective, and the color wheel is just another tool used in wine communication.

**Figure 3.11** Sparkling Wines. From Left to Right, Blanc de Blancs, Blanc de Noirs, and Rosé.

When the wine is poured, or after swirling, some still wines will reveal small bubbles that are usually the result of leftover carbon dioxide from the fermentation process. These faintly spritzy wines—such as many Vinho Verde wines from Portugal (see Chapter 9 on Portugal)—are often intentionally produced this way to provide a pleasant, cleansing effect on the palate. When judging the appearance of true sparkling wines it is the smaller bubbles and their persistence, the *perlage,* followed by the foam or head, the *mousse,* at the top of the glass that are the first signs of quality.

## Smell

A wine's smell may be the most important clue to its past, present, and future, as well as an important clue to its taste. While sweet, sour, bitter, and salty are the only four tastes our tongues can recognize, our sense of smell enables us to identify hundreds of other substances, sometimes by memory, sometimes by association. Smelling the wine is a skill that requires practice. In Chapter 2 on Wine Grapes we indicate that Sauvignon Blanc smells of green plums and Chardonnay of apples; the wine student would do well to try those products before and during a training session with those wines.

To tune up sensitivity to smells, go to the spice rack and sniff the cinammon, clove, and mint seperately. Take a walk in the woods and compare the scents of dead, brown leaves to live, green leaves. Go to a florist and try to distinguish between the smells of roses, violets, and magnolias. Pick up a pebble from a stream or lake and put it right under a nostril so the mineral or wet rock smell will be easier to recognize in a wine. These tricks may help you to train the nose and to be more proficient at identifying different smells.

Aroma messages are received through the front openings of the nose and in a **retronasal** manner through the back of the throat (see Figure 3.13). These smell and taste centers, the tongue, nose, and retronasal passage form our **palate.**

***How to Smell.*** When smelling or **nosing,** a wine, each person develops a comfortable "sniffing strategy." The wine should be smelled before and after swirling in the glass, because swirling aerates the wine, allowing the air to bring out the volatile elements in the nose of the wine. Sparkling wines, however, should not be aerated, as swirling breaks the bubbles in the wine.

A popular method of smelling a wine is first to give it a gentle sniff, then inhale more deeply, and finally inhale so heartily that you are virtually attempting to "taste" the wine with your nose. Others reverse this sniffing strategy, inhaling deeply first. The idea of "tasting with the nose" is not so far off the mark because of all the "taste analogies" your nose can decipher. Remember, your tongue can only taste four very general items, but your nose can identify and associate hundreds, even thousands of substances.

Whatever strategy for smelling wine you undertake, the important thing is to try to recognize and record first impressions, since **nasal fatigue,** a decreased sensitivity to smell, is bound to occur over time. Just as people

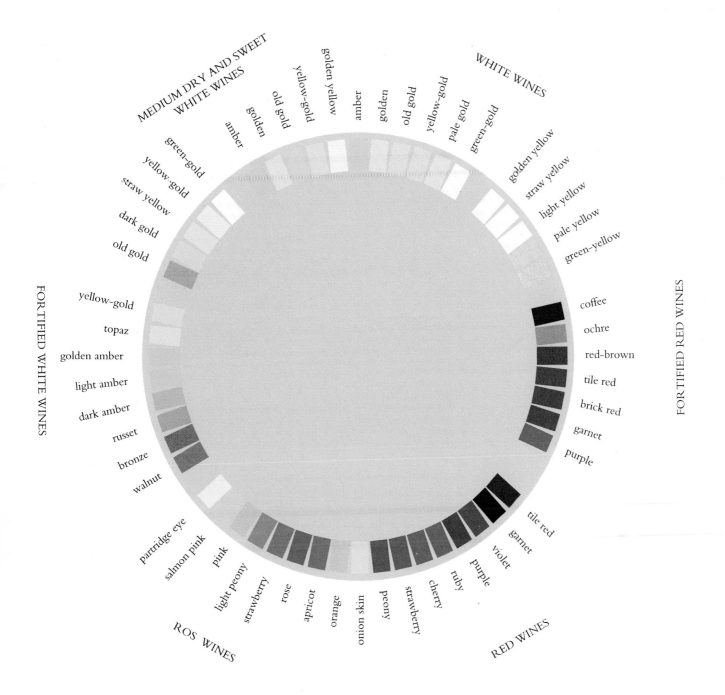

who wear perfume cannot really smell the perfume on their bodies after a while, so too our noses habituate themselves to the smells emanating from the wine glass, as time passes.

The nose of a wine may be shy at first, and then open up, releasing more of the volatile elements in the wine. **Closed** or **dumb** are two terms used when tasters are stymied by a lack of smells. Note the intensity of the wine's nose. Is it shy or powerful? Weak or intoxicating? The smells of a

**Figure 3.12** Davis Color Wheel. (Copyright held by the American Society of Enologists and Virticulturalists. A.C. Noble, et al Am. J. Enol. Vitic. 38: 143-46, 1987.)

**Figure 3.13** We Can Smell Aromas through the Front Openings of the Nose (Nostrils) and in a Retronasal Manner as Vapors Rise up through the Back of the Palate.

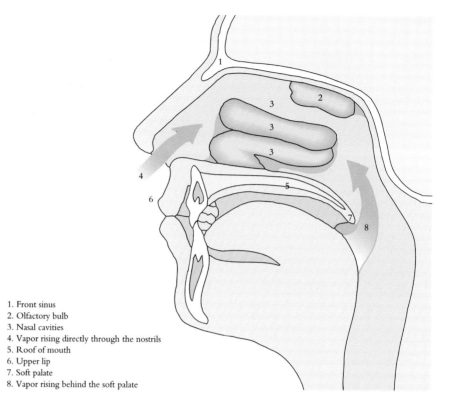

1. Front sinus
2. Olfactory bulb
3. Nasal cavities
4. Vapor rising directly through the nostrils
5. Roof of mouth
6. Upper lip
7. Soft palate
8. Vapor rising behind the soft palate

freshly poured fine wine will change in the glass over time. A simple jug wine will not really change much at all, no matter how much time passes, but a fine wine will show its breeding by going through waves of change in the nature and intensity of its smells that contribute to it being deemed "complex." The attraction and pleasure of just smelling such a wine allows some disciplined tasters to prolong this stage, and not put the wine to their lips until many minutes pass.

***What Do Smells Indicate?*** How can wine, made only from grapes, smell like a banana, rose, or bitter almonds, but almost never a simple blend of grapes and alcohol? The volatile substances that are the roots of these analogous smells result from **aldehydes, esters, ketones, alcohols,** and other chemicals. The volatile compounds include **piperonal** which smells of peach; a banana or pear drop smell indicates the presence of **isoamyl acetate;** tea rose is from **phenylethyl acetate; phenylpropionic aldehyde** gives the scent of lilac; and **acetoin** smells of almonds. Memorizing the names and properties of these chemicals is not as much fun as just trying to recognize the different smells and naming them. With experience, an aware taster will find that these associative smells are indicators of certain grape types, soils, wine regions, winemaking techniques, and other important factors.

Everyone has a different past and "taste memory," so for some wine tasters recognition of certain smells is easier than for others. There are companies that market smell kits that can be used to sensitize tasters to certain smells and to check the hunches of the taster's nose: "Was that really black-

currants I smelled?" Dried spices or flowers can be put in a solution, or fruit jams can be used to help train the nose to develop a memory bank of smells. Healthy people can train for smell, but a cold will block the olfactory cleft and make both smelling and tasting difficult. **Menosmia** is the term that describes an individual's inability to smell a particular smell. Every person has a different threshold at which he or she can distinguish a particular smell or one smell from another.

*Aroma vs. Bouquet.*    The smell of a young wine is an **aroma.** The **primary smell** is that of the grape type and the **secondary smell** is that of the wine after the fermentation process. An example would be a wine that has undergone malolactic fermentation and would have a lactic, or creamy, smell unrelated to the grape type. Experienced wine tasters can smell lychee nuts in a glass and know the wine is probably a Gewürztraminer, and definitely not a Muscadet because of aroma. Aroma should not be confused with **bouquet,** the **tertiary smell** of a wine, which develops with age. Bouquet is the product of the aging process of the alcohols, acids, esters, enzymes, and other chemical compounds in the wine both in cask and in bottle.  Nutty smells are always present in the bouquet of wines that are oxidized, such as Vin Santo of Italy or Sherry from Spain. The most ardent tasters can fill a page writing about the complexities of an aged fine wine's bouquet.

Unfortunately, there is no blanket statement for all wines regarding how much time is needed to be able to refer to the nose as the bouquet. Wines that have pronounced primary grape aroma and other smells, such as oak or alcohol, only suggest what the wine may achieve when time integrates the distinct parts into a more harmonius bouquet.

The Davis Aroma Wheel, developed at the University of California at Davis (UC Davis), gives some of the terms used for smelling wines, and their sources (see Figure 3.14), but these are not the only terms that can be used to describe the smell of wine. The idea of the aroma wheel and other aids to smelling wine is communication among the senses of the taster, so just about any mental association made from smelling wine is proper and correct. There is delight in a smell evoking a memory and opening a door. Walk through that door and allow the words to come out.

## Taste

***Tasting the wine.*** As we stated before, salt, sour, sweet, and bitter are the only four tastes the tongue can experience. Taste messages are sent to the brain from the **pappilae** on the surface of the tongue (see Figure 3.15). Each of the papillae has hundreds of taste buds, which envelop the taste cells and sensory hairs. **Filiform pappilae** are more sensitive to feeling than taste, and so are used to determine levels of hot and cold. **Circumvallate pappilae,** at the back of the tongue, are sensitive to bitterness, while **fungiform pappilae,** at the front tip of the tongue, are sensitive to sweetness. However, the sensory fibers that contact the taste buds are not solely sensitive to one taste message. Some of these fibers carry all four tastes, while others respond only to one. The general areas of the tongue where the four tastes are most acutely perceived are: bitterness at the back of the tongue, sweetness at the front tip, acidity on the middle to front sides and top, and salt at the front top and sides. In addition, there are areas of the tongue that are insensitive to taste.

Saliva production is stimulated by tasting, and the flow of saliva is certainly affected when tasting wine. Wines high in acid always increase saliva flow, while very astringent or tannic wines leave the mouth feeling dried out, making it hard to salivate.

One tastes a wine by moving it around the whole mouth. In this way the wine is warmed, hits more taste buds, and enters the retronasal passage, making flavors more evident. Ten to 30 seconds is a normal amount of time to swirl about an ounce of wine in the mouth before spitting. (It is always best to leave some of the wine in the tasting glass, in case you are instructed to taste, or want to taste, a particular wine again.) Quickly swallowing some wine may provide refreshment and pleasure, but to truly taste a wine takes a conscious effort. With practice, the processes of wine tasting become second nature.

The first taste of the wine is the **attack,** then the **middle,** then comes the **finish.** The attack refers to how powerful the wine is and what sensations are felt during the first five seconds the wine enters the mouth. The middle is the evolution of those sensations as well as new ones over the next ten seconds before the finish. The finish is the aftertaste of flavors and the length of time those flavors can be sensed on the palate.

A wine that feels **hot** on the taster's tongue has a high level of alcohol that is out of balance with the rest of the wine. A wine that has fruitiness, a hint of sweetness, oak, and alcohol, but lacks acidity to balance the other el-

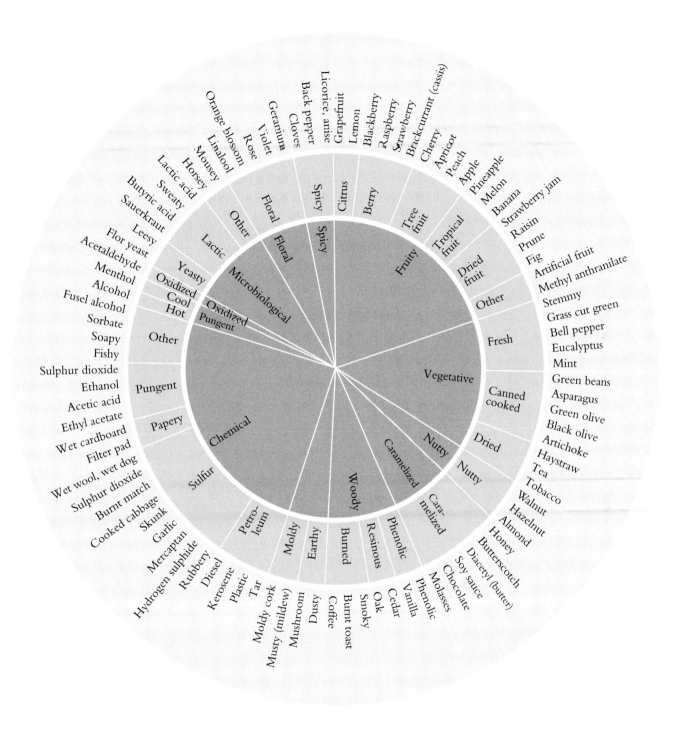

**Figure 3.14** The Davis Aroma Wheel.

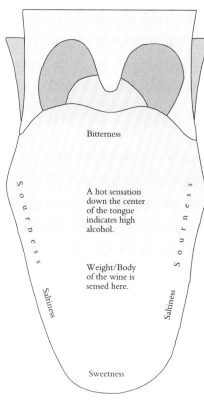

A hot sensation down the center of the tongue indicates high alcohol.

Weight/Body of the wine is sensed here.

Bitterness

Sourness

Sourness

Saltiness

Saltiness

Sweetness

**Figure 3.15** Tongue Sensitivity.

ements is said to be **flabby.** Wines which are unbalanced are inconsistent with the ideal of a fine wine: harmony of taste and nose, so that the total of the organoleptic elements in the wine is greater than its isolated parts. In other words, the sum should be greater than its parts.

How much perceived fruitiness, acidity, alcohol, or oak should there be? A wine should strike a balance of flavor components but be true to the grape type and the growing region it represents. A serious wine taster will become acquainted with the traditional tastes of the major grapes and wine regions of the world. This is a task that may take a lifetime, but this pursuit of knowledge and the attendant tastings provide pleasure. A wine-tasting novice may not like the green, high-acid flavors of a Sauvignon Blanc-based wine from Sancerre in the Loire Valley (see Chapter 6 on France), and may dislike the mineral nose even more. A taster familiar with the wine, however, will expect the mineral nose and acidity, and be disappointed if they are not present in the glass.

*Finish.* Brillat Savarin said of tasting, "While the wine is in one's mouth, one receives a pleasing but imperfect impression; it is only when you have finished swallowing that you can really appreciate the taste and discern the bouquet particular to each type of wine; and then a few more moments are required before the gourmet can say that's good, passable, or bad."

The finish or aftertaste is judged based on the elapsed time, after spitting or swallowing, that the flavors persist on the palate, and whether the lingering flavors are pleasant or not. White wines should have a finish underscored by acidity or they are described as flabby. Reds can more obviously overwhelm the mouth with their higher-tannin potential. If harmony is the goal, are the acidity, sugars, alcohol, or tannins so excessive that they dominate the finish? Any flavors or aromas that can be detected in the aftertaste should be noted. A wine that lasts only three seconds has a short finish, but may still be pleasant. A finish of seven to ten seconds is considered medium, and more than 15 seconds long, depending on the wine. Length of finish is the final measure of a great wine. Whether it is a short, refreshing, tart finish in a young white, or an immeasurably long, complex finish in an aged red, the finish is the final impression of a wine and prompts reflection on the overall quality of a wine.

## The Components of a Wine Tasting

The major components to isolate when tasting wine are as follows:

- **Alcohol.** The alcohol should be in balance with the other components because too much makes the wine taste "hot." The "heat" of a wine in its youth may diminish with time as other flavors evolve.

- **Residual sugar.** How much residual sugar is there? Many people confuse a wine that is fruity, with just a bit of residual sugar, with a wine that is sweet. The more residual sugar, the sweeter the wine (see Chapter 1 on How Wine is Made);

- **Oak.** Not all wines are fermented or aged in a barrel. If oak is tasted, how prominent is its flavor? Does the oak mask the fruit or perhaps a defect in the wine? American oak gives a scent of coconut in a wine while French oak smells more of vanilla. The red Reserva Rioja wines of Spain most often use American oak while the scent of French oak is found in many of that nation's finer wines such as those of Bordeaux. American wineries may use domestic or imported barrels.

- **Tannins.** Tannins come from the barrel in white wines and from grape skins, seeds, stems, and barrels in reds. Wood tannins are sensed more towards the back of the mouth, while grape skin tannins are sensed more at the front of the mouth. Tannin can make the mouth pucker and dry the palate, much like a cup of strong black tea that contains tannic acid.

  Astringency is the term used to describe this drying effect. The taste of tannins is bitter. Tannins as well as the anthocyanins (pigment) in a wine are both phenols that are natural antioxidants.

  Red wines that have a very high tannin level usually have low to medium acid levels so they are not overly hard or aggressively harsh. Aging reduces the effect of tannins in red wines. By contrast, lighter-weight reds with less tannins often have a higher acidity to provide an appealing freshness.

- **Acidity:** Tartaric acid is the main acid in wine and its presence in grapes is higher than in most other fruits. The hard taste of **tartaric acid** is accompanied by the green apple taste of **malic acid** and the citrus taste of **citric acid. Gluconic acid** occurs when rotten grapes

Students Studying Color, Smell, Body, Taste, and Finish During a Tasting.

are included in a wine. While the previous acids occur naturally in the grape, there are three other acids that occur because of bacteria or fermentation. **Lactic acid** has a sour cream type of taste while **succinic acid** is both salty and bitter and **acetic acid** is vinegary. Acidity keeps a wine fresh as it ages and provides balance to the fruit and alcohol components.

- **Carbon dioxide:** Sparkling wine usually contains about six atmospheres of presure. Some still wines may contain a slight amount of fizz that is retained from fermentation. A slight amount of effervescence is found in some Vinho Verde wines of Portugal and some of the northern Italian wines, such as Gavi.

- **Varietal character:** Is a specific taste, or tastes, of a grape type apparent? (See Chapter 2 on Wine Grapes.)

- **Off flavors:** Are there any unpleasant flavors, such as rancidity, rotten eggs, or mold?

- **Aromas in the nose and mouth.** How powerful are the wine's aromas? Are there floral or fruit indicators, such as violets or raspberries? Or perhaps vegetative or spicy aromas, such as bell pepper, black olives, or cinnamon? Any other indicators? The taster should focus on the flavors and aromas that are there, not those that are *supposed* to be there. For example, if a taster who thinks a wine could be based in Cabernet Sauvignon and perceives the classic bell-pepper aroma and tannin effect on the palate, he or she may easily imagine the blackcurrant/cassis flavors that should be there, even if they are not.

- **Body.** Body is the perceived "weight" of the wine in the mouth. It can be described as "watery," "very light," "light," "medium," "full," or "very full," or a combination of these terms, such as medium/full. As the "weight" of the wine progresses from light to full, the idea of the coating of the palate comes into play. A very light wine may actually cleanse the palate, whereas a full-bodied oak-aged wine may come close to deadening the palate.

    If water compares to a wine with a very light body, then a ginger ale could be the equivalent of a medium-bodied wine. A glass of whole milk could be compared to a full-bodied wine, while heavy cream might be the analogy for a very-full-bodied wine. Body is a feeling more than an actual taste and it is associated with the amount of power a wine has. The source of this power may be the alcohol, tannins, sugar, fruit, or a combination of two or three of these components. Wines high in alcohol have more glycerine which makes them feel slippery or full.

    Textural impressions may also be valid remarks on a wine's feel in the mouth. "Velvet" or "satin" imply smooth-feeling wines without harsh alcohol or tannic sensations while "loose knit" would refer to a wine whose taste components do not combine to make a balanced

A **hydrogen sulphide** smell is similar to rotten eggs and is created as yeast cells decompose and interact with any excess **sulfur dioxide** in the wine.

**Mercaptans,** formed by a breakdown of sulfur, imparts the smells of garlic, onion, or rubber to a wine, irritating the nose of the taster.

The chemical smell of iodine or a musty quality are attributed to using rotten grapes. A very slight iodine smell is not a fault in the wine, but may be the result of a wine made near the sea, or affected by noble rot *(Botrytis cinerea)*.

The smell of a so-called "corked" wine is a strong moldy smell that is the result of the chemical trichloranisole used in the process of preparing the cork.

A small amount of acetic acid or ethyl acetate occur naturally in wine but acetic bacteria can ruin a wine by increasing the amount of those substances. Over 150 milligrams per liter of ethyl acetate and 700 milligrams per liter of acetic acid will produce a wine which has an unpleasantly high level of *volatile acidity*. The wines will smell vinegary and dirty and have a harsh, sour taste.

If there are unpleasant odors a small taste of wine can be sampled. It is much easier to deal with a problem wine before all the tasters are seated than to have to remove glasses and replace wine in the middle of a tasting or seminar.

wine yet they are not individually well defined either. Figure 3.16 indicates the relationship and progression of elements associated with body, as well as providing a framework of reference for other aspects of wine tasting.

Finding pleasure in wine depends on its many components being in balance according to any individual's preferences. A taster may experiment using some simple solutions to define what those preferences are and to practice component identification. Start with a small glass of water and add a couple of tablespoons of lemon juice. Add sugar, a little at a time, and taste to feel when the beverage tastes good. The amount of sugar added to rectify the drink is a personal preference. The same process could be reversed starting with sugar and water then adding the citrus. To sample tannins, try a black tea steeped for a long period of time. One glass could be mixed with lemon juice and different amounts of sugar. Next, try the black tea with milk or cream and sugar, and notice how the tannin impression is less powerful.

**Figure 3.16** This Chart was Developed by M. Léglise from a Similar One by A. Vedel. It Uses the Intensity of the Main Components of Sweetness, Acidity, and Astringency to Indicate Balance in Red Wines.

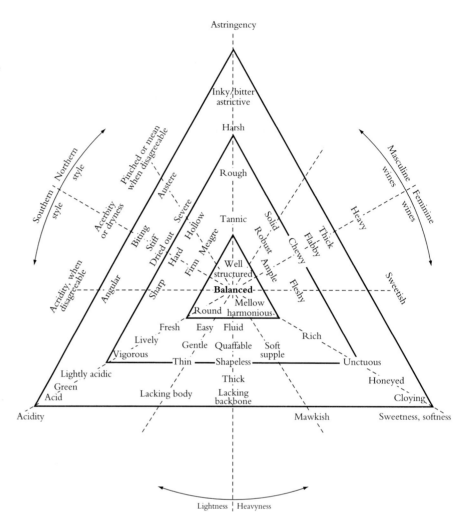

The components of wine should mesh. A young wine may be very aggressive in tannins, oak, and alcohol. However if there is enough richness of fruit and acidity, a taster will realize that in the future the power of the tannins and alcohol will diminish, bringing the wine into balance. The taster may appreciate the wine based not only on its *present* appeal, but on its possible positive *future*.

## Summary

The reasons for tasting wine vary but it is an acquired skill that begins as a discipline that may become a practice that leads to relaxation and pleasure. The tasting terms provided in the chapter are the framework that allows us to share our feelings about a wine with another. Opening our senses to a glass of wine may allow a recollection long forgotten or inspire a vision of the future. Euripides said, "He must be crazy who does not like to drink . . . wine invites us to the dance and makes us forget our ills."

Wine is an alcoholic beverage that may be used to slake thirst, relax, or enhance a meal. Wine may be taken for the aestethic experience of the heart and mind. As appreciation of music is universal regardless of origin so is the appreciation of a taste of wine. The next two sections of the book deal with the major wine-producing nations. The grape types, areas of production, laws, and cultures will be discussed. All this information is valuable background for consumers and professionals as to how these countries and their farmers and wine makers developed the wide range of wines that are available today. Wine lovers have an innate curiosity and wish to refine their understanding of the most civilized of beverages.

True wine devotees would never use their knowledge as a tool to intimidate another with terms a layman would find confusing or tedious. The tasting process and terms used are tools that help to define our preferences and share them. However, a fine bottle of wine shared with a boor or wine snob will be less appreciated than an average one consumed with good company.

# Wines of the New World

*Whether or not we accept the term "New World" as applying to the lands settled by Europeans in the past 500 years, the term is accurate in the world of wine. Grape growing and wine making were all but unknown outside of Europe and the Mediterranean basin until the grape vine was exported by European settlers. Now, wine is a part of every New World country where the climate allows the vine to prosper. Australia, New Zealand, South Africa, Argentina, Chile, Brazil, Mexico, the United States, and Canada all have healthy wine industries which strive to stand on their own merits.*

While it is true that the European settlers of many of these countries were looking to start a new life, free of the restrictions and encumbrances of the "old country," historical memories and cultural associations are evident in all aspects of life in the New World wine countries, in the form of language, food, and work habits. When it comes to wine, the New World pioneers admit to a reverence for the fine wines of the Old World while displaying a healthy disrespect for the glorification of the status quo and the limitations of Old World wine laws. Whereas it would be an exaggeration to say that New World wine makers have taken on the Old World wine establishment, it is true that, in New World wine making circles, experimentation and challenging the accepted are the norms.

Part 2 of our book looks at the current picture in each of the New World wine countries and the contribution of some of the trailblazers who have challenged the accepted truths of wine making and sometimes triumphed. The challenges for New World wine makers tend to fall into three categories:

- Grapes      which ones? grown where? grown how? how much total yield?

- Wine      what style? what fermentation method? how much wine maker interference?

- Appellations      geographic only? restrictions on grape varieties, yield, or minimum alcohol?

The pioneering nature of the New World wine maker and the freedom to experiment have resulted in some extraordinary changes. In some cases, challenges to the accepted wisdom are now everyday practice for wine makers in the New World and the Old. Who would have thought, for example, that grapes could be grown in the semiarid conditions of eastern Washington State in the United States, or in the Murrumbidgee area of southeastern Australia? But controlled irrigation has made the impossible possible, and large tracts of previously unproductive vineyard land in southern France are now productive thanks to large-scale irrigation. And who would have dreamed that wine could or should be made in anything other than a wooden vat or barrel, until the Australians and Californians perfected the temperature-controlled stainless-steel vat, which has completely changed the nature and style of modern wines?

For all of the brilliant and productive innovation of New World wine makers, there remains a recognition on their part that, even though Penfold's Grange Hermitage from Australia, and Beaulieu Vineyard's Georges de Latour Cabernet Sauvignon from California may be great wines, the history of fine wine making in Europe deserves reverence and respect. After all, without the European heritage, the New World wine makers would have no starting place or reference point.

Sometimes, however, the security blanket of reverence has clouded the view of the New World wine maker and consumer. One result is that all of the New World wine countries have ended up with an overabundance of plantings of Chardonnay and Cabernet Sauvignon, two of the grapes on which Europe built its claim to fame. Some would even say that there are plantings of Chardonnay in places where it will never produce good wine, let alone great wine.

In terms of appellations, the United States appears to have a more formalized and exact system than any other New World country, though it is a long way from the rigid controls most European governments impose on grape growing and wine making. The appellations in the United States cover much larger areas than do most of those in Europe, and there has been no attempt to restrict any appellation to certain grape varieties, as is the case in Europe. With the New World's love of the freedom to innovate, it seems unlikely that anything so elaborate as Europe's appellation system will ever evolve in the New World.

Certainly, the freedom to plant anything anywhere and to make the wine however one chooses has allowed New World wine makers to respond rapidly to changes in popular taste, which in itself is commendable. Where New World wine makers will be challenged is in avoiding a sameness of product, a world in which there is little or no difference between a Chardonnay from South Africa and a Chardonnay from Texas. After all, what has made wine so fascinating for so many people in the Old World and the New has been the seemingly endless array of different wines, from different grape types, grown by different growers, in different conditions, in different corners of this planet.

# North America

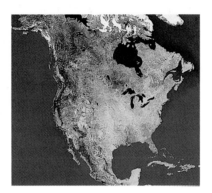

## Introduction

In the space of a quarter-century, the North American continent has emerged from relative obscurity as a wine producer to a position of prominence as a major producer of quality wines. Admittedly, there is a tendency, even within the United States, to think only of California producing good wine, but increasingly the international press focuses deserved attention on other areas of the United States as well as on Canada and Mexico as important and reputable producers of wine.

This chapter will concentrate on the United States as a wine-producing nation, providing a background to current attitudes toward wine, and a summary of the appellation system and label laws. After an overview of some of the important contributions made by U.S. wine makers, we describe the major wine regions within the United States, paying particular attention to California, Washington, Oregon, and New York. In these sections, we highlight the official appellations and some of the notable producers. Other states are also described in less detail.

The chapter concludes with a brief description of the wine regions of Mexico and Canada.

# United States

As a wine nation, the United States is a collection of contradictions and in-consistencies. Although the nation ranks as the fifth-largest producer of wine in the world, it ranks only 30th in annual per capita consumption (see Table 4.1). Whereas many U.S. wineries are proud to advertise the fact that their wines have been used at White House dinners, the controls imposed by government on labeling and merchandising wines are ridiculed by out-side observers. The United States is the only nation in the world that re-quires health warning labels on every bottle of wine sold (see Figure 4.1), whereas American wines exported to other nations are not permitted to carry the warning label. It is also the only nation in the world where many aspects of wine regulation are controlled by the same bureaucracy which oversees firearms (the Bureau of Alcohol, Tobacco and Firearms, or BATF).

Many Americans see the consumption of wine as one aspect of living well, yet there is also a strong sentiment throughout the nation that drinking is wrong. And, for all of the United State's consumerism, which allows any-body to buy and use the most complicated and technologically advanced machinery without knowing anything about how it works, there persists a

### TABLE 4.1   TOP TEN WINE-PRODUCING COUNTRIES, 1991 AND 1992*

| Rank | Country | 1991[r] | 1992[p] | % Change |
|---|---|---|---|---|
| 1 | France | 1138 | 1739 | 52.8% |
| 2 | Italy | 1594 | 1701 | 6.7 |
| 3 | Spain | 859 | 926 | 7.8 |
| 4 | CIS[a] | 480 | 480 | — |
| 5 | USA | 413 | 412 | −0.2 |
| 6 | Germany | 285 | 357 | 25.3 |
| 7 | Argentina | 387 | 307 | −20.7 |
| 8 | South Africa | 257 | 248 | −3.5 |
| 9 | Romania | 128 | 200 | 56.3 |
| 10 | Portugal | 267 | 193 | −27.7 |
| | Other | 1075 | 1121 | 4.3 |
| | **Total World** | **6883** | **7684** | **11.6%** |

*millions of gallons

[a]Commonwealth of Independent States, formerly the USSR. [r]Revised. [p]Preliminary.

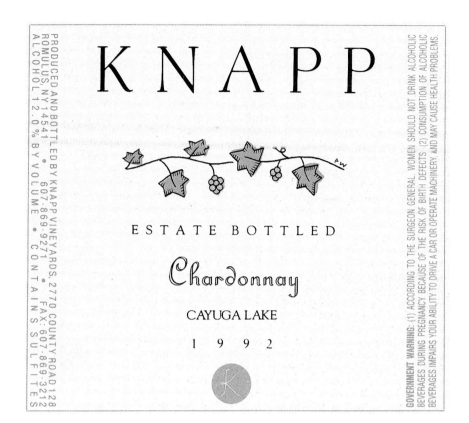

KNAPP

ESTATE BOTTLED

*Chardonnay*

CAYUGA LAKE

1 9 9 2

PRODUCED AND BOTTLED BY KNAPP VINEYARDS, 2770 COUNTY ROAD 128 ROMULUS, NY 14541 • 607-869-9271 • FAX: 607-869-3212 ALCOHOL 12.0% BY VOLUME • CONTAINS SULFITES

GOVERNMENT WARNING: (1) ACCORDING TO THE SURGEON GENERAL, WOMEN SHOULD NOT DRINK ALCOHOLIC BEVERAGES DURING PREGNANCY BECAUSE OF THE RISK OF BIRTH DEFECTS. (2) CONSUMPTION OF ALCOHOLIC BEVERAGES IMPAIRS YOUR ABILITY TO DRIVE A CAR OR OPERATE MACHINERY, AND MAY CAUSE HEALTH PROBLEMS.

**Figure 4.1** The Surgeon General's Warning. Many Producers in the United States Incorporate the Warning into Their Regular Label.

bizarre notion in the United States that in order to buy and enjoy wine, you have to know everything about it.

This chapter will attempt to define the place of wine in the United States by first looking at current attitudes and drinking trends, and then by describing the contribution of some North Americans to the world of wine. We will also provide profiles of the major vine-growing and wine-producing regions of the United States.

## *Wine Today*

At first glance, it may seem illogical that wine consumption in the United States has decreased steadily over the last decade to the point where annual per capita consumption is less than two gallons (eight liters) (see Table 4.2). But this trend parallels what is happening in the rest of the world (with the exception of Australia). There is another worldwide trend which partially explains why people all around the world are drinking less wine: wine producers are concentrating on higher-quality wines, and consumers have responded by purchasing and consuming higher-quality (higher-priced) wines, though in smaller quantity.

| Category | 1960 | 1970 | 1980 | 1990 | 1991 | 1992 | 1993 |
|----------|------|------|------|------|------|------|------|
| Beer | 95.8 | 117.4 | 139.5 | 131.1 | 126.2 | 124.1 | 122.2 |
| Wine | 5.7 | 8.3 | 12.1 | 9.2 | 8.8 | 9.3 | 8.9 |
| Spirits | 8.3 | 12.0 | 11.4 | 8.3 | 7.5 | 7.4 | 7.2 |

★Liters Per Person—21 and Over

An outstanding example of this move toward increasing sophistication in a shrinking market is the recent emphasis placed on premium quality wines by the Gallo wine company of Modesto, California. Still seen as the giant of the United States wine industry, producing more than all other U.S. wineries combined, Gallo is now emphasizing its line of wines from its properties in Sonoma, California. Their most prestigious wines sell for $45 to $60 per bottle, a far cry from the $1.99 Thunderbird which helped Gallo establish itself as the industry giant through the 1940s, 1950s, and 1960s. The U.S. wine industry appears to have accepted, even welcomed, this "drink less but drink better" trend, even though the long-term effect may mean reduced revenues for some companies.

Of the total U.S. population, approximately one-third does not drink alcohol at all. Of the remaining two-thirds, half were defined by a 1970s survey as "regular" wine drinkers, with the definition of regular being one glass of wine per *week*. Yet the dedicated wine drinker in the United States drinks one, sometimes two glasses of wine per *day*. By some estimates, as much as 90 percent of all the wine consumed in the United States is consumed by only 10 percent of the wine-drinking population (and remember that one-third of all Americans do not drink alcohol at all).

The profile of the American wine drinker is far different from the profile of the average European wine consumer. In Europe, most people at all socioeconomic levels drink wine, and not just one glass of wine per week, but at least one glass of wine at dinner every day. In other words, everybody drinks wine in the Old World wine-producing countries. In America, the higher a person's level of education and income, the more likely he or she is to drink wine (see Tables 4.3 and 4.4). The American wine industry therefore gears all of its marketing strategies to attracting the upscale, upmarket consumer. However, if the American wine industry wants to increase the sale and consumption of wine, it should broaden the base of those groups who consume wine, not just try to sell more wine to the existing wine drinkers.

***The Evolution of an American Wine Drinker.***  The majority of wine consumers in America today express a preference for white wine over red. This situation is very different from the consumption patterns of 20 or 30 years ago, when more Americans drank heavy red wines, especially sweet wines in

## TABLE 4.3   WINE CONSUMPTION ACCORDING TO LEVEL OF EDUCATION

| Type | Graduated College | Attended College | Graduated High School | Did Not Graduated H.S. | Total Adults |
|---|---|---|---|---|---|
| Domestic Table Wine | 43.3% | 33.2% | 23.6% | 15.0% | 28.0% |
| Imported Table Wine | 25.7% | 17.3% | 11.7% | 9.1% | 15.2% |
| Coolers | 21.9% | 24.6% | 22.2% | 16.2% | 21.5% |
| Champagne & Sparkling | 28.3% | 22.7% | 17.6% | 11.2% | 19.6% |
| Dessert & Fortified | 11.0% | 9.9% | 6.7% | 6.4% | 8.2% |
| Vermouth | 5.6% | 3.2% | 2.8% | 2.4% | 3.3% |
| Sangria | 5.4% | 6.8% | 6.4% | 6.8% | 6.4% |
| Aperitif & Specialty | 8.1% | 6.4% | 4.9% | 3.3% | 5.5% |
| **Adult Pop (mil)** | **36.5** | **44.3** | **66.7** | **38.3** | **185.8** |

*Source*: Impact Databank.

## TABLE 4.4   BEVERAGE CONSUMPTION ACCORDING TO INCOME

| Household Income | Total Beverages | Total Nonalcoholic Beverages | Total Alcoholic Beverages | Malt Beverages | Distilled Spirits | Wine[1] | Wine Coolers |
|---|---|---|---|---|---|---|---|
| Under $15,000 | 19.1% | 18.9% | 21.6% | 24.2% | 7.0% | 12.9% | 16.8% |
| $15,000–$24,999 | 15.7% | 16.0% | 11.4% | 11.6% | 7.6% | 16.2% | 18.3% |
| $25,000–$34,999 | 15.3% | 15.4% | 13.9% | 13.9% | 11.5% | 16.9% | 17.0% |
| $35,000–$44,999 | 17.9% | 18.1% | 14.1% | 12.9% | 19.9% | 16.6% | 19.7% |
| $45,000–$59,999 | 16.5% | 16.4% | 19.6% | 20.0% | 17.9% | 22.9% | 14.2% |
| $60,000 & over | 15.5% | 15.2% | 19.4% | 17.4% | 36.1% | 14.5% | 14.0% |
| **Total** | **100.0%** | **100.0%** | **100.0%** | **100.0%** | **100.0%** | **100.0%** | **100.0%** |

[1]Excludes wine coolers.
*Source*: Impact Databank.

a Port or Sherry style. But as our tastes in food have moved to lighter fare, so our preferences for wine have changed. If we highlight some of the best-selling wine brands over the last few decades, we will understand a lot about how individuals in America progress as wine drinkers, and how American tastes have changed (see Figure 4.2). In 1994 sales of Chardonnay in the United States reached 18 million cases (216 million bottles), overtaking White Zinfandel as the highest selling varietally-labeled wine.

***The Evolution of the American Wine Producer.***   Just as American wine consumers have changed over time, so the American wine producer has learned, adapted, and improved to the point where some parts of North America are now major producers of high-quality wines. Part of the North American psyche and character is an unswerving need to learn and understand, to experiment and improve, and this is as true for wine as for aeronautics. North American wine makers and researchers have made some major contributions to the world of wine knowledge. To understand these contributions, we need first to look at how the industry evolved.

For all of the early attempts at grape growing and wine making on the east and west coasts of North America, and notwithstanding the awards and gold medals from World's Fairs from the late 1800s through the early 1900s, serious world-class wine making did not emerge in the United States until the 1950s and 1960s. Earlier in this century, Prohibition existed as an amendment to the U.S. Constitution from 1919 to 1933. Even with its repeal in 1933 and the formation three years later of the Wine Institute, "to educate the American public about wine," many states, counties, towns, and villages retained some form of prohibition or restrictive licensing, and a similar situation existed in Canada. The beginning of the Great Depression

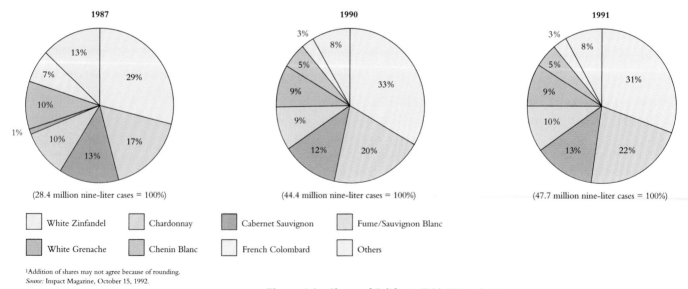

**1987**
(28.4 million nine-liter cases = 100%)

**1990**
(44.4 million nine-liter cases = 100%)

**1991**
(47.7 million nine-liter cases = 100%)

White Zinfandel  Chardonnay  Cabernet Sauvignon  Fume/Sauvignon Blanc

White Grenache  Chenin Blanc  French Colombard  Others

[1]Addition of shares may not agree because of rounding.
*Source:* Impact Magazine, October 15, 1992.

**Figure 4.2**  Shares of California Table Wines by Type.

was not the best time to borrow money to start up new wineries. In the 1940s, North American industry concentrated on helping to win a war, and it was not until the 1950s that the social and economic climate became ripe for any real development in wine production in North America.

This fact is highlighted by two staggering statistics. First, there were more acres planted with grapes in California prior to Prohibition than there are today. Second, the first new winery to open in Napa Valley following Prohibition was Joe Heitz's in 1962, 29 years after the repeal of Prohibition. Heitz was followed soon after by Robert Mondavi, who split from his family which runs the Charles Krug Winery, to open his own winery in 1966. At that time, two European immigrants, Charles Fournier from France and Dr. Konstantin Frank from Russia were pioneering the use of vinifera grape varieties in New York State. Since that time however, research and development have proceeded at a heady pace. Much of that development can be seen through the evolution of the standard label on bottles of North American wine.

## Naming the Wine

There are three main types of naming used on North American wine labels: proprietary, generic, and varietal (see descriptions below). This is in distinct contrast to the age-old practice in European wine countries, where many of the wines are named for the place where the grapes grow. There are also various descriptive terms used on North American labels. Some of these terms are defined in law, some are not.

**Proprietary Labels.** Throughout this century and still today, wine producers in North America have used *proprietary* names to label their wines. A proprietary name is one that is trademarked or copyrighted, and is for the sole use of one company. Early examples were as curious as the current crop of proprietary names, ranging from the early "Thunderbird" and "Night Train," to the more recent "Opus One," "Dominus," and Sutter Home's very recent "Fre" label for its nonalcoholic wines. The essential message here is to provide brand recognition and loyalty.

Proprietary labels (see Figure 4.3) also include those which use the name of the winery as the principal wording on the label, often followed by other descriptive words. Examples of this are the sparkling wines of Domaine Chandon and Domaine Carneros in California. There are even red and white Californian wines labeled simply "Lyeth," the name of the winery where the wines are made, but with no other name on the label.

Today's consumers are likely to know what they are buying when they buy "Opus One" or "Lyeth": they will probably know what grape varieties were used, where the grapes grew, and who made the wine. It is unlikely that consumers of "Thunderbird" were or are as informed. In other words, the producer of high-quality wines in North America today is dealing with a highly educated group of consumers.

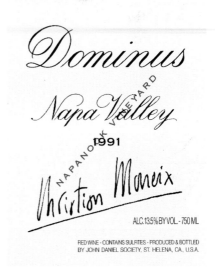

**Figure 4.3** Examples of Proprietary Wine Labels.

**Figure 4.4** Examples of Generic Wine Labels.

***Generic Labels.*** Generic labels have also been in use for many years in North America. The word "generic" refers literally to the fact that the name used reflects a *type* of wine. All of the generic names used on North American wine labels are European place-names, borrowed by North American wine makers, presumably in the belief or hope that their wine is of the type from that place in Europe. The most common examples of generic names used in America are:

**Chablis:** Used in North America to name any usually medium-dry white wine.

**Burgundy:** Used in North America to name any usually soft red wine.

**Champagne:** Used in North America to name any white wine with bubbles in it.

**Rhine:** Used in North America to name any medium-sweet white wine.

**Sauterne:** Used in North America to name any sweet white wine (notice that in crossing the Atlantic, the name *Sauternes,* a place in Bordeaux, France, has lost the final "s").

In practice, wines carrying these names bear little or no resemblance to the wines from the original place in Europe.

There has been an interesting development in generic wine labels (see Figure 4.4) with the introduction in California of the wine label term "Meritage," which indicates a red or white wine made in the style of Bordeaux red or white wines, and using the grapes used by Bordeaux wine makers. These grapes are mostly Cabernet Sauvignon, Merlot, and Cabernet Franc in various percentage combinations for the red wines, and Sauvignon Blanc and Sémillon in various percentage combinations for the white wines.

***Varietal Labels.*** Presumably in an attempt to bring more integrity and authenticity to wine names (as well as gain name differentiation), some U.S. producers, led by the Wente family in California in 1936, took the unprecedented step of giving their wines *varietal* names (see Figure 4.5). This means that the wine is named for the grape variety used to make the wine. As we now know, hundreds of varieties of grapes are used to make wine. Interestingly enough, the introduction of varietal labels has created the need and demand for a large body of legislation which controls when and how certain terms can be used on the label (see the following section on label laws). The most commonly used varietal names in North America are:

**Chardonnay:** *The* white wine, seemingly made everywhere.

**Zinfandel:** Named simply "Zinfandel" if the wine is red, but ironically called "White Zinfandel" if the wine is blush or white in color.

**Cabernet Sauvignon:** The famous red variety popularized by Bordeaux wine producers.

**Merlot:** Favored by some producers and consumers for its softer, fruitier character than Cabernet.

### Other Label Terms

*Estate-Bottled.* This term indicates that the activities of growing the grapes, making the wine, and bottling the finished product were essentially or substantially under the control of the same person or company. It is therefore assumed to ensure authenticity. The vineyards and winery must be located within any named appellation.

*Reserve.* This term is widely used to suggest wine blended from special vineyards, or wine aged longer than usual. In fact, this term may be used by any vintage-dated, varietally named wine.

*Late Harvest.* This phrase indicates that grapes were left on the vine to ripen for a longer period of time than usual, thereby developing a higher sugar content. The resulting wine, almost always white, will be very sweet.

*Botrytis.* When this term appears on the label, it indicates that the grapes have been attacked by the fungus of the same name (see the section on *Botrytis* in Chapter 2 on Wine Grapes). The resulting concentration of sugars in the grapes will make for an intensely sweet wine.

## The Laws Behind the Labels

**Varietal Names.** As soon as wine makers started using varietal grape names to label a wine, the U.S. government stepped in, demanding to know exactly how much of the grape named on the label was in the wine. (From an outsider's point of view, it is patently absurd that the U.S. government has never ruled on the use or misuse of terms such as "Chablis" or "Burgundy" by U.S. wine makers when the wines are obviously not from those places.) The immediate solution adopted by the BATF was to demand that at least 51 percent of the wine in a bottle labeled as Chardonnay be made from Chardonnay grapes. In other words, up to 49 percent of the wine could be made from *any* other grape variety, thereby dramatically reducing, even nullifying the Chardonnay character of the wine.

Responsible U.S. wine makers have always used 100 percent Chardonnay grapes in that wine, since the addition of even 3 or 5 percent of another grape variety noticeably alters the flavor of the wine. Those wine producers successfully lobbied for legislation to increase the minimum percentage of the named grape, and since 1983 legislation in the United States requires a minimum of 75 percent of the named grape variety be used in the production of a wine with a varietal label.

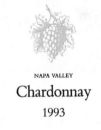

Cakebread Cellars

NAPA VALLEY

Chardonnay

1993

PRODUCED AND BOTTLED BY CAKEBREAD CELLARS
RUTHERFORD, CALIFORNIA, USA
ALCOHOL 14.1% BY VOLUME

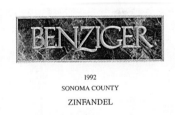

1992
SONOMA COUNTY
ZINFANDEL

ALCOHOL 14.0% BY VOLUME

**Figure 4.5** Examples of Varietal Wine Labels.

The 25 percent leeway allows producers to blend in a second or third grape when the wine maker considers that the wine will be improved by those additions. A good example is Cabernet Sauvignon wine. A wine made from 100 percent Cabernet Sauvignon is often too tannic and too intense for many consumers. A standard way of making the wine more appealing is to blend in wine from grape varieties which are known to have softer, less-aggressive characteristics. In the case of Cabernet Sauvignon, Merlot is often used as a blending grape. The wine maker is not required to state on the label exactly what percentage of any grape was used.

Any state is free to amend the federal legislation to require that a higher percentage of the named varietal be used, as in Oregon, where at least 90 percent of the grapes must be of the named varietal (except in the case of Cabernet Sauvignon, where 75 percent remains the minimum).

***Place Names.*** It is obvious that the makers of any product have competitors, and one way to gain an edge on the competition is to create some kind of differentiation, and to state that differentiation on the label. In the case of wine, one of the notable differences is the location of the vineyard, reflecting the belief that grapes grown in location A have different characteristics from those grown in location B. These differences are the accumulated effect of exposure to the sun, amount of rainfall, length of daylight, average temperatures, soil types, and so forth. (For more information on this, see the section on heat summation in this chapter, and the section on *terroir* in Chapter 6 on France.)

When some California wine makers wanted to suggest to the consumer that the use of grapes from Napa Valley made their wine somehow "better" than wine made from grapes grown elsewhere in California, the term Napa Valley began to appear on wine labels. The wine thus became not just Chardonnay, but *Napa Valley* Chardonnay. The same kind of place name differentiation is applied to Cheddar-type cheese made in the United States, where New York State, Vermont, and Wisconsin all vie for recognition as premium producers of "Cheddar" (even though Cheddar is a place name in England where that type of cheese was originally produced).

As soon as producers started using Napa Valley as a label term, the BATF stepped in to control the meaning of such terms. Currently, the law states that if a place name is used on a label, that place name must be an **appellation or AVA (Approved Viticultural Area,** sometimes also referred to as American Viticultural Area), approved by the BATF, and that at least 85 percent of the grapes used to produce the wine must come from the named AVA. Again, Oregon has gone beyond that requirement, to demand that 100 percent of any wine bearing an appellation name comes from that appellation. (For more on how the appellation system works in the United States, see the section in this chapter.) It is important to note that the appellation refers to where the grapes grew, not necessarily where the winery is located.

If an appellation is named on the label of a varietally named wine, at least 75 percent of the named grape variety must come from the named appellation. If a single vineyard is named in addition to an appellation, the single vineyard must lie completely within the named appellation, and 95 percent of any named varietal must come from the single vineyard.

***Vintage Dates.*** The other major legally defined term on U.S. wine labels is the vintage date. If a label on the bottle states a year, at least 95 percent of the wine must have been produced from grapes harvested in the stated year. For more complete information on the BATF regulations regarding minimum percentages, see Appendix C.

# North American Contributions

This section will look at some of the contributions made by Americans to the greater understanding of wine and how it is made. In particular, we will look at the concept of heat summation, wood aging, and the appellation system in the New World. This is not to suggest that only Americans have made advances in these areas, but they have certainly made significant contributions. Finally, in this section, we comment on some of the changes brought about by *phylloxera.*

***Heat Summation.*** We have already suggested that world-class wine making in America did not become a realizable dream until the 1950s. At that time, American wine makers were smart enough to recognize that the Old World countries had already had almost two thousand years of practice at making wine. Over that period of time, they have eventually reached a position where they have most of the right grapes growing in the right places. That situation was achieved more by trial and error than any other method. If one particular grape variety was not successful in one region, it has been torn out and replaced with another. As a result, today Cabernet Sauvignon and Merlot grow in Bordeaux, Nebbiolo grows in Piemonte, Riesling grows in Mosel, and so forth (see Part 3 of this book).

American wine makers knew they could not wait two thousand years to come up with the right answers; they wanted results in 20 years. The University of California at Davis (UC Davis) stepped in with a proposal to associate specific grape varieties with certain climatic conditions, specifically with the amount of heat exposure for the grapes, since there appears to be a direct relationship between the amount of heat exposure and the degree of ripeness of the grape at harvest.

Starting from the assumption that the minimum average temperature required to ripen a grape through the growing season is 50°F (10°C), the UC Davis team began measuring the daily temperatures between April 1 and October 31 in numerous locations throughout the California grape-growing regions. Over several years of data collection, they established a formula to determine the average amount of heat accumulation in any one area over and above the minimum required average temperature of 50°F (10°C). That formula is:

Daily average temperature - 50 = number of **degree days.**

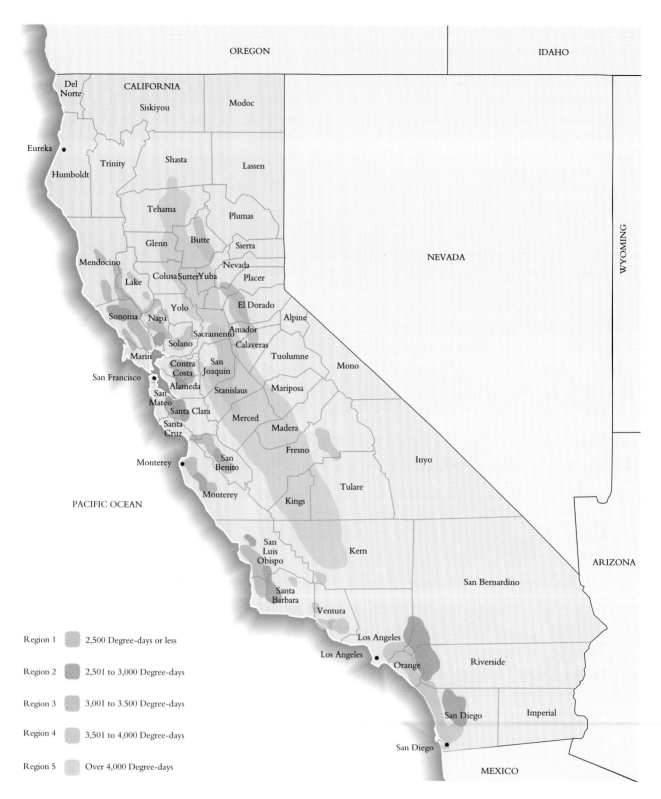

**Map 4.1** The Climatic Regions of California.

Region 1 · 2,500 Degree-days or less

Region 2 · 2,501 to 3,000 Degree-days

Region 3 · 3,001 to 3.500 Degree-days

Region 4 · 3,501 to 4,000 Degree-days

Region 5 · Over 4,000 Degree-days

When that calculation is made every day from April 1 to October 31, the result is a total number of degree days for that region. Regions throughout California were then classified according to the range of degree days measured. Map 4.1 shows the ranges of degree days for climatic regions 1 through 5, as determined by UC Davis.

Over the same period of time, UC Davis had conducted extensive research into the growing patterns of different vine varieties grown in different climates. They were then able to match specific grape variety recommendations to each climatic region. The principal recommendations are:

Region 1—Chardonnay, Pinot Noir, Riesling, Gewürztraminer

Region 2—Cabernet Sauvignon, Sauvignon Blanc, Merlot

Region 3—Zinfandel, Barbera, Syrah, Gamay

Region 4—Thompson Seedless, Malvasia

Region 5—Thompson Seedless, Dessert table grapes

The only role of UC Davis in creating this list is to provide recommendations. Grape growers remain free to plant any grape variety on any piece of land they choose.

The map created from all of this research shows that the cooler regions (regions 1 and 2) are all located near the coast. Those cool regions are exactly the ones which most people associate with high-quality wines from California: Napa, Sonoma, Carneros, Anderson Valley in Mendocino, Paso Robles in San Luis Obispo, and Santa Ynez Valley in Santa Barbara.

Table 4.5 gives a comparison of degree days for some of the notable locations in North America, the Southern Hemisphere, and Europe. It is well recognized that the degree day system of UC Davis is not perfect, and that many other factors are involved in choosing which grape variety to plant. For example, the system measures only heat summation over a period of time; it does not provide information on how much heat is accumulated at what point in the season. It seems to take no account of rainfall, either in terms of quantity or time. There is no reference to latitude, length of the growing season, or the number of daylight hours. It certainly avoids the question of soil, which Europeans have long regarded as a major factor. Despite these shortcomings, the heat summation system brought grape growing and wine making in California to a state of maturity much sooner than would have been the case without such a system.

On the topic of climate, fear and trepidation were evident throughout California in the early months of 1995 as storm after storm tore through various parts of the state. According to the Napa Valley Vintners Association and the Napa County Agricultural Commissioner, the main impact of the storms in Napa County has been property damage to trellissing systems and irrigation systems, as well as large amounts of debris to be cleaned out of vineyards. Up to 15,000 acres/6000 hectares faced an estimated $7.5 million

## TABLE 4.5  DEGREE DAYS COMPARISON

| | *Heat Units in Growing Season* | |
| | *In Degree-Days* *(Celsius)* *10° base* | *In Degree-Days* *(Fahrenheit)* *50° base* |
|---|---|---|
| **France** | | |
| Chablis | 950 | 1710 |
| Loire | 950–1100 | 1710–1980 |
| Champagne | 1050 | 1890 |
| Beaujolais | 1150 | 2070 |
| Côte d'Or | 1180 | 2210 |
| Alsace | 1230 | 2210 |
| Médoc | 1350–1400 | 2430–2520 |
| Hermitage | 1450 | 2610 |
| **Germany** | | |
| Mosel-Saar-Ruwer | 950–1150 | 1710–2070 |
| Baden | 1050 | 1890 |
| Rheinhessen | 1050–1100 | 1890–2070 |
| Rheingau | 1050–1200 | 1890–2160 |
| Pfalz | 1200–1250 | 2160–2250 |
| **California** | | |
| Monterey | 1200–1300 | 2160–2340 |
| Santa Clara | 1250–1300 | 2250–2340 |
| Livermore Valley | 1250–1400 | 2250–2520 |
| Napa | 1300–1450 | 2340–2610 |
| Sonoma | 1200–2000 | 2160–3600 |
| **Chile** | | |
| Maipo Valley | 1350–1400 | 2430–2520 |
| **South Africa** | | |
| Stellenbosch | 1300–1400 | 2340–2520 |
| Paarl | 1400–1450 | 2520–2610 |
| **New Zealand** | | |
| Canterbury | 900–1100 | 1620–1980 |
| Auckland | 1300–1350 | 2340–2430 |
| **Australia** | | |
| Coonawarra | 1150–1250 | 2070–2250 |
| McLaren Vale | 1300–1400 | 2340–2520 |

in property damage, while approximately 100 acres/40 hectares were washed away by flood waters and will have to be replanted.

In Monterey County, property damage will cost approximately $2.5 million, mostly for replacement of trellissing systems and irrigation systems. Throughout California, concern was still being expressed as late as May 1995 that the vineyards were still wet in many parts, making it difficult to bring machinery in to do routine work such as spraying. The first few weeks in May can be a critical time in parts of California as the vines flower and the grapes set, and it is important to be able to get into the vineyard for routine tasks.

*Wood Aging.*    In Chapter 1 we gave some examples of how the choice of a wooden barrel for making or aging wine might affect the final outcome. Much of the experimentation associated with wood aging was begun in the United States by wine makers such as Robert Mondavi who were not satisfied with blanket statements from Old World wine makers to the effect that one wood was better than another, but with no explanation. In fact, it quickly became clear to many Americans that most Bordeaux wine makers were not aware that a different type of barrel was used in Burgundy, nor did they care!

The Robert Mondavi Winery still conducts tastings which attempt to demonstrate the different effects on wine of different types of wood and of different lengths of time in wood. Such experimentation is now common to many large wineries in California, and yet we cannot help but be struck by the enormous investment of money and time which these experiments demand. Thousands of gallons of wine are involved for long periods of time, and some of that wine may never be sold. Thousands of barrels from various forests and coopers and of various ages will be used, all as part of the effort to understand more about wood aging, so that American wine makers can make better wine.

From our perspective, the efforts have been worthwhile. In the 1980s, for example, California had a reputation for making Chardonnays which were buttery, oaky, and with a sweet vanilla taste, all of which can be attributed to an overzealous approach to wood aging. Currently, the majority of Chardonnays from respected wine makers in California are much leaner, with less of the heavy oak treatment.

The experimentation which we have noted here in connection with wood continues in other areas, notably in vineyard management. Again, it is the larger wineries, such as Mondavi, Beringer, and Fetzer, that are most heavily involved in experiments to ascertain the optimum spacing for vines. This may seem simplistic on the surface, but there are endless variations involved in such experiments, all of them taking up land whose real estate value may be extremely high. A winery may experiment with spacing Merlot vines with two feet between the vines and five feet between the rows, then three feet between the vines and six feet between the rows, and so forth. Then, of course, they might have the same spacing variations for Cabernet Sauvignon and ten other grape varieties. These spacing experiments hope to establish guidelines for vine spacing which will result in improved yields and improved quality in the future.

**Map 4.2**  The Appellation System of California.

# Appellation System, or Approved Viticultural Areas (AVAs)

The appellation system (see Map 4.2) is not, of course, an American invention, although among New World countries, the United States has led the way in defining what appellations are. As the name implies, appellations in the United States are based in concept on the *appellation d'origine contrôlée* system which governs French grape growing and wine making. The U.S. system is not as extensive as the French system, however. In France, *appellation d'origine contrôlée* controls not only the delineation of any named area but also factors such as which grape varieties may be grown there, how many tons of grapes per acre may be harvested, minimum aging requirements, and minimum alcohol levels. In the United States the appellation system is restricted to a geographic definition of the named area.

To gain AVA status in the United States, the grape growers or wine makers of any region are required to petition the BATF. The petition must explain why and how the region is identifiable as a separate grape-growing area, and how it is distinct from any surrounding land. Usually, the petition will cite such factors as history, climate, soil, water tables, and so forth.

Of all the AVAs that have been approved in the United States, the most famous is undoubtedly Napa Valley in California. Ironically, Napa Valley was not the first AVA in the United States, nor is it the best defined. As appellations go, the Napa Valley is a very large area, encompassing many different climatic regions, a varied topography, and numerous soil types, and it was approved as the second AVA in the United States, only a short while after Augusta, Missouri was named as the first AVA in 1980.

Since that time, the number of AVAs has grown dramatically to the point where there are currently 125 distinct and defined grape-growing areas, 71 of which are in California. The system now involves the recognition of large umbrella appellations, as well as sub-appellations. The theory of this can best be understood in terms of concentric circles (see Figure 4.6). According to the label laws, if at least 85 percent of the grapes were grown in zone A, the wine may be labeled "zone A wine." If only 75 percent of the grapes were grown in zone A, and the remainder were

**Figure 4.6** Four Concentric Circles: A through D

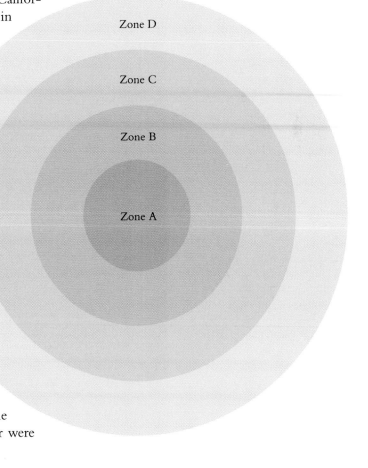

Zone D

Zone C

Zone B

Zone A

grown in zone B, the wine may be labeled "zone B wine" (since zone A falls *within* zone B, it naturally follows that at least 85 percent of the grapes were grown in zone B). If 50 percent of the grapes were grown in zone A, 25 percent in zone B, and 25 percent in zone D, the wine may be labeled "zone D wine" since at least 85 percent of all the grapes came from within zone D.

In practice, one of the best regions to look at is Sonoma County which contains several appellations (see Map 4.3). Using our concentric circles theory again, we could make the following assignments:

> Zone A = Russian River Valley
>
> Zone B = Northern Sonoma
>
> Zone C = Sonoma Coast
>
> Zone D = Sonoma County

The development of subappellations in Sonoma County, and more recently in Napa County, underscores an important tenet of the appellation system. Smaller appellations are drafted and adopted to make more specific delineations, with more precise recommendations for certain grape types. The smaller the appellation, the more likely it is that all of the grapes from that appellation will have similar characteristics. Thus it is true to say that smaller appellations usually produce more specific wines, and some people would suggest that greater specificity leads to better quality.

There are also appellations which encompass Sonoma County. The North Coast appellation groups together the counties of Napa, Sonoma, Lake, Mendocino, Solano, and Marin. Similarly, the North Coast appellation falls within the appellation of California, and California is surrounded by the "mega-appellation" of America.

The Sonoma County example is repeated throughout the state of California, with other large appellations encompassing smaller ones. In addition to the large appellation of North Coast, there are also the large appellations of Central Coast, subdivided into North Central Coast and South Central Coast, which are further split into counties and then into specific appellations.

Twenty-seven states now boast fully defined and registered AVAs, although only California has the degree of complexity of interlocking appellations described above. For a complete listing of AVAs throughout the United States, see Appendix C.

## Wine Regions of the United States—California

The Golden State produces far more wine than the rest of the states combined, much of this production coming in the form of bulk or jug wine from giant producers such as Gallo and Paul Masson. In many ways it can be argued that the true litmus test of any region's ability to make good wine should be measured by its ability to make good jug wine, or *vin ordinaire*.

**Map 4.3** The AVAs of Sonoma County.

*This map shows the large appellations of Northern Sonoma and Sonoma Coast within Sonoma County. Note that the two appellations overlap in the center of the county around the Russian River.*

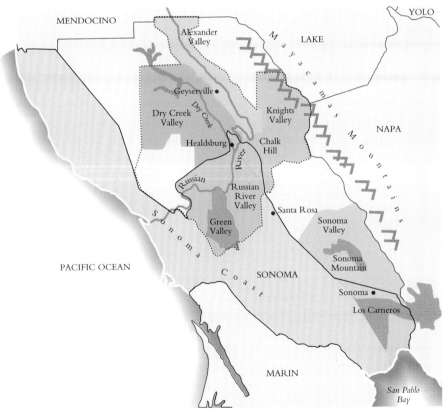

*This second map shows the smaller appellations which fall within the two larger ones.*

As early as 1985, producers knew that the seeds of disaster were taking root in the grape-growing areas around Napa and Sonoma. Some of the vines were sick and dying, and the culprit was *phylloxera*. Like many people with a potentially life-threatening disease, the initial response tended to be denial, or at least silent acceptance. As the symptoms of *phylloxera* became more noticeable, so the grape growers and wine makers began to admit the existence of *phylloxera* in the vineyards, and to talk hopefully about administering a cure. In the last five years, there has been full admission of the extent of the problem, and excited talk, not only about the remedy, but also about the opportunities that the remedy presents.

Grudgingly, it became accepted that the AxR1 rootstock, so highly recommended by the University of California at Davis as resistant to *phylloxera,* is no longer immune. Scientists have identified a new strain of *phylloxera,* biotype B, which AxR1 cannot withstand. It is also likely that the vinifera branch of the AxR1 parentage has proven to be a weak link, contributing to AxR1's susceptibility to biotype B *phylloxera.* The only solution is to replant entire vineyards on different rootstocks.

At least 12 counties in California show signs of infestation by *phylloxera,* and that number will only increase, unless sandy soil conditions keep *phylloxera* from establishing itself. The hardest-hit counties so far are are Napa and Sonoma, with Monterey showing increased symptoms of the pest. Both Sonoma and Monterey counties will likely see an even more rapid spread of *phylloxera* following the storm rains of early 1995, since the moving flood waters carried *phylloxera* from infested vineyards to previously unaffected sites. *Phylloxera* is already so well established in Napa County that the flood waters there had minimal effect on spreading *phylloxera*. The replanting process has been going on since 1987 in Napa and Sonoma counties, and will likely be spread over another 10 to 15 years. Costs will be in the millions of dollars, and there will definitely be shortages of certain grape types and wines, as the affected vineyards are torn out and growers wait three years for the new plantings to bear fruit.

The Napa County Cooperative Extension of the University of California has been monitoring the process of replanting for several years now, and recently published the following information. In Napa and Sonoma counties alone, it is estimated that about 65 percent of the vineyards were planted on the AxR1 rootstock. That amounts to about 22,000 acres (8800 hectares) in each county, at a replanting cost of around $30,000 per acre ($12,000 per hectare). To date, almost 9000 acres (3600 hectares) have been replanted in Napa County specifically because of the biotype B *phylloxera,* and almost 3000 acres (1200 hectares) in Sonoma County.

Since the only practical remedy is to replant, many growers have taken the opportunity to reassess which variety to grow and what rootstock to plant on, as well as what spacing and trellising to use. What appeared at first to be a major blow to the industry has been turned into a positive opportunity to further improve the quality of California wines by adopting more appropriate grape varieties and matching varieties and even clones to optimum sites, soils, and microclimates. Replanted vineyards are also using higher-density planting patterns, based on

Ounce for ounce, California's "lowliest" wines are as good as, if not better than, any other region's in the world. (The major challenger to this claim would be Australia.)

More and more, people are coming to realize that California's fine wines can also be the equal of those from the revered regions of the Old World. All too often, people have tried in the past to make direct comparisons of California's Cabernet Sauvignons to France's Bordeaux, or California's Pinot Noirs or Chardonnays to France's red or white Burgundies. Such comparisons are interesting, but should not define the direction of any producer, since the only thing that a Californian Pinot Noir or Chardonnay has in common with a French Burgundy is the *name* of the grape. Because there the spacing experimentations prevously undertaken by some of the large California wineries. Higher-density plantings should result in fewer, but higher-quality grapes on each vine, and an overall increase in yield per acre. As a preventive measure against similar problems in the future, vineyards have been replanted using a wide array of rootstocks, rather than relying so heavily on one type as was done in the past. Thus, if one rootstock develops any weakness to *phylloxera* in the future, the problem will not be so widespread or so dramatic.

Replanting of red varieties in Napa and Sonoma counties has concentrated on Merlot and Cabernet Sauvignon. Other red varieties showing modest acreage in recent replantings are Pinot Noir, especially in Napa, and Zinfandel and Sangiovese in Sonoma. Cabernet Franc has also taken significant acreage in both counties. For white varieties, the overwhelming preference shown in replanting has been for Chardonnay, while Sauvignon Blanc has maintained a reasonable rate of replanting. Napa and Sonoma growers have shown no inclination to replant Riesling or Chenin Blanc, but there has been some interest in Sémillon and Viognier.

Additional varieties planted in Napa County have included Malbec, Petit Verdot, Petite Sirah, and Primitivo as reds, and Muscat Blanc and Sauvignon Musqué as whites. In Sonoma County, other varieties have included Barbera, Cinsaut, Dolcetto, Gamay, Grenache, Malbec, Mourvèdre, Petit Verdot, and Petite Sirah, all red varieties. From this, it can be seen that, instead of replanting with the same variety, many producers have decided to take a completely different route. Thus we have seen an increase in the number of players in two important groups of growers and wine makers in California, the "Rhône Rangers," and the "Calitalians."

Even prior to the spread of *phylloxera,* the Rhône Rangers had great success planting and making wine from the broad array of grapes grown in the Rhône Valley in southern France, a distinctly hot climate region whose grapes may well be better to suited to some of California's climate than Chardonnay ever was. The Rhône grapes used in California for white wine production are Viognier, Roussane, and Marsanne. The Rhône grape used in California for red wine production include Syrah, Mourvèdre, Grenache, Carignane, and Cinsaut.

Important California producers of Rhône style wines (and their county locations) include Bonny Doon (Santa Cruz), Cline (Contra Costa), Concannon (Alameda), Geyser Peak (Sonoma), Guenoc (Lake), Marietta (Sonoma), McDowell (Mendocino), Joseph Phelps (Napa), R.H. Phillips (Yolo), Qupé (Santa Barbara), Ridge (Santa Clara), Swanson (Napa), and Zaca Mesa (Santa Barbara).

Among the Calitalians, the favored grapes for white wine production are Arneis, Cortese, Gargenega, Malvasia, Moscato, and Trebbiano, while Barbera, Dolcetto, Nebbiolo, and Sangiovese are being grown for red wine production. The prominent Italian-style producers (and their county locations) include Atlas Peak (Napa), Benziger (Sonoma), Bonny Doon (Santa Cruz), Chappellet (Napa), Cosentino (Napa), Estancia (Sonoma), Ferrari-Carano (Sonoma), Iron Horse (Sonoma), Martin Brothers (San Luis Obispo), Monteviña (Amador), Robert Pepi (Napa), Sausal (Sonoma), Seghesio (Sonoma), Shafer (Napa), and Swanson (Napa).

are many different clones of Pinot Noir and Chardonnay, there are many different Pinot Noirs and Chardonnays grown within Burgundy and within California. The real question then is not "How does this California Chardonnay compare with a white Burgundy?" but "In the world of wine, is this California Chardonnay good?" And the answer is increasingly a resounding "Yes!"

In any consideration of California's wine regions, certain names always spring to mind. In the North Coast region, Napa Valley has often been in the forefront, and is still renowned worldwide for some fine Cabernet Sauvignon and Chardonnay wines. One could even suggest that the Napa Valley comes the closest of any West Coast wine region to having its own history, longer and more packed with colorful characters than any other region. But Sonoma Valley too has pushed into the limelight, with a more-defined concentration on certain grape types, and a model appellation system. Both of these North Coast areas have been challenged recently by Mendocino farther to the north and by Arroyo Seco, Paso Robles, Santa Maria Valley, and Santa Ynez Valley in the Central Coast region.

The Californian wine regions run the gamut from the very cool, small coastal appellations where microclimates abound, to the predictable and huge Central Valley running from Bakersfield in the south to Sacramento in the north. This section of our book will concentrate on the most prominent regions and appellations, with special mention of important growers and wine makers. These regions are the North Coast, the San Francisco Bay Area, the North Central Coast, the South Central Coast, Southern California, the Sierra Foothills, and the Central Valley.

**North Coast.**   As already mentioned, the North Coast region is an official appellation or AVA. It is comprised of the six counties of Mendocino, Lake, Sonoma, Napa, Solano, and Marin. Undoubtedly, the first four are the most important, and some would contend that Marin is part of the Bay area, and that Solano is part of the interior. For all practical purposes, the debate may be academic, since Solano County produces little wine and Marin County even less.

*Mendocino.*   Mendocino County boasts four AVAs (see Map 4.4): Anderson Valley, Potter Valley, McDowell Valley, and Cole Ranch. Of the four, Anderson Valley is the best known, possibly because of the success of the sparkling wines from this appellation produced by Roederer Estate (owned and operated by the Roederer house of Champagne, France) and by Scharffenberger (now owned by Pommery, also a Champagne company). Its relative proximity to the coast allows for some fog influence in the western part of the valley where Pinot Noir and Chardonnay develop exactly the right qualities for *méthode champenoise* (classic method) sparkling wine. For some, this is also the place for California Gewürztraminer at its best. In the warmer, eastern end of the valley, Sauvignon Blanc grows well.

On the western edge of Mendocino County lies Potter Valley, with more vineyards than wineries, and a reputation for producing some fine Sauvignon Blanc as well as being a good source for Chardonnay grapes for use in classic-method sparkling wine. Also in the western part of the county is McDowell Valley, known for some old Zinfandel vines and for some Rhône varietals, such as Syrah and Grenache. Cole Ranch is situated near the Russian River as it flows south from Lake Mendocino to Hopland.

Aside from the official AVAs, Mendocino County enjoys a reputation as the home of many famous wineries, including Fetzer Vineyards (now moving more and more toward organic methods), Hidden Cellars, and Parducci Wine Cellars, who have long favored the rustic Redwood Valley and Ukiah Valley over the "more sophisticated" Napa and Sonoma.

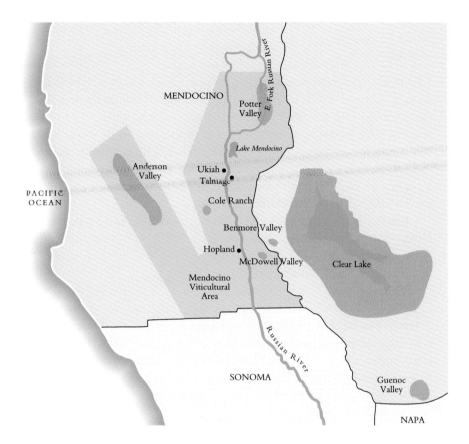

**Map 4.4**   Mendocino and Lake Counties' AVAs with Winery Sites.

*Lake.*    Again, Lake County boasts some little-known AVAs, and yet the county is well known for some famous names in the world of wine. The county is home to Kendall-Jackson Vineyards, Guenoc Winery, Konocti Cellars, and, most recently Steele Wines, established by Jed Steele, formerly wine maker with Kendall-Jackson.

With no coastal influence to bring really cool breezes into the vineyards, growers have wisely avoided Chardonnay and Pinot Noir, concentrating instead on Sauvignon Blanc, Cabernet Sauvignon, and Zinfandel. Recently, as elsewhere throughout California, growers have been experimenting with various Rhône varieties.

The very large AVA of Clear Lake covers almost 170,000 acres/68,000 hectares but has only slightly more than 3000 acres/1200 hectares of vineyards, with much of the land given over to fruit orchards, especially pears. The warmer climate of the Guenoc Valley AVA favors the growing of Syrah and Zinfandel. On the boundary with Mendocino County lies the Benmore Valley AVA, very close to McDowell Valley in Mendocino.

*Napa.*    In their rush to get federal approval for Napa Valley as an AVA (see Map 4.5) back in the early 1980s, the growers and producers compromised too much, too soon. The original proposal was to restrict Napa Valley to the drainage basin of the Napa river, but this was challenged by grape growers as far north and east as Pope Valley. The result is that the approved

Paul Dolan of Fetzer Vineyards.

## PAUL DOLAN OF FETZER VINEYARDS, MENDOCINO, CA

Like many happy and successful people in the wine industry, Paul Dolan came to wine as a second career. After earning a degree in business and finance from University of California at Santa Clara, followed by three years' service in the U.S. Army, the pull of Dolan's family history was too strong for him to consider anything other than a career as a wine maker. His father came from the Concannon family of Livermore, and his mother's family boasts three generations of wine makers at the original Italian-Swiss Colony winery in Napa.

Following a Master's degree in enology from Fresno State, Dolan joined the Fetzer family as wine maker in 1977, and worked closely with the Fetzers to build their impressive reputation for honest, well-crafted wines at reasonable prices.

When the Brown-Forman Company purchased the winery and the Fetzer name from the Fetzer family in 1992, Dolan became president of Fetzer Vineyards. He continues the philosophy laid by the Fetzers, concentrating on producing the wines in small batch sizes to emphasize varietal and vineyard character in the wines. He has also introduced an in-house barrel-building program, a complete recycling program, and he continues the path set by the Fetzers toward wines made from naturally farmed, organic grapes.

The jewel in the Fetzer Vineyards' crown remains the Valley Oaks Food & Wine Center at Hopland in Mendocino County, a conference center where chefs from the around the nation are encouraged to visit and spend time in the organic gardens where they can have their pick of innumerable varieties of fresh herbs, vegetables, and fruits. Perhaps the ultimate in food and wine pairing, the chefs are able to sample the fresh ingredients and the wines before deciding how best to combine the ingredients and what cooking methods to employ.

Listening to Dolan talk, one cannot help but feel that his professional life is a natural extension of his personal beliefs. "I want Fetzer Vineyards to continue to be recognized as *the* environmentally and socially conscious winery, committed to making the highest-quality, best-valued wines in the world."

Napa Valley appellation covers the whole of the county except Lake Berryessa and the northeastern corner. In this regard, Napa Valley as an appellation has less meaning than some purists might like. However, recent approvals of numerous subappellations are beginning to rectify the situation.

Undoubtedly, the county includes the most famous names connected with California wine: Krug, Inglenook, Beaulieu, Martini, Beringer, and Christian Brothers. Even the place names have become well known in the wine lexicon: Rutherford, Oakville, St. Helena, Yountville, as well as Napa itself, and the appropriately named Zinfandel Lane.

**Map 4.5** Napa Valley AVAs.

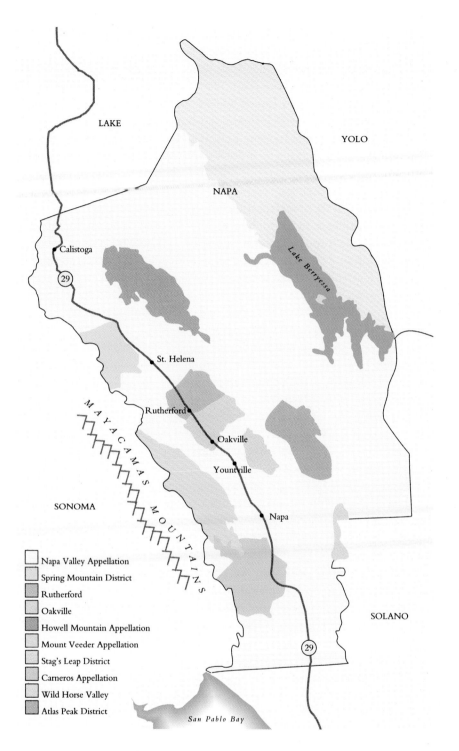

The valley floor runs approximately 30 miles/48 kilometers, from the city of Napa in the south to Calistoga in the north. It is bound on the west side by the Mayacamas Mountains (which separate Napa from Sonoma), and on the east side by the smaller ridge of Vacas hills which rise above the Silverado Trail.

Given its size, it is not surprising that several different climatic zones exist within the valley. A general overview suggests that cool ocean air and fog are pulled in from the Golden Gate Bridge into the San Pablo Bay and then north up the Napa Valley floor. The result is that the fog-enshrouded vineyards of southern Napa usually remain cooler than those in the north, which remain fog-free, or at least the fog burns off quicker farther north. Thus, the grossest generalization indicates that cool climate grapes like Chardonnay and Pinot Noir have done well in the Carneros District in the south, and warmer climate varieties such as Cabernet Sauvignon have prospered farther up the valley.

As attractive as this generalization is, it is really too simplistic to properly portray the seemingly never-ending stream of complexities and contradictions which flows through the valley floor. Inexplicable pockets of microclimates, and unknown, often earthquake-induced soil profiles mean that grape growing "rules" are broken every day. The net result is that, as important as soil and climate remain in determining the quality of the grapes and the wine, the personality of the wine maker also continues to play an important role in what style of wine is produced.

In an effort to make AVAs more meaningful, growers and producers in Napa Valley have pursued the idea of subappellations, though with different levels of commitment and cooperation. To date, there are nine approved subappellations within Napa Valley.

The first subappellation was approved in 1983, right after the original, cumbersome Napa Valley AVA was approved. The growers of grapes in the Carneros District, and the wineries who purchased them, moved very swiftly to distance themselves from Napa Valley and to establish their own identity, with great success. In fact, the players were so confident that they could go it alone without any reference to Napa that they had no qualms about the proposed boundaries crossing into Sonoma County which, at that time, was relatively unknown compared to Napa. However, this snub at historical rivalries and political boundaries ensured the integrity of Carneros as an AVA (see Map 4.6). This very cool district had been increasingly identified as *the* place in California to produce outstanding Pinot Noir and Chardonnay, and although other areas have since been identified as equally good at growing these two grapes, Carneros (sometimes called Los Carneros) continues to hold its own, amply demonstrated by such producers as Acacia, Saintsbury, Carneros Creek, Bouchaine, and Buena Vista.

The burgeoning classic-method sparkling wine industry was quick to recognize the potential of the Carneros District, and many producers purchased vineyard land there or developed long-term contracts with established growers. Those who established wineries for sparkling wine production there are Domaine Carneros (parent company Taittinger of Champagne, France), Gloria Ferrer (parent company Freixenet of Spain), and Codorniu Napa (parent company Codorniu of Spain).

In 1984, the Howell Mountain subappellation was approved, led by Ridge Vineyards, who favor the area for Zinfandel, and Dunn Vineyards, who trumpet the glories of Cabernet Sauvignon grown here. True to the inexactness of anything in Napa, relative newcomers, like the French-

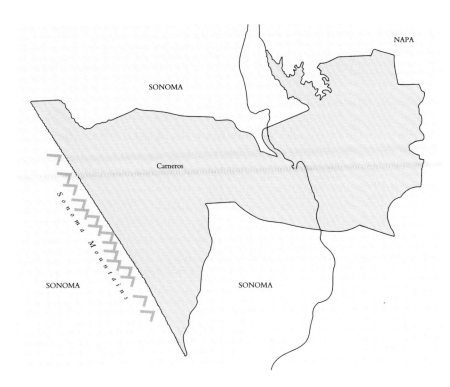

**Map 4.6** The Carneros District.

SONOMA

NAPA

Carneros

Sonoma Mountains

SONOMA

SONOMA

owned Chateau Woltner, claim that Howell Mountain is the ideal place to grow Chardonnay! Howell Mountain offers elevations to just under 2000 feet, ensuring good balance of acidity in the grapes, and southern and western exposure for afternoon and late afternoon sun to warm the vineyards.

The next approved subappellation, Stag's Leap District, has long been known as one of the best spots in California for Cabernet Sauvignon. One of the earliest plantings of Cabernet in the 1960s, the Fay Vineyard, remains a benchmark today. Later "pioneers" also saw the potential for Cabernet Sauvignon: as winery operators, Warren Winiarski of Stag's Leap Wine Cellars and Bernard Portet of Clos du Val were strong supporters of the push for separate recognition of the Stag's Leap District as a subappellation. The district was granted AVA status in 1984.

As in most areas where Cabernet Sauvignon thrives, Merlot, Cabernet Franc, and Sauvignon Blanc also do well, depending on the soil profile. Cabernet Sauvignon is better off in lighter, well-drained soils, and Merlot and Sauvignon Blanc in heavier soils.

Approved as a subappellation as recently as 1990, Mt. Veeder had its supporters back in the 1960s, when Mayacamas Vineyards was the only winery and vineyard tucked away in the hills between Napa and Sonoma counties. Now the Mayacamas Vineyards has a few neighbors, such as Mt. Veeder Vineyards and the Hess Collection Winery. All of the current tenants appreciate the elevation and sun exposure, and have variously found pockets where Cabernet Sauvignon or Chardonnay do extremely well.

One of the more recently approved subappellations in Napa is Atlas Peak, also a mountain site, though it sits across the valley floor from Mt. Veeder, above the small foothills which make up the Stag's Leap District.

Larry Brooks of Acacia Vineyards.

## LARRY BROOKS OF ACACIA VINEYARDS, CARNEROS, CA

Larry Brooks has never made any attempt to hide his love of fast cars, motorcycles, and racing bicycles. And so it seems strange in some respects that he is the guiding hand behind the enormously successful Chardonnays and Pinot Noirs of Acacia Winery which are held by some as models of wine making elegance and restraint.

Brooks has been with Acacia since the winery was founded by Michael Richmond in 1979, with complete responsibility for all wine making at Acacia since 1981. In 1986, Acacia was purchased by the Chalone Wine Group which also includes the Edna Valley winery in San Luis Obispo, the Chalone winery in Monterey, the Carmenet winery in Sonoma, and the recently acquired Canoe Ridge winery in Walla Walla, WA. Larry's title is now Managing Director of Acacia and Vice President in charge of production for the whole Chalone Group.

"I was already fascinated by Pinot Noir when I joined with Mike Richmond to open Acacia," says Larry, "and I felt that Carneros was the place to prove that California could make good Pinot Noir." That passion for Pinot Noir and for Carneros has not abated in the 15 years that Larry has been working there. "I just love Carneros," he says. "It is a true appellation in the sense that it has a uniformity of soil and climate. It does not follow any political boundaries of Napa or Sonoma County."

When Acacia was purchased by the Chalone Group in 1986, there was a danger that the emphasis would be on growth and expansion. Larry explains, "What has been good about Chalone is that any available money has been spent on improving what we have, so that each of the wineries in the Chalone Group has remained small and dedicated to doing one or two things well. At Acacia we concentrate on Pinot Noir and Chardonnay which, for me, is what Carneros is all about." The emphasis on small is also refelected in the Carneros Quality Alliance (CQA), a tight and effective grouping of Carneros wineries which works on promoting Carneros wines and on vineyard and winery research. "The CQA has been really useful in helping us through some difficult times," says Larry. "The big story of course is *phylloxera,* so, when we knew we had to replant, we also took a close look at clones, spacing, and trellissing. Although *phylloxera* will create a short-term supply problem, in the long-term it has allowed us to look closely at what we grow, and where and how we grow it. The CQA and all the wineries and growers here have worked together to find the best answers. The net result can only be even better wines in the future."

As Vice President in charge of Production for the Chalone Group, Larry acts as the main spokesperson on matters relating to vineyards and wine making. He is intent on letting each of the Chalone properties maintain its own style according to the soil, climate, and whatever grape varieties are deemed suitable.

As for velocity, Larry still races, though not with engines anymore. "Road-racing bicycles are enough danger for me now," he muses.

## CLASSIC-METHOD CLASSIC-VARIETIES SPARKLING WINES

Since the mid-1970s, a number of Napa Valley producers have been making some fine examples of sparkling wine, using the same grape varieties as those used by Champagne producers in France, and using the same long, labor-intensive methods of production. All of the Napa Valley producers have felt at least some degree of frustration with the attitude which persists in the marketplace that any sparkling wine not produced in Champagne, France is inherently inferior.

To attempt to change that attitude, some of the Napa Valley producers were instrumental in forming what is now a nationwide group dedicated to promoting U.S. sparkling wines made from the classic varieties (Pinot Noir, Chardonnay, and Pinot Meunier), using the classic méthode champenoise (see Chapter 1). The CM/CV (Classic Method/Classic Varieties) Society was established in 1990, with the principal goal of promoting awareness of the quality of U.S. sparkling wines produced within certain guidelines. Member wineries must comply with strict regulations as to grape varieties used, yield of juice per ton of grapes, vinification techniques, and the length of time the wine stays in contact with yeast in the bottle after the second fermentation.

There are currently seven member wineries of CM/CV. They are Domaine Carneros, Domaine Chandon, Maison Deutz, Roederer Estate, Scharffenberger, and Shadow Creek, in California, plus Gruet in New Mexico. Bottles of sparkling wine produced by member wineries will carry the CM/CV logo (see Figure 4.7).

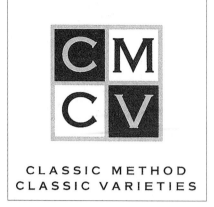

**CLASSIC METHOD
CLASSIC VARIETIES**

**Figure 4.7**   The CMCV Logo.

There is only one winery in this subappellation, Atlas Peak Vineyards, which set out intentionally to plant and produce Sangiovese-based wines. As such, this winery was one of the front-runners in what has become a new fascination among Californian grape growers and wine makers: deciding what will be the next big thing after Chardonnay and Cabernet Sauvignon. Some, as here, are betting on Italian varietals such as Sangiovese; others favor Rhône varietals such as Mourvèdre, Grenache, and Viognier. In addition to Atlas Peak Vineyards' Sangiovese plantings, some independent growers favor Cabernet Sauvignon on this site.

Two new subappellations in Napa are Rutherford and Oakville, both centered on the valley floor around the villages of the same names.

As new AVAs, both Rutherford and Oakville are brilliant examples of how difficult, and possibly how absurd, it is to draw lines on maps which represent differences and delineations in agricultural use. Some longtime residents argue the existence of a geological bench formation in both districts, and claim that the different soil structures which make up the gently sloping bench influence drainage and land use. Others deny the existence of any such bench. The debates will continue. But nothing will change the fact that vineyards in both Rutherford and Oakville are capable of producing

Dawnine Dyer of Domaine Chandon.

Having gained her initial winery experience with the Robert Mondavi winery and then at Inglenook, Dawnine Dyer joined Domaine Chandon in 1976 as a lab assistant with the specific task of setting up a quality control system. At that time, the Domaine Chandon company was using the facilities at Trefethen to make their wines, buying significant quantities of Chardonnay and Pinot Noir from the Trefethens. As was often the case in newly formed Napa wineries in the 1970s, she found herself performing all manner of chores around the winery, pitching in as necessary, and gaining invaluable hands-on experience in all facets of wine making. When Chandon's original wine maker, Sergio Traverso, left to do more consulting work, Dyer was asked by the company president to take on the role of head wine maker. In 1981 she was promoted to Vice President, and since that time she has had overall responsibility for all of the sparkling wines produced by Domaine Chandon. One of the most privileged and exciting aspects of her position has been to work in close cooperation with the blenders and wine makers from Moët & Chandon, Domaine Chandon's parent company. Dyer visits the Moët & Chandon headquarters in Champagne, France on a regular basis. With the advice and assistance of the Moët chief blenders such as Richard Geoffroy and the now retired Edmond Maudière, she has successfully developed a line of high-quality California sparkling wines.

When Dyer took over as wine maker, Chandon sold two distinct sparkling wines: the Brut and the Blanc de Noirs. As principal wine maker, Dyer has launched three new Domaine Chandon products: the Reserve label, the Etoile label, and a series of releases under the Club Chandon label, available only to members of the Club Chandon. Of those wines, Dyer says she is particularly pleased with the Reserve label since it is the realization of her personal conviction that California sparkling wines are capable of aging and developing. Against the opinion of her colleagues in Champagne, she kept aside a small quantity of what she felt were special wines from outstanding vintages, and later blended them to develop the Reserve category. As an endorsement of her blending skill and vision, her Moët colleagues were extremely impressed by her first version of Reserve, and it remains a special wine in the Chandon lineup.

Of all the harvests she has overseen, Dyer lists 1986 as one of her favorites. "The more I work at this, the more I feel that our situation is the opposite from the Champagne region. They get their best results from the warmer sites in the warmer years. Here we see finer wines from the cooler sites in the cooler years." 1986 was such a year in Napa, creating base wines for sparkling wine which were very lean, with high acid balance and a potential to be long-lived. In fact, it was wines from years like 1986 that convinced Dyer that a Reserve label was a viable option for Chandon.

Despite the increasing demands of her managerial position, Dyer still makes a point of spending as much time as possible in the vineyards and the winery, and admits a particular love for harvest time. "It's great to get out into the vineyards at harvest time to see and feel the excitement as the vineyard cycle ends and the winery gears up for nonstop activity over the next several weeks."

She is also proud of her recent work reshaping the Chandon Blanc de Noirs. "In my view, Blanc de Noirs is not just a rosé sparkling wine. It is a distinctly California product, emphasizing fresh red fruit qualities but without any hint of tannin." Part of the Blanc de Noirs reworking has been to use Pinot Noir from more specific vineyard locations, and to include more Pinot Meunier in the blend.

Perhaps surprisingly to some, Dyer does not feel that being a woman in the wine industry has been difficult. "You have to remember that 1974 was the beginning of a growth period in Napa, but there were very few fully qualified people around. Those who exhibited enthusiasm and initiative got ahead, regardless of gender." When she applied for her first position at Mondavi, she was fortunate enough to have been interviewed and hired by Zelma Long, who later became prominent as president and wine maker for Simi winery. "With Zelma as a role model, and the idealism of the time, I really felt that I could do anything if I worked hard enough at it," reflects Dyer.

Along with John Wright, Chandon's president, Dyer was active in making Chandon a founding member of the CM/CV Society, and she continues to work through various national organizations to promote the image and acceptance of wine in general and of California sparkling wines in particular.

Warren Winiarski of Stag's Leap Wine Cellars.

some of the finest wines in all of Napa. For many, they represent Cabernet Sauvignon at its California best, from the late 1880s' versions by Inglenook, from vines planted by Gustave Niebaum, through Georges de Latour's Beaulieu Vineyards versions in the early 1900s. The current renditions of Cabernet Sauvignon from Inglenook and Beaulieu Vineyards can be equally stunning, while relative newcomers such as Mondavi, Heitz, and Caymus have shown that their Cabernets can be impressive.

If there are any distinctions to be made between the two districts, they are those of individual style imposed by the wine maker, or they are a reflection of the broader span and more varied soil structure of Oakville. With the broader stretch of valley floor come different microclimates which, together with a larger number of different soil types, mean there is less concentration on Cabernet Sauvignon, and more room for Sauvignon Blanc or even Italian varietals such as Sangiovese.

## JACK CAKEBREAD OF CAKEBREAD CELLARS, RUTHERFORD, CA

Jake Cakebread of Cakebread Cellars.

Before wine became a way of life for Jack Cakebread, he ran a successful automotive service business in Napa. He also had a passion for photographing the Napa Valley. On one photography trip in the early '70s, he came across the ranch on Highway 29 which was later to become Cakebread Cellars. He spent the afternoon with the elderly couple who owned the ranch, and by the end of his visit he had talked himself into buying it. Cakebread Cellars was founded in 1973.

Today the Cakebread family is one of the mainstays of Napa, a solid family working together to produce quality wines. "We began small and we have always focused on quality. We started out with the idea of making one barrel, selling one barrel; making two barrels, selling two barrels."

Jack's wife Dolores has always been involved in the family business, planting the vegetable garden while Jack and his sons planted the vineyard. Today, good food and hospitality remain a fundamental part of the Cakebread business. Each year, they host the American Harvest Workshop at their property, featuring prominent chefs and sommeliers from around the nation and local purveyors of exceptional produce and foods.

Jack's sons are also active in the winery business. Bruce became wine maker in 1979, after studying at UC Davis and working with his father in the cellar for many years. In 1986, son Dennis joined the family team full-time with an MBA degree and many years experience in banking and finance.

Now as Chairman of the business, Jack still guides and directs with his inimitable but practical approach. When asked what rootstock he will be using to replant vineyards infected by *phylloxera* (see Chapter 2), he replies with a gleam in his eye, "You know, everybody has their own way of going broke in this business! We just take what advice we can get, and hope that it's right. We'll just have to wait and see." And, whereas he is pleased that the Rutherford and Oakville subappellations have finally been agreed on, there is still a smile on his face when he answers the question of where the famous Rutherford bench lies. "Well," he muses, "that depends on where your vineyards are!"

Currently, the Cakebread family owns and farms 75 acres/30 hectares of vineyards near their ranch, planted with Cabernet Sauvignon and Sauvignon Blanc. They also work closely with growers who provide them with grapes from other properties throughout the valley, including the Carneros District for some of their Chardonnay.

The Spring Mountain AVA lies above and to the west of the city of Saint Helena. The lower slopes of the hillside are home to the renowned Cabernet Sauvignon and Merlot vineyards of Cain Cellars and Newton, while Chardonnay is increasingly being planted in vineyards at higher elevations on the mountain. A few acres remain of Riesling vines which are capable of producing outstanding wine, though the public's apparent apathy for Riesling has made many growers opt for more lucrative varieties.

The final AVA in Napa County is the little-known Wild Horse Valley, situated in the southeastern corner of the county, and shared as an AVA with Solano County. The past and recent history of Napa shows a region still young, still developing, still defining its own character. We can only marvel at what could have been if Napa's early, farsighted pioneers had not been stopped in their tracks by the nightmare of Prohibition.

*Sonoma.*    Though the residents and, more especially, the wine producers of Napa and Sonoma like to trumpet their differences, such claims are mostly about good-natured rivalry. The counties do share similarities, as their inclusion together in the North Coast appellation suggests. However, what the two share most are the inconsistencies and inexactness in the climate and soil patterns which so greatly affect grape growing and wine making. Some parts of Sonoma frequently see fog over the vineyards, some areas hardly ever see it. Beds of volcanic, calcareous, and alluvial soil types are maddeningly interlaced, with no obvious pattern. The result is that, as in Napa, Chardonnay will grow inexplicably well right next to a plot of Zinfandel.

What did set Sonoma apart from Napa in the early 1980s was the county's pursuit of an appellation system that did and still does reflect differences in wine styles. In addition to Sonoma County as an AVA, the county also boasts the following AVAs and subappellations (see Map 4.3):

- Carneros, which extends eastward into Napa County

- Sonoma Valley, with the subappellation of Sonoma Mountain

- Russian River Valley, with the subappellations of Sonoma County-Green Valley, and Chalk Hill

- Dry Creek Valley

- Alexander Valley

- Knight's Valley

Two other large umbrella appellations exist:

- Northern Sonoma embraces the AVAs of Russian River, Dry Creek, Alexander, and Knight's Valleys

- Sonoma Coast includes most of the vineyards west of Russian River Valley, and some of the land near Sonoma Valley.

In Sonoma County, the Sonoma Valley AVA is the oldest and, perhaps because of that, the one which claims to be a good home to a broad array of grape types. Its sheer size is one reason for this, but it is also true that Sonoma Valley has much less floor than, say, Napa Valley, and many more hills with a multitude of exposures. Generally speaking, Chardonnay and Pinot Noir do well in the southern part of the appellation, near Carneros, where Buena Vista winery carries on the tradition started in the latter half of the nineteenth century by its founder, Agoston Haraszthy. Sonoma-Cutrer has also made a name for its Chardonnay in this area. Farther north, the appellation has produced good versions of almost everything from Gewürztraminer to Zinfandel.

The western part of the Sonoma Valley AVA contains the smaller subappellation of Sonoma Mountain, which excels in growing Cabernet Sauvignon of the highest order, with ripe fruit, good tannic structure, and balancing acidity. Fine examples are Kenwood, Benziger, and Laurel Glen.

The Russian River AVA and its two subappellations of Sonoma County-Green Valley and Chalk Hill are far easier to categorize, though still with some exceptions. This is Chardonnay and Pinot Noir country, with smatterings of other varieties. The Chardonnay and Pinot Noir are used for the production of excellent still wines, and very fine sparkling wines from this area. Some of the best Chardonnays come from Sonoma-Cutrer, Iron Horse, Jordan, and Chateau St. Jean. The last three of these producers are renowned for their sparkling wines as well. The masters of Pinot Noir in this appellation include Dehlinger and Rochioli, as well as Davis Bynum and Rodney Strong.

With a range of old and new wineries producing good to excellent wines from a broad array of Rhône varietals and from Cabernet Sauvignon, nothing can hide the fact that, for decades, Dry Creek Valley has produced the kind of Zinfandel to serve as a model for all others, as exemplified by Nalle, Quivira, and Pedroncelli. To the regret of the old-time Zinfandel fanatics, the Rhône varietals and Cabernet Sauvignon have shown promise here, and some of the Zinfandel acreage may be threatened. As for white wines, Chardonnay and Sauvignon Blanc are the standouts and, thus far, do not appear to be challenged to any great extent. As in many places throughout California, most of the wineries in this valley also bring grapes in from other locations to make their wines.

The Alexander Valley AVA has three mainstay grape varieties: Cabernet Sauvignon in the southern end, and Sauvignon Blanc and Chardonnay farther north. This does not rule out other grape varieties, with some old Zinfandel doing well and some new Rhône varieties showing promise. But, one strong indicator of the suitability of Chardonnay and Cabernet Sauvignon is the continued use by the Clos du Bois Winery of three single-vineyard sites in this appellation for Chardonnay (Calcaire, Belle Terre, and Robert Young vineyards) and one single-vineyard site for Cabernet Sauvignon (Briarcrest). Jordan, Simi, and Château Souverain also continue to make stunning examples of Cabernet Sauvignon and Chardonnay from this AVA.

Knight's Valley is essentially a one-winery appellation: Beringer Vineyards owns most of the vineyard property in this small valley almost on the

Barry Sterling of Iron Horse Vineyards.

## BARRY STERLING OF IRON HORSE VINEYARDS, SONOMA, CA

Barry and Audrey Sterling have lived, and continue to live, what many would consider a fine life. From Barry's prominent career as an international lawyer living in France and then England, the Sterlings took every opportunity in those countries to learn all they could about the culture, foods, and wines. Obviously, France helped Barry to pursue his passion for and fascination with food and wine at its best. He and his family traveled through France as often as possible, and dined at all of the finest restaurants, including those of Bocuse and Vergé.

At one time, Barry and Audrey were close to buying a wine château in Bordeaux. When that did not work out, Barry returned to his native California, and continued to work in corporate law in Los Angeles. He and Audrey spent many weekends traveling through the agricultural communities of the North Coast until, in 1976, they found the estate they were looking for—Iron Horse Ranch and Vineyards. The estate, house, and vineyards were in desperate need of renovation, and the Sterlings eagerly took on the project, working with Forrest Tancer who had been managing the estate when the Sterlings came to the rescue.

Forrest is now married to the Sterling's daughter, Joy, and Barry and Audrey's son, Lawrence, is also active in the workings of the winery. With Forrest as wine maker, Iron Horse Vineyards produces elegant Chardonnay, Pinot Noir, and Sauvignon Blanc, as well as Cabernet Sauvignon and a proprietary label "Cabernets," a blend of Cabernet Sauvignon and Cabernet Franc. More and more, Iron Horse is becoming known for its line of sparkling wines produced in the classic method used in Champagne, France.

Napa-Sonoma border. Beringer concentrates almost entirely on two grapes here: Cabernet Sauvignon and Sauvignon Blanc.

***San Francisco Bay Area.*** As the city of San Francisco has grown, many bedroom communities have developed at considerable distance from the city itself. Such is the case with the cities of Livermore and Pleasanton in Alameda County, and the development of these communities has threatened the vineyards in the historic Livermore Valley AVA (see Map 4.7).

Approved as an AVA in 1982, Livermore has a long history, much of it dominated by the Wente family, who still own and operate the Wente Bros. Winery here. Their neighbors include the Concannon Winery, Ivan Tamas Winery, and Stony Ridge Winery. Grape growing and wine making are still strong in the valley, and certainly the Wente family has no intention of giving up the ghost just yet. Along with their neighbors, they continue to produce still and sparkling wines which carry on the Livermore name. The rocky, gravelly soil has been a natural home to Sauvignon Blanc and Sémillon, and Chardonnay and Cabernet Sauvignon are also doing well here.

*North Central Coast.* The large chunk of land which makes up the North Central Coast region includes five counties: San Mateo, Santa Cruz, Monterey, Santa Clara, and San Benito. They all have AVAs of varying size, some of them as old as or even older than Napa Valley and Sonoma Valley. However, they have all been overshadowed to a greater or lesser degree by the counties in the North Coast region, and, in some cases, are only now gaining the recognition they deserve.

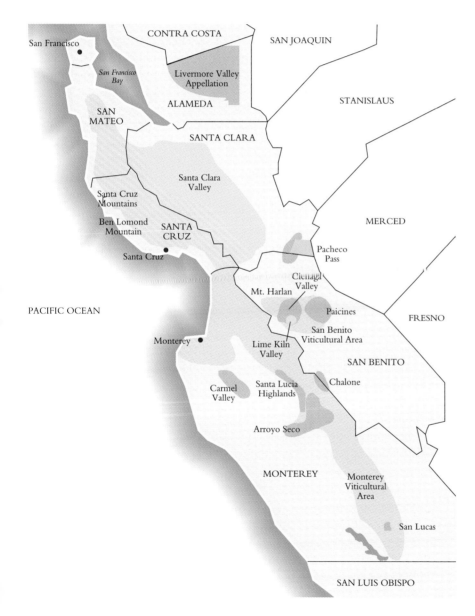

**Map 4.7** The Livermore Valley AVA and the North Central Coast Wine Regions.

Paul Draper of Ridge Vineyards.

## PAUL DRAPER OF RIDGE VINEYARDS, CA

The "Ridge" in the winery name refers to the Monte Bello Ridge in the Santa Cruz Mountains, home to the vineyards which originally gave the company its impetus and subsequently brought it fame and recognition. Paul Draper has been the wine maker at Ridge since 1969, and he lives with his wife and daughter on the ridge, overlooking the vineyards.

Draper proudly portrays his wine making philosophy as a hands-off approach. He will cheerfully admit that science and technology have brought great advances to wine making in the United States and around the world, but he prefers to maintain a natural and straightforward approach rather than a heavily technological one. Draper sums up his approach like this: "We begin with the most flavorful and intense grapes, intrude as little as possible on the natural process, and draw all the richness from the fruit into the wine." Draper is able to achieve such stunning results in his wines because of his dedication to the concept of single-vineyard wines, using sites where the soil, climate, and varietal are perfectly matched. All of the winery's vineyards have naturally well-drained soils, and the yields from each vineyard are kept low to intensify the fruit quality.

The natural process continues in the winery where Draper allows the fermentation to start from the presence of the yeasts that are naturally present on the grape skins. He does not introduce commercially purchased yeast strains. All of the wines go through natural malolactic fermentation, and are then racked, unfiltered, into small oak barrels.

Although the winery is located on Monte Bello Ridge in Santa Cruz, Draper works closely with the growers who own or manage single-vineyard properties throughout California that supply the grapes for the wines. In addition to Cabernet Sauvignon and Chardonnay from the Monte Bello Ridge properties, Draper also makes exceptional Zinfandel from the Lytton Springs, Geyserville, and Pagani vineyards in Sonoma County, and from a site in Paso Robles. Draper also uses fruit from the York Creek vineyard in Napa.

*Santa Cruz Mountains.*　This large AVA has only a small number of plantings. It dates from the early 1980s, and this may be a contributing factor to its size: the proponents were perhaps more interested in getting the appellation approved than in defining the region more accurately. Debates over the accuracy of the appellation linger, fired by the reputation of David Bruce's Pinot Noir from the hillsides which face the Pacific Ocean, and a similar reputation for Ridge Vineyard's Cabernet Sauvignon from its Monte Bello vineyard on the hillsides which face San Francisco Bay. Chardonnay plantings outnumber Pinot Noir and Cabernet Sauvignon throughout the AVA, with good versions again from Ridge Vineyards and from Mount Eden Vineyards.

# KEN VOLK, WILD HORSE VINEYARDS, CA

As a third-generation California native from San Marino, Ken Volk has always been fascinated by the exquisite fruit produce that comes from the Golden State. At college and university, he had concentrated on fruit science in general, and was headed for a career in managing citrus or avocado groves when he was bitten by the wine bug.

"I became fascinated by the idea that I could take a highly perishable fruit, and turn it into a product which, theoretically, could improve with age, so I began making wine in my garage at home." Starting with a baseball bat as a makeshift crusher, he fermented a batch of Gamay Beaujolais grapes in a garbage can. Following a few more successful batches at home, Volk signed on with the Edna Valley Vineyard to work the 1981 harvest and crush.

From these humble beginnings, Volk's progress has been dramatic. In 1982 he purchased 64 acres/25 hectares of vineyard property near Templeton in the Paso Robles appellation, and in 1983 he bonded his barn as the Wild Horse Winery. Fortunately for the Pinot Noir lovers of the world, Ken has a particular passion for this grape. "It's a difficult grape to grow and a difficult grape to make into wine," he reflects. "It's fickle, and you can never trust it to behave the way you think it will. Still I know that when I get it right, I can make great wine with Pinot Noir." Volk's track record at Wild Horse indicates that he has been right more often than not, having his winery named as "Winery of the Year" by *Wine & Spirits Magazine* in 1990, and he was named "Wine Maker of the Year" by the Central Coast Wine Growers Association in 1992.

Ken Volk of Wild Horse Vineyards.

*Monterey.* As a county, and as a very large AVA, it has been Monterey's misfortune to have been developed very quickly, with perhaps too-deeply rooted a belief in the ability of technology to make grape growing and wine making successful. Within a decade, Monterey's vineyards grew from less than 5000 to almost 40,000 acres (from 2000 to 16,000 hectares), with heavy investment in irrigation machinery and mechanical harvesters, but with little respect for topography and climate, let alone the existence of microclimates. Monterey is only now beginning to overcome the early criticisms of emphatic vegetable character in its wines, a result of the combined effects of overirrigation and incessant winds, which prevented the grapes from ripening fully. Part of the solution has been to create smaller subappellations, the most notable of which are:

- Arroyo Seco, suited mostly to Chardonnay, Riesling, and Gewürztraminer

- Chalone, developed as an AVA by Chalone winery, much respected for its Chardonnay, Pinot Blanc, and Pinot Noir

- Santa Lucia Highlands, showing increasing success with Chardonnay, Cabernet Sauvignon, and Merlot. Smith and Hook is a major producer.

**Map 4.8** The South Central Coast Wine Regions of San Luis Obispo and Santa Barbara Counties.

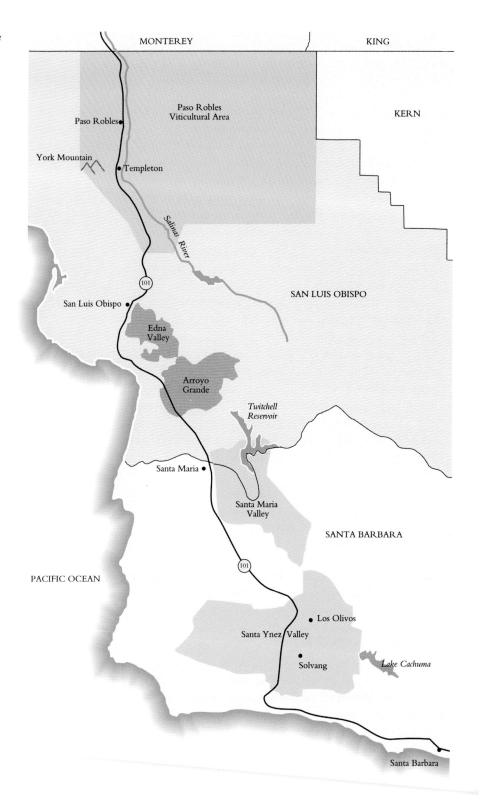

MONTEREY

KING

Paso Robles

KERN

Paso Robles Viticultural Area

York Mountain

Templeton

Salinas River

101

SAN LUIS OBISPO

San Luis Obispo

Edna Valley

Arroyo Grande

Twitchell Reservoir

Santa Maria

Santa Maria Valley

SANTA BARBARA

PACIFIC OCEAN

101

Los Olivos

Santa Ynez Valley

Solvang

Lake Cachuma

Santa Barbara

*San Benito County.* There are four small AVAs in San Benito County in addition to the general San Benito AVA. All of the small AVAs are the result of petitioning for regional recognition by individual wineries. In the case of the Cienega Valley AVA and the Paicines AVA, it was the large Almaden organization that identified and successfully petitioned for their approval, though Almaden has subsequently abandoned its plantings in these areas.

The Mt. Harlan AVA remains active today, having been developed by the Calera winery to define the extraordinary soil and topography of its highly acclaimed Pinot Noir vineyards. The winery also makes Chardonnay, and has recently ventured into Viognier.

**South Central Coast.** Despite their southerly location, the coastal areas of San Luis Obispo County and Santa Barbara County have cool stretches, and some of the ocean fog is drawn inland through the valley openings, creating microclimates in the inland valleys. Ironically, given that vines and wine were introduced to this part of California by Spanish missionaries long before Napa ever thought of growing vines, modern wine making is a very recent activity in these parts. Even so, five AVAs were approved early on, and one more recently.

*San Luis Obispo County.* The more northerly county of the two, San Luis Obispo is home to four AVAs (see Map 4.8):

—Paso Robles, the largest

—York Mountain, the smallest

—Edna Valley, the oldest

—Arroyo Grande, the newest.

A small section of the Santa Maria Valley AVA also stretches into San Luis Obispo County from Santa Barbara County (see information on that county on the following page).

Of the four, York Mountain is the easiest to define, because of its extremely cool climate, located as it is in Templeton Gap, a funnel which draws cold air in from the ocean throughout the growing season. Not surprisingly, Chardonnay is well represented here.

Situated farther to the south and closer to the coast, Edna Valley and Arroyo Grande enjoy a more maritime climate. Chardonnay dominates in both appellations, and, in Arroyo Grande, Pinot Noir is made into sparkling wine by Maison Deutz.

Playing what is now a familiar tune, the growers and producers of the Paso Robles AVA are now questioning the integrity and accuracy of their large area. The gently undulating hills in the west have so far produced some good Cabernet Sauvignon, in contrast to the steeper slopes in the east, which have been planted with Zinfandel for many years. But, again, this may be too simplistic a way of looking at the situation, and many would argue that there is a north-south differentiation as well, where the cool air from the Templeton Gap provides vineyards with a better chance of producing good Chardonnay or Pinot Noir, rather than Zinfandel or Cabernet Sauvignon. Leading producers in the region are Meridian Vineyards for Chardonnay, Wild Horse Winery for Pinot Noir from various sources, and Eberle Winery for Cabernet Sauvignon.

*Santa Barbara.* This county has two approved AVAs, Santa Maria Valley, and Santa Ynez Valley. Chardonnay and Pinot Noir dominate in Santa Maria, with some smaller plantings of Cabernet Sauvignon and Merlot farther inland. Au Bon Climat/Qupé, Byron Vineyards, and Cambria are major producers.

In the Santa Ynez Valley, Pinot Noir rules in the cooler western end, particularly as produced by Sanford Wines, while Sauvignon Blanc, Cabernet Sauvignon, and Merlot are found more in the eastern end.

**Southern California.** The general South Coast AVA stretches in a wide arc from just south of Los Angeles down to the city of San Diego and the Mexican border. Within this umbrella appellation are two small AVAs, Temecula and San Pasqual Valley, of which the former is the more well-known and more important. With a consistent soil structure and climate, the Temecula AVA offers a unified picture, although its wineries are anything but similar in size and philosophy. Cooled by ocean breezes that are drawn 25 miles/40 kilometers inland through Rainbow Gap, the vineyards in this area support mostly white varieties, such as Chardonnay, Sauvignon Blanc, and Chenin Blanc, with a small number of Cabernet Sauvignon plantings beginning to show promise. Callaway Vineyards & Winery is by far the biggest producer.

**Sierra Foothills.** The umbrella appellation of Sierra Foothills includes a large cluster of sizeable counties, and six smaller AVAs. At the heart of the Sierra Foothills vine country lie the counties of Amador and El Dorado, which are home to three of the region's more important AVAs (see Map 4.9). For the serious California wine lover, these vineyards are highly revered, since this is Zinfandel country through and through.

The three AVAs of El Dorado, Fiddletown, and California Shenandoah Valley all concentrate on Zinfandel, and most of it is produced in the old style: big, heady, hugely fruity and ripe, with soft tannins, masses of berry character, and enough alcohol to keep any wine from turning bad too soon. Without a doubt, this typically Californian vine thrives in the granitic hills and summer heat, with only elevation to keep the acidity high enough to maintain some structure and balance in the wines.

Many producers also make surprisingly well-balanced Sauvignon Blanc wines and, as elsewhere, just about everybody is experimenting with Rhône and Italian varieties. Major producers include Karly, Amador Foothills Winery, Monteviña, Santino Winery, and Shenandoah Vineyards.

*Central Valley.* The huge 300-mile-long/480 kilometers Central Valley cannot be overlooked in any consideration of California wine, and not only

**Map 4.9** The Sierra Foothills AVAs.

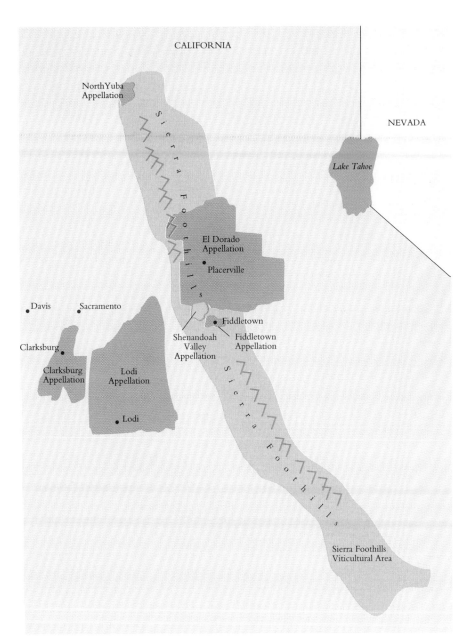

because of the quantity it produces. Here and there are pockets of wine making which rise far above the production of bulk table wines, particularly within the two AVAs of Lodi, just north of Stockton, and Madera in Fresno County, where Andrew Quady has built a strong reputation as a producer of fine dessert and port wines.

However, what really makes the Central Valley stand out is its jug wine production. Collectively, its larger producers have the capacity to produce 600 million gallons (22.5 million hectoliters) of wine per year; Gallo alone has a 300-million-gallon (11.3 million hectoliters) capacity. Many of the grapes used in the production of these wines, such as Emerald Riesling, French Colombard, Carnelian, and even Thompson Seedless, are unknown

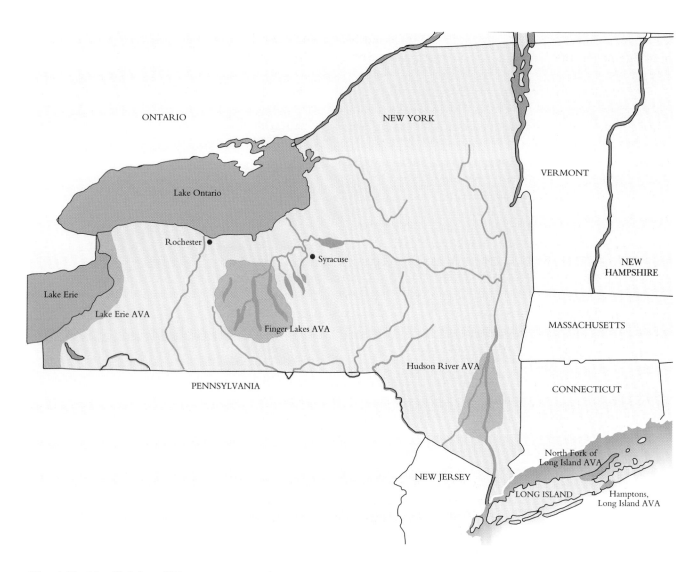

**Map 4.10** New York State AVAs.

ONTARIO

NEW YORK

VERMONT

Lake Ontario

NEW HAMPSHIRE

Rochester ●

● Syracuse

Lake Erie

Lake Erie AVA

Finger Lakes AVA

MASSACHUSETTS

Hudson River AVA

CONNECTICUT

PENNSYLVANIA

North Fork of
Long Island AVA

NEW JERSEY

LONG ISLAND    Hamptons,
Long Island AVA

today as varietal wines. As jug wines go, California's jug wines are among the best from any country.

In the northern end of the valley, around Lodi, a number of what used to be grower-cooperative wineries are now owned by famous families or investment groups who make midrange, highly acceptable varietal wines. Gallo, Sebastiani, Mondavi, and New York State's Canandaigua Wines are all new owners here. Most of the wines produced in these Central Valley facilities carry the "California" appellation.

## Northeastern United States—New York State

***Climate and Grapes.*** In a general sense, the climate of New York State's grape-growing areas can be classified as Region 1 and 2 in the UC Davis Heat Summation system. This immediately identifies New York as a cool climate grape-growing area, with an emphasis on white wine and sparkling wine production. Of the grapes grown in the state, the most common are

Chardonnay and Riesling in the vinifera family, and Seyval Blanc, Vidal, and Vignoles in the hybrid family (see the section on grape families in Chapter 2).

The tendency toward severe winter cold some years makes many New York State grape growers hesitant to work with vinifera grape varieties. They are generally not hardy enough to withstand such temperatures without a lot of labor-intensive care. Many growers prefer to work with hybrid varieties, which are more winter hardy and disease resistant. Some growers and producers continue to work with the extremely hardy native varieties, such as Concord, Catawba, and Niagara.

*Wine Styles.* The days when New York State produced mostly sweet red wines, such as the kosher brands of Manischewitz and Royal Kedem, and the nonkosher brands of Richard's Wild Irish Rose (from Canandaigua Wines), and Lake Niagara (from Widmer) are long gone. The range of wines currently produced in New York State is now much broader, including light, fresh Rieslings and Seyval Blancs, fuller Chardonnays, crisp sparkling wines, and full, dry Cabernet Sauvignons.

It comes as a surprise to most people to learn that New York State is the second-largest wine producer in the nation. More important, the quality of New York State wines is high enough to compete at a national and international level. Again, it is important to judge this region's wines not as direct comparisons to wines from anywhere else, but simply as wine. Using that as the sole criterion, New York State has nothing to be ashamed of, and much of which it can be proud.

*Regions.* There are six appellations (AVAs) in New York State (see Map 4.10). As with many of the recognized regions in Europe, what makes grape growing possible in an otherwise inhospitable climate is the existence of large bodies of water. In each case, the appellation relies on lakes, rivers, or the ocean to moderate the air temperature and make it possible for the early, tender buds and shoots to survive, and for the grapes to reach full ripeness with optimum flavor development.

*Lake Erie.* Located in the northwest corner of the state, this is the largest of New York State's AVAs, though it does not produce the most wine. The appellation continues southwest along the shore of Lake Erie, through Pennsylvania and into Ohio. The climate is strongly influenced by Lake Erie in a number of ways. Heavy snows, referred to as "lake-effect snow," are beneficial to the vines during the winter, since the snow acts as a layer of insulation against the very low temperatures.

In the spring, the lake stays cold for longer than the ground, keeping the air temperature lower than it otherwise might be. This retards the development of the buds, which helps reduce the possibility of damage by a sudden late cold spell or frost. In the fall, the lake stays warmer than the surrounding ground, keeping the air temperature higher and allowing the grapes to continue to ripen in the warmer air.

Vinifera varieties are in the minority in this region, and much of the harvest of native grapes now goes to jelly and juice production rather than

**Figure 4.8** A Label from a Dr. Konstantin Frank Johannisberg Riesling, 1976 Vintage.

wine production. Of the vinifera producers, Woodbury is the most prominent, winning numerous awards for its Chardonnay.

*Finger Lakes.* Though smaller in land area than the Lake Erie AVA, the Finger Lakes region produces more wine than any other appellation in New York. Finger Lakes vineyards have a larger percentage of hybrid and vinifera grapes planted for wine production, whereas the majority of Lake Erie's vineyards are planted with native varieties for juice and jelly production. The majority of the wineries are clustered around Keuka Lake, Seneca Lake, and Cayuga Lake, taking full advantage of the temperature moderation these lakes provide, and of the rolling hillsides which help to angle the vineyards into the sun and to minimize the risk of frost damage. The lakes, formed by glacial action during the ice age, are extremely deep in parts (up to 200 feet, or 60 meters), increasing their temperature moderating ability. The Finger Lakes AVA also includes a subappellation, Cayuga Lake (see Map 4.11).

The area owes much of its fame to some prominent names in the wine business, at least in the northeastern United States. For many years, the area's wine production was dominated by the giant Taylor corporation in Hammondsport at the base of Seneca Lake. The influence of Taylor is much less now, but, during its heyday, Taylor's Gold Seal label gained a reputation as one of New York State's finest sparkling wines. Charles Fournier, an immigrant from the Champagne region of France, and Dr. Konstantin Frank, a Russian immigrant, pioneered the planting of vinifera grape varieties in the region and recognized the potential of the land surrounding the lakes (see Figure 4.8).

Today, the Frank name is carried on by Dr. Frank's son, Willi Frank, and the sparkling wine tradition is continuing with fine products from such companies as Château Frank, Glenora, and Hermann Wiemer.

Not surprisingly, Chardonnay and Riesling are the most successful white vinifera varieties, and Vignoles and Seyval Blanc are prominent as white hybrid varieties. The production of red wine is much smaller, though some exceptional Cabernet Sauvignon is produced by the Dr. Konstantin Frank Winery and by Knapp Vineyards.

*Cayuga Lake.* The Cayuga Lake AVA is the only example in this state of a subappellation within a larger appellation. The growers and producers of Cayuga Lake feel that the slate and shale deposits which underlie this area make their growing conditions distinct enough to be singled out as a separate AVA. The wines tend to have a noticeably higher level of crispness. A prominent producer is Knapp Vineyards.

*Hudson River Region.* The Hudson River area boasts some of the oldest vineyards and wineries in America. There is evidence that Huguenot settlers planted grapes and made wine near New Paltz during the sixteenth century, and the Brotherhood winery has now incorporated the phrase "America's Oldest Winery" into its official name. It is the oldest winery in continuous operation, since it continued to produce sacramental wines

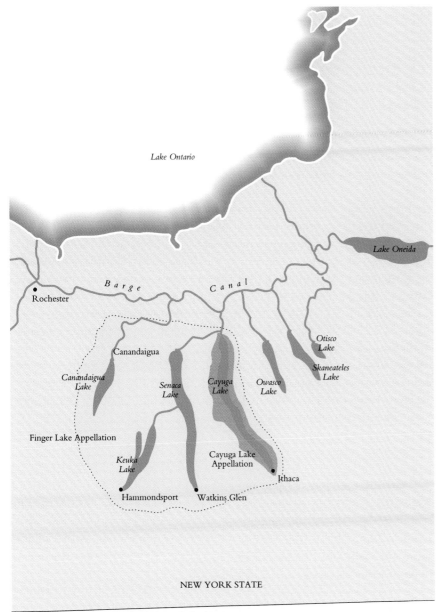

**Map 4.11** The Finger Lakes AVA and Cayuga Lake Subappellation.

Lake Ontario

Lake Oneida

*Barge* *Canal*

•
Rochester

Canandaigua

Otisco
Lake

Skaneateles
Lake

*Canandaigua*
*Lake*

*Seneca*
*Lake*

*Cayuga*
*Lake*

*Owasco*
*Lake*

Finger Lake Appellation

*Keuka*
*Lake*

Cayuga Lake
Appellation

•
Ithaca

•
Hammondsport

Watkins Glen

NEW YORK STATE

PENNSYLVANIA

through Prohibition. There are older wineries in America, but they closed during Prohibition.

The history of grape growing and wine making in this area is closely linked to the Concord grape and to other native varieties that have long been used to make juices, jellies, and the Manischewitz and Royal Kedem wines. The picture is very different now, with many acres planted with hybrid varieties, particularly at Benmarl, Cascade Mountain, and Clinton Vineyards. In the late 1970s, Clinton Vineyards planted some Chardonnay but has since abandoned the variety. In the 1980s, West Park Wine Cellars and Millbrook Vineyards also planted Chardonnay with greater success.

Anyone who listens to John Graziano talk about vinifera grape growing and wine making in the Hudson Valley can only come away with a reassurance that the future is secure for vinifera wines in the region.

"What fascinates me about wine making here," says John, " is the opportunity to continuously learn and to apply those nuggets of knowledge to the ongoing improvement of the whole grape growing and wine making process. For example, at a very basic level, we have learned that we can't grow Sauvignon Blanc and we can't sell Riesling, so we don't grow or make them anymore." Graziano also points to their adaptation of a lyre trellissing system to promote full ripening for some varieties and to increase airflow in the vines, thereby reducing the incidence of rot and mildew on the grapes.

John's attachment to the region is firmly established. He was born in Rye, NY, and attended Cornell University where he studied Fruit Crop Production, including courses in chemistry and viticulture. Cornell's proximity to the vineyards of the Finger Lakes gave John the excuse to indulge his interest in wine. After graduating from Cornell he worked for three harvests at the Rivendell Winery in New Paltz, NY. In 1984, he was asked by John Dyson to be the opening wine maker for Millbrook Vineyards. Dyson had previously been New York State's Commissioner of Agriculture and was determined to prove that good vinifera wines could be produced in New York. In John Graziano, Dyson has found a worthy and capable person to make the point.

The current repertoire of wines produced includes Chardonnay and Tocai Friulano as whites, and Cabernet Franc, Cabernet Sauvignon, Pinot Noir, Merlot, and Gamay Noir as reds. Surprisingly, Cabernet Franc represents Millbrook's largest production of varietal red wines. Over the years, Graziano has developed some preferences in grape types. "My favorite in the vineyard is Cabernet Sauvignon because of the orderly way in which it grows." Conversely, some would even say perversely, his favorite grape in the winery is Pinot Noir. "It's such a challenge to make good wine from. And when I do, I feel particularly proud."

The most notable progress in vinifera production has been at Millbrook Vineyards where they successfully grow and produce wines from Chardonnay, Pinot Noir, Cabernet Sauvignon, and Cabernet Franc. They also experiment with lesser-known varieties and have had good results with an Italian white variety called Tocai Friulano.

*North Fork of Long Island.* Out on the eastern end of Long Island, as potato farms disappeared in the 1970s, a few visionary people like Alex and Louisa Hargrave began buying the old farmland to plant grapes. The Hargraves have been followed by many others who share their dream of growing vinifera grapes in New York. Whereas the climate in the rest of the state meant that white vinifera varieties stood the best chance of success, the more moderate climate of Long Island means that red vinifera can finally be planted in greater quantities. The warmer climate comes from the more southerly latitude, the fact that the vineyards are almost surrounded by water, and from the position of the vineyards in the flow of warm, moist air which moves across the island in the fall and winter from the warmer southern states.

This is really the only part of New York State which fits comfortably into a Region 2 climate zone, and grape growers have had enough success with Cabernet Sauvignon, Merlot, and Cabernet Franc to claim to be

North America's equivalent of Bordeaux. While that claim may be an exaggeration, there are enough similarities that Bordeaux wine makers have shown an interest in consulting with some of the wineries on Long Island. Within the Long Island/North Fork AVA, the more prominent wineries are Hargrave, Palmer, Pindar, Bedell, Lenz, and Gristina.

*Hamptons, Long Island.* This smaller AVA in the southern part of the island has had a more checkered career, with financial woes closing some of the early starters. There are currently two major wineries, Duck Walk and Bridgehampton, both producing a wide range of vinifera wines.

**Other Northeastern States.** In addition to the large production of wine in New York State, many other states in the Northeast make wine, and some include recognized appellations. The more important ones are Pennsylvania, New Jersey, Connecticut, and Rhode Island. Vermont and Maine produce a number of good fruit wines from apples, pears, and blueberries.

**Climate.** In general, the northeastern states are all faced with the same kinds of climatic advantages and disadvantages as New York State, with the coastal regions enjoying the ocean influences on temperature. Like New York State, the other northeastern states have battled long and hard over the desirability and limited practicality of growing vinifera grapes in what can be a hostile climate. Even if a grower is lucky enough to propagate vinifera in the vineyard and to coax the fragile plants along for several years, high hopes can be dashed by a severe winter, as was experienced in 1980–1981, 1987, and again in 1993–1994, with temperatures sitting at −20°F (−30°C) for a week or two at a stretch. The resulting winter-kill, and subsequent need to replace up to 50 percent of the plants, are enough to make even the most persistent give up on vinifera and concentrate on hybrids.

## Major Wineries

*Pennsylvania.* Although the state boasts four AVAs, the wine-making industry here has never really flourished, despite some encouragement from the state government. In the northwest corner of the state, along the shores of Lake Erie, is Presque Isle Winery. In the southeast corner of the state, where temperatures are generally warmer, are Chaddsford Winery and Naylor Wine Cellars. Both of the latter have produced good Chardonnay and Cabernet Sauvignon, though both are also on record as suggesting that the red hybrid Chambourcin can make great Pennsylvanian wine.

The AVAs in Pennsylvania are Central Delaware Valley (along the border with New Jersey, where Central Delaware Valley is also an AVA), Cumberland Valley (which extends southward into the western part of Maryland), Lake Erie (shared with New York and Ohio), and Lancaster Valley, in the southern part of the state.

*New Jersey.* A long history of wine making and some recent state laws that encourage the development of small wineries are the basis of the current resurgence of interest in wine in New Jersey. Among those growing and producing cool-climate vinifera and hybrid wines are Tewksbury Wine Cellars, Alba Vineyards, and Renault Winery. The two AVAs in New Jersey are Central Delaware Valley (shared with Pennsylvania as the mutual boundary) and Warren Hills, in the northwestern corner of the state.

*Connecticut.* The Crosswoods Vineyards in the Southeastern New England AVA, and the Haight Vineyard in the Western Connecticut Highlands AVA are two leading examples of wineries facing the same challenges as growers and producers in neighboring states. Both are working hard to produce stylish Chardonnays, and Haight produces a number of hybrid varieties. The Southeastern New England AVA extends into the neighboring states of Rhode Island and Massachusetts.

*Rhode Island.* This tiny state is included in the large Southeastern New England appellation, but boasts some extraordinary microclimates with temperatures generally warmer than elsewhere in the region. However, this has not resulted in any major development of vineyards. One notable winery is Sakonnet Vineyards, making some good vinifera and hybrid wines.

## Northwestern United States

**Washington State.** Of the northwestern states, Washington State is the only one that can boast any substantial wine production before the 1970s. As early as the 1930s and 1940s, Washington State was producing large quantities of wine from native American grapes and other fruits, especially for the production of sweet, fortified wines of the sherry and port type. Today, any remaining acres of native grapes are used for juice or jelly production, while 11,000 acres (4400 hectares) of vinifera grapes produce in excess of 6 million gallons (226,500 hectoliters) of wine.

**Map 4.12** Washington State AVAs.

*Climate.* Washington State contains two distinct climatic regions for grape growing, separated by the Cascade Mountains. On the western side of these mountains, toward the coast, there is substantially more rainfall, and there are smaller swings between high and low temperatures. On the eastern side of the mountains, the climate approximates semidesert conditions, with much less rainfall, warmer days, and cooler nights. The lower rainfall means that vineyards must be irrigated, but it also means that there is less chance that rain at harvest time will increase the water content and lower the sugar content of the grapes, resulting in a thinner wine. The warm days make for good sugar and flavor development, while the cool nights help to keep acid levels high, maintaining clean, crisp, but ripe flavors in the wines. Overall, the climate is cooler than in California, but the daylight hours are longer, and the growing season is also longer. It is in the eastern part of the state where most grape growing occurs and where appellations have been approved.

## MIKE AND GARY HOGUE OF HOGUE CELLARS, YAKIMA VALLEY, WA

Mike Hogue of Hogue Cellars.

Nobody, least of all Mike Hogue, realized how big the Hogue Cellars winery would get when he planted the first vinifera grapes on the family property back in 1974. The Hogue story is a good example of how successful an enterprise can be if the product is good. From the 100 cases of Johannisberg Riesling produced in 1982 it was clear that the Hogues knew how to capture ripe Washington fruit and crisp acidity in a bottle. The gold medals have been almost incessant, and the winery today produces 250,000 cases (3 million bottles) of wine from over ten different varietals.

The Hogue family has been farming the fertile soils of the Yakima Valley for over 40 years. Their other agricultural products include bottled asparagus, sun-dried tomatoes, snap peas, sweet peppers, green beans, and carrots. When Mike and Gary decided to become commercial producers of wine, they had one simple goal: "To produce the highest-quality wine at the lowest-possible price." Even in the late 1980s, after several successful vintages, Gary admits "We still had a typical farmer's strategy to the business: Let's grow it and then see if we can sell it." Having lived up to their one simple goal, the Hogues have found that the critical acclaim heaped on their wines has brought customers to them, both wholesale and retail.

To deal with the wide range of grape varieties grown, the Hogues concentrate on the growing practices applied to each variety in the vineyard, altering the trellissing or pruning in order to maximize full ripeness and flavor development.

*Wine Styles.* Since Washington State concentrates almost entirely on vinifera grape growing, the wines are usually labeled by varietal names which are easily recognizable by most American wine consumers. The naturally crisp, fruity style favored by the climate is enhanced by cool, stainless steel fermentation for many of the white wines, especially Riesling, Sémillon, and Sauvignon Blanc. Occasionally, wood fermentation and aging is practiced on the latter two, and Chardonnay may be wood fermented and wood aged. However, any popularity of Washington Chardonnays has more to do with consumer fascination with the variety, and less to do with the wines' quality and character.

In red wines, Cabernet Sauvignon and Merlot can develop full-ripe-fruit flavors in the vineyard, backed up by substantial acid and tannin levels, which wine makers try to balance with oak flavors from aging. So far, the reds have shown attractive, vibrant flavors when young, and Merlot appears to show promise in the long run.

**Regions.** There are three AVAs in Washington State (see Map 4.12), ranging from Region 1 through Region 3 in the UC Davis Heat Summation System. The appellations are Columbia Valley, Yakima Valley, and Walla Walla Valley. Growers and producers concentrate on Riesling, Sauvignon Blanc, Sémillon, Chenin Blanc, Cabernet Sauvignon, Merlot, and Chardonnay. Some Washington producers also work with the red Lemberger grape (a red variety from Germany), though it still has to forge its own reputation in America. This may take some time since there are a variety of styles made, from easy going, light, fruity styles to full, oak-treated, tannic styles.

*Columbia Valley.* This is a huge AVA, covering 10.5 million acres (4.2 million hectares) with 6500 acres (2600 hectares) planted with vineyards, almost 60 percent of the state's total. The region encompasses two smaller subappellations with additional acreage, and it also extends southwards into the state of Oregon. By any measure, Columbia Valley is an oddity as an appellation. First, it covers many, many acres of land which are not and may never be vineyards, but the appellation was originally drawn to include some outlying vineyard areas. The land in between simply got included. Second, its size is somewhat at odds with the whole concept of appellations, which attempts in most places to identify small tracts of land that produce grapes and wines of definable regional character. To suggest that a wine is "typically Columbia Valley-style" would not convey much meaning. Third, some would argue that grapes should not be grown at all in the semiarid, almost desertlike conditions. It is only the technology of modern irrigation systems which allows the grapes to grow at all.

With irrigation, long growing seasons, and careful trellis selection, Columbia Valley vineyards are capable of producing consistently high yields of high-quality fruit, resulting in wines which are much admired around the world. Grape growing and wine production in the Washington State section of the Columbia Valley are dominated by the huge Stimson Lane organization which operates the Château Ste. Michelle, Columbia Crest, and Snoqualmie wineries. Stimson Lane has never sacrificed quantity for quality, even though Château Ste. Michelle alone produces in excess of 700,000 cases (8.4 million bottles) per year. Their consistently high quality wines and their price competitiveness enabled them, at least before White Zinfandel exploded onto the market, to sell more vinifera-labeled wine than any other American company. Château Ste. Michelle also markets a very good sparkling wine under the Domaine Ste. Michelle label.

At the other end of the spectrum from Stimson Lane, in terms of size, is the Hogue family, which has grown fruit in this area for generations. They started out with 100 cases (1200 bottles) in 1982, and now produce around 250,000 cases (3 million bottles) of wine every year, but they manage to maintain a family philosophy toward their grape growing and wine making. Where the Hogues and Stimson Lane are similar is in their commitment to quality. One other winery has been around as long as Château Ste. Michelle, and that is the Columbia winery, which continues to make quality vinifera wines, many of them now from vineyard-specific sites.

Within the Columbia Valley AVA are the two subappellations Yakima Valley and Walla Walla Valley. Yakima Valley has 4500 acres (1800 hectares) of vines planted within a defined AVA of just over half a million acres (200,000 hectares). The valley runs east–west around the towns of Wapato, Zillah, and Sunnyside, offering cooler temperatures overall than the rest of Columbia Valley. The Walla Walla Valley has only 60 acres (24 hectares) of vineyards within a defined AVA of almost 200,000 acres (80,000 hectares). The southern half of the Walla Walla appellation also extends into Oregon.

### Oregon

*Climate.* Whereas Washington State has its semiarid conditions in the Columbia Valley, the climate in Oregon's grape-growing regions is much more marine influenced, producing more marginal conditions for successful grape growing. The main grape-growing regions in Oregon are situated on the western side of the Cascade Mountains in river valleys that run north–south, only about 60 miles (100 kilometers) from the Pacific Ocean, with cooler temperatures and more rainfall than other West Coast grape growing regions (see Map 4.13). Some protection from the Pacific Ocean storms is provided by a small range of coastal mountains.

*Wine Styles.* As in Washington State, a small amount of fruit wine is produced, using fruit other than grapes. Otherwise, wine production is all from vinifera varieties. Oregon does not allow generic labeling of wine, and wines labeled by varietal must be made from at least 90 percent of the named variety (except Cabernet Sauvignon for which the minimum is 75 percent). Because their region is cool, Oregon growers and producers have concentrated on grape varieties recommended for Region 1 and have had great success with Pinot Noir. Chardonnay has not received the same kind of acclaim, probably because most growers started with the same clone of Chardonnay that had been widely used in California's warmer climate. New plantings of a more Burgundian cool-climate clone show great promise. Some growers and producers have also received acclaim for Riesling, Chenin Blanc, and Pinot Gris wines.

# DAVID ADELSHEIM OF ADELSHEIM VINEYARDS, WILLAMETTE VALLEY, OR

David Adelsheim

Before the wine industry became David Adelsheim's full-time occupation, he led the typically varied life of a youth of the 1960s. He attended universities in Berkeley, CA, Portland, OR, and Frankfurt and Berlin in Germany. After earning a Bachelor of Arts in German literature, he served in the U.S. Army, worked in a bank, built musical instruments, and constructed museum installations. Anybody who knows Adelsheim Vineyards' wines today will acknowledge that wine consumers owe David and his wife Ginny a great debt for eventually choosing to operate a vineyard and winery.

Like others who came into wine making in the early 1970s, Adelsheim recalls that it was an easy decision to make. "In 1971, my generation knew limitless bounds. It was very attractive to think that we would be operating a business which would be vertically integrated, quality oriented, and in touch with the land and nature." Today, he freely admits that he was in for a shock when idealism came face-to-face with the reality of business. "We had no business plan and no idea of the complexity of the business. We were hopeless at marketing and bookkeeping—the things that keep a business in business." Nevertheless, with a lot of help from friends, and with a quality product to sell, Adelsheim Vineyards has been and remains a successful and viable operation.

Now, as General Manager of Adelsheim Vineyards, David is very active in the overall direction of the vineyard and the winery. He was one of the first in the Willamette Valley to recognize that even the finest technology in the winery could not cover mistakes in the vineyard. As a result, together with his vineyard manager, he exercises a direct, hands-on approach to vineyard management, working closely with the Oregon State University and with UC Davis on clonal selection and evaluation. Much of his work has led to the adoption of Burgundy clones of Chardonnay that will be more suited to the cool, marine climate of the Willamette Valley than the California clones that were originally planted. He also recognizes the importance of timing the picking. "In the mid-'80s, I was lucky enough to be able to travel to UC Davis and to the Carneros District in California to taste the grapes as they were picking. From that experience, I learned that no matter what the sugar and acidity measurements are, there's no point picking Pinot Noir or Chardonnay unless they taste like Pinot Noir and Chardonnay." According to Adelsheim, the combination of more Pinot Noir and Chardonnay clones, and more knowledge and experience of timing the harvest can only result in better Oregon wines.

The Adelsheim Vineyard wines offer customers the choice of two distinct wine-making philosophies. The labels which carry an Oregon appellation are all wines blended from different clones, different vineyard sites, and different fermentation lots. The result is a pleasing, smooth wine with typical varietal character. The Reserve and Single Vineyard labels concentrate on capturing the unique character of Pinot Noir or Chardonnay from single vineyard sites, and are a reflection of the combination of grape variety, soil, climate, and vineyard techniques from that single location.

All of the Adelsheim labels are designed by Adelsheim's wife Ginny. The portraits on the blended Oregon appellation wines are of friends who helped the Adelsheims to construct their first winery and plant their first vineyards. The portraits on the single-vineyard wines are daughters, including the Adelsheims' own daughter Elizabeth.

David Adelsheim was instrumental in convincing the Burgundy firm of Drouhin to buy property in the Willamette Valley. "I think it was a positive step," says Adelsheim. "It focused attention on Oregon as a producer of top-quality Pinot Noir, and that can only be good for all of us in the long run." For all the advances and improvements that the Adelsheims have seen, he is quick to voice a much-repeated concern among United States vintners. "I am worried that we are not paying enough attention to creating a new generation of wine lovers. We have to make it easier for young people to enjoy wine."

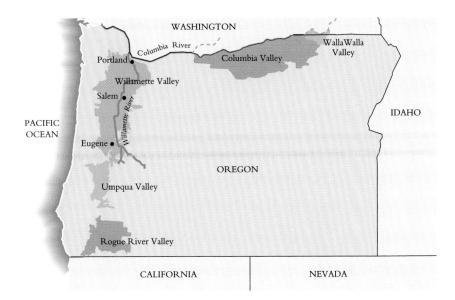

**Map 4.13**  Oregon State AVAs.

In years with enough sun and warmth, Oregon's Pinot Noirs develop vibrant, purple hues and attractive cherry fruit aromas and flavors, while the Chardonnays can occasionally display a ripeness of fruit which is surprising. Both varieties maintain good acid levels in the cool climate, providing backbone and structure. In recent years, the style of the Pinot Noirs has become more defined, offering more suppleness and smooth texture as some of the developmental wine-making problems have been ironed out.

*Regions*.  There are three AVAs lying entirely within Oregon, the Willamette Valley, the Umpqua Valley, and the Rogue River Valley. As the names imply, each one of the appellations takes advantage of climate and soil conditions provided by river valleys, with deeper and more complex soil profiles on the valley slopes, along with better sun exposure and frost and wind protection. Small portions of the Columbia Valley and Walla Walla appellations extend from Washington State into Oregon.

*Willamette Valley.*  This, the largest and best-known Oregon AVA, is home to some of the state's finest wineries, such as Knudsen-Erath, Sokol-Blosser, Adelsheim, and Eyrie. Both Robert Drouhin of Burgundy and Laurent-Perrier of Champagne own property here, along with Brian Croser of Australia's Petaluma winery. The finest areas within the appellation are acknowledged to be the Dundee Hills, and the Eola Hills. Pinot Noir and Chardonnay remain the most widely planted varieties.

*Umpqua Valley.*  Lying immediately south of Willamette Valley, the Umpqua Valley AVA has a slightly longer history of grape growing and was the site of Oregon's first winery, Hillcrest Vineyards. Hillcrest is still in operation and still produces some of the state's best Pinot Noir and Chardonnay.

**Map 4.14**  Texas Wine Regions and AVAs.

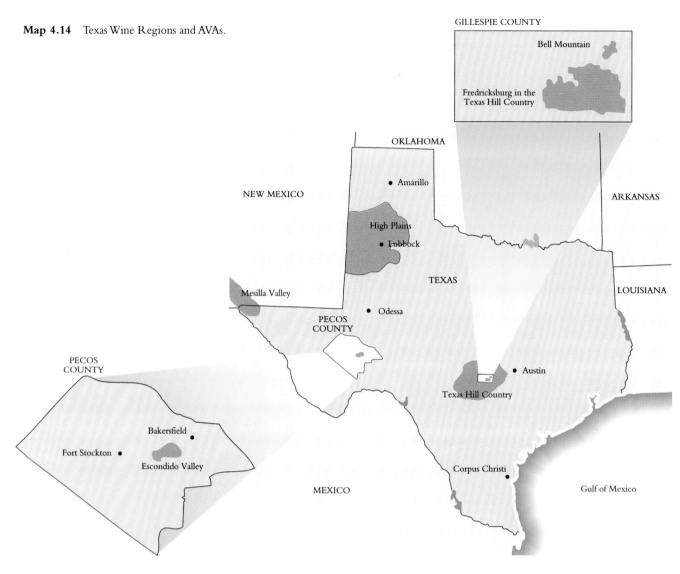

*Rogue River Valley.*  This newer AVA is in the southern part of Oregon, close to California. The climate is generally warmer, and high-elevation vineyards have produced some promising Cabernet Sauvignon, Chardonnay, and Chenin Blanc.

### Idaho

*Climate.*  The main grape-growing area in Idaho is at about the same latitude as the Umpqua Valley in Oregon and is situated just across the border from Oregon in the Snake River Valley. There is little rainfall in the generally warm summers, but the daylight hours are short, as is the overall growing season, making it difficult to achieve full ripeness and flavor development.

*Wine Styles.*  Region 1 grapes are the most suitable, but even Chardonnay has difficulty developing full varietal character. Riesling, Gewürztraminer, and Chenin Blanc have performed better, showing crisp, clean flavors and tart acidity.

The majority of all grape growing and wine making is located in the western end of the Snake River Valley, but there are no AVAs in Idaho. Ste. Chapelle is the largest producer.

# Southwestern United States

Covering a broad range of climates and microclimates, the whole southwestern corner of the United States has witnessed a revitalization of its wine industry, based mostly on careful selection of vinifera grape types according to climate and soil suitability. Many people believe that this area of the United States is too hot and dry for successful grape growing, but several wineries have proved in the last decade that this is a false image. Whatever climatic disadvantages may exist can be dealt with by site selection, especially using higher elevations to maintain cooler temperatures and thus ensure suitable acidity levels in the grapes and the wines. The problem of lack of rainfall is handled by irrigation, though any seasoned irrigated-vineyard manager will admit that the trick is knowing when to irrigate, and how much.

*Texas.*  By 1995, Texas had over 3000 acres (1200 hectares) of vineyards planted, with vinifera varieties in the majority. The state also had six AVAs (see Map 4.14). In the western part of the state, there are a number of wineries in the cool Texas High Plains AVA around the town of Lubbock. The most prominent wineries in the High Plains AVA are Llano Estacado and Pheasant Ridge, both producing some fine examples of crisp, fruity vinifera whites such as Riesling and Chardonnay, and lean but stylish Cabernet Sauvignon.

Three of the state's AVAs are in the Texas Hill Country region, to the west of the city of Austin. The number of wineries and the amount of land planted with vines in this region have been expanding rapidly. Most of the new plantings take advantage of the hill sites to develop full fruit character in the grapes while still retaining sufficient acidity levels. The AVAs are Texas Hill Country, Bell Mountain and Fredericksburg in the Texas Hill Country.

Among the wineries in this region, two well-established producers take advantage of the superior quality fruit from these AVAs. They are Fall Creek Vineyards, known for some fine vinifera varietal wines, and Moyer Champagne Cellars, making sparkling wine according to the classic method.

The fifth AVA is the Escondido Valley, situated in the Trans–Pecos region. This region is also home to Texas' largest winery, which bottles wines under the Ste. Genevieve label as a joint venture between the University of Texas and Cordier Inc. of Bordeaux. The Ste. Genevieve wines have received much acclaim as good examples of vinifera varietal wines.

The sixth AVA in Texas is Mesilla Valley, located in the far west corner of Texas around the city of El Paso on the border of Texas, Mexico, and New Mexico. This region extends northwards into New Mexico where it is also an AVA.

***New Mexico.*** The geographic and climatic combination of high elevations, warm days, and cool nights which have led to recognition for Washington State's and Texas' wine makers are also responsible for much of the praise which has recently been directed to New Mexico's wines. Two of the state's promising wineries are Anderson Valley Vineyards, making some excellent Chardonnay, and Domaine Cheurlin, where the Champagne/Burgundy heritage of the owners led them to concentrate on sparkling wines made from Pinot Noir and Chardonnay, with excellent results.

There are three AVAs in New Mexico. The Mesilla Valley AVA extends northwards from El Paso in Texas, where it is also an AVA. Farther west is the Mimbres Valley AVA, located around the city of Deming. Clustered around the city of Albuquerque in the center of the state is the Middle Rio Grande Valley AVA.

***Arizona.*** With similar concerns for the need for high-elevation vineyards, Sonoita Vineyards and RW Webb Winery have had success with vinifera wines in a state which is not usually thought of as a wine producer. The only AVA in Arizona to date is Sonoita, located directly to the south of Phoenix, on the Mexican border.

## Southeastern United States

Ironically, it is the mild climate of some of the southeastern states that is the biggest enemy to modern commercial wine production, particularly in Florida. The likelihood of year-round warmth and the resulting lack of a dormant period for the vine leave the plants highly susceptible to Pierce's Disease, a bacterial disease spread by insects that eventually kills the vine. Historically, the only grape truly resistant to this disease has been the Scuppernong Muscadine, the grape from which America's first wine was probably made by Huguenots in the 1560s. In more northerly states, such as Maryland and Virginia, wine makers have had more success using vinifera and hybrid grape varieties.

***Georgia.*** The wine industry in this state was given a tremendous shot in the arm in 1984 when a Frenchman agreed to be the wine maker at the Château Elan winery, originally importing juice from California to make the wine, but now making sound wines from homegrown Cabernet Sauvignon, Merlot, Chardonnay, Sauvignon Blanc, and Riesling, as well as a number of French-American hybrid varieties.

***North Carolina.*** Once again, French tradition and American technology have combined in the Château Biltmore wines, produced from vines grown on the famous Biltmore Estate. The winery has had some recognition for its Chardonnay, Cabernet Sauvignon, and sparkling wine.

***Virginia.*** Given Thomas Jefferson's famous endorsement of wine as a suitable beverage, it is perhaps strange that his state has not had an active wine industry in this century. However, recent ventures in the vineyard and winery business have taken advantage of local laws that encourage small winery development and of Virginia's proximity to Washington D.C. They produce some high-quality wines that can be sold to visiting tourists on site or marketed within the capital itself to restaurants that are anxious to support the local wineries.

The marketing and acceptance of Virginia wines will likely be helped by the existence of six AVAs, two of which make direct reference to the state's rich history. Monticello, around Charlottesville, is an AVA which recognizes Thomas Jefferson's contribution to the nation and to wine knowledge, and the lengthy AVA name of Northern Neck George Washington Birthplace, refers to Westmoreland County and the adjacent lands between the Rappahannock River and the Potomac River estuary.

The Shenandoah Valley AVA runs along the northern part of Virginia's border with West Virginia where the AVA is also recognized. Virginia's Eastern Shore AVA covers the vineyards located on the southern tip of the Accomac peninsula, taking advantage of the moderate climate of Chesapeake Bay. Farther inland the North Fork of Roanoke AVA relies on that river's influence on the grapevines, and directly to the north of North Fork Roanoke is the Rocky Knob AVA.

More and more of the wineries in Virginia are concentrating on vinifera wines, with almost 80 percent of all vineyard acreage planted to vinifera varieties, especially Riesling, Chardonnay, Cabernet Sauvignon, and Merlot. Principal wineries are Meredyth Vineyards, Ingleside Plantation, Rapidan River Vineyards, Oakencroft Vineyard, Barboursville Winery, and Montdomaine Cellars.

*Maryland.*   Maryland is one of the cradles of modern eastern grape growing and wine making, inasmuch as the state was home to Philip Wagner and his winery, Boordy Vineyards. Mr. Wagner wrote the book *Grapes into Wine,* which has been used by many eastern grape growers to better understand viticulture and vinification in this part of the United States. Though Mr. Wagner was a strong proponent of hybrid grapes for this climate, he relinquished control of Boordy Vineyards in 1980, and Boordy and a few other wineries now concentrate on vinifera. Some of the best producers are Byrd Vineyards and Catoctin Cellars. Maryland has three AVAs, all in the western part of the state. Cumberland Valley AVA is in the far western part of the state around the city of Cumberland; this AVA also extends northwards into Pennsylvania. The Catoctin AVA and the Linganore AVA are both near the city of Frederick.

# Mexico

In wine terms, Mexico is to the New World what Greece is to the Old: the starting-off point for grape growing and wine making, which eventually spread to other areas more suitable for those activities. Via Mexico came the Criolla grape, which was taken south where it became the basis of the early

**Map 4.15** Mexico's Wine Regions.

South American wine industry, and north to California, where it became known as the Mission grape and helped to found the early Californian wineries.

Despite limited local interest in wine, production has increased steadily over the past two decades. The main impetus has been the injection of capital and expertise from other countries, especially Spain, with familiar Spanish winery names such as Domecq and Osborne leading the way. The increasing use of modern wine-making equipment and methods is beginning to show dividends, moving Mexico's wine industry away from antiquated Spanish methods, which often resulted in heavy, dull, oxidized wines to methods that produce wines which appeal to the international market. The North American Free Trade Agreement (NAFTA) provides incentives for investment in Mexican wineries, with the promise of a concentration on higher quality and export marketability.

There are several grape-growing regions in Mexico (see Map 4.15). Of these, the North Baja California and the Querétaro regions have so far shown the greatest promise. The North Baja California region enjoys some of the fog-induced coolness for which the state to the north is so well known. This allows for some good flavor development and acid retention in vinifera grape varieties such as Riesling, Pinot Noir, and Cabernet Sauvignon, all of which have produced good wines from this region. Particularly important here is the area of Calafia in the Guadalupe Valley, where the Spanish-based company of Casa Pedro Domecq has produced some outstanding wines.

In the warmer, tropical part of the country lies Querétaro, where the Cavas de San Juan Winery relies on elevations of 6000 feet (1850 meters) and more to maintain acid balance in the grapes. Here some fine wines from vinifera varieties such as Cabernet Sauvignon, Chardonnay, and Pinot Noir are produced. The latter two grapes are also used to produce some sparkling wines that show exemplary crispness and depth of character.

A little to the north of Querétaro is the large region of Aguascalientes, home of the winery Vinicola de Aguascalientes, which produces more than one-tenth of the nation's total wine production, most of it in an easy-drinking, light, commercial style.

# Canada

Apart from some dry years in the 1920s and 1930s when the Canadian provinces attempted Prohibition, wine has been made in this country for most of this century, although very few people around the globe have ever heard of, let alone tasted, Canadian wine. The two main areas of production are the Niagara region and Lake Erie region in Ontario, and the southwestern part of British Columbia. Both of these regions experience cold winters and warm to hot summers and, just as in any other place where severe winter cold is a threat, grape growers and wine makers have had to learn how to handle the delicate vinifera varieties.

To encourage more wineries to concentrate on high-quality wines, both Ontario and British Columbia issue the Vintners' Quality Alliance (VQA) seal of approval to wines which successfully pass a taste test and chemical analysis. Though the system has shown some shortcomings, it is still a step toward a guarantee of quality and certificate of origin, bringing Canada into line with other quality wine-producing nations.

The VQA system allows for a separate VQA board in each of the two provinces that are responsible for the vast majority of Canada's wine production, Ontario and British Columbia. The VQA boards are made up of representatives from various segments of the wine and hospitality industries,

Karl Kaiser (left) and Donald Ziraldo of Inniskillin.

## KARL KAISER OF INNISKILLIN

Born and raised in Austria, Kaiser learned about grape growing and wine making while studying the subjects at a Cistercian monastery vineyard in his homeland. With his wife, he followed his parents-in-law to Ontario and began to look for work in the wine industry. In 1973, he was fortunate enough to meet up with Don Ziraldo who was about to achieve the impossible: get the first new winery license issued in Ontario in over 40 years. Against the Ontario industry giants of Andrés and Château-Gai, Ziraldo and Kaiser have shown through experimentation and perseverance that vinifera can prosper in the region, and that quality wines can be produced.

and they initiate and oversee regulations which govern appellations (known as Designated Viticultural Areas, or DVAs, in Canada), grape types, and labeling. The main regulations are these:

- Wines must be made from 100 percent vinifera varieties. (Currently, this is not a fully implemented regulation in British Columbia, though the VQA board appears to be moving in that direction.)

- All of the grapes used to make the wine must be from Ontario or British Columbia.

- When a grape variety is named on the label, 85 percent of the grapes must be that variety.

- If a DVA is named on a label, 95 percent of the grapes must come from that DVA.

- If a specific vineyard site is named on a label, the vineyard must lie completely within a DVA, and all of the grapes must come from that vineyard.

***Wine Styles.*** In earlier years, the Canadian wine industry was based on native grape varieties, and the practice of "amelioration" was common. This entailed adding water and sugar to the whole process to tone down the aggressive flavors of the native grape varieties. As in most other North American wine regions, Canadian producers now leave the native grapes for jelly and juice production, and concentrate on hybrid and vinifera grapes for quality wine production. Given the early onset of cooler temperatures in the fall season, the majority of the vinifera grapes grown are white varieties,

**Map 4.16** British Columbia's Wine Regions.

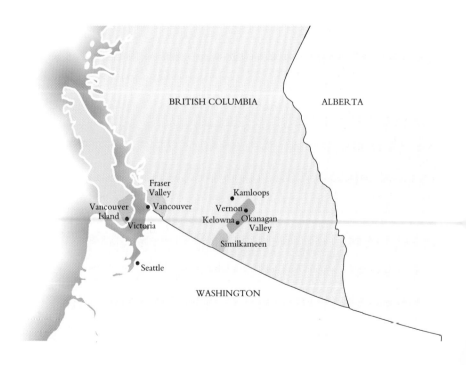

especially Riesling, Gewürztraminer, and Müller-Thurgau, as well as a number of the newer German crossings such as Bacchus and Optima. The favored hybrid grape is the Vidal, especially for ice wine, made as it is in Germany by leaving the grapes to freeze on the vine (see the section on Eiswein in Chapter 10 on Germany).

## Ontario

The Ontario wine region is centered on the gently sloping side of the Niagara escarpment, a strip of fertile soil adjacent to Lake Ontario, and on the north shore of Lake Erie. In both cases, the lakes help to moderate temperatures in the vineyards. The Vintners' Quality Alliance has operated in Ontario since 1988, and has approved three Designated Viticultural Areas (DVAs). These are Niagara Shore, Lake Erie North Shore, and Pelée Island. Since the concentration on quality vinifera wines is recent, most wineries are still learning where the best sites are for specific grape varieties. As a result, many wineries offer a wide array of wines made according to the personal preferences of the wine maker. As the quality wine industry matures, wineries will concentrate more on specific sites for each variety, and the less-successful varieties will be made in smaller quantity.

Even so, a number of Ontario wineries have already made a name for themselves. Allan Schmidt is a fourth-generation wine person, originally from British Columbia, but now making some fine Riesling at Ontario's Vineland Estate winery. At Château des Charmes winery, Paul Bosc makes some delicate Rieslings and oak-treated Chardonnay, and Inniskillin continues to impress with its Rieslings, Chardonnays, and Eiswein.

## British Columbia

The cradle of grape growing and wine making in British Columbia (see Map 4.16) is the Okanagan Valley DVA, a semidesert area similar to the Columbia Valley farther south in Washington State. Summers can be hot, but the summer nights and the winters can get very cold, and autumn frosts have caught many unsuspecting grape growers unawares. As in Ontario, a few industry giants controlled the wine industry for many years until the provincial government decided, in the 1970s, to allow small "cottage" wineries. Since then, a handful of wineries have had increasing success with Riesling, Müller-Thurgau, Pinot Gris, Pinot Blanc, and similar cool-climate varieties.

Lake Okanagan is the largest of a number of lakes in the Okanagan Valley, all of which help to moderate temperatures in the vineyards. More experience will help growers to identify the preferable sites which offer prolonged warmth and frost protection. Some of the outstanding wine makers are Ann Sperling of Cedar Creek winery, Harry McWatters of Sumac Ridge winery, John Simes, formerly from Marlborough, New

Zealand, but now with Mission Hill, George Heitz of Grey Monk Winery, and Ian Mavety of Blue Mountain Winery.

In addition to the Okanagan Valley DVA, three other DVAs have been approved. They are Similkameen Valley, Fraser Valley, and Vancouver Island. These areas offer wines in a similar style to those from the Okanagan Valley DVA. Most producers are concentrating on vinifera varieties suited to cool northerly climates.

## Summary

The vast land mass of the North American continent has made wine since European settlers arrived, and great strides have been made to bring North American wines to the point where they have earned respect in most other wine-producing nations. And yet many of the American regions are still in their infancy as wine growers, with much to discover and learn about the suitability of grape varieties and specific sites.

Within the United States, and particularly on the West Coast, the appellation system has advanced to the point that grape growers and wine makers rightly talk about regional characteristics, and the industry has matured to the point where competing with European wines is no longer the primary impetus. It is enough to know that individual regions can make high-quality wines which stand on their own merits. As the appellation system matures and evolves all around the United States and within Canada and Mexico, the industry can look forward to even better wines produced according to regional styles.

It is safe to say that North American wine has only just begun to show its true colors. With the American zeal for continuous improvement, we will see a refinement of existing growing regions, with a concentration on the sites that consistently produce high-quality wines. But there will also be brand new areas discovered which offer that magical combination of *terroir*, where soil type, microclimate, sun exposure, protection from wind and frost, grape type or clone, and vinification technique all come together to make truly great wine of extraordinary varietal and regional character.

Inside the winery, North Americans have made important contributions to understanding how to make better wine. Now, grape growers throughout the continent are working together with growers around the globe to understand more about vineyard techniques to produce grapes of optimum quality.

# The Southern Hemisphere

## Introduction

In this chapter we will describe the most important wine-making countries of the Southern Hemisphere: Chile, Argentina, and Brazil in South America; Australia and New Zealand, which comprise Oceania; and South Africa. For each country we will describe the most important wine regions, the types of grapes grown, and the best-known wines produced. We will also highlight some major growers.

The wines of all of these Southern Hemisphere countries have a distinct advantage over those of the Northern Hemisphere: they can appear in the marketplace about six months earlier, because harvest is in February and March, instead of September and October. In other words, the first 1994 wines reach Northern Hemisphere stores in the fall of 1994, instead of the spring of 1995. Until recently, Southern Hemisphere wines have been thought of as abundant in quantity but poor in quality. However, wine makers are moving away from fortified and jug wines toward premium, popular varietals. As the quality-to-price ratio improves, many Southern Hemisphere wines are gaining visibility and acceptance. The potential for growth, in both acreage and quality, is confirmed by the amount of investments recently made by Western European and California companies.

Southern Hemisphere producers are moving toward strict controls over varietal labels, which helps market share. After all, the average consumer looking for good value in wine is more comfortable buying a wine labeled "Chardonnay" than a wine labeled with an unknown place name. So varietal labeling helps sell the wines of the Southern Hemisphere.

The countries of the Southern Hemisphere, with far less land mass than those of the North, are all affected by the winds called the Westerlies, that blow over the surrounding oceans. The cold Western Australia Current, the Peru or Humboldt Currents which affect South America, and the Benguela, which affects South Africa, coupled with air pressure and cloud cover, create climatic conditions that can range from arid desert to frozen tundra.

As air masses travel south and are warmed they absorb moisture, but the Westerlies then push the moisture-laden air over cold ocean currents. Precipitation often occurs offshore, over the ocean, before it can reach the vineyards, many of which must therefore be irrigated. Most Southern Hemisphere vineyard areas began by the sea, where European immigrants settled, because these farmers benefited from the cooling breezes and the nearby markets to sell their wines. As in the Northern Hemisphere, most vineyards in the Southern Hemisphere are in the temperate zones.

# South America

## Chile

Chile is the world's tenth-largest wine producer and is recognized as the premier quality wine producer in South America (see Map 5.1). The growing conditions in this nation, 2,900 miles/4,831 kilometers in length and about 110 miles/183 kilometers in width, vary greatly. The Atacama Desert is in the north, the Pacific Ocean is to the west, and the Antarctic is due south. Because of its isolated geographic position, and the overwhelming presence of the Andes Mountains to the east, the *phylloxera* louse has never plagued the vineyards of Chile (see Chapters 3, 6, and 7). Chile's ungrafted vines are twice as old as those in France and California, which were uprooted at the turn of the century and are protected by American rootstock. With age comes quality, as the roots go deeper into the soil for nourishment. Another advantage to *phylloxera*-free vines is that new vines can be harvested after three years instead of four, since no time is needed for the graft from rootstock to vine to "take." Since these vines do not need to be grafted to foreign rootstock, they can grow by the *acodo mugron* system, which involves placing a branch from a growing vine in the earth, thus starting a new plant. As the vine matures, it is severed from the parent vine. These vines also provide the mixed blessing of higher yields, if the producer desires them.

GULF OF MEXICO

**Map 5.1** The Wine Regions of South America.

VENEZUELA

GUYANA
SURINAME
FRENCH GUYANA

COLOMBIA

ECUADOR

BRAZIL

PERU

BOLIVIA

PACIFIC OCEAN

PARAGUAY

ATLANTIC OCEAN

CHILE

ARGENTINA

Santiago •

URUGUAY

Mendoza

• Montevideo
Buenos Aires

Principal wine-producing regions

Other regions producing wine

# History

Vinifera vines were introduced to Chile by the Spanish explorer Cortez, circa 1523. Some commercial vineyards were planted as early as 1554, and there has been continuous wine production in the area surrounding Chile's capital, Santiago, for at least four centuries. Even though Spain, in a vain attempt to protect its export market, tried to ban new vineyards in Chile during the late seventeenth century, Chile developed a reputation for producing large quantities of inexpensive but drinkable wines by the early eighteenth century.

In the 1830s the Chilean government established the Quinta Normal, an experimental nursery for a wide range of plants including vinifera cuttings. The development of this agricultural station was a turning point in the Chilean wine industry, because it allowed Chile to isolate cuttings of vinifera vines just at the time when *phylloxera* was ravaging Europe.

During the nineteenth century the gentry of Chile established vinifera-based vineyards, more often than not employing French wine makers who

An Old Vine, between 60 and 100 Years Old, Untouched by *Phylloxera* and Still Bearing Fruit, at the Torres Vineyard in Chile's Central Valley.

A Young Vine, About 10 to 12 Years Old, at the Same Vineyard.

*Acodo Mugron*—the Bending of the Vine to Plant a New Vine, Without the Use of Nursery Rootstock. When the Vine Takes Root, it is Cut from the Parent. This Type of Planting Can be Done in Both Chile and South Australia, Because They Have Never Experienced an Outbreak of *Phylloxera,* and So Can Plant Vines on Their Own Roots.

The Torres *Manso de Varasco* Old Vines Vineyard in Chile's Central Valley.

were either financially wiped out or terrified by the *phylloxera* epidemic in their native country. The Chilean wine industry was quite healthy, especially in light of *phylloxera,* and began to be taxed heavily as the twentieth century arrived.

Because of taxation and political instability, by 1980 almost half of Chile's vineyards had been pulled out of the ground. Politically, Chile's bloody transition from the socialism of the late Salvador Allende to the military dictatorship of General Pinochet and his present-day successors has been detrimental not only to basic human rights but also to the country's vineyards. The return of the vineyards from collective to private ownership (beginning in 1982) has not been without some major problems. However, since 1987, more than 25,000 acres/10,000 hectares of new vineyards have been planted with premium vinifera grapes, with an eye to an ever-expanding export market, especially the United States.

## The Wines

Perhaps because of Chile's Spanish cultural roots and ancestry, Chile is primarily red wine country, and the wines can be charming, with forward fruit and aromas and flavors of red currants, strawberries, blackberries, and red plums. Chile's Merlot and Cabernet Sauvignon wines, extremely popular in the North American export market, lack the complexity of the finer wines of Bordeaux and California's North Coast, but they are food-friendly and usually approachable at an early age.

Chile's white wines span the spectrum of styles from oxidized wines heavy with the local *Rauli* oak flavors and little acidity and fruit, to delicate, fresh, high-tech white wines made by cool fermentation. The modern wines use Rauli oak only for storage and utilize 56 gallon/225 liter Alliers and Troncais barriques for aging (see Chapter 1 on How Wine Is Made). A good rule of thumb is to drink Chilean white wines within two years of their vintages (oak-aged Chardonnay can last three years). In addition to Chardonnay, Sauvignon Blanc and Riesling from Chile have found a home in the United States market. In the production of both red and white wines, Chile has a dual problem: permitting too-high yields in the vineyards and harvesting grapes from vines that are too young. Chile will have to deal with these issues if producers wish to break out of the low end of the international market, where they are presently (and profitably) ensconced.

The best wines of Chile are the so-called varietal/proprietary wines, with each producer using different names and criteria for their high-end products. For example, Santa Rita uses "Medalla Real," while Concha y Toro (Chile's largest winery, exporting 90 percent of their estate wines) uses both "Marques de Casa Concha" and "Don Melchor" as quality designations for their best varietal wines (for example, Cabernet Sauvignon "Don Melchor"). "Reserva Especial" seems to have no meaning, nor do minimum appellation standards apply to Chilean wines, although wines labeled by varietal must be 85 percent of the grape type. Estate bottling is ostensibly 100 percent, but vintage is not regulated, and if an appellation appears on the label, the "estate" can buy grapes from other viticultural areas.

Chilean wine laws stipulate that export white wines must attain a minimum alcohol level of 12 percent, and reds 11.5 percent. While "Reserva Especial" is a marketing term, the age requirement for **Especial** is two years, **Reserva** is four years, and **Gran Viño** is six years minimum.

"Finas" are varietal label wines made from government-recognized grape types, mostly vinifera, such as Cot (a clone of Malbec, best known as a blending grape in the red wines of Bordeaux), the Cabernets, and Pinot Noir for reds, and Sémillon, Sauvignon Blanc, and Riesling for whites. In contrast, Correntes are ordinary reds, made from red grapes such as "Pais" ("country") or Carignan, or whites such as Ugni Blanc (Italia), Muscat, or Torontel. The Pais is the most-planted common varietal, and Cabernet Sauvignon is the most popular "fina," followed by Cot/Malbec (sometimes labeled as Merlot). Wines based on French varietals go to quality production and the export market. The locals' everyday wine is Viño Pippero, made mostly from Pais. In a concerted effort to curb alcoholism, the government holds local consumption to a generous 10 gallons/40 liters per capita yearly. Production and grape yield quotas are enforced, and excess production is distilled into industrial alcohol.

## Wine Regions

The majority of Chile's premium wines are made between latitudes 32° and 38° S, placing the vineyards in the central part of the country (see Map 5.2), with the towering Andes having tremendous influence on growing conditions. The city of Santiago is at the northern end of the fertile basin between the Andes and the high plateaus of the coastal Cordillera mountain range.

**Map 5.2** The Wine Regions of Chile.

This basin is the Central Valley which, along with its hillsides, provides most of the grapes for Chile's fine wines. Here temperatures can reach 90°F/32°C during the day with lots of uninterrupted sunshine; however, temperatures can plummet at night. The Andes Mountains provide air drainage and sources of water, as do the Aconagua and Maule rivers. However, only about 20 percent of the 320,000 acres/128,000 hectares under vine in the Central Valley region are not irrigated.

The Central Valley, also known as the Regadio, is Chile's finest wine region. It contains the quality areas of Maule, Maipo, Aconagua and Rapel. Here the government has set up "Regiones Vitivinicolas," including Atacama, Coquimbo, Aconagua, Maipo, Rapel, Maule, and Bio Bio. The Maipo, Rapel, Maule, and Bio Bio areas may also print subregions on their labels. The Maipo Valley region is a desirable growing area, because its mild winter and spring seasons mean that frost is not a problem. Its dry autumn and summer seasons relieve the fear of mildew in the vineyards. Maule soils contain more clay and less sand than the Maipo region. Maule's cool climate makes it an attractive area for white wine production, while Rapel is a desirable region to produce red wines.

Chile's Regadio vineyards, in addition to being *phylloxera*-free, are also largely free of downy mildew, a fungal disease that attacks the leaves of the vine and interrupts photosynthesis. Later in the growing season downy mildew leaves its mark by depressing grape sugar levels, and fruit ripeness. Because the Central Valley (along with California and Western Australia, neither of which have this fungal disease in their vineyards) receives little rainfall in the spring and summer, it creates an inhospitable climate for downy mildew.

Five percent of the 176 million gallons/704 million liters of wine produced annually in the Central Valley are exported to the United States. Foreign investments, such as the vineyards of Miguel Torres (see Chapter 8 on Spain) and Bordeaux's Château Lafite-Rothschild indicate that both production and export numbers will be increasing in this area.

Quality producers include Concha Y Toro, St. Morillon, Cousina Maucul, José Canepa, Santa Rita, Miguel Torres, Undurraga, Los Vascos, Linderos Valdivieso, Erraruiz-Panquehe, Santa Carolina, and San Pedro.

## *Argentina*

Argentina (see Map 5.1), with 900,000 acres/360,000 hectares under vine, ranks fourth in the world in wine production. Argentina's thirsty domestic market, with a per capita consumption of 13 gallons/50 liters per year, is important to its wine industry, yet exports to other regions are also increasing. Quality is the paramount issue in Argentina. A great deal of Argentina's grape musts and concentrates, produced from high-yielding vineyards in warmer areas, are exported for blending. The finished wines are often labeled as products of the importing country; the United Kingdom, Japan, and Venezuela are major customers. At the same time, Argentina's finer wines, its *"Vinos Finos,"* are gaining respect and market share in North America and Western Europe, because of their high quality and affordability.

Cooler fermentation and export market demands are inducing a less oaky, less alcoholic, fresher range of wines.

Argentina's *Instituto Nacional de Viniviticultura (INV)*, the federal regulatory body, controls pruning methods, harvesting schedules, transport of grapes, release dates of finished wines, alcohol percentages, and the planting of new vines. The INV also sets prices. Neither appellation nor varietal labeling is regulated, but vinos finos, Argentina's best wines which account for about ten percent of total production, are under strict government and industry controls. Like so many other countries where the climate is warm, chaptalization is forbidden in Argentina.

West of Argentina's capital city, Buenos Aires, lies the Pampas, grassy plains known for their *gauchos* (cowboys), cattle, and grains. The Colorado River is south of the capital; south of the Colorado the Antarctic-cooled Patagonia begins, while to the north, the tropical river winds warm the vineyards. The problem of scant rainfall, only about eight to ten inches/20 to 25 centimeters annually, is solved by utilizing the regional rivers and the runoff from the Andes Mountains as sources of irrigation. Gravity brings the rain and snow from the Andes down through porous rocks and underneath the surface of the soil. Dams and canals at the base of the Andes and over 30,000 boreholes for wells supply much needed water to the vines. This intricate system began in the 1800s, and today some wells are still filled by natural water pressure. Since most vineyards are on flat land, often composed of alluvial soil, the water has also been used to flood the vineyards in order to drown the *phylloxera* louse. The long roots of Argentina's ungrafted vines, planted in deep soil, obtain ample nourishment. Irrigated fields can produce 1830 gallons of wine per acre/18,000 liters per hectare, but vinos finos yields are lower.

Criolla is the historic grape of Argentina, introduced by the Spanish *conquistadores,* circa 1550, and it is the principal varietal used for making rosé wines, which account for about 15 percent of total production. The Criolla, when ripe, is actually pink-skinned. Red grapes include Malbec, Cabernet Sauvignon, Syrah, Pinot Noir, Cereza, Tempranillo, Nebbiolo, Bonarda, Barbera, and Sangiovese. Some of these varieties reflect their influence of the huge influx of Spanish and Italian immigrants who came to Argentina in the 1820s. These immigrants, along with a second wave of settlers arriving from Spain, Italy, and France just before 1900, founded and developed Argentina's wine industry. Their taste for red wine (and the beef of the Pampas) still predominates Argentina's wine culture. Important white grapes include Sémillon, Chardonnay, Ugni Blanc, Sauvignon Blanc, Riesling, Sylvaner, Muscat of Alexandria, Pedro Ximénez, and Torontel.

Argentina's major wine regions include Mendoza, San Juan, Rio Negro, and La Rioja. Mendoza is centered on the Mendoza river valley, a 60,000 square mile/96,000 square kilometer area of which about 40 percent is under vine. Grapes from the Mendoza region produce about 70 percent of Argentina's wine. The 40,000 small farmers in the region utilize more than 1000 *bodegas* (wineries) to make wine, but the dozen largest corporate landholders make 25 percent of all the wine from the region.

Of the 642,000 acres/256,800 hectares under vine in Mendoza, only 100,000 acres/40,000 hectares are planted with white grapes. The red Malbec does particularly well in northwestern Mendoza. Mendoza's finer wines come from grapes grown in the Andes foothills and the basins of the rivers, where approximately 12 inches/30 centimeters of rain fall annually as opposed to the eight inches/20 centimeters that fall near Buenos Aires. The INV headquarters for wine control are located in the city of Mendoza, and the area has the potential to store one billion gallons/four billion liters of wine.

San Juan, the second-largest growing area, accounts for 160,000 acres/64,000 hectares, only ten percent of which are planted in red grapes. Of the grape musts and concentrates Argentina sends to other countries for blending, 80 percent come from this warm area, which produces wines with good sugar levels but low acidity. This region also produces good Sherry-style fortified wines. San Juan is north of Mendoza, and is warmer with less rainfall; summer temperatures can exceed 100°F/40°C, and annual rainfall can be as scant as six inches/15 centimeters per year.

Rio Negro is Argentina's third-largest wine region, with 45,000 acres/18,000 hectares and 3500 vineyards, the best of which are located on the river banks. Rio Negro is south of Mendoza and its longer, cooler ripening period produces grapes with more acidity and balance. Therefore the area has the potential to produce vinos finos, including base wines for *méthode Champenoise* sparklers. Rio Negro has been pegged as the Argentine wine region most likely to attract foreign investment in the near future.

Finally, La Rioja, Argentina's oldest wine region, with less than 14,500 acres/5800 hectares in quite warm conditions, produces bulk wines. There is not enough water for irrigation in La Rioja, so it will continue to be a minor wine-producing area.

Argentina's quality wineries include Weinert, Trapiche, Proviar Moët & Chandon, Crillon and Bianchi (both owned by Seagram's), Flichman, Navarro Correas, Bodegas y Vinedos Giol, and Bodegas y Vinedos Penaflor.

## Brazil

Brazil (see Map 5.1) was first made known to Europeans in 1500 by Pedro Alvares Cabral of Portugal, and vines have been planted here since 1532. It was not until the 1970s, however, that high-quality wines began to be produced in Brazil. The warm, humid climate made growing vinifera, such as the Criolla, difficult, so native American grapes and hybrids have been planted since the mid-1800s. Concord, Delaware, and Niagara are examples of the *vitis labrusca*; Isabella is an important hybrid grown in Brazil. In fact, hybrids account for half of all vine plantings.

In the 1870s, Italian immigrants to Brazil found a more hospitable area for vinifera in the higher grounds north of the Jaqui River, where they introduced Barbera, Bonarda, Nebbiolo, and Trebbiano. Today, however, most wine comes from the south. Rio Grande Do Sol is the largest region, with fully 40 percent of the nation's wine production. A southern subregion with extensive vinifera plantings is Santana do Livramento, which is the Palomas district of Rio Grande Do Sol. Bordering Uruguay, Santana do Livramento encompasses Brazil's newest wine region, Frontera. Since 1975, Frontera has been planted with more than 1900 acres/800 hectares of vines, all of them vinifera.

The first Brazilian wine cooperative was begun in 1911. The Aurora Co-operative, Brazil's largest, was formed in 1931. Aurora has over 1000 members and also owns vineyards. In total, Brazil has 180,000 acres/72,000 hectares under vine and produces about 92,750,000 gallons/3.5 million hectoliters of wine per year, most of it undistinguished.

In 1973, the Brazilian government, responding to the promise of foreign investment and the possibility of an active wine-export industry, established federal wine regulations. These regulations stipulate that Brazil shall produce three categories of wine:

- Vinho de Consumo Corrente (local table wines)

- Vinho Especial (wine typical of a particular region)

- Vinho Fino, which must be made from vinifera, must contain a minimum of 60 percent of the varietal stated, and must be aged.

In addition, *Origem Controlada* indicates that the wine comes from a controlled, geographically delimited area. *Vinhos finos* account for about 20 percent of total production.

National Distillers, an American company, and the European companies of Moët & Chandon, Remy, Cinzano, and Martini & Rossi have invested in Brazil, perhaps lured by the high yields or the improved quality of wines made from Barbera, Cabernet Franc, Merlot, Sémillon, and Riesling grapes. Brazil's annual per capita consumption, in this nation of 130 million, is only 0.7 gallons/3 liters. Obviously, the potential domestic market is enormous. The export market, especially in North America, is also being targeted for the sale of the *vinhos finos* wines.

Brazil is the third-largest wine producer in South America, and the fifteenth largest producer in the world, with about 100 square miles/166 square kilometers of the nation's 3.3 million square miles/5.5 million square kilometers planted with grapes. Through investments in its vineyards and cellars, coupled with government quality controls, Brazil's importance in the world wine market is sure to increase. Quality producers include Aurora, Palomas Santa Rosa, Heublein do Brasil, Garibaldi, Monaco-Vinhedos, Moët/Provifin, Viniccia Armando Peterlongo, and Vinicola Riograndense.

# OCEANIA

## Australia

Australia (see Map 5.3), the world's eleventh-largest wine producer, has produced wine for almost two centuries, but the present focus on dry table

**Map 5.3** The Wine Regions of Australia.

wines dates only from the 1960s. Like other wine-producing nations in the Southern Hemisphere, such as New Zealand and Chile, Australia can send its vintage wines to markets in the Northern Hemisphere six months before its Northern competitors, because harvest takes place in March and April. Australia's wine industry is largely modern and high-tech, producing wines with clean flavors and strong varietal character. There are 15 million people in Australia, and wine consumption is reasonably high; about five gallons/20 liters per capita, annually, and growing.

## Contemporary Australia

Almost all of the major varietals are grown in Australia's wine regions, whose soils and climates are quite diverse. Australia's major disadvantage is that more than half the country is desert, and many other areas have low rainfall and very hot weather. So, although high sugar levels in the grapes are almost never a problem, low acid levels are an issue. Chaptalization is illegal in Australia, but adding acid during fermentation is common. Mechanical picking at night and keeping the must cool also helps to maintain acidity and freshness in the wines. The cooler areas, which are mostly close to Australia's coasts, provide the best climates for viticulture. South Australia produces more than half Australia's wines, and the southeastern states and growing areas produce almost all of the rest. Tropical winds heat the northern parts of the country, while Antarctic winds cool the southern areas. Coonawarra actually has a cooler average temperature than the Côte d'Or of Burgundy.

THE TASTING CELLAR

Throughout Australia, Wineries Maintain Public Tasting and Sales Rooms. In South Australia, for Example, There are More Than 400 Wineries within an Hour's Drive of the City of Adelaide. Many of the Wineries Rely on Their "Cellar Door" Sales as a Means to Develop Brand Loyalty.

Michael Hill-Smith is Australia's First Master of Wine, and Proprietor of the Universal Wine Bar in Adelaide. His Family Owns the Legendary Yalumba Winery in the Barossa Valley, and He is a Partner in Shaw and Smith Winery, Which Produces an Incomparable Unoaked Sauvignon Blanc.

The Murray River and its tributary, the Murrumbidgee, provide much needed irrigation for many of the drier areas, as the average rainfall is under 30 inches/75 centimeters. However, rainfall can be fairly unpredictable from vintage to vintage; 1993 saw more than 50 inches/1.25 meters of rain deluge South Australia. The Great Dividing Range, about 7300 feet/2400 meters at its highest point, and other hills and mountains help to provide a cooler climate for growing wine grapes. The melting snows also provide irrigation, and cloud cover can reduce the scorching of the grapes in some areas. Beneficial, cool maritime breezes in some of the newer and cooler growing areas have allowed for the production of balanced and crisp, dry wines.

Australians have proven they have the equipment and knowledge to make fine wines from their traditional areas and grapes, but nowadays the industry emphasizes good site selection and growing methods to produce the best fruit. Philosophically, many Australian **vignerons** (growers) are trying to "make the wine in the vineyard," relying less on technology at the winery. The historic areas of Adelaide Hills and Swan Valley are losing vineyard acreage due to urban sprawl, while the cooler and finer soil-type areas, such as Coonawarra and Keppoch in South Australia, Margaret River and Mount Barker in Western Australia, and Geelong and Yarra Valley in Victoria, as well as the state of Tasmania, are rapidly increasing in acreage. The New South Wales areas of Mudgee and Hunter Valley are showing slower growth, and the Barossa, after years of decline, is coming back as an important region, slowly increasing its acres under vine.

The raisin industry uses about half of Australia's grape production, which explains why the Sultana (Thompson Seedless) is the most planted grape with the Muscat Gordo (Muscat of Alexandria) second. Other white grapes of importance include those used for Sherry- and Port-style wines. As the industry responds to worldwide customer demand by planting in

Some Examples of Australian Varietal Wine Labels. Shiraz is the Syrah Grape, Native to the Rhône Valley. Rhine Riesling Indicates the True White Riesling Grape, and Not Just a Riesling-style Wine. Hermitage, Named for the Famous Wine from the Northern Rhône Valley, is Really an Alternative Name for Shiraz. Notice the Label Reads "100 Percent" Hermitage.

cooler sites, Riesling (the best is labeled as Rhine Riesling), Chardonnay, Sémillon, Sauvignon Blanc, and Traminer are destined to become the most important varietals for quality white wines. Shiraz (Syrah), which can produce wines of great elegance and long life, is the most-planted red grape, with Cabernet Sauvignon a distant second. Grenache and Mataro (Mourvèdre) are losing acreage to Merlot, Cabernet Franc, and Pinot Noir.

## History

The history of wine in Australia is the history of the European immigrants who settled the country and brought their wine culture with them. In 1791, vinifera cuttings from the Cape of Good Hope and Rio de Janeiro were introduced at Sydney, followed in 1832 by the introduction of vinifera vines from Spain and France. Over the years, British, Swiss, German, Yugoslavian, Italian, and Polish immigrants came to Australia, constantly expanding its wine industry. Significantly, Australia has no native grapevines, and neither hybrids nor crossings have ever been planted; Australia's wine industry is virtually 100 percent European vinifera-based.

When *phylloxera* hit the classic growing regions of the world at the turn of the century, South Australia was not affected due to rigorous controls of plant material that are still in effect. Australia's other wine regions were decimated by the disease, including its then most-productive wine region, Victoria. After World War I, soldiers were used to replant vines, and the industry, comprised of both private companies and cooperatives, began to grow again. By 1930, South Australia was Australia's most important wine region, producing more than 75 percent of Australia's wine.

Because South Australia has a warmer, Mediterranean climate than cooler Victoria, from the 1930s to the early 1950s, the industry focused on "stickies," usually sweet, Port- and Sherry-style fortified wines. South Australia's Barossa Valley also produced highly alcoholic red table wines. Due to its membership in the British Commonwealth, Australia became the premier exporter of wine to the United Kingdom, outpacing even France.

By the 1950s Australia had found its place in the modern wine world, focusing on inexpensive varietal wines. With the advent of cool fermentation of white wines and barrel-aging of red wines, the focus of the Australian wine industry shifted to the production of dry white and red table wines. By 1990, "stickies" accounted for only six percent of sales; of the remainder, 50 percent consisted of dry white wines, 13 percent dry red wines, and sparkling and dessert wines about ten percent each.

With some exceptions, like the famous Grange Hermitage wines (see the section on South Australia in this chapter), the production of good-quality, mid-priced wines continues to be Australia's marketing and export strategy. In the United States, the great majority of Australian wines are priced between $7 and $13. Exports, especially of Chardonnay and Cabernet/Shiraz blends, grew by leaps and bounds in the 1980s and have continued steadily. Today, foreign and Australian corporate investment in the wine industry is a driving force and will continue to be so in the foreseeable future.

# Wine Laws

Australia does not have a system of wine laws like the Appellation d'Origine Contrôlée in France (AOC) or Denominazione di Origine Controllata (DOC) in Italy. Instead, Australia, through its federal Wine and Brandy Corporation, relies on a Universal Recording System, an auditing system which is used to track production and the movement of grapes made into wine. The Wine and Brandy Corporation enforces Australia's Label Integrity Programme (LIP), which guarantees the following:

- A minimum of 85 percent of the grape variety stated on the label must be used.

- If two different types of grapes are used in a blended wine, and neither grape represents 85 percent of the blend, both grapes must be mentioned on the label in order of importance (i.e., a wine labeled Cabernet/Shiraz has more Cabernet than Shiraz).

- If the name of a growing area, region, or district is placed on the label, a minimum of 85 percent of the grapes must come from that place (e.g., Coonawarra).

- If a vintage is stated on the label, a minimum of 95 percent of the grapes must have been harvested during that vintage.

- If the term "Show Reserve" is used on the label, the wine has won a medal at a tasting competition (Australian vignerons take their competitions and medals very seriously).

- If the terms "Reserve Bin" "or Bin #" appears on the label, it usually distinguishes a premium or higher-quality wine. For example, some producers make several Shiraz-based wines but with several different bin numbers at different prices, indicating that a particular bin is higher quality than another.

- If the term "wood-matured" appears on the label, it indicates that the wine has an oaky taste, because of time spent in new or relatively young casks.

There is an ongoing controversy in Australia over whether the federal government should define the boundaries of each wine region. Among the wine producers there is general agreement as to what boundaries an appellation encompasses, and legislation seems sure to follow. This is an especially important issue in dealing with the European Community. Australia's best wine producers know that their export market, which now accounts for 10–15 percent percent of production, is growing steadily and that their wines must conform to European Union (EU) wine laws (see the Introduction to Part 3). Australian wine laws are highly self-regulated by an extremely competitive wine industry, and much like the industry itself, the laws are progressive in approach and strong in execution.

# Wine Regions

**New South Wales.** This region (see Map 5.4) is located about 100 miles/166 kilometers north of Sydney, and although some areas of New South Wales are very hot, cloud cover helps to moderate heat in the vineyards, which are planted on volcanic soils. A benchmark for Australia occurred in 1980, when Murray Tyrrell's 1976 Pinot Noir emerged victorious over French Burgundies in a Paris tasting. Obviously, New South Wales (NSW) benefited from the ensuing positive press. "Hunter Honey" is the compliment paid to the excellent Sémillon produced in NSW's Hunter Valley. This region is second only to South Australia in acreage under vine and total wine production.

Mudgee, called the "nest in the hills," has an average elevation of 1800 feet/600 meters, providing a long, cool, ripening period. The focus in this region is on quality. In 1979 local producers decided to claim their own self-regulated Mudgee appellation. Some vineyards are planted on flat land and some on slopes. Though Marsanne and Nebbiolo-Barbera blends are found in Mudgee, it is Cabernet, Shiraz, Sémillon, and Chardonnay wines that are most prominent.

The Hunter Valley is Australia's oldest wine-making region. The Brockenback Range provides a cooling influence, along with afternoon clouds to combat the heat and humidity. Irrigation is not needed in Lower Hunter, as there is adequate rainfall which, when coupled with the region's humidity,

**Map 5.4** The South Australia, New South Wales, and Victoria Regions of Australia.

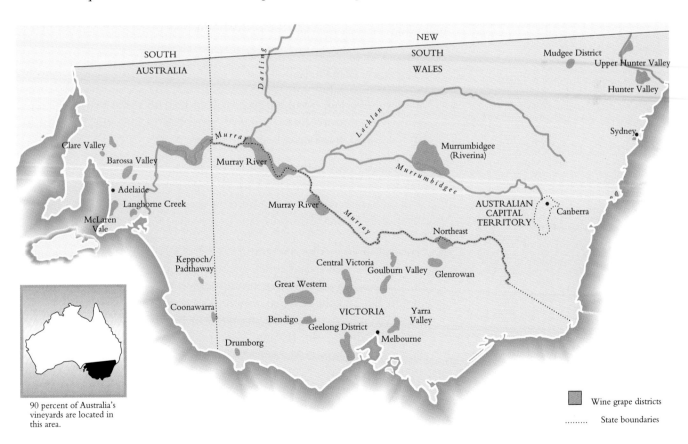

90 percent of Australia's vineyards are located in this area.

Wine grape districts

......... State boundaries

makes mildew a threat; lime and copper sulphate sprays seem to control the problem. The volcanic soil is rich and especially good for ageworthy whites, such as Sémillon and Chardonnay. Lindemans, established in 1870, is still is a major producer in Lower Hunter.

The fertile soils of the Upper Hunter Valley produce Chardonnay and Sémillon that can be drunk young. Unlike the Lower Hunter, irrigation is a necessity in this region. Australia's corporate giant, Penfolds, began production in Upper Hunter in the 1960s, but the most successful export wine from the region is Chardonnay from Rosemount.

***Victoria.*** Swiss immigrants pioneered wine-making in Victoria, which was Australia's premier wine region before the *phylloxera* epidemic, and today is third in total production. Annual average rainfall is about 22 inches/55 centimeters but thanks to the moderating influence of the Murray River, which flows through both Victoria and South Australia, fairly high-volume production is possible.

Victoria (see Map 5.4) includes what may be Australia's most promising wine region, Yarra Valley, which is the coolest vineyard area on the mainland; only Tasmania is cooler. Located east of Melbourne, Yarra features both adequate rainfall and rich soils, good for the production of high-quality Riesling, Chardonnay, Shiraz, Cabernet, and arguably Australia's best Pinot Noir. Domaine Chandon (see Chapter 4 on North America) produces very fine sparkling wine in Yarra, and noted wine writer James Halliday, a partner in Coldstream Hills, produces elegant Pinot Noir and Chardonnay.

Other significant growing areas and producers of Victoria include the following:

- *Avoca Vineyards:* Taltarni makes Bordeaux-style Cabernet Sauvignon and Sauvignon Blanc here.

- *Bendigo:* Möet & Chandon has invested here to make sparkling wine, and Cabernet and Shiraz produced here often include eucalyptus notes in the nose. Chardonnay is also produced.

- *Glenrowan:* also called Glenrowan-Milawa North East, this area is known for dessert wines and for Cabernet with notes of blackcurrant and strong character. Arid conditions also help to produce late harvest Muscat and Tokay from Muscadelle, as well as fortified wines.

- *Goulburn Valley:* Australia's historic Château Tahbilk was first produced here in 1860. Château Tahbilk continues to make wine as it always has, in the most traditional way. Its no-compromise wines need plenty of bottle age, and the original winery is one of the treasures of the Australian National Trust. Today, better than half of the world's Marsanne grapes, native to the Rhône Valley of France, are planted here, with Michelton a popular Marsanne producer.

- *Great Western:* The nineteenth-century gold rush brought settlers to this cool region where the Great Dividing Range provides cloud cover, rains, and high elevation. Seppelt makes a famous sparkler here.

- *Murray River:* The region's namesake provides good irrigation and mostly bulk wines.

- *Corowa Rutherglen:* On the banks of the Murray River, Corowa Rutherglen enjoys a good reputation for fortified Muscat de Frontignan, which may be barrel-aged for up to 50 years. There is a new emphasis on lighter style white table wines in this region.

**Tasmania.** Since 1986, the Tasmania appellation on the wine label guarantees that 100 percent of the grapes are grown here and that the wine has been tasted and evaluated. One of the world's coolest viticultural areas, at latitudes 41° to 43° S, it is located further south than most New Zealand regions. A noteworthy recent development is that the French Champagne house, Louis Roederer, has joined forces with a local producer, Heemserk, to produce sparkling wines. Pinot Noir, Chardonnay, Riesling, Gewürztraminer, and Cabernet grapes are grown, with much of the production shipped across the Bass Strait to be crushed and vinified on the mainland. Tasmania has two distinct growing areas: Hobart is cooler than Launceton, which has no frost problem.

**Queensland.** Most Queensland vineyards are close to the New South Wales border in the Granite Belt, which is about 23 miles/38 kilometers long and 9 miles/15 kilometers wide, with high elevation and a long, cool growing season. Australia's Great Dividing Range gives some protection to the area, but rainfall here in the far north is heavy. A favorite wine of Queensland is Balandean Nouveau, a light wine made by carbonic maceration, usually with Shiraz in the blend.

**Western Australia.** Perth is the capital of this state, whose eastern half is dessert. Western Australia has produced some impressive wines, stressing low yields in the vineyards.

Swan Valley, at the base of the Darling Ranges, was historically important for jug and fortified wines, because of its warm climate. Cooler fermentation techniques may lead to improvements in wine-making, but with dry summer days at over 100° F/ 40°C, low acid levels are a problem.

The Margaret River is sandwiched between Cape Leeuwin and Cape Naturaliste on the Indian Ocean, which causes some problems with salinity from sea breezes. Rye grass is planted to prevent wind damage, and sunflowers to keep birds from eating the grapes. Margaret River receives about 35 inches/88 centimeters of rain annually, and in 1978 was the first area in Australia to establish an appellation system. Some of the vineyards are planted at elevations as high as 3000 feet/1000 meters, but frost is not a problem. Planted in a mix of sand and gravely soil, Cabernet Sauvignon has established a track record in the Margaret River region, and hopes are high for quality Pinot Noir, Chardonnay, Sémillon, Sauvignon Blanc, Merlot, Zinfandel, and Cabernet Franc. Cape Mentelle is the best-known producer in the Margaret River region.

Mount Barker, also called Franklin River or the Lower Great Southern Area, averages about 30 inches/75 centimeters of rain and elevations of

Brian Croser, Trained at the University of California at Davis, is the Owner and Wine Maker at Petaluma Vineyards in the Adelaide Hills. He Makes Fine Varietal Wines at Petaluma, as Well as Making Croser, a World-class Méthode Champenoise Sparkler.

Brian Croser Also has a Second Label, Bridgewater Mill, Named for the Old Mill House Which Serves as an Elegant Tasting Room and Restaurant.

1000 feet/330 meters. This is the coolest region in Western Australia, where loam soils and long ripening conditions allow for the making of quality Rieslings that can age.

***South Australia.*** This region, which currently produces between 50 and 60 percent of Australia's wine, has never been attacked by *phylloxera,* and it is not uncommon to produce fine wines from Riesling and Shiraz vines that are more than 100 years old. With the first vines planted around South Australia's major city of Adelaide in 1837, the region produces what is arguably Australia's finest wine. In the 1950s, Max Shubert, then wine maker for Penfolds, produced Shiraz-based Grange Hermitage, which continues to rank as one of the world's finest red wines. "Grange" can age for 30 to 40 years, depending on the vintage, and is one of the best expressions of the full-bodied and fruit-rich Shiraz/Syrah grape.

South Australia's major wine-producing regions include Adelaide Hills, Barossa Valley, Coonawarra, Clare Valley, and Padthaway/Keppoch. The Adelaide Hills region, with elevations from 1250 to 2380 feet/420 to 775 meters, receives an average of 30 inches/75 meters of rain per year, but precipitation can be highly variable from vintage to vintage. The Piccadilly Valley produces fine Chardonnay, as well as Pinot Noir, which is used almost exclusively for fine sparkling wine. The dominant producer in the region is Petaluma which, under the guidance of Brian Croser, an oenology graduate of both Adelaide's Roseworthy College and the University of California at Davis makes fine table wines under the Petaluma label and its second label, Bridgewater Mill. Croser produces extraordinary sparkling wine under his own name. The French

The Barossa is home to two outstanding producers who share a love for the valley, but could not be more different in their approach to wine making. Robert O'Callaghan's Rockford Winery produces a unique "Basket Press Black Shiraz" that is blended from grapes grown on up to 30 different properties in the Barossa. After O'Callaghan makes 30 separate wines and ages them in American oak for a year, each grower is invited to taste all of the wines, as they are lined up on "Rocky" O'-Callaghan's blending "bench." By mutual consent with the growers, O'Callaghan chooses the best of the best to go into his finished wine, which he urges customers to age for ten years. Rockford wines are made by hand, including a Riesling made from vines that are at least 100 years old. The most modern equipment O'Callaghan uses is more than 50 years old, including a 100-year-old basket press—just a large basket full of grapes, placed under mechanical pressure. Rockford also produces about 500 bottles of a memorable sparkling Shiraz.

At the other end of the spectrum is the "Baron of the Barossa," Peter Lehmann, who grew up in the region when it produced "stickies," fortified Ports and Sherries. Now approaching 70 years old, Lehmann has seen the wines of the Barossa change from these early, unctuous, high-alcohol products to refined table wines. The darling of the local growers, Lehmann owns no vineyards, but buys grapes on a handshake and a toast with each of his growers. Unlike Rockford, Peter Lehmann produces a wide range of wines—Cabernet, Shiraz, Merlot, Riesling, Chardonnay, Sauvignon Blanc, Sémillon, among others—and keeps focused on the export market. A larger-than-life character, Lehmann, when asked why he makes so many wines from so many different varietals grown in the Barossa, answers, "Because I can."

Robert "Rocky" O'Callaghan Owns and Makes Rockford Wines in the Barossa Valley. His Wine Making Facilities Are Between 50 and 100 Years Old, as are the Vines for His Basket Press Black Shiraz, One of the Best Red Wines Made in Australia.

Champagne house Bollinger owns 28 percent of Petaluma, and the group also produces very good sparklers in Oregon, under the Argyle label.

Along with the Hunter Valley in New South Wales, South Australia's Barossa Valley is probably the most famous wine region in Australia. Settled by German immigrants, the Barossa produces fine Riesling from old vines. The Eastern Ranges, with altitudes of about 2000 feet/600 meters, yield grapes higher in acid than those grown on the valley floor at 820 feet/275 meters. The valley is 8-by-20 miles/13-by-32 kilometers, and one of the strengths of the region and a reason for its return to wine-making primacy in Australia is that it can successfully grow many different red and white varietals. This fact provokes controversy in this tradition-laden area, where Shiraz and Riesling are the grapes of history.

Coonawarra, the "Bordeaux of Australia," is a one-by-eight mile/1.6-by-13 kilometer strip of land with a "terra rossa" soil—a calcareous-limestone porous base with red topsoil. Thanks to cool sea breezes, Coonawarra has the lowest heat summation in South Australia. Coonawarra's water table provides the right amount of moisture and the area is known for producing perhaps the best Cabernet Sauvignon in Australia, as well as buttery, oaky Chardon-

The "Baron of the Barossa," Peter Lehmann Has Been Making Wine for More Than 50 Years, and is as Well Known For His Hospitality as He is for Being an Informal Ambassador for the Quality Wines of Australia.

Jane Mitchell of Mitchell Wines Ripped Out Her Chardonnay Vines to Plant Riesling in the Clare Valley. Her Rich, Ripe, Rhine Riesling, Which Can Age For at Least Ten Years, is Considered the Benchmark by Which All Others are Judged.

nay. Some producers, like Petaluma, label red wines simply "Coonawarra," much like a wine from the Médoc area of Bordeaux, assuming that buyers will know that Cabernet is in the bottle.

About 50 miles/83 kilometers north of Adelaide, with soil conditions sometimes similar to Coonawarra, the cool growing area of Padthaway/Keppoch makes white wines a priority. Chardonnay does especially well here. Finally, the Clare Valley grows Rhine Riesling in the Mount Lofty Ranges and the Camel's Hump Ranges. At 1100 to 1300 feet/255 to 325 meters, these hills provide shelter from wind and rain, as well as calcareous subsoil. Very fine wines are produced by Mitchell and by the neighboring Skillogalee winery.

When buying Australian wines, good value is just about guaranteed. The wines, like almost all of the wines of the New World, feature varietal labels, and the wines are true to the taste characteristics of each varietal. At the same time, Australia is developing its own style with certain grape types and varietal blends.

In Australia's export market (in which the United States and Canada are becoming increasingly important clients) wine consumers can easily find the following wines:

*White Wines:* Chardonnay, Sauvignon Blanc (sometimes called Fumé Blanc), Rhine Riesling, Sémillon, Sémillon/Chardonnay blend, Chenin Blanc, Marsanne.

*Red Wines:* Cabernet Sauvignon, Shiraz, Cabernet Sauvignon/Shiraz blend, Shiraz/Cabernet blend, Gamay, Pinot Noir.

Australia also exports some fine sparkling wines, made by the méthode Champenoise, and some interesting Port-style fortified wines. Some of Australia's best export wines include those made by: Brown Bros., Cape Mentelle, Château Tahbilk, Hardy, Henschke, Lindemans, Mitchell, Mitchelton, Orlando, Padthaway Estate, Penfolds, Petaluma, Peter Lehmann, Rosemount, Seppelt, Taltarni, Tyrrells, Wyndham, and Yalumba.

## New Zealand

New Zealand (see Map 5.5), the thirtieth-largest wine producer in the world, is a country with modern wine-making equipment and technology, good soils, and good climate, and so can compete with the finest traditional wine regions of the world. Exports account for more than ten percent of production, and local consumption has tripled in the past two decades to better than 4 gallons/15 liters per capita annually. The North and South Islands, stretch 932 miles/1553 kilometers, from 34° to 47° S. The two islands are separated by the Cook Strait, and vintage conditions vary from island to island, due to opposing air masses: dry and sunny to the west, versus wet and cloudy to the east.

The islands are small enough that all areas are affected by the maritime climate, creating a generally hospitable climate for viticulture. There is something of a problem with heavy autumn rainfall, which contributes to high humidity, rot, and mildew in the vineyards.

David and Diana Palmer of Skillogalee Vineyards in Australia's Clare Valley Make Fine Wines from Clare Valley Fruit. Diana also Runs an Informal Restaurant at the Vineyard.

**Map 5.5** The Wine Districts of New Zealand.

NORTHLAND PENINSULA

Whangarei

Great Barrier Island

TASMAN SEA

AUCKLAND • Auckland

NORTH ISLAND

WAIKATO

*Waikato*

POVERTY BAY

• Gisborne
Poverty Bay

HAWKE'S BAY
Napier •
Hastings •

• Hawke's Bay

MAHIA PENINSULA

*Wanganue*

Wanganui •

Cook Strait

MARLBOROUGH

Nelson •

WAIRARAPA

Bleuheim

• Wellington

SOUTH ISLAND

CANTERBURY PLAIN

• Christchurch

SOUTH PACIFIC

*Waitaki*

*Clutha*

*Mataura*

Dunedins •

Stewart Island

Wine districts

The most prized growing areas in New Zealand are those with relatively less rain, less-fertile soils, good drainage, long, cool growing seasons, but plenty of sunshine. These ideal conditions provide grapes with good levels of acidity and adequate sugars.

***Contemporary New Zealand.*** In the early 1900s farmers from Germany brought cuttings of Müller-Thurgau grapevines to New Zealand, as climatic conditions promised success with this varietal, a biological cross between Riesling and Silvaner. Although Müller-Thurgau is still the most widely planted *vinifera* grape in New Zealand, the world market's demand for other quality varietals makes this status temporary. In the 1980s, the New Zealand government paid farmers the equivalent of about $800 per acre/$2000 per hectare to uproot unpopular grape varieties. Many farmers used the money to upgrade their vineyards with French varietals that have export potential. Chardonnay, Cabernet Sauvignon, Merlot, Muscat, Chenin Blanc, Sauvignon Blanc, Riesling, Gewürztraminer, and Pinot Noir are gaining ground in New Zealand, and wines made from these grapes are finding increasingly appreciative audiences in the export market. New Zealand, like other Southern Hemisphere growing areas, has a natural advantage in the world market, since its grape harvest is in March and April.

*History.* Just before the turn of the century, New Zealand's first commercial wines were made with the American hybrid, Isabella, which was known locally as Albany Surprise. Other hybrids, such as Baco Noir and Seibel, were a major part of the young industry. These grapes were mostly used to make fortified wines. New Zealand imposed Prohibition from the early-to-mid 1900s, and then an outbreak of *phylloxera* wiped out most of the vines. By 1923 only 180 acres/72 hectares of vines remained. Yugoslav immigrants from Dalmatia started replanting and new wineries were built, but local taste was geared toward fortified and sweet wines. New Zealand was not a wine-conscious nation; until about 30 years ago restaurants could not legally sell wine with food.

By 1960 there were only 1000 acres/400 hectares of vines in New Zealand, but a new appreciation for table wines began to emerge. Between the years 1970 and 1983 national consumption figures reversed, from 70 percent dessert wines to 70 percent table wines. Although a good deal of wine made in the 1970s was of the "liebfraumilch" style, straightforward and fruity, plantings of Sauvignon Blanc also began in the early 1970s. Today, New Zealand has better than 14,000 acres/5600 hectares under vine, and 90 percent of these are vinifera vineyards. The recent free trade agreement with Australia promises increased investment and a larger market for New Zealand wines.

Currently, wine producers of New Zealand are able to operate with a minimum of governmental regulation. Wine quality is guaranteed by intense competition, especially in the export market. What regulations there are seem to mirror those enforced in Australia. New wine laws guarantee that wines labeled by varietal, vintage, or area contain at least 85 percent of what is indicated on the label. Boundaries for districts and regions are also being formalized. Generic labels, such as "Burgundy" or "Chablis" are forbidden under these new laws.

## Wine Regions

*North Island.* Today, the North Island contains 70 percent of New Zealand's population. The area west of Auckland used to have three-fourths of the nation's vines, but because of rising land costs and urbanization, only seven percent of the country's vines are now planted there. Grapes are brought to the North Island to supply New Zealand's three largest wine producers, Montana, Corbans, and Villa Maria, which together are responsible for more than 75 percent of New Zealand's total wine production. Auckland is a broad appellation, but Kumeu River, Henderson Valley, Kumeu-Huapai District, and Henderson-Kumeu may also appear on labels; they are all northwest of Auckland. New plantings are taking place in the cooler and drier areas surrounding Waimauku. Other areas in and around Auckland are Waiheke, Riverhead, and Ihumatao.

While the entire Auckland area and appellations total only 700 acres/280 hectares under vine, Poverty Bay (also called the Gisborne District) has 4400 acres/1760 hectares of fertile soils. The ground conditions, along with wet and warm summers, make Poverty Bay a high-quantity producer.

Hawke's Bay, southeast of Auckland, the area surrounding the Art Deco city of Napier, is one of the most promising viticultural regions of New Zealand. It has comparatively less rain, more sun, and lighter soils with good drainage. Currently Hawke's Bay has 3200 acres/1280 hectares under vine, mostly classic red and white Bordeaux varietals. Interest in the wines of Hawke's Bay is increasing, and it should soon become the largest wine region on the North Island, usurping Poverty Bay. The Wairarapa appellation area has good drainage, sunshine, and low rainfall in autumn. The Pinot Noir-based wines from the neighboring Martinborough vineyards have been praised as the finest from New Zealand.

*South Island.* Montana Winery began to plant Sauvignon Blanc on the South Island in 1976 and released its Sauvignon Blanc from the Marlborough region in 1980, to enthusiastic reviews and excellent consumer response. Today, Marlborough has more than 5000 acres/2000 hectares under vine, mostly on stony and gravel soils, planted in Sauvignon Blanc, Chardonnay, Riesling, and Gewürztraminer.

Marlborough, on the northeast coast of the South Island, and centered around the city of Blenheim, has long, sunny summers and moderate rainfall: 30 inches/75 centimeters per year, compared to Poverty Bay's annual average of 40 inches/one meter. The slow ripening period in Marlborough is a result of lots of sunshine, without scorching heat, throughout spring, summer, and fall. Chardonnays are made in a lighter style than in Hawke's Bay, and Rieslings are made in both fruity and crisp styles as well as late harvest/*botrytis.*

Sauvignon Blanc from Marlborough has caught the attention of the wine world. The nonoaked versions have drawn the highest acclaim, because of their clean gooseberry, grassy, tropical fruit, and herbaceous varietal smells, with their lively citric attack on the palate. They are enjoyable in their youth, while the North Island examples, usually made in oak, may age longer. Cloudy Bay and Montana Sauvignon Blanc wines are considered the finest from this region.

OLIFONTSRIVER

KLEIN KAROO

PAARL

DURBANVILLE

ROBERTSON

Cape Town •
CONSTANTIA
Constantia •

STELLEN-
BOSCH

OVERBERG

*Cape of
Good Hope*

SOUTH ATLANTIC OCEAN

▨ Wine producing area

----- Delimitation of Wine of Origin

**Map 5.6**   The Wine Regions of South Africa.

# South Africa

South Africa (see Map 5.6) is trying to increase its wine exports by moving out of the market for bulk and fortified wines and brandy and into that of high-quality vinifera wines. Problems that face the South African wine industry are a 15–year waiting period imposed by the government that delayed availability of new plants to farmers, a local population whose consumption is only 3 gallons/11 liters of wine per year, a warm climate producing grapes with low acidity, tendencies to plant too many vines for

The Best Vineyards in South Africa are Located Close to the Coastal Regions of the Cape of Good Hope.

higher yields and, perhaps most importantly, social and political policies which have resulted in sanctions and resistance to almost all the products of the country. Because South Africa, by virtue of its failed apartheid policy, isolated itself for so long, its wine industry has been out of touch with most state-of-the-art production methods and contemporary trends in the wine industry. Today, however, cooler fermenting, night harvesting, and keeping the grapes and must cool are improving the freshness and acidity of the wines.

South Africa has more than 250,000 acres/100,000 hectares under vine and produces around 225,250,000 gallons/8.5 million hectoliters of wine per year, making it the eighth-largest wine producer in the world. Most wine makers belong to the *Kooperatieve Wijnbouwers Vereniging (KWV)*, which issues licenses to grow grapes and sets official quotas of production. KWV, founded in 1917, is the cooperative wine growers' official organization, and it works with the government's Wine and Spirit Board.

## Wine Laws

In 1973, the South Africa Wines of Origin System was adopted, with government rankings applied to regions, districts, wards, and estates, in ascending order of specificity. The South African government issues a sticker indicating a wine's origin. Until recently, neck labels on table wines were color-coded to indicate levels of quality, but this labeling approach has been abandoned. Essentially, the quality wines of South Africa must contain at least 75 percent of both the stated varietal and vintage year. The country's finest wines, which formerly received gold neck bands, are tasted and approved by a government-appointed tasting panel. South Africa's finest wines

Meerlust Estate, a 200-year-old Stellenbosch Winery Owned by the Myburgh Family, Produces Some of the Finest Bordeaux-style Red Wines in South Africa.

are its Estate wines, grown at prestigious properties. There are about 80 recognized estates across the country.

South African sparkling wines made by the méthode Champenoise are labeled as *Cap Classique,* the country's new label term indicating sparkling wine made by the classic method.

## Vineyards and Grape Types

Most of South Africa's vineyards are within 100 miles/166 kilometers of Capetown in the southwest of the country. To the east are a series of mountain ranges, but most vines are grown only from sea level on the coast, up to the foothills of these mountains. The Westerlies keep the vineyards of the coastal plain wetter and cooler than those of the Little Karoo (Drakenstein Mountains to Swartberg/Black Mountain). The coastal plain, with about 34 inches/85 centimeters of rain a year, is not irrigated, while Little Karoo, with only eight inches/20 centimeters of rainfall, needs the extra water. The majority of vines in both regions are planted on flat land and, as in Australia, new sites with higher elevations are sought for the cooler climate and better acid levels in the grapes. Overberg is the most southern vineyard area in the Cape and the coolest; Constantia and Stellenbosch are the next coolest regions.

The Cinsault grape, here called Hermitage, is the premier red grape, accounting for about 15 percent of all vines planted. A biological cross of the Cinsault/Hermitage with Pinot Noir produces Pinotage, which makes a

The Fleur du Cap Winery is Located in the Lush Stellenbosch Region. Fleur du Cap is One of the High-quality Wines Produced by the Large Wine Group, The Bergkelder.

light- to medium-bodied red wine. Cabernet Sauvignon, Merlot, and Syrah are also widely planted, as are grapes to make port. The Chenin Blanc grape, often called Steen in South Africa, accounts for 25 percent of total vineyard acreage, and produces fruity table wines and sweet late harvest wines. Other important grapes are Sémillon (nicknamed "Greengrape"), Riesling, Palomino, Ugni Blanc, and Clairette. Chardonnay is planted on about one percent of total acreage under vine, but as export demands increase so should its plantings.

Vineyard areas include the following:

- *Stellenbosch:* Stellenbosch is a well-known area with the greatest number of registered estates, such as Alto, Simonsig, Overgaauw, and Kanonkop. The Bergkelder is a large, quality-oriented wine company which makes its own wines—Fleur du Cap and the Stellenryck Collection are the best known—and is a négociant for 18 Stellenbosch estates. As négociant, the Bergkelder acts a broker; it buys grapes and finished wines, blends them to create a particular style, and then markets and exports those wines. Hannes Myburgh's historic Meerlust Estate produces excellent red wines, and boasts the Cape's only Italian wine maker, Giorgio della Cia. The university in this region contains the country's oenology and viticultural school. Cabernet/Merlot blends, such as Meerlust's Rubicon, do well here, as does Mulderbosch Sauvignon Blanc.

- *Paarl:* Known for its white wines and sherries made by the **solera** system (see Chapter 8 on Spain), Paarl is on the same latitude as southernmost Spain. Ports are also made here.

- *Constantia:* Constantia is a promising area for Sauvignon Blanc and Riesling wines from Klein Constantia vineyards, and for Cabernet Sauvignon from Groot Constantia.

- *Overberg:* Hamilton Russell Vineyards in the Walker Bay area produces fine wines here.

- *Little Karoo or Klein Karoo:* Whereas the previously mentioned vineyard areas lay in the Coastal Plain, mountain ranges up to 5000 feet/1600 meters block the maritime influence in this region. The soil is schist, rather than the sandstone with mixed granite and clay found in the Coastal Plain. Tinta Barocca red wines do well here.

# Summary

Wines produced in the Southern Hemisphere have become an increasingly important part of the international wine scene. In the United States wine imports from both Australia and Chile have risen significantly—an average of about 25 percent per year—since 1990. There's no mystery as to why these wines enjoy such popularity in the marketplace; they provide good value. In addition, as with most wines of the New World, easy to understand varietal labels help the American consumer to buy the wine with minimal intimidation.

While wines from Australia and Chile are increasingly popular in the United States, we also see some good wines from New Zealand, especially Sauvignon Blanc, in the American market. Perhaps most exciting are the wines from the "new" South Africa which, after so many years of international isolation, has hit the ground running with some very fine wines at some very attractive prices.

MAR
DEL
NOR
The North Hemi: sphere
New found land
Afores or Westerne Iles
Sommer Ilands or Bermuda
S. Anna
Sept citez
Hesperides or
Gorjons Iles
Islas de C.
Hispaniola
Sombrero
Anguille
Barbada
S. Bernardo
La Trinidad
Caribana
SOUTH
AMERICA
BRASIL
OR PERU
Timbuia
R. S. Augustin
A. Trinidada
S. Barbara

# Wines of the Old World

For many wine lovers, both novices and the more experienced, Old-World wine conjures up myriad romantic images. All of the images would be "old" in some way: old bottles, old wine makers, old vines, old cellars. But such images themselves are old, and probably inexact memories representative of a past world which has changed dramatically in order to survive. In the Old-World wine countries, the only old things left are a decreasing number of old bottles stored in wondrously, magically old cellar buildings in fairy-tale old villages. Many of the vines are new, the wine makers are certainly new, the machinery and equipment are new, and some would even say that the wine made there is somehow new.

Part 3 of our book will look at the major wine-producing countries of the European continent and the Mediterranean basin, the countries and civilizations which distributed the vine over thousands of years and nurtured and perpetuated the age-old mysteries of wine making. We will concentrate on the current state of grape growing and wine making in those countries, every one of which has undergone dramatic changes in recent years.

In the past 50 years, the Old-World wine-producing countries have seen more change than during the previous eight millennia of wine-making history. The changes have been rapid, and have brought previously insular communities roaring headlong into the twenty-first global century.

Faced with the challenge of aggressive wine makers in the New World, and with an evermore educated and more questioning consumer, Old-World wine makers have had to change or perish. Again, as in the New World, the changes and challenges have been in the areas of:

- *Grapes* Where to grow them? How to grow them? How to maximize yield?

- *Wine* How to make it accessible to the majority of consumers, in terms of availability and in terms of taste?

- *Legislation* Can quality be assured by label legislation?

The results have been nothing short of astounding. Whereas Old-World wine makers were once secretive, old-fashioned, and distrustful of anything new or different, today's Old-World wine makers, from France to Romania and from Germany to Algeria, are more likely to be cooperative, open-minded, and eager to try any innovation. As a result, the traveler in European wine countries today is likely to see stainless steel tanks where before they were unheard of, or an aggressive oak-barrel program with barrels of various ages from brand new to three years old, where before all of the barrels were so old that nobody could remember.

More importantly, Old-World grape growers and wine makers are more open to developing their own innovations as well as importing ideas from outside. Various areas have experimented with heating and cooling the must or grape juice before fermentation starts to extract more color, or to bond the tannin molecules into longer molecular chains, resulting in a softer overall texture on the palate. In the vineyard, obsolete vine varieties have been replaced, and vineyard areas have been expanded. In some areas vine spacing, the trellis system, or the pruning system have been changed, and all of this in countries where the vine had been grown in the same manner for thousands of years.

From the consumers' point of view, far-reaching changes have been enacted in national wine legislation, especially in Europe. There are examples throughout history of laws or guidelines being drafted to ensure that a wine would be made according to a particular method, but the first formalized, national system undoubtedly came from France in the form of the Appellation d'Origine Contrôlée system (see Chapter 6 on France for a full explanation of this system). Other European countries have since enacted their own legislation, based on the French system. Since the late 1950s, when the six European nations of France, Germany, Italy, Belgium, Luxembourg, and the Netherlands embarked on the road toward a limited European Union, the intent has always been to slowly but effectively align the wine laws of all European countries so that they all have similar categories, similar requirements, and similar limitations.

Having progressed from a European Economic Community in the 1960s and 1970s, to a European Community in the 1980s, and a European Union in the 90s, the wine nations have all updated and amended their wine laws to bring their legislation in line with an overall framework. The result is that France, Italy, Germany, Spain, Portugal, Austria, and Greece all have appellation laws which fit that framework. In a general sense, the philosophy and policy of the European Union legislators have been to create two broad categories of wine *vin de table* (often referred to as "jug wine," or "box wine," or "plonk" in other countries), and *vin de qualité produit dans une région déterminée*. In addition, the overall objective of the European Union has been to encourage a reduced production of *vin ordinaire* in all European countries, and an increased concentration on quality wine production. Twenty years ago, this seemed like an impossible task, yet great strides have been made toward reducing, if not completely eliminating, the huge quantities of surplus vin ordinaire produced, particularly in France, Italy, and Spain.

## COMPARISON OF APPELLATION SYSTEMS IN EUROPEAN WINE-MAKING COUNTRIES

|  | *France* | *Italy* | *Spain* | *Portugal* | *Germany* |
|---|---|---|---|---|---|
| **Quality Wines** or Vin Provenant d'une Région Déterminée (VQPRD) | Appellation d'Origine Contrôlée (AOC) | Denominazione di Origine Controllata e Garantita (DOCG) | Denominación de Origen Calificada (DOCa) | Denominação de Origem Controlada (DOC) | Qualitätswein mit Prädikat (QmP) |
|  |  | Denominazione di Origine Controllata (DOC) | Denominación de Origen (DO) |  | Qualitätswein bestimmter Anbaugebiete (QbA) |
|  | Vin Délimité de Qualité Supérieure (VDQS) | Indicazione Geografica Tipica (IGT) |  | Indicação de Proveniência Regulamentada (IPR) |  |
| **Table Wines** | Vin de Pays |  | Vinos de la Tierra | Vinho de Mesa Regional | Landwein |
|  | Vin de Table | Vino da Tavola | Vino de Mesa | Vinho de Mesa | Tafelwein |

When studying the appellation laws of the various countries, it is helpful to remember that the categories in each country fit the overall framework, which is based on the French system (see the table above). At the same time, however, it must be pointed out that the objective of the appellation system of any country is to *ensure authenticity* by legislating that certain grapes are grown in a certain place to produce a wine. An appellation system *cannot* guarantee quality, since quality is a perception of the consumer. Having said this, we would have to agree that the very existence of an appellation system encourages the production of quality wines.

Wine consumption in Old-World wine-producing countries has always been substantially higher than in the United States. The history of wine in Europe and its acceptance as a beverage for daily use have resulted in a set of unwritten laws about when and how to drink wine. It is more or less assumed that all family members will drink wine, sooner or later. But it is also understood that the consumption of wine takes place with meals, so that the wine is enjoyed as a beverage with, or as an accompaniment to, food. It is not the norm that anybody in an Old-World wine-producing country drinks wine for the explicit purpose of getting drunk. Moreover, one of the roles of the small social group of family or village in Old-World countries is to supervise consumption of wine to ensure that excess consumption does not occur on a regular basis. When it does, the individual is reminded of his or her obligation to respect wine as a beverage: drunkenness is not glorified.

Even so, per capita consumption in all Old-World countries is declining, at the same time as production of higher quality wines in those same countries is increasing. For all of the changes which have already occurred in wine making in the Old World, more are still to come as production of high-quality wine continues to increase. In particular, the Eastern European countries will see astounding changes as their economies settle and flourish following the political upheavals of the late 1980s and early 1990s. There are exciting possibilities ahead for all Old-World wine countries, and increased pleasures for wine lovers from all over the world.

# France

## Introduction

In France's many wine-growing areas, trial and error have determined which varieties could thrive for the production of wines of quantity or struggle to produce the most interesting and rare examples. It is for this reason that in this chapter soil types, climates, and exposures will be discussed in more detail than elsewhere. The *terroir* of a vineyard location refers to its soil, exposure to the sun, its drainage of air and water, and its shelter from such elements as wind and rain. It is the understanding of terroir that has allowed French farmers and wine makers to produce many of the finest expressions of a grape variety in the world, or to blend to make up for what one area and grape type cannot accomplish alone. As a general rule, the warm *Mediterranean* areas tend to blend together different grapes to make more interesting wines, while in the cooler *Continental*-climate growing regions it is possible to make fine single-grape-type wines.

The French have also had centuries of experience in matching the proper grape types with the best locations. Many of the new regions of the world are just beginning to understand what to plant and where. In

**Map 6.1**  The Wine Regions of France.

the United States, the heat summation theory depends on average temperatures rather than soils as a guide to planting different grape types.

The stability of France as a nation and culture has allowed its wines to be recognized and respected for centuries. (See Map 6.1 for the wine regions of France.)

Poets, artists, and epicures have paid homage to the delicious foods and wines of France. The preeminent position they have enjoyed for centuries is the result of generations of farmers, viticulturists, chefs, scientists, and legislators devoted to providing the best the land can offer. The gastronomic contribution of such chefs as Taillevent, Carême, Escoffier, and Point were, for the most part, paired with French wines. The level of sophistication achieved by the service of fine foods and wines in the wealthy homes and courts of France were emulated by their counterparts in the Western world. Today the finest delicacies, such as foie gras and cheeses, and French wines and spirits are exported for all who enjoy the pleasures of the table. Throughout the western world the birth of a child, a wedding, a sporting event win, or any other celebration calls for a glass or bottle of Champagne.

True Champagne is a product from a region east of Paris, just as Chablis is, and they both share similar soil types and climates. Confusing to some wine drinkers is the fact that the generic terms "Champagne" or "Chablis" may be found on bottles of wine produced in other nations from grapes grown in climates and soils different from the original regions.

# History

Arriving at the port known today as Marseilles, the Greeks brought their expertise in viticulture to the south of France around 600 B.C. Vineyard expansion under the Romans was followed by the export of the wines from Gaillac and the Rhône areas to Rome. After Roman rule, Gaul, as France was called, was invaded by tribes from the north and then the Moors from the south. A great expansion of northern grape-growing regions in the sixth and seventh centuries was due to the wealth of the market there and the influence of the Church. Charlemagne's father, Pépin the Short, had been the General who defeated the Moors, and Charlemagne was crowned Emperor of the Holy Roman Empire in the year A.D. 800.

Charlemagne brought political stability to France and enacted wine laws. He forbade the foot trodding of the grapes and transport of the wine in animal skins. His legislation also led to the production of better wine presses and the need for more coopers (barrel makers). Charlemagne was based in the north, at Aachen, and increased the vine's presence in the north as well as the export of wines. The still wine of Champagne was used for the coronation of Charlemagne's son Louis in 816. In the cathedral of the town of Reims, in 987, Hugh Capet became the first of 37 successive kings to be crowned there. This established Champagne as the beverage of celebration. However, it would not become the sparkling wine known today until the seventeenth century.

The year 1152 saw the marriage of Eleanor of Aquitaine to Henri of Anjou, who later assumed the throne of England as King Henry II. Their powerful alliance of lands and the taxes from their subjects allowed the wine business to develop and prosper. Entrepreneurs from Britain, Scotland, and Ireland, as well as French merchants, used the port of La Rochelle on the Atlantic coast to ship the wines of Bordeaux. Casks of wine made to drink young were transported by the large British naval fleet to an appreciative market that could afford the fresh "clarets." Wines were also shipped to Amsterdam and from there to other northern European ports. The King of France (Louis IX) captured the port of La Rochelle in 1224 and the British were forced to concentrate their exports out of the port of Bordeaux. The Bordelais people prospered, along with the British, until the return of Aquitaine to the French in 1453.

The Dutch were the next naval power to extol and export the wines of Bordeaux. Meanwhile in Burgundy, more legislation had been passed to restrict yields of lesser grapes from the area, but Burgundy's location made its wines less accessible. *Complant* and *métayage* were the French systems whereby peasants would develop and share crop vineyards with the landowners. Monasteries tended to begin and maintain vineyards themselves. The Burgundian vineyards were for the most part being developed and surveyed by monastic orders. Legislation by the Council of Aachen in 816 dictated that each cathedral have a vineyard that would be worked by the clergy. The monks had the education, time, and resources to develop vineyards and record their experiments and results.

Wine was France's most important export during the Middle Ages and many prospered from its popularity. The effect of Napoléon and the French Revolution's ideals of *liberté, egalité, fraternité* (liberty, equality, fraternity) at the close of the eighteenth century, was to appropriate the vineyards and châteaux from the rich, who included the nobility and the church. There was also a fragmentation of vineyard holdings. Large plots of land held by the church or individuals were broken up. The prices and popularity of France's wines did not diminish after the Revolution. Natural catastrophes, however, devastated the vineyards. The eighteenth century saw a powdery mildew, oidium, destroy many vineyards and in the latter half of the century the louse *phylloxera* wrought destruction again. The *phylloxera* louse could not effectively attack vitis vinifera that were grafted onto American rootstocks so most farmers imported American vines to replant their vineyards. More vineyard problems such as *peronospera* (downy mildew) and black rot fungus occurred in the late nineteenth century.

The University of Bordeaux began its Institute of Oenology (wine studies) in 1880. The work of Louis Pasteur was combined with the efforts of the Institute's professor Ulysse Gayon and others to begin to control the problems and to create a modern wine industry based on science, not just tradition. The Institute's creation allowed the French to research and utilize the best grapes and techniques for each distinct terroir and climate. The Institute continues to train wine makers and to assist in controlling the production and authenticity of wines produced in France. Émile Peynaud, an author, educator, and consultant, joined the Institute in 1949 and is credited as being the most significant influence on the present style of Bordeaux wines. The Institute is currently run by the great grandson of Ulysse Gayon, Pascal Ribérau-Gayon, has educated wine makers from all over the world. The Appellation d'Origine Contrôlée wine laws that began in the 1920s, the scientific achievements of the Institute of Oenology, and the quality and cost of France's wines served as a model that other wine-producing nations continue to follow. The destruction of France's vineyards and the loss of lives during the world wars has been followed by a half century of replanting and building the current wine industry.

## The Current Wine Trade

The average amount of French wine produced annually has been about 1700 million gallons (64.4 million hectoliters). An illustration of the effect of vintage variation was the difficult 1991 vintage when spring frost reduced the crop by a third. The French are among the top wine consumers per capita, with about 17.7 gallons (67 liters) consumption per capita each year. As in most other nations there has been a decline in quantity consumed over the past three decades but an increase in quality and price of the average bottle sold. Production now exceeds demand, creating a surplus of wine which has a limited life span. The drop in consumption worldwide from 1979 to 1991 was from 75.5 million gallons (286.5 million hectoliters) to 62 million gallons (234.5 million hectoliters). France now has over 5.3 million gallons (20 million hectoliters) of wines in warehouses and must do battle in a global marketplace where it is being challenged at all levels, from the simple good-value everyday drinking wines, to those which are most expensive.

An exciting result of the shift in consumption patterns has been the uprooting of high-yielding grape types planted in less desirable areas and their replacement with higher-quality vinifera in better locations. The 222,390 acres (90,000 hectares) of Ugni Blanc (Trebbiano in Italy) make it both nations' most-planted white grape. In France, Ugni Blanc makes inexpensive white wines and is used for brandies such as Armagnac and Cognac. Chardonnay, by comparison, accounts for under 49,400 acres (20,000 hectares). The Carignan, with over 494,000 acres (200,000 hectares) planted, is the nation's leading red and is also used for inexpensive table wines, while the noble Cabernet Sauvignon covers 59,280 acres (24,000 hectares) of land. With the trend of consumption shifting toward less quantity and more quality, it is certain that in the near future plantings of Ugni Blanc and Carignan will be replaced by higher-quality grape types, and laws are already in place to enforce changes. The switch has been partially financed by the European Community (EC) and also by entrepreneurs. The investment is due to the European surplus of wine known as the "wine lake." Wine is a perishable commodity and the Europeans must react swiftly to international customers' preferences.

The average consumer who has not read a wine book may not be familiar with such place-names as Meursault or St. Julien but can more easily relate to a wine labeled Chardonnay or Cabernet Sauvignon at a price under ten dollars. The myriad wine styles available, and the many-tiered price levels, are what makes the French wines so important to consumers and professionals associated with the business of wine and food.

There are, however, some concerns about the present wine industry of France. The past decades have seen some appellations' boundaries extended to include areas that cannot produce wines as representative of the appellation because of less-suitable soil types or exposures. The permitted yields have been increased for many areas and a PLC (plafond limité de classement) allows a producer to ask permission for 20 percent over those higher yields. The density of plantings per acre has also increased in many locations, causing less nutrition per plant, resulting in other problems. As will be mentioned elsewhere in this book, the producers with integrity are not seduced by these temptations to make more wine of a lesser quality. They continue to harvest low yields from the best locations and vines, in a manner that would make their ancestors proud.

# French Wine Laws

French wines may be separated into four official levels. They are, in ascending order, *vin de table* (table wines), *vin de pays* (country wines), *vin delimité de qualité supérieure* or VDQS (quality wines from a limited area), and *Appellation d'Origine Contrôlée* or AOC (higher-quality wines from a controlled area). *Appellation d'Origine Contrôlée* wines, which are at the top of the quality pyramid, are now the largest category produced with over a third of total production. The AOC wines may also achieve an officially recognized higher status identified by a term such as *Grand Cru* (great growth) in some regions. The lowest-quality *vin de table* now account for over a fifth of production. In between are small amounts of *vin délimité de qualité supérieure* and about a fifth of the nation's wine comes from larger production zones, the *vin de pays*. A fifth of the country's grapes are destined for the production of spirits.

The wine laws of France and the EC are enforced by the **Institut National des Appellations d'Origine** or **INAO.** The INAO is further assisted by control boards in each of the major regions. INAO began in 1935 to control AOC wines. It is now also in control of VDQS wines, cheeses, and other agricultural products from specific locations such as lavender oil from Provence.

***Appellation d'Origine Contrôlée Laws.*** Wines under AOC must meet the following conditions to use the name of the area on a label:

- The wine must be 100 percent from approved grape types. A wine may be from as many as 13 grape types (such as Châteauneuf-du-Pape) or from as few as one (such as La Romanée-Conti).

- The wine must be from a limited zone or area of production; generally the smaller the area or the more specific the calling of origin the higher the quality wine. An example would be the Romanée-Conti AOC which is a 4.46-acre (1.8-hectare) vineyard. It is rated as Grand Cru (loosely, "Great Growth") and is one of a few superior vineyards within the larger AOC Vosne-Romanée which contains 243.6 acres (107 hectares) and is sold at lower cost.

- The grape variety has to achieve a minimum level of must weight and alcohol levels. An example would be the *vins doux naturel* (naturally sweet wines) of France which are required to have a minimum of 8.8 ounces per 0.264 gallons (252 grams of sugar per liter) of must. Another example would be the minimum alcohol level for a Côtes-du-Rhône regional wine is 11 percent while the Châteauneuf-du-Pape appellation wines within the same region must achieve a minimum of 12.5 percent alcohol. In some areas a maximum alcohol level may also be indicated.

- The wines may not exceed a maximum yield. Generally, the more specific the area, the lower the permitted yield, thereby assuring the consumer that the higher-quality wines will be made from grapes with more concentrated flavors. The lowest yield in the nation is for the appellation *Quarts de Chaume* in the Loire which may not produce over 581.24 gallons per 2.47 acres or 22 hectoliters per hectare. By contrast, a *Coteaux du Layon* appellation, which is the larger appellation that contains Quarts de Chaume, may be 792.6 gallons per 2.471 acres or 30 hectoliters per hectare, and the larger appellation *Anjou* that contains them both may produce 1,321 gallons per 2.471 acres or 50 hectoliters per hectare.

- The methods used in the vineyards and wineries are regulated. Examples of this are methods of pruning, the minimum density of vines, vine training systems, and the Champagne method for the production of its sparkling wines.

- The wine must pass a tasting test to confirm it has the traditional taste of wines of the place of origin.

- The wine must be bottled in the same region as the appellation. An example is Champagne, which by a 1919 law must be bottled in the region of La Champagne.

***Vin Délimité de Qualité Supérieure.*** The VDQS began in 1949 and today represents about one percent of all wines. The wines are under the jurisdiction of INAO and most follow similar rules but are generally allowed higher yields and lower minimum alcohol requirements. These wines aspire to be approved and elevated to AOC level in the future.

***Vin de Pays.*** Vin de pays are "country wines" made in large production zones, such as the Midi. The global challenge has been confronted in another manner in the nation's largest producing region, the Languedoc-Roussillon or "Midi." This warm southern area produces more wine than all of the United States. The determining factor for which types of grapes to grow in the area was the resistance of each grape to problems associated with warmer conditions, and ability to give high yields. In 1979 a government ruling allowed for a revolution to take place; the labeling of wines by grape name on country wines or "vin de pays." While the Carignan will not disappear, domestic and foreign investors are banking on the popularity of the Chardonnay, Viognier, Cabernet Sauvignon, Syrah, and other types in demand that are replacing lower-quality varieties. The move has been a success and more details on wines of the Midi are found later in this chapter.

The 1979 laws for vins de pays stipulated the label should have the name of the region where the grapes were grown. The three possibilities for place-name are the **département** where it is made, a smaller area within the département, or a larger region such as a grouping of départements. There are 95 administrative divisions, known as départements, in France. The wines must also achieve a minimum of between nine to ten percent alcohol for the Mediterranean regions, and pass a tasting analysis.

Eighty-five percent of vin de pays are from the Mediterranean area of France. A few years ago 90 percent was labeled by smaller zones but today more varietal wines are being labeled under the three large areas which are the *Jardins de France* (gardens of France—around the Loire), *Comté Tolosan* (southwest), and *Pays d'Oc* (south).

***Vin de Table.***   Vin ordinaire (ordinary wine grown anywhere in France) has no limits on the amount of yield permitted. More red than white wine is produced in this category that accounts for a little over a fifth of national production. Most is produced in the warmer southern growing areas. The EC requires a portion of vin de table to be distilled and is pressuring France to decrease the acreage of vineyards producing these lower-quality wines because of the "wine lake" or surplus mentioned earlier.

# Wine Regions of France

## *Champagne*

The word "Champagne" brings to mind notions of success, glamour, and celebration. No other beverage is so universally identified with joy and festivity.

The Champagne region (see Map 6.2) is an Appellation d'Origine Contrôlée located 90 miles/144 kilometers northeast of Paris. It is France's northernmost wine region. While the Champagne method is utilized worldwide for the production of the finest sparkling wines, true Champagne comes only from this one area.

France is divided into many *départements* and the wine regions of the nation often encompass numerous départements. The Champagne appellation vineyards are mostly in the Marne département. The three major subregions of Champagne within the Marne are the Côte des Blancs, Montagne de Reims, and Vallée de la Marne. The other départements within Champagne are the Côte de Sézanne (Sézannais), Haut Marne, Aisne, Seine et Marne, and the Aube. There are 72,500 acres (29,290 hectares) planted with the sole white grape permitted, Chardonnay, and the permitted red varieties Pinot Noir and Pinot Meunier.

***History of Champagne.***   Henri IV was the first to serve Champagne at court in the sixteenth century and the fashion spread to other European nobility. The region was known for its still wines until the late seventeenth century, when sparkling wines were first produced. The wines made in this cold climate often could not finish their fermentation because of low temperatures, but the warmth of spring would renew fermentation and the bubbles were captured in the bottle. By the end of the seventeenth century, British glass makers had produced a bottle strong enough to contain the bubbles without breaking.

Dom Pérignon was a monk who served at the Abbey d'Hautvillers from 1668 until his death in 1715. He did not invent sparkling wine but did enhance its quality by the judicious blending of different grapes and vine-

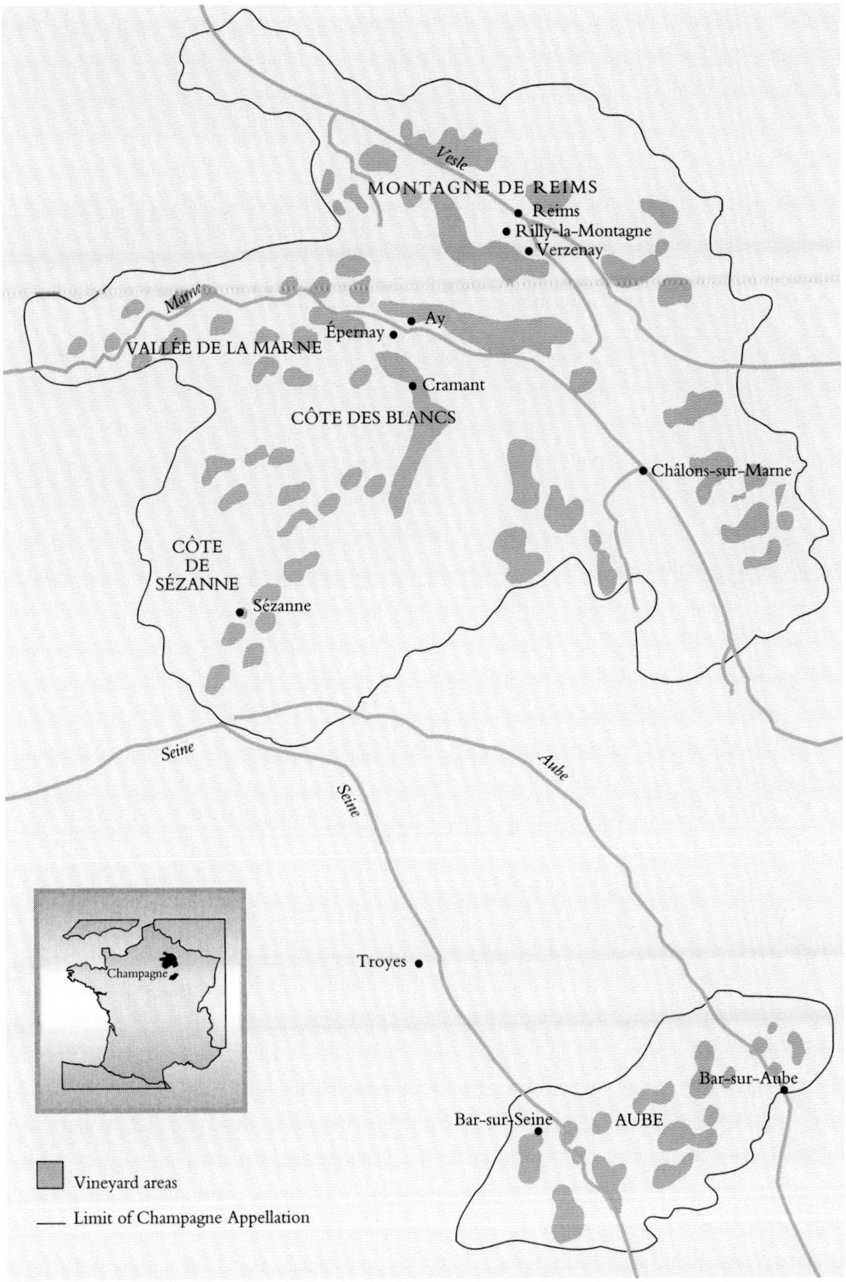

**Map 6.2** The Champagne Region of France.

Map 6.2 The Champagne Region of France.

yards to produce clearer lighter-colored wines. The use of cork as a stopper was a final touch for consistency. By 1735 King Louis V had a law insisting on the use of cork stoppers.

Circa 1825, an employee, Antoine Muller, and the proprietor of the Champagne house of Veuve Clicquot-Ponsardin, developed a system to remove the deposits formed in the bottles after fermentation. *Rémuage* (riddling) was the name given to the process of twisting and raising the bottles to move the deposit toward the neck where it could be frozen and removed

Champagne Vineyards.

(See Chapter 1 on How Wine Is Made). The labor-intensive process of clarification made Champagne, with its fine bubbles, more visually attractive. *Gyro-palettes* are automatic riddler machines utilized by some Champagne houses today.

The invention of the *gluco oenometre* in 1836 by André François allowed the amount of sugar needed to produce the required bubbles to be more accurately measured and made the cellars less hazardous as fewer bottles were lost to explosions. A formula to produce sparkling wines of five or six atmospheres of pressure in a bottle was now available. During the nineteenth century exports expanded with different labels and levels of sweetness used for specific markets. The Scandinavians and Eastern Europeans demanded, and were sent, sweeter styles than those for the domestic market or Britain. The Bollinger company sent a semidry wine to England in 1865 which was followed by the first true Brut sent by the Pommery Marque (firm) in 1874. Champagne consistency and quality increased and so did sales, and with a range of dry-to-sweet products its use at the table was elevated. Champagne was often paired with other luxury items such as caviar or foie gras and also consumed as an apéritif, cocktail, and with desserts. In 1908 Champagne included only the wines of the Marne and Aisne départements but demand led to the expansion of the area and by 1927 vineyards of the Aube département, located 70 miles (112 kilometers) southeast of the Marne, were included.

During World War II a local control board named the *Comité Interprofessionel des Vins de Champagne* or CIVC was created. One of its important functions was to set the *échelle de cru* or rating of the communes. Until recently prices for each grape varietal were legally fixed each year. The vineyards of each of the 312 communes have been numerically categorized and farmers are paid according to the annual price set for the varietal and the percentage of that amount the commune is granted. The échelle de cru rat-

**Figure 6.1** A Variety of Champagne Labels.

ing system, updated in 1985, ranges from 80 to 89 percent for the lowest-level Deuxième Cru, 90 to 99 percent for the 38 Premier Cru communes, and the 17 Grand Crus are rated at 100 percent. Premier Cru translates as "first growth" and "deuxième" as second growth. Each of the regions in France uses a different system to classify their wines in order of quality. In Champagne, Grand Cru wines are from the most esteemed village's vineyards. As mentioned earlier in this section, the prices are no longer enforced by law by but still serve as a reference point. As example would be that in 1993 a Grand Cru vineyard's reference price was 20.5 French francs (about $4 U.S.) for 2.2 pounds (one kilogram). A buyer or farmer would use that figure as a starting point for negotiations. There are 312 crus in Champagne and the 17 Grand Crus are Ambonnay, Avize, Äy, Beaumont sur Vesle, Bouzy, Chouilly, Cramant, Louvois, Le Mesnil sur Oger, Mailly, Le Marne, Oger, Puisieulx, Sillery, Tours-sur-Marne, Verzenay, and Verzy.

The Grandes Marques of Champagne had always dominated exports but after World War II the domestic market began to grow in importance. Today over 60 percent of sales are within France and a large portion are from coopératives or producers other than the Grandes Marques. Union Champagne is a coopérative that supplies wines to the Grandes Marques as well as selling its own wines both on the domestic and export markets under a variety of different brand names. Marne et Champagne is a company which makes Champagne for other firms who wish to have their own brand on a label. Over 300 companies and ten million bottles are produced by this firm. The initials *MA (Marque d'Acheteur)* will appear on the labels of brands produced for buyers.

The most powerful company of the region is Louis Vuitton Moët Hennessey. This consortium owns the firms Moët et Chandon, Veuve Clicquot, Ruinart, Mercier, and Lanson which collectively produce 40 percent of the region's exports. See Figure 6.1 for several examples of Champagne labels.

***The Champagne Trade.*** There are 20,000 farmers who grow grapes to sell to others or to make their own wine. *Récoltants-Manipulants* is the term found on labels for farmers who make their own wine. Although they farm 87 percent of the land, the growers sell their own wines mostly to the domestic market and have only seven percent of exports. The bulk of their harvests are used by coopératives and *Marques* (companies) that may own some vineyards but buy much of the grapes they use for blending. The Marques only own about ten percent of the region's vineyards. The Marques are also known as *Négociants-Manipulants,* meaning they are permitted to supplant their own vineyard sources by buying grapes. Coopératives are used by half of the growers and they may just press the grapes or actually make the wine and sell it or return it to a grower to be sold under that grower's own label. The Marques are mostly located in the towns of Reims, Ay, and Épernay. There are over 100 Champagne Marques. The Grandes Marques are the long-established major firms that are legally required to have a presence in the international market. The largest of the Grande Marques is Moët et Chandon which produces 24 million bottles of wine in an average year. Moët was instrumental in stopping the legalized fixing of grape prices for each year. Since 1990 prices for each grape type are indicated annually but the Marques are not legally bound to pay those prices. Champagne and the Grandes Marques have a profound effect on the French economy, because although the vineyards amount to only three percent of national plantings, they represent about one-quarter of all wine and spirit exports, one-third of AOC output, and 0.6 percent of the nation's export business. The United States and Great Britain, the top export markets, each consume about 15 million bottles of Champagne per year.

At the turn of this century Champagne prices were out of reach of the average French family, yet today 60 percent of each year's production is consumed within France. At the lower-price end of the market, there has been a surplus of wine, perhaps because of increased competition from other sparkling wines within France or from around the world. The Grandes Marques have reacted to this by elevating quality. In 1993 they agreed to use only *la cuvée* (first press) of grapes. Grapes are usually pressed from 8800 pounds (4000 kilograms) to give 704 gallons (2666 liters) of juice with the first la cuvée yielding around 541.5 gallons (2050 liters). *La première taille* and *la deuxième taille,* the subsequent pressings, which amount to 162.75 gallons (616 liters), will now be sold off to others. The first pressing produces a finer wine than the following presses as it is less tannic and has less color.

One way the Champagne producers, other than the Grand Marques, have decided to prove the worthiness of their products was to enact a law in 1992 that forbids the use of a "deuxième taille." By forbidding the third press there is a loss of quantity of wine produced, yet a higher-quality product.

Champagne producers are designated by initials on a label. *CM (Coopérative-Manipulant)* on a label indicates the wine was made by a coopérative. *NM* is used for *Négociant-Manipulant* or houses that may buy grapes. *MA (Marque Auxiliare)* is for secondary brand names. *RM (Récoltants-Manipulants)* are the farmers who make their own wines but may purchase up to five percent of grapes from another source. The term *sur lattes* refers to Champagne wines that are resting and waiting to have the deposits removed and the dosage added. Any merchant may purchase these bottles and label them as their own. Négociants that use these wines would be cautious to buy sur lattes bottles in a style similar to their own.

Mechanical harvesting and irrigation are forbidden. The *Chartre de Qualité* is a mission to further control the production of Champagne by analysis of the vineyards, grape clone selections, as well as the type and quality of the wine presses.

***The Soil and Climate of Champagne.***   Laws dictate which grapes may be planted in specific sites. For example, the Grand Cru, Cramant, is only authorized for Chardonnay. Trial and error have allowed the vignerons (vine growers) to discover the grape types best suited for each zone of production. In the Vallée de la Marne, the fruity and hardy Pinot Meunier is the most-planted varietal. Montagne de Reims, which contains the prestigious Bouzy site, is where Pinot Noir predominates. The Côtes des Blancs, as its name hints, is exclusively for the white Chardonnay and contains the Grand Crus Le Mesnil sur Oger and Cramant. When a wine is made from a single commune (village) it is known as a *monocru*.

Throughout these areas the elevation is over 328 feet (100 meters) and woods offer some protection, yet average temperatures (50°F/10°C) are just above the minimum needed to allow grapes to ripen. The low temperature allows for high levels of natural acidity yet reaching a sufficient level of ripeness is difficult (see Chapter 1 on How Wine Is Made). The harvest dates are set by each village and the wines must achieve a minimum alcohol level of eight percent. Chaptalization and the secondary fermentation both increase the alcohol content, and the final wines are released at about 12.5 percent.

Both Champagne marques and foreign producers of fine sparkling wine seek out property in cooler zones such as Carneros in Napa, California, U.S.A., Penédes in Cataluña, Spain, or Tasmania in Australia. With their best efforts to use the Champagne method, similar grape types and similar cool climate, these producers realize they are making different wines. This is because of the high concentration of chalk in the soil of Champagne.

The chalk contributes heat retention, brings out the grape's acidity, and allows both surface water drainage and subterranean water storage. The two types of chalk soil are Micraster and Belimnita Quadrata and the latter type is found only in Champagne. The topsoil is clay and the chalk, which is a kind of limestone, may reach depths of 800 feet (243 meters). The low fertility of chalk soils produce fewer leaves on a vine canopy. This allows more sun exposure of the fruit and better air circulation than a dense canopy. The variations in soil composition and the minerals they provide to the vines is one of the factors that determines the taste of Champagne.

The size of the annual harvest varies greatly due to temperature, rainfall, and hail. About 250 to 285 million bottles are sold annually. Spring frosts occur in one out of three harvests, and freezing cold in one winter out of seven. In the past, smudge pots or heaters were put in vineyards to help, but today *aspersion* is a more common solution. It consists of continually misting the grapes with water so they are protected from damage. A problem of aspersion is that strong winds may blow the water on to a neighboring vineyard, leaving the grapes susceptible to rot. Alsace, also a cool region of France, has the Vosges mountains as protection from rainfall. The Champagne region has no such protection, and the high average annual rainfall of 25.6 inches (650 millimeters) can cause problems, such as the grapes swelling from too much rain and diminished pollination. These problems aside, when things do go right the permitted yield is 177 gallons (65 hecto-liters) per 2.47 acres (one hectare), a high figure considering other French wine yields in similar price ranges. Legislation is underway that will officially reduce yields but the conscientious producers already yield less than officially permitted. In Champagne, a region that traditionally keeps large stocks of wine in reserve for blending in with future wines, there is too large a surplus even though the region sold over 200 million bottles in 1993 of which one-third was for export.

**The Styles of Champagne.**   Champagne is fermented dry (see Chapter 1 on How Wine Is Made). The *assemblage* (blending of still wines before second fermentation) and the *dosage* (wine and sugar added after the second fermentation and aging) are two critical steps in perpetuating the house style. Variations on the perfume of the wine, weight on the palate, and flavors showcased by each producer are part of the intrigue of exploring wines by different producers. A tasting of the most popular dry or Brut style made by a half dozen Marques is a good way to reveal the wines' similarities and differences. Just as a conductor brings a personal interpretation to a classical piece regardless of the orchestra and location, so must the *chef de caves* (cellar master and wine maker) reflect the style of the house using grapes from different sources or vintages.

Pinot Meunier is prohibited from Premier and Grand Cru vineyards yet still occupies the most acreage in the region. It has red fruit aromas and flavors and gives structure in its youth. The Pinot Noir is second in plantings and is also responsible for adding weight or power to a *cuvée*, or along with raspberry and strawberry scents. Although Chardonnay can produce some of the world's most full-bodied dry wines, here it is used to contribute delicacy and elegance to the cuvée. The Chardonnay offers apple and spice aromas when young but with age develops complex scents. These three grapes all have the ability to ripen in this cool climate, but the wines they produce are high in acidity. Therefore, some of the Marques choose to have their wines go through a malolactic fermentation in November or December to lessen the aggressive acidity. Krug and Bollinger are examples of two Grandes Marques who still ferment their wines in oak and avoid the malolactic fermentation.

As with other wines, soil, climate, grapes, and methods all contribute to the final product, but in Champagne there is also consistency. The vagaries of vintage present a puzzle to the afficionado of a specific Bordeaux château or Burgundy commune, but in Champagne the majority of wine produced is nonvintage and made in a style consistent to each specific producer. Large producers use limestone caves to store millions of gallons of wine from different sites and grapes for blending purposes. Wines are blended by the chef de caves to make the still wine that will undergo a second fermentation and thus become Champagne. (See Chapter 1 on How Wine Is Made). Consumers who find a house style they enjoy may be assured that a near replica of that style will be available for as long as the company exists.

The following is a list of Champagne products labeled by their sugar content.

*Extra Brut, Brut Sauvage, or Ultra Brut.* These products are bone dry with under 0.6 percent of residual sugar per liter.

*Brut.* Brut is by far the most popular style of Champagne and has under 1.5 percent residual sugar. Brut nonvintage wines are the mainstays of the Champagne business.

*Extra Dry.* Extra-dry wines range from semidry to semisweet as companies may produce products between 1.2 and two percent residual sugar per liter.

*Sec.* The range for Sec is 1.7 to the sweeter 3.5 percent.

*Demi-Sec.* Sweeter still is the demi-sec style which contains between 3.3 percent to five percent residual sugar per liter.

*Doux.* The sweetest style of Champagne has a minimum of five percent of residual sugar per liter.

Following is a list of other types of Champagne which are usually made in a Brut style even when not indicated on the label.

*Nonvintage.* A nonvintage Champagne must be aged at least one year before release. A majority of Champagne is made as nonvintage, which allows blending not just locations but vintages as well to produce the house style.

*Vintage.* A vintage-dated wine must be aged a minimum of three years before its release. Conscientious producers age their nonvintage or vintage products longer than the minimum. Vintage wines are not made every year and even when a producer decides to make a vintage there are still more nonvintage bottles made. In a year a producer makes a vintage, a maximum of 80 percent can be declared as such. This is to ensure that sufficient amounts will be reserved for future blending into nonvintage wines. Vintage wines must contain at least 80 percent grapes of the declared year and have a minimum of 11 percent alcohol. All Champagne corks are stamped with the word "Champagne," and vintage products have corks marked with the vintage.

*Blanc de Blancs.* A Blanc de Blancs is Champagne that is made exclusively from Chardonnay grapes resulting in the most delicate of Champagnes. As only 25 percent of the region is planted in Chardonnay, these wines will be more expensive than nonvintage products blended with red grapes as well. The wines repay their cost with a green apple citrusy aroma in youth that evolves into more nutty butterscotch tones with age. The previous examples are only a few of the scents that Chardonnay can offer in a well-crafted Champagne. The delicacy of the Blanc de Blancs wines refers to their weight on the palate which allows many to have finesse and complexity as well. In a dinner serving several Champagnes in successive courses, the Blanc de Blancs usually precede heavier wines such as Blanc de Noirs or Rosé.

*Blanc de Noirs.*    Blanc de Noirs (white of blacks) refers to wines made from only the red grapes. Bollinger makes a Blanc de Noirs from Pinot Noir vines never affected by *phylloxera* called Vieilles Vignes. Blanc de Noirs will generally be fuller in body than those wines which contain Chardonnay in a blend. The red berry scents and flavors on the palate are accompanied by a rich finish in balance with the region's traditional high acidity.

*Côteaux Champenois.*    Côteaux Champenois are the still wines of the region and amount to only one percent of annual production. The wines may be labeled with a name of a single vineyard. Rosé des Riceys are dry, still "blush" wines.

*Rosé.*    Rosé Champagnes are mostly made by blending red wine into a cuvée (blend) of white wines. Some producers may use a brief skin contact time to release pigments, a method commonly practiced for still rosé table wines. Rosé Champagnes are not in a semisweet style as many "blush" wines are. They are full-bodied, elegant, and expensive wines that vary in color from pale salmon to black cherry. The color of Rosé Champagne is one of its attractions but a blindfolded taster might have a hard time discerning a rosé from a brut. Again, it is house style that will determine how much red wine is added during the assemblage, and the balance of components in the wine.

*Recently Disgorged.*    *Autolysis* refers to aging of the wine with the lees, and it contributes richer flavors and a fuller-bodied wine. Bollinger is one of the companies known for "RD," that spends about eight years on the lees. The extra aging contributes to a greater complexity of the wine and the Bollinger firm's practice of fermenting in oak also gives this wine an extra dimension of power and interest.

*Cuvée de Prestige or Tête de Cuvée.*    Cuvée de Prestige or Tête de Cuvée are the top of the line from each Marques and most are vintage dated. Krug is an example of a Grandes Marque which does not include the year for their Grand Cuvée.

Champagne is released ready to drink but the vintage, recently disgorged, and cuvée de prestige products can be cellared for a decade or more if the buyer seeks more complexity, rather than the forward fresh fruit and crispness the wine offers when released. The above styles are all in the most popular brut or dry style.

Some of the major Marques are listed here, followed by a "GM" if they are one of the Grande Marques or a "Coop" if applicable. The names of their Prestige Cuvée follows the • symbol

## CHRISTIAN BIZOT, CHAMPAGNE BOLLINGER

Christian Bizot is the President of Champagne Bollinger, in the town of Ay. Mr. Bizot has maintained and elevated his firm's reputation and the quality of their wines. He and his nephew Guy, who is assuming more of the responsibilities as Christian prepares for retirement, issued a charter of quality in 1992 to provide customers with detailed information on the source of their grapes and their vinification and aging. An example is revealing that 60 percent of the Special Cuvée nonvintage and 62 percent of the Grande Année and RD are from the *Pinot Moret* clone of the Pinot Noir of which 35 percent come from Ay. The balance in their special cuvée is 25 percent Chardonnay and 15 percent Pinot Meunier while the vintage products are 35 percent Chardonnay and three percent Pinot Meunier with all grapes coming exclusively from the Marne district. The nonvintage is fermented in stainless steel while the vintage wines are fermented in 53 to 106 gallon (200- to 400-liter) oak casks. The nonvintage is aged three years before disgorgement—the Vintage Grand Année five, and the RD eight years. The longer-aged vintage wines are aged with cork rather than a metal capsule so the wines will be able to develop their aromatic potential. Complex aromatics develop after the second fermentation when the resulting bubbles protect the wine from oxygen and the wine is in a *reductive state*. The Bizot family also closely monitors its wholesalers to ensure the wine will be shipped and stored in ideal conditions.

A. Charbaut • Certificate Blanc de Blancs

Alain Thiénot • Grande Cuvée

Alfred Gratien • Cuvée Paradis

André Jacquart • Le Mesnil Grand Cru

Ayala, GM, • Grande Cuvée

Barancourt, • Grande Cuvée

Beaumont des Crayères, Coop, • Cuvée Spéciale Nostalgie, Cuvée de Prestige

Besserat de Bellefon • Grande Cuvée Blanc de Blancs

Billecart-Salmon, GM, • Cuvée Columbus

Bollinger, GM, • Année Rare RD, Vielles Vignes Francaise Blanc de Noirs

Bruno Paillard

Canard Duchêne, GM, • Cuvée Charles Septième Brut

Charles Heidsieck, GM, • La Royale

De Castellane • Cuvée Florens de Castellane

Delamotte • Nicolas Louis Delamotte

Deutz, GM, • Cuvée William Deutz, Rosé Cuvée William Deutz

Devaux, Coop • Cuvée Spéciale

Drappier, • Grande Sendrée

G.H. Mumm, GM, • Mumm de Cramant, René Lalou, and Grand Cordon Rouge

Gosset, • Cuvée Grand Millèsime

Heidsieck Monopole, GM, • Cuvée Diamant Bleu

Henri Abelé, GM, • Blanc de Blancs Réserve du Répas

Henriot, GM, • Cuvée Baccarat and Réserve du Baron Phillipe de Rothschild

Jacquart • Blanc de Blancs Cuvée Nominée

Joseph Perrier,G.M. • Cuvée de luxe Josephine

Krug, GM, • Grande Cuvée, Clos de Mesnil Blanc de Blancs

Lanson, GM, • Noble Cuvée

Laurent Perrier, GM, • Grande Siècle, Grande Siècle Alexandra Rosé

Louis Roederer ,GM, • Cristal

Mercier, GM, • Bulle D'Or

Moët et Chandon, GM, • Dom Pérignon and Dom Pérignon Rosé

Oudinot

Perrier Jouët, GM, • Belle Epoque Brut and Belle Époque Rosé

Philliponat

Piper Heidsieck, GM, • Rare

Pol Roger,GM, • Cuvée Winston Churchill and Réserve Spéciale Pol Roger Brut

Pommery Greno, GM, • Louise Pommery, Rosé Louise Pommery

Ruinart Père et Fils, GM, • Dom Ruinart Blanc de Blancs

Salon, GM, • Cuvée S (the only wine made)

Taittinger, GM, • Comtes de Champagne Blanc de Blancs and Rosé, Collection

Union Champagne, Coop, Pierre Vaudon Blanc de Blancs

Veuve Clicquot Ponsardin, GM, • La Grande Dame

Vilmart • Coeur de Cuvée, Grand Cellier D'Or

# Burgundy

Burgundy shares with Bordeaux the historical and present distinction of producing some of the most illustrious and expensive dry wines in the world (see Map 6.3). The cooler climate is responsible for greater swings in vintage quality than Bordeaux. Wines of Bordeaux are generally blended, while the finest Burgundies are the result of a wine maker working with a single grape type planted in a specific location. *Climat* is the term used for a specific vineyard in Burgundy and while one climat may have multiple owners, a Bordeaux château has only one. The finest Burgundy vineyards have been officially ranked as either Premier Cru or the highest-quality level of Grand Cru. The superlative climats in Burgundy are judged to be superior because of *terroir*. *Terroir* refers to the sum of a vineyard's components, including soil type, drainage of water or air, protection from winds or rain, and exposure to sun. Premier and Grand Crus are Burgundy wines that have attained the higher status and follow the more stringent production methods imposed on them. The most exquisite examples are those crafted from the low-yielding older Pinot Noir and Chardonnay vines. A producer may include the name of a nonclassified climat on a label if they believe the vineyard merits attention and should be considered for classification. The challenge Burgundy presents is to discover, by experience, which producers are best for wines from these smaller sites and which are good-value wines from the larger areas.

*Wine Making.* The négociant or wine merchant name is an important consideration when purchasing Burgundy. The region contains 52,800 acres (22,000 hectares) farmed by over 10,000 growers or *vignerons*. Small landowners often sell their products to a négociant or coopérative who is financially able to market the wines effectively. *Propriétaire-Recoltants* are independent wine growers who sell under their own label. *Mise en bouteilles au domaine* (bottled at the wine-growing estate) is a category that has only been popular since the 1960s. The American wine writers and importers, Frank Schoomaker and Alexis Lichine, recognized the appeal of artisan-produced wines of limited supply from distinct vineyards and promoted their production and sales in France and in America. Today about half of the Côte D'Or wines are domaine bottled.

*Négociants-Éleveurs* are merchants who may purchase grapes or wines from growers which will be aged and bottled in the cellars of the négociants. The wines may be blended from different sources or remain as a wine from one source or site. It is

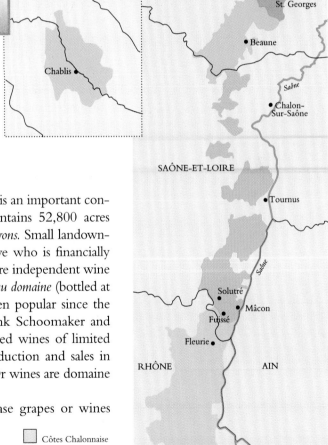

**Map 6.3** The Wine Regions of Burgundy.

Legend:
- Chablis
- Côte de Nuits, Hautes Côtes de Nuits
- Côte de Beaune, Hautes Côtes de Beaune
- Côtes Chalonnaise
- Mâconnais
- Beaujolais

difficult for one négociant to master and produce excellent wines from a number of different villages or climats and relatively easier for a single viticulteur or vigneron whose family makes only a small amount of wine. Yet, large négociants may have the financial means to choose and invest in better lots of grapes from a variety of sources and to upgrade their wineries with new equipment. The négociants benefit from having sufficient stock and consistent house styles that make their wines attractive for export markets or wider distribution within France. There is no guarantee that an estate-bottled wine is superior to one bottled by a négociant or coopérative.

The finest whites are made from the Chardonnay grape. The less-expensive wines are fermented in stainless steel while the better wines are made in oak. The coolest region of Chablis makes wonderful wines that have very little evidence of oak in the smell or taste. This is because very large older oak casks known as *feuilletes and foudres* are used. There are some producers who use smaller barrels and want some oak expression in their wine. The most powerful, complex, and long-lived dry whites in the world are produced in the Côtes d'Or from Chardonnay fermented in small new oak barrels. New oak contributes more tannins than used barrels do. The wines get rich creamy flavors both from the malolactic fermentation and from *batonnage* or stirring the *lees* in a barrel (see Chapter 1 on How Wine Is Made). Wines are usually bottled within one to two years. Good-quality white wines are also produced in the Mâconnais and Chalonnaise regions but they do not attain the complexity or demand the prices of the finest Chablis and Côte d'Or wines.

Red wines from the Gamay grape will be discussed in the section on Beaujolais, where they dominate plantings. For the other Burgundy regions it is the more noble Pinot Noir that is the key ingredient. Although the thin-skinned disease-sensitive Pinot Noir poses problems for wine makers around the world (see Chapter 2 on Wine Grapes) they take the risk because it is also capable of making the most delicious wines that may be complex and long lived. Because of the thinner skins wine makers attempt to maximize the color and tannin extraction from the juice. There is no one recipe used by all Burgundian wine makers to produce red wine. Some leave the stalks in with the juice and skins and macerate them all together for a couple of days before fermentation.

Another technique used is *saignée* or bleeding. This involves removing some of the juice so there is no more than twice the amount of solids. The lesser amount of juice benefits from more color and tannin extraction from the solids. During fermentation, a cap of solid matter is formed at the top of the must or juice. Pushing the cap down into the juice with sticks or spraying the juice from underneath over the top of the cap results in more extraction of color, tannins, and flavors. The temperature of fermentation is another factor as warmer temperatures will result in more extraction as well. Some believe that Pinot Noir is too delicate a varietal and is overwhelmed by aging in new oak barrels while others disagree. The wines generally spend a year to two in oak before bottling. Some producers believe in fining and filtering the wine (see Chapter 1 on How Wine Is Made) while others avoid these practices with the hope of retaining more flavors. Fining and filtering add stability but some négociants go a step further and pasteurize their wines for stability. Pasteurization robs wine of a chance to improve in the bottle and is not practiced by most négociants for fine wines.

These are some of the decisions wine makers make but the most important quality issue has already occured in the vineyard. The best clones of Pinot Noir, from low-yielding vines in the best sites, make the finest wines. It is up to the wine maker to preserve the identity of the grapes from the specific vineyard locations.

***History of Burgundy.***  Evidence of vineyards in Burgundy begins in 300 B.C. During the era of the Holy Roman Empire, nobility often donated vineyards to the church and records of the influence of the monasteries producing wines in Burgundy date back to the sixth century. The monks had sufficient holdings of vineyards and were able to taste and analyze the wines and keep records of the styles of wines produced by the different plots of land. The Cluny monastery of Benedictine monks dating from the tenth century and later the Citeaux monastery of Cisterian monks founded at the end of the eleventh century both expanded vineyards in Burgundy. Detailed maps of the best vineyards were drawn, with *climats* sometimes walled-in. These climats were known as *clos*.

The popularity of Burgundy wines increased when they were used by the popes at Avignon, in the south of France, in the early fourteenth century. Philip the Bold, Duke of Burgundy, wanted to maintain the high quality of the wines and issued an edict at the end of the fourteenth century. The decree forbade the use of the high-yielding Gamay grape and overfertilizing the soils which would increase yields. Landlocked Burgundy had to maintain a reputation for quality as its wines were not as easily exported as those of its rival Bordeaux.

The vineyards of the church and nobility were confiscated and sold after the French Revolution at the end of the eighteenth century. Prior to the Revolution primogeniture required whole vineyards to be passed on to the eldest son of a family. Under the laws of Napoléon, vineyards were typically equally divided among the children of the deceased owner. The Napoléonic code has led to a fragmentation of vineyards over the past 155 years.

Burgundy was hurt by the disasters of the oidium and *phylloxera* in the nineteenth century just as Bordeaux was. Another similarity was that the best vineyards of Burgundy were first classified in 1855, the same year the best châteaux of the Médoc in Bordeaux were rated. The Burgundy classification did not have as strong a commercial impact as that of Bordeaux because of the multitude of small growers who did not have the financial means to promote their small parcels of land. It was not until the Appellation d'Origine Contrôlée system came into effect in the 1930s that the ratings of the best climats were universally accepted and respected.

***The Appellations of Burgundy.***  Burgundy is comprised of subregions contained in départements. The AOC subregions, followed by their départements in parentheses, are Chablis (Yonne), Côte de Nuits and Côte de Beaune (Côte D'Or), Côte Chalonnaise and the Mâconnais (Saône-et-Loire), and Beaujolais (Rhône). These six regions and the communes or towns within them will be covered in more detail later in this section. The

Hautes Côtes de Nuits and Hautes Côtes de Beaune are regions west of the Côte D'Or at an altitude of 984 to 1312 feet (300 to 400 meters). Because of the altitudes there are colder growing conditions which expose vines to a higher risk of frost. Wines made here tend to have less richness of flavor, less color, less alcohol, but more acidity and can be a good value.

The cool climate and grape types of Burgundy are conducive to the production of *Crémant de Bourgogne* sparkling wines which are made by the Champagne method.

Regional wines labeled simply *Bourgogne* (Burgundy) are the least expensive and are made from a broader range of grape types with higher permitted yields. The reds and rosé wines are from Pinot Noir and Gamay, with the César and Tressot permitted in the Yonne. White wine grapes permitted are Chardonnay, Pinot Blanc, Pinot Gris, Aligoté, and Melon de Bourgogne. Bourgogne Aligoté is a tart, light-bodied, dry wine from the Aligoté grape with 15 percent Chardonnay permitted in a blend. *Bourgogne Passe-Tout-Grains* is a blended dry, fruity, light-bodied red with a minimum of a third Pinot Noir and the balance from the Gamay grape.

The quality of the wines begin with the larger regions within Burgundy and peak with the smallest climats. These wines may be subdivided into the following categories:

*Regional.* A wine from any region within Burgundy. An example is the Côte de Nuits or Côte de Nuits Villages. In a region some communes are considered to offer better grapes but not good enough to have their own communal appellation. A négociant could blend wine from the different villages approved within the Côte de Nuits and sell a Côte de Nuits Villages for a slightly higher price than a regular Côte de Nuits.

*Commune (village, town, or hamlet).* A commune wine has a separate appellation and the grapes come from a demarcated area around the town. Lower yields and higher minimum alcohol levels must be followed to ensure the grapes are more concentrated in flavor and are ripe. Vosne-Romanée is an example of a communal wine and its name appears on a label prominently.

*Premier Cru.* The commune name is followed by the name of an approved climat. An example is Vosne Romanée "Les Malconsorts." A common practice is to blend wines from different Premier Crus to enable a négociant to bolster quantity available of a single product. The Premier Cru (see Figures 6.2 and 6.3) distinction is based on the terroir of a particular climat and by blending that unique character is lost. However, the consumer is protected as to the quality of the wine because lower yields and higher minimum alcohol levels than a commune wine must still be met.

*Grand Cru.* These superlative sites are not required to list their commune on a label as they have their own appellations (see Figure 6.4). There are 30 Grand Cru sites in the Côte d'Or but the words Grand Cru need not appear on the label either. An example is Romanée-Conti, a vineyard in the commune of Vosne-Romanée. The wines of Chablis follow different rules. In Chablis, the term Grand Cru does appear on a label, alone if blended

**Figure 6.2** A Chablis Premier Cru Label.

**Figure 6.3** A Volnay Santenots Premier Cru Label.

from different Grand Cru climats, or with the name of the specific vineyard if made exclusively from that source. There are no Grand Cru wines in Mâconnais, Châlonnais, or Beaujolais.

***The Wine Regions of Burgundy—Côte d'Or.*** The Côte d'Or is considered by many to be the world's finest growing area for Chardonnay and Pinot Noir. Thirty miles (48 kilometers) long and under two miles (3.2 kilometers) at its widest (see Map 6.4), yet there are myriad nuances in style that depend on the soil, rainfall, exposure to sun and wind, drainage, and the grower's and wine maker's approach. The Côte de Nuits half produces mostly red wines while the Côte de Beaune to its south is celebrated for both white and red wines.

Elevation is between 721 and 984 feet (220 and 300 meters) for most vineyards. The hillsides shield the vineyards from excessive rain, and the southern rain-bearing clouds often dissipate moisture before reaching the Côtes. The east, southeast, and south-facing slopes are usually the best exposures. The

**(a)**

**(b)**

**Figure 6.4 a and b** Labels from a Grand Cru and a Premier Cru Wine from the Gevrey-Chambertin Commune.

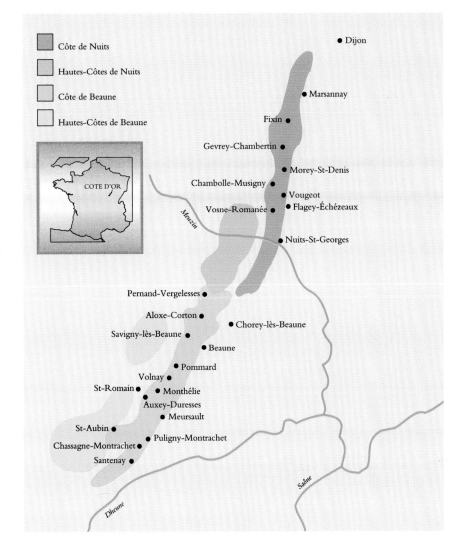

**Map 6.4** The Côte d'Or.

Chambertin, One of Nine Grand Cru
Vineyards in Gevrey-Chambertin.

relative humidity, sunshine hours, and rainfall are similar to Bordeaux, yet the area is cooler and subject to hailstorms and frost. A good summer would have a dry warm June during flowering, as rain could harm the flowers or the grapes formed from them. A dry warm July allows *véraison* (color change) to occur and sugar levels to increase in the grape. A little rain is welcome in early August but too much rain throughout the month could lead to rot or diluted grapes.

Soil types vary but are mostly limestone, chalk, marlstone, and clay. The white wines are often planted higher up where there are more stones and chalk. Clay is more common lower on the hillsides. Small stones assist drainage and absorb heat while finer clay particles aid the fertility of the vine. The Premier and Grand Cru sites are those with the best exposures, best-drained soils, and higher elevations.

The Pinot Noir grown on chalk or limestone soils is not as heavy in structure as when grown in clay-based soils. Change trace elements, such as potassium or nitrogen, in different sites and the character of the wine shifts slightly. The whole question of soil types is integral to understanding why this relatively small growing region has developed such an intricate web of sites or "climats."

***The Wine Regions of Burgundy-Côte de Nuits.*** The Côte de Nuits produces some white wine and rosé but is revered for its red wines. The major communes from north to south are Marsannay, Fixin, Gevrey-Chambertin, Morey-St. Denis, Chambolle-Musigny, Vougeot, Flagey-Échezaux, Vosne-Romanée, and Nuits-St. Georges.

*Marsannay.* The commune of Marsannay is most famous for rosé wines, which may be labeled as Marsannay or as AOC Bourgogne-Marsannay. The rosés tend to have an orange tinge and a floral and strawberry blackberry nose. To enjoy their fruit and power, they are best drunk within three years. Domaine Clair Dau, which started the rosé style in 1919, still produces fine examples today. A 1987 AOC decree has brought standards up for the whites and reds as well.

*Fixin.* Fixin consists of 488 acres (197.5 hectares) of vineyards that often sell their products as Côte de Nuits-Villages, an easier-to-pronounce and more recognized appellation. Of these 488 acres, 265 acres (107.7 hectares) make wines that may be sold under the name of the commune Fixin. The wines are firm, tannic, and earthy, and the soil benefits from limestone content along with the clay. They are similar to their more-famous neighbor Gevrey-Chambertin but more rustic and less expensive. With age a cassis bouquet develops. Clos du Chapitre and Clos de la Perrière are the largest of the six Premier Crus; there are no Grand Crus. A little white wine is produced from Chardonnay and Pinot Blanc grapes.

*Gevrey-Chambertin.* The historic town of Gevrey-Chambertin is known for producing the most powerful Burgundies from its variety of soils and exposures. The village wines tend to come from flat land or from the base of the hills, while the Premier and Grand Crus are on slopes with the best sun exposure and drainage. There are over 1200 acres (485.5 hectares) of land entitled to the commune appellation and about a fifth of the acreage is Premier Cru and Grand Cru status which are large areas by Burgundian standards. This is not only the largest village appellation in the Côte de Nuits, it also boasts 25 Premier Crus and the largest number of Grand Crus (nine) in Burgundy.

All the wines are reds made from Pinot Noir grapes. Depending on site, yield, and methods of vinification, they range from medium weight to the most powerful and rich examples. Yet "powerful" Pinot Noir often means bright fruit flavors combined with a full texture, without the force or tannin of a Cabernet-based wine. Over 1.2 million bottles of Gevrey-Chambertin appellation wines are made in an average year, and they can be enjoyed within three to ten years. The prices of Premier and Grand Crus can be justified not only by their refinement but also by their aging potential. They should show well after five years and the best, though delicious after a decade of cellaring, may improve and live to be enjoyed after 30 or 40 years.

Of the Premier Crus, Clos Saint-Jacques, Varoilles, Les Cazetiers, and Combes au Moines are considered the finest examples. The Grand Cru vineyards that may add the name Chambertin to their own are Charmes, Chapelle, Griotte, Mazis, Mazoyères, Latricières, and Ruchottes. Although Charmes-Chambertin produces the largest volume of wine (Mazoyères is usually sold as Charmes today), it is not considered the best-situated Grand Cru and its wine matures more quickly than that of other Grand Crus.

The finest of the Grand Crus is Chambertin. Clos de Bèze is another Grand Cru that may use its own name or opt to be sold as Chambertin. These vineyards produce firm, fuller-bodied versions of Pinot Noir that have the power, fruit, and acidity to age well.

Leaving the Village of Vosne-Romanée.

*Morey-St. Denis.* Morey-St. Denis produces wines of finesse, with an aroma of violets and strawberries. The communal wines and Premier Crus are medium weight, the Grand Crus more forceful. The area produces mostly reds, but some whites are made too. Grand Crus include Clos de la Roche, Clos St. Denis, Clos des Lambrays, and a small portion of Bonnes-Mares shared with the Chambolle-Musigny commune to its south. The limestone soil of Chambolle-Musigny and Gevrey-Chambertin to the north is also evident in Morey-St. Denis. At Clos de la Roche the enrichment of marlstone gives the wines more body and longevity. Mommessin négociants have a *monopole* (monopoly) of the Grand cru Clos de Tart. They own all 18 acres (7.28 hectares) and produce a wine not as deep in color or full in body as Clos de la Roche but with a fine intensity of flavors. Clos St. Denis has similar character and finesse as Clos de Tart while the Clos des Lambrays matures quickest of the four Grand Crus and may be drunk from five to ten years after the vintage. A fine Premier Cru is the Clos de la Bussière which is a monopole owned by Domaine Georges Roumier. Of the 25 Premier Crus some other fine examples are Le Clos des Ormes, Les Sorbés, Les Charmes, and Les Monts Luisants. The latter produces a rarity: a fine full-bodied white wine from a mutation of the red Pinot Noir grape. The communal wines of Morey-St. Denis offer wines with greater balance and a style between the more powerful Gevrey-Chambertin wines and the lighter style of Chambolle-Musigny.

*Chambolle-Musigny.* If Gevrey-Chambertin is known for the weight and power of its wines, then Chambolle-Musigny provides the most silky, elegant, and delicate of styles which has the advantage of being approachable and enjoyable at an earlier date than its peers. The effect of mostly limestone soil with less clay is apparent in the lighter weight of these wines. The seductive bouquet of the finest examples offer violets, cherries, raspberries, with a counterpoint of earthiness. Of the Premier Crus, Les Amoureuses

and Les Charmes are the finest. The elegant aspects of the Grand Crus Bonnes-Mares and Musigny are accompanied by great intensity and depth of flavor. Musigny is the more delicate of the two. The fine producer, Domaine Comte Georges de Voguë, own about 18 of the 26 acres (7.27 of the 10.5 hectares) of Musigny and also produce a complex full-bodied white wine from under three-quarters of an acre (one-third of a hectare) of Chardonnay. Bonnes-Mares is a fabulous Grand Cru which is a firmer, fleshier red wine needing a decade to begin to show its best qualities. The smell of wildflowers and ripe wild berries are a prelude to the concentrated flavors of both Musigny and Bonnes-Mares.

*Vougeot.*    The Grand Cru vineyard Clos de Vougeot was established by Cistercian monks about 1100 and by 1336 the 124 acres (54.5 hectares) were surrounded by stone walls. The vineyard had one owner in the 1880s but today it is split up among 80 owners. The variables among grower practices and location within this largest single vineyard in Burgundy account for wide variations in style. Apart from the Grand Cru, there are another 44 acres (17.7 hectares) of Premier Cru and commune wines. The best examples will have a floral truffle nose and good weight on the palate.

*Flagey-Échezeaux.*    No commune wines are made in Flagey-Échezeaux. The 74 acres (29.9 hectares) of Échezeaux and 24 acres (9.7 hectares) of Grand Échezeaux are both rated Grand Cru. As the name indicates, the Grand Échezeaux is more revered. The vineyard is contiguous with Clos de Vougeot, but these wines possess a more complex nose of violets and raspberries on the palate and they combine richness with balance.

*Vosne-Romanée.*    Perhaps the most representative and famous examples of Pinot Noir in the world, and certainly the most expensive, come from this commune. About 33 acres (13.3 hectares) of wines made in Flagey-Échezeaux wines may be sold under the commune name of Vosne-Romanée as well. The wines are in a style somewhere between the sturdy power of Gevrey-Chambertin, and the delicacy of Chambolle-Musigny, and they are known for their textural qualities. Descriptors such as "satiny" or "silky" are often used. The complex perfumed nose of the best examples is another cause for their reputation. The former Premier Cru La Grand Rue, a monopole of Domaine Lamarche, shares with Clos de Lambrays of Morey-St. Denis the honor of being elevated to Grand Cru status in the 1980s. Although both wines are fine examples, neither has attained the level of complexity of the other Grand Crus of their communes. The Grand Crus of Vosne-Romanée range from the lightest in body and quickest-maturing Romanée St. Vivant to the most massive, rich, and generous Richebourg. La Romanée is medium bodied and with two acres (0.84 hectares) is the smallest appellation in France. There are some who would cite Richebourg as a personal favorite but most would give the honor to either Romanée-Conti or La Tâche. The latter is considered most consistent in quality of the Grand Crus, even in lesser vintages. The 4.5-acre (1.8-hectare) Romanée-Conti is less than a third the size of La Tâche. Romanée-Conti and La Tâche are monopoles owned by the Domaine de la Romanée-Conti, and they both are complex wines with great elegance, the quintessential expressions of Pinot Noir. The Premier Crus of Les Malconsorts, Les Chaumes, and Clos de Réas (monopole of Jean Gros) are richer than the Suchots and Beaumont's Premier Crus farther north.

*Nuits-St. Georges.* This commune, which covers 800 acres (323 hectares), include such fine Premier Crus as Les St. Georges, Vaucrains, Les Cailles, Les Porrets, Les Boudots, Les Murgers, and Clos de la Maréchale. There are 41 Premier Crus, the largest number in Burgundy, but no Grand Crus here. The northern vineyards in this commune make fine perfumed wines from the stonier soils while the southern vineyards with more clay produce firm fuller-bodied examples.

***The Wine Regions of Burgundy—Côte de Beaune.*** Côte de Beaune is twice as large as the Côte de Nuits and is known for its great white wines and fabulous reds. The communes from north to south are Ladoix, Pernand-Vergelesses, Aloxe-Corton, Savigny-lès-Beaune, Chorey-lès-Beaune, Beaune, Pommard, Volnay, St. Romain, Monthélie, Auxey-Duresses, Meursault, St. Aubin, Puligny-Montrachet, Chassagne-Montrachet, and Santenay.

*Ladoix-Serrigny.* The Ladoix AOC produces primarily red wines of good acidity. Some of the best Premier Crus are entitled to use the Aloxe-Corton name, and some vineyards are included in the Corton or Corton Charlemagne Grand Cru.

*Aloxe-Corton.* Aloxe-Corton produces primarily red wines. Wines of the Corton Grand Cru may be red or white. Wines from the best 28 vineyards of Ladoix, Pernand-Vergelesses, and Aloxe-Corton may be used in the

Grand Cru Corton. Corton, which consists of 300 acres (323 hectares), is the largest Grand Cru in Burgundy and the only red Grand Cru in the Côte de Beaune. The Corton Grand Cru may also add the name of the climat after Corton, such as Corton Les Bressandes. Among the finest of the red Grand Crus are Les Renardes, Le Clos du Roi, and Les Perrières. The red Grand Crus are found on heavier soils with some chalk but more clay and marl. The Grand Crus seem to combine the power of the finest Côte de Nuits wines with the graceful style of the Côte de Beaune reds. The Premier and Grand Crus need time to open up, will be best after a decade and will improve for two decades more when from a good vintage. The white Corton-Charlemagne Grand Cru is planted at higher elevations on thinner soils of stones and chalk. It has scents of almonds, fruits, spices, and flowers and is rich and full bodied on the palate. The wines should not be drunk for at least three years but the finest may last 20. The Chardonnay grape is the dominant variety but Pinot Blanc is planted as well. About 150,000 bottles of Corton-Charlemagne is produced in an average year which is less than half the Corton Grand Cru red production. A small amount of Corton (Blanc) Grand Cru is also made from Chardonnay and Pinot Blanc grapes.

*Auxey-Duresses, Monthélie, and Chorey-Lès-Beaune.* These communes offer good-quality traditional whites and reds that are most often less expensive than similar wines from the more renowned communes.

*Pernand-Vergelesses.* Pernand-Vergelesses produces white wines with forward fruit qualities and good acidity from Chardonnay and Aligoté grapes. Whites are planted in the fields high in chalk content. More red wines are produced from vineyards where the clay soil is enriched by iron. The reds have a raspberry aroma and need some age to lose their coarse edge of youth. Many of the red-wine vineyards do not have the more favorable south or eastern exposures and as a result of less sunshine the grapes do not always reach full ripeness. Iles de Vergelesses is the finest of the five Premier Crus, all of which need at least five years to show well.

*Savigny-lès Beaune.* Savigny-lès Beaune produces mostly red wines. Vineyards geographically closer to Pernand-Vergelesses have a lighter style than those closer to Beaune. Of the 22 Premier Crus, Les Dominodes and Marconnets may be the best example of the more powerful, rounder style, while the Aux Vergelesses and Aux Serpentières display finesse allied with fruit on the palate and a floral nose.

*Beaune.* Beaune, the largest commune in the Côte de Beaune, is also the center of the wine trade. There are over 13,000 acres (5252 hectares) of vines. Only five percent of production are white wines which have a nutty and acacia smell and are medium bodied, while the reds have the floral character of roses. The wines are best drunk within four to ten years. There are 42 Premier Crus covering 795 acres (321 hectares), but no Grand Crus. The wines from the northern section tend to be rounder, fuller, and longer lived than those from the south. Monopole Premier Crus from the south include the Clos des Ursules (Louis Jadot), and Le Clos de la Mousse (Bouchard

Frank Grux, Wine Maker of Olivier Leflaive Frères (left) and Olivier Leflaive (right).

Père et Fils). The Clos des Mouches vineyard produces both red and white wines; Joseph Drouhin use Chardonnay grapes from this vineyard to make a fine example of an aromatic, full-bodied white Burgundy. Le Clos du Roi, Les Perrières, and Bressandes are Premier Crus in the north that couple good fruit with power. The lighter sand- and gravel-based soil of Les Grèves makes it a lighter-style Premier Cru from the north.

*Pommard.* Pommard has 832 acres (332.5 hectares) of vines, making it the second-largest wine-producing area in the Côte de Beaune. In the past the area was maligned for overproduction, falsified labels, or for heavy, dull wines. Today's conscientious négociants produce better-balanced wines, yet wines from Pommard are still more earthy and darker in color than those of Beaune. All the wines are red and many have aromas of animal hide, berries, and plums. The fuller-bodied wines are from the bottom of the slopes with medium-bodied sturdy examples produced from vineyards higher up. The weight of the wines and their astringency in youth may be attributed to the red clay soils enriched by iron oxides. Les Rugiens is one Premier Cru example in such soil and is known for its depth of flavor, deep red color, and power. Of the 28 Premiers Crus, Les Epenots is in a softer style but will still benefit from cellaring for over a decade. Other fine Premier Crus are Clos de la Commaraine (a monopole of Jaboulet-Vercherre), Les Arvelets, Le Clos Blanc, Les Bertins. Of the commune wines the Clos des Epenots is a fine example as is the 50-acre (123.5-hectare) vineyard at Château de Pommard which is the largest family-owned vineyard in the Côte d'Or.

*Volnay.* For those searching for elegance and charm in the Côte de Beaune, Volnay is the commune to choose. The wines are known for a violet and raspberry nose, silky texture, and harmonious flavors. The consistent high quality in the vineyards is shown by the fact that of the 527 acres (213 hectares) planted, 284 (115 hectares) are of Premier Cru status. The Premier Cru Les Caillerets is considered the benchmark style of the 34 Premier Crus and is prized for its finesse. Its chief rivals for top site are the Clos des Ducs (monopole of Domaine Marquis d'Angerville) and Clos de la Bousse d'Or (monopole of Domaine de la Pousse d' Or). Clos des Chênes is the largest Premier Cru, followed by Champans which is the second largest. Wines from a half dozen vineyards of the bordering commune Meursault, may sell their reds as Volnay-Santenots. Whites from these vineyards are labeled as Meursault Premier Cru or Meursault Santenots.

*Meursault.* Meursault produces mostly white wines from calcareous soil rich in iron and magnesium. When yield is kept low and the wines are given a few years to develop, they offer a wonderful hazelnut, cinnamon, and toffee-apple smell and a rich mouthful of flavor. La Goutte d'Or is a Premier Cru that typifies the full rich style, and was a favorite of Thomas Jefferson. Les Perrières and Les Genevrières are perhaps the top Premier Crus. Both demonstrate fine balance and persistence of flavors but are not as buttery as La Goutte d'Or. Les Charmes is the largest of the Premier Crus and is richer in style than Les Poruzots, the smallest Premier Cru.

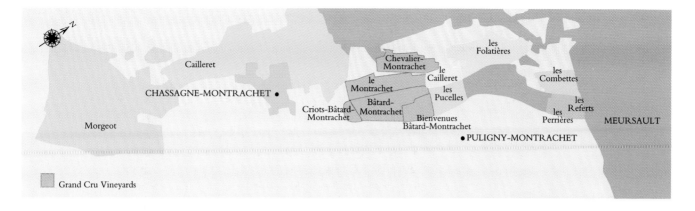

Grand Cru Vineyards

*Blagny.* Blagny is located between Meursault and Puligny-Montrachet. The earthy red wines may bear just the town name, but whites are sold as either Puligny-Montrachet or Meursault.

*Puligny-Montrachet.* Puligny-Montrachet produces steely, powerful white wines in a leaner, more concentrated style than those of Meursault. The aromas tend to be more floral, fruity, and almond rather than the pronounced hazelnut nose of Meursault. Le Cailleret, Les Folatières, Les Perrières, and Les Pucelles are top Premier Crus with typical Puligny style, while the Les Combettes and Les Referts situated near Meursault share attributes of both villages. The superlative Grand Cru Montrachet was added to the commune name of Puligny in 1879. Puligny-Montrachet shares the Grand Cru Montrachet vineyards as well as the Grand Cru Bâtard Montrachet with the commune of Chassagne-Montrachet to its south. The Chevalier-Montrachet and Bienvenue-Bâtard Montrachet are Grand Cru grown entirely in Puligny-Montrachet (see Map 6.5).

**Map 6.5** The Grand Cru Vineyards that Lie between the Villages of Puligny-Montrachet and Chassagne-Montrachet Produce Some of the Greatest White Wine in the World. They are Chevalier-Montrachet, Le Montrachet, Bienvenues-Bâtard-Montrachet, Bâtard-Montrachet, and Criots-Bâtard-Montrachet. Some of the Prominent Premier Cru Vineyards are also Labeled.

Le Montrachet, the Vineyard That Produces the Most Expensive Dry White Wine in the World.

## GRAND CRUS OF BURGUNDY

*Côte de Nuits*

Chambertin, Chambertin Clos de Bèze, Charmes-Chambertin, Chappelle-Chambertin, Griotte-Chambertin, Latricières-Chambertin, Mazis-Chambertin, Mazoyères-Chambertin, and Ruchottes-Chambertin are reds from Gevrey-Chambertin.

Clos des Lambray, Clos de Tart, Clos St. Denis, Clos de la Roche, and part of Bonnes Mares are reds from Morey St. Denis.

Most of Bonnes Mares which is red and Le Musigny which is mostly red, with a little white wine as well, are from Chambolle-Musigny.

Clos de Vougeot is red from Vougeot.

Grand Échezeaux and Échezeaux are reds from Flagey-Échezeaux.

Richebourg, Romanée-Conti, Romanée St. Vivant, La Romanée, La Grand Rue, and La Tâche are reds from Vosne-Romanée.

*Côte de Beaune*

Corton-Charlemagne and Charlemagne are whites from the communes of Aloxe-Corton and Pernand-Verge-lesses.

Corton is mostly red and a little white both made from the communes of Ladoix-Serrigny and Aloxe-Corton.

Chevalier-Montrachet white is exclusively from the commune of Puligny-Montrachet while a part of the white wines Montrachet and Bâtard-Montrachet also come from the commune of Puligny-Montrachet.

Criots Bâtard Montrachet white is exclusively from Chassagne-Montrachet and part of the white wines Bâtard-Montrachet and Le Montrachet also come from the commune Chassagne-Montrachet.

*Chablis*

The seven white wines with Grand Cru status within Chablis are Blanchots, Bougros, Les Clos, Grenouilles, Les Preuses, Valmur, and Vaudésir.

The best vintages of Grand Cru whites of the Côte de Beaune have the potential to age for over three decades. The 19.75-acre (8-hectare) Le Montrachet vineyard produces the most expensive dry white wine in the world. The best examples display a bouquet of nuts, flowers, fruit, and honey and combine these qualities with a firm texture, elegance, and a long finish. When properly handled in the field and winery they are the quintessential Chardonnay. The other Grand Crus of Puligny and Chassagne, as well as Corton-Charlemagne or Meursault-Perrières, when made by a more-skilled and conscientious producer, may surpass Le Montrachet in quality and yet be lower priced. The age of the vines used and the nuances of flavor expressed by each producer are part of the quality search that fascinates lovers of fine Burgundy. These fine white wines of the Côte de Beaune need at least five years before they begin to open up and display their charm and complex scents and flavors.

*Chassagne-Montrachet.*    Chassagne-Montrachet whites share the acidic, mineral, and fruit qualities of Puligny but may have a creamy quality. Le Morgeot is a fuller-style white Premier Cru than Les Grandes Ruchottes or La Grande Montagne. The 3.9-acre (1.52-hectare) Criots-Bâtard-Montrachet is a Grand Cru exclusively in Chassagne-Montrachet. It is an elegant wine, though not as full-bodied as the two other Grand Crus, Montrachet and Bâtard-Montrachet, that Chassagne shares with Puligny-Montrachet. Red wines of Chassagne-Montrachet are earthy and firm with a spicy aroma and are best from sites with gravel, marl, and limestone soils. Chassagne-Montrachet produced more red than white until recently. World demand for Chardonnay from this famous commune has led to the planting of some vines in soils better suited for Pinot Noir. Puligny and Chassagne-Montrachet whites are best planted in limestone and silica soils. There is more magnesium at Chassagne-Montrachet; Puligny-Montrachet has more clay.

*Saint-Aubin and Saint-Romain.*    Saint-Aubin is prized for white wines with finesse and typical nutty scents at more affordable prices than Meursaults or Montrachets. The commune also makes fresh reds that can be drunk young to enjoy their attractive strawberry aromas and tastes. The richer Premier Crus need some aging. Saint-Romain has no Premier Crus and the wines are not expensive; here chalk soil and high elevation result in whites and reds with high acidity.

*Santenay.*    Santenay produces mostly earthy, perhaps coarse, red wines from vineyards rich in marl. They are good value wines with typical Pinot Noir fruit and some have "barnyard" type aromas. When produced from a top site and vintage the reds need a decade to soften. A small amount of white wine is produced as well.

**The Wine Regions of Burgundy—Chablis.**    For Chardonnay drinkers who appreciate high acidity in a wine this is the perfect wine. The cold climate provides the high acidity for the Chardonnay grapes grown here. A tinge of green to the straw color is the first indication of a classic Chablis. The smell of flowers, flint, hay and green apples is evident in the finer examples. The taste should be tart with good fruit balance along with a complete middle palate and persistent finish. All of these qualities are found in the best category Grand Cru or the second-best, Premier Cru.

The traditional way to ferment and age the wines of Chablis is in *feuillette,* a 34.87-gallon (132-liter) oak cask. Some growers use *foudres,* larger casks. Although some still vinify and age in wood, others choose stainless steel. The sense of oak should not diminish the smell and taste of fruit, and oak does not play as large a role here as it does elsewhere in Burgundy. Experiments on the effect of oak for the higher-quality wine continues with some négociants convinced it enhances fine wines and others definitely opposed to using oak. J. Moreau, A. Régnard, J. Durup, and Louis Michel are producers who avoid oak and W. Févre, J. Drouhin, Raveneau, and R. Dauvissat are proponents of using oak. Those using oak are doing so in varying

Christian Moreau, Producer of Fine Chablis in a Traditional Style.

degrees of influence. La Chablisienne, the large coopérative of the region, uses oak for some of its cru wines.

In Chablis, frost is combatted by using heat from stoves or torches in the vineyards or by using water sprinklers. The water sprayed on the grapes ensures that temperatures do not fall below 0°C or 32°F, unless strong winds alter the direction of the water. Water sprinkling is a much less expensive procedure than heat. The best sites face south, southeast, and southwest and are between 393.6 to 822.5 feet (120 and 250 meters) in elevation.

The first appellation law in the area was promulgated in 1919. In 1920 the Kimmeridgian soil was specified as an important part to qualify wines as Chablis. Kimmeridgian soil, which consists of clay, limestone, and fossilized shells of oysters, produces the finest wines of the region. Today, the permitted boundaries of the appellation have been expanded to increase production, and vines are planted on hard limestone Portlandien soils as well.

Because of the global respect for the wines of the area, some countries use the name Chablis to indicate a generic dry white wine, although such wines have little in common with well-made examples from the appellation. Chablis is made exclusively from Chardonnay. Some Aligoté, Pinot Gris, Sacy, Pinot Noir, César, Tressot, and Sauvignon Blanc grapes are found in the region but they are not permitted to be labeled as Chablis. Examples of other labels include the Sauvignon de St. Bris from Sauvignon Blanc and Irancy from Pinot Noir with some César and Tressot.

### Quality Levels of Chablis

*Petit Chablis.* Petit Chablis is a simple fresh wine that is the least-expensive product of the region. It is best consumed within three years of the vintage. The minimum alcohol level a Petit Chablis must attain is 9.5 percent with the same required maximum yield as the superior Chablis or Premier Cru appellations. Today there are about 500 acres (200 hectares) of Petit Chablis planted, but a much larger area for planting has been approved. It is doubtful investors will take advantage of expanding acreage at the lowest quality level.

*Chablis.* These wines must have a minimum alcohol of ten percent. The basic Chablis category is where a lot of the vineyard expansion has occurred and it now includes over 6000 acres (2424 hectares) of vines.

*Premier Cru.* These vineyards are those 40 climats judged to have better exposure and soils than plain Chablis. To simplify recognition, these are often labeled under the names of the 12 most-renowned sites. Montée de Tonnere, Vaulorent, and Fouchaume are age-worthy examples that are situated just east of the Grand Crus vineyards Blanchots and Valmur on the superior right side of the Serein river. Montmains and Vaillons are two others with good fruity qualities that are on the left bank of the Serein river. Fourchaume and Beugnons have appeal at a younger age, yet most of the Premiers should be consumed at least three years after the vintage. A Premier Cru must achieve a minimum of 10. 5 percent alcohol level.

*Grand Cru.* Seven sites were granted the highest classification of Grand Cru Chablis in 1938. Wines from these vineyards made by the best producers can be enjoyed after four or five years or cellared and then savored after one or two decades. Producers who ferment and store these wines in wood will create wines with more color and body than those using inert vats. The nose of these wines may be of acacia, hay, flint, grapefruit, green apple or pears, and honey. The Grand Crus are all on a well-drained slope just east of the town of Chablis. The seven Grand Cru wines also benefit from facing southwest where vines receive the most sunshine, allowing them to ripen. There are about 250 acres (101 hectares) of Grand Cru Chardonnay which produce about 500,000 bottles in an average year. The yield is lower than the other wines of the region and the minimum alcohol content is higher at 11 percent. Each author or critic may champion a favorite site, attracted to the honey-apple nose and depth of Les Clos or the finesse of Les Preuses, or the structure of Vaudésir. The wines of Bougros are on a very steep incline and are firm and expansive on the palate. The nose of Valmur is part of its appeal and its balance another. Grenouilles are fuller examples than Blanchots, yet Blanchots wines still have good texture and a long finish.

### The Wine Regions of Burgundy—Côte Chalonnaise.
The Côte Chalonnaise is 15 miles (25 kilometers) long and about 4.3 miles (seven kilometers) wide (see Map 6.6). The soils are similar to the Côte d'Or, based on limestone with some clay and sand. About two-thirds is planted with Pinot Noir; Chardonnay, Aligoté, and Gamay provide the balance. The wines are beginning to be acknowledged in the export market, as quality Burgundies at reasonable prices. Most wines are made to be enjoyed from two to six years after the vintage. They are meant to be drunk young and most are not made to be cellared. Bourgogne Aligoté de Bouzeron is the best example of this grape. It is the only village allowed to include its name with that of Aligoté. It is dry with a citrus taste. The four villages with their own appellation are Givry, Montagny, Rully, and Mercurey. Chardonnay is used for the whites and Pinot Noir for reds.

*Rully.* Rully produces 1.25 million bottles of communal wine and another 250,000 bottles of Premier Cru wines. The whites have a spicy apple aroma, full body and color, with good fruit and acidity, and may be drunk young. Some négociants are using oak barrels to give the wines more character. The Premier Cru reds have a ruby color, strawberry aroma, and are medium bodied. Les Cloux and Les St. Jacques are two of the Premier Crus.

**Map 6.6** The Wine Regions of the Côte Chalonnaise, the Côte Maconnais, and Beaujolais. The Cru Villages of Beaujolais are Italicized.

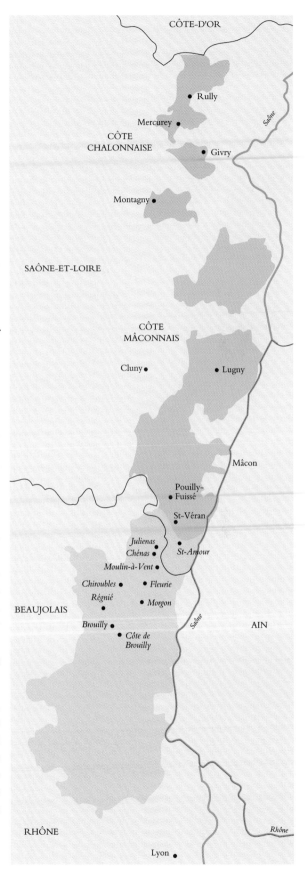

*Mercurey.* Mercurey, the most renowned commune of the region, has had AOC status since 1936. The soil of clay, limestone and iron makes fine Pinot Noir which can smell of violets, cassis, and strawberries. These reds are more firm than others from the Chalonnaise and should be drunk between four and eight years after the vintage. Three and three-quarter million bottles of red are made in an average year and only 125,000 of white wine. Some of the top Premier Crus are Le Clos du Roi, Clos des Fourneaux, Clos Marcilly, and Clos Voyens.

*Givry.* Givry produces 625,000 bottles of light-bodied dry reds that may be enjoyed after two years. About 60,000 bottles of fresh crisp whites are also made in average vintages. The area contains no Premier Crus.

*Montagny.* In Montagny, the criteria for Premier Cru status is not the site but achieving 11.5 percent minimum alcohol level. Annual production is 750,000 bottles of dry, light- to medium-bodied white wines intended for early consumption.

**The Wine Regions of Burgundy—Mâcon/Mâconnais.** The region stretches 31 miles (50 kilometers) from north to south and is 9.3 miles (15 kilometers) wide. The Saône River flows through the region and then on through Beaujolais as well. Whereas vines dominate agriculture in the Côte d'Or the farms of Mâcon grow other fruits and vegetables and have livestock as well. The area is known primarily for white wines with over two-thirds of its acreage devoted to Chardonnay. The climate is warmer than that of Chablis, the other subregion that concentrates on whites. The topsoil is varied from clay sand to granite, but the subsoil is mostly limestone. The white grapes Aligoté and Chardonnay are planted where there is more marl; Pinot Noir is planted on more chalky sites. Gamay is grown on heavier clay soils and those of granite with sand. The east-facing slopes are preferred to those of the west, which have fewer plantings. The density of plantings is about one-quarter less than in the Côte d'Or. The hills provide good drainage and are protected from wind and rain by trees planted on the top.

The regional wines are good value, and those labeled *supérieur* simply guarantee an extra percent minimum alcohol (11 versus the ten for wines labeled just Mâcon).

*Mâcon-Villages.* This is an appellation which consists of 43 villages. The wines may include the name of the town if the wine is exclusively from that commune. Examples are Mâcon-Lugny or Mâcon Viré. Reds which are made from mostly Gamay and some Pinot Noir are labeled Mâcon plus the name of the commune.

*Pouilly-Fuissé.* This is the finest appellation of the region, and its fame is international. The commune's 2100 acres (848.4 hectares) accounts for about 10.5 million gallons (40,000 hectoliters) of wine a year. The best examples display a straw-green color, a nose of flowers, apples, and nuts, and are dry, rich, and round on the palate. The wines are made from the communes of Chaintré, Fuissé, Vergisson, and Solutré. The latter contains the village Pouilly and a famous crag of limestone rock. The vineyard soils beneath the rock contain thousands of bones of horses and other animals that were driven over the crag by hunters. These bones date from 20,000 B.C. (Solutréen period) and are said to be responsible for the more powerful taste of the Pouilly Fuissé from the Solutré section. A Pouilly-Fuissé may be enjoyed at between two to seven years old, depending on the vintage and producer. Although there are no Premier Crus the name of a specific climat may be included on a label. New oak barrels are expensive and are not common for the more affordable wines of Mâcon but are sometimes used for Pouilly-Fuissé.

*Saint Véran, Pouilly-Vinzelles, Pouilly-Loche.* Saint Véran was introduced as an appellation in 1971. It's chalk-based vineyards used to produce Beaujolais whites and Mâcon-Villages. Saint Véran produces about half the quantity of Pouilly-Fuissé and is most often made in a fresh lighter style that may be drunk after only a year. It is sold at a more affordable price than Pouilly-Fuissé. Pouilly-Vinzelles and Pouilly-Loche are alternative choice whites, also in the lighter, early-consumption style.

***The Wine Regions of Burgundy—Beaujolais.*** There are 150 million bottles produced annually from about 49,420 acres (19,893 hectares), mostly in the Rhône département and some in Saône-et-Loire. This amount surpasses the total production of all the other regions of Burgundy.

The wines are labeled, in ascending order of quality as *Beaujolais AOC, Beaujolais Supérieur* (higher minimum alcohol; mostly for the domestic market), *Beaujolais-Villages,* and *Cru Beaujolais* (from specific villages). The vast majority of wine is red from the Gamay grape. Most are best appreciated

The Beaujolais Region.

young and served chilled (around 50°F/10°C). The cru wines have the edge in interest and body and can be enjoyed at 58 or 60°F/14.5 or 15.5°C and between two to eight years after the harvest, depending on the vintage and village. The region benefits from hills that form a shield from the winds from the west and a warmer growing season than other parts of Burgundy. The best vineyards consist of granite-schist-based soils with some clay and sand topsoil in the Haut-Beaujolais or northern part where the Cru Beaujolais and most Beaujolais-Villages wines are from. The nouveau and plain Beaujolais appellation wines from the south are grown on clay and limestone. Some white wines from Chardonnay and Aligoté are made but most are sold under the St. Véran appellation of Mâcon rather than as Beaujolais Blanc. Rosé wine is allowed but very little is produced.

The Beaujolais *Nouveau* or *Primeur* is about half of the yearly production. The nouveau wines are the first wines to be consumed of the vintage, are traditionally served "Frais" (slightly chilled), and are known for their fruity and refreshing style.

Carbonic maceration is used to make nouveau wines (see Chapter 1 on How Wine Is Made). The grapes are put whole into a container, to which carbon dioxide is added. The absence of oxygen results in an intercellular fermentation with a reduction in malic acid and a small amount of alcohol created. Then a regular fermentation with oxygen takes place. *Primeur* or *Nouveau* wines, picked in late September and released for sale the third Thursday in November, offer the growers and négociants a quick sale and the customer an easy drinking (*gouleyant*) fruity wine that is simple and refreshing but not complex. Light simple wines like Beaujolais Nouveau are usually best consumed within the region, yet half of the Nouveau production is exported. The regulations for Nouveau stipulate it must have less than 0.07 ounces (two grams) of sugar and 0.175 ounces (five grams) of acidity per 0.26 gallons (liter) and may not exceed 13 percent alcohol.

The color of Beaujolais varies from the translucent pink-purple of the Nouveau wines to a ruby red cherry-violet range for the Crus. The smells are floral with red fruits and peaches. The wines are light bodied. Of the ten crus, *Moulin-À-Vent,* which benefits from magnesium concentration in the granite soil, may be the finest. The rose, violet, and red fruit nose of youth develops into a mushroom/gamy smell with age and the wines have more weight and depth than other Crus. The name is based on 300 year old

## WINE PRODUCERS OF BURGUNDY

The skills and integrity of the many growers and producers is a complex web further complicated by the fact that some are more respected for the wines of one site or village over another. For a basic list of producers we offer the following with the caveat that not every quality producer is listed and those that are have their strengths and weaknesses also. Those listed with asterisks are families or firms that have more than one company.

*Amiot-Bonfils, *Arnoux, A. Bichot, *Bachelet, Baron Thénard, *Boillot, J. C. Boisset, Bonneau du Martray, *Bouchard, L. Carillon, Chanson, *Chartron, Château Fuissé, *Chauvenet, *Chevillon, M. Chignard, *Clair, J. F. Coche-Dury, F. Coffinet, Clos des Lambrays, *Dauvissat, Joseph Drouhin, Drouhin-Laroze, G. Duboeuf, *Dugat, Domaine Dujac, René Engel, Faiveley, S. Fessy, W. Fèvre, Château Gris, *Gros, H. Gouges, Hospices de Beaune, Hospices de Nuits, Jaboulet-Vercherre, Château des Jacques, Louis Jadot, Jaffelin, *Jayer, F. Jobard, Labouré-Roi, A. Lichine, Lamarche, *Lamy, Laroche, Louis Latour, *Leflaive, Leroy, *Lignier, Lupé-Cholet, Joseph Matrot, *Michelot, Moillard, Mommessin, Mongeard-Mugneret, J. Moreau, *Mugneret, Patriarche, La Reine Pédauque, A. Pic, Château de Pommard, Ponsot, Domaine Jacques Prieur, Prosper-Maufoux, Domaine de la Pousse d'Or, Ramonet, *Raveneau, Remoissenet Pere et Fils, D. Rion, Domaine de la Romanée-Conti, Ropiteau, G. Roumier, A. Rousseau, *Roux, E. Sauzet, *Trapet, Château de la Tour, Domaine Vincent, *Voarick, Comte Georges de Vogüé

## GRAND CRU

A partial list of some of the most famous of the Grand Cru classé vineyard sites followed by their size and the varietals they are recognized for includes:

Altenberg de Bergheim (64.2 acres/25.6 hectares Riesling and Gewürztraminer), Brand (140 acres/56 hectares Riesling, Gewürztraminer, and Pinot Gris), Geisberg (21 acres/8.4 hectares Riesling), Goldert (111.9 acres/44.7 hectares Gewürztraminer and Muscat), Hengst (187.2 acres/74.8 hectares, Gewürztraminer, Pinot Gris, and Riesling), Kitterlé (63.7 acres/25.5 hectares Riesling, Gewürztraminer, and Pinot Gris), Rangen (46.4 acres/18.5 hectares Riesling, Gewürztraminer, and Pinot Gris), Schlossberg (197 acres/78.8 hectares Riesling).

---

windmill, and the area is between the towns of Romanèche-Thorins and Chénas.

*Juliénas* and *Morgon* both have medium bodies and aromas of cherries and raspberries. *Chénas* is also medium in body and is known for such floral aromas as peonies. Red fruit aromas are present in the *Côte de Brouilly* which is fuller in style than *Brouilly.* Brouilly is the largest of the Crus and has aromas of blueberries. *Régnié* is the newest Cru, elevated to that status in 1988. The northern section of the commune closer to Morgon produces more concentrated examples than those from the sandier soils to the south by Brouilly. The lighter-bodied *Saint-Amour* has aromas of stone fruits such as nectarines and apricots. *Chiroubles* and *Fleurie* are also lighter-bodied wines and as the name suggest Fleurie offer aromas of flowers such as violets.

The minimum alcohol level for Beaujolais is ten percent and the Villages and cru wines must attain 10.5 percent naturally. It is common to find Beaujolais at close to the 13.5 percent maximum alcohol level because of chaptalization. The addition of sugar, in an area warm enough to allow the grapes to ripen naturally, is done to compensate and give weight to wines produced from high yields in the densely planted vineyards. Because of their

**Map 6.7**  Alsace.

lighter, fresher, fruitier style the alcohol content may not be apparent. Consumers should be wary as it is easy to overindulge as the charm of these wines belies their alcohol level.

## The Wine Regions of Alsace

Alsace is a region of about 74.5 miles (120 kilometers) long and 2.5 miles (four kilometers) at its widest (see Map 6.7). The Vosges mountains protect the vineyards from the winds and moisture from the west, and the Rhine river provides a moderating influence to the east. A long, dry growing season allows the grapes to ripen slowly and develop aromatic qualities. Vines grow in a variety of soil types and the best vineyard sites face south where grapes in this cold region can benefit from the heat of the morning and afternoon sunshine.

Located in the Haut Rhin and Bas-Rhin départements, its northeast position made it susceptible to invasions by Swedish forces (1633) and repeatedly by the Germans. Although Alsace was officially part of France in 1918, the area's viticulture was not regulated by INAO until 1945, and further regulations regarding yield, ripeness levels, and label terms continue to be updated.

Alsace is the only AOC region to label wines by their grape name. Exceptions to this are Edelzwicker or "noble blend," Gentil which is a proprietary blend from the producer Hugel, and sparkling wines which are labeled Crémant d'Alsace. The latter are produced by the *méthode champenoise* and account for about 13 million bottles annually.

The minimum alcohol requirement is 8. 5 percent in Alsace, but many wines are chaptalized (see Chapter 1 on How Wine Is Made) because the region has a cold climate and has the highest-permitted yield in France, at 2642 gallons per 2.47 acres (100 hectoliters per hectare). The best growers anywhere in the world always try to curtail yield to improve quality. The 31,000 acres (12,524 hectares) of vineyards in Alsace are owned by over 9200 farmers, so there is a temptation to make the most of small holdings. Coopératives and négociants buy grapes and market about two-thirds of the wine; the balance is estate bottled.

The local wine board determines harvest dates and, as in Champagne, all wines must be bottled within the region. A term that may appear on a label is *élevé en fûts,* indicating oak aging.

The distinctive bottle used is known as *la flûte du Rhin* (flute of the Rhine). The local "Weinstub" cellars feature wine tastings with regional foods. The wine route is known not only for the wines themselves but also for the gastronomy and beauty of this area.

The wines of Alsace are usually fermented dry and have good structure. The most noble of the grape types, and the only ones permitted to bear the highest-quality designation of Grand cru are the Gewürztraminer, Pinot Gris, Muscat, and Riesling. Yield for these is lowered to 1848 gallons per acre (70 hectolitres per hectare) and the minimum alcohol is 11 for the two former and ten for the two latter. About 50 sites produce single-varietal, single-vineyard wines and the name of the cru will be on the label along with the grape name.

Some producers choose not to label wine from Grand cru sources as such but to include other label terms indicating quality, such as Réserve, or some proprietary or historic name. Examples include the Cuvée Jubilee from Hugel and the Cuvée Frédéric Emile from Trimbach. About ten percent of the vineyard acreage in Alsace has been awarded Grand cru status but, as in Burgundy, the name of an unclassified site sometimes appears on a label.

Another similarity to Burgundy is the use of the term *clos* for superior vineyards that have been enclosed by walls. These wines may be equal to or superior to wines labeled as Grand cru even if not classified as such. Some of the famous are the Clos des Capucins, Clos Gaensbroennel, Clos Saint Hune, Clos Saint Immer, Clos Saint Landelin, Clos Rebgarten, Clos de Schlossberg, Clos Saint Urbain, Clos Windsbuhl, and Clos Zissel.

The warmer vintages with sunny days that extend ripening produce two other categories of wine which by law are never chaptalized. *Vendange Tardive* means "late harvest" and produces semidry to sweet wines. *Sélection de Grains Nobles* means "selection of noble grapes." These wines are rich, full-bodied sweet rarities. Wines labeled as Sélection de Grains Nobles must be affected by the *pourriture noble (Botrytis cinerea)* and they continue to develop over a decade or two. Although these Sélection de Grains Nobles are higher-alcohol, sweeter wines, the northern climate provides good acidity for balance.

Production is around 120 million bottles annually, 95 percent of which is white. Pinot Noir is used for reds and rosés and it has increased to about 6.5 percent of acreage, giving wines with fruity aroma and taste along with good acidity. Some oak-aged reds are being made with more weight on the palate to handle stronger food preparations. Certainly the white wines made from Riesling, Gewürztraminer, and Pinot Gris are the most full-bodied examples of these varietals in the world and their style has developed along with the rich and flavorful cuisine of the region. Malolactic fermentation (see Chapter 1 on How Wine Is Made) is avoided to maintain high acid levels to balance the wines. The following white grapes are important in Alsace:

*Riesling.* The finest and the most-planted (20 percent) variety in the region. The varied soils produce wines with aromas from mineral to floral and fruity. Vines planted on lighter sandy soils yield wines that are faster maturing and lighter in body than those planted on heavier limestone soils. In Alsace's long, cool growing seasons, Riesling is known for its balance of fruit and acidity.

*Gewürztraminer.* Some prefer the distinctive spicy, floral, fruity powerful nose and taste of this grape to that of Riesling. It occupies almost as much total acreage as Riesling, even though its yield is less. Clay limestone soils that benefit Riesling also do well for Gewürztraminer. This pinkish-hued grape produces wines with more power and color than most white grapes.

Weinbach Vineyards in Alsace.

Schlumberger Vineyards in Alsace.

*Pinot Gris (Tokay d'Alsace).* Less fruity and floral than the preceding grapes with a more nutty nose, the finest examples of Pinot Gris have a scent of violets. Pinot Gris is known as the "Sultan" of Alsace because of the Turkish presence in Hungary where it originated. Legislation has been passed that makes it mandatory for the Pinot Gris name to appear on labels either alone or in conjunction with Tokay d'Alsace. The wines are very rich and full in body. Pinot Gris accounts for about five percent of total plantings.

*Muscat.* The musky floral fruit aromatics of this wine are more powerful than the body, which is often light to medium when vinified dry, with just a hint of residual sugar. The late-harvest versions though will be heavier in body. The Muscat accounts for only three percent of plantings.

**Figure 6.5** A Pinot Blanc Label.

*Sylvaner.*    Sylvaner grapes yield light-bodied fresh wines for early consumption without the intensity of the previous four. Second only to Riesling for acidity, Sylvaner accounts for about 20 percent of plantings.

*Pinot Blanc.*    Pinot Blanc (see Figure 6.5) makes dry wines with more body than Sylvaner. Pinot Auxerrois, even though it is a different grape, may be labeled Pinot Blanc or Klevner. In either case both ripen early and, combined account for 19 percent of plantings.

*Chasselas.*    Chasselas, often blended into Edelzwicker, is being replaced by the above varieties that have more acidity, structure, and flavor.

***Wine Producers of Alsace.***    Producers include: L. Beyer, A. Boxler, M. Deiss, Dopff au Moulin, Dopff et Irion, Hugel, Domaine Klipfel, M. Kreydenweiss, Kuentz Bas, M. Laugel, Jos Meyer, Meyer-Fonne, Muré-Clos St Landelin, C. Schleret, Domaine Schlumberger, P. Sparr, F. E. Trimbach, Domaine Weinbach, Domaine Zind Humbrecht. The largest co-op is Cave Vinicole Eguisheim-Wolfberger.

## The Loire Valley

The Loire is the longest river (635 miles/1022 kilometers) in France and was once connected to the Seine (see Map 6.8). Fruits, vegetables, spices, flowers, dairy products, meats and, of course, wine were transported on this important commercial route and supplier of goods to Paris. The wines were also exported to the Dutch and British. The fish and seafood from the Atlantic Ocean and the rivers contributed to the evolution of wine styles of the region. In the Loire, while still white wines dominate, sparkling wines, rosés, and light- to medium-weight reds are also produced.

The region's four Grand crus are Chenin Blanc wines with two being dry and the other two sweet. Dry wines are more in vogue and in the past three decades vineyards in the region of Anjou have replaced some Chenin Blanc with the more stylish white Muscadet or Chardonnay grapes. The Chenin Blanc, known as Pineau de la Loire, does not have the popularity of Chardonnay. Both Chenin Blanc and Sauvignon Blanc from the Loire are capable of making fine light- to medium-bodied wines with cleansing high acidity. The expansion of Muscadet, known as Melon de Bourgogne, may owe more to its price, resistance to cool temperatures, and suitability to light fare than its complexity. Those searching for rare white grapes can slake their thirst for bone dry white with the Romartin grape used at Cheverny or the Gros Plant, also known as Picpoul or Folle Blanche, from the Pays Nantais region. The Aligoté and ubiquitous Chardonnay of Burgundy are

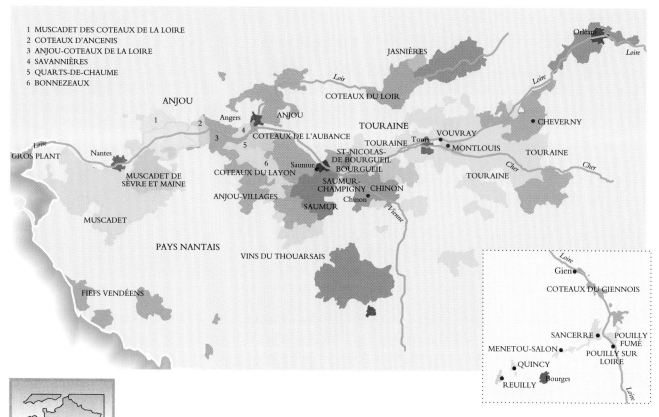

1 MUSCADET DES COTEAUX DE LA LOIRE
2 COTEAUX D'ANCENIS
3 ANJOU-COTEAUX DE LA LOIRE
4 SAVANNIÈRES
5 QUARTS-DE-CHAUME
6 BONNEZEAUX

**Map 6.8** The Loire Wine Region of France.

also present, as is the Pinot Gris, also known as Pinot Beurot, Tokay d'Alsace, and Malvoisie.

The Muscadet (Melon de Bourgogne) is the most important grape in the western portion of the region, known as the Pays Nantais. Sauvignon Blanc is the best white grape for the eastern vineyards or Upper Loire. Chenin Blanc is the best grape for the central regions of Anjou, Saumur, and Touraine, with Sauvignon Blanc second in importance. Loire white wine makers traditionally avoid malolactic or oak fermentation but as in other regions around the world some are experimenting with these techniques.

Flowering is an important time for wine makers here as there is the risk of spring frost. Over two-thirds of the crop was destroyed by frost in 1991. The beginning of the last week of June is the usual flowering time in the Loire, and when it happens earlier wine makers will think of producing sweeter wines where possible. The years 1990, 1989, and 1988 were warmer vintages which enabled wine makers to make some dessert wines, especially in the warmer subregions of Anjou and Touraine, along with dry wines.

The Cabernet Franc (Breton) is the region's most-planted red grape. It ripens well in the cool central region of the Loire where it makes medium-weight wines with some complexity. The Gamay is used for the simple, lighter-bodied wine of the central region. The Pinot Noir does best in the eastern zone or Upper Loire. Other red varieties grown in the Loire are Cabernet Sauvignon, Malbec (Cot), Pinot Noir (Auvernat Noir), Chenin Noir (Pinot d'Aunis), Pinot Meunier, and Grolleau.

A good deal of sparkling wine is made in the region, owing to the suitability of the grape types, soils, and climate, especially in cooler years.

Whether under a specific appellation or as Crémant de la Loire they are appreciated within France and widely exported.

Vins de Pays du Jardin de France is used for wines outside a declared appellation or those wines made from grapes not permitted in the appellation they are grown.

**Figure 6.6** A Muscadet Label.

# Wine Regions of the Western Loire

**Nantes.** The Nantes, or Atlantic region, in the westernmost part of the Loire, is cool and ideally suited to the Melon de Bourgogne or Muscadet grape, which ripens early and is cold hardy. Over three-quarters of Muscadet (see Figure 6.6) produced comes from the Sèvre et Maine area where the wines have more balance than the tarter examples from the Coteaux de la Loire or the simpler Muscadet area. (Muscadet is both the name of the area and the commonly used name for the grape Melon de Bourgogne.) *Sur lie* is a popular technique of leaving the wine on its lees until it is ready to be bottled without racking it to another container, which preserves the freshness of the wine and gives a prickly quality, which is most apparent when the wine is young. Muscadet has been successfully exported as a good apéritif or first-course wine, particularly with oysters or simple appetizers. A maximum alcohol level of 12.3 percent is set for Muscadet to maintain a lighter character and discourage overchaptalization of this popular wine. The Gros Plant grape is also made sur lie and this wine shares a similar light-bodied, dry style with the edge for aromatics going to Muscadet and green tart acidic tastes to the Gros Plant. Below AOC are the VDQS wines which include dry reds, rosés, and whites from Fiefs Vendéens and Coteaux D'Ancenis regions. The latter is known mostly for Gamay wines and varietal labeling.

# Wine Regions of the Central Loire

The Central Loire is divided into two provinces; Anjou and Saumur will be covered first and then the Touraine region will be explored.

**Anjou and Saumur.** The area is going through a shift in plantings and styles. As the popularity of rosés and sweet white wines declines, vignerons are emphasizing drier whites and reds. White wines dominate production near the Layon River while more reds and sparkling wines are produced in Saumur.

Anjou and Saumur are the basic appellations for dry whites, rosés, and reds. Anjou Villages are red wines from Cabernet Franc and Cabernet Sauvignon. Rosé d'Anjou is a semisweet wine made from the tart, high-yielding Grolleau grape. Cabernet de Saumur and Cabernet d'Anjou are dry or sweet rosés and are superior to the simple Anjou appellation rosés.

*Savennières.* The high quality of Savennières is due to Chenin Blanc grown on schistous slate soil, with some volcanic rocks. Two Grand cru whites, Château de La Roche-aux-Moines and Coulée de Serrant, are produced here as are many other fine wines. Savennières wines need time to develop balance between the aggressive acids and the fruit flavors. After a half dozen years the wines begin to display floral, honey, mineral, and spicy qualities in the bouquet and complex and intense flavors on the palate. The wines can improve for decades and are the finest examples of dry Chenin Blanc made.

*Coteaux du Layon.* These are Chenin Blanc-based semisweet to sweet wines. The name of the best communes may be added to Coteaux du Layon wines. They are Beaulieu sur Layon, Chaume, Faye-D'Anjou, Rablay du Layon, Rochefort sur Loire, St.-Aubin de Luigné, and St. Lambert du Lattay. Moulin Touchais is a company that bottles its wines under the Coteaux du Layon appellation for domestic use and as AOC Anjou for export. These wines are very rich in flavor and can live for decades. The wines gain in color and complexity in the bottle. The Coteaux du Layon produces some of the finest dessert wines in France. Their high acidity balances their sweetness and the bouquets evolve over ten or 20 years.

*Bonnezaux and Quarts de Chaume.* These are two Grand cru appellations within the Coteaux du Layon. They are the finest examples of the floral-honeyed nose and luscious sweetness balanced with acidity that the Chenin Blanc can produce with the right soil, climate, and low yields. Both are over 13 percent alcohol and may be consumed young but will repay cellaring for over a decade. Quarts de Chaume's character is partially related to a high percentage of iron in the soil. The appellation has the lowest permitted yield in the nation, set at 580 gallons (223 hectoliters) per 2.47 acres (one hectare).

The sweet wines of the Loire rival those of Bordeaux, although the noble rot forms more regularly in the warmer region of Sauternes than in the cooler, more northerly Loire. The sweet wines of the Loire are most often bottled young and allowed to mature in the bottle, while Sauternes are matured in cask.

*Coteaux de L'Aubance.* Semisweet and sweet wines are produced from the Chenin Blanc grown on the banks of the Aubance river. The dry still whites, reds, and rosés made are sold under the broad Anjou appellation.

*Saumur-Champigny.* Saumur-Champigny, the finest red of the area, is made from Cabernet Franc grown on south-facing slopes with chalky limestone soil. The wine can age for a decade or be consumed after a couple of years.

*Crémant de la Loire, Saumur Mousseux, and Anjou Mousseux.* These are dry white or rosé sparkling wines made by the Champagne method.

Dry sparkling and still wines are made as the VDQS Vins du Thouarsais with Chenin Blanc used for whites; Cabernet Sauvignon, Cabernet Franc, and Gamay are the red grapes planted.

A portion of the dry Rosé de Loire, which must be a minimum of 30 percent Cabernet, is produced here as is some of the Rosé d'Anjou Pétillant which has a light effervescence.

*Touraine.* This fertile region consists of about 28,400 acres (11,360 hectares) and is referred to as the "Garden of France." The Sauvignon Blanc is the most widely planted white grape here, perhaps because it ripens before the Chenin Blanc. Chenin Blanc is used for both still and sparkling wines. Gamay is the most important red grape, followed by the Cabernet Franc and Cot (Malbec).

Still wines with the regional Touraine appellation may bear the name of the grape as well. Touraine Mousseux sparkling wine is made by the Champagne method as are the Crémant de la Loire and the more specific Vouvray Mousseux and Montlouis Mousseux. These sparklers are good value alternatives to Champagne.

*Bourgueil and Chinon.* These are the two best reds of the region and are made from Cabernet Franc with some Cabernet Sauvignon. The most powerful versions are medium- to full-bodied and are produced from south-facing slopes on volcanic clay limestone "tufa" subsoil with some gravel and clay on top. A Chinon from a top producer, such as Charles Joguet, will improve over a decade. Or, just as a Saumur-Champigny, these Loire reds offer bright red berry fruit and wild flowers in the aroma along with good fruit and acidity on the palate when drunk young.

*Saint-Nicolas-de-Bourgueil.* This is a similar-style red wine appellation to that in the northwest of Bourgueil. Rosés are also made in these Loire appellations.

*Vouvray.* Vouvray, a Chenin Blanc grown by the right bank of the Loire, may be either still or sparkling, in a range of sweetness that depends on how long and warm the season is. The terms used are *moelleux* for sweet, *demi-sec* for semidry, and *sec* for dry. The *pourriture noble (Botrytis cinerea)* is not common in the area but those vintages, such as 1945 or 1955 when it was widespread, produce the most luscious long-lived examples.

*Montlouis.* This area is across the river from Vouvray and was granted its own appellation in 1938. Before that, the wines were sold as Vouvray. The wines are similar, but slightly lighter and may be drunk younger.

*Jasnières.* Under 200,000 bottles of dry wines, with high acidity produced from low yields, are made annually. These Chenin Blanc wines offer a range of smells from floral, quince, and melon to mineral that are part of their appeal. The town of Jasnières is located close to the Loir River, a tributary of the Loire River, and is a separate appellation within the Coteaux du Loir.

*Coteaux du Loir.* Coteaux du Loir produces about the same amount as Jasnières but makes more reds and rosés for early consumption than white wines. The red grapes used include Pineau D'Aunis which is a Chenin Noir, Cabernet Franc, and Cot, the local name for Malbec.

*Cheverny.* An appellation since 1993, Cheverny produces sparkling, rosés, reds, and whites best drunk young. The white grapes include Chenin Blanc, Sauvignon Blanc, Chardonnay, or the local variety Romartin. These crisp wines may include a varietal name on the label.

A Sauvignon Blanc Vineyard in Pouilly-
sur-Loire.

## Wine Regions of the Upper Loire

Many restaurateurs, chefs, and owners believe Sauvignon Blanc is a better match for a wider variety of foods than Chardonnay. Sauvignon Blancs are typically more tart than Chardonnay wines and their higher acidity cleanses the palate (see Chapter 13 on Wine and Food). Sauvignon Blanc wines of the Loire are the benchmark style by which others are judged. These wines have mineral, herbal, and gooseberry aromas, medium weight on the palate, and explosive acidity. Pouilly-Fuissé is a popular Chardonnay-based wine from Mâcon, Burgundy. Here in the Loire, Pouilly-Fumé is one of the finest examples of Sauvignon Blanc. Confused by the similar-sounding names? There also exists Pouilly-sur-Loire grown in the same region as Pouilly-Fumé, but using the Chasselas grape to produce a simpler, less-tart wine.

*Pouilly-Fumé.* Fifteen hundred acres (600 hectares) of Sauvignon Blanc vines are planted in mostly limestone-based soils in the Pouilly-Fumé appelation. The grape musts are fermented in stainless steel or old oak barrels. The largest estate is the 128-acre (51.2-hectare) Château de Nozet which produces a high-quality, more-expensive product, "Baron L," in the best vintages. Another producer, Didier Dageneau, also produces fine wines which, as the Baron L, may improve with some cellaring but are not as age worthy as Savennières. Most wines of the region should be drunk from two to five years from the vintage. The Sauvignon Blanc grape is known as Blanc Fumé because of its smoky or flint-like aromas when grown in the area. This inspired Robert Mondavi to begin labeling his Napa Valley Sauvignon Blanc wines as Fumé Blanc and many other American wineries have adopted the name.

*Sancerre.*  Sancerre is a larger area than Pouilly-Fumé with 4000 acres (1600 hectares) in 14 communes, and more variations in its soil types. The whites are similar in style to Pouilly-Fumé but occasionally a sweet *vendange tardive* (late harvest) is made. Sancerre also produces dry light-bodied reds and rosés from Pinot Noir under its appellation. Most Sancerre wines are best drunk young within three years while the fruit and acidity are still lively.

*Quincy.*  Quincy is a dry Sauvignon Blanc with herbaceous and gooseberry aromas. The vineyards are on the banks of the Cher, a tributary of the Loire.

*Ménétou-Salon.*  Ménétou-Salon offers dry whites, rosés, and reds from Sauvignon Blanc and Pinot Noir. The wines are similar in style to Sancerre and may be found at a lower price as they are not as well known.

*Reuilly.*  Reuilly has a similar limestone-based soil as Ménétou-Salon. Sauvignon Blanc, Pinot Noir, and a small amount of Pinot Gris are used to produce dry white, rosé, and red wines.

**VDQS Wines of the Loire.**  VDQS wines of good value include Côtes Roannaises, Châteaumeillant, Côtes de Gien, Côtes D'Auvergne, Vins de L'Orléanais, Côtes de Forez, and Saint Pourçain Sur Sioule. The Sauvignon and Chenin Blancs are used along with Burgundy varietals such as Chardonnay, Aligoté, and Tressalier (Sacy) for whites. Gamay is the major grape for red wines while some Pinot Noir is used for rosés and reds.

**Wine Producers of the Loire Valley.**  Loire producers include Ackerman-Laurance, Aubert, G. Audebert, Domaine des Baumard, Donatien Bahuaud, Château de Belle Rive, Bouvet Ladubay, M. Brédif, Couly-Dutheil, Dageneau, Delaporte, Château de Fesles, Domaine Filliatreau, Drouët, Druet, G. Huet, Charles Joguet, Joly (Coulée de Serrant), Lamé-Delille-Boucard, Domaine de l'Hyvernière, Mardon, Masson-Blondelet, Louis Métaireau, Meunier-Lapha, Château Moncontour, Marquis de Goulaine, Monmousseau, Moulin Touchais, Château de Nozet-Ladoucette, H. Pellé, Pipet, Prince Poniatowski, M. Redde, Remy-Pannier, Reverdy, Château de la Roche aux Moines.

## Jura and Savoie

These mountainous regions are located east of Burgundy. Their small amount of wines produced are seldom exported, perhaps because they are well appreciated by the locals, perhaps because of confusion over the different grape types and styles produced. Varietal labeled wines are increasing. The regions produce more white and sparkling wines with some rosés and reds produced as well as the specialties *vin jaune* or *vins jaunes* and *vins de paille.*

# Jura

In Jura, the vines are planted on slopes usually facing south or southeast to get maximum sunshine. The cold winters and high altitude (800 to 1600 feet/244 to 488 meters) are ameliorated by generally dry and warm autumns, which allow the grapes to ripen.

The Savagnin, the main white grape, is a late-ripening variety that can contribute a nutty nose and medium- to full-weight to a wine. The Poulsard and Trousseau are the indigenous red grapes most used. The Poulsard is a thin-skinned grape sensitive to problems in the vineyards such as *coulure* (grape drop after flowering) and spring frost as it is an early bloomer. It also oxidizes, or loses color, easily. However, the aromatics of the grape and its ability to be used for blending and to produce rosés have maintained its importance. The Trousseau gives a darker color and can achieve high sugar levels and yields. The thick-skinned grape is the same as the Bastardo of the Douro in Portugal, a much warmer growing region, and it is being replaced by the Pinot Noir which does well in cooler climates. As the Jura roughly runs parallel to Burgundy, Pinot Noir and Chardonnay, the finest grapes of that region are found in the Jura as well. Chardonnay now accounts for 45 percent of the region's acreage. The Jura wines include:

*Vin Jaune.*   Vin jaune (yellow wine) is made from late-harvested Savagnin grapes. The fermented wine spends at least six years in oak, with air contact, before it is released. As in Jerez, Spain, the *flor* yeast provides a protective layer on the surface of the wine so it does not brown (see Chapter 8 on Spain). The typical nutty smell of oxidation evident in a Sherry is also present in these wines, and their flavor has been compared to that of a fino Sherry. While finos are best drunk young, vins jaunes can last for decades. *Clavelin* is the local name for the squat bottles used for vins jaunes.

*Château Chalon.*   This appellation is comprised of four communes producing vin jaune. It is also the name of a town. The permitted yield is a low 792 gallons per 2.47 acres (30 hectoliters per hectare).

*L'Étoile.*   The appellation produces dry white and vin jaune from Savagnin and Chardonnay. Poulsard is permitted but rarely used.

*Vins de Paille.*   Vins de Paille (straw wines) are another specialty of the area. The grapes are dried on straw mats or hung until they lose some of their water content, as in the *Passito* system in Italy (see Chapter 7 on Italy). The loss of liquids and concentration of sugars in the grape results in a dark-colored, luscious dessert wine with scents of dried fruits and nuts. Vins de Paille are rare and expensive and most are sold in half bottles.

*Arbois.*   The Arbois is an appellation within the Côtes du Jura. Production includes a range of styles from dry to sweet whites, rosés, light, medium, and heavy reds as well as the paille and jaune wines.

***Côtes de Jura.*** A similar range of wines as the Arbois appellation are made as well as a Mousseux (sparkling wine).

The Arbois and Côtes de Jura produce vins gris (gray wines) and vins corail (coral wines) which are both dry rosés with good structure. The color and body style may be attributed to extended skin contact with the juice. The dry reds are light cherry in color and medium bodied. The whites, from Savagnin, Chardonnay, and Pinot Blanc grapes, tend to have a deep color and are well rounded

# Savoie

Savoie's climate is affected by its many mountains and lakes. The area produces 70 percent white wine. As in Jura, vines are grown on slopes at high altitudes with southerly exposures. The Jacquère is the most planted white grape and, like the Savagnin of the Jura, it is a late ripener. The grape tends to produce light-bodied dry white wines with a smoky scent. The lower-yielding Roussette, also known as Altesse, is another late ripener. It produces wines with a spicy aroma that are richer and fuller than those from the Jacquère or the third important white grape, Chasselas.

***Vins de Savoie.*** Vins de Savoie include white, sparkling, rosé, and red styles, and the 17 cru communes add their names to the label. In that case, lower yields and higher minimum alcohol level are required. The principal red grapes include the Burgundian Pinot Noir and Gamay as well as the Mondeuse. The Mondeuse adds color, weight, and peppery flavors to a blend. Some wines may be barrel fermented. Wines made with more Gamay and up to 20 percent white grapes are served cool as a Beaujolais nouveau is. Sparkling wines are made by the *méthode champenoise* using local and Burgundian varieties. The whites are typified as being dry with good fruit concentration and refreshing acidity.

***Seyssel.*** Seyssel, the first appellation of the region, covers Mousseux (sparkling) and white wines. The vineyards are on the banks of the Rhône River. The Molette, a high-acid white grape, is the dominant grape for the Mousseux, with some Altesse blended in. Seyssel Mousseux is made by the Champagne method and is the smallest appellation for sparkling wine in the nation. The Roussette de Seyssel dry white is distinguished by floral scents and good acidity and is meant to be drunk young.

***Roussette de Savoie.*** The Roussette de Savoie is pure Roussette only when the names of the communes Frangy, Monterminod, Monthoux, or Marestel are on a label. Otherwise the wines may legally have as much as 50 percent Chardonnay blended with the Roussette.

***Crépy.*** Chasselas vines are planted south of Lake Geneva to produce light-bodied dry whites which may have a hint of effervescence when bottled off the lees.

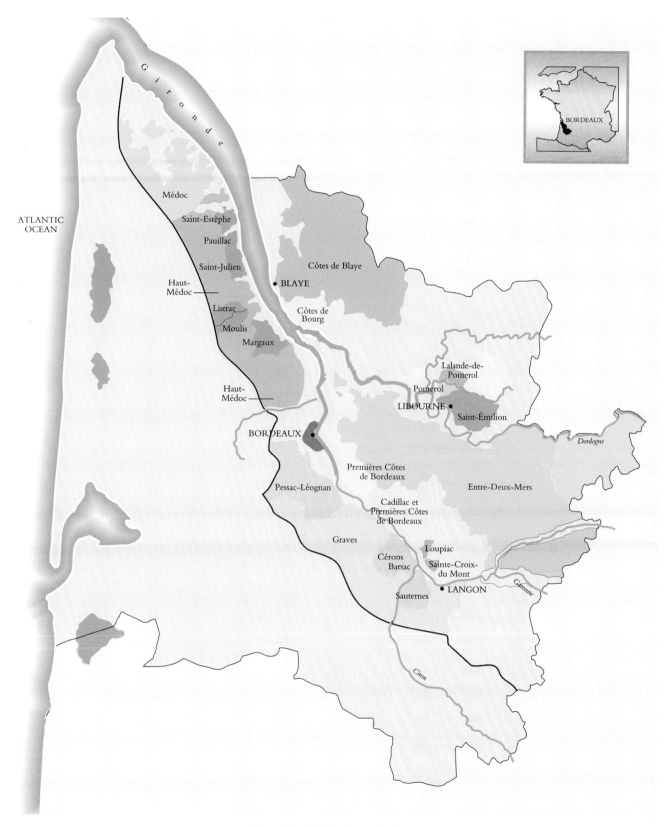

ATLANTIC
OCEAN

*Gironde*

Médoc

Saint-Estèphe

Pauillac

Saint-Julien

Haut-Médoc

Listrac

Moulis

Margaux

Haut-Médoc

BORDEAUX

Pessac-Léognan

Graves

Cérons
Barsac

Sauternes

Côtes de Blaye

BLAYE

Côtes de
Bourg

Lalande-de-
Pomerol

Pomerol

LIBOURNE

Saint-Émilion

*Dordogne*

Premières Côtes
de Bordeaux

Entre-Deux-Mers

Cadillac et
Premières Côtes
de Bordeaux

Loupiac

Sainte-Croix-
du Mont

LANGON

*Garonne*

*Ciron*

BORDEAUX

**Map 6.9**   The Bordeaux Region.

# Bordeaux

***Introduction.*** The region of Bordeaux (see Map 6.9), as the name implies, is bordered by waters, which moderate the extremes of temperatures. In addition, the Gulf Stream-warmed Atlantic Ocean and the Gironde, Garonne, and Dordogne Rivers have been the conduits by which Bordeaux wines have traveled to foreign markets. Those markets helped establish the region as the largest fine wine-making area in the world.

Bordeaux has built its reputation on its red wines and the most famous regions within it exclusively for red wine production are Médoc, St-Émilion, and Pomerol. The Graves region produces both dry red and dry white wines while the Sauternes region is exclusively for sweet wines. These appellations and smaller zones within their boundaries as well as the other regions of Bordeaux will be covered in more detail later in this chapter.

The authorized grape types for red Bordeaux are the Cabernet Sauvignon, Merlot, Cabernet Franc, Malbec, Carmenère, and Petit Verdot. The authorized white grapes are the Sauvignon Blanc, Sémillon, Muscadelle, with up to 30 percent of Merlot Blanc, Ondenc, Mauzac, Colombard, and Ugni Blanc for some regional wines. Characteristics of these are found in Chapter 2 on Wine Grapes.

The red grape Carmenère is less astringent than the Cabernets but is used sometimes because it contributes color. It is used for regular Bordeaux and for Médoc and St-Émilion wines. The Malbec, also known as Cot or Pressac, is used for regional Bordeaux and in the right bank areas of St-Émilion and Pomerol to add both color and body. The Petit Verdot is a late-ripening grape with high acidity and is used for regional Bordeaux as well as in the left bank regions of Médoc and Graves.

The Muscadelle is third in white plantings and there are 4940 acres (2000 hectares). Muscadelle gives high yields as well as fruity flavors and floral aromatics to blends. It is more often used for the semisweet and sweet wines of Bordeaux than the dry whites. The other minor grapes are used because of their resistance to vineyard problems and their high yields rather than for contributing specific attributes to a finer wine.

Cabernet Sauvignon may be the first grape one thinks of when discussing red Bordeaux, but Merlot plantings total 98,800 acres (40,000 hectares) compared to Cabernet Sauvignon's 61,750 acres (25,000 hectares). There are 32,110 acres (13,000 hectares) of the third most important variety, Cabernet Franc.

Bordeaux wines are, for the most part, blended. Generally speaking, the Cabernet Sauvignon is the dominant grape on the left bank of the Gironde River, in the Médoc and Graves. St-Émilion and Pomerol wines are on the right bank of the Gironde River, and are made from mostly Merlot and Cabernet Franc.

The Sauvignon Blanc (11,115 acres/4500 hectares) is the dominant grape for the best dry white wines. Sémillon (29,640 acres/12,000 hectares) is the most important grape for sweet whites. The different varietals ripen and are harvested at different times and are then fermented separately. The

*assemblage* is the blending of the different grapes from different parcels of land. This takes place around the end of December. In dry blends Sémillon gives structure while Sauvignon Blanc provides acidity for sweet wines.

The Bordeaux appellation produces an average of 660 million bottles a year from 283,395 acres (113,356 hectares) of vines. Red wine production is triple that of the white wines and sparkling, rosé, and brandy are made in the region as well. The 54 appellations of Bordeaux supply about a quarter of the national AOC output. The business of Bordeaux wine involves 60,000 people, including over 13,000 "vignerons" farmers (5000 of them belong to one of the 60 coopératives), 400 *négociants,* and 150 *courtiers.* The courtier acts as an intermediary between sellers of wine and the buyers and is not involved in the production or storing of wine before shipping.

Coopératives range in size from the 60,000-case Cave Coopérative La Rose Pauillac to the six-million-case Sovicop Producta. Cooperatives and négociants are the primary producers of regional wines. Regional wine labels, such as Bordeaux, one of its subregions Médoc, or a commune in the Médoc such as Pauillac may also feature a prominent brand name, such as the popular Mouton Cadet, in addition to the regional name.

A Château wine on a label indicates both the brand name of the product and the producer. During the assemblage the quality of the individual barrels is assessed. Top châteaux will decide which barrels are of a high enough caliber to be labeled with the name of the château and which are sold under a secondary label or just as regional wines. Another option open to the château owners is to sell the wine off to négociants.

The words *mise en bouteilles au château* on a label indicate the wine was bottled on the property rather than being shipped by cask to be stored and bottled by a négociant later. *Mise en bouteilles dans nos caves* indicates "bottled in our cellars," and is wine bottled by a négociant or coopérative.

Château wines offer the most complexity and fetch the highest prices. Over 9,000 châteaux in Bordeaux produce wines in different styles and price ranges. Of these, only a small percent have been granted the status of *Grand cru.* Unlike Burgundy, where the specific vineyard site and *terroir* was the basis for *Premier* or *Grand cru* status, here it is the courtiers, négociants, and the wine's popularity and prices that determined which château received ranking. However, the best châteaux in Bordeaux have also gained their accolades because of their superior locations. Over time, châteaux classified at one level have lost or added vineyard acreage, perhaps from a château at a lower level, without losing their ranking. Debates continue over the merits of the ranking system yet consumers are protected against faulty wines by the control measures of INAO and accredited tasting panels who sample all wines before they may be sold.

### History of Bordeaux.

Evidence of viticulture in Bordeaux dates from the first century A.D. Romans, who also brought new vines, dubbed the region's wines *"vinum clarum"* because of their light and clear appearance. The red wines resembled a dark rosé rather than the opaque black cherry-color style associated with the region today. Whites and reds were often blended together and the skin contact time was short to produce the *clairet,* or light, style. The British used the term *claret* to refer to red Bordeaux. The 1152

marriage of Eleanor of Aquitaine from the southwest (Gascony) and Henri of Anjou from the northwest was a powerful alliance. Henri became the first Plantagenet king of England. Their wealth and Britain's large fleet of ships soon allowed the claret of Gascony to become the preferred wine throughout the British Isles. French farmers delivered barrels of wine to Irish, Scottish, Welsh, and British businessman who shipped them first from the Atlantic coast port of La Rochelle and then from the river port of Bordeaux to Britain. Laws stipulating that Bordeaux wines be shipped before those of other regions and be excluded from the *Grand Coutume* tax further helped establish Bordeaux wine exports to England. The British affection for claret wines continued until their expulsion from Bordeaux in 1453.

The Dutch were the next powerful influence on the development of Bordeaux. There was a general expansion of new vineyard areas, as the Dutch had need for more than high-quality claret. With seafood a major part of the Dutch diet, many of the new plantings were of white varieties that were used to make both dry and sweet table wines as well as the base wine for brandies. In the fifteenth century, the Dutch navy was the largest in Europe, and was used to transport the different styles and quality levels of wines from Bordeaux to the ports of northern Europe. In the seventeenth century the marshy Médoc region was dredged and made arable by Dutch engineers. The Médoc, and its châteaux, were destined to become the most-renowned wines of Bordeaux.

Most exports were sold as simple Bordeaux. The use of a specific château name, or the notion of wine as a valuable investment that would increase in complexity, was the next development. In 1666 the owner of Chateau O'Brian (today Chateau Haut-Brion in the Graves), Monsieur de Pontac, sent his son to London to open a restaurant to sell their wine. The maneuver was a success and rekindled Britain's love of claret. Unfortunately in 1688 King William of Orange, who preferred the heavier wines of Spain and Portugal, increased taxes on French wines and they became too costly for most of Great Britain's consumers.

Jacques de Ségur was the first major wine grower around the town of Pauillac in the Médoc. His son Marquis Nicholas Alexandre de Ségur was the first president of the parliament of Bordeaux. The wealthy owner of Châteaux Lafite, Latour, and Calon was referred to as "Prince des Vignes" (Prince of Vines). During the eighteenth century, attempts were made to elevate the wines by using the superior grape varieties and lowering yields. Glass bottles and cork stoppers were introduced to protect wines from oxidation while being stored in cellars. Négociants from Ireland, England, Holland, and other nations set up shop on the Quai des Chartrons on the Garonne River where they used *chais* to store the wines. The négociants did not deal exclusively with wine but prospered from other exports and imports as well. Wine, weapons, and other goods were traded in Africa for slaves, who were shipped to the West Indies to harvest goods destined for Europe. The wealth from international trade allowed the city to expand and build fine mansions, theaters, restaurants, and hotels. Classifications of the châteaux, such as the one published by the Tasset-Lawton firm, were used to recognize the producers achieving a higher-quality product than the fresh clarets.

A level of sophisticated lifestyle in Bordeaux led by the courtiers, négociants, château owners, and nobility created an equally sophisticated level of communication used to describe the character of the wines and their uses at the table with various foods. By the 1790s, the finest wines were labeled with the name of the château on the bottle and were made in a heavier style that would benefit from cellaring. The French Revolution and subsequent Napoléonic Wars slowed the expansion of the Bordeaux trade.

Classifications by Jullien in 1816 and 1822 preceded the *syndicat des courtiers* definitive rating of châteaux in 1855 still used today. The Médoc was classified and the aforementioned Graves wine Château Haut-Brion, because of its price and popularity, could not be excluded. The five communes of Sauternes were also classified. Critics of the system argue that the classification is antiquated, but, with the exception of elevating Château Mouton Rothschild in 1973, the Bordelais have resisted change.

The British market boomed again because of the lowering of taxes by the 1860 Anglo-French Treaty negotiated by the British Chancellor of the Exchequer William Gladstone. The latter half of the nineteenth century was a difficult period for the Bordelais as *oidium,* a powdery mildew, and then the louse *phylloxera vastatrix,* destroyed most of the vines. Wines from the North African colonies were brought in to try to keep the wine business afloat and many of the Bordelais tried to make up for their losses by overproducing from the healthy vines remaining. The quality of the wines and Bordeaux's image suffered. The creation of governmental regulatory boards to control aspects of production from vineyards to the chais of the châteaux restored the quality and the reputation of Bordeaux wines. The world wars took their toll on the business of Bordeux, and sales fell. During the 1950s the regions of Graves and St-Émilion were officially classified and the importance of the latter on the export market increased. The winter of 1956 was so cold it devastated about a quarter of the Médoc vineyards, a third of the vineyards of the Graves, and over 85 percent of the St-Émilion vines were lost. During the next decade, the varieties of clones planted and the selection of how much wine from the young vines could be included in the blend for the fine wines led to shifts in style among the châteaux. Both the rootstocks and clones used for replanting since the terrible frost of 1956 were chosen by conscientious producers to improve quality rather than quantity. Those estates using a higher proportion of young vines made wines with less concentration. During the 1960s, North America became an important export market. Baron Phillipe de Rothschild's regional Bordeaux, Mouton Cadet, led the way in sales and Ab Simon of Châteaux and Estates (Seagram's fine wine division) was a major figure in the importation and promotion of the Château wines.

The 1960s in Bordeaux was a period of replanting, expanding markets, and rising prices. In the 1970s the high prices for lesser vintages such as 1972, 1973, and 1974 finally met consumer resistance. The 1980s produced many great vintages and the lighter 1980, 1984, and 1987 vintages provided useful wines that were priced lower. Nineteen-ninety was one of the hottest years ever in Bordeaux and with a dry August, produced a rich, age-worthy vintage. 1991 was a disaster for the right bank areas of St-Émilion and

Pomerol because of frost. The left bank of Médoc and Graves made some decent light wines. The 1992 and 1993 wines were also lighter vintages not suitable for aging. If the Bordelais keep yields and prices down these wines will find a place on the market.

The volume of Bordeaux wine sales increased by 55 percent over the dozen years between 1981 and 1993. The red wines of Bordeaux remain popular in America but sales of white wine have plummeted. The Conseil Interprofesionnel du Vin de Bordeaux spent about $4 million (22 million francs) from 1990 to 1993 promoting the white wines of the region, yet sales lag behind 1988 and 1989 figures by 40 percent. The message has been received by the wine makers as well. There are some white wines of the top châteaux that have complexity, power, and the ability to age, but the majority of white wines produced today are in a fresh, light, dry style without the oxidation, residual sugar, or overuse of oak that was evident in some past examples. Another positive effort has been to promote a more casual approach to these lighter whites and utilize them as an apéritif or with ethnic foods.

Négociants have lowered some prices to generate cash flow and to compete with the new world wines and those of Eastern Europe. Another ploy is to provide varietal information for markets, such as the United States, where customers shop by grape type. Tags hung from the necks of bottles will allow Americans to know that the Médoc they are considering is mostly Cabernet Sauvignon while the St-Émilion next to it is primarily made from Merlot. In the vineyards, chais, and the marketplace, the Bordelais are responding to international feedback from sales representatives and consumers. Exports in 1993–94 reached 20 million cases, recovering from previous declines and demonstrating the efficacy of these programs.

***Wine Making in Bordeaux.*** Bordelais select and vinify separately the grape varieties, from various plots of land and pressings. Long, cool fermentation in stainless steel vats produces the charming, fresh style of dry white wines. A more complex age-worthy white results from the use of oak. Both styles benefit from macerating grape skins before fermentation to increase the wine's aromatics. Bordeaux white wines range from fresh non-oaked dry Entre-Deux-Mers to sweet, extended wood-aged Sauternes.

Today, reds as well as whites may be fermented in stainless steel vats. Château Haut-Brion was the first to install them for better control of fermentation temperatures and many have followed suit. The fermentation of the red wines will last up to ten days during which the juice is often pumped up and over the cap to extract more color and tannin in the wine. Tannin is also increased during a *cuvaison* period after fermentation when the wine is left in contact with the skins for one to two and a half weeks. The top châteaux may use brand new oak barrels each year, giving the wine even more intensity from wood tannins. The classified top-quality red wines often spend 18 to 24 months in oak before being bottled.

Red press wine may be added to the regular free-run wine to provide more color, flavor, and tannin. In warm years with good fruit the decision to use vin de presse adds weight and longevity to the wine but can also make a wine tough and unapproachable in its youth. A vacuum-like machine used to concentrate the juice before fermentation was used by the Premier Grand cru Château Lafite Rothschild in the 1992 vintage. This *concentrateur* may spread in popularity and replace the *saignée* ("bleeding") method of removing some of the liquid from the juice and skins to concentrate color, fruit, and tannins. The rain-affected 1992, 1993, and 1994 vintages provide the opportunity to compare the benefits of the concentrateur versus the saignée method. Wine makers are not permitted to chaptalize if they use a concentrateur.

## The Wines of Bordeaux

Wines are labeled by location with the individual château as the smallest source for wines. An example is Château Latour. It is in the commune of Pauillac, in the Haut Médoc portion of the Médoc, in the region of Bordeaux.

The classified château wines generate the most excitement and the highest prices but it is the regional wines that generate the most volume and these will be covered first.

*Bordeaux.* Bordeaux, the most general appellation, is required to contain between 9.5 and 12.5 percent alcohol for reds and rosés. Dry whites must contain 9.5 to 13 percent, with under 0.14 ounces (four grams) of sugar per 0.264 gallons (liter) to be labeled *Bordeaux Sec.* Whites with over 0.14 ounces (four grams) of sugar and between 10.5 and 13.5 percent alcohol are under the Bordeaux appellation. Yield is a maximum of 1452 gallons per 2.47 acres (55 hectoliters per hectare) for reds or rosés and 1716 per 2.47 acres (65 hectoliters per hectare) for whites. *Bordeaux Mousseux* or *Crémant de Bordeaux* are sparkling wines made by the Champagne method. *Bordeaux Clairet* falls somewhere between a rosé and a light red and, because of lower tannins, can be served lightly chilled.

*Bordeaux Supérieur.* Bordeaux Supérieur has 0.5 percent higher minimum alcohol, lower yields, and excludes the subsidiary grape types that could make up to as much as 30 percent of simple Bordeaux appellation whites. Bordeaux Supérieur may be followed by a subregion. A red example would be the Merlot-dominated reds of Bordeaux Supérieur *Côtes de Castillon* and Bordeaux Supérieur *Côtes de Francs.* Sweet white examples of Bordeaux Supérieur subregions are the *Loupiac, Cérons,* and *Sainte Croix de Mont* areas.

*Premières Côtes de Bordeaux.* The southern portion of the *Premières Côtes de Bordeaux* is also known for sweet wines which may be labeled with the area Cadillac. The Premières Côtes de Bordeaux is 37 miles (60 kilometers) long and the northern part of the appellation is planted with mostly red grapes.

*Bourg and Blaye.* North of the Premières Côtes de Bordeaux, still on the east side of the Garonne, are the regions of *Bourg* and *Blaye,* where 90 percent of the wines are red. The *Blaye* and *Côtes de Blaye* appellations are used mostly for white wines but the *Premières Côtes de Blaye,* with 0.5 percent more alcohol and made from only the classic grapes, produces aromatic, medium-weight reds. Merlot dominates the red vineyards while Sauvignon Blanc the whites. The Bourg has heavier soils and more gravel than Blaye, and the resulting Merlot-dominated wines have more force. Some whites, both dry and sweet, are made, and the *Côtes de Bourg* appellation is used for both reds and dry whites.

*Entre-Deux-Mers.* The *Entre-Deux-Mers* ("between two seas") appellation produces only dry whites. These cool-fermented crisp, light- to medium-bodied wines from clay and gravel-based soils can be drunk young and are often drunk with a first course or local seafood.

*Graves de Vayres.* The *Graves de Vayres,* to the north of Entre-Deux-Mers, makes both whites and light reds.

*Néac, Lalande-de-Pomerol, and Fronsac.* Farther north still, across the Dordogne River near the town of Libourne, are the red wine areas of *Néac, Lalande-de-Pomerol,* and *Fronsac* that also use Merlot as the principal grape, along with Cabernet Franc.

*Canon-Fronsac.* The *Canon-Fronsac* subregion produces age-worthy wines with more color, body, and complexity than most Fronsac, but both offer good value.

The wines of Bordeaux covered thus far offer the consumer an alternative to the more renowned Bordeaux regions and their exalted chateaux. In the remainder of this section, we survey the most respected regions of Bordeaux and their best-known châteaux. Throughout the following communes the authors have identified cru bourgeois–classified chateaux which provide the traditional flavors of each commune at affordable prices.

**Médoc.** Medio Acquae, the area "between the waters" of the Atlantic Ocean and the Giron de Estuary, was an area the Romans considered too marshy to be useful. Today pine forests protect the 49.6-mile (80-kilometer) stretch of vineyards from the winds. Rainfall is about 34.5 inches (875 millimeters) a year and frost is rare. Warm years with too much moisture can cause problems such as gray rot, to which the Merlot grape is particularly vulnerable. The years with warm dry Augusts usually produce the best vintages for laying down to develop. In Médoc they say "Aout fait le mout" ("August makes the ripeness"), meaning that the warmth of August ripens the grapes for harvest, which most often takes place from the end of September to the beginning of October.

Cabernet Sauvignon is the most important grape of the Médoc because of the well-drained soils with more gravel and rocks than clay. It ripens well and produces wines that are more austere or reserved than opulent rich examples from the new world (see Chapter 4 on North America). These Médoc reds have a track record of warranting cellar time to mature and reveal their complexities and grace. The Merlot, with its high sugar content, thinner skin, forward fruit flavors, and low acidity, is also important but is prone to problems here, not only of gray rot but also of frost damage and coulure. Coulure is when the grapes fall off the vine just after flowering. It usually occurs because of cold temperatures or too much rain during the flowering period. The Cabernet Franc is prized for the fragrance it gives and the Petit Verdot for color and tannins.

The *Haut-Médoc* subregion is superior to the Médoc, the simplest regional designation, and extends from the town of St.-Seurin-de-Cardoune south to Blanquefort. The appellation includes 15 communes. Of these the ones situated closer to the river, such as Macau or Blanquefort, have more gravel and alluvial soil, producing more elegant wine because of better drainage of the vineyards. The Médoc saying is "Les meilleures vignes regardent la rivière" which translates as "the best vines see the river." Saint Sauveur and Saint Laurent du Médoc are two communes farther inland that produce sturdier reds.

The six communes most respected in the Haut-Médoc often label wines under their own names which are from north to south, *St-Estèphe, Pauillac, St. Julien, Listrac, Moulis,* and *Margaux.* The latter is unique among the six as there is a specific Château Margaux within its boundaries. The large (2718 acres/1087 hectares) AOC *Margaux* includes the communes of Arsac, Cantenac, Labarde, Margaux, and Soussans.

In 1855, the finest wines were given Grand Cru Classé status in five levels with corresponding numbers from Premier Grand Cru Classé (first great classified growth) through Cinquième Grand Cru Classé (fifth great classified growth). The classification is listed in the appendix. The 1855 ranking had 61 châteaux, 55 from the Haut Médoc.

Château Margaux Premier Grand Cru Classé.

# MÉDOC CLASSIFICATIONS

*The Syndicat de crus Bourgeois.* The 1855 classification was an attempt to organize the wines in a hierarchy based on the quality and price of the châteaux. Because Château Haut-Brion was a well-known, high-quality, and expensive wine its red wine was included at the top of the classification in spite of its location in Graves. Aside from price the locations of the châteaux were considered. The drainage of water and cold air benefit the best châteaux situated closest to the Gironde River. Again it is the gravelly soil and some elevation which allow the drainage. In 1932 this syndicate added three levels to the 1855 classification; in ascending order they are *cru bourgeois* (a minimum of a 17.3-acre/seven-hectare vineyard), *grand bourgeois* (adds oak aged), and *grand bourgeois exceptionnel* (adds "mise en bouteilles au chateâu" and from the Haut-Médoc). These wines are representative of their areas, offer good value, and mature more quickly than the Grand Cru classé wines. Examples of cru bourgeois from the Médoc include Château Greysac and Château Loudenne, while Haut-Médoc examples include Château Larose Trintaudon and Château Coufran. The absence of the cru bourgeois rank is not necessarily an indication of a poor wine, just as the absence of a *consorzio* label in Italy does not indicate an inferior wine (see Chapter 7 on Italy). Château Lannesan and Château Gressier Grand Poujeaux are just two examples of good Médoc wines granted cru bourgeois status in the 1932 ratings but denied it by the *Syndicat* when rankings were revised in 1978. A recent EC ruling will only allow the term *Cru Bourgeois* to be used; the terms *grand bourgeois* and *grand bourgeois exceptionnel* will not be permitted.

*Margaux.* It is the only Médoc appellation with châteaux included in all five levels of Grand cru. The gravely soil with some marl, pebbles, sand, and limestone produce the most elegant wines of the Médoc. Floral and ripe fruit aromas and tastes combine in a medium-weight wine, not as powerful as those from the northern communes of Pauillac and St-Estèphe. The Premier Grand Cru Château Margaux is the ultimate expression of this area's wines, and is made with 75 percent Cabernet Sauvignon, 20 percent Merlot, and the balance is Petit Verdot and Cabernet Franc. The wine is fermented in large oak vats and aged in Tronçais oak. As Médoc is a red-only appellation, the fine white wine "Pavillon Blanc" from 24 acres (ten hectares) of Sauvignon Blanc planted at Château Margaux, is entitled to the appellation Bordeaux not Margaux. The area's cru bourgeois wines include Château Siran (Labarde), Château d'Angludet (Cantenac), and Château Labégorce Zédé (Soussans).

*Moulis.* Moulis is a small area with varied soils producing medium-weight wines with good fruit. The best-ranked cru bourgeois include Château Chasse Spleen, Château Maucaillou, and Château Gressier Grand Poujeaux.

*Listrac.* Listrac wines have good fruit, yet they are heavier than those of Moulis and need a little more time to soften. Listrac cru bourgeois include Château Fourcas Hosten, Château Clarke, and Château Cap Léon Veyrin.

*St.-Julien.* The gravely soil with some clay and a limestone subsoil of St. Julien offer good drainage and allow vine roots to go deep for nourishment. Seventy-five percent of the production are Grand crus with an elegant style. They are deep-colored, balanced wines with sumptuous fruit. One of the most prized is Château Léoville Barton which is planted with 70 percent Cabernet Sauvignon, 15 percent Merlot, 8 percent Petit Verdot, and 7 percent Cabernet Franc. Château Léoville Las Cases is 65 percent Cabernet Sauvignon, 18 percent Merlot, 14 percent Cabernet Franc, and 3 percent Petit Verdot. Another of the great châteaux is Château Ducru Beaucaillou consisting of 65 percent Cabernet Sauvignon, 25 percent Merlot, and 5 percent each of Petit Verdot and Cabernet Franc. Château Gloria, Château Hortevie, and Château Moulin de la Rose are cru bourgeois examples.

*Pauillac.* This port on the Gironde river is the capital of the Médoc. The land consists of iron-rich gravel over clay and limestone plateaux to the north and south, with the Gahet Valley in the center. The vineyards have good drainage and produce wines that are firm in structure and are often described as having a "lead pencil" scent along with the traditional cassis aroma. Pauillac boasts three of the five Premier Grand Cru Classé wines.

Château Lafite-Rothschild is considered to be the most aromatic of the Pauillac Grand crus offering violets as part of the Pauillac panoply of smells. Château Lafite actually has some of its land in the St-Estèphe appellation and its vineyards total 222 acres (90 hectares), making it one of the biggest chateaux. Lafite is comprised of 70 percent Cabernet Sauvignon, 20 percent Merlot, five percent Cabernet Franc, and five percent Petit Verdot.

Recognized as the top of the second growths in the 1855 classification, Château Mouton-Rothschild, which always fetched higher prices, was elevated to Premier Grand cru in 1973. Baron Phillipe de Rothschild was the first proprietor to château bottle the entire harvest. He created a magnificent wine museum at the property, and starting in 1945 commissioned different artists to design a new wine label each year (see Figures 6.7 and 6.8). Mouton is planted with 85 percent Cabernet Sauvignon, five percent Merlot, and ten percent Cabernet Franc. The wine is barrel fermented, as is Lafite. Baron Nathaniel de Rothschild purchased Mouton in 1853 while his brother James bought Lafite in 1868.

The other member of the trio of Premiers Grands Crus Classés is Château Latour made from 80 percent Cabernet Sauvignon, ten percent Merlot, five percent Cabernet Franc, and five percent Petit Verdot. Latour is considered the most consistent and heaviest of the Pauillac Premiers Grands Crus. Latour is fermented in temperature-controlled stainless steel vats, then aged in new oak for about two years, after which it is bottled without filtration. These three Premiers Grands Crus are most expensive in powerful vintages that last for decades.

**Figure 6.7** A Château Mouton Rothschild Label Designed by Dorothea Tanning.

**Figure 6.8** A Château Mouton Rothscild Label Designed by John Huston.

Château Pichon-Longueville de Lalande and Château Pichon-Longueville Baron are respected Deuxiéme Grands Crus that differ in style. The former has lighter soil than the Château Pichon-Longueville Baron to its north and an unusual grape mix. The wines are made from 45 percent Cabernet Sauvignon, 35 percent Merlot, 12 percent Cabernet Franc, and eight percent Petit Verdot, whereas Baron's breakdown is 75 percent Cabernet Sauvignon, 23 percent Merlot, and two percent of Malbec. The fuller-bodied style of Baron can be attributed to the higher percentage of Cabernet Sauvignon and the heavier soil.

A less expensive alternative to the Grand Cru wines of Pauillac are the secondary wines they produce. Examples are Les Forts de Latour (Château Latour), Carruades de Lafite (Château Lafite Rothschild), Réserve de la Comtesse (Château Pichon Lalande), Les Tourelles de Longueville (Château Pichon Baron), and Haut-Bages-Avérous (Château Lynch Bages). Cru bourgeois wines include Château Pibran, Château Fonbadet, and Château La Couronne.

*St-Estèphe.* The northernmost fine-wine appellation is the largest commune, but only six percent of its plantings (five châteaux) were included in the 1855 classification. Here the soil contains gravel rocks, some chalk, and sand on the surface, over a deep gravel and clay subsoil. There are also fossilized oysters and limestone subsoils that allow deep penetration of the roots. St-Estèphe used to be known for sturdy or meaty wines that took a very long time to soften and allow the fruit to show. Today however, because of increased plantings of Merlot and updated winery techniques, the wines display softer tannins and richer fruit flavors while still retaining the longevity and weight expected of a St-Estèphe. The only cooperative in the commune produces one-quarter of the appellation wines, the Grand crus one-fifth, and the rest is made by cru bourgeois and smaller châteaux. All share the characteristic dark color, earthy, oaky and cassis nose, and full body. The finest of these wines are the second-growths Château Cos d'Estournel (50 percent Cabernet Sauvignon, 40 percent Merlot, and ten percent Cabernet Franc) and Château Montrose (65 percent Cabernet Sauvignon, 25 percent Merlot, and ten percent Cabernet Franc), each of which produces about 25,000 cases per year. Bruno Prats, owner of Cos d'Estournel, has the grapes harvested at optimum ripeness to emphasize the fruit. Some of the wines are stainless steel fermented, and only in the richest years are all-new oak barrels used. Château Calon Ségur, a third growth and the most northerly Grand cru in the Médoc, is made with 50 percent Cabernet Sauvignon, 25 percent Merlot, and 25 percent Cabernet Franc. Cru bourgeois include Château Meyney, Château Les Ormes-de-Pez, Château Phélan-Ségur, Château de Pez, Château Marbuzet, and Château Bosq.

The St-Estèphe wines are closest to the powerful style of Pauillac, while St-Julien and Margaux, to the south, both stress elegance and fruit.

**Graves.** The Graves region extends southward from the Médoc beyond Langon near Sauternes. As the name suggests, the soil is mostly gravel and the pebbles, which facilitate drainage, range from white to a yellowish color.

**Figure 6.9** A Graves Label.

Jean Bernard Delmas, Director and Wine Maker of Château Haut Brion Since 1961. Mr. Delmas' Skill in Selection of Rootstocks and Clones As Well as His Expertise in Wine Making Enable This Château to Produce One of Bordeaux's Finest and Most Consistent Wines Regardless of Vintage Conditions. The Wines Are a Testament to the Potential of the Graves Area and the Abilities of Its Wine to Compete with Those of the Médoc.

The subsoils are sand and clay and, as in the Médoc, pine forests to the west offer protection from winds. The area is about 34 miles long and 12 miles wide (54.5 kilometers long and 19.25 wide) and covers around 7400 acres (3000 hectares) of vines. The area first achieved fame for its reds and later became known for whites as well. Today the appellation Graves applies to both (see Figure 6.9).

The finest dry whites and reds come from the communes of *Pessac* and *Léognan* in northern Graves. The alluvial deposits there have been built up over time and created a more gravely rolling landscape with better drainage. Fifty-five châteaux are in the *Pessac-Léognan* appellation created in 1986. Mineral, floral, tobacco, smoke, red fruit, and chocolate are among the scents of the finest red wines, which also possess an earthiness and firmness on the palate. Château Haut-Brion was included in the 1855 classification. The Graves area's first rating was in 1953 which became official in 1959. Among the finest properties are Château La Mission-Haut-Brion, Château de Fieuzal, Château Haut Bailly, Château Pape Clément, and the vineyard of Domaine de Chevalier. All of the cru classé châteaux are in the Pessac-Léognan appellation. White wines from the Pessac-Léognan appellation must contain a minimum of 25 percent Sauvignon Blanc by law, but it is most often the dominant grape in the blend. It provides such aromatics as redcurrant, gooseberry, and citrus along with its natural high acidity on the palate. The Sémillon adds a richness and structure on the palate as well as suggestions of honey in the scent of the blends. The Sémillon is the dominant grape in Graves vineyards of the south and also in the wine regions of Bordeaux that produce sweet wines. The Graves classification is found in the Appendix.

The historic Château Haut Brion is a 98.6-acre (40-hectare) American-owned property in Pessac planted with 55 percent Cabernet Sauvignon, 25 percent Merlot, and 20 percent Cabernet Franc. It produces 2000 cases per year, including its second label Bahans Haut Brion. Jean Bernard Delmas succeeded his father as wine maker and has kept the wine at the forefront of the Grand crus. He favors a short hot fermentation to extract color and fruit and keep the tannins soft enough to produce a wine that is medium to full in body and enjoyable after five years. The full-bodied dry white wine made from 55 percent Sémillon and 45 percent Sauvignon Blanc, is barrel fermented and aged. Only 1000 cases of the white are made annually, and the complexity and rarity of the wine accounts for its high cost. The white became a cru classé in 1960.

Château La Mission-Haut-Brion consists of 42 acres (17 hectares) planted with 60 percent Cabernet Franc, 35 percent Merlot, and five percent Cabernet Franc. The estate has the same owners as Haut Brion but the wines are different, with La Mission the more powerful of the two but both having the cassis and mineral aromas of Graves and the ability to age gracefully.

Domaine de Chevalier in Léognan, a single vineyard surrounded by woods, was planted in 1770. Five thousand cases of red (Cabernet Sauvignon 65 percent, Merlot 30 percent, Cabernet Franc five percent) and 800 of white are produced (Sauvignon Blanc 70 percent, Sémillon 30 percent) each year. Both wines are balanced, offer complex smells and tastes, and great finesse. The barrel-fermented white wine is aged 18 months before bottling and is best savored after seven years and may last over 20 years. The Bernard family, who acquired the property in 1983, make successful wines even in lesser years. In good years their wines are consistently among the top wines of Bordeaux.

Château Bouscaut is unusual in being the only Grand cru that has more Merlot than Cabernet Sauvignon on the left bank. The vineyards are planted with 60 percent Merlot, 30 percent Cabernet Sauvignon, and five percent Cabernet Franc. Chateau Pape Clément has the distinction of being the first vineyard named in Bordeaux. It is planted with two-thirds Cabernet Sauvignon and one-third Merlot.

Château Couhins Lurton is 100 percent Sauvignon Blanc. Owned by André Lurton, this barrel-fermented and aged white should be drunk within three years. Other Lurton-owned properties include the nonclassified Château La Louvière, Château du Cruzeau, and Château Rochemartin. Château de Landiras and Domaine de la Graves are produced by Peter Vinding-Diers, formerly the wine maker for Château Rahoul, known for its full-bodied dry white made exclusively from Sémillon. These Graves wine makers are among the leaders in the evolution of Bordeaux wines.

***Sauternes.*** The Sauternes region, which adjoins the southeastern portion of Graves, has mostly gravel and clay soils. The region is subdivided into the communes of *Sauternes, Bommes, Fargues, Preignac,* and *Barsac.* The Barsac commune has limestone along with gravel and sand and produces wines lighter in body. Barsac may be sold under its own appellation or as Sauternes. The Sémillon is the most important of the permitted grape types due to its sensitivity to *pourriture noble* (noble rot or *Botrytis cinerea*). The noble rot occurs during ripening if there is sufficient humidity in the vineyard. The *pourriture noble* is a fungus that causes the skins to shrivel and concentrates the sugars, glycerine, and acids of a grape. The resulting wine is a viscous nectar with a roasted nut-honey, citrus, tropical fruit, and floral bouquet, and is luscious on the palate in the vintages most affected by *botrytis.* Although they are delicious while young, the best can last for decades.

The warmer Garonne River is cooled by the Ciron River, creating the morning dampness so the fungus may form. The sun later in the day dries off the grapes. The late grapes are gathered in many *tries* (pickings) to ensure either *botrytis* or the ripest grapes possible. The finest vintages are those with widespread *botrytis.*

Rain at harvest dilutes the concentration of sugars and a *cryoextraction* technique is now being used to reduce the water in must in wet vintages. Cryoextraction also assists a wine maker when there are lower levels of ripeness in the grapes. The grapes with the most water freeze before those with a higher sugar content. The *must* is then obtained from pressing the nonfrozen sweeter grapes. The lower the temperature during cryoextraction, the lower the yield and the greater the concentration of sugar in the must. The minimum sugar level for a Sauternes is 7.73 ounces per quart

(221 grams per liter), the minimum alcohol is 12.5 percent, and the maximum yield is 660 gallons per 2.47 acres (25 hectoliters per hectare) Sauternes wines must be sweet: dry wines made in the region are sold as Bordeaux or Bordeaux Supérieur.

When Sauternes was classified in 1855, *Château d'Yquem* was the only wine accorded the Premier Grand cru status. The wine is made from 80 percent Sémillon and 20 percent Sauvignon Blanc. It may be the finest dessert wine in the world and its success can be attributed to the soil, grapes, and wine maker, as well as the commitment of the Comtes Alexandre de Lur Saluces, who owns the château. Harvesting extends over numerous *tries* (pickings) to ensure only *botrytis*-affected grapes are selected. The yield is an astoundingly low 221 gallons per 2.47 acres (eight hectoliters per hectare), which equals roughly one glass of wine per plant. The wines are never chaptalized. They are barrel fermented and aged for three years in new oak. In an average year 3300 cases of this rarity are made. Most years the winery makes 2000 cases of a dry wine from equal parts Sémillon and Sauvignon Blanc. This wine, called simply "Y," is sold as a Bordeaux Supérieur. Château Raymond-Lafon is a cru bourgeois made by Pierre Meslier, the same wine maker at Château d'Yquem. Château Gilette is not classified as it began production in the 1930s but it is one of the finest and most expensive wines of the region. It is 85 percent Sémillon and 15 percent Muscadelle from low-yielding vines and is only produced in exceptional vintages. The wine spends from 15 to 20 years in tanks rather than barrels before bottling. The best vintages are labeled *"Crème de Tête"* and are golden in color and rich and full on the palate.

A Sauternes by a négociant provides a less-expensive introduction to these sweet wines. The Sauternes classification is included in the Appendix.

***St-Émilion and Pomerol.*** *St-Émilion* and *Pomerol* are on the right bank of the Gironde River, and north of the Dordogne River and its port Libourne. St-Émilion and Pomerol, along with the lesser-known Fronsac to the west, are referred to as *Libournais,* or Right Bank, wines. Many of the best vineyards are on sheltered, south-facing slopes. The best vineyards are of limestone with varying amounts of sand, gravel, and clay as a base. Alluvial sandy topsoils are also responsible for the distinct character of some châteaux. The vineyards on the slopes have better air drainage and are less susceptible to spring frosts. When hit hard by the frosts, such as in 1991, the top châteaux sell their wines off as regional wines.

The Merlot and Cabernet Franc are the principal grape types for these red wine regions with Cabernet Sauvignon, Carmenère, and Malbec in supporting roles. The Cabernet Sauvignon does not fare as well in this area because of the generally cooler climate and different soils than the Médoc.

The wines of St-Émilion and Pomerol are often the first wines to entice a wine consumer to drink Bordeaux reds because of their softer tannins, forward plummy fruit flavors, and ability to be enjoyed in their youth or with age.

***The Right Bank Wine Regions of Bordeaux—St-Émilion.*** St-Émilion is one of the most respected fine wine regions in Bordeaux. The region is bor-

dered by the Dordogne River to the south and the Isles River to the north; Pomerol is to the west. Excellent wines are from terraces of gravelly soil mixed with sand, while the most-powerful examples are grown on the hills and plateaus with clay- and limestone-based soils. The former are traditionally referred to as the *"Graves"* wines of St-Émilion and the latter are known as the *"Côtes"* wines.

The region was first classified in 1954 and again in 1984 in two categories; 11 Grands Crus (subdivided into A and B levels) and St-Émilion AOC. The outskirt, or satellite, appellations have the same yield and alcohol requirements as St-Émilion. These appellations include *Montagne–St-Émilion, Lussac–St-Émilion, St. Georges–St-Émilion,* and *Puisseguin–St-Émilion.* These wines offer good value. Château St. Georges (50 percent Merlot, 50 percent Cabernets) and Château Corbin (65 percent Merlot, 35 percent Cabernets) are fine age-worthy examples.

Château Cheval Blanc, one of the two "A" Grands Crus, is grown near Pomerol on the Graves section of St-Émilion. The wine comes from 86.5 acres (35 hectares) planted with 65 percent Cabernet Franc and 35 percent Merlot. It is aged in new oak barrels each year and the high percentage of Cabernet Franc makes this one of the most exotic of the crus of Bordeaux. The wine is approachable in its youth because of its rich fruit flavors but it may be cellared for decades. Château Figeac included the present Cheval Blanc vineyard until their separation in the 1830s. It is a Grand Cru "B" estate using about equal parts of Cabernet Franc, Merlot, and Cabernet Sauvignon. These two properties are similar in style to their neighbors in Pomerol. The other "A" Grand Cru, Château Ausone is in the "Côtes" section of St-Émilion. It is planted in half Cabernet Franc and half Merlot and is aged in new oak each year. Its wines are known for their aroma, concentration, and finesse and have regained their former prominence under wine maker Pascal Delbeck, who arrived in 1975. The vineyard's altitude and exposure allowed it to survive the 1956 frost without the damage that destroyed most of Cheval Blanc's and Figeac's vines.

The regional wines of St-Émilion are generally medium-weight dry wines that can be drunk within five years before their fruity quality diminishes.

The Union des Producteurs de St-Émilion has about 20 percent of the region's one thousand growers as members and bottles both single-estate wines and regional wines. The St-Émilion classification is included in the Appendix.

***The Right Bank Wine Regions of Bordeaux—Pomerol.*** Pomerol is an area of 1800 acres (727 hectares) with over 170 growers compared to St-Emilion's 12,850 acres (5200 hectares) of vineyards not counting the 7200 or so acres (2909 hectares) in its satellites. Although Pomerol has never been officially classified, their limited production, compared to other fine areas, and the quality attained by the best producers, has resulted in price levels often exceeding the classified growths of the Médoc. The INAO requires the must weights here to be six ounces per quart (171 grams per liter), higher than those of Pauillac which is 5.6 ounces (162 grams). Merlot occupies three-quarters of the vineyards. Cabernet Franc (called "Bouchet" here) is second in importance, and the Malbec (Pressac) plays a minor role. The soils vary with clay, sand, and gravel and the base is either *molasse,* sedimentary rock, or *machefer,* iron. Iron is one of the reasons for the richness of the wines produced. Merlot yields high-sugar, lower-acid wines that can be drunk within four years or aged a couple of decades, again depending on vintage and property.

Château de Sales, largest of the properties, yielding 20,000 cases per year makes wine in a lighter style due to its lighter sandy soils with some gravel. It is made from 65 percent Merlot with the balance divided equally among the Cabernets.

The undisputed star of Pomerol, and of the Merlot grape worldwide, is the 28-acre (11.2-hectare) Château Petrus. There, five percent of the vineyard is planted with Cabernet Franc (not always used for the final product) which amounts to about 4,000 cases of the most expensive Merlot-based wine in the world. The soils are clays with some sand and gravel. The grapes are harvested when they are fully ripe. There is no dilution due to rainfall or morning dew, as the propeller blades of a low-flying helicopter just before the harvest removes surface moisture. The wines are made from a mix of the free-run *vin de goutte* and the *vin de presse* in cement vats. No filtering is done and the wines are aged in new oak. The wine is deep in color with complex scents of fruits and spices as well as rich fruit flavors on the palate and lots of texture. The average age of the vines is over 40 years, which accounts for the complexity and balance the wines achieve. The winery is co-owned by Madame Lacoste Loubat and the Jean Pierre Moueix Établissements. The wine maker is Jean Claude Berrouët. Christian Moueix, the son of Jean Pierre, is director here as well as at Château La Fleur Pétrus, another high-quality property. The Moueix firm makes Château and regional wines as well as "Dominus," an American proprietary wine from the Napa Valley.

Christian Mouiex, Director of Fine Properties in Pomerol, Bordeaux Also Produces a First-Class Proprietary-Labeled Wine Domnus in the Napa Valley of California.

The Vineyards of Château Petrus.

The Merlot Grape Produces Exquisite
Wines at Château Petrus in Pomerol.

Other reputable Pomerol wines include Château Certan de May,
Château Clinet, Château La Conseillante, Château L'Évangile, Château La
Fleur de Gay, Château Gazin, Château Lafleur, Château Le Pin, Château
Bon Pasteur, Château L'Église Clinet, Château Latour a Pomerol, Château
Petit Village, Clos René, Château Trotanoy, and Vieux Château Certan.

## Côtes-du-Rhône

**Introduction.** The Rhône Valley, between the Alps and the Massif Central
Mountains, is 125 miles (200 kilometers) long from Vienne in the north to

Avignon in the south. The Rhône River begins in the Swiss Alps and gathers force from melting snows and streams as it makes its way south to the Mediterranean, passing first through Burgundy and then on through the vineyards of the Côtes-du-Rhône. The river serves as a moderating influence and, as in other fine wine regions, the best vineyard sites are closest to the water. The *mistral,* the name of the powerful wind that sweeps through the valley, can blow hard enough to strip vines of their shoots, leaves, and fruit. As a result, many of the best vineyard sites are protected by cypress or poplar trees. One positive effect of the mistral is to decrease the risk of mildew or rot by drying the plants.

The *Septentrionales* region in the north is about 36 miles (57.6 kilometers) long. Traveling south, vines are scarce for 30 miles (48 kilometers) until the *Méridionales* (south) region begins south of the town of Montélimar. The Méridionales extends 36 miles (57.6 kilometers) south to the city of Avignon. The wider Méridionale produces much more wine than the Séptentrionales. The Mediterranean influence in the south is seen in fields of lavender, thyme, garlic, and olives. The north has a continental climate with colder winters and warmer summers than the south. Most of the Séptentrionales vineyards are close to the river on terraced granite-based slopes. Precipitous slopes are less common for Méridionales vineyards where limestone soils exist.

The Côtes-du-Rhône is the second largest wine region in France after Bordeaux. Reds account for 95 percent of the region's average annual production of almost 80 million gallons (three million hectoliters). Sparkling wines, rosés, and whites, from dry to sweet, are also produced in the Rhône. The Syrah is the sole red grape in the north while the Southern vineyards are planted with an assortment, including Grenache, Cinsault, Mourvèdre, and Syrah. Clairette, Marsanne, Bourbelenc, Roussanne, Grenache Blanc, and Ugni Blanc are the white grapes that do well in this warm region. The minimum alcohol level set for both red and white wines is 11 percent.

***History of the Rhône.*** Wine has been produced here for over 2500 years. Wines were first popularized by the papal court, which had moved from Rome to Avignon in 1309. Pope Clément V was the first of six popes to reside in the region which led to the designation of the area as Chateauneuf-du-Pape some 500 years later. The Saône River was the passage to northern markets but the dukes of Burgundy forbade the entry by a decree that began in the mid-fifteenth century and lasted over a century. The development of new routes such as the Canal du Midi and the abolition of taxes led to the opening of more markets such as Russia and Great Britain by the end of the seventeenth century.

Sometimes the powerful and deep-colored red wines of Hermitage in the northern Rhône were even blended in to weaker Burgundies or Bordeaux. "Bordeaux Ermitage" labels told customers the Bordeaux blend had been strengthened. By a 1727 law the most famous area of the southern Rhône guaranteed that the grapes used for its wines of Châteauneuf-du-Pape had to come from a defined area. This was the precursor to the national AOC laws that were promoted by this same area a few centuries later.

The Baron Le Roy de Boiseaumarie was the owner of Château Fortia in Châteauneuf-du-Pape. He pushed for recognition and regulation of the wines of his region in 1923 and spearheaded the development of the present wine law system of France. Producers also branded "CDR" initials on casks so their Côtes-du-Rhône wines were easily identifiable at the northern ports of what today are the Netherlands, Belgium, Germany, and England. The *phylloxera* that hit at the end of the nineteenth century destroyed most of the vineyards.

The Rhône region again struggled to rebuild after the world wars and it is only in the last 30 years that consumers and critics are discovering and praising the wines of the region.

*Wine Making in the Rhône.* Regional wines made by simple Côtes-du-Rhône wine cooperatives tend to be destemmed, quickly pressed, and fermented without a long maceration of grape skins. Those wines are fruity, forward, and can be drunk young. One variation destems during a mechanical harvest and then uses whole-berry fermentation in a modified version of carbonic maceration (see Chapter 1 on How Wine Is Made). Some producers both in the north and the south leave the stems on and do not crush all the red grapes before fermentation.

In the north a common technique is to bring wooden crates with whole grapes to be emptied into an open wooden vat. During fermentation, a cap of solid matter, mostly grape skins, is formed and floats over the liquids. The cap is pushed down repeatedly to get more juice in contact with these solids so that more color and flavor intensity are achieved, as well as giving the wine a longer life from the higher tannin level. The wine makers may start submerging the cap with their feet and this is known as *pigeage*. They are supported by wooden planks, and they then lower themselves into the open vat. When the cap becomes thinner, as it is submerged and mixed with more juice, the wine maker uses poles to keep pushing the cap down. These techniques are used to increase the power of the wine. Even the grapes not completely crushed are releasing their pigments as carbon dioxide creates an anaerobic situation with enzymes causing a fermentation within the grape itself.

In the southern Rhône whole berries are passed through rollers narrow enough to press some grapes yet leave others intact. Cap submersion is accomplished in the south by *remontage* or pumping the juice from the bottom of the closed-top cement or stainless steel vats over the top of the cap. As Grenache, a principal grape in the South, is prone to oxidize, it must be protected by the closed-top vats. Temperature-controlled stainless steel vats allow wine makers to better guide each of the grape types that will be fermented separately and then blended together and aged.

*Pièces* and *demi muids* are the small- and medium-sized oak barrels that are commonly used for aging in the north; while in the south the larger *foudres* casks are used. New barrels are more often used in the north than the south. As in other major wine regions of the world, experiments with techniques both in the fields and the wineries continue and allow for stylistic differences among producers.

Since the 1950s the Rhône appellation area has expanded from 40,000 to 150,000 acres (16,000 to 60,000 hectares). The selection of better rootstocks, vinifera clones, and temperature-controlled fermentation has improved the overall quality of wines. In the past, field blends of different grapes were often harvested and fermented together in the south. Today, the better producers harvest and ferment each grape variety separately, and the subsequent blend defines the producer's style.

### Appellations of the Côtes-du-Rhône

*Côtes-du-Rhône.* The simple Côtes-du-Rhône appellation wines come from 163 communes with approximately 99,000 acres (39,600 hectares) of vines. The Vaucluse, in the south, produces the most wine of the six départements within the Rhône. With over 200 million bottles produced annually, quality varies, and choosing a reliable négociant or cooperative is important. Forty percent of Côtes-du-Rhône is made by 422 local négociants, 40 percent by négociants from outside the region, and 20 percent by cooperatives and unions. Côtes-du-Rhône may be lighter bodied and fruity or medium bodied and more rustic. Côtes-du-Rhône reds must use a minimum of 70 percent Grenache, Mourvèdre, Cinsault, and Syrah combined; the balance is comprised of Counoise, Carignan, Vaccarèse, Terret Noir, Muscardin, and Camarèse. Meditteranean growing regions, such as the southern Rhône, often use a variety of grapes as each contributes different elements to a blend. Cinsault is an early-ripening grape that contributes good fruit flavors and spicy scents as well as high yield. The Counoise is more difficult to grow but adds finesse along with fruit and interesting scents of flowers, fruit, and spices. Vaccarèse and Muscardin also add complexity to the bouquet of a wine. Black pepper is one scent offered by both, and the Muscardin imparts more alcohol and weight to a blend. The Terret Noir adds tartness to a wine. The contributions of Syrah, Grenache, and Mourvédre are covered in Chapter 2 on Wine Grapes.

*Côtes-du-Rhône Villages.* This appellation requires lower yields and higher minimum alcohol levels than the basic Côtes-du-Rhône wines. Sixteen of the best villages may add their commune name on labels. The villages include Rasteau and Beaumes de Venise, which are also known for their *vins doux naturel* (sweet fortified wines). The other 14 villages are Cairanne, Chusclan, Laudun, Roaix, Rochegude, Rousset les Vignes, St. Gervais, St. Maurice sur Eygues, St. Pantaléan les Vignes, Sablet, Séguret, Valréas, Vinsobres, and Visan.

*Communes.* The best wines of the Rhône are labeled by the commune appellation and some include the *lieux dits* also known as *mas,* or vineyard site, on the label. Although no Premier or Grand cru system exists in the Rhône the best lieux dits wines command prices comparable to the finest Bordeaux or Burgundy wines. The communal wines, such as Hermitage in the north, are often referred to as the crus of the Rhône.

# Wines of the Séptentrionales or Northern Rhône

Grapes from a single vineyard may be used to add complexity to a blended wine of the commune or sold under the name of the commune with the mas name as well. The best vineyard sites, on steep granite slopes close to the river, are used for the commune-named wines, which account for 25 percent of Rhône production. The northern half of the Séptentrionales (see Map 6.10) produces wines with slightly higher acidity and lower alcohol than the southern half. Ridges to the west of the river protect the better sites from the drying winds. Farther south some of the vineyards are on calcareous soils or plateaux or granite slopes. Clay, sand, and iron create variations similar to the many subtle differences found in Burgundy to the north. As in Burgundy, where the finest wines come from a single grape variety and location, the variations in soils and exposures has a profound influence on each grape variety. Viognier is the white grape of choice in the northern portion while Roussanne and Marsanne are better grown in the southern portion of the Septentrionales. The Roussanne is the lower yielding of the two and is also sensitive to fan leaf virus and oidium, so farmers tend to play it safe and rely more on Marsanne. The Syrah is the dominant red grape throughout this region and, as will be indicated in the rest of this section, it produces wines of different character in each location.

Moving from north to south the crus or communes of the Séptentrionales are *Côte Rotie, Condrieu, Château Grillet, St. Joseph, Crozes Hermitage, Hermitage, Cornas, St. Péray,* and *Brézème.* The latter is an appellation south of Valence producing a small amount of Syrah-based wines. The other communes are described here:

*Côte Rotie.* The Côte Rotie, or roasted slopes, produce reds of great power and finesse from grapes grown on steep southeastern-facing slopes. Unfortunately the area was expanded in 1966 to include vineyards on the plateau whose wines do not have the same intensity of flavor. Today the area encompasses about 320 acres (128 hectares), planted mostly in Syrah but including some white Viognier, which by law may comprise up to 20 percent of the red wine. Most Côte Rotie wines contain only a little of the white grape, which adds aromatics and finesse to the blend. *Arzelle* is the local name for the topsoil, which is comprised of broken mica schist and pebbles. The precipitous incline of the vineyards led the locals to construct *cheys,* or stone walls, to protect vineyard soils from erosion.

The vineyards of the *Côte Brune* section in Côte Rotie have darker, heavier, iron-rich clay soils and make more powerful wines than the *Côte Blonde* section, where the vines are planted in limestone, chalk, and sand. The Côte Blonde wines are approachable at a younger age. Both sections' vineyards are at a gradient of about 35 degrees. The Blonde or Brune names appear on labels when wines from the two areas are used separately while some producers prefer to blend the two. There are over 50 mas in the Côte Rotie and the Guigal company is fortunate to own two of the best, La

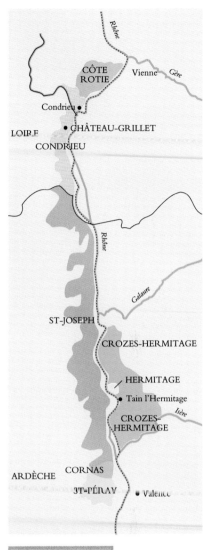

**Map 6.10**
The Northern Rhône Region.

Côte Rotie.

Mouline in the Côte Blonde and La Turque in the Côte Brune. Other fine *mas* include *La Landonne, La Garde, La Chevalière,* and *La Châtillone.*

Most wines of Côte Rôtie are medium- to full-bodied, with violet, spicy, oaky, roasted, blackcurrant, and raspberry aromas and concentrated fruit flavors. Individual mas display other complex aromas and tastes and most wines have a long finish.

*Condrieu.*    The Condrieu appellation refers to white wines made from 200 acres (80 hectares) of Viognier grapes on the left bank of the Rhône River. The wines used to be made in semidry to sweet styles, but today the wines are dry and are much in demand for their pear, peach, banana, honey, and floral scents and lush fruit flavors. These are viscous full-bodied wines that tend to lack acidity and so are best drunk between 15 months to four years to enjoy all the forward fruit flavors.

*Château Grillet.*    The smallest appellation in the Rhône, with less than ten acres (.4 hectare) within the Condrieu area, Château Grillet consists of a steep granite-based Viognier vineyard. The wine is similar in style to Condrieu but more expensive. Château Grillet is fermented in enamel vats and then aged 1½ years in oak before it is filtered and bottled. Although it is a fine wine, the price may be based on the small amount produced and the fact that it can age a little longer than Condrieu.

*St. Joseph.*    The area stretches 40.3 miles (65 kilometers) along the Rhône River and produces about 80 percent red wine with the balance in white wines. Because the boundaries have been expanded to include sites without the best southern exposure, the wines are less alcoholic and tannic than other Syrahs from the southern half of the Séptentrionales. They are best drunk from two to six years. The wines have cherry/berry flavors and

Gérard Jaboulet is the President and Managing Director of Paul Jaboulet Aîné, a firm that has produced fine Rhône wines since 1834. Gérard is assisted by Phillipe Jaboulet who is in charge of the 215 acres (86 hectares) of vineyards they own. Jacques Jaboulet, the wine maker for the firm, also purchases grapes from other sources. They make affordable, fun, fruity wines with some weight such as their Côtes du Ventoux and Côtes-du-Rhône as well as luxurious world class wines such as Hermitage "La Chapelle." La Chapelle's power comes from the Syrah grown in the granite and schist of Les Bessards mas at the top of the Hermitage slope. The Syrah of the slightly sandier calcareous soils of le Méal section provides aromatics.

The grapes for La Chapelle are destemmed and then fermented at about 70 degrees Fahrenheit (29 degrees Celsius). The wine is then left to macerate with the skins for five weeks followed by aging in Nevers or Allier oak barrels for up to 20 months. The wine needs at least six years to begin to open up and may be enjoyed for three or four decades. With time the opaque deep purple color goes through various hues of red and the black pepper, blackberry smells evolve into scents of leather, truffles, dark fruits, spices, and violets. Each vintage matures at a different pace, and La Chapelle's combination of power, elegance, and complexity makes it one of the greatest of French wine treasures.

are medium bodied. The whites are mostly from Marsanne, with some Roussanne included, and the best can have peach and floral aromas and concentrated fruit flavors. Again, because of low acidity, most are best drunk fairly young. J. L. Grippat and J. L. Chave are two producers offering lush aromatic examples.

*Crozes Hermitage.* Crozes Hermitage comes from 11 communes totaling 2200 acres (880 hectares) around the town of Tain l'Hermitage; 4.5 million bottles of red wine and 500,000 of white wine are produced annually. Crozes Hermitage wines are similar in style but not as concentrated in flavor as the more revered Hermitage wines. Appellation boundary expansion now includes the less-desirable plateau vineyards south of Tain l'Hermitage. The wines of Crozes Hermitage are made from Syrah with up to 15 percent Marsanne and Roussanne permitted. These wines are a less-expensive alternative to Hermitage. The finest *mas* may be the 86-acre (34.4-hectare) *Thalabert* owned by the négociant Paul Jaboulet Aîné. Low yields, older vines, and barrel aging combine to produce a wine with floral, fruit, and spicy notes that is rich on the palate and can be enjoyed between three to ten years after the vintage. White wines of the commune are best drunk from one to three years after the vintage.

*Hermitage.* Hermitage, the most famous wine of the northern Rhône, comes from 380 acres (152 hectares) of steep granite-based vineyards with some sand and pebbles. The southwest-facing vineyards retain the sun's heat and provide good drainage. Over 75 percent of the plantings are Syrah, the balance are Marsanne and Roussanne. The red wine may include up to 15 percent white grapes, but as in Côte Rôtie, most producers desire the pure expression of Syrah. The vineyards were first planted by the Phoenicians in 400 B.C. and the current name is derived from a hermit who planted grapes after returning from being a knight of the crusades in the thirteenth century. Hermitage became popular in the seventeenth century when bottles were sent to King Charles the Second of England by his cousin King Louis the Fourteenth of France. By the nineteenth century Hermitage was the nation's highest priced wine.

The commune's highest section is at about a thousand feet (304 meters) above sea level. The mas or lieu dit *Bessards* is highest, below is *Méal,* and then *Greffieux.* Although all Hermitage wines are deep-colored and powerful, the heaviest and most tannic are from Bessards. The mas *Murets* to the east is less steep, and with more clay in the soil is better suited for the white varieties, as is Greffieux. Wine makers harvest separate mas and ferment the wines individually to be blended later. An example is Gérard Chave, acknowledged as one of the master blenders and producers of Hermitage. His cuvée is sourced from such lieux dits as *Les Bessards, Méal, Beaumes, Diognières, L'Hermite, Les Roucoles,* and *Péléat.* Paul Jaboulet Aîné produces one of the richest, most complex wines of the area, known as *Hermitage La Chappelle,* named after the chapel atop the slope of Hermitage. This wine is also made from a blend of the finest mas and needs at least six years of cellar time before it begins to release its complexities of scents and flavors. *Chevalier de Sterimberg* is the extraordinary white wine of Jaboulet, honoring the hermit Henri Gaspard de Stérimberg, and it should also be cellared for a couple of years. Guigal also produces an age-worthy white Hermitage as does the négociant Chapoutier whose *Chante Alouette* white is made exclusively from Marsanne. Guigal's red Hermitage and Chapoutier's *de la Sizeranne* are among the finest examples of the commune.

Hermitage red wines undergo extended maceration and usually spend a year to two in small barrels before being bottled. The opaque black plum–colored wines have a range of scents that may include spices, cassis, other fruits, and even tar. The great depth and variety of flavors in these full-bodied wines is followed by a rich fruit finish. The white wines can also be aromatic, with scents of apricots, nuts, flowers, and honey and offer a fuller body when oak aged. Reds from a fine vintage can last a couple of decades. Most whites are best between three to nine years after the vintage but those from the finest producers and vintages improve for 20 years. There is a very small production of *vins de paille,* or straw wines, made by drying the grapes on straw mats to produce a sweet oxidized wine.

*Cornas.*   One of the most tannic and powerful of the world's wines is made from the 173 acres (69.2 hectares) of Syrah grown on the steep slopes of Cornas. The vines are shielded from the mistral winds, and the best are grown on terraced vineyards of granite with limestone. The word *Cornas* derives from the Celtic word for "scorched earth" and the heat-retentive soils and Syrah grape combine to make a wine with deep color and choco-late, tar, prune, and other fruit aromas, and rich fruit and oak flavors. Not a wine for the timid, Cornas has been called too rustic by some. A few pro-ducers are destemming the grapes in order to make less-tannic examples. August Clape and Noël Verset are traditional producers who continue to make some of the richest-scented and flavorful wines of the world.

*St. Péray.* St. Péray consists of 150 acres (60 hectares) that produce white and sparkling wines from Marsanne and Roussane grapes. These whites, from the southern extreme of the Séptentrionales, are not as rich or complex as their neighbors made from the same grapes. The sparkling wines are made by the *méthode champenoise* and are moderately priced.

### Die-Central East Rhône

*Clairette de Die.* Die is located in the eastern Rhône region along the Drome River. It lies between the northern and southern regions and is known for sparkling *clairette* wines made by two distinct methods. In the tra-ditional *méthode Dioise,* Muscat and a little Clairette are bottled before fully fermented, to retain gas. The wine has no yeast added but goes through a continued fermentation in the bottle due to the natural sweetness of the Muscat. After four months or more the wine is decanted off the lees and bottled without adding a dosage and is labeled *Clairette de Die. Clairette de*

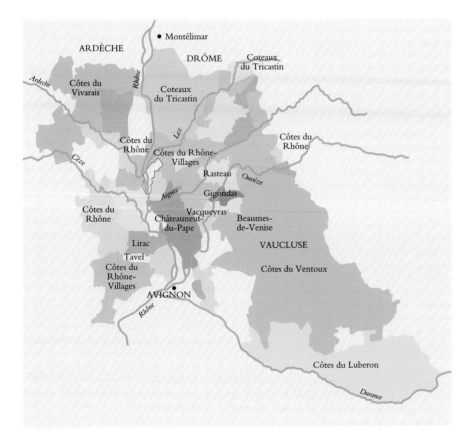

Map 6.11 The Southern Rhône Region.

**Figure 6.10** Muscat de Beaumes de Venise, with Its Lovely Smell of Peaches and Orange Blossoms, Is Best Enjoyed within Three Years.

*Die Brut,* which lacks the seductive Muscat smell, is made by the Champagne method which includes adding sugar and yeast for a second fermentation and then a dosage. Some dry still Clairette-based wines are also made.

## Wines of the Méridionales or Southern Rhône

The Méridionales (see Map 6.11) has more variations in soil, landscape, and grape types than its northern neighbor. The appellations from north to south include the *Côteaux du Tricastin, Côtes du Vivarais, Rasteau, Gigondas, Vacqueyras, Muscat Beaumes-de-Venise, Châteauneuf-du-Pape, Lirac, Tavel, Côtes du Ventoux,* and *Côtes du Lubéron.* We describe the best-known appellations in the sections that follow.

*Côteaux du Tricastin.* Côteaux de Tricastin produces mostly pleasant, medium-bodied reds from a blend of the traditional Grenache, Syrah, Mourvèdre, Cinsault, and Carignan red grapes. Up to 20 percent white grapes may be included. Some rosé and a small amount of dry whites are also made.

*Rasteau.* In Rasteau, the best wines are the sweet *vins doux naturels* made from Grenache. The wine is fortified with alcohol to arrest the fermentation process before all the sugar is converted. The resulting sweet wines contain about 21 percent alcohol. One style leaves the skins in contact with the fermenting must, resulting in a darker, tawny-colored wine. The wine, named *Rancio* Rasteau, is aged in casks at least two years before bottling. The hot conditions under which casks are stored impart a unique scent to the wines. The grapes for the Rasteau fortified wine may come from the Rasteau commune itself or two other villages, Sablet and Cairanne. Two-thirds of the region's production consists of still red, white, and rosé wines, mostly full-bodied reds at moderate prices. *Garrigue* is the local term for the heat-retentive stony soil.

*Gigondas.* This appellation gets its name from the Latin *iocunditas,* or happy town. The soil is red clay with some gravel and pebbles. Gigondas is to the south of Rasteau at the foothills of Dentelles de Montmirail limestone-rich mountains. The wine has a minimum alcohol level of 12.5 percent but often attains 14 percent. These full-bodied reds are from a mix that is a maximum of 80 percent Grenache with the balance provided by Syrah, Mourvèdre, and Cinsault. The wines are among the most powerful of the Rhône and have a dark plum color and a nose that can include rich aromas of fruit, spice, minerals, and smoke with jam/fruit flavors. Rosés have a minimum of 15 percent Cinsault and maximum of 60 percent Grenache, producing dry wines with aromas of nectarines and good weight on the palate.

*Muscat Beaumes-de-Venise.* The sweet vin doux naturel has a lovely smell of peaches and orange blossoms and is best enjoyed within three years (see Figure 6.10). As in Rasteau, the wine is made by *mutage* (addition of alcohol). The result is a medium-bodied sweet white wine with at least 3.85

ounces (110 grams) of residual sugar per liter and 15 percent minimum alcohol. Simple still table reds are also made with medium weight and spicy berry flavors.

*Vacqueyras.* Vacqueyras was promoted to AOC status in 1989. The wines are deep in color with fruit, floral, and spice aromas, and medium weight on the palate. The reds are made from a blend of Grenache, Mourvèdre, Syrah, and Cinsault. A small amount of white and rosé wines are also produced in the area.

*Châteauneuf-du-Pape.* The qualities of the wines of the most famous appellation of the southern Rhône are primarily due to the exposure and soil. Heat-retentive large pebbles, or *galets,* from a few inches to a few feet thick, cover reddish clay alluvial soils. The appellation covers 7500 acres (3000 hectares) and there are also some vineyards in sand, chalk, gravel, and clay mixes. The vineyards of Châteuneuf-du-Pape, at about 393.6 feet (120 meters) high, are not as steep as those of the famous Hermitage to the north, but they still provide good drainage. Even though there are trees for protection, the vines here may be planted at an angle leaning into the *mistral* so that when they mature, they will be blown straight. About three percent of Châteauneuf-du-Pape production is white, with Clairette and white Grenache the most important varietals. Roussanne, Bourbelenc, and other grapes are also used to varying degrees by different producers. In this warm growing region, lack of acidity is a problem and, with few exceptions, the wines are best drunk young. In an attempt to preserve acidity producers try to prevent malolactic fermentation (see Chapter 1 on How Wine Is Made).

The appellation is best known for reds and their laws are among the strictest in France. The permitted yield is 924 gallons per 2.47 acres (35 hectoliters per hectare), with a minimum alcohol of 12.5. Chaptalization is illegal here, unlike many other areas of France. Further, five percent of each vintage must be declassified each year to ensure that the less-ripe grapes are not included.

There are two basic styles of reds: a leaner, fruit-forward type that is drinkable from two to six years after the vintage and the *vins de garde,* age-worthy wines that just begin to soften up when the former style is fading. The color of the red wines can range from garnet to mahogany with orange hues. Among the descriptors used for smells are cinnamon, coffee, fig, leather, violets, bay laurel, tar, and cedar. The high alcohol level assures a generous wine whose flavors vary according to the source of the grapes as well as the blend of varieties used. The following examples illustrate the range of blends (because of space limitations not all fine estates are listed.)

*Château Fortia:* 70 percent Grenache, 12 percent Syrah, 3 percent Mourvèdre, 6 percent white grapes

*Château de Beaucastel:* 30 percent Grenache, 30 percent Mourvèdre, 10 percent Syrah

*Chante Perdix:* 80 percent Grenache, 20 percent Muscardin

*Vieux Donjon:* 80 percent Grenache, 10 percent Cinsault, 10 percent Syrah

*Château de la Gardine:* 60 percent Grenache, 23 percent Syrah

*Château de la Nerthe:* 60 percent Grenache, 30 percent Mourvèdre

*Domaine du Vieux Télégraphe:* 70 percent Grenache, 10 percent Syrah, 8 percent Cinsault, 5 percent Mourvèdre

*Domaine de Mont Redon:* 65 percent Grenache, 15 percent Cinsault, 15 percent Syrah, 5 percent Mourvèdre

*Clos des Papes:* 70 percent Grenache, 20 percent Mourvèdre, 8 percent Syrah

*Domaine de la Solitude:* 50 percent Grenache, 20 percent Syrah, 15 percent Mourvèdre, 10 percent Cinsault

*Château Rayas:* 100 percent Grenache (low-yielding, very old vines)

The main grape is the Grenache, but recent planting trends favor Mourvèdre instead of Syrah. Only Domaine de Mont Redon and Château de Beaucastel utilize all 13 permitted grape types. The permitted red grapes are Grenache, Mourvèdre, Syrah, Cinsault, Counoise, Muscardin, Vaccarèse, and Terret Noir. Clairette, Bourbelenc, Roussanne, Picpoul, Picardin, and the white version of the Grenache are the permitted white grapes.

Only those estates which both grow and bottle their own wine are entitled to emboss the bottle with the coat of arms with the papal seal of crossed keys.

*Lirac.*  East of Châteauneuf-du-Pape is Lirac, which produces mostly medium-weight reds and rosés from a minimum of 40 percent Grenache. The small amount of white wine, blended with at least one-third Clairette, is prized for its light body and perfumed bouquet. All Liracs should be drunk young.

*Tavel.*  A clay-based soil with lots of stones gives the rosés of Tavel a medium to full body. They are made with at least 15 percent Cinsault and at most 60 percent Grenache. The oak-aged examples have more tannins and orange highlights than the fresher, fruitier, pinker, newer-style wines. The rosés have been famous since their use at the seventeenth-century court of Louis XIV.

*Côtes du Ventoux.*  Côtes du Ventoux produces lighter-style to medium-bodied dry reds, rosés, and whites from limestone-based soils. The fresh style of wine here is due to the 6232-feet-(1900-meter-) high Ventoux mountain which blocks the mistral and provides cooling breezes. La Vielle Ferme and Paul Jaboulet Âiné offer good examples of these inexpensive reds.

*Côtes du Lubéron.*  South of the Ventoux, the Côtes du Lubéron has similar soils and it's wines are good values as well. The Grenache and Syrah are the main red grapes, with Ugni Blanc and Clairette leading the whites. These dry wines have fine floral aromas and are best drunk young.

***Côtes-du-Rhône Producers.***   With a region this large we cannot list all the producers of wine but some of the important ones are: M. Chapoutier, J. L. Chave, Barge, Château de Beaucastel, B. Burgaud, J.F. Chaboud, Château d'Aquéria, Château de Montmirail, B. Faurie, Château Fortia, Château Grillet, Château Rayas, Château la Nerthe, A. Clape, Clos des Papes, R. Michel, Clos du Mont-Olivet, J.L Colombo, Délas, Domaine de Coyeux, Domaine de Mont Redon, Domaine de la Solitude, Domaine du Vieux Télégraphe, J. Fayolle, Vidal-Fleury, A. Graillot, J. L. Grippat, E. Guigal, P. Jaboulet Aîné, J. Jamet, R. Jasmin, M. Juge, Père Anselme, A. Perret, E. Pochon, R. Rostaing, H. Sorrel, R. Trollot, G. Vernay, N. Verset, La Vielle Ferme.

# The South of France

Many Mediterranean lands exported their culture, foods, and products to the south of France. The Spanish grapes Garnacha, Cariñena, and Mataro became the Grenache, Carignane, and Mourvèdre, respectively, which today are heavily planted and thought of as French varietals rather than Spanish. The Greeks established the city of Massalia (Marseilles) and planted vines, as did the Romans after them.

High-yielding grape types, resistant to heat and humidity, were planted in fertile and easy-to-harvest areas following the *phylloxera* plague. Quantity was pursued over quality. Today there is a movement to upgrade quality to produce wines worthy of AOC status. Others have chosen to produce varietal-labeled Vin de Pays, not always from traditional grapes but directed to the current stylistic preferences of the consumer.

The AOC wines have improved over the past two decades because of an investment in planting *vinifera* types in better locations such as hillsides and by curtailing yields. The increased use of fermenting at cooler temperatures in stainless steel preserves the fruit aromatics and flavors in contrast to the hot, alcohol, baked-fruit smells and tastes that were common in some of these wines before. Today, many of the southern appellations are smaller, reversing the trend of expanding boundaries as in many of the famous wine regions of France. Unlike the cooler northern regions which prize south-facing slopes for maximum heat and ripening, some of the southern producers value other exposures to preserve acidity in the grapes and resulting wine.

The south includes four regions: *Provence, Languedoc-Rousillon (Midi), Southwest,* and *Corsica.*

***The Wine Regions of the South of France—Provence.***   This area (see Map 6.12) has a history of supplying vacationers with refreshing simple rosés made from mostly Grenache and Carignan. Today, 60 percent of the region's production is rosé and about 35 percent is red. The trend is to replace vineyards of high-yielding Carignan with the popular Cabernet Sauvignon, Syrah, and Mourvèdre. The Sémillon and Rolle white grapes are being planted along with the traditional white grapes, Clairette and Ugni Blanc.

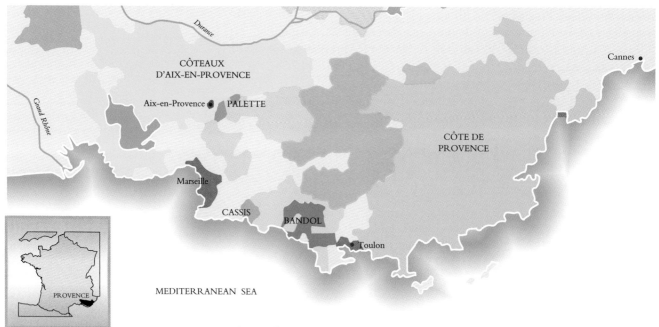

MEDITERRANEAN SEA

**Map 6.12** The Region of Provence.

Vineyard acreage in some seaside locations has given way to lodging for the tourist trade.

The Mediteranean climate offers these varietals over 3000 sunshine hours to ripen. Rainfall is low and the mistral wind dries the vines of any excess humidity.

### Appellations of Provence

*Côte de Provence, Côteaux d'Aix en Provence, and Côteaux Varois.* The Côte de Provence encompasses 44,500 acres (17,800 hectares) and is the largest appellation of the three. Today, Syrah and Cabernet Sauvignon each may account for up to 30 percent of a blended wine while the Carignan is held to a maximum of 40 percent. Serious producers are investing in new oak barrels and using higher proportions of Cabernet Sauvignon, Syrah, and the local reds, Tibouren, Calitor, and Mourvèdre, to make finer wines.

There are four small appellations in Provence, *Bandol, Palette, Cassis,* and *Bellet.*

*Bandol.* Reds and rosés are the majority of production with some dry whites. The reds can have up to 20 percent white grapes added but by law must contain at least 50 percent Mourvèdre. Grenache and Cinsault are the other main grapes for reds and rosés. The reds can offer spicy, red fruit scents and a medium to full body. The best can improve over a decade. The rosés tend to have an orange-red color and are made bone dry to slake the thirst in hot weather. Whites are made from such local southern grapes as Ugni Blanc, Bourbelenc, and Clairette with Sauvignon Blanc used to add acidity. Domaine Ott and Domaine Tempier are both producers whose wines are found in the U. S market.

*Palette.* Palette is a small appellation based on limestone soils that produce more whites than reds and rosés.

*Cassis.* Whites are about three-quarters of the production and are based on Clairette, Sauvignon Blanc, Ugni Blanc, and Marsanne. The Cap Canaille Cliff shelters the vineyards from the mistral wind.

*Bellet.* Bellet is 111 acres (49 hectares) of cooler, terraced vineyards that produce lighter-style reds and rosés. Whites from Rolle and Chardonnay grapes are full bodied and aromatic.

### The Wine Regions of the South of France—Languedoc-Rousillon or Midi.
The Languedoc and Rousillon areas, also known as the Midi (see Map 6.13), contain 40 percent of the nation's vineyards but only produce ten percent of the total AOC production. It is an area traditionally associated with simple table wines. Recent investments and improvements have led to an increase in quality. Here, the emphasis has been on vins de pays or country wines. The largest area for country wines is Vins de Pays d'Oc and its subregions. Eighty percent of the nation's vins de pays are produced here from the Gard, Hérault, Aude, and Pyrénées-Orientales départements.

The wine industry is based mostly on farmers with small holdings who sell their wine to négociants or cooperatives. Domestic and international investors have established large wineries with stainless steel tanks for controlled fermentation and oak barrels for aging. Fortant de France is the label used by the Skalli négociants for a line of varietal-labeled wines. Domaine de la Baume also produces a line of varietal wines as Vins de Pays de l'Hérault and they are owned by the Australian firm, Hardys. Les Salins de Midi have been innovators in the region for four decades. Their estates are experimenting with organic farming and new varietals. Other importers include Les Jamelles, Val d'Orbieu, and Réserve St. Martin.

The new grape varieties and improved equipment have transformed the style of many wines. Aramon was a popular red grape until the 1960s when Carignan became the most-planted grape type, followed by Grenache. To lessen the natural tannins of the Carignan, many producers are using carbonic maceration to make medium-weight reds with fresh fruit flavors. The wines with deeper color, and more complex aromas and tastes are made with Cabernet Sauvignon, Syrah, Mourvèdre, and Cinsault. The white grape types traditional to the area, Bourbelenc, Maccabéo, and Picpoul, are being replaced by the more aromatic Viognier, Sauvignon Blanc, Chardonnay, Rolle, and Marsanne. Some 85,000 acres (34,300 hectares) of vineyards have been converted to the more promising red and white varieties from 1983 to 1993.

Mild winters and warm summers allow the grapes to fully ripen. The best vineyards tend to be on slopes and in the foothills of the mountains. The flat land of the plains is used for high-yield table wines. An overabundance of wine in warehouses has led to pressure from the European Community to replace these vineyards with other fruit crops. The *vignerons* are putting their efforts into producing less quantity and higher-quality wines. A good share will be sold under the varietal name rather than appellation name because many of the new varieties are not yet authorized for AOC status.

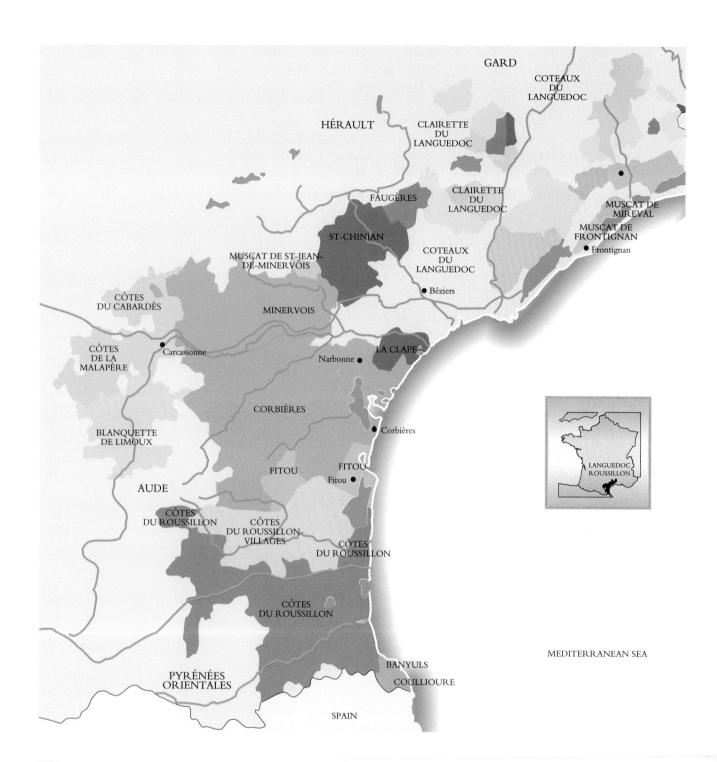

GARD

COTEAUX
DU
LANGUEDOC

HÉRAULT

CLAIRETTE
DU
LANGUEDOC

CLAIRETTE
DU
LANGUEDOC

MUSCAT DE
MIREVAL

FAUGÈRES

MUSCAT DE
FRONTIGNAN

• Frontignan

ST-CHINIAN

MUSCAT DE ST-JEAN-
DE-MINERVOIS

COTEAUX
DU
LANGUEDOC

• Béziers

CÔTES
DU CABARDÈS

MINERVOIS

CÔTES
DE LA
MALAPÈRE

• Carcassonne

LA CLAPE

Narbonne •

BLANQUETTE
DE LIMOUX

CORBIÈRES

Corbières •

FITOU

FITOU

Fitou •

AUDE

CÔTES
DU ROUSSILLON

CÔTES
DU ROUSSILLON-
VILLAGES

CÔTES
DU ROUSSILLON

CÔTES
DU ROUSSILLON

MEDITERRANEAN SEA

BANYULS

COULLIOURE

PYRÉNÉES
ORIENTALES

SPAIN

LANGUEDOC
ROUSSILLON

**Map 6.13**   The Region of Languedoc-
Rousillon.

## Appellations of the Midi

*Côtes du Rousillon, Côtes du Roussillon Villages.*   Côtes du Rousillon
may produce red, rosé, or white while the Villages appellation is for red
wines only. These require lower yields and higher minimum alcohol levels.
With over 25 million bottles annually, quality varies but the reds from the
better villages can last four years while others are made to be in a lighter

style and are best enjoyed within a year. Carignan is the dominant red grape but Syrah and Mourvèdre combined must account for at least 30 percent of the blend. Maccabéo, Marsanne, Roussanne, Malvoisie du Roussillon, and Rolle or Vermentino are white grapes used to produce simple wines best consumed within a year of the vintage.

*Coteaux du Languedoc.*    This large appellation stretches from Narbonne to Nîmes and includes 91 villages, most of which are in the Hérault département. Red wines dominate production and by law must have a minimum of 20 percent Grenache, ten percent each of Mourvèdre and Syrah, and no more than 50 percent of Cinsault and Carignan. Rosés and white wines are also made and the Ugni Blanc, Bourbelenc, and Grenache Blanc are the most-planted white varieties.

The better villages of the area, allowed to add their own names to a label, have applied to be raised to AOC status. Some examples are La Clape (fine whites as well as reds), St. Saturnin, and Montpeyroux. Faugères and St. Chinian are two that have recently been elevated to have their own appellation. To accomplish this, the lesser sites of St. Chinian were not approved and the area was reduced by approximately 20,000 acres (8080 hectares).

Within the boundaries of this AOC is one of the Midi's most expensive wines, even though it is still only a Vins de Pays de l'Hérault. Mas de Daumas Gassac is over 75 percent Cabernet Sauvignon with the balance of Syrah, Cabernet Franc, Malbec, Pinot Noir, and Tannat. Aimé Guibert, the proprietor, does not fine or filter the wines before bottling. The property is situated on soils similar to those of some of the finest châteaux of Pauillac in the Médoc subregion of Bordeaux. The wine was first released in 1978 and won respect for its style which was reminiscent of Bordeaux. The wines have an opaque dark plum color, the smell of blackcurrants, and a full body. Their white wine is based mostly on Chardonnay, Viognier, and Petit Manseng with Muscat, Marsanne, Roussanne, and Bourbelenc. Whereas the red can mature and be enjoyed over a dozen years, the small amount of white produced is best enjoyed young.

Although double or triple the price of most other Midi wines, the quality is consistently high and the wine provides the opportunity to drink the best wine of a region at a price significantly less than the best products of the other major regions of France.

*Minervois.*    The wine of this region is named after the goddess of wisdom and the town Minerve. The area is south of the Montagne Noire (Black Mountain) and has many terraced vineyards among the 61 villages it encompasses. Some 9800 acres (3920 hectares) are planted mostly in red grapes. New legislation is forcing farmers to reduce the amount of traditional Aramon, Alicante Bouschet, and Carignan and increase the use of Mourvèdre, Syrah, and Grenache. Some producers are destemming to produce less-tannic wines and the best examples of the area's potential come from the higher-elevated vineyards using lower yields. White wines vary in quality more than the reds but some producers are making aromatic full-bodied white wines using oak barrels. A small amount of sweet fortified

Muscat de St-Jean-Minervois made in the northeast portion of the zone has its own AOC.

*Corbières.*   The reds (90 percent of production) are fuller in body than Minervois and the best are aged in oak and may be cellared for five years. Carignan still dominates the blend which may also include Grenache, Mourvèdre, Syrah, and Cinsault. With about 30,000 acres (12,000 hectares), it is the largest of the Midi appellations. To attain AOC status the acreage was reduced and the best sites have applied for Grand cru status. Eleven sites have been nominated and await official recognition. Examples are Boutenac, Fontfroide, and Sigean which are well suited for the Mourvèdre while Syrah is best grown at Serviès. The range of soil types, exposures, altitudes, and grapes used is expressed in the wines from individual domaines.

*Fitou.*   In 1948, Fitou became the first table wine to gain AOC status in the Midi. The laws stipulate the wines must be red and aged at least nine months in oak barrels or vats. Carignan and Grenache are the dominant grapes but, as elsewhere in the Midi, Mourvèdre and Syrah are increasing in acreage. The appellation covers over 6100 acres (2440 hectares) with a portion on the coast and the rest inland separated by the Corbières appellation.

*Costières de Nîmes.*   Although 62,500 acres (25,000 hectares) have been approved for AOC status only 3000 acres (1200 hectares) are used for that purpose. The emphasis in this area is on using popular varietals to produce vins de pays. A maximum of 40 percent Carignan is allowed for the AOC red wine and Grenache must account for at least 25 percent of a blend. The soil is covered with large pebbles similar to many vineyards in the Rhône which it borders.

*Coullioure.*   Grenache and Mourvèdre combined may account for a minimum of 60 percent of a blend that may also include Syrah, Carignan, Counoise, and Cinsault. On the steep slopes of this area low yields are the norm and the small amount of wines produced here have rich fruit flavors and a full body. A maximum alcohol level of 15 percent and a maximum residual sugar of .175 ounces per quart (five grams per liter) are required for this appellation. The wines can be cellared and appreciated after a decade but may also be enjoyed two years after the harvest. In their youth they are opaque dark-colored wines with powerful sweet fruit aromas and taste. Dr. Parcé, of Dr. Parcé Mas Blanc, is a respected producer who led the way for AOC status with his high-quality wines. Mourvèdre is the dominant grape in his blend which also includes Syrah and Counoise. Collioure is located next to the village of Banyuls and its wines used to be sold as Banyuls Sec, while today dry wines of Banyuls may be sold as Collioure.

*Banyuls.*   Banyuls is a vin doux naturel based on a minimum of 50 percent of black Grenache. A Banyuls Grand cru must use a minimum of 75 percent Grenache. The juice is fortified and the wine is left on the skins for about a month to develop aromatics and gain color. The wine is then transferred to glass containers, known as *bonbonnes,* or to oak casks. The Grand crus must spend at least two and a half years in oak before bottling and some are aged longer. Some producers keep the wines in cool conditions while others do not. Left in barrels that are not filled completely and are exposed to seasonal variations in temperature, the wines oxidize, turn brown, and take on the style known as *Rancio.* Rancio has a complex bouquet including scents of dried fruits and nuts. These full-bodied sweet wines may be enjoyed up to 30 years after the harvest. Producers include Dr. Parcé Mas Blanc, Le Mas St. Louis, and the Cave Coopérative L'étoile.

*Other Vins Doux Naturels.* The residents of Rousillon identify with their Catalan neighbors just across the border in Spain; vins de pays from the southern part of the area is labeled Catalan, while the northern wines are labeled Côtes Catalan. Arnau de Villanova from Catalan is credited with discovering the fortification process in the thirteenth century to produce vins doux naturel. Banyuls, as discussed, is an appellation within the Roussillon that specializes in the sweet vins doux naturels. Other vins doux naturels appellations include *Maury, Muscat de Frontignan, Rivesaltes, Muscat de Lunel, Muscat de Mireval, and Muscat de Frontignan.* Mas Amiel is the finest producer of Grenache-based Maury. The wine spends at least a year in glass bonbonnes and then is aged in oak to produce six-, ten-, or 15-year-old examples. The latter has characteristics similar to a tawny Porto. Over two-thirds of the nation's production of vins doux naturels is labeled *Rivesaltes* and it is produced throughout the Roussillon and in part of the Aude. The grapes used for the Rivesaltes appellation include Muscat, Maccabéo, Malvoisie du Roussillon, and Grenache Noir, Gris, or Blanc. The Rivesaltes may be white without any skin contact, red with extended maceration of the skins, or tawny with age. Rivesaltes made exclusively from Muscat has the appellation *Muscat de Rivesaltes.* A Rivesaltes Rancio style is produced as well as a Porto style made by bottling the fortified wine young and allowing it to mature in the bottle rather than the cask.

**The Wine Regions of the South of France—Southwest.** The area (see Map 6.14) covers 70,000 acres (28,800 hectares) with over half of the vines producing AOC wines from a variety of grape types, wine-making techniques, soils, exposures, and climatic influences. The Atlantic Ocean moderates the climate for those vineyards closest to it, while vineyards farther inland have warmer growing conditions.

The area is overshadowed by Bordeaux, the world's largest fine-wine area to its north, and the Midi to the east, France's largest production area. There are some good-value sparkling, rosé, dry, and sweet whites, as well as medium- to heavy-weight red wines in this zone. Comté Tolosan is a large vins de pays area producing mostly red followed by rosé and some whites. The local red grapes are Tannat and Fer. Cabernet Sauvignon, Cabernet Franc, and Merlot are increasing in acreage along with Sauvignon Blanc and Sémillon.

The AOC appellations of the Southwest are *Limoux, Cahors, Côtes de Duras, Buzet,* and *Côtes du Marmandais.*

**Map 6.14** The Southwest Wine Region of France.

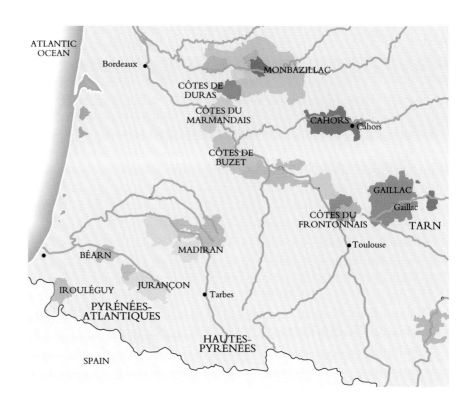

*Limoux.* Limoux is a cool region producing mostly white and sparkling wines located southwest of the medieval fortressed city of Carcasonne. The nation's first sparkling wines fermented in the bottle were made here at the Abbey of St. Hilaire in 1531. The dry sparkling wine *Blanquette de Limoux* must contain at least 90 percent of the Mauzac grape, known locally as the Blanquette. Blanquette is a late-ripening variety with aromas and flavors of quince and apples, high acidity, and high sugar levels. In the Blanquette Méthode Ancestrale technique (100 percent Blanquette), wines are not disgorged to remove the dead yeast cells. In addition, these wines are sweeter than Blanquette de Limoux, with less carbonation. The dry sparkling *Crémant de Limoux* is made with Chardonnay, Chenin Blanc, and a maximum of 60 percent Blanquette.

The former appellation Limoux Nature for dry still white wines has been changed to simply *Limoux*. The wines must be made from Chardonnay with some Chenin Blanc and Blanquette permitted. The wines must be barrel fermented and stored in oak at least until the January after the harvest. Stirring of the lees during barrel aging is also mandated by law.

*Cahors.* Dubbed the "black wine" for its opaque dark purple hue, Cahors must have a minimum of 70 percent Malbec (Auxerrois here), with Merlot and Tannat. The best Cahors have a richness of plums and dried fruit, both in the nose and flavor of the wine and a full body. The traditional-style wines can improve over a decade. A recent trend by some producers is to opt for lighter-style wines that can be drunk young.

*Côtes de Duras.*   The area has had AOC status since 1937. The best sites are on hilltops and south-facing slopes with clay or calcareous clay soils. The Bordeaux-style white wines dominate and offer good value. The Sauvignon Blanc grape must be at least 25 percent of a blend if that much Ugni Blanc is used. Sémillon, Mauzac, Chenin Blanc, and Muscadelle are also used for whites which are produced in dry to semisweet (moelleux) styles. Reds, from traditional Bordeaux grapes, are easy-drinking wines to be drunk young.

*Buzet and Côtes du Marmandais.*   Red wines dominate here and are produced from traditional Bordeaux varieties. The wines may be best from two to ten years after the harvest, depending on vintage and producer. Only a small amount of rosé and white are made and they are also based on Bordeaux varietals.

### Bergerac

*Bergerac.*   Bergerac is a region on the eastern frontier of Bordeaux and uses similar grape types. The red wines are medium weight in style; the less-tannic wines have good fruit flavors. Within Bergerac are the appellations *Pécharmant, Montravel,* and the sweet whites of *Saussignac* and *Monbazillac.*

*Pécharmant.*   Pécharmant wines have a higher minimum alcohol and lower yield than Bergerac. The wines have more intense aromas and flavors of cassis without being heavy. They can be cellared for a decade. The white wines labeled *sec* (dry) have .14 ounces (four grams) or less residual sugar per liter by law, while *moelleux* wines are those with higher residual sugar levels.

*Montravel.*   Montravel produces dry whites from Bordeaux varieties Sauvignon Blanc, Sémillon, and Muscadelle. *Côtes de Montravel* and *Haut Montravel* are appellations using the same grapes to produce semisweet to sweet wines.

*Monbazillac.*   This region's luscious white wines, from the same grapes as Sauternes, offer a less-expensive alternative. As in Sauternes, the grapes are handpicked in successive *tries.* When affected by *botrytis* the wine is rich with honeyed smells and tastes and the alcohol level often reaches 20 percent. The wines can be drunk after two years but the best improve over 20 years from the harvest.

### Pyrénées

*Jurançon-Jurançon Sec.*   The sweet wine Jurançon is made from low yields of late-harvested grapes whose sugars have become concentrated by *passerillage* (grapes dried on the vines by the sun) due to the warm, dry winds from Spain and cool nights. The cool nights are a result of the vines being planted at altitudes close to 1000 feet (304 meters) above sea level. The Petit Manseng is the principal grape for these wines which have aromas and tastes of spices, honey, and pineapples, and good acid balance. Gros Manseng is the main grape used for the sec (dry) version that is permitted twice the yield allowed for sweet wines. The sec are best within three years of the harvest but the sweet wines can be delicious after 15 years of age.

*Madiran.* Madiran red is another heavyweight contender from the southwest with an opaque dark color, rich fruit smell, and lots of power on the palate. The Tannat is the grape used for 40 to 60 percent of the blend. Cabernet Sauvignon, Cabernet Franc, and Fer make up the balance. Traditionalists use mostly Tannat, while others rely more on the Bordeaux Cabernets. As in Cahors, the power of the wines matches the richness of the hearty local fare and the best wines improve up to a decade.

*Pacherenc du Vic Bihl.* This appellation is for dry and semidry white wines made in the same area as the red wines of Madiran. The Gros Manseng, Petit Manseng, and Courbu are used along with the local Ruffiac grape, as well as Sauvignon Blanc and Sémillon.

*Irouléguy.* This area is in the Basque section of the Pyrénées mountains. The vines are planted at elevations up to 1300 feet (395 meters) above sea level. Red wines are based mostly on the tannic, deep-colored Tannat with Cabernet Sauvignon and Cabernet Franc also used. The reds can have a deep color and spicy red fruit flavors, and account for two-thirds of the production from terraced vineyards. Rosés are characterized by an orange-red color with a fruity aroma, a dry taste, and a medium to full body.

*Béarn.* This Basque area produces mostly rosés and reds from Tannat, up to 60 percent, as well as other local grapes such as Fer, Manseng Noir, and Courbu Noir, and Cabernets. The Béarn wines may come from other appellations that do not permit reds, such as Jurançon, or rosés, such as Madiran. The former is known as *Rouge de Béarn* and the latter *Rosé de Béarn*. A third source for the appellation is around the town of Bellocq and whites, reds, and rosé wines from there are labeled as *Béarn Belocq*. These are easy-drinking light wines with good fruitiness that are best drunk young.

# Corsica

The island has some of Europe's oldest vineyards. The sunshine and warm weather allow the grapes to ripen completely and temperature-controlled fermentation in stainless steel vats produces fresher-style wines. As in the Midi, there is a movement to plant more Cabernet Sauvignon, Syrah, Mourvèdre, Chardonnay, and Viognier. These new grape types are not permitted for AOC wines and are labeled by varietal and as Vins de Pays de L' Ile de Beauté. Red grapes are better suited to the climate than whites which only amount to a tenth of production. Nielluccio and Sciarello are the island's best indigenous red grapes. Vermentino (Malvasia) and Russula Bianca (Ugni Blanc) are the major white grapes used.

*Patrimonio.*    Patrimonio was the first AOC on the island and its reds are made from a minimum of 90 percent Nielluccio. The small amount of white wine produced is made from Vermentino when dry, and from Muscat for sweet vin doux naturel. *Ajjacio* is an appellation based mostly on Sciarello with Grenache, Carignan, and Cinsault blended in. The styles of these two appellations are medium to full in body, with the Patrimonio's chalk-based vineyards being the richer of the two. *Vins de Corse* is a large appellation of almost 2500 acres (1000 hectares) and the best include the name of a specific site or town on the label. *Vins de Corse Coteaux de Cap Corse* on the northern portion of the island produces rosés, and dry to sweet white and red wines. Muscat du Cap Corse is a new appellation for Muscat-based vins doux naturel. The total AOC output is about an eighth of the island's total production.

# Summary

For most of this century, French wines dominated wine lists in fine restaurants in America, and as late as the 1970s most French restaurants in the United States continued to offer only French wines. Today, French wines must compete with wines from around the world, due in large part to the popularity of recognizable varietal grape names on labels in contrast to the place-names used for most AOC wines. The French wine community, including national and regional wine-trade associations and their public relations firms, have responded to the challenge. Tastings for retailers, restaurateurs, and consumers demonstrate the versatility of French wines with a wide range of food—from Asian cuisine to American barbecue.

The Traditional Bottle Shapes of France. From left to right: Rosé from Provence, Muscadet from Loire, Beaune from Burgundy, Gewurztraminer from Alsace, and Graves from Bordeaux.

Wine-producing nations are crafting wines to cater to current taste preferences according to market research. The vins de pays of southern France may be doing that as well, but there it is an improvement in quality over the simple table wines that dominated production before. In France's Appellation d'Origine Contrôlée areas, an emphasis on taste characteristics derived from the *terroir* of a particular site is still evident in most wines. The mineral and gooseberry smells of a Sauvignon Blanc from Sancerre, the barnyard and raspberry bouquet of aged Pinot Noir from Chambertin, the roasted, spicy, black-fig aromas of Syrah at Côte Rôtie, are indicative of those grapes in those soils and are welcome landmark scents of a maintained tradition.

The *Institut National de Recherche Agronomique* continues to work with the *Institut d'Oenologie de Bordeaux* to improve techniques in the vineyards and wineries throughout the nation. INAO maintains quality control over French wines, and the government subsidizes the promotion and export of French wines. In every corner in France people associated with wine are finding their own way to contend with the realities of the global market. There are those who would deal with it simply as a business and those who are *artistes* devoted to creating magic. Most fall somewhere in between and are finding a way to maintain the best parts of tradition, understand the taste preferences of current consumers, and prepare for the future.

# Wine in Contemporary Italy

## Introduction

It is impossible to make a blanket statement about the wines of Italy today. We cannot use the term "modern wines of Italy," because this would apply to a fraction of the country's enormous wine production, most of which is made by traditional, even outmoded, methods. It would also be a mistake, however, not to focus on the best wines of Italy, some produced with great success and old technology, and some just finding an audience, but made by the most innovative methods.

Italy is the world's largest producer, exporter, and consumer of wine (see Table 7.1). Very little of this is fine wine. About two-thirds of Italy's export wines are shipped in bulk for blending, especially to France and Germany, and the amount of wine that is distilled into industrial alcohol exceeds the entire wine production of the New World. So, while Italy's production is prodigious, the amount of wine that makes it into bottles with labels is about 25 to 30 percent and, of this total, far less than half is classified under Italy's **DOC (Denominazione di Origine Controllata)** system. As a result, classified wines account for approximately 13 percent of total production, just a slightly smaller percentage than the AOC wines of France (see Chapter 6 on France).

View of Toscana.

Italy's best wines appeal to the sophisticated wine drinker, as well as the novice, for they are food-friendly, appealing, and full of personality. During the last 20 years, Italy's export wines (see Table 7.2) have gone far to help erase their image of inexpensive jug wines, a view that is still all-too-prevalent and, unfortunately, sometimes true. Among those who love the fine wines of Italy, a common question is "Why does Italy still produce lousy wines, when they are capable of such high achievement?"

Within this relatively small amount of recognized wines—if more than 125 million gallons/500 million liters of wine can be considered small—the majority are of average quality, and there are even some undistinguished, unlikeable wines. However, about ten percent of DOC and some newer DOC-equivalent wines are remarkable for their high quality. Connoisseurs look to these noble wines, some of them traditional, some new, some rediscovered, as the benchmarks by which all other Italian wines of any promise should be compared. Some of the fine wines are made by solitary artisans, some by large cooperatives. They may be distinctive or soulful, elegant or earthy, red or white, still or sparkling, known throughout the world or known only in a hometown province.

### TABLE 7.1 ITALIAN WINE PRODUCTION, EXPORT, AND CONSUMPTION

- produces about 1.6 billion gallons/6.4 billion liters of wine,

- exports approximately 375 million gallons/1.5 billion liters, and

- consumes 17.25 gallons/70 liters per capita (down from 22.5 gallons/90 liters about 20 years ago).

Italy has been a single nation-state for little more than a century; indeed, the top of the "boot" was not truly complete until 1954. Since World War II, Italy has seen 56 governments come and go, with no sign of political stabilization in sight. It is no wonder that the wines of semianarchistic Italy vary so greatly from region to region, province to province. This profile is the exact opposite of the stable French model which, due largely to social and political continuity, allows France to focus on Europe's worldwide wine trade. If Italy demonstrated political stability and a more national identity, its wine trade might exhibit similar traits. Of course, regional and provincial identity is what makes every Italian wine so distinctive from every other Italian wine. If this attitude were to change . . . well, it just would not be Italy.

Starting in 1963, when Italy's wine laws were passed, the modest stirrings of a national commitment to quality could be sensed. These laws, which have been updated and amended every few years, allow Italy to take its place on the European stage with the other premium producers of the European Community (EC). The EC has set strict agricultural and land-use laws for its members (see the Introduction to Part 3), and Italy, while it is ahead of Spain and Portugal in its wine legislation and regulation, still is playing catch-up with the stars of the show, France and Germany. The EC has offered Italy's vineyards and wineries financial help in upgrading their properties and production methods, sometimes sending out a double message to increase yields while improving quality, which is a difficult trick. Overall, however, the DOC laws and EC oversight have helped Italian wines in their improvement process.

With hundreds of native vinifera grapes, and dozens of imported ones, Italy makes an enormous array of wines. Its climate, which at its extremes can mimic North Africa in the south and Switzerland in the north, allows

## TABLE 7.2   ITALIAN WINE EXPORTS BY VOLUME (1992)

- 1.6907 billion gallons/63.8 million hectoliters produced

- 328.6 million gallons/12.4 million hectoliters exported

| | |
|---|---|
| Germany | 38 percent |
| France | 25 percent |
| United Kingdom | 9 percent |
| United States | 9 percent |
| Switzerland | 7.6 percent |
| Holland/Austria/Sweden | 3.4 percent |
| Belgium/Luxembourg | 2 percent |
| Canada | 1.7 percent |
| All Others | 5 percent |

almost every known grape to thrive. Soils are as varied as the weather, and fine wines are made in almost every one of the 20 wine-producing regions, often from native grapes, sometimes from French and German vinifera. The reputation of the producer is paramount, as the same grapes from the same region, even the same town, can make very different wines. In the hands of a vigneron committed to quality, the wine can sing a classic aria, but if a producer committed only to profit gets his or her hands on those same grapes, the wine will sing off-key, and all we will hear will be flats and sharps.

The portrait of Italy's wines is unpredictable, changing almost daily, but unmistakably changing for the better. It has been said before, but it bears repeating: Italy is not so much a country as it is one gigantic vineyard.

## History

When the Phoenicians, traveling from Persia around 2000 B.C., landed in what is now Puglia in southern Italy, they found that grapes were being grown and wine was being made and sold. Later, when the Greeks conquered Sicilia and a good part of southern Italy, they introduced grapes that are still being grown in modern Italy. Farmers and slaves in ancient Campania grew Greco (Greek), Aglianico, Moscato, and Malvasia—all vinifera grapes that continue to be planted in modern Campania. The Greeks embraced the wine culture of their new colonies in Magna Graecia, and what is now Italy came to be called Oenotria, the "Land of Wine."

While the Greeks began an active wine trade in the south, the Etruscans focused their energies in central Italy, especially in what is now Toscana and Umbria. Both peoples developed their own methods of viticulture, which

Greek Tablet, Celebrating the Wine Harvest.

Ancient *amphorae,* Greek Wine Vessels.

Roman Ruins.

Greek Ruins at Pastum.

were later synthesized and improved upon by the Romans, whose greatest poets and scholars wrote about the wonders of wine. Although they planted vines in Sicilia, the central coast provinces, and the Alps, the Romans did their best work on their home turf. The area around the ancient city of Pompeii became the center for the wine trade, and it was here that new production methods originated, including primitive but successful attempts at aging the wine, making lighter, drier versions of what had been flat, alcoholic wines, and stopping fermentation by utilizing cold-water baths, a precursor to temperature-controlled cool fermentation.

Roman Wine Plaque in Ceramic Relief.

The Roman wine trade spread to every part of the empire, as wines were traded across what is now Italy, France, Germany, parts of North Africa, Spain, and England. Wine traders from what is now the Piemonte region introduced wooden barrels for transport and, by extension, aging. All of this occurred before the first century A.D.

As if predicting Oenotria's future, the Roman Emperor Domitian, around A.D. 100, decreed that, due to overproduction, whole vineyards would have to be uprooted. This was forward thinking on the part of Domitian, who realized the inverse relationship between quality and quantity, but the fall of the Roman Empire had begun, and Italy's wine culture would not surface again—except for the wines needed for sacred rites of the Catholic Church—until the end of the Middle Ages.

The early Romans had written about wine with passion and erudition, and their viticultural records survive to this day. The same cannot be said for the period from the Middle Ages to the Renaissance. We do know that in the fourteenth and early fifteenth centuries sweet wines were well liked in Europe, and wine was also used as food to sustain daily life. With the coming of the Renaissance, wine enjoyed a resurgence as a subject of the arts, especially painting and poetry. The little technical knowledge we have about wine making in the sixteenth century indicates that due to a desire for good wines by the richest Italians and other Europeans, quality generally improved, but the former Oenotria was still far from the days when its beloved Bacchus was the only god of food or drink.

Beginning in the late seventeenth and early eighteenth centuries, Toscana became the center of Italy's wine culture, and the beginnings of modern wine laws began to take root. However, the rest of the independent provinces that make up contemporary Italy, feeling the effects of war and widespread poverty, had little or no part in developing a modern wine trade. At this point France, a culturally and politically unified country, assumed control of Europe's international wine trade, a role it continues to enjoy today.

Starting in the mid-nineteenth century, however, the provinces of a reuniting Italy began to enter the modern age. With a nod in the direction of France, the Italians began to age their drier red wines in Chianti and in Barolo (where Italy's first commercially produced dry wine was made in the 1850s). Sparkling wines were produced around Asti, based on the methods learned in the Champagne region, and Marsala was introduced by J. Woodhouse, an Englishman who owned a Port house. As Italy became a unified and somewhat more prosperous country, red, white, and sparkling wine producers developed international markets for their wines. Italy was back on the quality map, as a true rebirth of its wines had begun.

Just before the turn of the twentieth century, Italy's impressive wine industry was dealt a blow from which it has never completely recovered. Both the vine louse *phylloxera* and the powdery mildew, oidium (see Chapters 2 on Wine Grapes and 6 on France), decimated Europe's vineyards. Italy was hit particularly hard by these dual pests, for two essential reasons. First, before *phylloxera*, promiscuous plantings—the planting of grapevines alongside other crops— was the norm in Italy, so not only vines but a great deal of

Italy's total agricultural output was damaged. Second, before the destruction of Italy's vineyards, 2000 different local grape varieties were used to produce wines. Since the only way to subdue *phylloxera* was to plant the vines on American rootstock, a painstaking and expensive process, marginal producers making artisan's wines were wiped out, as were their historic grape types. In place of the native vines many French and German vinifera grapes were planted, along with high-yielding native grapes that, with the help of the long growing season in southern Italy, could produce wines of high alcohol but little complexity.

This reputation for frivolous wines, sometimes dressed up in silly bottles, has been hard for Italy to shake, but the image of Italian wines *is* changing. One of the most important reasons for this change is Italy's wine laws, but the integrity, passion for quality, and increasing financial strength of Italian wine producers should not be underestimated.

## Wine Laws

Since the early Romans, Italy has had wine laws. In 1716, the Grand Duke of Toscana proposed the idea of delimited wine zones for Chianti, Pomino, Carmignano, and Valdarno di Sopra. Fine wines have been made in Italy for hundreds of years, and the variety of wines and grape varietals has often appeared virtually endless.

After World War II, with prosperity and the attendant optimistic view of Europe as an economic and political confederacy, France and Italy, as the world's leading producers of wine, both agreed that a pan-European approach to enforceable wine laws would be necessary. Perhaps foreseeing the coming of the European Community, the two nations planned to provide equivalent laws for each wine-producing nation in Europe. Certainly, if Italy wanted to become a part of the modern wine industry, the adoption of modern wine laws was necessary. This was especially true because after World War II, in an effort to recover economically, Italy began to develop a worldwide reputation as the leading producer of inexpensive, low-quality bulk, or jug wines. Producers, especially in the southern and central areas of the country, took advantage of the long growing season and the sunshine to produce wines high in alcohol, but with little depth. Although fine wines were still being produced in Italy, they were overshadowed by the cheap one-dimensional wines that flooded the international market.

In 1963 the Italian Parliament adopted the Demonazione di Origine law, effective in 1966 and modeled after the French Appellation Contrôlée laws. This law established the **Denominazione di Origine Controllata (DOC)** category, guaranteeing the origin of a particular wine. The purpose of the DOC laws was to ensure that Italy would regain its place as a producer of consistent, high-quality wines. Since the passage of the original DOC laws, the controversial legislation has been continually updated, with sweeping changes made in 1992 (these changes are commonly called the "Goria Laws," named for the Minister of Agriculture who was instrumental in their passage).

In 1980, the category of **DOCG (Denominazione di Origine Controllata e Garantita)** became an important part of Italy's wine legislation. The DOCG regulations were part of the original law but not activated for 17 years. The first DOCG zone, Brunello di Montalcino from Toscana, was followed by Barolo and Barbaresco from Piemonte. DOCG established the tradition of a "guarantee," an even higher level of regulation for the very few wines considered to be highest in quality and reputation from a given DOC area. At present, there are a total of 13 DOCG wines in Italy, with a few more awaiting this highest designation.

The purpose of the DOC law was to uphold and improve the reputations of Italy's wines by establishing geographically delimited zones. There are roughly 240 DOC and DOCG zones spread throughout Italy's 20 wine regions. Each region is an independent political unit, similar to the constituent states in the United States, and the DOC-approved zones within the regions produce a total of more than 850 wines—white, rosé, red, sparkling, and fortified. These zones can vary widely in size: the entire Abruzzo region contains only two contiguous DOC zones, covering over 19,920 acres/8300 hectares, while all of Piemonte contains 37 DOC zones, including four DOCG zones, on less than 84,000 acres/35,000 hectares.

While the DOC/DOCG wines of Italy often include the finest wines produced in the country, these wines still represent only 13 percent of Italy's wine production, with a current national goal of 20 percent. Italy's wine production is still excessive, and the DOC laws are just one tool in lowering production levels.

Of course, as with all members of the European Community, Italy's DOC laws must adhere to the EC wine laws (see the Introduction to Part 3). Wines that are DOC or DOCG quality may also bear the symbol VQPRD (for sparkling wines, VSQPRD), a European Community designation. Also, Italy must recognize the import laws of other countries. For example, any Italian wine shipped to the United States must have the words "Product of Italy" on the label (see the section on labels in this chapter). As with virtually all wine laws in Italy, the EC regulations are controversial for their lack of standardization. The best Italian wine makers pride themselves on the fact that their wines are not chaptalized, unlike their French counterparts; chaptalization is illegal in Italy under both DOC and EC laws. However, the question becomes this: Why should an Italian wine maker go to jail for doing what French wine makers do all the time: adding sugar to grape must during fermentation to raise alcohol levels?

The structure of the DOC laws encompasses all Italian wines, including the thousands of different wines that do not achieve DOC/DOCG status. As in most countries, but especially in Italy, wine laws are helpful, but the reputation of the producer is the most reliable guide to quality. Much like the French wine laws, the following categories of Italian wines (listed here from lowest to highest quality) have been established.

**Vino da Tavola.** Translated as "table wine," the Vino da Tavola designation includes wines that never reach bottles. Much of these wines are used for blending in inexpensive bulk wines, and most of the wine that is distilled for industrial alcohol. Beginning with the 1995 harvest, if the wine is bottled, the label can designate only color (i.e., "vino da tavola rosso") and the name of the producer. Grape variety, recognized geographical designation, and vintage year may not be listed on the label. "Fantasy" or proprietary labels, as well as names of vineyard estates or atypical geographic designations (not covered by law) are allowed in this category, however.

*Indicazione Geografica Tipica (IGT).*    Each IGT wine is typical of the large growing area in which the grapes are grown and the wine is made. Until 1992, these wines were informally designated "Vino Tipico." Far less restrictive than DOC, the IGT law allows many of the Vino da Tavola wines to "graduate" to this higher category. It is the fervent, though idealistic, hope that eventually 40 percent of Italy's wine production will fall into the IGT, DOC, or DOCG categories.

The newest category, IGT includes a wide range of very fine wines (many from Toscana), formerly vino da tavola or vino tipico, that rely on the reputation of the producer as a sure sign of quality. For instance, a producer in the Chianti Classico region might make a wine from 100 percent Sangiovese grapes. Legally this wine cannot be called Chianti or Chianti Classico; currently the maximum percentage of Sangiovese allowed is 90 percent. So the producer may decide to give the wine a proprietary name (such as Monte Vertine's "Le Pergole Torte"), or, if 100 percent varietal, simply call the wine by the grape name, Sangiovese (or colloquially, "Sangioveto," as produced by Badia a Coltibuono). Alternately, should wine maker Piero Antinori decide to blend 85 percent Cabernet Sauvignon, a nontraditional grape in Chianti, with 15 percent Sangiovese, he is no longer producing Chianti, but a wine with a proprietary designation (vineyard site name: Solaia). Many of these high-quality wines are among the most expensive Italy offers, and, at least within the confines of the DOC laws, some of the most controversial. Since these wines can be the finest expression of the wine maker's art, the IGT designation has developed a certain panache, especially since quite a few of these wines have met with commercial success in the export markets.

*Denominazione di Origine Controllata (DOC).*    A wine that is designated DOC is made from approved grape varieties and grown in approved vineyards located in demarcated geographical zones. Each of the 240 DOC zones can be as large as an entire region, or as small as part of a commune or town. Subregions, such as a **classico** region, may be demarcated, some of the best known being Valpolicella Classico, Orvieto Classico, and Soave Classico. Aside from the broad strokes painted by the DOC laws, local consortia of growers and producers further define the qualifications for each particular DOC. For example, the growers' *consorzio* in Valpolicella Classico meets to decide yields per hectare in each particular vintage, within the limits set forth by the national DOC criteria. Nominations for new DOC regions are made by the consortia and local chambers of commerce, submitted to regional DOC representatives, and then forwarded to the federal DOC commission, which is part of the Ministry of Agriculture.

Each DOC controls the following aspects of wine produced within its boundaries:

- Grape types permitted and in what percentages. For some wines, minimum and maximum elevations for planting.

- Yield per hectare of grapes and pruning methods to be used in the vineyard.

- Total gallons/hectoliters of wine produced.

- Vinification method for some wines.

- Aging methods and length of aging for some *riserva* (reserve) or *vecchio* (old) wines. These wines must be aged for a minimum period of time. Each wine has its own minimum aging requirements.

In addition to these regulations, chaptalization is not allowed in the production of these wines.

In a practice begun in 1990 in Piemonte, but not yet in place in other Italian wine regions, each DOC is supposed to meet certain minimum standards of color, aroma, and flavor, all of which are controlled by tasting commissions. Also, each wine must pass stringent chemical analyses for minimum alcohol percentage by volume and for total acidity. In some cases, minimum and maximum residual sugar levels are set, especially for wines that are made in a particular DOC area, but in different styles. For example, Orvieto, a white DOC wine from Umbria, ranges from dry to semisweet to sweet, and sugar levels are set for each wine. All of the wine regions are expected to follow Piemonte's lead and incorporate scientific and organoleptic testing within the next few years.

***Denominazione di Origine Controllata e Garantita (DOCG).*** The highest level attainable within the DOC laws, DOCG wines must be sold in bottles smaller than 1.25 gallons/5 liters, and an official numbered tag must be placed on the bottle across the cork's capsule. It is not uncommon for the bottles to also be numbered by the producer. DOCG wines must submit to even more stringent organoleptic analysis—a serious judging of their appearance, nose, and taste—than DOC wines. Some producers from DOCG regions have had their wines publicly rejected by the tasting commissions; in such cases, the wines must be declassified as vino da tavola. As of 1994, there were ten red DOCG wines: Barbaresco, Barolo, and Gattinara from Piemonte; Chianti, Vino Nobile di Montepulciano, Brunello di Montalcino, and Carmignano from Toscana; Torgiano Rosso Riserva and Sagrantino di Montefalco from Umbria; and Taurasi from Campania. The three white DOCG wines are: Albana Di Romagna from Emilia-Romagna; Vernaccia di San Gimignano from Toscana; Moscato d'Asti/Asti from Piemonte, including both the world-renowned sparkler (formerly Asti Spumante) and the almost-still wine *(frizzantino),* made with just the slightest prickle of bubbles. Wines expected to join the DOCG pantheon soon are Orvieto and Greco di Tufo; white wines from Umbria and Campania, respectively.

## CONSORZIO

Throughout Italy, the consorzio system is a voluntary association of producers, from a DOC/DOCG zone, and each consorzio offers technical and marketing assistance to its membership; Chianti Classico's consorzio is the best known and best organized. Some of the Italian consorzi enjoy government approval, and maintain standards that are higher than those set by DOC/DOCG, as demonstrated by their laboratories and tasting panels. These consorzi seem to work well, if for no other reason than what the alternative seems to be: lots of arguing and bickering among growers and producers.

***Naming Italian Wines.*** In Italy, there is no distinct pattern to how wines are named. Often, the wines are given a place name associated with the region of production, or are named for principal grape variety used (a varietal label); sometimes a combination of both is used: grape name and place name. The combination label often, but not always, symbolizes better quality than the simple varietal label. Proprietary labels are also used. In addition, descriptive terms like *classico, riserva, vecchio, novello, secco, amabile, abboccato, dolce, superiore, frizzante, spumante, passito, recioto, amarone,* and *liquoroso* may appear. The names of significant single vineyards are not often found on Italian labels, and there are no legal vineyard rankings under DOC law. Naming the **cru** (growth) is considered by most Italians to be ostensibly French, but it is finding some favor in the Piemonte region, and to a lesser extent, in Tuscany.

Table 7.3 shows some well-known labels of each type: place names, grape names, combination names, and proprietary labels.

The EC also requires that the percentage of alcohol-by-volume appear on the label (*e.g.,* 12.5 percent), and that if the bottle is the standard 750ml/75cl size this number appear on the label, followed by the letter "e" if the wine is to be sold within the EC. This quirk is due to the fact that, prior to EC standardization, some Italian bottles contained 72cl.

If the wine is estate bottled, an approved phrase, such as *imbottigliato dal produttore all'origine* ("bottled by the producer at the source"), often followed by the name of the producer, appears on the label. This is the equivalent of the phrase *Mise en bouteilles au château* from Bordeaux (see Chapter 6 on France). If the wine is produced and bottled by a cooperative or a group of cooperatives, the phrases *imbottigliato dalla cantine sociale* or *imbottigliato dai produttori riuniti* may appear. *Imbottigliato nella zona di produzione* ("bottled in the production zone") lets the buyer know that the wine is not estate bottled, but simply bottled within the legal limits of the particular DOC zone.

# Italy's Wine Regions

Italy is divided into 20 wine regions (see Map 7.1), each a political unit with provincial subregions that bear the name of the province's major city (*e.g.,* in the province Lazio, the eponymous subregion and city are both named

### TABLE 7.3

*Place Names*

Chianti, Chianti Classico, Chianti Classico Riserva

Orvieto, Orvieto Abboccato, Orvieto Secco, Orvieto Classico

Frascati, Frascati Superiore

Valpolicella, Valpolicella Classico Superiore, Recioto della Valpolicella

Barbaresco, Barbaresco Riserva, Barbaresco Riserva "Santo Stefano"

Asti

*Grape Names*

Pinot Grigio

Moscato

Barbera

Dolcetto

Chardonnay

Teroldego, Novello di Teroldego

*Combination Grape Names and Place Names*

Moscato d'Asti

Nebbiolo d'Alba

Sangiovese di Romagna

Cortese di Gavi

Brunello di Montalcino

Greco di Tufo

*Proprietary Names*

Le Pergole Torte

Sassicaia

Tignanello

Cabreo La Pietra

Rubesco

**Map 7.1** The Wine Regions of Italy.

Rome). Each region contains anywhere from one (in Basilicata) to 38 (in Piemonte) DOC or DOCG zones. Taking a look at the map of Italy (see Map 7.1), we can readily divide the country into four parts, each containing smaller constituent regions: (1) Southern Italy (Sicilia, Sardinia, Calabria, Basilicata, Puglia, and Campania); (2) Central Italy (Lazio, Molise, Abruzzo, Marche, Umbria, and Toscana); (3) Northwest Italy (Emilia-Romagna, Liguria, Lombardia, Piemonte, and Valle d'Aosta); and (4) Northeast Italy (Veneto, Friuli-Venezia Giulia, and Trentino-Alto Adige).

## Southern Italy

While the vineyards of Southern Italy (see Map 7.2) prompted the ancient Greeks to call their colonized area Oenotria, or "Land of Wine," and the Roman poets Virgil and Horace sang the praises of the intoxicating Falernum, today this region is better known for its huge production than for its minuscule amount of fine table wines. The wine lake continues to flow, just barely abated, in the South. Indeed, Southern Italy accounts for almost 40 percent of Italy's total wine production, with Puglia producing more than any other single region, and Sicilia a close second. Because much of this wine is being used for blending bulk wines or for distilling into industrial alcohol, the whole of Southern Italy accounts for under ten percent of DOC production. A significant portion of the DOC wines of the South can be accounted for by one justly famous fortified wine, Marsala, which produces well in excess of 5.83 million gallons/220,000 hectoliters each year, accounting for about 75 percent of Sicilia's DOC production. On the other hand, Sicilia's best dessert wine, the DOC wine Malvasia delle Lipari, accounts for only 6625 gallons/250 hectoliters total production. But this is a mere drop in the ocean, when one realizes that the total production of wine from the South now approaches 795 million gallons/30 million hectoliters per year.

Often we hear that because the climate of Southern Italy is so hot, so sunny, it can never be a premium viticultural area. This is just not true. While much of the South is drenched in sunlight, the coastal and mountain regions can be quite cool, allowing for the production of good wines. Climate is really not the problem in Southern Italy, but human nature just may be. While the EC and the Italian government have provided funds to improve the wines in the south, and the EC pays a premium to growers who decrease their acreage in vines, mismanagement and corruption are commonplace. Add to this a tradition of making high-alcohol, full-bodied, one-dimensional wines designed to boost the thinner wines of the

**Map 7.2**  Southern Italy.

northerly regions, and a certain geographical isolation (particularly in Sicilia and Sardinia), and you have a situation that does not welcome change, including the attempt to make wines of higher quality.

And yet, even in the South, there are several shining stars: wine makers and producers whose commitment to quality is high and whose product is glorious. While these producers hardly represent a revolution in the wines of Southern Italy—some of them have been making quality wines for many generations—they are, at least, living proof that fine wines can be made successfully here.

*Sicilia.* It is no exaggeration to say that the DOC laws just have not caught on in Sicilia, since there is so little DOC production in this region, which battles with Puglia for the title of Italy's largest wine producer. In fact, DOC is so unimportant to much of Sicilia's wine industry that the quality designation for much Sicilian wine is a simple "Q" printed on the bottle label, but it is not an objective guarantee of quality.

On the other hand, the best-known and most highly regarded table wines from Sicilia made by Corvo/Duca di Salaparuta are vino da tavola wines. The Corvo group has led the way in wine making technology and export marketing with their ubiquitous white and red, well-made, reasonably priced table wines. Their Duca Enrico, however, a red wine first produced from the 1984 vintage and made from 100 percent local grapes (Nero d'Avola) grown on 15-year-old vines, is aged in French oak barriques for 18 months. While quite expensive, the wine has met with great critical success and consumer response, proving that great wines can be made in Sicilia. Corvo/Duca di Salaparuta also produces the more moderately priced Terre D'Agala, also made from local varietals, and also a major success in ex-

The Island of Positano, Near Sicilia.

port markets. Another important wine producer is Regealia, whose Rosso del Conte is an outstanding red wine.

Total wine production in Sicilia averages about 237 million gallons per year. About 15 percent of this total is derived from about 240,000 acres/96,000 hectares, half of which is planted in the Catarrato grape, used to make Alcamo and Etna white wines (both DOC), as well as the famous fortified wine, Marsala. The newest plantings in Sicilia are white grapes that are made into light- to medium-bodied wines. The growers are still planting mostly native grapes, but some Sauvignon Blanc, Pinot Bianco, and Pinot Grigio, as well as Chardonnay, are being planted, though none of these fit the present DOC profile in Sicilia. While Sicilia, like the other Southern regions, has problems with its wines' reputations, recent trends seem to indicate a slow move toward lower production and toward higher quality.

*DOC Wines.*    Of Sicilia's ten DOC zones, one (Moscato di Siracusa) produces no wine (a good reason to review the granting of DOC zones, none of which have ever been withdrawn). Two zones (Faro and Moscato di Noto) produce only a few hundred bottles annually, with most of the production at Noto supervised by a state-run experimental station. Cerasuolo di Vittoria, produced on the southeast section of the island, is a local red wine made from Frapatto, Calabrese, and Grosso Nero grapes. Only 39,750 gallons/1500 hectoliters are produced. A fairly small amount (92,750 gallons/3500 hectoliters) of Moscato di Pantelleria is made as a fresh, sweet white wine, and as the sun-dried Moscato di Pantelleria Passito. Both wines are made on the tiny island community of Pantelleria, from Zibibbo, the colloquial name for the large Moscato grape that produces Italy's best raisins.

The Island of Capri, Near Sicilia.

*malvasia delle lipari*

*denominazione*
*d'origine controllata.*
*Imbottigliata da*
*Hauner Carlo srl*
*in Salina, Italia*
*lit.0,750e  13,5%vol.*
*vendemmia 1987*

# Hauner

**Figure 7.1** Carlo Hauner Produces Malvasia delle Lipari in the Town of Lipari, Sicilia.

Another tiny island, this one northeast of Sicilia, is home to the town of Lipari, where wine maker Carlo Hauner produces his Malvasia delle Lipari (see Figure 7.1). Also made in passito (sun-dried, raisinated grapes) or liquoroso (sweet and fortified) style, his standard sweet Malvasia is rare, but imported to the United States, where it has many admirers. Total production is only 66,250 gallons/250 hectoliters. On the northeastern part of the main island, 212,000 gallons/8000 hectoliters of Etna is produced yearly as bianco, bianco superiore (said to be the best example of the wine from this picturesque town), rosso, and rosato, all made from native grapes.

In western Sicilia, Alcamo produces 636,000 gallons/24,000 hectoliters of white wine bearing the name of its commune. Quality here is strictly dependent on the producer, and the wine can be very fine or quite ordinary. It is a wine made to accompany fish, made from local grapes, but with up to 20 percent Trebbiano Toscano allowed in the blend. The best producer is Rincione.

Western Sicilia is also home to Marsala, the fortified wine with so much history, a wine that at one time was the equal of Sherry and Madeira. Since the key to the production of a great Marsala is aging of the wine in local oak barrels, the finest Marsala is the dry Vergine or Soleras, which is made by blending wines from various vintages, much like the solera method for making Sherry (see Chapter 8 on Spain). Marsala Vergine ranks among the finest fortified wines in the world. During the last century, however, Marsala, which is made in a variety of styles—*secco, semisecco,* and *dolce,* along with *superiore* and *riserva* designations—has been largely relegated to the kitchen as an important ingredient in egg- and coffee-based dishes, as well as desserts and pastry (zabaglione and marzipan), due to its assertive flavor and lack of nuance. Also, Marsala has many imitators, and inferior fortified wines in the Marsala style have been made in other countries for many years. In 1986, the DOC laws for Marsala were rewritten, with far more restrictive regulations, so that it may one day regain its place as one of the fine fortified wines of the world.

Quality levels of Marsala are *Fine* (aged one year), *Superiore* (aged two years), *Superiore Riserva* (aged four years), *Vergine* or *Soleras* (no sweetened musts are allowed, and must be aged five years), and *Vergine Stravecchia* or *Vergine Riserva* (aged at least ten years).

**Sardinia.**   Sardinia is the most isolated area of Italy, an island of about one million inhabitants, about 150 miles/240 kilometers from the mainland. Spanish, Basque, Corsican, and Arabic influences abound, reflected in several different dialects and unique island lifestyle. Although the island is surrounded by Italy's largest seacoast (a total of about 1500 miles/2400 kilometers), the people still tend their sheep, pastures, and farms in the hills.

Sardinia is home to 18 DOC zones, but little of its wine is distinguished. In a country with so many fine wines, hunting for a good Sardinian wine may not be worth the effort for most people. Production methods in Sardinia reflect an inharmonious blending of the old and new. Wine is largely made by cooperatives utilizing modern technology and turning out ordinary, impersonal wines, or by traditionalists who do not appear interested in changing unscientific production methods. While the future of Sardinian wines is unclear, the single standout producer is Sella & Mosca, whose wine estates produce light white wines of singular character and good quality, none of them DOC, made from the respected Torbato grape.

The most highly regarded white wines of Sardinia are Vermentino di Galluria, a dry wine from the far north, the sweet Malvasia di Bosa from the central west coast, and the almost Sherry-like Vernaccia di Oristano, which is made in dry, sweet, and fortified versions. Many favorite Sardinian red wines are based on the Cannonau, derived from the Grenache grape. The Cannonau di Sardegna DOC zone takes in most of the island, making various wines that vary from dry to sweet to fortified styles, with Riserva and Superiore designations.

*Calabria.* While the Greeks had Calabria in mind when they called this part of the world Oenotria, modern Calabria bears little resemblance to that ancient land of wine. Wine takes a backseat in Calabria's economy to olive oil, grains, citrus, and vegetables. Also, while the wines of Calabria are for the most part undistinguished, production does not meet the demand of the citizens and tourists, who seem to enjoy drinking the local wines from the utilitarian **demijohns.** So there really is little incentive for the Calabrese to make better wines, unless they want to expand their wine markets, which does not seem to be a regional priority.

Calabria is home to eight DOC zones, the most famous being the small coastal zone of Ciró, which produces dry whites, rosés, and reds, some with Riserva status. Ciró is the stuff of legend; it, or rather its progenitor, Krimisa, was drunk by the athletes celebrating their victorious performances in the ancient Olympics. Modern Ciró has come a long way, utilizing temperature-controlled fermentation, and making a wine with lower alcohol. The whites, made from the Greco grape, are quite fresh and appealing.

Adjoining Ciró is the Melissa DOC, making similar wines from more or less the same grapes. Calabria's finest wine is Greco di Bianco, a rare, sweet wine produced on the southern coast, which is very hard to find, even for the most dedicated wine enthusiasts.

*Basilicata.* Bordered by Calabria, Campania, and Puglia on three sides, with a small outlet to the Ionian Sea on the fourth side, Basilicata (sometimes known by its ancient Roman name, Lucania) produces only 196,100 gallons/7400 hectoliters of its single DOC, Aglianico del Vulture, which accounts for only about two percent of Basilicata's total wine production. The Aglianico grape produces a dry red wine, with Vecchio and Riserva versions, as well as a sweet sparkling wine.

A very poor region of Italy, Basilicata can point to the Aglianico del Vulture, grown on the high slopes of Monte Vulture in the northeast, with justifiable pride, since this area produces one of Italy's finest wines from more than 1000 small DOC-registered plots. Aglianico del Vulture (DOC), in its best Riserva style, is full-flavored, and shows very deep extract of color, allowing it to age for easily five and perhaps as much as ten years.

Basilicata also produces under-appreciated Malvasia and Moscato-based wines, from grapes grown in the Vulture hills, and some good Sangiovese-based red wines, all of which are legally designated as vino da tavola.

***Puglia.*** Puglia produces more wine than any other Italian region, vying with Sicilia for this questionable honor. Quality, however, is not the focus of this region, although since the 1980s there has been a lot of talk about up-grading these wines. While the talk may be serious, it was during the 1980s, paradoxically, that Puglia eclipsed Sicilia's total wine production.

Surprisingly, Puglia has been granted 24 DOC zones, three more than Toscana, but only two percent of the region's production is classified. In fact, a substantial amount of the more than 250 million gallons/one billion liters of wine produced annually from this region is either distilled into industrial alcohol, or made into concentrated musts, used for blending and to increase alcohol and flavor levels, taking the place of illegal sugar. A bit more than 20 percent of Puglia's wine finds its way into bottles, and overproduction was a problem even before *phylloxera* struck Italy.

In general, the outlook for the wines of Puglia is not bright, but there is at least one shining star on the "heel of the boot." On the Salento Peninsula in the southeast is the prominent DOC zone Salice Salentino. A hit in the export market, particularly in the United States, the red Riservas from Dr. Cosimo Taurino have made a minor splash as a best buy for daily enjoyment. Made mostly from the local workhorse Negroamaro grape, the wine is full bodied and rich in fruit. Salice Salentino is, at its best, an age-worthy red of consistent quality that mellows nicely for five to six years. A very fine dry rosato is also produced in this DOC zone, but not widely exported.

***Campania.*** While rich in wine history—the ancient Romans and Greeks greatly prized the vineyards of this region—contemporary Campania is not a haven for quality wines. In fact, less than one percent of total wine pro-

Campania Vineyard.

duction is DOC (the lowest percentage in Italy), and only about five percent of the agricultural output of the region is attributable to grapevines. With just under six million people, and with commercial activity centered around the poor coastal city of Naples (Napoli), this is Italy's second most highly populated region. Campania actually imports more wine than it exports, and with no regional commitment to improving its wine picture, this physically beautiful and agriculturally lush area is unlikely to realize its fine wine potential any time soon.

## Central Italy

The six regions of Central Italy (see Map 7.3) produce a great deal of wine—25 percent of the country's total production, and about one-third of Italy's DOC/DOCG wines. This is an exciting time for wine making in Central Italy, as the area finds itself at a crossroads, having to make a critical choice between tradition and innovation. Happily, many producers are following the lead of Toscana and are trying to upgrade their wines. While the DOCG red wines of Toscana—Chianti, Brunello di Montalcino, Vino Nobile di Montepulciano, and the newest, Carmignano—are well known to lovers of Italian wines, there are other treasures to taste in these regions. Central Italy is divided by the Apennines mountain range into two distinct subsections, geographically, culturally, and viticulturally. The west, or the area that borders the Tyrrhenian Sea, includes Toscana, Lazio, and Umbria. The east, defined by its proximity to the Adriatic Sea, is made up of Marche, Abruzzo, and Molise. The wines produced in the east and west are quite different in style, quality, and constituent grape varieties.

Toscana is thought of as a center of Italian red wine production, but high-quality white wines are also produced here. The Vernaccia grape, for

Mastroberardino Headquarters, Campania.

Antonio Mastroberardino.

## THE MASTROBERARDINO FAMILY

While it is true that much of Campania is a wine wasteland, one producer is redefining the wines of the region, producing wines of good and sometimes great quality, with elegance largely unimagined in the rest of Southern Italy. The Mastroberardino family, whose wine-producing history began in the early eighteenth century, make their best wines from ancient Greek and Roman varietals. Their vineyards, centered around the town of Avellino, produce a total of about 75,000 cases of wine per year. They make an interesting vino da tavola, Lacryma Christi (Tears of Christ) del Vesuvio in dry white, rosé, and red versions (see Figure 7.2). Mastroberardino's best DOC white wines, however, are Greco di Tufo (only 312 acres/130 hectares under vine), and Fiano di Avellino (7680 acres/3200 hectares). Both are full-bodied wines that age well for anywhere from three to ten years, depending on the vintage. The family's flagship red wine is Taurasi (528 acres/220 hectares planted), which is produced from the powerful Aglianico grape and is one of Italy's finest age-worthy reds. Taurasi is one of Italy's newest DOCG designates, an honor that is well-deserved and due to the labors of *la familia* Mastroberardino, which, by its commitment to producing quality wines from low-yielding ancient grape types grown in volcanic soil, stands apart in the Campania wine world.

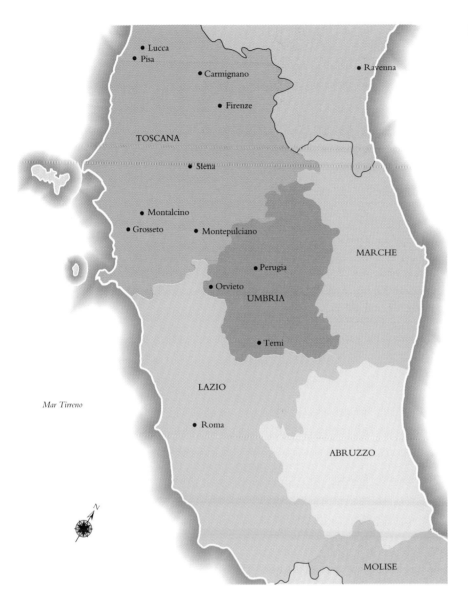

**Map 7.3**  Central Italy.

example, produces a good wine, especially in the vineyard areas surrounding the town of San Gimignano. As a matter of fact, Vernaccia di San Gimignano was named the first white DOC of Italy, and was awarded DOCG status in 1993. Also, Trebbiano and Malvasia grapes, sometimes on their own, and sometimes blended, can produce good to very fine wines. These same workhorse grapes appear in the classic DOC wines of Lazio, home to Italy's capital city of Rome. Regional favorites such as Frascati and Est! Est! Est! di Montefiascone are made primarily from blends of local clones of Malvasia and Trebbiano.

In Umbria, a soon-to-be DOCG white wine, Orvieto, dominates. Orvieto is made from Malvasia and Trebbiano, along with local varietals. The exciting red wines of Umbria—Sangiovese-based Torgiano Rosso Riserva and Sagrantino di Montefalco, made from the elegant local Sagrantino—come from two of Italy's new DOCG zones.

**Figure 7.2** Lacryma Christi del Vesuvio is a Delicious Vino da Tavola Made by the Mastroberardino Family.

Along the Adriatic seacoast, there are two important local varietals: the red Montepulciano from Abruzzo (not to be confused with the town, Montepulciano, in Tuscany), and the white Verdicchio from the Marche region. Sangiovese and Trebbiano, which are used to make wines on their own, as well as blended wines, fill out the picture in the central and eastern regions. Currently, Molise is not an important wine area, most often growing Montepulciano and Trebbiano grapes for the blended wines of Abruzzo.

***Abruzzo.*** Abruzzo is comprised of two DOC zones; Montepulciano d'Abruzzo and Trebbiano d'Abruzzo. The red Montepulciano is consistently underrated, probably because it is so little known. The wine is consistently good, with mouth-filling fruit and full-bodied character. Approachable when young, it can age quite nicely. The well-known cooperative, Casal Thaulero, makes a wonderful version of the wine, widely available in the United States, and always at a fair price. When grown in the mountainous inland areas, the Montepulciano yields grapes with less extract and power, and so a good DOC rosé wine, Cerasuolo di Montepulciano d'Abruzzo, is often made from these grapes. In Abruzzo, the local version of the Trebbiano grape most often makes a simple, straightforward wine that should be drunk fresh, usually with fish. Molise, not known for its wines, makes some in the style of Abruzzo, from similar grape varieties.

***Marche.*** The citizens of Marche consume more wine per capita than those of any other region of Italy, no mean feat in a country whose national consumption per person is probably the highest in the world. The most famous wine produced by these happy, healthy folks is Verdicchio, a wine of often stellar quality, sometimes overlooked due to its easy availability. Like the Loire Valley's Muscadet (see Chapter 6 on France), Verdicchio is the ideal accompaniment to a great variety of seafood. There are two DOC Verdicchio zones; Matelica and Castelli di Jesi. The latter zone encompasses Fazi-Battaglia's 84 acre/35 hectare single vineyard, Le Moie, which produces a Verdicchio of unparalleled quality. The wine from both DOC zones is enjoying a resurgence in popularity, due largely to improved fermentation techniques—the increased use of temperature-controlled stainless steel has increased the wine's freshness and acidity—and smaller yields per hectare. While 20 million bottles of still Verdicchio are produced each year (Soave from the Veneto region is the only white wine exported in greater quantity to the United States), the sparkling Verdicchio is a local favorite. This is most often made by the **charmat** (tank) process, but small amounts are produced by the **metodo tradizionale** (see Chapter 1 on How Wine Is Made). Another important DOC is Bianchello del Metauro, producing mostly white wines.

The majority of the wine produced in Marche is red, and the two best wines—Rosso Conero, based in the Montepulciano grape, and Rosso Piceno, based in Sangiovese—produce medium-bodied wines that are meant to be drunk within about three years. **Governo** (adding must to create a second fermentation) is widely practiced in production of red wines from Marche.

Vineyards, Umbria.

*Lazio.*   It may come as a surprise to the world's urban dwellers that the city of Rome, which contains four DOC zones, including Frascati, produces more than 10,600,000 gallons/400,000 hectoliters of delimited white wine. With the Roman metropolis as its anchor, Lazio, where tremendous yields appear to be commonplace, produces about 90 percent of all the white wine of central Italy. With regional and local clones of Malvasia and Trebbiano grapes accounting for most of Lazio's whites, the wines range from the simple to the undistinguished, and can border on the miserable. High yields produce wines so fragile that they can hardly travel less than 20 miles from the vineyards into the center of Rome without being bruised and shocked. The Frascati wines that are exported bear little resemblance to the frothy, tangy, quaffing beverage consumed locally. Est! Est! Est! is also popular, but it is a wine with no real distinction, especially in questionable export versions.

The best red wines of Lazio come from two of its 17 DOC zones. Aprilia, which makes mostly white wines from the Trebbiano grape, also produces some good reds wines from Merlot grapes, and red and rosé from Sangiovese. In the Cerveteri DOC zone, red wine is made from Montepulciano grapes.

*Umbria.*   Landlocked, and surrounded by Toscana, Lazio, Abruzzo, Marche, and Emilia-Romagna, Umbria has managed to make wines with its own regional personality. Lush vineyards are planted in Umbria's magnificent green hills and watched over by the spirit of its own Assisi native, Saint Francis. Wine, however (and the region's heady olive oil), accounts for only a small percentage of Umbria's agricultural output, with tobacco, grains, and dairy products far more important to the Umbrian economy. Umbria is best known for its white Orvieto, produced along the Tuscan border, sometimes by Tuscan producers (e.g., Ruffino, Antinori, Cecchi, Barone Ricasoli, and Melini). A DOC since 1971, and with upcoming DOCG status, Orvieto ac-

Lungarotti's San Giorgio Vineyard in Umbria.

Le Tre Vasselle, Owned by the Lungarotti Family, Includes a Wonderful Wine Museum, Inn, and Restaurant in the Umbrian Town of Torgiano.

counts for about 60 to 70 percent of Umbria's classified wines. Very popular in export markets, Orvieto can be produced in *secco* (dry), *abbocato* (semi-dry), *amabile* (semi-dry to semi-sweet), and *dolce* (sweet) versions. There is also an Orvieto Classico district, where the best wines are produced, especially the dry and semi-sweet ones. Stylistically, Orvieto is going through an identity crisis. Originally based in the local Grechetto and Malvasia grapes,

Lungarotti's Rubesco Vineyard, Where the Grapes for Torgiano Rosso (DOC) and Torgiano Rosso Riserva (DOCG) are Grown.

Orvieto was a soft, honeyed wine, made by old methods. While there seems to be a small resurgence of this style, today most Orvieto is produced as a dry wine, the product of cold fermentation of the free run juices of the Trebbiano grape. The Florentine producer Antinori is producing a high quality vino da tavola at Castello della Salla, within the Orvieto zone.

Among the reds of Umbria, the area around the provincial capital, Perugia, boasts two of the newest DOCG wines, the Sangiovese-based Torgiano Rosso Riserva, and Sagrantino di Montefalco. The most prominent producers of the red Torgiano are Dr. Giorgio Lungarotti and his stepdaughter, the highly accomplished Teresa Severini. Severini, with her mother, Dr. Maria Grazia Lungarotti, have established an elegant inn and lovely wine museum, Le Tre Vasselle (The Three Wine Jugs), in the town of Torgiano. Producing the wine under the name Rubesco, Lungarotti has brought international attention to the red wines of Umbria, to the point that the Rubesco brand name is better known than the entire Torgiano zone. Rubesco Riserva, a red wine made from grapes grown at the Monticchio vineyard of about 27 acres/11 hectares, is one of Italy's finest wines, aged in French oak for eight years prior to release, and certainly worthy of a DOCG designation.

Though it may be made as a sweet passito wine from sun-dried, raisinated grapes, the dry Sagrantino di Montefalco, with its nose of blackberries and its full body, is getting international attention. Sagrantino di Montefalco must contain at least 95 percent Sagrantino grapes. In contrast, three times as much DOC Montefalco is produced. This wine may contain up to 75 percent Sangiovese and as little as ten percent Sagrantino grapes.

*Toscana.* Toscana (see Map 7.4) is Italy's best-known wine region, and, with Piemonte, its most important. Toscana is home to four red DOCG zones: Brunello di Montalcino; Vino Nobile di Montepulciano; Car-

**Map 7.4** The Region of Toscana, Showing the Defined Area for Chianti.

**(a)**

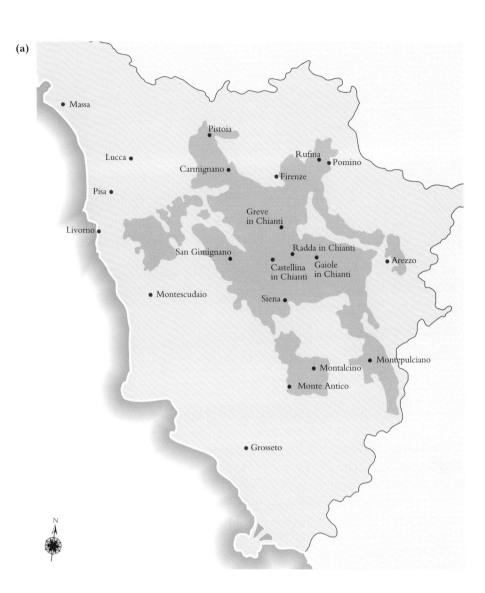

View of Toscana's Hills.

**(b)**

Lucca •

Carmignano  • Firenze

Pisa •

Chianti Region

Livorno •

Chianti
Classico

Vernaccia di
San Gimignano

• Siena

Vino Nobile di
Montepulciano

Brunello di
Montalcino

Sangiovese Grapes, the Backbone of Virtually All of Toscana's Red Wines.

**Map 7.5**   Chianti.

**Figure 7.3**   The Best Chianti is Often Shipped in Brown or Green Bordeaux-shaped Bottles.

mignano; and, of course, Chianti (which includes seven legally defined districts, all with the prefix *Chianti:* Classico, Colli Aretini, Colli Fiorentini, Colli Senesi, Colline Pisane, Montalbano, and Rufina. All of these wines are based on clones of the Sangiovese grape (although Carmignano can contain between 10 and 15 percent Cabernet Sauvignon). Toscana also produces two white wines of note, the dry Vernaccia di San Gimignano and the luscious, sweet Vin Santo. Add to this equation some of Italy's finest, fanciest, and most expensive vino da tavola, all with exotic, evocative names, and you have a region that prides itself on quality; the leader in the renaissance of Italian wines on the world stage.

***Chianti.***   Chianti (see Map 7.5), which encompasses Siena to the south and stretches north to the hills of Florence, is Italy's most famous wine, and perhaps its most controversial (see Figure 7.3). Depending on the precise area where it is produced, as well as on the producer, grapes, soil, and climate, the wine can be thin and insipid, elegant and rich, age-worthy or ready to drink when bottled, light and delicate, or a virtual powerhouse of a wine. Chianti just may be the most accurate viticultural expression of the organized anarchy that is Italy, as the personality of the wine depends heavily on the personality of the producer. With about 25 million gallons/950,000 hectoliters of wine produced annually, there is still plenty of simple, and even a bit of questionable, Chianti to go around. However, DOCG status has contributed to lower yields on the vine and better wine in the bottle. Gone are the days of the decorative wicker baskets which enveloped a demi-amphora of bitter, thin red wine. Today the best Chianti, like the best Rioja of Spain (see Chapter 8 on Spain), is shipped in brown or green Bordeaux-shaped bottles, and the wines, especially those from the Classico district in their Riserva versions, can be world class.

Chianti's primary grape is Sangiovese, and the best wines utilize its historical progenitor, the Sangioveto; the two names are often used interchangeably in conversation. Legally, Chianti from any district must be between 75 and 90 percent Sangiovese, no more and no less. The wine may also include up to ten percent Canaiolo Nero and is supposed to include at least five percent white grapes—Trebbiano or Malvasia. Up to ten percent other red varieties are allowed, recently including up to five percent Cabernet Sauvignon. Several of the modern producers illegally forego the white grapes, and use up to ten percent Cabernet, as even a small amount of this assertive grape can appreciably enhance the character of a good Chianti. Interestingly, if a producer, say in the Classico district, wants to make a fine wine from 100 percent Sangiovese, from a prized vineyard, the wine would not be entitled to the Chianti appellation, and would have to be declassified.

While chaptalization is illegal in Italy, the closest thing to it is practiced in Chianti, though not by all producers. *Governo alla Toscana* was, until recently, practiced throughout Chianti to introduce a secondary fermentation to the multi-grape wine. Since the grape percentages of the Chianti blend are standardized, the musts are often blended and fermented together. When the wine has almost stopped its initial fermentation, legal grapes, often the Colorino varietal, which have been dried in the sun *(passito)*, are added just as they begin to ferment, creating a very slow refermentation. While the chemistry of governo is not totally understood, it produces a Chianti that is

The Monsanto Estate in the Chianti Classico DOCG Zone.

Harvesting in Chianti Classico.

softer and lower in acid. When bottled young to be drunk fresh, a bit of the carbon dioxide produced by the governo process gives the wine a slight but pleasant spritz, creating *Chianti di pronta beva*. However, the governo process is used not only for young Chianti but also sometimes for riserva wines that will age in wood for a minimum of three years, and produce at least 12.5 percent alcohol. As these wines mature, they develop more aromas and a rich toasted character, with none of the youthful fizz. The governo process, which can be expensive when employed by a quality producer, is enjoying a resurgence in Chianti, and is no longer looked down on as a way to get around the law against chaptalization.

***Chianti Classico.*** While Chianti is legally subdivided into seven delimited districts, it is usually only Chianti Classico, and once in a while, Chianti Rufina, that include the name of the district on the bottle label (at least for export). All of the districts are capable of producing fine wines, and just about all of them have decreased yields and improved technology since 1984, when DOCG status was granted to the entire Chianti zone. It is Classico, however, which lies between Siena and Florence, that has made the greatest strides in quality and enjoys the greatest international reputation. The largest district in Chianti, Classico has applied for its own DOCG, and many would argue that Chianti Classico, the traditional and historical heartland of the Chianti zone, deserves nothing less.

Many Chianti Classico producers are members of the regional consortium, or consorzio. The Chianti Classico consorzio is also called "Gallo Nero" in honor of its symbol, the black rooster ("rooster" in Italian is "gallo"), which appears on the neck label of each bottle of member wines. In 1992, California's Ernest and (the late) Julio Gallo won an acrimonious Goliath versus David lawsuit based on their name and trademark. The consorzio was forced to drop the name "Gallo Nero" in the United States only, where it is now called Consorzio del Marchio Storico.

**Figure 7.4** Ruffino is One of the Larger Producers in the Chianti Classico Zone.

The best producers in the Chianti Classico zone include Badia a Coltibuono, Brolio, Castellare, Castello di Ama, Castello di Volpaia, Fontodi, Isole e Olena, Monsanto, Monte Vertine, and San Felice. Larger producers of fine wines with worldwide distribution include Antinori, Cecchi, Melini, and Ruffino (see Figure 7.4).

***The "Super Tuscans."*** The Chianti Classico region is the birthplace of many of the high quality but non-DOC "Super Tuscan" wines. In the mid-1970s, Piero Antinori and his wine maker of 30 years, Dr. Tachis, produced the Sangiovese-Cabernet blend, Tignanello, aged in *barrique.* Antinori followed this upscale vino da tavola with Solaia, in which Cabernet dominated the blend. Other producers then began to produce wines blended with Bordelais grapes. Some forward-thinking traditionalists traveled a different path by producing pure Sangiovese/Sangioveto wines, beginning with Le Pergole Torte, first produced in 1977, by the well-respected Chianti Classico producer Sergio Manetti of Monte Vertine. While these expensive wines and others based on largely French varietals have provoked much discussion in the wine world, they have had one unmistakably positive impact: their success and reputation has helped upgrade the image and quality of the original, modest grandparents—Chianti in general, Chianti Classico in particular.

Chianti Classico producers have petitioned the Italian government to allow all Chianti to be made from 100 percent Sangiovese. Not yet approved, it probably will be, as it will upgrade even more the image of Chianti, and bring back wines like Badia a Coltibuono's "Sangioveto" and Monte Vertine's "Le Pergole Torte" into the Chianti Classico fold.

To bring some semblance of order to the new unclassified wines of Toscana, with an eye to DOC recognition, some of the better-known producers, led by Ruffino and Frescobaldi, formed a voluntary group to define the types of new wine. If a producer is a member of this **Capitolare** (formerly Predicato) group, the following phrases might appear on his or her wines.

**Figure 7.5** Sangioveto is One of a Group of Red Wines Made from Sangiovese.

Marketing Director Emmanuela Stucchi-Prinetti at Badia a Coltibuono in the Chianti Classico Zone. Emmanuella's Brother Roberto, Trained at the University of California at Davis, is the Wine Maker. Their Mother, Lorenza de Medici, Runs a Cooking School at the Former Abbey.

*Capitolare di Biturica.* This label applies to red wines based in Cabernet Sauvignon, with up to 30 percent Sangiovese and ten percent other grapes allowed. Examples are Sassicaia, produced by Tenuta San Guido and Tignanello, produced by Antinori.

*Capitolare di Cardisco.* This label applies to red wines made from Sangiovese, with up to 10 percent other red grapes, but no Cabernet or Merlot allowed. Examples are Sangioveto from Badia a Coltibuono (see Figure 7.5), made by Roberto Stucchi-Prinetti, Spargolo from Cecchi (see Figure 7.6), and Le Pergole Torte from Monte Vertine.

**Figure 7.6** Phrases like *Capitolare* (Formerly Predicato) *di Cardisco* are Being Used to Give Some Order to the New, Unclassified Wines of Toscana.

**Figure 7.7** The American-owned Castello Banfi is One of the Newer Producers of Brunello di Montalcino.

**Figure 7.8** Castello Banfi is also Producing Rosso di Montalcino.

*Capitolare del Muschio.* This label applies to white wines based in Chardonnay or Pinot Bianco, with up to 20 percent Riesling, Müller-Thurgau, or Pinot Grigio grapes allowed. For example, Cabreo La Pietra, produced by Ruffino, is an oak-aged Chardonnay wine.

*Capitolare del Selvante.* These are white wines made from Sauvignon Blanc, with up to 20 percent of the same blending grapes allowed in Capitolare del Muschio. An example of this style is Borro from Antinori.

### Other DOCG Zones

*Brunello di Montalcino.* Almost always Italy's most expensive wine, sometimes it is also its best. The wine was created just before the turn of the century, and just after the *phylloxera* disaster, by Fernuccio Biondi-Santi. His grandson, Franco, has continued the family tradition of making wine exclusively from a local clone of the Sangioveto Grosso, a grape with a rusty brown skin and medium-large berries. While older vintages of Biondi-Santi reservas can match and often exceed the prices brought by old first-growth Médoc wines, Brunello's prices have recently almost come back down to earth. Some of the newer producers, such as Barbi, Poggio Antico, Il Poggione, Caparzo, and the American-owned Castello Banfi (see Figure 7.7), are producing big, age-worthy wines of elegant grace and complexity.

The small hill town of Montalcino also encompasses the DOC Rosso di Montalcino (see Figure 7.8). With only one year of aging required as opposed to four years for Brunello, this younger sibling delivers consistently high-quality and fantastic value at about the same price as a midrange Chianti Classico. Moscadello di Montalcino, a DOC wine based on the

A Vertical Tasting of Biondi-Santi Brunello di Montalcino, Whose Older Vintages are Legendary.

The Arno River Flows Through Florence.

Siena (above) and Florence are the Major Cities in Toscana.

Moscato Bianco grape, is a sweet white wine, sometimes frizzante. With a large investment from the American-owned producer and importer Banfi, it seems positioned to challenge Asti.

*Vino Nobile di Montepulciano.* This is made mostly from yet another Sangioveto clone, Prugnolo Gentile. The wine is produced in a hilly commune due east of Montalcino. This DOCG wine suffers from an identity crisis, always compared favorably with Chianti Classico, but almost never

Franco Biondi-Santi, Whose Grandfather, Ferrucio, Isolated the Brunello Clone of the Sangioveto Grosso in 1888.

Villa Capezzana, a Famed Estate in Carmignano.

considered a match for Brunello di Montalcino. Producers of this wine are currently upgrading production methods, trading in their old Slovenian oak and chestnut barrels for French barriques. Vino Nobile is rebuilding its reputation, and following the lead of Brunello, its producers are also making a reliable new DOC wine, Rosso di Montepulciano. Fine producers are Avignonesi, Fassati, Boscarelli, Poizano, and Tenuta Trerose.

*Carmignano.* One of the wines mentioned by the Grand Duke of Toscana in 1716 as worthy of its own delimited area, is Toscana's newest DOCG. Produced within the Florentine hills of the Chianti Montalbano district, Carmignano has long symbolized commitment to quality. With a maximum production of 500,000 bottles (about 350,000 annually is the norm), true Carmignano is produced on 11 estates, most of them formerly controlled by the Medici family. To achieve DOCG status, the wine must be approved at an annual public tasting. With up to 15 percent Cabernet Sauvignon or Cabernet Franc in the blend, Carmignano is worthy of long aging, yet approachable when young. Capezzana, a producer whose vineyards are located in the hills overlooking the city of Prato, has been instrumental in bringing attention to this wine and securing its DOCG status. Carmignano also produces a small amount of rosé and Vin Santo, both DOC wines.

### White Wines

*Vernaccia di San Gimignano.* This is produced from a vine that can trace its ancestry back to at least the thirteenth century and was named Italy's first DOC white wine in 1966. In its first year of DOC status, annual production was about 18,550 gallons/700 hectoliters, but has grown to more than 1.06 million gallons/40,000 hectoliters. While Vernaccia enjoys a good reputation, relatively few producers have sacrificed higher yields for higher quality, and much of the wine is sold to thirsty tourists who descend on the beautiful hill town of San Gimignano, with its many towers overlooking the

Older Vintages "Jailed" at Frescobaldi.

breathtaking countryside. Vernaccia di San Gimignano from Falchini, San Quirico, and Strozzi, as well as the oak-aged Terruzi and Puthod's Terra di Tufi, are examples of this wine at its best; complex, medium bodied, but with refreshing acidity. Also popular on the regional level is Vernaccia spumante, produced by the charmat process.

*Vin Santo.* The holy wine of Toscana, made by producers large and small. Originally a dry wine, legend has it that Vin Santo was made into a sweet nectar so that children could sip it during mass. True Vin Santo is made in small batches, and by a painstaking process, which includes carefully selected passito grapes, long fermentation, and maturing in chestnut or oak barrels (caratelli), for perhaps five years. Vin Santo is traditionally served as an aperitif, or with biscotti for dessert. The biscuits, which in Toscana are called cantucci, are dipped into the wine; the wine-soaked crumbs are happily consumed. The DOC status of Vin Santo is confusing, as it is controlled in seven DOC zones, including Carmignano and Pomino, and is classified as vino da tavola everywhere else in Toscana. The best Vin Santo is truly sainted wine, luscious, sweet, and expensive. Frescobaldi and Tenuta Trerose make excellent Vin Santo (see Figure 7.9).

**Figure 7.9** Vin Santo is the Holy Wine of Toscana.

## Northwest Italy

The five regions of Emilia-Romagna, Liguria, Lombardia, Piemonte, and Valle d'Aosta make up the northwest sector of Italy (see Map 7.6). While these Alpine regions have a common geography, their culture and their wines are quite different from each other. Because the region is so close to France and Switzerland, French and Germanic influences can be felt throughout the Northwest, especially in Lombardia's capital, Milan. In Valle d'Aosta, where the language is, depending on loyalties, either an Italian-pep-

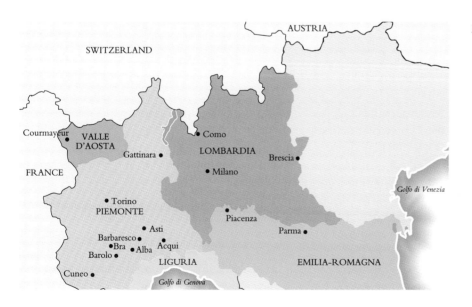

**Map 7.6** Northwest Italy.

Nebbiolo Grapes Make the Age-worthy
Red Wines of Piemonte.

pered dialect of French, or a spicy French dialect of Italian, wine labels might be written in either language, along with some in German, just for good measure.

As Italian wine lovers will attest, the red wines of Piemonte, especially the "king and queen" of Italian reds, Barolo and Barbaresco, speak to a simultaneous sense of tradition and quality that is hard to find in modern Italian wines. These were among the very first DOCGs and are made only from the revered Nebbiolo grape. A newer DOCG wine, Nebbiolo-based Gattinara, as well as the DOC wines Barbera and Dolcetto from around Alba and Asti, round out the famous red wines of Piemonte. The sometimes-elegant Gavi, made from Cortese grapes, and the ancient Arneis, are two white wines of note. The Piemonte region is best known for Asti (formerly Asti Spumante), a sweet sparkling wine, second only in popularity to Champagne. This renowned sparkler is made from the Moscato grape, as is its almost still counterpart, Moscato d'Asti (and both are now DOCG). And speaking of bubbles, Brachetto d'Acqui is a rarity, an excellent sweet, red, sparkling wine.

The wines of Emilia-Romagna are mostly frizzante, and Emilia is best known for its secco and amabile versions of the very popular Lambrusco, which accounts for about 25 percent of all of the import wines purchased in the United States. Romagna has its own very fine Sangiovese-based wines, as well as some sparklers. Unlike the serious wines of Piemonte, most of the wines from Emilia-Romagna are simple, fun to drink, and a perfect match with the rich food of the region. Lambrusco is especially coveted as an aid to digesting two rich staples of the local diet, prosciutto di Parma and Parmigiano Reggiano, and is said to cut the cholesterol of these items. Sangiovese di Romagna is a DOC wine quite different from Tuscan reds, and is beginning to develop a following in the wine world. Italy's first white DOCG, Albana di Romagna, produces wines that, despite their lofty status, are nothing special, at least in their dry export versions.

Lombardia produces some very good wines, few of which are appreciated in the home region. For example, Valtellina (DOC) produces better than 750,000 cases of wine per year, all made from the Nebbiolo grape. The neighboring Swiss, who love good wine, import almost all of this production, with most of what is left finding its way to the United States. The Franciacorta DOC produces some of the best metodo tradizionale sparkling wines in Italy. Oltrepò Pavese, in the south, produces 15 different types of DOC wines, from still to sparkling, from dry to sweet, from white to red, from miserable to excellent quality.

Liguria and Valle d'Aosta produce little wine. In Liguria, because of the mountainous terrain, there are only about 750 acres/300 hectares of DOC vineyard. What local wine there is to enjoy is fine, but not much is seen beyond the French and Italian Alps. While the wines of Valle D'Aosta are neither French nor Italian in character, the small amounts of DOC wine produced—only 35 acres/14 hectares have DOC designation—dictate that to taste the wine you must visit this beautiful region.

*Emilia-Romagna.* A compelling argument can be made that Emilia-Romagna is the culinary capital of Italy. The cheeses and dairy products, pasta, hams, and sausages produced in this region are some of the best in the world. Prosciutto di Parma and Parmigiano Reggiano both enjoy rare DOC status, as does Emilia-Romagna's vinegar, *aceto balsamico* (balsamic vinegar), which by law must be made from cooked grape musts and aged for a minimum of 12 years in small wooden barrels. While the foods of this region are superb, no one would ever argue that Emilia-Romagna is the viticultural center of Italy.

Emilia-Romagna produces more wine than any other region except for Sicilia and Puglia, but little of it is distinguished or exciting. Of the nearly 238.5 million gallons/nine million hectoliters of wine produced here, only about 1.855 million gallons/700,000 hectoliters have DOC or DOCG sta-

Balsamic Vinegar Aging in Oak Barrels in Modena, Emilia-Romagna.

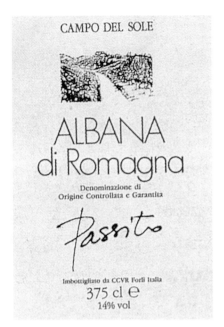

CAMPO DEL SOLE

ALBANA
di Romagna

Denominazione di
Origine Controllata e Garantita

*Passito*

Imbottigliato da CCVR Forlì Italia

375 cl ℮
14% vol

**Figure 7.10**    Albana di Romagna is Italy's Most Unlikely DOCG.

tus, and various Lambrusco DOC zones account for about half of that production. This frizzante, happy wine, made in white, red, and rosé, dry or amabile, is produced from grapes grown mostly in the plains of Emilia. The locals prefer the drier versions of the bubbly Lambrusco, but the myth that the sweeter types were created solely for the American market is not true (even though Lambrusco Reggiano is the most popular DOC wine in the United States). Both sweet and dry Lambrusco have been around for a long time, and both are produced from local clones of the Lambrusco grape. In the hilltop vineyards of Emilia, especially Colli Piacentini, DOC wines are being made in still and sparkling styles from native grapes, as well as from French and German varietals.

The hill country of Romagna is home to Italy's most unlikely, and probably unworthy DOCG, Albana di Romagna (see Figure 7.10). Its inclusion in such an exalted class has led to suggestions that the entire DOCG structure is suspect, with talk of political pressure and, at the least, poor judgment by the DOC governors. Albana di Romagna just does not measure up to the standards set by the other DOCG members. The wine is pleasantly fruity with some overtones of toast, but that's about it. Locally, there are some good frizzante, amabile, and passito versions of the wine, but the export market is exposed mostly to the dry Albana. The other prominent DOC white from this area is Trebbiano di Romagna.

The true success story in Romagna's hills is its Sangiovese di Romagna. This wine is overshadowed by the Sangiovese-based wines of Tuscany, but it deserves more exposure, especially in the riserva style. Always good value, this red wine can be truly elegant: a delicate balance between generous fruit and soft tannins. The riserva from Umberto Cesari, a perfect food wine, is often available in a dramatically oversized three-liter bottle, just the thing for an informal, festive dinner party. If any wine from Emilia-Romagna should be considered for DOCG status, it is Romagna's Sangiovese, not its Albana.

*Lombardia.*    Due largely to the influence of its cosmopolitan industrial capital, Milano, the Lombardia region is not immediately identified with fine wines, especially by the Lombardians themselves. Although the residents of the region look to neighboring Piemonte, Veneto, and (sacrilegiously) to France for their best wines, they are missing some very good ones in their own backyard. While only about 15 percent of Lombardia's total wine production is DOC, the zones of Valtellina, Franciacorta, and Oltrepò Pavese produce some very good wines.

The DOC zone of Valtellina, with its superiore subzones of Inferno, Grumello, Valgella, and Sassella, produces high-quality wines based on the esteemed Nebbiolo grape, whose colloquial name in Lombardia is Chiavennesca. Inferno and Grumello are worth searching for in the United States, but the best bottlings go over the border to Switzerland. Indeed, the Swiss have invested heavily in the vineyards of Valtellina, and have come to almost think of the wine as their own. While the Nebbiolo has a reputation as a powerhouse grape in its native Piemonte, in Valtellina it shows its delicate, lighter side, making a wine with less concentration of tannins, and a far leaner structure than Barbaresco or Barolo. Sforzato is a Valtellina Superiore made from passito Nebbiolo grapes, producing a wine with a minimum of 14.5 percent alcohol. The best of these Valtellina wines, whatever the style, can age, and tasting an older riserva is quite a lovely experience. Look for Valtellina wines from Nino Negri and Rainoldi.

From the Franciacorta DOC zone, centered around the city of Brescia, Lake Garda, and Lake Iseo, comes some of the finest metodo classico sparkling wines Italy has to offer. Made from a blend of Pinot Bianco, Chardonnay, and Pinot Noir, sparkling Franciacorta from Berlucchi, Ca'del Bosco, Bellavista, or other excellent producers are a match for their progenitor, Champagne. The still wines from Franciacorta are also of the highest quality, with whites made from the Pinot Bianco and Chardonnay grapes, and reds made from a curious but successful blend of Cabernet Franc, Barbera, Nebbiolo, and Merlot.

Oltrepò Pavese, located in the southwest sector of Lombardia produces more than 26.5 million gallons/one million hectoliters of wine each year, or about half of Lombardia's total production. The wines of this area are not held in the highest regard, but some good examples of Barbera, Pinot Bianco, Riesling, and Moscato are produced. Much of the wine is blended or sold to bulk spumante producers in other regions, so Oltrepò Pavese, centered around the city of Pavia, and just south of the Po River, has an image problem that will not improve overnight. Some producers are striving for quality, and are using modern techniques in the production of French white and red varietals. The wines of this area are little known in export markets, and virtually unknown in the United States.

*Piemonte.*   The Piemonte region produces two of the finest traditional red wines of Italy, a fact recognized by the Italian government when it awarded the second and third DOCG zones to Barolo and Barbaresco, respectively. Made from Nebbiolo grapes, these full-bodied wines represent a level of excellence to which other Italian wines, including other DOCGs, can only aspire. Piemonte is known by wine lovers as the quintessential premium red wine region of Italy. Although 30 of the 38 DOC and DOCG zones in Piemonte produce red wines only, Piemonte is also home to four interesting white wines of high quality. We will discuss these before we move on to the better-known reds.

### White Wines

*Gavi.*   Piemonte's dry white table wine, made from 100 percent Cortese grapes, can sometimes achieve great complexity, though recent versions emphasize its acidity and subtle fruit. Gavi is a testament to the wine makers of southeastern Piemonte, because whether the wine is barrique aged or the product of cool fermentation in stainless steel, it is almost always well made, and a fine accompaniment to fish. Some of the best Gavi producers include La Scolca, Villa Sparina (see Figure 7.11), and Michele Chiarlo. There are a couple of other Cortese-based DOC zones in the Piemonte that enjoy a strictly regional reputation.

**Figure 7.11**   Villa Sparina is One of the Best Producers of Gavi, the Dry White Table Wine of Piemonte.

**Figure 7.12** Asti is a Frothy, Refreshing Wine That is Fun to Drink, Low in Alcohol, and Moderately Priced.

*Arneis.* A fairly new DOC white wine, the Arneis grape is grown mostly in Alba's Roero hills. The name of the grape in Piemontese dialect translates as "rascal," because Arneis has a centuries-old reputation of unpredictability. With its energies harnessed by modern wine making methods, Arneis, which surprisingly for Italy is a white wine of singular character, can be a fruity pleasure, with a touch of almonds in the finish. Arneis from Ceretto's Blangé estate is good quality.

The DOC zone Erbaluce di Caluso makes still and spumante dry white wines, as well as luxurious sweet wines in passito and liquoroso versions. The sweet, fortified liquoroso must have a minimum sugar content of 30 percent and must be aged for five years before its release.

While wine connoisseurs pine for the red wines from the hills of Langhe, and applaud the Gavi from Monferratto, Piemonte is still best known as the home of sparkling Asti (formerly Asti Spumante—see Figure 7.12). Made from the Moscato grape, and grown in the areas surrounding the towns of Asti and Cuneo, this bubbly sweet wine has been the victim of invidious comparisons to Champagne, which it outsells in the American market. The fact is that Asti, along with its not quite still counterpart Moscato d'Asti, has received DOCG status. It is a frothy, refreshing wine that is fun to drink, low in alcohol (7–9 percent), and moderately priced.

Sparkling Asti (the term "spumante" no longer appears on the bottle, since its elevation to DOCG) is not produced by the méthode Champenoise, and unlike sparklers made by the charmat process or transfer method (see Chapter 1 on How Wine Is Made), most often does not go through a secondary fermentation at all. The grapes are harvested early to emphasize acidity in the wine, and then quickly crushed, so that minimal oxidation can occur. The must is then filtered and stored in stainless steel tanks, at temperatures just shy of freezing, so that it does not ferment. Because Asti is very

Moscato Vineyards in the Hills Surrounding Asti in Piemonte.

delicate, and largely a nonvintage product, it is fermented in batches, so that it is fresh when purchased. In a fermentation process that takes a little more than a month, the must is introduced to the wine maker's yeasts and fermented in anaerobic stainless steel vats (to create carbon dioxide naturally), which are quickly chilled when the must produces the requisite alcohol and residual sugar (3–5 percent). The wine is filtered, bottled, finished with a champagne cork and cage, and shipped almost immediately.

Moscato d'Asti is a *frizzantino* (a tiny sparkling) version of Asti, and is made by a slightly different process. The finished wine has a light, well-defined spritz but is usually somewhat lower in alcohol and slightly higher in residual sugar than Asti. The best Moscato d'Asti comes from small producers, and it can be quite expensive, while the most reliable sparkling Asti usually comes from those shippers with an active international market, like Gancia, Cinzano, and Martini & Rossi, to ensure that the wine has not been sitting in a warm warehouse for too long.

Moscato d'Asti/Asti is the name of the new DOCG, which includes both the sparkling and the spritzy Moscato-based wines.

### Red Wines

"Wine is red" is an old Piemontese adage that has contemporary resonance, because this region takes its red wines seriously. All of Piemonte's reds, whether light and fruity or massive and tannic, strive to define what the constituent grapes are capable of producing. Piemontese wine makers struggle to work almost exclusively with native varietals —Nebbiolo, Barbera, Dolcetto, Grignolino—in a market that thirsts for Cabernet Sauvignon and Pinot Noir. Whether Piemonte wines are produced in the traditional style (big, complex wines that need much aging) or in a more-contempo-

The Picturesque Southeastern Langhe Hills Contain the Two Classic DOCG Wine Zones, Barolo and Barbaresco.

Stainless Steel Tanks at Ceretto Winery in Barolo.

rary version (maintaining complex character, but approachable sooner) elegance is their signature.

***Barolo and Barbaresco.*** While Piemonte is steeped in tradition, it is not standing still. Barolo and Barbaresco, in the southeastern Langhe hills, share DOCG status, awarded in 1980. Historically these wines, especially Barolo, were made from very ripe grapes and fermented in contact with their skins for months, usually in large chestnut casks, where the wine aged for years before bottling. These wines, much appreciated by connoisseurs, but not accessible to the general wine-drinking public, have virtually disappeared from the Langhe. Today, Barolo and Barbaresco are just as likely to come from Nebbiolo grapes grown in cooler areas within the delimited zone, and skin contact is limited to weeks, not months. Most important, both alcoholic and malolactic fermentations take place in stainless steel temperature-controlled vats, producing wines of fine structure and balance, without hard tannins (see Chapter 1, on How Wine Is Made).

Truly progressive producers, like Angelo Gaja, and the Ceretto brothers—Marcello and Bruno—have taken to aging their Barolo and Barbaresco wines in barriques, which makes them ready to drink in two to three years. Their wines still improve in the bottle for ten to 20 years, depending on the vintage. Wine produced from the Nebbiolo grape, but not from the Barolo or Barbaresco DOCG zones, is classified as Nebbiolo d'Alba, a DOC zone that encompasses ten communes in the Langhe. The wine is medium bodied, with moderate aging potential. Often showing the best traits of its DOCG progenitors, Nebbiolo d'Alba is always a good value.

***Barolo.*** Barolo is considered to be the most assertive and complex DOCG wine in Italy, though this profile is moderating as modern wine-making methods take hold in the zone. With softer tannins, the "king" of wines, made

# THE LEGACY OF
# RENATO RATTI

Renato Ratti, a wine producer, writer, and man of great intellectual depth, developed the map that defines the neighboring Barolo and Barbaresco vineyards and carefully pointed out those growing areas whose quality or historical significance needed to be recorded for posterity. Ratti, who died in 1988 at age 53, remains the spiritual son of the Langhe, and his maps remain unchanged, the reference points for the great wines of the Langhe. Ratti believed that, much as the Grand crus of Burgundy define the best properties in that region, it was important for historical and commercial reasons to recognize the superior vineyards of Barolo and Barbaresco.

This approach is sometimes called *cru* in Piemonte, but the specific local terms are *sori* (sunny vineyard), *bricco* (hilltop vineyard), or simply, *vigneto* (a single vineyard). Naming the best vigneti goes against DOC law and spirit, which does not recognize the concept of cru (see Chapter 6 on France). However, this kind of recognition is now a full-scale movement in Piemonte, somewhat akin to the "Super Tuscan" trend in Chianti, and is gaining strength. In fact, the 77 vineyards that make up the DOC zone Dolcetto di Diano (d'Alba) comprise the only DOC zone in which each vineyard is recognized on the label, though not ranked for quality (see Figure 7.13). These Dolcetto wines are the first legal crus of Italy, and have helped to move the discussion of single-vineyard recognition rank forward, perhaps making Renato Ratti's vision a reality in Piemonte and other regions of Italy.

**Figure 7.13** Renato Ratti Played a Major Role in Defining the Areas of Barolo and Barbaresco.

Bricco Rocche, a One-Hectare Site Owned by Bruno and Marcello Ceretto, Who Make an Expensive and Sought-after Single-vineyard Barolo Here.

Bruno Ceretto.

Figure 7.14 Ceretto is One of the Producers of the New, More-approachable Style of Barolo.

from 100 percent Nebbiolo grapes, has become more benevolent, and is no longer reserved for drinking in the winter, accompanying only the most-exaggerated styles of cooking and the oldest cheeses. Contemporary Barolo, which comes from its namesake town, as well as the communes of La Morra, Serralunga, Monforte, and Castiglione Falletto, is likely to be a well-balanced wine, redolent of violets, spices, tobacco, and the heady white truffles for which the region around Alba is so well known. With a medium-black cherry color and intense structure, its soft tannins give the wine an edge that makes it an ideal accompaniment to rich foods and sauces. Barolo is an ideal wine for a great meal's cheese course, but also is wonderful with game, braised stews, and roasts. Traditional Barolo is available from the producers Fontanafredda, Pio Cesare, Mascarello, and Vietti, while the more- approachable, new style of Barolo (see Figure 7.14) is made by Ceretto (whose Bricco Rocche is one of the finest wines of Italy), Aldo Conterno, Renatto Ratti, and Luciano Sandrone. Cru wines made by the enigmatic Bruno Giacosa, a private man who makes expansive, generous wines, are in a class by themselves, are hard to come by and, even by Barolo standards, very expensive.

***Barbaresco.*** Until recently, Barbaresco had to be content to live in the shadow of its regal neighbor, Barolo, but those days are over. While the wine is, like Barolo, pure Nebbiolo, in the Barbaresco zone the grapes ripen sooner and maintain a bit of acidity lacking in the more ponderous Barolo. While by no means a light wine, Barbaresco seems not as intense on the palate as "the king," and is, in the best Italian tradition, one of the great food-friendly wines. However, depending on the vineyard, Barbaresco can be fuller bodied, though more graceful, than some Barolo. Barbaresco, Treiso, and Neive are the three communes that comprise the DOCG zone, with the best single vineyard sites located in Barbaresco itself.

Fine Barbaresco is produced by Ceretto, I Paglieri, Marchese di Gresy, Pio Cesare, Fratelli Giacosa, Mascarello & Figlio, Prunotto, Renato Ratti, and Vietti. However, the growing success of Barbaresco, which is now widely recognized as Italy's most consistently fine wine, is due in no small

Bartolo Mascarello, One of the Finest Wine Makers in the Langhe.

Vineyards in Barbaresco.

## ANGELO GAJA

Gaja, whose *vigneto*-based wines are the benchmark of quality and price in Barbaresco, operates on the principle that he, with his enologist, Guido Rivella, is making some of the finest wines in the world, and that such wines deserve the high prices that he asks. The world has embraced this approach, as Gaja's best wines are sold on an allocation basis, with a waiting list. The Barbaresco wines from the Sori Tildin, Sori San Lorenzo (see Figure 7.15), and Costa Russi *vigneti* are sold in the United States for $100 or more per bottle, depending on the vintage and demand. Gaja, who in 1988 purchased a once-great Barolo vineyard in serious decline, Marenca Riv ette in Serralunga, has begun to market his Barolo, using the same strategy as his Barbaresco.

Although he has brought attention to the traditional wines of the Langhe, Gaja is also a modern producer, making two very expensive vino da tavola, a Chardonnay from the Gaia e Rey vineyard, and a Cabernet Sauvignon from the Darmagi estate ("Darmagi" translates as "what a shame," the phrase Gaja's father repeated over and over again as he saw his beloved Nebbiolo vines replanted with the Bordelaise varietal). Angelo Gaja wants to prove that he and, by extension, the Langhe region of Piemonte, can successfully compete on the world stage with the rest of Italy, and with France and California. As if to amplify this idea, Gaja recently bought a large Brunello di Montalcino vineyard in Toscana, where he will produce yet another DOCG red wine. Gaja also markets and distributes some of the most prestigious French and Californian labels, as well as the much-admired Riedel glassware from Austria.

Angelo Gaja.

**Figure 7.15** Angelo Gaja's Barbaresco Wines, Such as Sorì San Lorenzo, are Sold on an Allocation Basis.

## PRODUTTORI DEL BARBARESCO

Just up the road from Gaja, and across the street from the landmark Barbaresco church tower, is the unassuming Produttori del Barbaresco, presided over by director Celestino Vacca and his son, Aldo, who is in charge of marketing the wines made by this co-op. Aldo Vacca, a charming, serious young man steeped in the history and culture of the Langhe, seems poised to inherit the mantle of pride passed down from Renato Ratti. He is tireless in his efforts to promote not only the Produttori wines but the Langhe as well.

Aldo Vacca.

The single-vineyard wines of the Produttori del Barbaresco—Rio Sordo, Montestefano, Montefico, and Asili—are some of the best wines produced, challenged only by Gaja and the winemaking skills of Bruno Giacosa. The Produttori also makes a fine collective Barbaresco, but the estate wines are remarkable not only for their quality, but for their fair prices. Often one-third and sometimes one-quarter the price of Gaja wines, it is no exaggeration to claim that while the styles may differ, the wines are often Gaja's equal. Yet Aldo Vacca, who worked for his neighbor for a few formative years, would be the first person to credit Gaja with enhancing the image of Barbaresco overall, encouraging every producer in the zone to make better wines.

part to two formidable powers, a producer and a wine-making collective. Located in the Barbaresco town square, within five minutes walking time of each other, are the renowned Angelo Gaja, who has brought the wine world's attention to Barbaresco by producing incredible wines at incredibly high prices, and the Produttori del Barbaresco, a wine-making collective that produces great wines that are great values.

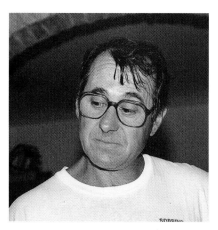

Luciano Sandrone, One of the New Breed of Langhe Wine Makers.

***Gattinara.*** Much like Italy's first white DOCG wine, Albana di Romagna, Gattinara must have been awarded this exclusive status based on its potential to improve its historically important wines. Gattinara encompasses the northernmost growing area for the Nebbiolo grape and is always a decent wine and, because of its location, a wine with good acidity, but it is very rarely distinguished. To include Gattinara in the company of Barolo and Barbaresco, Italy's first DOCG zones, is unfair to all three. Gattinara's recent wine history includes quite a bit of chicanery, with not much attention being paid to the delimited zone and its laws. However, with DOCG status comes a lot more supervision, and all Gattinara must now pass stringent tasting and chemical analysis. So Gattinara wine makers, unless they want their wines declassified to *Spanna* (the colloquial name for Nebbiolo), will have to awake from their recent slumber. At its best, Gattinara can be highly attractive, lighter than most Piemontese Nebbiolo-based wine, and worthy of DOCG status. Incidentally, the forementioned Spanna del Piemonte can be a fine vino da tavola. Gattinara includes only 216 acres/90 hectares of vineyard, so Spanna and several other minor DOC zones surrounding Gattinara should now become more prominent.

### Dolcetto, Barbera, and Grignolino

***Dolcetto.*** Dolcetto grapes, the "little sweet ones," produce a dry red wine, usually medium bodied and fruity, although Dolcetto d'Alba can be mouth filling and complex and may benefit from some aging. Dolcetto is often, but erroneously, compared to Beaujolais (see Chapter 6 on France), which is a lighter and simpler wine. There are actually seven Dolcetto DOC zones; five of the best are centered around the town of Alba, the two lesser areas are close to Asti. Dolcetto, whose tannins are usually very light, is a "crossover" wine, an appropriate match for lighter meats, poultry, fatty fishes, vegetarian dishes, and various pastas, like ravioli filled with veal in a light cream sauce, or pasta primavera. Light Dolcetto wines may benefit from a bit of chilling. Good Dolcetto is made by good Barbaresco and Barolo producers: Ratti, Gaja, Giacosa, Sandrone, Conterno, Ceretto, and Vietti.

***Barbera.*** Alba (see Figure 7.16), Asti, and Monferrato are the three DOC zones that make wine from Barbera grapes, with Asti held in the highest regard. After generations of poorly made, oxidized wines, contemporary Barbera is a refreshing, lighter wine with good acidity and balance, usually made for early consumption. The quality of this wine has been improved by cool fermentation and malolactic treatment, and a handful of Langhe producers make wines of real elegance. The *vivace* (lively) style of Barbera is sparkling and sweet, but U.S. consumers are more likely to see the dry, still wine, sometimes aged in barrique, but just as often in the bottle. Good Barbera producers include Bava, "Mariuccia" Borio at Cascina Castelet, and Michele Chiarlo.

**Figure 7.16** The Best Barbera Wines in Piemonte Come from the Alba or Asti DOC Zones.

***Grignolino.*** With DOC zones in both Asti and its native Monferrato, the Grignolino grape produces brick red wines with refined aromas and light

The man most responsible for the new respect afforded Barbera is the late Giacomo Bologna, who died in 1991. His Bricco dell'Uccelone (named for the loon, a bird who is said to have nested in the hilltop vineyard), aged in French oak and very expensive, established Bologna as the Gaja of Barbera. His Bricco della Bigotta (named for the gossips who sit in their chairs on the streets of Rocchetta Tanaro) and Barbera from his La Monella vineyard are wines to which all other Barbera should aspire. With his capable young daughter, Raffaella, at the helm, Bologna's vision will outlive him. Giacomo Bologna was so loved and respected in Piemonte that 6000 people attended his funeral.

body but astringent, hard tannins. The best Grignolino is full of herbal and spicy notes, but can be hard to find. Grignolino, more than any other Piemontese wine, is sensitive to the vintage year, so buying Grignolino is an exercise in *caveat emptor* ("let the buyer beware"). Due to its fruitiness and structure, Grignolino is often served cool, which brings out the wine's sparse acidity. Good producers are Giacosa, Cossetta, and Pavese.

***Other Wines.*** Two unusual red wines are Freisa and Brachetto, made in areas surrounding the towns of Asti and Acqui, respectively. Freisa is dry but fruity, with a light cherry color and a raspberry flavor. Surprisingly, the serious Angelo Gaja makes a charming and inexpensive Freisa, whose froth makes it fun to drink. Fun also is the bubbly Brachetto, a sweet spumante wine. With more than five percent residual sugar, and up to five percent Moscato Nero (Black Muscat) in its blend, Brachetto is the red answer to sparkling Asti. Unlike the white sparkler, however, Brachetto is hard to find, and only about 39,750 gallons/1500 hectoliters are produced annually. Banfi imports a good, refreshing Brachetto, and a rarely seen wine of fine quality is made by Giacomo Bologna's family.

Ruché is a rare red grape that produces a wine with a nose of white fruits: quince, orange blossom, peaches, figs, and apricots. The wine has a good fruit/acid balance, with just a hint of bitterness. Roberto Bava is well known as a producer of fine Ruché, and he also makes a sacramental, late-harvest wine based on Malvasia grapes. Bava's labels often have illustrations of musical instruments on them—brass for white, strings for red. His Barbera "Stradivario" is a fine example of this grape's potential.

# Northeast Italy

Comprised of three regions, Veneto, Friuli-Venezia Giulia, and Trentino-Alto Adige, northeast Italy (see Map 7.7) is, by any measure, the most technologically advanced and the most quality conscious wine-making area of all of Italy. The white, red, and sparkling wines made in these regions are impressive and might be considered the most cosmopolitan and least "Italian"

**Map 7.7**  Northeast Italy.

**Map 7.8**  Veneto.

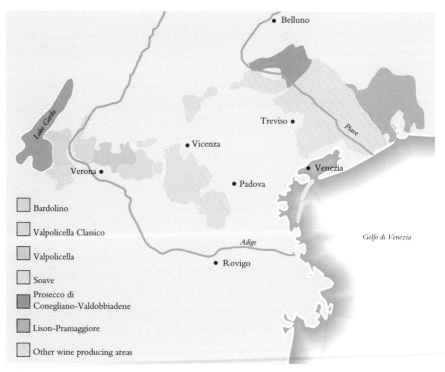

Bardolino

Valpolicella Classico

Valpolicella

Soave

Prosecco di
Conegliano-Valdobbiadene

Lison-Pramaggiore

Other wine producing areas

of any Italy has to offer. The wines of the *Tre Venezie* (the three regions are sometimes called this, because of their ancient historical links to Venice) are wordly, because the wine makers toil to make wines that will please the thirsty palate of the wine world, especially outside Italy. Perhaps this bow to foreign markets accounts for the surprising fact that there is not one DOCG zone in any of the three regions of the northeast.

The Grand Canal, Venice.

**Veneto.**   Veneto (see Map 7.8) is Italy's largest producer of DOC wines, with about 40 to 42 million gallons/160 to 170 million liters of classified wine produced yearly. Soave, one of the the most popular DOC wines in the United States, and two popular reds, Valpolicella and Bardolino, account for a total of more than 25 million gallons/100 million liters each year. Eastern Veneto, presided over by Venice, produces 350,000 gallons/1.4 million liters of Italy's beloved Prosecco, a refreshing semidry frizzante wine that is just now finding an audience outside of Italy. As part of the modern approach of the Tre Venezie, Veneto also produces a great deal of DOC wine from an international array of varietals, both red and white. For example, the DOC zone Lison-Pramaggiore lists 12 types of legal grapes: Cabernet Franc, Cabernet Sauvignon, Merlot, Chardonnay, Sauvignon Blanc, Riesling, and six local varietals.

Piazza San Marco, Venice.

One of the Hundreds of Narrow Canals in Venice.

Arrigo "Harry" Cipriani, Owner of Harry's Bar, a Landmark in Venice, and Famous for the Refreshing Bellini. The Drink is Made from Prosecco—a *Frizzante* Wine from Veneto—and French White-peach Concentrate.

Veneto produces a vast amount of quality wine from delimited zones. Soave, Valpolicella, and Bardolino, along with Toscana's Chianti, are Italy's main representatives in international markets, especially the United States. Other DOC zones, such as Bianco di Custoza, Colli Berici, Colli Euganei, Piave, and the newly combined Lison-Prammaggiore, each make up to 12 different wines, from as many grape types.

*Soave.* No, the full name of this wine is not Soave Bolla, though it is completely understandable why Americans might think so. Bolla, and the powerful cooperative Cantina Sociale di Soave, are the major producers of Soave, with more than 1000 growers under contract to provide Garganega and Trebbiano grapes for the wine. Wildly successful in export markets, Soave, precisely because of its popularity, is also often misunderstood. Many people dismiss Soave as an "industrial" wine, predictable and bland, pleasant but without much character. In many cases this profile is correct, but there are several Soave producers working successfully to upgrade the wine's image.

It is a shame that the world of thirsty Soave drinkers rarely gets to taste a Soave Classico, or better yet, one of the cru wines from the hilly Classico subzone. Soave's best wines come from its Classico area, where yields are traditionally lower, and there is generally more Garganega in the blend (usually around 80 percent; the legal minimum is 70 percent). Soave Classico, when made by a producer like Anselmi, Allegrini, or Pieropan, can be everything people who enjoy light white wines look for: fresh and fruity, with bracing acidity. On the other hand, Soave Classico Superiore, with a minimum alcohol level of 11.5 percent (Soave DOC is 10.5 percent), and minimum aging of eight months, kind of misses the point of Soave at its best. While the additional alcohol provides more body, the aging of the wine works against Soave Classico's true character, which emphasizes freshness and delicacy.

*Recioto Wines and Amarone.* Recioto di Soave (see Figure 7.17) is a sweet wine made from semidried Garganega and Trebbiano grapes. These

Terraced Vineyards in Soave, Veneto.

Recioto di Soave, a Sweet Wine Made from Semidried Grapes, Aging in Bottles at the Anselmi Winery.

**Figure 7.17** Recioto di Soave is a Sweet Wine Made from Semidried Garganega and Trebbiano Grapes.

topmost grape bunches, the ones that have gotten the most sun, are dried on wicker racks before pressing. The equivalent of a German Auslese (see Chapter 10 on Germany), because the grapes are "out-picked" from special bunches, the shriveled, *botrytis*-affected grapes produce a wine of 14 percent alcohol and 2.5 percent residual sugar. Spumante and fortified liquoroso versions are also produced. In the Valpolicella DOC zone (see the following section on Valpolicella) a sweet Recioto della Valpolicella is produced. An age-worthy, full-bodied, sweet red wine made from dried Corvina,

Grapes Drying on Racks at the Masi Winery, to Make Amarone, a Dry, Recioto-style Valpolicella.

**Figure 7.18** Amarone is a Powerhouse Wine, Full of Fruit and with a Pleasantly Bitter Finish.

Rondinella, and Molinara grapes, the finished styles are the same as Recioto di Soave.

Amarone (Recioto della Valpolicella Amarone) is made from the same process, but the grapes are pressed somewhat earlier than for the sweet Recioto della Valpolicella. The wine is vinified dry, reaching about 14–15 percent alcohol, and is a powerhouse, full of fruit and a pleasantly bitter finish. Amarone is best with heavy meat, game dishes, and fine cheeses, or appreciated in place of Port after dinner. Good producers include Tommasi, Alighieri, Zonin Masi (see Figure 7.18), and Quintarelli.

*Valpolicella.* A perfect match to the traditional American Thanksgiving dinner, Valpolicella is an unsung member of the Italian pantheon of fine wines. Like its neighbors, Soave and Bardolino, Valpolicella can be overlooked because it is so readily available. The charm of this wine is its modesty; Valpolicella does not overwhelm the palate, but sings a soft tune as background music to good food. The Corvina, Rondinella, and Molinara grapes in the classic blend create a wine that is light, with the resonance of cherries, and eminently drinkable. As a matter of fact, Valpolicella is a good "crossover" wine, because its tannins are quite soft, almost imperceptible. As with Soave, the best wines are made from grapes grown in the Classico district. Unlike the white wine of Veneto, however, the best wines from this area can be those labeled Classico Superiore, with a minimum of 12 percent alcohol, and one year aging.

The best examples of Valpolicella are the single-vineyard wines from the Classico area. Paolo Boscaini makes a tasty wine from his Marano vigneti, while Sandro Boscaini and Serègo Alighieri of Masi winery, and the Allegrini family estate, also contribute masterful cru wines from the Valpolicella Classico area, some of which can age quite nicely for two to three years. These wines are among the greatest red wine values in the American market, and when the inevitable price-to-quality comparison is made, single-vineyard Valpolicella Classico Superiore stands alone.

*Bardolino.* Located along Lake Garda, Bardolino can be *rosso* (dry, light red), *chiaretto* (dry rosé), or *novello* (fruity, young red made in the Beaujolais style, and Italy's first DOC-approved novello). The *rosso* and *chiaretto* Bardolino can also be made in sparkling versions. An older style, Bardolino Classico Superiore (see Figure 7.19), is not often seen in the United States. Also comprised of Corvina, Rondinella, and Molinara grapes, Bardolino is by nature lighter than Valpolicella, even though the soil and climate are quite similar. More than a million cases of Bardolino are produced each year. As in Valpolicella, Boscaini is a name that means quality in Bardolino.

A producer of fine dessert wines in Bardolino is Maculan, whose Torcolato is one of Italy's best. Torcolato is a blend of local grapes, is oak aged, and may be *botrytis* affected. With a nose of honey, ginger, dried pineapple, and papaya, and a viscous but clean taste, Torcolato has developed an international following. Maculan also produces good Chardonnay and Cabernet Sauvignon-based wines.

**Figure 7.19** Boscaini is a Name that Means Quality in Valpolicella and Bardolino.

***Friuli-Venezia Giulia.*** Friuli-Venezia Giulia, which borders Austria and the former Yugoslavia, is home to Italy's most technologically advanced wines. Friuli plants French and German varietals alongside the native Tocai Friulano, Riesling Italico, Refosco, Verduzzo, and Ramandolo grapes. Known primarily for white wines, Friuli producers emphasize freshness and, unusual for Italian dry whites, fruitiness. One of Friuli's most celebrated and recently rediscovered sweet white wines is the vino da tavola Picolit, which compares favorably to fine Sauternes. Spumante wines, some made in the metodo classico from Chardonnay and Pinot Noir grapes, are beginning to take hold in this region. Red wines are being produced from local grapes, plus Bordelaise varietals and Pinot Noir. Aging reds in barriques has become commonplace.

Friuli-Venezia Giulia was under Austrian control until after World War I, and its vineyards were decimated during the battles of World War II. Its capital, Trieste, a port city, was ceded to Italy, but much of the rest of the former region of Istria was eventually awarded to (then) Yugoslavia in the early 1950s. Culturally, however, Friuli is influenced more by Italy than by Austria and the former Yugoslavia, and its DOC white wines are, much like Italian design, a testament to modernism in the vineyards. Since only about 25 percent of Friuli's vineyards are planted on steep slopes, mechanical harvesting is the norm, as is temperature-controlled cool fermentation in stainless steel vats. Producers insist on low yields, even though Friuli produces 50 million cases of DOC wine per year.

In Friuli, DOC designations take second place to grape varieties, and Friuli is home to dozens of varietals, about a third of which are native to the region. So, when discussing the DOC wines of Friuli, we must also include the grape types, as many wines have varietal labels. No single variety dominates the region, and some grape types are DOC approved, some are not: Cabernet Franc, yes; Cabernet Sauvignon, no; Sauvignon Blanc, yes;

Vineyards in Collio Orientali del Fruili.

Chardonnay, no in Collio, yes in Collio Orientali. In addition, some of Friuli's best wines are *vini da tavola,* like the esteemed wines of young maverick Silvio Jermann. Jermann would rather name his Chardonnay "Where the Dreams Have No End," after a song by the rock group U2, than to be confined to DOC nomenclature. Sparkling wines, most made by the charmat method, are also unclassified.

Of the eight DOC zones of Friuli-Venezia Giulia, the most important are Collio, Collio Orientali del Friuli, and Grave del Friuli.

***Collio.*** The hills bordering the former Yugoslavia contain the vast Collio DOC zone, sometimes called Collio Goriziano for the border town of Gorizia in the southeast. The most important producers include Marco Fellugia, Mario Schiopetto, Livio Felluga, Pighin, and the rock music-loving Jermann. With the exception of Collio Bianco, which is a blend of Ribolla, Malvasia, and Tocai Friulano grapes, all the DOC wines are 100 percent varietal. Legal varieties are Cabernet Franc, Malvasia, Merlot, Pinot Bianco, Pinot Grigio, Pinot Nero, Riesling Italico, Sauvignon Blanc, Tocai Friulano, and Traminer. Note that the Riesling and Tocai used are not descended from the German, Hungarian, or Alsatian varietals, but from local grapes.

The Collio Orientali del Friuli region is famous for the sweet but rare vino da tavola, Picolit, and for more assertive DOC red wines. In this geographic continuation of Collio Goriziano, the wine makers insist that their wines are different from their neighbors'. There are some cru vineyards in the zone, and approved varietals are Cabernet Franc; Merlot; Picolit; Chardonnay; Malvasia; three Pinots: Bianco, Nero, and Grigio; local Riesling; Tocai Friulano; Traminer; and the unique Ramondolo, Ribolla, and Verduzzo. To qualify for varietal labeling, the wines must be a minimum of 90 percent of the stated grape, with the other 10 percent made up by a grape of the same color. The producer most recognized in the United States is Collavini.

Grave del Friuli is Friuli's largest DOC, located on elevated plains. More than half of the region's DOC wines come from Grave, which, like the Graves appellation in Bordeaux, is named for its gravely soil. While quite a bit of Tocai is produced in this zone, Pinot Grigio takes precedence in the export markets, with the French classics, Sauvignon Blanc and Chardonnay, making inroads. Although Friuli is best known for its dry, crisp white wines, red Merlot grapes dominate the Grave vineyards. Wines from Grave tend to be less expensive than those from the two Collio DOC zones, but no well-known producers sell to the United States market, as so much of Grave's production is consumed in the EC countries. Varietal labels are based on a minimum 85 percent of the labeled grape, and 15 percent other DOC-approved grapes. Grape types include Cabernet Franc; Cabernet Sauvignon; Chardonnay; Merlot; the three Pinots: Bianco, Nero, and Grigio; Traminer; Sauvignon Blanc; local Riesling; Tocai Friulano; Refosco Rosso; and Verduzzo.

***Trentino–Alto Adige.*** Bordering Austria and Switzerland, Trentino-Alto Adige may be a region only for the sake of convenience. While Trentino's culture is undoubtedly Italian, officially bilingual Alto Adige (Südtirol in German) has a predominantly Austrian culture, as Austria ruled this area from 1363 to 1920. Trentino has been linked to Alto Adige as a political unit so that Italy can exercise some control over the region, many of whose citizens think of themselves as Austrians. Whatever the practical difficulties of folding a Germanic culture into a Latin country, the wines of this Alpine region are phenomenal. More than half the wine produced is DOC, and a third of that production finds its way to export markets. The 12 DOC zones of Trentino-Alto Adige are not terribly significant, for here it is the grapes that differentiate one well-made wine from the other. The Alto Adige (Südtiroler) DOC designation allows 19 varietals, the Trentino DOC designation allows 20. All of Trentino Alto-Adige's wines, including some fine,

**Figure 7.20** Alto Adige is a Large DOC Zone in Trentino Alto-Adige.

expensive sparklers and its ubiquitous Pinot Grigio, are among the best made in Italy.

Of the 12 DOC zones in Trentino-Alto Adige (of which ten have both Italian and German names) four are of significance in the world market: Alto Adige (see Figure 7.20), (Südtiroler), Santa Maddelena (St. Magdalener), Trentino, and Teroldego. Important native red grapes are Schiava (Vernatsch), Lagrein, and Teroldego Rotaliano. Significant red and white foreign grapes include the Bordeaux and Burgundy varietals, and Müller-Thurgau, the most widely planted grape in Germany (see Chapter 10 on Germany).

***Alto Adige (Südtiroler).*** Alto Adige (Südtiroler) is a large zone, using the Teutonic town of Bolzano (Bozen) as its northernmost anchor. The wine makers of Südtirol are known for their ability, and two firms—Lageder and Kettmeir—stand out among them. In addition, one man, Georgio Grai, is a legend in Italian wines. Alois Lageder is best known for his modern approach to making wines from single vineyards at the winery founded by his great-grandfather. Lageder's barrique-aged Chardonnay and Cabernet are exquisite wines, while his Pinot Grigio is perhaps the best from the region. Franco Kettmeir is known in the United States for a range of quality wines produced in a fresh, crisp style. Santa Margherita is Alto Adige's largest producer of Pinot Grigio, for which it gets inexplicably high prices in the United States. This firm also produces other DOC wines, and a good Chardonnay. Grai makes powerful, long-lived wines, very few of which are exported. In fact, a good portion of his wines are sold at his wine bar in Bolzano, an important stop on any wine lover's search for the Grail.

DOC wines are labeled by varietal (mostly 95 percent minimum), except for spumante, which is a blend of Pinot Bianco or Chardonnay with Pinot Nero or Pinot Grigio, most often made in the metodo tradizionale. Red varietals include Lagrein Scuro (Lagrein Dunkel), a red Malvasia, Merlot, Pinot Nero (Blauburgunder), and Schiava (Vernatsch). Whites are Chardonnay, Moscato (Muskateller), Müller-Thurgau, Riesling Italico and Renano (Welschriesling, Rheinriesling), Sauvignon Blanc, Sylvaner, and Gewürztraminer.

***Santa Maddalena (St. Magdalener).*** This is considered to be one of the finest red wines of northeastern Italy. It is made in the Southern Tyrol from the Schiava (Vernatsch) grape. Schiava means "slave girl," reflecting the grape's ability to bend to the will of the wine maker, while always maintaining a certain delicacy. Santa Maddalena is considered to be the best example of the Schiava grape, since the wine shows medium body, good ruby color, and moderate aging potential. We see very little Santa Maddelena in the United States, because most of the wine is consumed by the Swiss, Austrians, and Germans.

***Trentino.*** The best-known producers in Trentino, the Italian part of the region, are Ferrari, a producer of world-class sparkling wines, and Càvit, a group of cooperatives that has banded together to market good wine at fair prices. The house of Ferrari started the wine-making renaissance in Trentino by producing one of the finest brut sparkling wines outside of Champagne. The Ferrari spumante wines are in a class by themselves, and are often more expensive than most nonvintage Champagnes. The Cantina Viticotori—Càvit for short—is a forward-looking group, making wines from many different DOC-approved varietals and marketing them the world over. The Càvit Pinot Grigio is best known in the United States. A well-made wine, it sells for one-third the price of Santa Margherita. Càvit also makes a tasty brut spumante by the classic method.

There are 16 wines with varietal labels produced in Trentino, all made from 100 percent of the grape, in addition to a DOC white, red, and a luscious dessert wine. The white varietals are Chardonnay, Moscato, Müller-Thurgau, Nosiola, Pinot Bianco, Pinot Grigio, Riesling Italico and Renano, and Traminer Aromatico. The reds are Cabernet Sauvignon and Cabernet Franc, Lagrein, Marzemino, Merlot, and Pinot Nero.

Teroldego Rotaliano is considered Trentino's finest red wine, with a full body and flavor, and age-worthy character. Recent versions of Teroldego have emphasized a lighter style to make the wine more accessible in its youth. Not only has Teroldego rosé begun to develop a following, but novello versions of this once mighty wine have been approved by the DOC. While purists may bemoan the loss of stature in this wine, it must be said that Novello di Teroldego from a well-known producer (Zeni is perhaps the best example for the American market) is a fruity mouthful, with gentle acidity. A good alternative to Beaujolais, the Novello di Teroldego can easily outshine its French counterpart.

# Summary

A major tributary of the "wine lake," Italy produces some of the finest wines in the world, and many of them are available in the American market. The quality wines of Toscana and Piemonte are the most highly regarded Italian wines, but wines from Umbria, Trentino Alto-Adige, Veneto, Friuli-Venezia Giulia, Lombardia, Marche, Sicilia, and Camapania can also be excellent. These wines represent a small fraction of Italy's prodigious output; the actual number of wines available to the consumer can be staggering. A good rule of thumb when buying any Italian wine is to purchase based on the strength of the reputation of the producer.

Like the food of Italy, the wines of Italy are full of regional and local personality and spirit; they speak to the soul. Italian wines are so diverse that they are perfect "food wines," for everything from hors d'oeuvre to dessert.

# Spain

## Introduction

Spain has more acres of land under vine than any country and is the third largest producer and exporter of wine in the world—a distant third, however, after France and Italy. The per-capita consumption of wine in Spain is about 20 gallons/80 liters, or about two glasses of wine per person per day, including wines made by farmers for home consumption. Although Spain produces some of the finest wines in Europe, traditional Spaniards are more apt to drink their local wines, or *vino corriente,* on a daily basis. For example, Spain is world renowned for its Sherry, produced in Jerez de la Frontera in southern Andalucía (Andulusia), but very few Spaniards living in northern Spain drink this fortified wine. Spaniards are most likely to drink a fine **Rioja** at a special occasion or during a meal at an expensive restaurant. The best-known wines of Spain are reserved for the large export market.

Twenty to 30 years ago, it was still a common event to walk into a wine shop in Spain with an empty bottle and fill it from a cask of local *tinto, clarete,* or *blanco.* During the late 1970s, however, in the waning years of the Francisco Franco regime, Spain experienced a rise in its middle class, and with it a more sophisticated approach to wine. Today, Spain is a prosperous nation, an important member of the European Community (EC). The current generation of Spanish wine producers understands that the future of Spain's wine industry lies in the production of quality wines for consumption throughout Europe and the rest of the world.

The Sierra Cantabria Mountains in Rioja Alavesa.

A Tapas Bar in Madrid, Where the Spanish Relax with Light Food and a Cool Sherry.

On a Daily Basis, Traditional Spaniards are Likely to Drink Their Local Wines.

Spain has Some Wonderful Restaurants. At *El Olivo*, in Madrid, in Addition to Tasting More than 350 Sherries at the Tapas Bar, You can Taste up to 45 Spanish Olive Oils with Your Dinner.

# History

Grapes were cultivated in Spain as early as 4000 B.C. and starting about 1100 B.C. the Phoenicians, who founded Cadiz as an important Atlantic port, introduced commerical wine making to Spain. The Carthaginians, natives of the ancient North African city Carthage, followed the Phoenicians into Cadiz, and ruled southern Spain for about 900 years. From 264 to 146 B.C. the Carthaginians and the Romans (who ruled parts of northern Spain along the Ebro River) fought the three Punic Wars. Rome emerged triumphant and expanded the Spanish wine trade by exporting mostly bulk wines of low quality to Gaul (modern France), England, Germany, and to Rome itself.

As the Roman empire crumbled, Spain was invaded by barbarians, first by the Suevi, and later by the Visigoths; still the wine trade prospered. In 711 A.D. the Moors, followers of Islam, overthrew the Visigoths, but did not impose their Moslem beliefs on the commerce and culture of the vine. Officially, production of wine was prohibited, yet the Moors imposed an excise tax on its sale.

In Andalucía, viticulture flourished under Arab rule. Gradually, vines spread to the inland's temperate zones, and later the valleys, slopes, and foothills, with plantings of vines as high as 3000 feet/1000 meters above sea level.

By the mid-thirteenth century, Spain was almost entirely under Christian rule, with Granada the only province still ruled by the Moors. The wine trade in Spain began to flourish in the late fifteenth century, as the Moors were defeated and the country was united as a Christian monarchy in 1492. With Christopher Columbus' discovery of the West Indies in that same year,

Vines Have Been Planted as High as 3000 Feet/1000 meters Above Sea Level.

Pope Alexander VI decreed that the New World would be divided between Spain and Portugal. Spain was granted possession of virtually all of Latin America, except for Brazil which became a Portuguese colony.

The Inquisition (it, too, was declared in 1492), which effectively expelled all observant Jews from Spain, led to political hegemony between Spain and other European countries, culminating in the defeat of the Spanish Armada—Spain's much-admired navy—by the English in 1588. A year later Spain declared war on England, seizing British ships in the ports of Jerez. The effect on Spanish wine exports was devastating, especially because duties on wines were dramatically increased by England and its allies. Portugal was the beneficiary of Spain's problems, because it was granted favorable duty rates on its exported wines.

By the late eighteenth century Spain was on its way back to prosperity, with new wine merchants and importers, both Spanish and British, reinvigorating the wine trade. The early- to mid-19th century was particularly profitable for the wines of Jerez and Málaga. In the 1800s, when *phylloxera* attacked French vines (see Chapter 2 on Wine Grapes), new markets for Spanish wines were opened worldwide. Many French growers, especially from Bordeaux (just 300 miles/480 kilometers from Rioja), settled in Spain's best wine districts and brought with them their skills and wine-making techniques. During the scourge of *phylloxera* in France, Rioja alone shipped millions of gallons of bulk wines through Bordeaux, helping to both keep the French wine industry alive and to broaden Spanish wine markets. When *phylloxera* crossed the Pyrenees into Spain, its wine industry was decimated, leaving a permanent scar on the history of Spanish vines and, thanks to the tradition of promiscuous plantings (vines, plants, and trees planted on the same small plot of land) on all of Spanish agriculture.

After the tragedy of *phylloxera,* and a painful and fractious political history dominated by the 50-year reign of Generalissimo Francisco Franco, which ended with his death in 1975, Spanish producers were in economic turmoil.

Jerez Vineyards.

Growers, however took advantage of a warm climate and long growing season, and Spain came to be widely known for inexpensive bulk wines that were full bodied, alcoholic, and undistinguished in quality. But as early as 1926, when Rioja was demarcated (followed by Jerez in 1933 and Málaga in 1937), Spain began to institute controls and laws designed to improve Spanish wines and, consequently, Spain's standing in the international wine community.

As new wine-making technology, including closed stainless steel vats and cool fermentation, was introduced to Spain, some excellent wines were made. In 1972, the Ministry of Agriculture formed the **Instituto de Denominaciónes de Origen (INDO),** the equivalent of the French AOC and Italian DOC (see the following section on Spanish Wine Laws). Today, as a member of the EC, Spain must also adhere to new pan-European laws governing production, distribution, and land use.

Spain has an ongoing tradition of small-land holdings, so grapes are often but one crop of the family farm. It is not uncommon, even today, to find olive trees, fruit groves, and vineyards intermingled on a small piece of land.

## Wine Laws

Spanish wine-making laws date back as far as the Middle Ages, but it was not until 1926, when Rioja was proclaimed a demarcated region, that modern regulations took hold in Spain. Today, there are 39 official wine-making regions in Spain, and two island regions. Each region is governed by its own *Consejo Regulador,* a joint regional-federal body with a strong local identity that regulates the growing, making, and shipping of the regional wines.

Spanish wine laws entered the modern era in 1970 with the adoption of the *Estatuto de la Viña, del Vino y de los Alcoholes,* a complex set of federal wine regulations stating that all Spanish wines had to adhere to certain qual-

**Figure 8.1** The Back of a Rioja Cosecha Label.

**Figure 8.2** The Front of a Rioja Cosecha Label.

ity standards and wine-making procedures, methods of viticulture, transport, distribution, sale, and export. This government decree was followed in 1972 by the formation of the Instituto de Denominaciones de Origen (INDO), to oversee and coordinate the activities of the various Consejos Reguladores. In addition to the general regulations specified in the Estatuto document of 1970, the INDO, in concert with the regional regulators, governs boundaries of the wine regions, grape varieties, yield-per-hectare, pruning methods, vinification and aging methods, and minimum alcohol content. Some laws are specific to each growing region; others apply to all of Spain (e.g., sparkling wine laws). In Cataluña, which includes four provinces (Barcelona, Gerona, Lérida, and Tarragona) that revived their local autonomy shortly after the death of Franco, the *Instituto Catalan de Vino* (IN-CAVI) is the equivalent of INDO.

Fine Spanish wine-producing regions are entitled to the **Denominación de Origen (DO)** designation, much like the wines and regions of France (AOC) and Italy (DOC). As of 1986 the category **Denominación de Origen Calificada (DOCa)** was added to Spain's wine laws, to recognize truly superior wine regions, much like Italy's DOCG designation. So far, the only DOCa is Rioja. Because Spain is a member of the EC, quality designations for all Spanish wines are approved by the **Office International du Vin (OIV).**

## INDO Quality Designations

INDO has established the following quality designations for Spanish wines, listed in ascending order of quality.

**Vino de Calidad.** Quality wine from one of the 39 specific regions. Equivalent of French vin de pays or, perhaps, VDQS (see Chapter 6 on France).

**Vino de Cosecha.** Vintage wine, with at least 85 percent of the wine made from grapes harvested in the stated vintage (see Figures 8.1 and 8.2).

**Figure 8.3** The Back of a Rioja Crianza Label.

**Figure 8.4** The Back of a Rioja Reserva Label.

**Figure 8.5** The Front of a Rioja Reserva Label.

***Vino de Crianza.*** Wine that is released to the market in its third year, having spent at least six months in small oak barrels. In Rioja, *crianza* wines must have at least one year barrel aging, plus one year bottle aging (see Figure 8.3).

***Reserva.*** Red wines aged at least three years, one year of the three in **barrica.** White wines aged at least two years, including six months in oak barrels. American oak is most often used in Spain (see Figures 8.4 and 8.5).

***Gran Reserva.*** Red wines aged two years in the barrel plus three years in the bottle, or three years in

**Figure 8.6** Rioja Gran Reserva Labels.

**Figure 8.7** The Front of a Rioja Gran Reserva Label.

the barrel and two in the bottle. Gran Reserva (see Figures 8.6 and 8.7) red wines may not reach the market until six years after the vintage. White wines must be aged four years, including six months in oak barrels. Gran Reservas are made only in exceptional years (see Figure 8.8).

# Spain's Wine Regions (see Map 8.1)

## Northern Spain

The great majority of Spain's table wines are produced in the northern provinces, because the climate is relatively cooler, although the summers are quite hot. Using the heat summation approach (see Chapter 2 on Wine Grapes), northern Spain would contain regions 2, 3, and 4. The Atlantic Ocean attracts rain to the northern coastal regions, and the Ebro and Duero rivers carry the cool breezes from the Pyrenees to the vineyards.

The DO areas of northern Spain (DOCa in the case of Rioja) are listed below as appellations of their host regions:

- *Cataluña:* Alella, Ampurdán-Costa Brava, Penedès and Cava, Conca de Barberà, Tarragona, Priorato, Terra Alta, and Costers del Segre.

- *Aragón:* Somontano, Cariñena, Calatayud, Campo de Borja, Rioja, and Navarra.

- *Basque Country:* Chacolí de Guetaria and Rioja Alavesa.

- *Castilla y León:* Ribera del Duero, Rueda, Toro, Bierzo, and Cigales.

- *Galicia:* Valdeorras, Ribeiro, and Rías Baixas.

**Figure 8.8 a&b** Read Labels Carefully. The Same Producer Makes Both Reservas and Gran Reservas. Gran Reservas are Made Only in Exceptional Years.

**Map 8.1**  The Wine Regions of Spain.

We shall discuss each of the major DO or DOCa areas more or less in order of its importance to the Spanish wine industry and its presence in the world market.

***Rioja.***  With a total of about 108,000 acres/45,000 hectares under vine, Rioja, Spain's most important fine-wine producing region (see Map 8.2), lies along the Ebro River in central northeastern Spain. Rioja is about 2000 square miles/5000 square kilometers, and includes parts of the autonomous regions, or *autonomías,* of La Rioja, Navarra, and the Basque Country.

Rioja's climate is regulated by its position, halfway between the Atlantic Ocean and the Mediterranean. The Atlantic provides cool breezes in a generally temperate zone, to lend a touch of acidity to the wines. The Mediterranean's breezes are warmer, giving strength and body to the wines. Rioja has produced quality wines in the bottle for more than 100 years, relying on the varietals Tempranillo and Garnacha and, secondarily, Mazuelo and Graciano grapes, to make highly regarded red wines. Viura, Malvasia, and Gar-

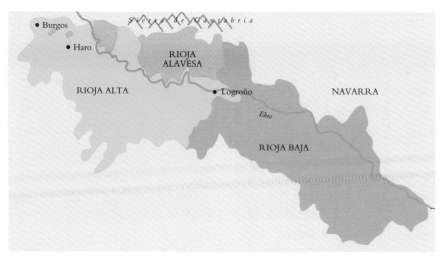

**Map 8.2**  Rioja.

**Figure 8.9 a&b**  Rioja Wines are Bottled in Both Bordeaux (left) and Burgundy-style Bottles (right), Traditionally Indicating the *Clarete* and *Tinto* Styles, Respectively.

nacha Blanca are the approved white grapes in the Rioja region. As of 1992 all Rioja wines must be bottled; no bulk wine sales are permitted under law (see Figure 8.9). This is a giant leap forward in quality for Rioja, and it is consistent with its distinction as the only wine region granted DOCa status by the Spanish government.

Important producers in the Rioja district include Marqués de Caceres, Marqués de Riscal, Bodegas Lan, Montecillo, Marqués de Arienzo, Paternina, La Rioja Alta, Campo Viejo, Muga, Marqués de Murrieta, Remelluri, Contino, CVNE (Compañia Vinícola del Norte de España), and Martínez Bujanda.

Rioja is known throughout the world for the quality of its red wines, made from four red varietals. Each grape provides unique aromatic and flavor characteristics in the finished blend.

Rioja.

Neighbors in Rioja Alavesal. Telmo Rodriguez (left) of Remelluri Vineyards, Whose Bordeaux-style Rioja Reserva has Received International Acclaim, Pictured with Issac Muga (right), Whose Classic Wines are Legendary Among Rioja Lovers.

**Figure 8.10** Tempranillo Grapes.

**Figure 8.11** Garnacha Grapes.

**Figure 8.12** Mazuelo Grapes.

**Figure 8.13** Graciano Grapes.

Luis I. Vallejo, President of CVNE (Known as Cune) in his Cellars. Luis and his Cousin, José Madrazo, also Own Contino, One of Rioja's Finest Single Vineyard Wineries.

## Red Grapes

**Tempranillo.** Tempranillo is the finest grape in Rioja, with a thick skin and a black color (see Figure 8.10). It yields from 10.5 to 13 percent alcohol, with good levels of acidity. Tempranillo ages well, especially when blended with the less-delicate Garnacha and Mazuelo. Most red *reserva* and *gran reserva* wines in Rioja are dominated by Tempranillo.

**Garnacha.** Garnacha Tinta is closely related to the Grenache grape, native to the Rhône Valley in France. The grape is thick skinned and resistant to oidium (see Figure 8.11), the powdery mildew that attacked Rioja along with *phylloxera* at the turn of the century. Fermented Garnacha musts may contain up to 16 percent alcohol, and are blended with Tempranillo to add body and alcohol, and to help the Tempranillo age in the cask and bottle. Garnacha is the most widely planted red wine grape in Spain, partly because its yield-per-hectare is high.

**Mazuelo.** Also called Cariñena, Mazuelo is the same as the Carignane varietal grown in France (see Figure 8.12). Mazuelo vines yield large grapes that produce musts with deep color and extract, along with high levels of tannin. While strictly a blending grape, Mazuelo is valuable to the finished wine, because fine Rioja spends so much time in wood.

**Graciano.** Graciano is strictly a blending grape (see Figure 8.13), adding freshness and aroma to the wines, and yielding only about 11 percent alcohol. Because of its low yields, little Graciano is found in modern Rioja vineyards.

Rioja also produces a large quantity of white wines (see Figure 8.14), much of it consumed within Spain. These wines, which can taste oxidized and overly oaky to the American palate, rarely attain the elegance of Rioja's reds.

# White Grapes

*Viura.* Also known as Macabeo in other regions of Spain, the Viura grape yields about 11 percent alcohol (see Figure 8.15). High in tartaric acid, this varietal makes light and fruity wines when processed through stainless steel cool fermentation. Viura is the basic, and sometimes the only, grape in more than 90 percent of Rioja's white wines.

*Malvasía.* This grape (see Figure 8.16) does well in oak-aged white wines, which are almost a thing of the past in Rioja. Malvasía is quite a vigorous grape and is sometimes blended with the more acidic Viura to produce the best, rare riserva white wines of Rioja.

Carlos Martínez Bujanda (above) and his Brother Jesús, Produce 150,000 Cases of Estate-bottled Wine in Rioja from 1536 Acres/640 Hectares of Their Own Vineyards (the Average Holding in Rioja is about Two Hectares). Their Conde de Valdemar Wines has been Quite Successful in the International Market. Martínez Bujanda also Produces French Varietal Wines, and Ages Their Best Wines in French oak barrels.

**Figure 8.14 a&b** Rioja also Produces a Large Quantity of White Wine.

*Garnacha Blanca.* This grape (see Figure 8.17) produces one-dimensional, high-alcohol, low-acid wines and, though still a legal varietal, it is not used much in Rioja any more.

For the export market, Rioja concentrates on red wines with a Bordeaux style, largely owing to the influx of French wine makers during the early part of the *phylloxera* epidemic. These export wines are aged mostly in American oak, because the small American barrels have thicker staves, which means slower, more-controlled oxidation of the wine. However, the more expensive French oak barrels, which impart softer aromas and flavors, are gaining in popularity in Rioja.

**Figure 8.15** Viura Grapes.

**Figure 8.16** Malvasía Grapes.

**Figure 8.17** Garnacha Blanca Grapes.

Export Wines are Aged Mostly in American Oak.

The Wine Cellars of Rioja are Filled with Millions of Bottles.

To make reserva and gran reserva Rioja wines, bottle aging is at least as important as barrel aging, so the cellars of Rioja are often filled with literally millions of bottles of wine waiting for their release dates. Theoretically, the wine producers of Rioja age the wines for the consumer. All Rioja wines—crianza, reserva, and gran reserva—are supposed to be ready to drink when sold, although some of these wines can last a decade or more. Most of the grape tannin-based sediment in the wine is left in the barrel, and these wines should not have to be decanted.

The red wines of Rioja that are consumed in the region's restaurants, bars, and homes are quite different from the export versions, though the quality is high. These wines are produced by what can best be described as a modified carbonic maceration technique (see Chapter 1 on How Wine Is Made), but in *uncovered* concrete vats. This *vino de cosechero,* "wine maker's wine," is fruity, fragrant, and meant to be drunk young.

***Subregions.*** Rioja is subdivided into three subregions: Rioja Alta, Rioja Alavesa, and Rioja Baja.

*Rioja Alta.* Rioja Alta, the northernmost subregion, lies closest to the Atlantic Ocean, with 40,800 acres/17,000 hectares under vine. The soil is largely clay, with some alluvial silt. Red wines from this subregion are of high quality. They consist of about 50 percent Tempranillo, blended with Garnacha, Mazuelo, and sometimes Graciano. The wines of Rioja Alta are generally about 10 to 12 percent alcohol, good for some aging in both cask and bottle. In fact, the wines of this subregion are usually the longest lived wines in all of Rioja. White wines are blends of Viura and Malvasía.

*Rioja Alavesa.* Rioja Alavesa is a hilly, chalky area on the north bank of the Ebro, with 16,800 acres/7000 hectares under vine. The climate is temperate, and the vineyards are planted on the south-facing slopes of calcareous clay, beneath the Sierra Cantabria mountain range. This area arguably produces Rioja's best red wines, generally composed of about 80 percent Tempranillo grapes. The wines are mouth filling, fruity, and soft, and usually do not age as long as the wines from Rioja Alta, though many fine reserva and gran reserva wines come from this subregion. White wines are about the same quality as Rioja Alta, with the same grapes in the blend.

*Rioja Baja.* The largest and southernmost subregion of Rioja, with 50,400 acres/21,000 hectares under vine on clay and silt, Rioja Baja is close to the Mediterranean Ocean. This subregion has a semiarid climate, and the Garnacha grape dominates. Red wines from Rioja Baja tend to be full, aro-

Rioja Alavesa.

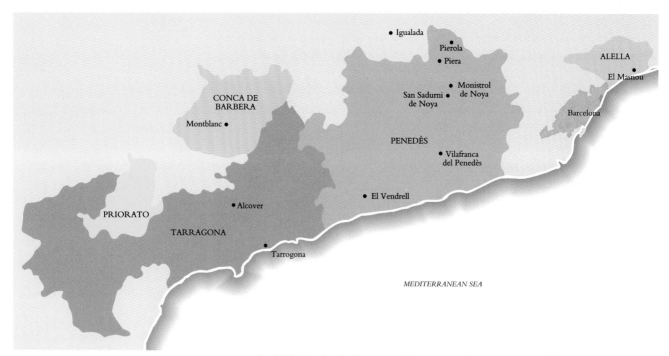

**Map 8.3** Cataluña.

matic, high in alcohol, somewhat coarse in texture, and low in acidity; they also oxidize quickly. Some adventurous producers are planting Tempranillo in the higher elevations with good results. White wines are low in acid, and can even be flat and flabby.

***Cataluña.*** Located in the northeast corner of Spain, Cataluña (Catalonia) includes the province and city of Barcelona and six Catalan DO zones (see Map 8.3). Ampurdán–Costa Brava is close to the border with France; Alella, which is part of Barcelona province, is situated on the Mediterranean coast; Penedès, also part of the Barcelona province, lies farther south and inland, centered around the city of San Sadurni de Noya, and is the official center of the Cava sparkling wine region; Tarragona, in Southeast Cataluña, is the largest DO in the region; Priorato is a small, mountainous area, whose DO area is within Tarragona; Terra Alta, in the mountainous southwest, is one of the newest demarcated wine regions in Spain.

Cataluña produces fine red wines, some good white wines, *rancío* dessert wines (old white wines, purposely oxidized, and sometimes fortified), sweet *mistelas* (fortified), and rosé wines. This region also produces more sparkling wine—*cava*—than the entire Champagne region of France. There has been some successful experimentation in Cataluña with vitis vinifera grapes from France (Cabernet Sauvignon, Merlot, Sauvignon Blanc, Chardonnay, and Gewürztraminer) and from Germany (Riesling and Müller-Thurgau). Use of these grapes is authorized by the Consejo Regulador, but still almost all of the grapes in Catalan wines are native to Spain. The Mazuelo, Garnacha, Garnacha Blanca, Tempranillo, and Malvasía grapes of Rioja are also important in Cataluña. Other important native grapes:

*Monastrell.* Native to Cataluña, Monastrell is the second most-planted red wine grape in Spain, after Garnacha. Wines made from the Monastrell

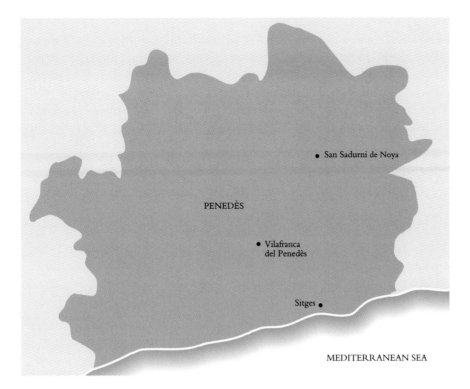

**Map 8.4** Penedès.

PENEDÈS

• San Sadurni de Noya

• Vilafranca
del Penedès

Sitges •

MEDITERRANEAN SEA

grape can have high levels of alcohol, deep color, elegant flavor and nose, and good aging potential. This grape also produces good rosé and fortified wines.

*Macabeo.*   Known as Viura in Rioja, Macabeo produces fruity, well-balanced wines, resistant to oxidation, and so is a good candidate for cold fermentation. Along with Xarel-lo and Parellada (see below), this varietal is one of the three classic white grapes of Cava (see Sidebar on Cava in this chapter).

*Xarel-lo.*   Native to Cataluña, this grape (pronounced "Sharel-yo") makes wines of medium strength and medium acidity. It is also called Pansá Blanca.

*Parellada.*   With musts that are high in acidity and low in alcohol, this white varietal is used for its fresh, fruity bouquet and flavor in still white wines and Cava. Parellada is said to be the best white wine grape in all of Cataluña.

*Pedro Ximénez.*   Grown widely in Andalucía to make sweet Sherries, and in Montilla, where it makes a dry wine, this warm-weather lover is grown in small amounts in Priorato and Terra Alta to be added to the musts of other grapes, probably to raise alcohol levels, and to increase sweetness to make rancío dessert wines.

*Penedès and Conca de Barbera.*   Penedès (see Map 8.4) has a long and successful history of exporting wines (see Figure 8.18), and it has 54,000 acres/22,500 hectares under vine, including French and German varietals.

**Figure 8.18 a&b** Penedès has a Long and Successful History of Exporting Wines.

**Figure 8.19** Gran Vina Sol is an Elegant Chardonnay/Parellada Blend.

**Figure 8.20** Torres Gran Coronas Reserva is a Blend of Cabernet Sauvignon and Merlot.

## THE TORRES FAMILY

Perhaps the most important producer of still table wines for export from Penedès is Miguel Torres, a Bordeaux-trained wine maker who introduced French vinifera to Penedès. Torres produces a wide range of wines, both in type and cost. Viña Sol, which is 100 percent Parellada, is a fresh, clean wine that represents great value. Gran Viña Sol is an elegant Chardonnay/Parellada blend (see Figure 8.19). Torres makes several Penedès vinifera/French vinifera blends, both white and red. Torres Coronas (see Figure 8.20), a blend of Tempranillo and Cabernet Sauvignon, retails for less than $10, but the winery also produces a Gran Coronas Black Label, made exclusively from Cabernet Sauvignon, that retails for anywhere from $30 and up, depending on the vintage available. With his son, Miguel, Jr., Miguel Torres has also established vineyards and wineries in Chile. His daughter, Miramar, produces a fine Chardonnay in California's Sonoma Valley.

## CAVA

Cava (see Map 8.5), formerly Champaña, is the name of a class of sparkling wines, the relatively new DO, and the *bodegas,* or cellars, in which the wines are made. Cava is also the name given to the *méthode champenoise* process utilized to make the sparkler. About 90 percent of the wine is made in Penedès, and close to 100 percent comes from provinces within Cataluña. More Cava is made than any other sparkling wine, and more than 40 million cases of Cava were exported worldwide in 1994.

In descending order of dryness, Cava is labeled as **Brut de Brut, Brut Natur, Brut, Seco, Semiseco, Semidulce,** and **Dulce.** Traditionally made from the three white grapes, Parellada, Macabeo, and Xarel-lo, some cavas now contain Chardonnay in the blend. A small amount of Cava is made in Rioja, Aragón, and Navarra, but without DO status.

The best-known producers of Cava include Freixenet, who sells well over one million cases of Cava per year in the United States. Freixenet, producer of the ubiquitous Cordon Negro Brut, also owns Gloria Ferrer, a good sparkling wine vineyard and winery in Sonoma. Cordoníu (see Figure 8.21), who also owns a Napa Valley winery, produces tens of millions of bottles of Cava per year, and blends traditional Champagne varietals with classic Cava grapes. Cordoníu's cellars and winery, built in the style of the Spanish architectural visionary, Gaudi, can accommodate more than 120 million bottles underground. Other important Cava producers are Juve y Camps, Chandon (owned by Moët et Chandon), Cavas Masachs, Paul Cheneau, Marqués de Monistrol, and Heredad Segura Viudas (owned by Freixenet).

**Map 8.5** Cava.

The white wines are pale, green, and acidic, with 11–12 percent alcohol and what has been described as an apple-skin bouquet. The red wines, which are light in texture with subtle flavors, take to oak aging and can be excellent.

Much like Rioja, Penedès is divided into three subregions: Bajo Penedès, Medio Penedès, and Penedès Superior. The Bajo and Superior regions are, respectively, the warmest and coolest growing areas, with Riesling, Muscat, and Gewürztraminer growing in Penedès Superior. About 60 percent of the wine of Penedès comes from Medio Penedès, a moderately warm area. Quality producers includes Miguel Torres, René Barbier, and Jean León.

**Figure 8.21 a&b** Cordoníu is One of the Best Known Producers of Cava.

Conca de Barberà, the small DO just west of Penedès, with 17,760 acres/7400 hectares under vine, provides wine for the Penedès Cava producers, as well as Chardonnay, Cabernet Sauvignon, and Pinot Noir grapes for the best Torres wines. This DO has almost no regional identity and is often thought of as a subdistrict of Penedès, whose name appears on the labels of Penedès-based producers, even though the contents of the bottle may be made from grapes and wine grown and produced in Conca de Barberà.

*Priorato.*   Located in the highlands of the Mediterranean province of Tarragona, Priorato has only 4320 acres/1800 hectares under vine. The soil is rugged, full of slate, and located on mountain slopes to absorb the heat of the sun; the climate is semiarid. Priorato produces red wines from Garnacha and Cariñena grapes, with a legal minimum of 13.5 percent alcohol, but the wines are well balanced, if a bit overpowering. Some deep yellow rancío dessert wine is also produced in Priorato. The most important producer in this region is Cellars Scala Dei, who make cool-fermented wines, emphasizing freshness and fruit, while still adhering to the high minimum-alcohol standard.

*Tarragona and Terra Alta.*   Tarragona and Terra Alta, with about 94,000 acres/39,000 hectares under vine combined, make white, red, and dessert wines. Tarragona is best known for its dessert wines, which contain 23 percent alcohol and for the production of sacramental and aromatized wines. Terra Alta makes table wines, mostly sold through the regional cooperatives, while 30 percent of Tarragona's white wines are sold in bulk to Cava producers in Penedès. The most visible producer in both areas is Pedro Rovira, who makes traditional wines of good quality.

*Ampurdán-Costa Brava.*   After *phylloxera* hit the Ampurdán-Costa Brava region, much vineyard land was permanently lost, making it a very small DO. The entire denominacíon consists of about 7200 acres/3000 hectares on the Pyrenees border with France, with the highest rainfall in all Cataluña. The area produces mostly reds and rosés that are fresh and fruity, with a delicate bouquet. In the 1980s modern cooperatives were established here with modern wine-making methods, and there is much new planting of French varietals in this wine region.

*Allela.*   Allela has lost more than 2400 acres/1000 hectares to the urban expansion of Barcelona, and now is only 840 acres/350 hectares. The denominación is famous for white wines with good acidity (often made from Chardonnay) and light, fresh red wines.

### Other Northern DO Regions

*Costers del Segre.*   The Costers del Segre denominación was created to accommodate one producer, Raimat, owned by the Raventós family, owner of the gigantic Cava producer, Cordoníu. In 1915, Manuel Raventós purchased the Raimat estate, building a town, church, school, railroad station, and a magnificent Gaudi-inspired wine cellar cooled by water running over its roof. A futuristic winery was completed in 1988. Wines from the Raimat estate (see Figure 8.22) are of very fine quality and include still and sparkling Chardonnay, as well as the red Abadia, which is a blend of Tem-

**Figure 8.22**   Wines from the Raimat Estate are of Very Fine Quality.

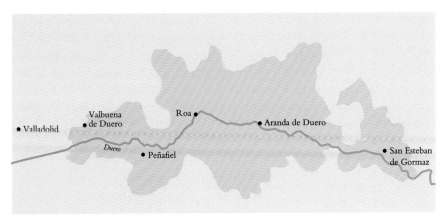

**Map 8.6** Ribera del Duero.

pranillo and Cabernet Sauvignon. Raimat also produces varietal Merlot, Cabernet Sauvignon, and Pinot Noir wines.

*Castilla y León.* Spain's largest *autonomía*, Castilla y León, covers the northern half of the country's central plateau and includes nine provinces. The city of Valladolid is the vortex of wine making in Castilla y León, and the best wines are made in the DOs encircling the city. The two most important denominaciónes in this region are Ribera del Duero and Rueda, located on opposite banks of the Duero River. Cigales, best known for rosé wines; Bierzo, making red wines from the local Mencía grape; and Toro, situated on the Galicia border, are minor denominaciones in the region.

*Ribera del Duero.* A relatively new DO, Ribera del Duero (see Map 8.6) has 28,800 acres/12,000 hectares under vine on dry highlands. Here the vines literally cling to the earth to protect themselves from burning summers and bitter cold winters. This extreme microclimate is softened by the shelter and moisture of the Duero River valley. On the upper slopes, the soil is rich in chalk, while the lower slopes are alluvial clay.

Ribera del Duero produces almost no white wine and makes some bone-dry rosés. It is famous, however, for its red wines aged in oak, the best of which is Vega Sicilia, an extraordinary wine made from a blend of local Tempranillo (here called Tinto del País) and Garnacha, as well as classic Bordeaux varietals (Cabernet Sauvignon, Merlot, and Malbec) which account for about 30 percent of the finished wine. Vega Sicilia's *Unico*, never released before aging ten years in oak and two more in the bottle, commands prices in excess of $100 per bottle. Vega Sicilia has been famous as perhaps Spain's greatest red wine for more than 100 years, and has only improved with time. Since 1982, the winery has been owned by the Alvarez Diaz family, who has expanded the cellars, cooperage, and wine-making facilities. Describing the taste of a mature Vega Sicilia is a bit like explaining a sixth sense; it is a great wine, full of black currants and velvety texture, but it is almost beyond formal description—a revelation.

Nearby, at a far more reasonable price, Alejandro Fernandez has been making Pesquera since about 1976 (see Figure 8.23), with great critical

**Figure 8.23** Pesequera has been Made Since About 1976.

**Figure 8.24** Viña Mayor is a Fine Wine from Ribera del Duero.

**Figure 8.25** Marqués de Riscal, a Famous Rioja Producer, has Major Holdings in Rueda. The Handmade Bottle Netting on All Marques de Riscal Wines is Traditional; It Originated as a Way to Fight Counterfeiting of the Wine by Unscrupulous Bulk Wine Producers.

praise since the 1982 vintage. Fernandez has opted to make his age-worthy wine from the local Tinto del País/Tempranillo. Another fine wine from this region is Viña Mayor (see Figure 8.24), also 100 percent Tempranillo, and made by the Barcelo family. At less than one-sixth the price of Vega Sicilia, both Pesquera and Viña Mayor are shining examples of what Ribera del Duero is capable of producing.

*Rueda.* Famous since the seventeenth century for its white wines, Rueda is located at the southwest tip of Valladolid along the Duero River. With 12,000 acres/5000 hectares under vine on soil of sand and clay, the wines are made in two distinct ways. The classic Rueda is Viura and Palomino-based, 15 percent alcohol, amber in color, with a natural *flor* yeast (see section on Sherry later in this chapter). The wine is allowed to mature in a modified solera and tastes like a coarse Sherry. The new Rueda white wines, vinified in stainless steel, are fresh, with about 12 percent alcohol, greenish-yellow, and with a fruity bouquet. The dominant grape in Rueda's new styles is the native Verdejo. Some Chardonnay and Sauvignon Blanc has recently been introduced to Rueda, to blend with Verdejo and to be made as varietals, especially by the leading export bodega of the region, Rioja-owned Marqués de Riscal (see Figure 8.25).

*Galicia.* If anyone wants to find a wine revolution in Spain, they need only look to Galicia. Two of its three denominaciónes, Ribeiro and Rías Baixas, today produce some of the best white wines in all of Spain, but until the mid-1980s their wines were nothing special. What happened to account for this quick turnaround?

*Ribeiro.* Ribeiro had for centuries relied on the Palomino grape, the grape of Sherry, to make its white wines. These wines tended to be heavy and oxidized, and very little was bottled. With the help of a regional research station and the encouragement of the local Ribeiro cooperative, many Palomino vines were replaced with two native varietals, Treixadura and Torrontés. The cooperative pays about double the price for these grapes as it pays for Palomino, whose planting it is actively discouraging.

Treixadura and Torrontés, when vinified with cool fermentation techniques, make a wine that is light to medium bodied and refreshing, with appealing aromas. Since the late 1980s, the Ribeiro cooperative has invested millions of dollars in stainless steel tanks and filters for must, with results that are nothing short of outstanding The wines, made either by the co-op or the Caves do Ribeiro company, are wonderful with fish, and are appearing in increasing number on the export market.

*Rías Baixas.* Like those of its neighbor Ribeiro, the white wines of Rías Baixas have gone from total obscurity to celebrity status. Rías Baixas, a fairly new DO, also invested heavily in new high-tech equipment and found itself a new grape: Albariño. While it is difficult to grow this grape in this wet region, the effort is worth it. Albariño is produced under its own varietal label, and has taken the wine world by storm. Albariño from Rías Baixas is at least 12 percent alcohol, medium to full in body, with a complex nose and flavor. The Albariño revolution took place almost overnight, and this revolutionary wine is fetching high prices in wine shops and restaurants.

Wines labeled "Albariño" are 100 percent varietal. The denominación also produces a wine labeled as "Rías Baixas," which must have at least 70 percent Albariño grapes in the blend. Good producers of Albariño include Morgadio, Valdamor, Marqués de Vizhoja, Santiago Ruiz, Martin Codax, and Fernandez Cervera Hermanos.

## Central Spain

Central Spain (see Map 8.7) includes the following DOs: Valdepeñas, Almansa, La Mancha, Méntrida, Vinòs de Madrid, Bullas, Yecla, Jumilla, Alicante, Levante, Valencia, and Utiel-Requena. Central Spain is best known for its bulk wines and its white Airén grape, which holds the dubious distinction of being the most planted grape in the world. If a grape could be a weed, Airén would be one. There are pockets of improvement in the area's wine industry, especially in the delimited areas of Levante and Valencia, and most of the other DO growing areas have come to realize that modernizing their approach to wine making and distribution is a matter of financial survival. Central Spain, however, with its warm climate and long growing season, has a long way to go before it is considered an important wine region in world markets. In this section we briefly survey four important denominaciones.

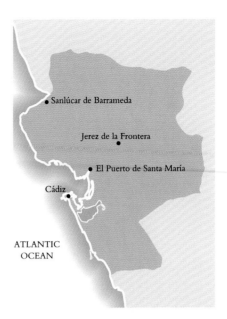

**Map 8.7**  Central Spain.

***Valdepeñas.***  Located in Castilla-La Mancha, the southern half of Spain's high central plateau, the climate of Valdepeñas is dry and sunny. Valdepeñas, like most of Central Spain, produces table wines that are fruity, with not much acidity. Valdepeñas has been famous for producing wines since the sixteenth century but today, of 250 bodegas in the DO, only 40 bottle their wine. It is said that the best wines are tasted in the jug or demijohn, when the wine is fruity and fresh. Grown on hilly terrain of reddish-brown chalky soil, the primary red grape is Cencibel (the colloquial name for Tempranillo), along with some Garnacha. The dominant white grape is Airén, which has a thick skin to protect it against the sunshine. About 90 percent of the red wine from Valdepeñas is made from the ubiquitous Airén grape, but the intensity of the color and extract from the Cencibel and Garnacha is such that the finished wine is a deep ruby color.

***La Mancha.***  The largest part of the entire region, and at 1.152 million acres/480,000 hectares under vine, La Mancha is the largest DO in all of Spain. The soil is clay with chalk subsoil, and the dominant grape is Airén. Typical wines are high in alcohol—13–14 percent—low in acid and have little fruit. A lot of this wine is sent to other regions for blending, and much of it is distilled for spirits. Although less than 30 percent of the wine produced in La Mancha is bottled, some encouraging signs, such as increased production of bottled red wines made by carbonic maceration, and more sparkling white wine production, have been observed in the land of Don Quixote.

***Valencia.*** The Valencia DO is 115,200 acres/48,000 hectares and is located on the Mediterranean coastal strip that runs from below Cataluña to just south of Alicante, consisting of sandy, mountainous highlands. Valencia produces more white than red wine, almost all of it quite earthy, assertive, full bodied, and low in acid. Cool fermentation is helping to make the wines more palatable in their youth, and rosé and red wines made from the local Bobal grapes show some promise. The DO Utiel-Requena maintains close commercial links with the wineries of Valencia, and is often considered a subdistrict of Valencia.

***Alicante.*** An area with little rainfall, hot summers, and mild winters, Alicante has 81,600 acres/34,000 hectares under vine, producing mostly red and rosé wines made from the Monastrell grape. This grape has never been seriously affected by *phylloxera* and is not widely grafted onto American rootstocks here in this region. The red wines are deep in color and extract, with some spice, and they age well. Alicante also produces sweet wines made from white Moscatel grapes, as well as a range of rancío-style dessert wines. Two producers, Salvador Proveda and Bodegas Eval, make red wines of good quality.

## The South and Islands

The south and the islands comprise the following denominaciones de origen: Jerez, Málaga, Montilla-Moriles, Manzanilla-Sanlúcar de Barrameda, Condado de Huelva, Binissalem (the Balearic Islands), and Tacoronte-Acentejo (the Canary Islands). The South is dominated by the Andalucía autonomía, which includes the provinces of Cadiz, Córdoba, Granada, Jaén, Málaga, and Sevilla. These are the romantic Moorish regions of Spain, home to the Alhambra, castanets, flamenco dancing, and the sun-drenched, whitewashed buildings that reflect the hot sun. To wine lovers they are the home of Sherry and of dry and sweet wines of Sherry-like character. Southern Spain is one of the warmest classic wine-growing regions, and the important wines, no matter their denominación, are fortified (like Málaga), or so naturally high in alcohol that they need no fortification (like Montilla-Moriles). Table wines are strictly local, and much wine from the south is sold in bulk to add strength to a blend.

The Balearic Islands (DO: Binissalem), whose capital is Mallorca (Majorca), and the Canary Islands (DO: Tacoronte-Acentejo), are of interest only insofar as they produce wine at all. A few small producers make bottled wine, some of it decent, none of it yet exported.

***Sherry.*** Jerez, the home of Sherry, is Spain's southernmost region, where annual rainfall totals only about 22 inches/56 centimeters. Sherry is produced from 43,200 acres/18,000 hectares of vineyards on Andalucía's southern Atlantic coastline. Here the DO is named after the capital of the province, Jerez (or Xeres) de la Frontera, whose corrupt English form is "sherry." Sherry has long been associated with England, ever since Sir Fran-

**Figure 8.26** Palomino Grapes.

*Albariza* Soil, Full of Chalk, Acts Like a Sponge, Absorbing the Scant Rainfall in Jerez during Cool Months, Distributing it to Palomino Vines during the Hot Summer.

Palomino Vines in Jerez.

cis Drake raided Cadiz in 1587 and carried off almost 3000 pipes (110 gallon barrels) of the wine. To this day the names of many famous Sherry houses are of British origin, and many are British owned.

Sherry is a fortified wine (see Chapter 1 on How Wine Is Made), whose alcoholic strength is increased by the addition of grape brandy after fermentation. The wine is purposely oxidized by storing it in wooden barrels only two-thirds full with wine, with a loose stopper in the barrel hole, allowing air to invade the wine.

Ninety percent of all Sherry is made from the Palomino grape (see Figure 8.26), which grows on albariza soil (soil that is at least 40 percent chalk. The white, chalky soil acts like a sponge, storing the scant rainfall and releasing it to the vines during the harsh summer months). The Palomino grape produces a base wine of approximately 10 percent alcohol, with good fruit, average acidity, and coarse character. The other important grape in Jerez is Pedro Ximénez (named after Peter Siemons, a German who introduced the

# SHERRY VINIFICATION

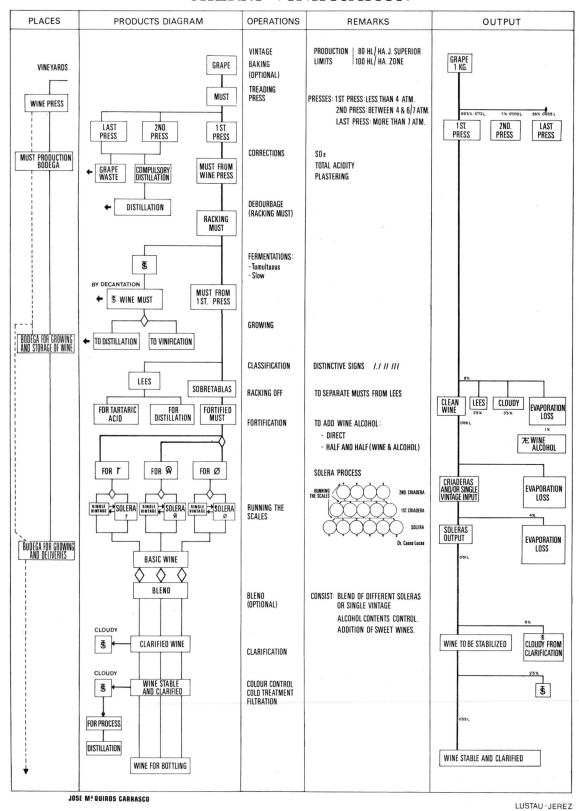

JOSE Mª QUIROS CARRASCO

LUSTAU-JEREZ

**Figure 8.27** A Sherry Vinification Chart.

The Vineyards of Jerez.

José Ignacio Lopez, Director of the John Harvey *Bodega* in Jerez, Conducting a Tasting of a Variety of Sherries.

grape to Spain), which is used mostly for the production of sweet Sherries, or for sweetening and coloring the wine before bottling. The Pedro Ximénez grape is grown on *barros* soil, which is richer in clay, and on *arenas,* soil that is sandier than either the *albariza* or arenas, and not as good, though highly productive. Moscatel grapes are also grown in these soils, and are used for sweetening and color, as well as for making inexpensive dessert Sherries.

While the Pedro Ximénez and Moscatel grapes are dried in the sun to concentrate their sugars, Palomino grapes are no longer treated this way, since the object in modern Sherry making is to obtain a must with low sugar and tannin content, but with the highest possible degree of acidity. The biggest problem in the steps between harvesting the Palomino grapes and the formal start of fermentation is the uncontrolled oxidation of the must (see Figure 8.27). Modern methods and devices have been introduced to help predict the right moment to harvest and to minimize oxidation of the must before it reaches the bodegas. Today the grapes are trucked from

*Flor* on the Surface of the Wine.

Barrels of Sherry.

the vineyards in refrigerated tanks to slow down the oxidation and fermentation process.

After fermentation, all Sherries are dry white wines with 11 to 14 percent alcohol. This new wine from the current vintage, called añada wine, is stored in 60-gallon/220-liter American oak barrels. The wine maker adds neutral grape spirits to the añada to increase the alcohol content to about 15.5 percent. While the wine is stored over the winter, it is watched and tasted carefully, and classified as either *fino* or *oloroso.* Fino is very pale, delicate, and dry; oloroso is heavy and dark. It is nature that classifies the wines more than it is the wine maker, since no one can predict which characteristics each barrel will develop.

The most important element in the development of fino character is the natural occurrence of a dense, white, frothy yeast on the surface of the wine. This yeast is called *flor,* and its formation restricts the amount of air that gets to the wine, thereby keeping the wine pale and delicate under a virtual blanket of yeast. Fino (and manzanilla, a fino made in Sanlúcar de Barrameda) is kept from oxidizing by the *flor.* Oloroso, for some reason not completely understood by wine makers or scientists, does not develop the yeast. Sometimes, after the *flor* presents itself, it diminishes and disappears, allowing oxidation and creating yet a third classification of Sherry, *amontillado.* This wine becomes slightly fuller and darker than a fino, but not nearly as heavy and dark as an oloroso.

Once the Sherries are classified, they are placed in soleras, the system devised to age Sherry and ensure a consistent quality and style. Each category of Sherry has its own solera, which is a network of large barrels, all of them two-thirds full, through which the wine passes during the aging process. The solera consists of several rows of barrels stored in a criaderas (tier) system. There are typically nine to 14 criaderas in a solera system, although some manzanilla Sherries can be made from as many as 19 tiers. The

Osborne's High-tech Approach to Making Some of Its Sherries, Using Stainless Steel Tanks.

A Four-tier Solera at Domecq. Notice That This Solera Contains the Añada (the New Wine), Two Criaderas (the Name For Each Row of the Solera), and the Solera—the Oldest Wine in the System. It is the Bottom Row (the Solera), That will be Bottled.

bottom row, called the solera, represents the oldest blend of wines in the system. The top tier is two-thirds full of the youngest blend of wines. When a producer wishes to bottle a fino Sherry, for example, up to one-third of the wine will be removed from each barrel in the bottom row in the fino solera.

To replenish the bottom row, wine is drawn from the row above it, leaving the barrels in the second row with some wine missing. To replenish the second row's wine, more wine is taken from the third row, immediately above it, and so on up the scale of each tier, until finally, to replenish the top row, añada is taken from the original barrels.

The solera system provides for consistent style and flavor, consistent quality, maturation of the young wine as it takes on the characteristics and qualities of the older wine in the system, and rejuvenation of the older wines by the young wines. Since the classic solera system is used throughout the whole Jerez region, there is really very little vintage Sherry, though some is made. In a modified solera, wines from one vintage are aged in barrels, and after more than 20 years of aging, are blended together to make a vintage Sherry. Should you see a bottle of nonvintage Sherry with a solera date on it ("Solera 1872," for example), this is the date of the oldest wine in the solera, and even today a few molecules of that wine may be present in the bottom barrels. After the wine has been taken from the solera, it is fined (traditionally using egg whites, sweetened or colored as necessary with Pedro Ximénez and Moscatel grapes), and fortified again to achieve stability.

Following are the basic marketing categories of Sherry:

**Fino.** Pale, dry, and delicate, with 15.5 to 17 percent alcohol.

**Manzanilla.** A fino from the coastal port town of Sanlúcar de Barrameda. It is said to take on a slightly salty tang. Manzanilla has the same alcohol content as fino.

Lustau's *Almacenista* Sherry.

**Amontillado.** Slightly fuller and darker with a nutty flavor and a slight hint of sweetness; 16 to 18 percent alcohol.

**Palo Cortado.** A rare Sherry, almost a freak, with little or no flor; palo cortado has the nose of amontillado and the flavor and color of oloroso. Contains 18 to 21 percent alcohol.

**Oloroso.** Full bodied, rich, and dark; up to 20 percent alcohol.

**Cream.** Very sweet oloroso, made by blending with Pedro Ximénez and Moscatel grapes or a sweet grape concentrate. Less-sweet cream Sherry is sometimes called *amoroso*.

Barrels of Amontillado. Manuel Arcila, Director General of Emilio Lustau, Pictured with Lustau's Famous *Almacenista* Solera.

A Butt of *Palo Cortado*, a Rare Sherry That Falls Somewhere between the Amonfillado and Olovoso Styles. It is Relatively Fresh, but Rich in Flavor.

A Tasting of 22 of Lustau's Sherries.

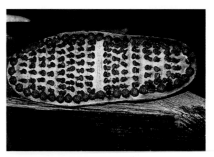

*Zapatos de Pisar* are the Cowhide Nail-studded Boots which were Used Traditionally to Press the Grapes for Sherry. They are Still Used by Hobbyist Wine Makers and for Public Festivals.

A Traditional Three-tier Solera at Osborne, in Jerez.

Tasting the Sherry Using a Venencia, a Silver Cup on the End of a Long, Flexible Whalebone or Bamboo Handle. Small Amounts of Sherry are Drawn from Casks and Whipped into a Small *Copita*, a Sherry Taster. Using the Venencia Successfully is a Real Skill.

**Pedro Ximénez/P.X.** Dark brown, very sweet and viscous, made exclusively from Pedro Ximénez grapes.

Perhaps Andalucía's finest Sherry producer is Emilio Lustau, whose *Almacenista* (shareholder's) Sherries are unique. Produced in several styles, the almacenistas are made from small batches of Sherries purchased each year from hobbyists and connoisseurs, and blended by Lustau. Lustau produces about 40 different Sherries, all of them worth tasting. Other quality producers include Osborne, Pedro Domecq, Antonio Barbadillo, Gonzalez Byass, Bobadilla, House of Sandeman, and Valdespino. John Harvey & Sons is best known for its popular Harvey's Bristol Cream.

# Summary

Spain produces some of the world's most highly esteemed wines, especially the classic red table wines of Rioja, and the fortified Sherries of Jerez. Penedès is an exciting wine region, producing wines made from blends of Spanish, French, and German varietals. Sparkling cava has become a highly successful bubbly that is well made, widely available, and great value. Some of the wines from lesser-known denominaciones such as Albariño from Rías Baixas, the red wines of Ribeira del Duero, and the whites of Rueda and Ribeiro, show real promise in the export market.

Like the rest of the European/Mediterranean wine-producing countries, Spain produces a lot of wine, not all of it memorable. Central and south-central Spain still produce a great deal of bulk wine, with the emphasis on quantity, not quality. Virtually none of these wines are produced for the export market. Small pockets of wine improvement in central Spain are worth watching, especially among some young, fresh, appealing white wines.

Luckily for American consumers, the great majority of wines exported from Spain are very good. At the very least, these wines are drinkable, at best they are among the world's finest. Unique in the wine world, Rioja producers actually age their wines for the consumer. Prices for most Spanish wines are fair, and in many cases, real bargains can be found. Spain's best wines, especially the country's best reds, marry well with a wide range of foods from around the world.

# Portugal

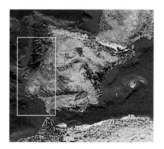

## Introduction

Portugal is in the midst of a revolution in its vineyards, wineries, and world image. The seventh-largest wine-producing nation, Portugal has an average annual production of 264 million gallons/10 million hectoliters. In 1991, consumption was at 16.3 gallons/62 liters per person. However, following the current trend in Europe, per capita consumption has declined in Portugal to 13.4 gallons/51 liters. By comparison, this amount is seven times higher than the current consumpsion level in the United States.

When one thinks of Portugal, semisweet rosés which are inexpensive and known throughout the world, immediately come to mind. Next, one thinks of the higher-quality fortified wines like Madeira and Porto. The Portuguese promote the quality of their red and white label wines as well as their sparkling wines on a global basis. While the international market is awash with Chardonnay and Cabernet Sauvignon varietal-labeled wines, the Portuguese focus on their native grapes which can produce aromatic, complex wines in a wide variety of styles. The Alvarinho may be considered one of the finest white grape and the Touriga Naçional one of the finest reds; but those varietal names are not often found on Portuguese wine labels.

Typical Portuguese Blue Tile.

The same grape type may go by a different name in a different region when this occurs the synonym will sometimes be in parentheses following the local name for the grape variety. Applying different names to a grape type is not unique to Portugal, it is common throughout Europe.

In the past, Portugal like other European countries with a relaxed attitude toward wine, had many promiscuously planted vineyards, where a number of different grape types would coexist with other fruits or vegetables in a field. Although different grape varieties ripen at different times, farmers harvesting three or four varieties of grapes would choose a "compromise" date. As a result, some of the varietals were not fully ripe and others would be overly ripe. The different grape varieties of the field would be pressed and fermented together to make one wine. Today however, many farmers are encouraged to modernize their vineyard and plant the varieties in separate plots. Farmers receive a premium for bringing in higher-quality grapes from separate locations in smaller containers. Each varietal can be pressed and fermented separately. This process gives the wine maker the option to make a final blended wine from the different grape types and areas. However, there are still some producers in Portugal who believe that complexity is gained through maintaining field blends, so they continue this practice. In a nation of growers and wine makers with a passion for their product, both styles of vineyards will coexist and consumers will make their own decision as to which wines they prefer.

Building on the unique tastes of indigenous grape varieties with the potential to produce excellent world-class wines, the Portuguese want to develop an international market. The government is working with wine producers to educate consumers through promotional advertisements, literature, and tastings. Place names such as Bordeaux, Chianti, and Rioja have historically established their presence in the export market and are more readily recognized by most wine consumers than the Dão, Minho, and Bairrada regions of Portugal.

A similar predicament in marketing Portuguese wines is the absence of a national culinary identity for Portugal. Portuguese wine styles evolved with the typical dishes prepared in their respective regions. While there are many French, Italian, and an increasing amount of Spanish restaurants in America, there are few Portuguese restaurants. The wide range of wines produced in Portugal may accompany an equally wide range of foods from around the world (see Chapter 13 on Wine and Food.)

# History

After King Alfonso III defeated the Moors in 1249, he created a parliament with people's representatives. Expanded agriculture and commerce led to the Treaty of Windsor in 1385, formalizing the alliance between Portugal and Britain. Wines were shipped to England in exchange for fishing rights. Subsequently, during the fifteenth and sixteenth centuries, the Portuguese prospered in the shipping trade and colonization. However, in 1580, the Spanish were at war with Britain. With ease, the Spanish defeated the Portuguese and left them weak and isolated. By the next century, the British and the Dutch took over Potugal's maritime trade and many of its colonies. In exchange for protection, foreign goods, and funds, the Portuguese gave the British control of locations such as Ceylon (Sri Lanka) and the ports of Tangiers and Bombay. In 1680, the British had imposed extremely high taxes on French wines. In comparison, Portuguese wines were attractively priced, and sales to Britain boomed.

The Methuen Treaty of 1703 further cemented the Portuguese-British relationship. The British shipped salt cod, wool, and textiles in exchange for wine. Foreigners with capital, such as the British, were better financed than most local Portuguese producers and as a result gained riches and power. During the mid-eighteenth century, the Marquis de Pombal succeeded in temporarily wresting power from the foreigners and creating laws to increase the quality of the wines. By 1786, however, the British regained some of their influence and established the Factory House in Oporto. This building was built only for the British firms dealing in wine. The members of this powerful agricultural club still meet every Wednesday as they have for over two centuries, to discuss the state of the Porto business and the actions of the farmers, producers, and governmental agencies.

The British influence is perhaps best exemplified by James Forrester. One of the most influential Englishmen in the history of the Port trade, Forrester emigrated to work for the family firm in Oporto in 1831. His contributions include very detailed writings on the growing and maintaining of grapes and on the sites within the Douro. His detailed maps of the region's topography and the hydraulic maps of the Douro were a boon to the trade. In 1861, after 30 years in the area, he drowned when his boat hit a rock in the river. The weight of his gold-filled money belt sunk him while his lady companions, buoyed by the hoops under their crinoline dresses, floated to shore.

While the English maintained a presence in Portugal for centuries, other European merchants were involved in trade development as well. For example, in the seventeenth century, Scottish, German, and Dutch entrepreneurs were involved in the commerce of the Duoro, as were the wealthy farmers. By the mid-eighteenth century it was common practice to fortify Porto and store it in lodges for a year or two before exporting it. This prosperous practice continued, making the nineteenth century a period of expansion with many new Porto firms being established. Trade expansion extended to the North and South American markets. Unfortunately, new vineyards were planted only to be devastated by the powdery mildew, oidium, and *phylloxera* at the end of the century.

The early twentieth century was marked by a period of political turmoil in Portugal. The assassination of King Carlos in 1908 was followed by pressure on his successor, Manuel II, who was forced to abdicate his throne. One of the last acts under the monarchy was to establish wine laws. The regions of production for Dão, Moscatel de Setúbal, Carcavelos, Vinhos Verdes, and Colares were demarcated. New boundaries for the Douro were set. Other attempts followed to improve quality by controlling which grapes and areas were to be used, but the political instability made consistent policies impossible. There were over 60 ministers of agriculture during the Republican period of 1910–1926.

Political stability returned with the military takeover in 1926 and the appointment of Antonio de Oliveira Salazar, first as Finance Minister and then as Prime Minister in 1932. His regime took the nation out of debt and he immediately set up control boards to regulate the wine industry. Export was controlled by the Grémios dos Exportadores do Vinho do Porto, and both the *Casa do Douro* and the *Instituto do Vinho do Porto* (IVP) regulated the Douro. *Federações dos Vinicultores* were regional federations set up around the country. The *Junta Naçional do Vinho* began in 1937 as a higher authority to most of the regional federations. These control boards helped to establish and control cooperatives to better organize the wines of the many individual farmers. Although the cooperatives did meet an acceptable quality level, there were few fine wines produced.

The political revolution of 1974 ousted many of the private owners, and the farmers who took over did not always have the means to maintain, or improve, the quality of the vineyards and cellars. The election of 1976 was the start of Portugal's reclaiming and rebuilding efforts. Currently, domestic as well as international investments and support from the European Community (EC) are focused on quality rather that quantity.

## Wine Laws

Grapes and wines are controlled by the official board *The Instituto do Vinha e do Vinho (IVV)*—The Institute of Vine and Wine. The IVV is the governing body that is also responsible for awarding the demarcated areas within larger zones their official designations. However, the IVV does not govern Porto; it is controlled by the *Instituto do Vinho Do Porto* which, in turn, checks on the *Casa do Douro* which represents the growers.

*Associação dos Produtores dos Engarafadores de Vinho Verde* is an example of one commission controlling and promoting its local wines while working with the IVV which regulates the production and exportation of wines of Portugal. The Portuguese system organizes wine areas in accordance with the EC system. Wines from a demarcated area may use the place name on a label. The smallest zones of production produce higher-quality, more expensive wines because supply is limited. Wines from an individual vineyard site must have unique character because of a specific soil and climate.

The hierarchy of place names on labels includes:

- *Vinho de Mesa.* The lowest level of domestic wines are these table wines, which may not state a vintage year.

- *Vinho Regional.* These regional wines are from large areas such as Alentejo, Beiras, Estremadura, or Ribatejo. Some producers opt to market higher quality wines in this category because larger regions sometimes receive broader customer awareness or acceptance.

- *Vinhos de Qualidade Produzidos em Regiões Determinadas (VQPRD).* These wines come from smaller defined regions with the potential of more specific character. The wines were also given IPR status and producers may use either designation.

- *Indicação de Proveniência Regulamentada (IPR).* These are VQPRD wines. The term translates to Indication of Regulated Provenance. Examples of the 26 IPRs include Alenquer and Valpaços.

- *Denominação de Origem Controladad (DOC).* This highest echelon is equivalent to the French AOC, Italian DOC, or Spanish DO (see Chapters 6 on France, 7 on Italy, and 8 on Spain). The older term RD, for *Regiões Demarcadas,* still appears on older bottles of wine. The DOC regions that are most important are *Madeira* (fortified wines), the *Douro* (known for both table wines and the fortified Porto), and the table wines of *Bairrada, Dão,* and *Vinho Verde.* Portalegre and Reguengos in Alentejo are two of the newest to be elevated to the DOC status. When the Vinho Regional category was set up, many subregions of the IPR were also granted within them, and the producers had an option of how to label the wines. The waiting period for an IPR area to be elevated to DOC status is five years.

Portugal's higher-quality wines are subject to stringent controls on production and taste, just as in other European countries. These classifications are fairly recent and are updated continuously. New areas may be defined and boundaries changed, as in France, the role model for the system. Quality terms commonly found on Portuguese wine labels include:

- *Garrafeira.* Red wines aged a minimum of two years before bottling and then another year before release. Whites wines aged a minimum of one year which includes six months in the bottle. A slightly higher minimum alcohol than a simple regional wine must be achieved. *Velho* (old) is another term for an aged wine.

- *Reserva.* The wine must have 0.5 percent higher minimum alcohol than the region's required minimum. The term should be used for better products from better vintages and may be used in conjunction with the term "garrafeira."

- *Escolha* or *Grande Escolha.* Sometimes used for a producer's choice, or top selected wine.

- *Superior.* Higher minimum alcohol by at least 0. 5 percent.

- *Engarrafado na Origem.* Wine bottled at the estate. A *garrafa* is a bottle.

- *Engarrafado na Região.* Bottled in the region where the grapes were grown.

- *Adega.* A winery.

- *Quinta.* An estate farm, or vineyard.

- *Vinho.* Wine.

- *Casta.* Grape.

- *Seco.* Dry, with residual sugar under four grams per liter.

- *Doce.* Sweet.

- *Solar* or *Palacio.* A vineyard and fine home similar to the French château. Most often the term *quinta* is used instead.

- *Armarazem* or *Lodge.* A storage facility for Porto, Madeira, or table wine.

- *Colheita.* Vintage.

- *Branco.* White.

- *Tinto.* Red.

- *Espumante.* Sparkling.

**Map 9.1** The Wine Regions of Portugal.

## Wine Regions

Portugal (see Map 9.1) is roughly 120 miles/200 kilometers wide and 360 miles/600 kilometers from north to south with varied terrain and climatic conditions. Joining the EC meant defining demarcated areas as most European wines are labeled by place of origin. Porto has been defined since

1756, but many less-famous subdistricts were content to have the name of a larger, more recognizable region on their labels. Although the government has already recognized 26 IPR areas, some producers still label by larger area. For example, the nation's oldest branded table wine, Periquita, has its vineyards bisected by two zones—the IPRs of Arrabida and Palmela. Using grapes from both IPR zones, Periquita must use the broader area Vinho Regional term Terras do Sado. With 26 IPRs and 18 DOCs, most consumers outside of Portugal will need time before the IPR or DOC designations on labels help identify a wine style. While four DOCs in the sun-baked Algarve seems a disservice to other DOC zones that are deserving of the distinction because of their quality wines, this chapter focuses on the regions most often represented in the export market.

# The Wine Regions of Portugal

## Douro

The source of the Douro River is 400 miles/680 kilometers inside of Spain, where it is known as the Duero. The Portuguese Douro area is comprised of 685,000 acres/272,712 hectares and the grape types were chosen not only for the character they give the wine, but also for their ability to withstand the hot temperatures of the area. Although best known for its fortified wines, about half of the production is in table wines. The lower altitude vineyards are warmest and produce superior Porto. At higher altitudes, the cooler climate allows the grapes to maintain their acidity and make fine table wines. The steeply sloped vineyards have a variety of exposures. In most cases, walls separate rows of vines and prevent rain from washing the soils away. The principal soil type is schist (crystalline metamorphic rock with minerals arranged in parallel layers), which in some locations is 60 feet/18 meters deep. The hard schist must be broken to a depth of 5 feet/1.5 meters to plant vines. After five years of growth, the vine is able to penetrate the fissures in the rocky soil to get water stored in the subsoils of volcanic rock and granite.

Before the *phylloxera* epidemic early in this century, each row had its own stone wall. When the replantings were done after the scourge, there were five to ten rows per wall. Growers continue to experiment with the number of rows between stone terraces and with the density of plantings. The cost of maintaining the stone walls led to systems called *patamares* in which terraces were bulldozed out of the slopes. Another system is *vinha ao alto* in which rows are planted up and down the slopes rather than laterally. Both systems remove the need for stone terraces so that mechanical harvesting is possible. Tractors can be used up to an incline of 30°, but not on the precipitous slopes at 45°. Erosion is a problem when planting without stone walls. The traditional density of plantings was 2400 plants per acre/6000 plants per hectare to force the vines to suffer and compete for nourishment, but with the patamares only half the plants fit; each vine must yield almost double. Because schist-based soils are low in organic materials and do not

The Torta Valley in the Douro Region.

produce large yields of grapes, experiments continue to find ways to increase production while maintaining quality.

The climate of the Douro varies by subregion but is essentially hot in the summers and cold in the winters. Schist retains heat, causing the farmers to concentrate on thick-skinned red grapes. They use drip irrigation in harsh, dry conditions.

Older vines that penetrate deep extract more minerals from the soil, which results in a wine of more complexity. About five percent of the Douro is planted in granite-based soil, and **esteva**—a rockrose gum cistus—can be found throughout the region. The plant gives off a perfume which some people detect in the wines as well. The Serra do Marão, a 4592

An Example of the Soil Found in the Douro Region.

The Douros Vinha ao Alta or Up-and-Down Planting System.

feet/1400 meters mountain, provides some protection from winds, hail-storms, and excessive rainfall.

There are 28,000 growers in the Duoro, farming 81,000 acres/32,400 hectares of vines in three major subdivisions. The Baixo, or Lower Corgo, is downstream from the Corgo River which joins the Douro River by the town of Régua. Without the protection from the Serra do Marão, the area has the most rainfall; thereby diluting the grapes and producing wines with less power. Another reason for a lighter style is that the Baixo Corgo is the coldest of the three areas so the grapes do not reach high grape sugar levels.

The Cima Corgo or Upper Corgo is north of the Baixo and considered the finest of the three regions. The warmer, drier area also benefits from the

The Three Methods of Planting in the Douro: Old, Patamares, and Vinhao ao Alto.

## THE BENIFICÍO RATING SYSTEM

There are 83,000 individual vineyards in the Douro, graded according to the *Beneficío* system from A to F. The Casa do Douro in the town of Régua controls the Benefíco rating system. Just as the Médoc classification of 1855 in France was challenged, so is the Beneficío system, which was introduced in 1947.

In the Douro region, vineyards are rated by quality in categories from A to F. The system not only officially ranks vineyards by points but it also sets production limits. Points are given for geographic position, altitude, soil, steepness or gradient angle, age of vines, maintenance of the vineyard, position with relation to climatic conditions, production, and grape quality for a possible total of 1680 points. For example, an A-rated vineyard may produce 184 gallons/700 liters of Porto wine from 1000 plants. An E-rated vineyard is permitted to make only 80 gallons/300 liters per 1000 plants, an F rating or 201 points or less forbids production. The best sites are in the Upper Corgo and the Douro Superior.

moderating influence of other smaller rivers such as the Pinhão. An approximate comparison of yields would show that 1000 vines in the Baixo would yield 528 gallons/2000 liters of juice but only 145 gallons/550 liters in the Cima Corgo. Lower yields always translate to more concentrated flavors in the wine produced.

About ten percent of the region's production comes from the Douro Superior which is the eastern portion of the Douro. Some of the vineyards in the zone are flatter and easier to harvest mechanically. With colder winters, hotter summers, and lower rainfall than the Baixo Corgo, the Douro Superior is able to produce wines with concentration and power.

*Associação Para o Desenvolvimento da Viticultura Durense* (ADVID) is an association of top producers that was founded in 1982 for grape and vineyard research, the same year the World Bank made grants available to Portugal. The grants were offered on the condition that the money would be used to create high-quality vineyards that would grow the best of the 88 grape varieties permitted. The list of grapes permitted for World Bank financing is based on the research done by ADVID and is much shorter than the list of grapes allowed by the Portuguese government for production in the Douro. The top five grapes for quality are the Touriga Naçional, Tinta Roriz, Tinta Barroca, Tinto Cão, and Touriga Francesa. The most-planted grapes in the Douro, for reason of quality or quantity, are:

* *Touriga Naçional.* This small grape has a high skin-to-juice ratio and gives dark-colored, tannic wines with good acid balance (see Figure 9.1). Raspberry, blackberry, and mulberry fruit, as well as game and violets, are some of the aromas in the table and Port wines produced with a

**Figure 9.1** The Touriga Naçional is One of Portugal's Top Red Grapes.

high percentage of this grape. While yields are very low compared to other grapes, a new clone, R110, shows promise for its higher sugar levels and yield.

- *Tinta Roriz.* This grape produces an aggressive wine with lots of sugar, body, astringency, and longevity. The nose may be floral, herbal, and spicy. The Tinta Roriz can be planted in warmer sites as it is an early ripener and gives the best results in rich soils. It produces more than twice the yield of Touriga Naçional. This is the grape that the Spanish call Tempranillo (see Chapter 8 on Spain.)

- *Tinta Barroca.* This grape produces wine with softer tannins and higher yields than Touriga Naçional or Tinta Roriz. Tinta Barroca adds good color and a floral, fruity nose to a blend but is not particularly aggressive on its own. Acid levels are relatively low. The grape grows best in the cooler sites along the Douro.

- *Tinta Cão.* This grape works well in cooler areas. While Tinta Cão takes a long time to develop and show its qualities, it aids the longevity and complexity of a blended wine. The Tinta Cão does not have the weight or fullness of color of Touriga Naçional but shares the trait of low yield. Tinta Cão produces a wine with fine floral and fruit flavors with some spiciness as well.

- *Tinta Amarela.* This grape does well in the warmest areas and is similar to the Tinta Barroca, but spicier. Although it is not one of the top five varietals it remains popular. Ferreira company, for example, does not use the Tinta Cão but does use Tinta Amarela for their Portos and still wines.

- *Touriga Francesa.* This grape contributes good sugar, acid, and fruit qualities, such as strawberry and orange. Floral aromas, such as roses, are followed by earthy tastes on the palate. Touriga Francesa is a good varietal to plant in the moderate temperature zones. The Touriga Francesa is **not** the same grape as Tinta Francisca, another Douro variety, or Pinot Noir, as is sometimes suggested.

- *Bastardo.* This grape may comprise up to 60 percent of a Porto blend, but is not permitted to be planted in new vineyards because of its high yield and high sugar levels. Bastardo is known as *Trousseau* in the Jura region of France.

## Porto

Porto is a fortified wine. It is made by transferring the fermenting wine to casks containing clear grape spirit of 77 percent alcohol/154 proof. The ratio is 116 gallons/440 liters of wine to 29 gallons/110 liters of spirits, making the cask size known as a *pipe*. The 145 gallon/550 liter pipe was the size shipped to the lodges for storage by the *barco rabelo* boats. These flat-bottom boats transported the wine so it could be stored in the cooler lodges at Vila Nova de Gaia. Today, wines are transported by rail or truck but the lodges maintain the *barco rabelos* for the tourists to appreciate and for promotional events. Other sizes of pipes are 169 gallons/640 liters, 191.5 gallons/725 liters, and for export shipping 141 gallons/534 liters. The fermenting must is added to the *aguardente* (grape spirit) when the fermentation achieves six or seven percent alcohol. The final Porto product ranges between 18 and 20 percent alcohol.

Porto was not always made with a high alcohol content. Prior to the 1700s, the wines were fortified with up to three percent additional alcohol to better handle the rigors of transportation by boat. Wines from a single, unblended year were recognized in 1734. After the devastating earthquake of 1755, which destroyed much of Lisbon, the Marquis of Pombal, Sebastião Carvalho de Melo, was named chief minister by King Joseph. The Marquis established a board to regulate the production and sale of the wines of the Douro. The laws of the Marquis elevated the quality of Porto but made him many enemies, particularly among the British and other foreign entrepreneurs, who had been prospering by controlling most of the production and export of wines as well as the warehouses used for aging. Their collective strength also helped to force the farmers to accept lower prices. These enemies were more interested in doing business as they wished, making quick profits, than developing one of the great dessert wines of the world. Maria, Joseph's daughter, was influenced by those against the Marquis and the first thing she did was to pardon all the political prisoners against the Marquis of Pombal. Her next action was to remove the 83-year-old gentleman from his position of power, and after a trial, he was banished from Lisbon. Some of the positive achievements under the Marquis were the reduction of the area where Porto could be made, the restriction on adding manure to increase the yields per plant, and the ending of the practice of adding elderberries to wine to give darker color and more fruit flavor.

The wines of this period were shipped in bulk, or were put into bottles which did not have the cork in contact with the liquid and would sometimes spoil. The first vintage-dated bottles appeared in 1775, and the bottle shape used today was first seen in 1784. The superior bottle design allowed the wines to be cellared for longer periods. By the mid 1800s, standard practice was to fortify Porto to around 20 percent alcohol, leave the wine in casks for four years, and then let it mature slowly in the bottle. Most of the vintage-dated wines were bottled in England, the primary market.

The *phylloxera* began to destroy the vines in 1868, and there was more destruction from flooding in 1909. In 1914 the Portuguese and British signed a treaty which officially defined Porto. Even today, wines from other areas or nations may not legally call their product Porto as that name is reserved for the wines bearing the *selo de origem* (seal of origin) from the Douro. Since the 1930s the domestic controls for growing are granted by the Casa do Douro, located in the city of Régua. They control the Benefício system of ranking vineyards and determining permitted production levels. In the past, they were the sole sellers of the *aguardente* (brandy) used to fortify Porto and they still buy much of the excess wine of the region and turn it into aguardente. The Instituto do Vinho do Porto (IVP or Port Wine Institute) is a government-empowered association that checks the records of the shippers and the quality of the wines stored at lodges. They are located in Oporto. The Porto companies are required by law not to sell off more than a third of their wines in stock each year. This regulation is to insure the companies have sufficient aged wines for blending. The agents of the IVP taste and analyze the wines before issuing the *selo do origem*. The Associação dos Expatadores do Vinho do Porto (AEVP) is in charge of export controls.

The chief concern when the grapes arrive to a quinta is to get the maximum amount of color extraction from the skins before the addition of the clear aguardente. When they arrive at the winery a portion of the grapes or all of them may be crushed in rollers. Stems are usually removed, because their tannins are too bitter.

A small amount of the best Porto is made in the traditional manner in large stone troughs or *lagares*. They measure 18 feet square/1.6 square meters and are three feet/1meter high. They may be made of granite or of slate and can hold a couple of dozen people. Once their feet are inspected for cleanliness, they are set to the task of the *corte*, a controlled treading of the grapes by foot for several hours. The idea is to get the most extract from the *manta*, or cap, and not to crush the grape pits, which would contribute overly bitter tannins. (The manta comprises the skins which contain the pigments so vital to maintaining the dark color of Porto.) Eventually the pits rise to become part of the manta. Once the fermentation is under way, wooden planks are put over the top of the lagar. Workers stand on the planks and continue to push the cap down with wooden plungers.

The same result can be obtained mechanically by an autovinifier. The autovinification method (known as the Ducellier system in Algeria where it began) uses large closed vats. The buildup of carbon dioxide pressure is used to pump juice up and over the manta to extract color and tannins. Autovini-

The Large Stone Troughs in Which Porto is Made.

**Figure 9.2** There are Four Types of Indicated-age Tawnies of Porto Available: 10-year, 20-year, 30-year, and 40-year Versions.

fication is less labor intensive than the system using lagares. The first vats used were concrete, but stainless steel is more commonly used today and temperatures can be controlled. Some producers are now doing a combination of *remontage* (pumping over) followed by autovinification.

The autovinification system relies on the natural powers of the carbon dioxide during the fermentation process, does not require electricity, and allows for a good deal of color and tannin extraction in a short, hot fermentation before fortification. Today, precautions are taken to ensure that fermentation stays within 55.8°F (31°C) and 74°F (29°C).

Porto may be made from one vintage or a blend of years. It is the aging period that determines the wine's style and how it may be labeled. The two main types are the *ruby*, or *vintage style,* which is bottled young and the *wood,* or *tawny style* which is aged in a cask. The wines in casks are racked at least once a year (see Chapter 1 on How Wine Is Made) and over time the precipitation of the sediments and the slight oxidation that takes place in the cask results in light-colored, softer Portos that may be consumed when released. Wines must be submitted to a tasting panel for approval and for chemical analysis by the Intituto do Vinho do Porto.

The styles of Porto include:

**Tawny.** True tawny Porto ages at least six years in the cask before release. When the bottling date is given, the consumer should enjoy the product within a couple of years from that date. These wines, served cool at 40 to 45°F (4.5 to 7°C), have a sweet and nutty nose, but the taste is not as rich and sweet as the ruby or vintage styles. The majority of tawnies are only three years old and made by the lighter-style techniques to give the trade a less-expensive high-volume cash product. Commercial, inexpensive tawnies are made by using red wines with less color extraction or by blending together white and red Porto to get a tawny color. The commercial-grade tawnies and simple rubies comprise over 80 percent of each year's production.

**Indicated-Age Tawnies.** The four products available are the ten-year, 20-year, 30-year, and 40-year versions. The wines are made from a blend of vintages and the indicated age for each is the average age of the blend of wines used for each type (see Figure 9.2). The average age is an ideal set by the Instituto do Vinho do Porto, but the key is taste, and if the wine does not pass, it will not receive the seal from the IVP. House styles among producers and the different complexities of a 30-year old or a 40-year-old compared to a ten-year old make the indicated age category a favorite of many consumers and people in the trade. They can be the most elegant of the Portos. The ten-year old is the least expensive and the 40 the most expensive.

Producer Bruce Guimarens begins to set aside selected lots after four or five years for blending into his Fonseca, and his Taylor, Fladgate, and Yeatman wines of this style. On the other hand, João Nicolau de Almeida keeps a *madre,* or mother blend, of each of the 10s, 20s, 30s, and 40s. When he draws a portion from a madre to bottle, it is then replenished. de Almeida never depletes the entire stock of his madre in order to maintain his company's style.

Bruce Guimarens, Technical Director of Both Taylor, Fladgate, and Yeatman, and Fonseca Porto.

Both men are after a consistency in house style. Indicated-age tawnies must carry the date of bottling on the label.

***Colheita.***    Colheita is an aged tawny from a single vintage. The wines are usually cask aged for a minimum of seven years, up to as long as 50 years. They vary in style by both vintage and house but, like indicated-age tawnies, they acquire a softer fruit and lower tannin character with an intriguing bouquet. Some of the firms specializing in colheitas include Kopke, Niepoort, Cálem, and Burmester. They are not as commonly found as the indicated-age blends, and are ready to enjoy when released.

***White.***    White Portos are made in sweet to semidry styles. The sweetest is *lagrima*. They are served chilled, most often as an aperitif. Grapes used include the Malvasía, the Gouveio, the Viosinho (for its sweet nose), and the Rabigato for its high acidity.

***Ruby.***    Ruby Porto is a blend that spends up to two to three years in stainless steel or wood before it is bottled. Sweetness, spiciness, and fruit are present both in the nose and taste of the wine.

***Crusted.***    Crusted Portos are blended wines bottled young with some of the character of vintage Porto. Like vintage Porto they always are decanted when served and are dark and powerful in youth.

***Vintage Character*** and ***Super Ruby.***    These Portos are aged four to six years from blends, but they are usually made with less maceration time than vintage Portos. They have more body and fruit than tawnies but less concentration and complexity than vintage Portos. These are very good value wines for those not prepared to invest in vintage or indicated-age tawnies. They are from finer sources and contribute about 12 percent of total annual production. Sandeman's Founders Reserve, Warre Warrior, Graham 6 Grapes, and Fonseca Bin 27 are examples of Portos that choose not to include the term Super Ruby or Vintage Character on the label.

***Single-Quinta.***    Single-quinta is Porto made from only one vineyard. It is made in both tawny and vintage styles.

***Late-Bottled Vintage.***    This Porto is from a single vintage, bottled between July 1 of the fourth year and December 31 of the sixth year after the vintage. Most of the wines are similar in style to vintage character but come from a single vintage. Late-bottled vintage Porto has been racked more often than true vintage style and therefore throws less sediment. The best are made as vintage is, without fining or filtering. A bottle of 1927 the authors sampled at a quinta in 1994 was still delicious, dispelling the myth that late-bottled vintage port wines cannot age.

***Vintage.***    The rarest and most expensive of styles (see Figure 9.3). Only the finest vineyard sites and grapes are used. The wines must be declared and sam-

João Nicolai de Almeida, Wine Maker of Adriano Ramos Pinto.

## MAJOR PORTO PRODUCERS

The firms of Porto include: Adriano Ramos; Pintos; Barros Almeida; Borges and Irmão; Burmester; Cálem; Churchill Graham; Cockburn Smithies; Croft; Da Silva; Delaforc; Dow; Ferreira; Fonseca Guimaraens; Gonzalez-Byass; Gould Campbell; W. and J. Graham; Kopke; Martinez-Gassiot; Niepoort; Offley Forrester; Quarles Harris; Quinta do Infantado; Quinta do Noval; Quinta do Vesuvio; Real Companhia Velha; Robertson (also bottled as Rebello Valente); Royal Oport; Sandeman; Smith Woodhouse; Taylor, Fladgate, and Yeatman. Van Zellers; Warr; Wiese and Krohn.

The term *quinta* usually refers to a single vineyard but may also be a company name as well, such as the Quinta do Infantado and Quinta do Noval listed above. It is difficult to summarize a company's vintage products in a few words but each house does try to maintain a style of its own.

Fonseca makes its vintage from 50 percent foot-trod grapes sourced from its own vineyards in the Cima Corgo. The result is a lush, voluptuous style with medium weight. Owned by the same firm, at Taylor, Fladgate, and Yeatman, the goal is for a more austere style with great concentration and power. The firm uses grapes from the Douro Superior as well as the Cima Corgo. The single estate Quinta de Vargellas provides complexity to their vintage Porto and a portion is bottled as a single quinta wine. Delaforce has a quicker-maturing, light- to medium-weight style. Cockburn and Sandeman offer medium weight.

José Soares Franco is the wine maker at Ferreira which is the top-selling brand within Portugal. Ferreira produces softer-style medium-weight vintage Porto. Dow is one of the most powerful and rich examples as well as one of the driest. Graham is as full bodied as the Dow, but is in a sweeter style. The full-bodied Warre is owned by the Symington family, who are also proprietors of Dow, W and J Graham, Quarles Harris, Smith Woodhouse, and the Quinta do Vesuvio. Among the quintas owned by Symington are Quinta da Cardavinha (Warre) and Quinta dos Malvedos (Graham). The Symington family has been able to maintain high-quality standards for its wines while bottling over a million cases of Porto a year.

**Figure 9.3** A Vintage Porto is Best Drunk After 20 Years.

ples approved by the IVP. The wines must be bottled between July 1 of the second year and June 30 of the third year after the harvest. The more companies that declare a vintage, the more likely it is a given year will be accepted as superior by collectors and the trade. For example, in 1970, 39 companies declared vintages; in 1952 only two companies did. Outstanding vintages from this century include 1985, 1977, 1970, 1963, 1955, 1948, 1945, 1935, 1931, 1927, and 1908. The wines are bottled young, when they are an opaque, dark-purple color with very high tannins and fruit concentration. Over years in the bottle, the coloring matter and tannins form sediments; therefore they must be decanted before serving (see Chapter 15 on Wine Service). The wines should project a sense of harmony or balance allowing the complexities of bouquet and taste to be enjoyed. A vintage Porto is best after 20 years.

The best producers use a selection of the top ten grape varieties from the best quintas for their high-end wines. However, only eight percent of Porto is made in those categories and the bulk of business is done in ruby and simple tawny styles. In the past two decades annual production of vintage Porto has doubled to about nine million cases of wine, with the United States and the United Kingdom are the top markets. The biggest markets in volume sales are, in order, France, Belgium, Portugal, Holland, and Britain.

Porto is most often consumed at the end of a meal with cheese, nuts, or dessert, or as a dessert unto itself. Northern European countries also use Porto as an aperitif.

## Still Wines

The nonfortified wines of the Douro are most often made in locations that are rated low on the beneficío system. The more-temperate climate zones and the areas with higher elevations that are not ideal for fortified wines make table wines. The still wines were given DOC status in 1982. The Viosinho and Gouveio are the most prevalent grapes for dry whites; the Malvasia contributes floral and fruity scents. Raposeira, the #1 sparkling-wine brand in the country, is made here as well. The cellars at Lamego make two and a half million bottles annually using the méthode Champenoise for Chardonnay, Pinot Noir, Pinot Blanc, and local grapes such as Cerceal, Códega, and Malvasia. Touriga Naçional, one of the nation's top grapes, is used in combination with other reds described in the previous section on Porto.

Barca Velha, a red wine made by the Ferreira company, is considered by many to be the nation's best table wine (see Figure 9.4). The first vineyard on the estate in the Douro Superior was planted in 1888, yet the first vintage of this noble wine was 1952, when Fernando Nicolão de Almeida returned from Bordeaux. He made the wine at the Quinta do Vale do Meão in the hot Douro Superior. In the past, temperature-controlled fermentation was difficult to achieve, as it required bringing ice up from Oporto. Today there are stainless steel vats for fermentation, after which the wine rests in new 71-gallon/270-liter Portuguese oak casks. The present blend is 60 percent Tinta Roriz, ten percent Tinta Barroca, ten percent Tinta Amarela, and 20 percent Touriga Francesa. Barca Velha is not made every year.

The nose of Barca Velha has been described as violets, blackberries, figs, damson, and spice. Although the wine is full bodied, it has rich fruit and good acidity to support the weight. The label Ferreirinha Reserva Especial is used for those vintages that do not make the very best wine for long aging.

Esteva is a lighter-styled red wine made by Ferreira from Touriga Francesa, Tinta Roriz, and Tinta Barroca. It is named for the gum cistus plant found throughout the vineyards of the Douro.

At the estate Quinta do Côtto, red wines with mostly Tinta Roriz and Touriga Naçional grapes are made by Miguel Champalimaud. The best wine produced at the quinta is labeled Grande Escolha. It is fermented like Porto by the autovinification system to spray more juice over the cap to extract color and tannins. The wine spends one and a half years in new oak before release. A dry white is also produced from local grapes.

Quinta da Pacheca makes both whites and reds from indigenous and French varietals. The vineyards are not on slopes, yet the varietal-labeled wines have a following in Portugal.

Sogrape are proprietors of the Barca Velha red and Ferreira Porto, Mateus Signature wines with the DOC Douro, and other Douro wines under the brand name Vila Regia. There in the Douro, the Planalto label is a crisp white made from the Viosinho, Gouveio, and Malvasia grapes. Red wines are also produced from such local grapes as the Touriga Naçional, Tinta Roriz, Tinta Amarela, and Touriga Francesa. Wines come from cool, elevated

**Figure 9.4** Barca Velha is Considered by Many to be Portugal's Best Red Table Wine.

growing sites and are cool fermented, making wines with better fruit-acid balance than is generally associated with an area as warm as the Douro.

# Other Wine Regions of the North

## *Minho*

This is Portugal's largest demarcated wine region with over 60,000 acres/24,000 hectares of vines. It is named after the River Minho which traverses the Spanish border to the north.

This region has a longer wine-making tradition than the Douro and has been exporting its wines for 700 years. Although the landmass is only 9.2 percent of the nation, over 20 percent of the population lives in this verdant area. The first capital of Portugal, under its first king, Alfonso Henriques, was in this province at Guimarães. The region is known internationally for its white wines, and even the Portuguese joke about the very tart style of the red wines. The local people have no problem consuming most of the red wines within their own region. The wines are best served cool. When poured from a few inches above the ceramic cups used, the wines froth up as they are already spritzy. The Vinho Verde red wines are under ten percent alcohol and are ready to drink within several months of the harvest. Seventy percent of production is red wine from such indigenous grapes as Espadeiro, Vinhão, Borraçal, and Tinto Azal. As in many of the world's wine regions, a simple local wine with local fare and good company can be a memorable experience. A chilled red Vinho Verde with its redberry flavors, high acidity,

The Enforcado System in the Minho Region.

low alcohol, and slight effervescence compliments a broad variety of dishes beyond the regional foods. Although the area was first demarcated in 1908, the *selo de garantia* control and approval system begin in 1959.

The white Vinhos Verdes have light body, high acid, low alcohol levels, and good fruit flavors. These wines are among the world's best-value summer wines because of their low alcohol and fruit-acid balance. The minimum acidity is 0.2 ounces per gallon/six grams per liter by law. The whites are not only useful apéritifs but their spritzy, tart, and cleansing qualities make them useful companions to a wide range of foods (see Chapter 13 on Wine and Food). They are appreciated abroad and represent about five percent of the nation's export volume.

The six subdivisions of the Minho are *Monção, Amarante, Penafiel, Basto, Ponte de Lima,* and *Braga. Monção,* the most northern of the six regions, is the one zone where the superior white grape the Alvarinho (Albarino in Spain) thrives. The thicker-skinned Alvarinho produces wines with more body than the average Vinhos Verdes. The scent of an Alvarinho-based Vinho Verde is of apples and lime with some floral hints as well. The Vinhos Verdes ("green wines") get their name not because of color but by their ability to be enjoyed young when they are fresh and not *maduro* (mature or aged). Most Vinhos Verdes are delightful, tart, fruity, and fresh and are to be consumed within a year or two without serious analysis. They often do not carry a vintage date.

Over 100,000 farmers cultivate an assortment of grape types for Vinhos Verdes. Azal and Pedernão are white grapes prized for their natural high acidity while the Avesso is less tart and can be grown in warmer zones. The Loureiro is the most expensive of the grapes south of Monção with its scents of bay laurel, quince, and orange blossoms. The Trajadura grape has forward fruit smells such as lemon or lime. The largest producer of Vinhos Verdes is the Guedes family-owned Quinta da Aveleda. The Quinta da Aveleda (see Figure 9.5) is as committed to maintaining their glorious gardens as they are to enhancing the quality of their wines and distributing them around the world. The Quinta de Aveleda produces varietal wines labeled Loureiro or Trajadura as well as two other brands, Grinalda and Casal Garcia. The latter is a bit sweeter in style than the others.

Single-varietal Loureiro (see Figure 9.6) is also made by the Solar das Bouças. A Loureiro-dominated blend is made by the family-owned Casa de Sezim. Tâmega is another popular company which uses a variety of white grapes. The Champalimaud family has Paço de Teixeró which is primarily of the Avesso grape. Gatão is a top-selling brand on the domestic market and is a blend made by Borges and Irmão. The most famous of the Monção producers are the Palácio da Brejoeira, Alvarinho de Monção Cepa Velha, and Soalheiro. The Alvarinho grape yields wines in the Monção Vinhos Verdes region that are richer without being heavy, can live up to four years, and are more expensive. Alcohol levels of a Monção are controlled at 11.5 percent minimum to 13 percent maximum compared to the common 8.5 percent average of the wines produced in the other regions.

The principal soil type for growing vines in these regions is granite. Cool breezes from the Atlantic moderate the climate. The area is planted

**Figure 9.5** Most Vinhos Verdes do not Carry a Vintage Date.

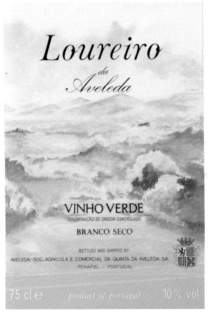

**Figure 9.6** The Loureiro is the Most Expensive Grape South of Monção.

Antonio Guedes in the Garden of Quinta da Aveleda.

Loureiro Vines Grown by the Cruzeta System.

with an abundance of Australian gum trees. Primarily harvested for paper products, these trees deplete the soil of moisture needed to grow grapes. Therefore, irrigation is permitted and practiced. Average rainfall is four times that of the Douro. The days are hot and the nights are cool. This environment allows vines a chance to mature slowly.

A sixteenth-century law forced farmers to grow grains and other food crops. Grapes could be planted only on the periphery of fields, where some can still be found today. There are numerous ways to plant the vines for Vinhos Verdes, but they all involve height. The advantages of this are protection from insects, spring frosts, and rot; leaving room for second crops or fruit and vegetables; and preventing extra heat from reflecting onto the grapes. In cooler climates, where grapes have difficulty ripening, low-bearing systems are used in heat-retentive and heat-reflective soils.

*Enforcado* is the term used for forcing the vines upwards, often on tree trunks, and then stretching them across branches to other trees. Variations on the higher systems of plantings include the *ramada* or *latada* version which are trellises supported by posts. The *cruzeta,* or cross, system has posts over six feet/1.8 meters high and double rows of wires used to support the grapes. The leaves on top also provide a canopy of shade. A lower-planted single-wire system, called *bardo,* is being tried to make mechanical harvesting possible.

The harvest may be done early to ensure high quality. The wines are usually bottled from the original vat in which they were fermented so they do not oxidize. They also retain a spritzy or prickly quality ("pétillance") from the captured gas of the original fermentation. Stainless steel or epoxy-lined vats allow for cooler fermenting than does wood. Malolactic fermentation is not practiced, since most producers want to retain high acidity. Adding carbon dioxide before bottling is permitted and the amount is usually one atmosphere per liter (approximately one atmosphere per quart), compared to a Champagne which naturally produces about six atmospheres.

The simple wines of the Vinhos Verdes DOC offer the consumer an inexpensive and refreshing dry wine that is usually nine percent alcohol or less. With concerns about alcohol consumption, and given the wine's ability to go with hot and spicy dishes (see Chapter 13 on Wine and Food) these wines should develop a following. The single-variety wines and more complex blends are sought after in Portugal and have a bright future in the international market as well.

## Tras os Montes

The name Tras Os Montes translates to "behind the mountains." As a result of its rainshadow protection and location, this is one of the driest parts of the nation. Granite soils dominate the northern portion, while schist is more common in the warmer southern portion. The three IPRs are the Valpaços, Chaves, and Planalto-Mirandes subregions. The most-respected winery in this region is Valle Pradinhos, which uses local grapes and French vinifera varieties. The winery, which is run by João Nicolao de Almeida who is also wine maker for Adriano Ramos Pinto in the Douro, makes wine only in the best years. It is in the IPR zone of Valpaços, but because of the high percentage of the nontraditional Cabernet Sauvignon used, it is marketed as a Vinho Regional.

The main red grapes used are the Bastardo, Tinta Carvalha, and Tinta Amarela; whites include Gouveio, Malvasía, Codéga, and Boal. It is in the northeastern portion of the nation.

# Central Regions

## Beira

The large Beira region is split into the Littoral near the Atlantic Ocean and the Alta (upper) and Baixa (lower) inland areas. The area is mountainous and has many steep-sloped vineyards. It separates the Douro and Minho areas from the central and southern regions of Estremadura, Ribatejo, and Alentejo. The IPRs include Cova de Beira and Lafões, but it is the DOCs in the Littoral, and Dão in the Alta, that are known internationally.

## Bairrada

Most Portuguese wines are made from blends. However that is not the case in this 45,000 acre/18,000 hectare region, which produces over 6.5 million cases of wine a year, over 80 percent of which is from the red Baga grape. The Baga is a thin-skinned grape filled with pits giving the wine its high tannin and high acidity. Sixty percent of the nation's sparkling wines are made in this region. Of the white grapes used, the Maria Gomes (also known as Fernão Pires), occupies over half of the white vineyard acreage and is important for both sparkling and still wines. Maria Gomes has an orange zest and peppery aroma. The Bical is second in plantings, gives structure or body, and is used more for sparklers. The Cerceal is the grape highest in acidity of the region and has a lanolin-type aroma. The Rabo de Ovelha (also known as Rabigato), is an early ripener that gives a light style.

The *barro* (clay) soil dominates the area, and the nearby Atlantic Ocean provides moderating climatic influences and rainfall. The region runs from the city of Aveiro in the north to Coimbra in the south. Over 20,000 farmers grow grapes, mostly to sell to cooperatives or other large producers.

Luis Pato is one of the most visible quality wine makers of the area, and he believes the Baga must be grown on chalky soils to develop balanced wines. He produces a white with a very crisp character and makes his rosé wine with ten percent Cabernet Sauvignon, a softening agent when used with the harsher Baga. His rosé sparkler is made by drawing off some of the juice from the red wine. It is a full-bodied, garnet-colored sparkling wine with firm structure, fruit, and acidity. The oak-aged reds from Pato or other producers, such as Caves Alliança, Quinta do Carva linho, Caves São João,

"Bacalhau" Codfish is a Specialty Throughout Portugal.

Riddling Sparkling Wines at the Bairrada School.

and Sogrape, are now being destalked to avoid the harshest tannins. Other methods used to make the wines less tannic include carbonic maceration, less maceration time, and cooler fermentation temperatures. By law the reds must contain at least 50 percent Baga but many contain 100 percent. The rich fruit scents of berries and plums are coupled with a very rich fruit taste and finish.

Estacão Vitivinicola, the research station for viticulture founded in 1887, provides local students a three-year course in viticulture and oenology. Recent research has led to reintroducing the Castelão local grape, which was abandoned for its sensitivity to *coulure* (grape drop after flowering), and to introducing Chardonnay and Cabernet Sauvignon because of their international status. The vineyards of Bairrada were once destroyed in 1756 to prevent the local wines from being blended into those of the Douro. The region was recognized in 1979 and the wines are increasingly found in the export market.

# Dão

The Dão area, located to the east of Bairrada, is also primarily a red wine region. The Dão area is warmer than Bairrada and has mostly granite-based soil that is poor in organic and mineral sources. However, this is where red grapes do best. Some lighter wines are made from the flatter, sandier sections that are to the west. Where there is more fertile schist-based soil, farmers prefer to plant the white grapes. The area is more mountainous with vineyards often at 1640 feet/500 meters or more. The mountains offer protection from winds. The steepest elevations have terraced vineyards which are labor intensive. There are many forests of pine and eucalyptus in this region.

About two-thirds of the region's production is red. Touriga Naçional, Jaen, Alfrocheiro Preto, Bastardo, Tinta Pinheira, and Tinta Roriz are the authorized red grapes. The most popular brand, both domestically and abroad, is the Grão Vasco, made by Sogrape.

Encruzado is the top white grape for quality but, like Touriga Naçional, it does not produce a large yield. The wine has a nutty aroma. Other white grapes are Assario Branco, Cerceal, and Borrados dos Moscas. The latter name means "fly droppings"; this grape is known by the less-whimsical name Bical in Bairrada.

A problem in the area until the 1980s was that over 100,000 farmers worked the 50,000 acres/20,000 hectares of land. The small holdings led the government to try to control quality by insisting that the wine be made at one of the cooperatives. An exception to that was the producer Casa de Santar, which made its own wine under the brand name Conde de Santar. Although co-ops can make fine wines in Portugal, in this area the results were of mediocre quality. With Portugal's entry into the European Community (EC), this practice was discontinued. Privatization offers the potential for superior wine making.

One company with the financial strength to bring modern wine making to the area is Sogrape. Their multimillion-dollar investment at Quinta

The Quinta dos Carvalhais Winery.

dos Carvalhais was in conjunction with the EC. The winery is an anomaly amid the region's dated wine production facilities. A main concern of José Soares Franco, Sogrape's wine maker, is that the grapes result in a wine produced by the natural force of gravity rather than through an automated process. The key word for Soares Franco is "soft," and he intends to make less-rustic wines by controlling fermentation temperatures and maceration. The lighter reds will have some carbonic maceration, while the more-complex reds will receive from 12 to 18 hours of cool maceration before fermentation in oak.

The techniques in the winery can only succeed, however, if the fruit brought in is of the highest quality. As in other burgeoning wine areas around the world, the local farmers are rewarded for bringing in better varietals with lower yields from distinct vineyards. The Sogrape Duque de Viseu brand whites and reds are wines with more intensity than the good-value Grão Vasco made

Microvinification at Quinta dos Carvalhais.

**Figure 9.7** Red Wines are Primarily Produced in the Dão Area.

at the same facility. The whites are barrel fermented from Encruzado, Assario Branco, and Cerceal after some skin contact. José Soares Franco uses the local red grape varieties and ages them in nontoasted Portuguese and French oak barrels. The reds get good acid levels from the Jaen and Alfrocheiro Preto grapes and complexity and power from the Touriga Nacional.

The José Maria da Fonseca Successores firm is best known for their wines in the Setúbal region, but they also produce a Dão wine labeled as Terras Atlas. Cabernet Sauvignon has been planted at the Quinta Casa da Insua (see Figure 9.7) for 60 years, and a fine single quinta wine is made by Fonseca's wine maker Domingo Soares Franco. The Carvalho, Ribeiro, and Ferreira company based in the Estremadura region also owns and produces a single-quinta Dão de Quinta do Serrado.

# The Southern Regions

## *Setúbal*

José Soares Franco, Wine Maker for Sogrape in the Dão and the Douro.

The Setúbal area is located south of Lisbon. The Atlantic Ocean as well as the Tagus and Sado rivers, provide a moderate climate. The port town of Setúbal is on the Sado. Terras do Sado is the Vinho Regional term for wines from within the Setúbal peninsula. Serra da Arrábida and Palmela are the IPR subregions. Soil types range from sandy to limestone based. Traditional wines of these regions, with long-established reputations, use traditional grapes and techniques. There are also new-wave wines, some from indigenous grapes and others from the popular international types such as Chardonnay and Cabernet Sauvignon.

Vineyards have existed in the area for centuries, but it was in the 1830s that casks of wines were first exported. By 1849, the bottled wines were sold in the Americas, Asia, Africa, and throughout Europe. The force behind the international drive for success was José Maria da Fonseca who came to the area in 1834. He was the first to commercialize and export the region's wines. He improved vineyard quality, mechanized winery production, and founded organizations to coordinate exports of wines and spirits from the mainland and Madeira in association with other producers.

The company was split in three with his descendants Domingo and Antonio Soares Franco running the original section, José Maria da Fonseca Successores, based in Azeitão. Domingo Soares Franco is one of the few Portuguese wine makers to have studied at the University of California at Davis. J. M. da Fonseca Internacional is owned by the IDV branch of Grand Metropolitan Company and was built on the success of the rosés of the Lancers brand.

João Pires and Filhos, (now named J. P. Vinhos), is run by Antonio d'Avillez and makes a wide range of wines including sparkling, still, and fortified (see Figure 9.8). The Fonseca Successores, Fonseca Internacional, and J. P. Vinhos are the most important producers of the region and all maintain a strong international presence.

The principal local white grapes for dry wines are the Fernão Pires, Arinto, and Esgana Cão, which translates as "dog strangler." Arinto and Esgana

Domingo and Antonio Soares Franco of José Maria da Fonseca Successores.

**Figure 9.8** Loridos Sparkling Wine is Only Produced in the Best Vintage years.

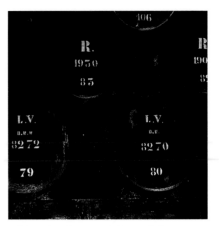

Old Casks of Moscatel de Setúbal.

Cão are prized for their refreshing high acidity. Chardonnay is also grown; a fine example is the barrel-fermented Cova da Ursa made by J. P. Vinhos. The Muscat is used for semidry to sweet, still, and fortified wines.

*Moscatel de Setúbal,* a fortified wine-producing region, was demarcated in 1907. It was the first of the local wines to be exported. Southern exposures are often preferred in other parts of Europe for more sunshine and ripeness, but here the northern-exposed hillside vineyards yield the finest grapes. The Muscat of Alexandria is fermented, then spirits are added to arrest fermentation. The final alcohol level is about 18 percent. What makes the product so special is a five- to six-month skin-contact period, used to develop aromatics and flavors, followed by further wood aging. Wines tasted from cask at 50 and even 80 years of age were incredible nectars. The old treasures were dubbed "Torna Viagem" when casks were shipped beyond the equator and then returned. It was believed the voyage would enhance the wines' quality.

The hue of these wines ranges from orange-red to chestnut to walnut color for the oldest versions. Another clone of Muscat, called the Roxo (purple) is also vinified in small amounts, and its varietal is listed on the label (see Figure 9.9). Up to 30 percent of Arinto, Esgana Cão, Rabo de Ovelha, Tamarês, or Roupeiro may be legally included in the blend. When age is indicated, such as five or 20 years, the wine is often a blend. The given age indicates the youngest wine taken from the barrels as in Madeira.

Moving from the sublime to the simple, the popular Lancers brand still has a large following for its semidry rosés made from mostly the Castelão Francês or Periquita grape. The local grapes are supplemented by product from the Estremadura and Ribatejo regions to make over 1.5 million cases a year.

The Periquita, or "parakeet," is the most important red variety in the region (see Figure 9.10). The Castelão Francês grape was brought from the Ribatejo region by José-Maria da Fonseca to be planted at a vineyard he purchased in 1846 called Cova de Periquita. The wine was labeled Periquita (see Figure 9.11), and its popularity accounts for the fact that both names are used for the grape. Other grapes included in the branded-name wine Periquita are Es-

**Figure 9.9** The Roxo is Another Clone of Muscat.

**Figure 9.10** The Periquita is the Most Important Variety of Red Grape in the Setúbal Area.

**Figure 9.11** The Periquita Wine is Named for the Popular Name of Grape Variety.

**Figure 9.12** The Cabernet Sauvignon Grape is Used to Make Quinta da Bacalhâo.

padeiro, Monvedro, and Bastardo. The wine has rich berry flavors along with a medium to full body and may be enjoyed for three to 12 years. A small amount of Reserva is made in exceptional years.

Other local red grapes found in the region include the Touriga Naçional, Alfrocheiro Preto, and Moreto. Cabernet Sauvignon is the grape for the Quinta da Bacalhâo by J. P. Vinhos (see Figure 9.12). The Quinta da Camarate blend by Fonseca Successores has a quarter Cabernet Sauvignon and the balance is Castelão Francês. Merlot is also grown in the region.

## Estremadura

*Estremadura,* or *Oeste,* is, as the name implies, on the west coast of the country (see Map 9.2) Recently, the term Oeste has been abandoned for use with wine and the name Estremadura is found on demarcated wines. Estremadura produces the largest volume of wine in the nation. Over 30 different grape types are grown, and much of the wine is made at cooperatives.

The *Alenquer* IPR is a promising subzone that has been growing Periquita and other local grapes for reds and Arinto, Vital, and Fernão Pires for whites. Alenquer is protected from excessive dampness by its position east of the Montejunto mountain, and from extremes of temperature by the Tagus river. The Quinta da Abrigada, Quinta dos Platanos, and Quinta de Pancas are quality producers. The latter is experimenting with French varietals under the guidance of wine maker João Portugal Ramos.

Some small DOC zones around Lisbon include:

**Bucelas.** This region produces crisp whites, mostly from Arinto, with Esgana Cão, Rabo de Ovelha, and Cerceal permitted up to 25 percent of the blend. A varietal labeled Arinto is made in a fresh style at Caves Velhas. The Quinta da Romeira is a restored estate that is also producing a balanced wine exclusively from Arinto labeled as Prova Regia.

**Carcavelos.** The region maintains only a small production of fortified sweet white. The vineyard area is shrinking as Lisbon expands.

**Colares.** Lisbon has also taken over former vineyards here, and production is small. The historic site produced wines even in the times of *phylloxera,* as the louse could not attack the vines grown on sand dunes. The Ramisco is the main red grape used, and the low yields can result in an extraordinary wine that can improve over 20 years. The rich fruit and floral bouquet comes with time, as does the softening of tannins.

## Ribatejo

Ribatejo is another large zone with fertile soils and commercial wines that benefit from the proximity of the river Tagus and Atlantic Ocean. The area produces the second largest volume of wine in Portugal, most of it white. The Trebbiano of Italy is widely planted and is here called Tália. The Vital and Fernão Pires are the most-planted local grapes. The João de Santarém is the local name for the Periquita of Setúbal and the Baga of Bairrada is known here as

Poeirinha. They are the principal red grapes along with the Trincadeira and Camarate. They may be used for bulk wines but also can be a portion of a producer's garrafeira blend. IPR regions include Cartaxo and Alheirim. In the latter, a family-run estate, Herdeiros de Dom Luis de Margaride, produces quality wines from local grapes and is experimenting with French varietals. Carvalho, Ribeiro, and Ferreira is a large company intent on quality which recently brought in an American wine maker, Jerry Luper. João Portugal Ramos is the consultant and wine maker for the high-quality local producers Falcoaria and Quinta da Lagoalva de Cima. The latter produces wine from indigenous varieties and also from those varieties blended with the estate-grown Syrah.

## Alentejo

This vast agricultural area, comprising about one-third of the nation's land mass, stretches from the river Tagus east to the border with Spain. The plains are planted with grapes, grains, fruits, and vegetables, and are the largest source of cork trees in the world. The area is home to both traditional grapes and traditional vinification methods. Grapes are pressed by foot in lagares, sometimes fermented in *talhas* (clay amphorae), and aged in both chestnut and Portuguese oak casks. Recent financial investments include a new wave of French varietal planting, modern, controlled stainless steel tanks for fermentation, and French oak barrels for aging. Although the majority of wines are made by cooperatives, a number of individual estates provide fine wine.

The central figure in wine making in the region is João Portugal (J.P.) Ramos, who is wine maker or consultant at over a dozen of the most-important estates and cooperatives.

The IPR subregions include Évora, Granja-Amareleja, and Moura. Recent promotions from IPR to DOC include Borba, Redondo, Reguengos de Monsaraz, Vidigueira, and Portalegre. In Portalegre, the northernmost subregion, vines grow on the granite-based slopes of the São Mamede mountain. The cooperative recently received $800,000 from the EC and came up with $400,000 of its own to enhance quality. Terras de Baco is the label used for some wines. This is one of the co-ops managed by J. P. Ramos. Red wines are best here, as they are in the Estremoz and Reguengos areas farther south. The cooperative at Borba also modernized at a similar cost.

The principal red grapes used in the Alentejo are the Trincadeira (Amarela) for aroma, body, and taste, Aragones (Roriz) for elegance, Periquita for blackberry and anise scents and red berry tastes, Alicante Bouschet and a hybrid, the Grand Noir, for color. For whites the Alva (Roupeiro) gives structure, Arinto gives high acidity, and Fernão Pires gives alcohol and high yields. The Manteudo, Diagalves, and Assario are also used.

Vidigueira, the area where J. P. Ramos got his start at wine making, is a warm area making mostly white wines which tend to lack acidity. Although the area is hot, there are some sections with soil types which maintain high acidity in the wine, and efforts are being made to vinify the wines in a crisper style. Although the acidity levels for whites would be higher in the

**Map 9.2**  The Vinho Regional, Which Includes Estremadura, Ribatejo, Alentejo, and Algarve.

João Portugal Ramos with Traditional *Talhas,* Clay Amphorae.

The Quinta do Carmo Estate.

cooler Portalegre to the north, their vineyards are mostly used to make finer red wines which command higher prices than white wines. The domestic market consumes most of the region's white wines while reds have appeal to the export market. The Moura IPR has authorized use of up to five percent Chardonnay and 20 percent Cabernet Sauvignon, which are also promoted for export.

Château Lafite-Rothschild recently purchased a one-half controlling interest in Quinta do Carmo. This estate was built by King João IV in the seventeenth century for his mistress. The very fine wines from the estate (see Figure 9.13) are made mainly from the Alicante Bouschet, a grape type that is usually associated with high alcohol and yields, but not necessarily high quality. The reds are all estate bottled from 173 acres/70 hectares with more plantings underway. Unfortunately the best soils are where the cork trees are planted on the 2500 acre/1000 hectare property. By law, cork trees can not be uprooted. The wines here were made in the traditional manner, including lagar pressing, under J. P. Ramos. However, a new wine maker and technical director, Arnaud Warnery, was hired by the Rothschilds from the Montpellier region of France. Ramos is experimenting with different rootstocks, techniques, and grape blends for the different soils. For example, he is destemming the grapes for a softer style and using French oak for some lots. The density of new plantings will be 1335 per acre/3300 per hectare so mechanical harvesting can be done. From this process, the reds have deep color and rich blackcurrant and black fig smells and are full bodied without being overly tannic.

The Herdade de Cartuxa is a 593 acre/240 hectare estate by Evora, producing quality wines, approximately two-thirds red with the balance in white. Coffee and spicy notes, as well as dark fruit flavors, are found in reds which are made with Periquita, Aragonez, Trincadeira Moreto, Tinta Caiada and a little Cabernet Sauvignon, and Alicante Bouchet.

The 74 acre/30 hectare Tapada do Chaves in Portalegre has a national reputation for its excellent reds made with 90 percent Trincadeira. The tapada term means a "walled vineyard" as "clos" does in Burgundy, France. Although the winery dates from 1900, the first commercial bottling was in 1965 when J. P. Ramos joined the winery and he switched from 1320 gallon/5000 liter barrels to 132 gallon/500 liter for more intensity. Further, he prefers temperature-controlled fermentation in stainless steel. He has also successfully used amphorae, at times, such as for the small 1988 vintage. The reds have a raspberry-cherry spicy nose and good fruit on the palate with a silky feel after aging.

The Herdade do Esporão is a modern winery with over 4940 acres/2000 hectares of vines, over 1000 barrels, and a production that exceeds two million bottles a year. Indigenous grapes are used with French vinifera. J. P. Vinhos, mentioned earlier in the Setúbal region, are also producers of quality wines here.

In Portalegre, Morgado de Reguengo is a Trincadeira, Periquita, and Aragonez 111 acre/45 hectare vineyard. Spicy red-fruit flavors are found in this wine made by Domingos Soares Franco of Fonseca Successores for his cousin. He also makes Tinto Velho in amphorae from a blend of mostly Trincadeira and Periquita in Reguengos. The wine has rich fruit flavors and is medium to full in body.

The Alentejo, with examples such as the Morgado de Reguengo, Tapada da Chaves, and Quinta do Carmo, produce some of the nation's finest and most complex red wines. There are fruit and floral aromatics as well as rich textural impressions on the palate that make these wines worth seeking out.

## Algarve

The Algarve area is better known for its beaches than for the quality of its wines. Assigned four seperate DOC designations, these designations are not, for the most part, taken seriously. The area produces 97 percent red wine from grapes that withstand the heat and produce a high alcohol product.

## Madeira

The island of Madeira, located about 400 miles/680 kilometers west of Morocco, was claimed by the Portuguese captain Zarco in 1418–1419. The legend is that he set fire to the island to discover what goods it could provide for Portugal and the resulting ash enriched the volcanic soil. The island has terraced vineyards up to 2625 feet/800 meters above sea level. The rainfall is heavy, yet vines benefit from an elaborate irrigation system. Irrigation is necessary because of the porous soil. The vines are trained high to reduce the risk of rot. The best sites have a southern exposure. Funchal, the city

**Figure 9.13** The Evolution of the Quinta do Carmo Label.

The Island of Madeira.

where most of the company lodges are located, is the home of the Instituto do Vinho da Madeira (Madeira Wine Institute) control board.

The original Madeira wines were powerful but not fortified as much as wines of the present day (just as Porto wines evolved to a higher alcohol level). The wines were originally shipped to the East Indies and other ports to the east. As wine is sensitive to changes in temperature and movement, it is odd that this wine, rocking in casks in the hold of ships and then transported across the Equator, were not ruined. By the seventeenth and eighteenth centuries, Madeira, fortified and made in the style known today, became quite popular in the United States and Great Britain. The twin disasters of oidium and *phylloxera* (see Chapter 2 on Wine Grapes) in the latter half of the nineteenth century devastated the crops here, as they did in most parts of Europe. Many farmers, not wishing to suffer such losses again, planted wild American grapes or resistant hybrids. These hybrids and wild vines have been outlawed. However, it will be some time before the transformation to higher-quality grape types is complete. The change is possible, however, because of financial grants from the EC and investments by the companies who buy the grapes to make their wines.

James Andrew Symington came from Scotland to Oporto in 1882. As mentioned earlier in this chapter, the Symington family is the top producer of Porto. In the late 1980s they became majority owners of the Madeira Wine Company, the largest producer on the island. Their commitment to quality, proven in Porto, should help make Madeira a more consistent, higher-quality product. Another important producer of Madeira is Henriques and Henriques.

The wine making process contines to evolve. No longer is it necessary to send the wines halfway round the world to get the heating and cooling effect. Wines are heated and cooled by **estufagem**; heating is done either by steam pipes in a room with casks or by placing the wine in large fiberglass-lined concrete tanks. A *solera* process (see the section on Sherry in Chapter 8 on Spain) is used, and the wines spend at least one and a half years in large casks before bottling. The solera blending system was found to be difficult to monitor by government officials and has been outlawed for the future.

In the past the wines were fortified with spirits made from sugarcane; but, this process was banned in 1973 and now *aguardente* (grape brandy) must be used. A minimum of 85 percent of the grape type must be used for varietal-labeled wines. The Tinta Negra Mole still represents over half of vineyard acreage. It will now be used for younger-style wines with an indication of sweetness. Seco will be the most dry and doce the sweetest. The Tinta Negra Mole, Malvasia Roxo, Verdelho Tinto red grapes, and the Moscatel white are classified as *Castas Boas* (good varieties) which are considered better than the *Castas Autorizadas* (authorized varieties). The red grapes in the latter category are Tinta Madeira, Triunfo, and Complexa, while the whites are Boal do Porto Santo and Rio Grande. The highest-quality grapes are *Castas Nobres* (noble varieties): they are the Sercial, Verdelho, Bual, Malmsey (Malvasia), and Terrantez white grapes and the Bastardo red grape. The American wild grapes and hybrids are now forbidden in Madeira.

The best wines are made from the Sercial, Verdelho, Bual, and Malmsey (Malvasia) grapes and their name is found on the label. The plantings tend to follow elevation with Sercial at the highest altitudes. These finer grapes, such as the driest Sercial and semidry Verdelho, are allowed to ferment out most of their sugars before the addition of aguardente. The sweeter versions are fortified earlier while still in their skins. They are not baked in *estufas* (ovens) but rather are stacked in attics where natural swings in temperatures over a long period of time allow them to develop gracefully. *Vinho de Canteiro* is a term sometimes used for the wines naturally aged on racks *(canteiros)*. The Sercial is the local name for the Esgana Cão, which is known for high acidity. The Verdelho is semidry, Bual is a sweet dessert wine, and Malmsey makes the darkest-colored and sweetest of styles.

Just as the Porto industry needs volume sales of ruby and tawny, so Madeira depends on *Granel,* the youngest style. It is a two-year-old product that is used more for cooking than for drinking. It represents over a third of total sales. Rainwater, also commonly found in kitchens, is a semidry blend. The three-year-old *"Finest"* and five-year-old *"Reserve"* categories are based mostly on Tinta Negra Mole grapes. To bear a varietal name, a Madeira must be at least five years old and have a minimum of 85 percent content of the named grape type. *"Special Reserve"* guarantees a minimum age of ten years in cask; *"Extra Reserve"* guarantees a minimum of 15 years. The highest quality of all is *"Vintage,"* which comes entirely from the grapes harvested in the stated year and must spend a minimum of 20 years in cask and two in bottle before being sold.

Madeira can have an incredibly long life. After surviving the fortification, heating and cooling stages, and extended aging, they are hardy enough to last a century. A small wine glass holding about three ounces is the way to appreciate it, the drier versions chilled and the sweeter at room temperature. The less-expensive styles are useful in the kitchen but the finest examples are often served as an aperitif, with a soup or dessert course, or on their own to end a meal.

The Madeira Wine Company represents over two dozen of the top producers and includes such firms as Blandy, Cossart-Gordon, and Leacock.

## Summary

In Portugal, as discussed in the previous chapters on Spain and Italy, there is controversy over the use of wood for aging. The older generations of Spanish, Italian, and Portuguese wine drinkers preferred wines that were maduro, or well matured, which meant long aging in the cask, usually at the expense of fruit flavors. The present generation of wine makers is working to preserve the rich fruit flavors the wines can express. Controlled fermentation temperatures for each type means better-quality wine without the "hot" taste associated with warmer growing regions. Stainless steel or epoxy-lined tanks can be used to control temperature, but the question of oak storage still remains along with many associated questions: Large old oak casks as aging vessels or smaller new ones that contribute more tannins and vanillins to a wine? Traditional Portuguese oak, or American and French barrels? These are some of the questions and experiments that are under review as the Portuguese entry into the EC pushes the nation to compete in the international market with both its fellow member nations and those outside the block.

International market demand brings wine makers from the United States, Australia, and France; but the native wine makers educated in Portugal are still producing most of the wines. Leaders in the field are José Soares Franco, responsible for Ferreira Porto and the Dão and Douro wines of Sogrape in the north. In the central and south, Domingos Soares Franco of Fonseca Successores, and Joaõ Portugal Ramos, consultant/wine maker in the Alentejo, are the best-known wine makers.

New legislation and investments should allow Madeira to gain respect and popularity, while high-end Porto continues to be valued as an ideal way to end a meal.

Vinho Verde may lead the way for consumers to experiment with other whites. Most are low alcohol, tart, fruity, fun wines with a slight effervescence. Aside from most being inexpensive, the low alcohol makes them an ideal choice for an apéritif in hot weather or as a match with hot and spicy dishes (see Chapter 13 on Wine and Food). Matéus and Lancers continue to sell in large volume. Portugal's red wines hold great promise for the future. As traditional techniques using lagares and talhas continue to produce some fine wines, technology has enhanced the quality of many others. The challenge is getting these wines, with their unique flavors, and outstanding value, into the glass of the international consumer.

# Germany

## Introduction

The place of wine in Germany is far different from that in the southern European countries of France, Italy, Spain, and Portugal. The national alcoholic beverage of Germany is beer, with a per-person consumption of 38 gallons (144 liters) per year. In the southern European countries, where wine is the most common daily alcoholic beverage, the production triangle (see Figure 10.1) shows a relatively small (45 percent) production of quality wines, while around 50 percent of total production is ordinary everyday table wines. In Germany, since beer is the common alcoholic beverage, there is far less demand for ordinary everyday table wine and the triangle is inverted, with at least 90 percent of all wines produced often fitting into the quality category. In fact, the 1994 vintage shows an astonishing 98 percent of all wines produced from that harvest in the quality category.

Because Germany sits on the northernmost boundary for grape growing, it experiences dramatic shifts in weather patterns from year to year, resulting in inconsistent levels of production at any given quality level. Sometimes the very highest-quality level represents 25 percent of total pro-

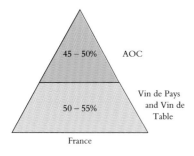

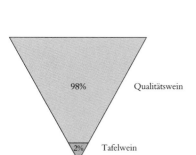

Though Germany produces far less wine in total than France, the vast majority of Germany's wine production falls into the Quality Wine category.

**Figure 10.1** Production Triangles.

| Year | Total Per Capita Consumption of Wine in Germany | Per Capita Consumption of German Wine in Germany |
|------|--------------------------------------------------|---------------------------------------------------|
| **TABLE 10.1 WINE CONSUMPTION IN GERMANY, IN GALLONS (LITERS)** | | |
| 1979–80 | 6.8 (25.6) | 3.2 (12.1) |
| 1989–90 | 7.0 (26.4) | 3.4 (12.9) |

duction; sometimes it is 75 percent. During the last decade, more and more young people in Germany have been drinking more wine, and, as in many countries around the world, the consumption of good quality wines is increasing (see Table 10.1).

The current status of German wines in export markets around the world is a complex one, and there have recently been signs of change. Historically—certainly in North America—consumers have thought of all German wines as sweet, white wines. In fact, 15 percent of Germany's wine production is red; of the 13 officially designated quality wine regions, three—*Ahr, Franken,* and *Württemberg*—specialize in red wine production. The notion that all of Germany's wines are sweet probably stems from the association of **Liebfraumilch** as being the typical German wine. The middle 1960s through to the late 1970s saw a very widespread acceptance of light, fruity, slightly sweet, white wines, typified by the brand Blue Nun. Many other labels followed suit, most of them only poor imitators of Blue Nun, and consumers worldwide quickly assumed that all German wines had the same slightly sweet characteristics as their favorite Liebfraumilch.

This assumption gained currency during the period when American consumers' taste preferences were changing from full, heavy, strong, often sweet red wines (Port-type wines and "monster" Zinfandels) all the way across the taste spectrum to light, dry whites. The light, slightly sweet, fruity wines of Germany were an interim step in this transition, and consumers remembered them for those characteristics. The same transition in consumer preferences has occurred in most wine-consuming countries at one time or another.

When the majority of consumers around the globe declared that their stated preference was for *dry* white wines, especially for Chardonnay, the sales of German wines outside of Germany began to plummet, because many consumers wrongly assume that Germany does not make dry wines. In fact, almost 40 percent of German wine production is dry or half dry (see the section on Wine Making in this chapter).

For most of the 1980s, German wine export figures to the United States fell dramatically from a high point that indicates consumers' widespread acceptance of Blue Nun and other brands. A string of excellent vintages at the end of that decade focused renewed attention on what German wine makers had been up to. Current export and sales figures show a small, but healthy increase, as seen in Table 10.2.

| TABLE 10.2  GERMAN WINE IMPORTED INTO THE UNITED STATES (THOUSANDS OF 12-BOTTLE CASES). | | | | |
|---|---|---|---|---|
| *1970* | *1980* | *1990* | *1991* | *1992* |
| 1162.7 | 4903.9 | 1690.7 | 1317.7 | 1419.9 |

*Source:* U.S. Department of Commerce, and Impact Databank

Many consumers still hesitate to try German wines because they have trouble, at the post–Blue Nun stage, understanding German wine labels (see the section on Labels in this chapter).

# Climate

Germany's wine-producing regions (see Map 10.1) are some of the coolest in the world, because of their position in high northern latitudes, with a summer sun that remains relatively low in the sky. Even though summer daylight hours are long, the indirect sunlight means that careful site selection is needed to grow grapes that will provide full, ripe flavors. Rivers, which moderate climate by heat retention and light reflection, play a fundamental role in the most northerly regions where steep riverbanks provide elevation and angling of the vineyards into the sun's light and heat.

All of these factors provide for a long, slow maturation period, resulting in fully developed, yet delicate, fruit aromas and flavors. The lack of extreme heat and the continued presence of cool night temperatures, however, leave the ripe grapes with good to exellent sugar levels but high acid levels.

The Vineyards at Schloss Johannisberg in the Rheingau Region.

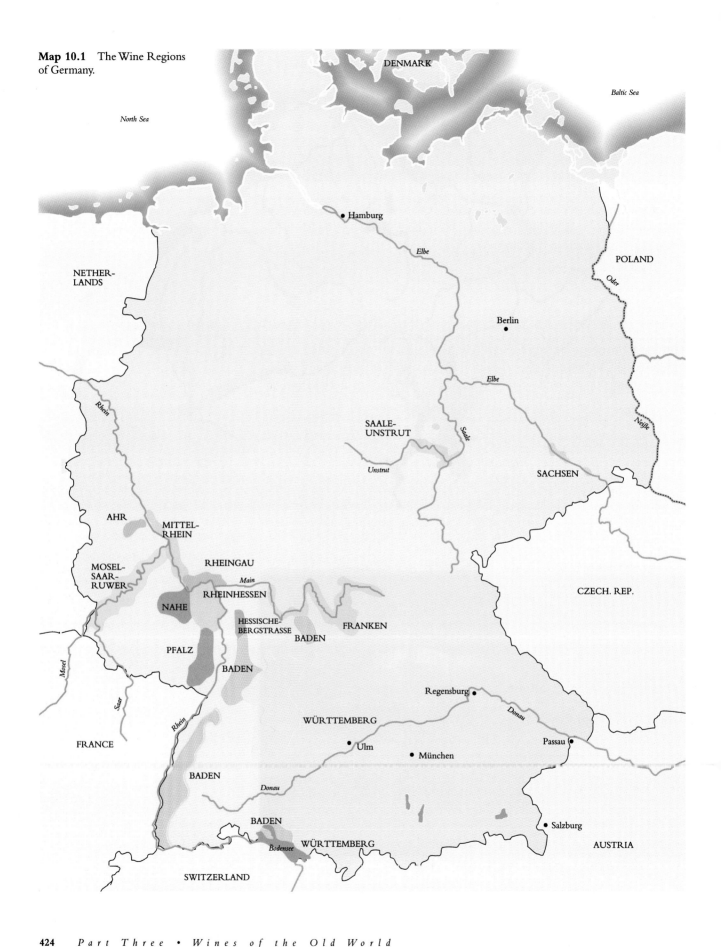

**Map 10.1** The Wine Regions of Germany.

DENMARK

North Sea

Baltic Sea

Hamburg

Elbe

NETHER-
LANDS

POLAND

Oder

Berlin

Rhein

Elbe

SAALE-
UNSTRUT

Saale

Neiße

Unstrut

SACHSEN

AHR

MITTEL-
RHEIN

RHEINGAU

Main

CZECH. REP.

MOSEL-
SAAR-
RUWER

RHEINHESSEN

NAHE

HESSISCHE-
BERGSTRASSE

FRANKEN

BADEN

PFALZ

Mosel

BADEN

Saar

Regensburg

Donau

WÜRTTEMBERG

Rhein

Ulm

München

Passau

FRANCE

BADEN

Donau

Salzburg

BADEN

WÜRTTEMBERG

Bodensee

AUSTRIA

SWITZERLAND

## Wine Styles

Germany's cold climate has two major effects on the styles of wine produced:

- The majority of Germany's wines are white (86 percent), with most of the wines produced from Region 1 grape varieties (see Chapter 4 on North America). These include Riesling, all of its cousins, and subsequent biological crossings (see the section on Grape Varieties in this chapter).

- Most of the white wines are fresh, lively, fruity, and neither strongly alcoholic nor assertively forward or aggressive (nine percent alcohol by volume is average for many German wines).

The cold climate also makes Germany a natural site for the production of sparkling wines, the best of which are labeled *Sekt,* or *Deutscher Sekt* if all of the wine's grapes are grown in Germany. Sekt (the *S* is pronounced more like a *Z* in English) has been in use as a term to identify German sparkling wine since the Treaty of Versailles in 1918 restricted the use of the term "Champagne" to France, at least within Europe.

Like many nations, Germany makes both low-end and high-end sparklers. The bulk of Sekt is in fact produced by using surplus French and Italian wines as a base, with the addition of approximately 20 percent German wines. However, some producers do label their product as Deutscher Sekt, indicating the exclusive use of grapes grown in Germany. In addition, if a label states a grape variety, a vintage year, or a region, the wine must be made from at least 75 percent of grapes of the stated variety, year, or region.

Most Sekt is produced using the **charmat** method, and some is produced by the **transfer method** (see the section on sparkling wines in Chapter 1 on How Wine Is Made).

# Wine Making

The clean, fresh, crisp, aromatic style of many of Germany's wines is achieved by long, cool, slow fermentation in inert containers. Stainless steel fermenters are now commonplace in Germany, though many of the older wineries still use very old large oak barrels. These are generally not being used to give oak character; their age means that they have very little oak character left, and many of them are lined with an inert layer of epoxy. In other words, they are convenient but inert containers used for fermentation, or for storage of wine prior to bottling. However, some of the new generation of German wine makers have been experimenting with the use of newer oak barrels of different sizes, for fermentation and for aging. So far, results are inconsistent, but some wines show great promise, especially when made from less-famous grapes, such as Pinot Gris.

**Figure 10.2** Riesling Grapes.

In addition to the advanced technology of refrigerated, temperature-controlled stainless steel fermentation tanks, German wine makers take full advantage of German expertise in building precision-engineered centrifuges. Using the refrigerated stainless steel containers to chill the fermenting wine below 38°F (3°C), the wine maker can stop the fermentation at exactly the point where he or she has the desired level of residual sugar left in the wine. The wine can then be placed in a centrifuge which spins the wine at high speed and expels the solid yeast particles from the liquid, but leaves the dissolved sugars as residual sugar. If a centrifuge is not used, wine makers can achieve the same effect by passing the wine through a micropore filter which will extract all of the solid yeast cells from the wine. In both scenarios, since the yeast cells have been removed, the wine will not referment as it warms up, even though there is sugar present.

Also important to watch as a recent trend in German wine styles is the use of the word *trocken* on the label. Trocken means "dry" in German, and the wines are made dry by ensuring that all of the sugars present in the grape juice are converted into alcohol (see Chapter 1 on How Wine Is Made). In some ways, this can be seen as an obvious attempt to recapture market share by positioning Germany's finest wines alongside the presumed dry wines of France, California, Italy, and other important growing regions. On another level, Germany's wine makers insist that Germany's wines have always been produced dry, and the phenomenon of sweet, fruity Liebfraumilch wines was simply an aberration. Whatever the historical truth may be, Germany's finest wine makers are now making waves, and a name for themselves, with their distinctly dry, wood-treated white (and in some cases red) wines.

Because of Germany's climate disadvantages, and the occasionally low grape-sugar levels, chaptalization is a regular practice at lower-quality levels of German wine. Chaptalization is forbidden at the highest-quality level, and prestigious producers scorn the practice. Also permitted, at all quality levels, is the addition of **süssreserve** (sweet reserve) to the finished wine. Süssreserve is unfermented sterile grape juice, equal in quality to the wine. In other words, before fermentation of the grape juice begins, a wine maker can separate out a small quantity of juice, and render it sterile so as to prevent fermentation. The remainder of the juice is allowed to ferment completely dry, and, at the end of the fermentation process, the süssreserve juice can be blended in, giving the wine a fruitier, even sweeter character. The addition of süssreserve is widely practiced in German wine making, but is frowned on by many top-quality producers.

It is, of course, ironic that Germany remains famous as a producer of some of the world's finest sweet wines, and it is similarly ironic that the mostly inhospitable, cold climate is also responsible for some of Germany's greatest sweet wines. Cool, misty conditions toward the end of the growing season often promote the development of *botrytis* (see Chapter 1 on How Wine Is Made), allowing the production of rich, concentrated, very sweet wines.

**Figure 10.3**  Silvaner Grapes.

## Grape Varieties

Germany's climate is best suited to the recognized cool climate grapes. Most of the vineyards are planted to white Region 1 varieties, and approximately 12 percent of plantings is given to the lighter red varieties, such as Pinot Noir.

*Riesling.*  The noble Riesling grape (see Figure 10.2) is assumed by many people to be Germany's most widely planted grape, but it is not. It is, however, highly revered by all German grape growers and wine makers for its ability to produce wines of outstanding beauty and delicacy, that taste incredibly fresh when first made but are capable of extensive aging and development.

Despite its glowing reputation, Riesling faces a major problem, especially in Germany's cold climate. To fully ripen, Riesling needs a long, slow growing season, because the grape is an early budder and late ripener. Riesling's internal clock leaves it quite susceptible to spring and fall frosts. It is not the most practical grape to grow in Germany's cold vineyards. Surprisingly, Riesling is the dominant grape in the northern region of *Mosel-Saar-Ruwer,* but specific microclimates there allow it to do well.

*Silvaner.*  The Silvaner (Sylvaner in Alsace) was previously widely planted throughout Germany (see Figure 10.3). It was popular as a workhorse grape that made ordinary to good wines, but rarely exceptional ones. The advantage of the Silvaner grape, and what made it so popular with growers, is that it is late budding and early ripening. This translates into a short growing season, or a vine type which, in practical terms, is well suited to Germany's climate.

***Müller-Thurgau.*** In what turned out to be a successful attempt to capture the delicacy and ripeness of Riesling in a shorter growing season, a Professor Müller, in 1893, created a crossing of Riesling and Silvaner. The resulting new grape variety, called Müller-Thurgau, has many of the fruit and acid balance characteristics of Riesling but is less likely to be exposed to early or late frosts. Given the grape's practicality from the growers' point of view, and its attractive flavors and balance from the wine makers' point of view, it is not surprising that the Müller-Thurgau is now the most widely planted grape throughout Germany. Since that landmark clonal crossing in 1893, many more crossings have been developed from various grape varieties and clones, all specifically engineered for a cold northern climate. As Germany rebuilds its international wine-export markets, consumers around the world can expect to see more of the hitherto little-known varieties such as Müller-Thurgau, and more recent crossings such as Bacchus, Optima, Rieslaner, and Scheurebe.

***Other Grapes.*** Despite its German-sounding name, the Gewürztraminer is not widely grown in Germany, and it is probably not a "native" German grape anyway. The markedly pungent aroma and flavors of "Gewürz" tend to be too strong for many German wine makers, who prefer to concentrate on the delicacy and finesse of Riesling or Müller-Thurgau.

Pinot Gris is now becoming widely used by wine makers who want to produce barrel-treated dry wines, with higher alcohol levels and fuller flavors. It is also referred to as the Grauburgunder or Ruländer. The same is true of the Pinot Blanc or Weissburgunder. In addition, the seemingly ubiquitous Chardonnay was approved by the German wine authorities in 1991 as a permitted grape variety to be grown in any of the following regions: Ahr, Mosel-Saar-Ruwer, Mittelrhein, Nahe, Rheinhessen, Pfalz, Württemburg, and Baden.

Finally, whenever red wines are produced in a cold climate, Pinot Noir will usually be the grape of preference. In the regions of Ahr and Baden the Pinot Noir is capable of producing some very fine red wines, though they are not often exported. Pinot Noir is also known as the Spätburgunder.

# Wine Laws

Germany's wine laws have been evolving for centuries, and they continue to evolve today as legislators and producers attempt to keep pace with rapidly changing technology and world markets. Of all the European wine-producing countries, Germany has been the most active in accepting the need for laws to govern grape growing, wine making, and labeling, and the need to review and, if necessary, change those laws.

Prior to the 1970s, Germany, France, and Italy were the movers and shakers in the European wine scene. These countries had already embraced the vision of a "United States of Europe" in some form, with common wine laws in each constituent country. Until the 1970s however, the wine laws of

## GERMAN WORD USAGE

Within the German wine laws, and on German wine labels, there are some words which need to be understood if we are to figure out what is in the bottle. The following language hints may help.

The terms *Qualitätswein bestimmter Anbaugebiete* and *Qualitätswein mit Prädikat* are respectively abbreviated to QbA and QmP (see the following section on Wine Categories for definitions of these terms). The reason for the use of uppercase and lowercase abbreviations is that, in written German, all nouns are spelled with uppercase initial letters. *Qualitätswein, Anbaugebiete,* and *Prädikat* are all nouns, whereas *bestimmter* and *mit* are prepositions.

Also, plural forms are different. The plurals of *Grosslage* and *Einzellage* are *Grosslagen* and *Einzellagen*. But the plurals of *Bereich* and *Anbaugebiet* are *Bereiche* and *Anbaugebiete*.

Within the QmP category, the six subcategories, or distinctions, are all compound words, utilizing various combinations of seven key words. Those key words, with their *literal* translation are:

| Key Word | Literal Translation |
|----------|---------------------|
| *lese* | picked |
| *spät* | late |
| *aus* | out |
| *beeren* | berries, grapes |
| *trocken* | dry, dried |
| *eis* | ice |
| *wein* | wine |

Lastly, the suffix *er* in German means "from." Thus *Bernkasteler* means "from Bernkastel" in much the same way a "New Yorker" is someone from New York. This suffix may also appear at the end of the vintage year (*e.g.,* "1989er"), meaning "from the 1989 vintage."

each of those countries tended to be inward-looking and parochial, rather than international in scope.

In 1971, Germany became the first European nation to enact a radical reformation of its wine laws. With only minor alterations and updates since then, the laws of 1971 remain the basis for Germany's reputation as a premium-quality wine producer.

In many ways, the practical embodiment of the any nation's wine laws, from the consumer's point of view, is the label on the bottle, which also acts as the primary selling agent for any bottle of wine. Germany's wine labels are a fine example of a curious paradox: They are the worst selling agents of any wine from anywhere, but they are also the most accurate and most informative reflection of the wine laws and culture that govern wine production. If only we all could recognize and understand a few key German words and phrases, and decipher Gothic script, the average German wine label would tell us everything we want to know about the origin, style, and taste characteristics of the wine! For most people, however, especially Americans used to simple varietal labels, German wine labels are all but impossible to understand (see the section on Labels in this chapter).

What distinguishes Germany's wine laws from those of any other nation is the fact that a heavy emphasis is placed on the natural sugar content of the grapes at harvest. The grape sugars must be measured and recorded, and there are specified levels of grape sugar which must be achieved if a producer wants to classify his or her wine in any of the legal categories. In addition, certain descriptive words are allowed to be used on the labels, *but only* if a predetermined sugar level was reached at harvest time. The laws and categories listed below reflect the fact that the two former German states were reunited in 1992. The reunification brought only a small area of vineyards in the former East Germany under the German wine laws.

## Wine Categories

Like all member nations of the European Community (EC), Germany recognizes two broad types of wine (see the Introduction to Part 3):

- Ordinary wine, often referred to as *Vin de Table* or Table Wine.

- Quality wine, officially referred to throughout Europe as VQPRD (Vin de Qualité Produit dans une Région Déterminée).

Within those two broad groups, Germany has four main categories of wine, two of them in the ordinary wine group, and two of them in the quality wine group. These four categories parallel the systems used to classify wines in all other EC countries. In ascending order of perceived quality, Germany's main categories are

- *Tafelwein* (table wine) and *Deutscher Tafelwein* (table wine whose grapes were grown in Germany) (see Figure 10.4)

- *Landwein* (regional wine)

- *Qualitätswein bestimmter Anbaugebiete,* or QbA (quality wine)

- *Qualitätswein mit Prädikat* or QmP (highest-quality wine)

In the following sections, we describe each of these categories. In general, the regions identified for Tafelwein are very large. The regions for Landwein are smaller and fall within the larger Tafelwein regions, and the regions for Qualitätswein are smaller still.

***Deutscher Tafelwein.*** Wines in this category (English translation: "German table wine") are the daily consumption of the average German wine drinker, and very few of them ever reach an export market. The laws that

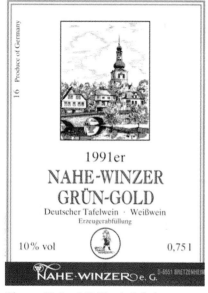

1991er
NAHE-WINZER
GRÜN-GOLD
Deutscher Tafelwein · Weißwein
Erzeugerabfüllung

10% vol          0,75 l

NAHE-WINZER e. G.   D-6551 BRETZENHEIM

**Figure 10.4**   A Tafelwein Label.

govern production of wine in this category are fairly broad, but they do stipulate a minimum natural grape-sugar content at harvest, and they identify four main regions. One of the region names appears on the label to indicate where the grapes were grown. Those regions are:

- Rhein und Mosel (divided into two subregions—Rhein and Mosel; the producer may choose to identify the subregion on the label)

- Bayern

- Neckar

- Oberrhein (divided into two subregions—Römertor and Burgengau; the producer may choose to identify the subregion on the label).

Given that more people drink beer than wine on a daily basis in Germany, and the consequent minor emphasis placed by German wine makers on the production of ordinary wine, it is understandable that, in some years, the majority of the grape harvest goes to the production of high-quality wines, leaving a shortage of ordinary wines for daily consumption. To fill this gap the German wine laws allow for wines from other European countries to be imported and sold in Germany as simple "Tafelwein," not "Deutscher Tafelwein." These imported table wines may or may not have been blended with German table wine, but most are bottled in Germany. They often carry the phrase *Wein aus mehreren Mitgliedstaaten der Eg* ("Wine from EC countries") on the label.

**Landwein.**    Landwein, or "regional wine," is assumed to be better-quality table wine because the laws that govern its production are more stringent, requiring higher levels of grape sugars at harvest, and requiring that the grapes used to make the wines come from one of 19 designated Landwein regions, all smaller than the four Deutscher Tafelwein regions. The particular region is specified on the label (see Table 10.3).

## A GEOGRAPHIC NOTE

We mentioned previously that rivers play an important role in German viticulture. The Neckar and the Mosel (*Moselle* in French) are tributaries flowing into the Rhein (Rhine in English) River as it flows northwards and westwards from the Bodensee in southern Germany to the North Sea, which separates Britain from northern Europe. The Rhein flows through the Oberrhein region, and the Main River defines Bayern.

### TABLE 10.3    LANDWEIN REGIONS

| | |
|---|---|
| Ahrtaler Landwein | Starkenburger Landwein |
| Rheinburgen Landwein | Landwein der Mosel |
| Landwein der Saar | Landwein der Ruwer |
| Nahegauer Landwein | Altrheingauer Landwein |
| Rheinischer Landwein | Pfälzer Landwein |
| Fränkischer Landwein | Regensburger Landwein |
| Schwäbischer Landwein | Unterbadischer Landwein |
| Südbadischer Landwein | Taubertaler Landwein |
| Bayerischer-Bodensee Landwein | |
| Sächsischer Landwein★ | Anhaltiner Landwein★ |

★Both the Sächsischer Landwein and the Anhaltiner Landwein districts were part of the former East Germany.

***Qualitätswein bestimmter Anbaugebiete (QbA).*** Wines in this category (the English translation is "Quality wine from designated areas of origin"), are often referred to simply as "Qualitätswein" or "QbA." This category usually encompasses the largest amount of German wines.

The grapes of QbA wines must be varieties approved by German wine authorities, and must be sufficiently ripe at harvest to reflect the natural flavor characteristics of the grape and the region. The German wine laws allow QbA wines to be "enhanced" by the addition of süssreserve (see the section on wine making in this chapter).

The grapes used to produce the QbA wines must be grown in one of 13 ***Anbaugebiete,*** or specified regions (see Map 10.2). These regions are then subdivided as shown in Table 10.4. In order of greater and greater specificity, the subdivisions are region, district, collective vineyard site, and

**Map 10.2**   The Qualitätswein Regions.

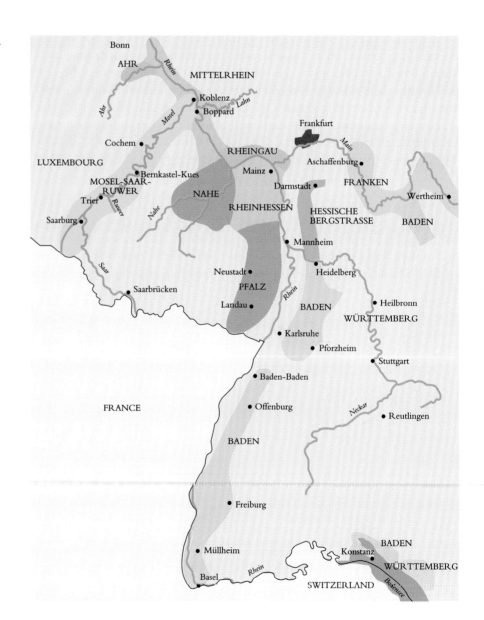

*For the location of the Sachsen and the Saale Unstrut regions, refer to Map 10.1.*

The names of most German wines are based on the regional designations described in the Wine Laws section in this chapter. As in some parts of France, some wines carry a regional name, indicating that the grapes come from any mix of vineyards within that region. Other wines carry a smaller district name, and still others bear the name of a specific vineyard site. A regional wine might, for example, be labeled Mosel-Saar-Ruwer Riesling, indicating that the wine was made from Riesling grapes harvested from anywhere within the Mosel-Saar-Ruwer Anbaugebiet, or region (see Map 10.2).

For district names, each of the 13 Anbaugebiete is split into smaller *Bereiche* or subregions. A wine from a Bereich might, for example, be labeled as Bereich Bernkastel Riesling, indicating that the wine was made from Riesling grapes harvested from vineyards within the Bereich, or district of Bernkastel, which surrounds the town of Bernkastel in the Mosel region.

Each Bereich contains several *Grosslagen,* or collective vineyards. A wine from a **Grosslage** might, for example, be labeled as Bernkasteler Badstube Riesling, indicating that the wine was made from Riesling grapes harvested from any combination of the single vineyards which make up the Grosslage named Badstube, which is in the town of Bernkastel. The wine is called a Bernkastel*er* because it comes from the town of Bernkastel. This type of wine is usually produced at QbA or QmP level. If it is a QmP wine it will also list on the label one of six classes described on pages 434–435, such as Kabinett.

Each **Grosslage** is made up of several *Einzellagen,* or individual vineyards. A wine from a specified **Einzellage** might, for example, be labeled as Bernkasteler Doktor Riesling, indicating that the wine was made from Riesling grapes, all of which were harvested from the *Einzellage,* or well-known single vineyard named *Doktor,* located within the town of Bernkastel. Again, this wine would be made at QbA or QmP level.

In any of the above examples, if the word trocken appears on the label, the wine is dry. If not, the wine will probably show the delicate balance of fruit sweetness and acidity for which German wine producers have become famous.

## TABLE 10.4 QbA CLASSIFICATION OF A SAMPLE WINE

**13 Anbaugebiete (*e.g.,* Mosel-Saar-Ruwer)**

(specified wine regions, each with its own name)

**34 Bereiche (*e.g.,* Bernkastel)**

(small districts, each with its own name, within a region)

**152 Grosslagen (*e.g.,* Bernkasteler Badstube)**

(collective vineyard sites, each with its own name, within a district, grouping together several smaller vineyard sites)

**2600 Einzellagen (*e.g.,* Bernkasteler Doktor)**

(very small plots of land which are individual vineyard sites, each with its own name)

individual vineyard site. Table 10.4 shows how this system is used to classify one particular QbA wine.

***Qualitätswein mit Prädikat (QmP).*** At this quality level (translated into English as "quality wine with special distinction, or special attributes") it becomes glaringly obvious that Germany's wine laws and label terminology are not based on historical perspective, soil considerations, or vineyard classifications, but simply on the degree of ripeness of the grapes at harvest and the measurable sugars in the juice of those grapes. In theory at least, *any* vineyard in any of Germany's 13 Anbaugebiete, given suitable weather during the growing season, could garner enough sugars in the grapes to qualify for QmP, the highest rung on the ladder of German wine classification.

It is also theoretically possible (and it happens in practice) for one vineyard to go through several successive pickings, with each subsequent picking yielding grapes that are higher in sugar than the grapes from the previous picking. By this method it is possible for one vineyard to produce two or (rarely) three classifications of the same wine within the same harvest year (the QmP classifications and distinctions follow).

The QmP category is subdivided into six classifications or distinctions. Again, to qualify for any of these distinctions, the wine maker or grape grower must be able to show that the original grape sugars at harvest were sufficiently high to meet the predetermined standard. Remember that, in achieving higher sugar levels, the grape growers also achieve fuller ripeness of the natural grape flavors. Thus the objective is to produce clean, natural varietal character within the balancing parameters of acidity, alcohol, and sweetness. Even though the grape sugars at harvest increase for each distinction, most of these wines remain at alcohol levels of seven to ten percent by volume. For any wine deemed QmP, one of the six classifications described below must be printed on the label.

*Kabinett.* **Kabinett** wines are usually fine, relatively light wines, made from "fully ripe" grapes. Remember that "fully ripe" in a German/cold climate context is not the same as, say, in a Californian/temperate climate context. Here it means very fresh, just-ripe flavors, with plenty of acidity still present. Kabinett wines may or may not show a hint of sweetness.

*Spätlese.* **Spätlese** literally means "late picked" or "late harvest" but, again, this should not be equated with a Californian "late harvest" designation (see Chapter 4 on North America). To make this wine, the grapes are left on the vine slightly longer than for Kabinett, allowing them to reach higher sugar levels. They show fuller flavor and more concentration. They are not necessarily sweeter.

*Auslese.* **Auslese** translates as "out picked," or selected, indicating that, at harvest, some bunches of grapes were selected as showing very full ripeness or obvious signs of *botrytis*. The resulting wines are usually intense in aroma and taste. They are usually sweet.

*Beerenauslese.* The term **Beerenauslese** is often abbreviated to BA when spoken, though not on the label. The literal translation is "berries out picked," suggesting that, at harvest, the pickers select and pick from the grape bunches those individual grapes that are considered overripe or that show signs of extensive *botrytis* rot. The wines made from these grapes are very rich and luscious. Only a small number of wines are made in this style in very small quantity, and they are relatively expensive.

*Eiswein.*    **Eiswein,** or "ice wine," has recently become a separate distinction within the QmP category, although the measured sugar content at harvest must be at least equal to Beerenauslese standards. Eiswein from Germany is rare and expensive, and it represents one of the purest renditions of the essence of grape varietal character (see Figure 10.5), unblemished by *botrytis.*

To qualify as Eiswein, the grapes are left on the vine, often into December, until a sudden drop in temperature freezes the water content of the grapes. The attendant risks involved are as great as, if not greater than, with **Trockenbeerenauslese** (see below), since the grapes used to make Eiswein *cannot* show any sign of *botrytis,* or any other kind of rot, and should have no breaks in their skins. The objective is to allow the varietal characteristics of the grape to develop to their maximum. Because the grapes are not affected by rot, they maintain an optimum balance of sugars and acids. That balance can then be shown off to the highest degree by harvesting the frozen grapes and pressing them so gently that the frozen water content is left untouched. Thus all that drips from the press is pure, concentrated, "liquid grape character." The resulting wines are usually sweet, though not excessively so, but they are very concentrated renditions of the sugar/acid balance of the grapes.

**Figure 10.5** Eiswein Grapes.

*Trockenbeerenauslese.*    By now it should be clear that many German words are compounds of three or, in this case, four shorter words. Pieced together, this tongue twister simply means "dried berries out picked," or selected raisins. That is to say, the grapes used to make this wine are selected at harvest for the fact that they are probably covered with *botrytis* and have also shriveled to raisins while still on the vine. Many wine makers and grape growers take enormous risks (the grapes are exposed to frosts, high winds, hail, rainstorms, and natural predators, such as birds, deer, and appreciative children) to leave the grapes on the vines as late as November or December in order to get these prized grapes. Since they are shriveled raisins, they contain very little juice, but that juice is extremely rich and concentrated in natural grape sugars. It makes a wine that comes close to pure nectar, an incredibly concentrated essence of the grape variety. Fine TBA wines are rare, often age worthy, and very expensive. (Trockenbeerenauslese is usually abbreviated to TBA in speech.)

# The Quality Control Process

As in all European wine-producing countries, Germany operates a system of checks on wines which are to be sold as quality wines. At the vineyard level, the German wine laws do the following:

*   Stipulate which permitted grape varieties can be grown

*   Define the growing regions (appellations of origin)

*   Set the minimum sugar levels that grapes must reach in order to qualify for the various label designations.

At the postproduction level, the laws require that any quality wine go through an analytical and a tasting test. The analytical test measures the wine's content of alcohol, residual sugar, and acidity, and also tests for any fraudulent additions to the wine. The tasting test is done by experts familiar with the region where the grapes were grown. The tasters expect to be able to identify the "correct" characteristics derived from the grape, the region, and the vintage.

If a wine passes these tests it is given its *Amtliche Prüfungsnummer* (usefully abbreviated to A.P. No.) which must be printed on the label, and which can be used in the future to identify the exact origin of the wine. Two bottles of each wine are kept sealed by the wine authorities for at least two years, in case complaints are leveled against the wine.

If a wine is judged *not* to meet the panel's standards, the panel *may* approve a lower status for the wine than the one requested by the producer, or it may refuse the wine outright. If a wine is rejected, the producer can blend it in with another wine, or initiate legal proceedings against the decision.

## DRYNESS IN QMP WINES

In this chapter we have pointed to the trend to "revert" to the tradition of drier styles of German wine. To help consumers identify which wines may be made in a dry style, the German wine laws were recently amended to allow the use of one of two words on the label to indicate a sweetness level. Those two words are:

- **Trocken,** indicating a dry wine, showing little if any sign of residual sweetness.

- **Halbtrocken** (half dry), indicating a wine which might be described as only slightly sweet.

Theoretically, either of these descriptive terms could be used on the label of *any* classification of German wine, from Tafelwein to QmP Trockenbeerenauslese. In practice, the categories of wine made with *botrytis*-affected grapes (Auslese and up) would very rarely be made in a dry or half-dry style.

# Labels

Even the most protective German wine makers would, or should, admit that one of the biggest barriers to increased sales of German wines is the German wine label. To the average wine consumer around the world, a German wine label is not only daunting but intimidating.

The irony is that, of all wine labels in the world, German wine labels are the most accurate and informative, telling the consumer not only where the wine comes from, but usually indicating the grape variety used and offering hints as to the wine's style and taste characteristics.

All German wine labels indicate the quality level which the wine falls into (from Tafelwein—see Figure 10.5—to QmP Trockenbeerenauslese), and then go on to present information about the bottler or shipper, the bottle contents, the wine's geographic origin, grape variety, vintage year, and description of the grape's sweetness level at harvest. Table 10.5 shows what information must be shown for wine of each quality level.

## THE VERBAND DEUTSCHER PRÄDIKATSWEINGUTER (VDP)

As in many walks of life, in wine production there are groups who favor the old way of doing things, stressing that they are maintaining the style, character, and quality of times gone by. In German wine making, the VDP is such a group. Its members are all single-estate wine producers, all committed to producing high-quality wines that continue to exhibit the distinctiveness of their regional and varietal origin.

The movement began at the beginning of this century and has grown from small regional groups to a national association with 171 member estates. All members abide by regulations which go beyond the standards set by the German wine laws.

VDP members are, for example, bound by these guidelines:

- no chaptalization

- lower yields in the vineyards

- a higher concentration of Riesling plantings

- reduced use of chemicals

- higher sugar content at harvest

- premium vineyard sites.

VDP member wines can be identified by the association logo printed on the capsule on the bottle neck.

## WINE AND FOOD

Many people assume that German wines are too sweet to be compatible with food. In fact, at levels up to Spätlese, their balance of fruit, sweetness, and acidity is so masterful that they make excellent accompaniments to many light appetizers and entrées.

Kabinett wines make a good match with seafood, cold meats, light poultry, veal or pork dishes, and vegetarian stir-fry. Spätlese wines, with their fuller body and bracing acidity, work well with cream sauces, pork dishes, galantines, and patés. Auslese wines, served in small quantities, match fruit-based desserts and foie gras. Beerenauslese and Trockenbeerenauslese wines are best savored on their own, especially before or after dinner. For more information, see Chapter 13 on Wine and Food).

# Wine Regions

With the reunification of Germany, there are now 13 recognized Anbaugebiete producing wines at QbA and QmP level, including two new regions from the former East Germany. The total number of acres under vine in these 13 regions is just shy of 246,400 (100,000 hectares). From all perspectives, particularly that of the U.S. export market for German wines, four regions would be considered much more important than the others. These are Mosel-Saar-Ruwer, Rheingau, Pfalz (formerly Rheinpfalz), and Rheinhessen. We will discuss these four regions in some depth, after summarizing the salient facts about all 13 wine-producing regions in Germany. Remember that each Anbaugebiet is comprised of anywhere from one to eight Bereiche (smaller districts within the region), each of which contains from one to 25 Grosslagen, and from 43 to 506 Einzellagen. (See Table 10.4.)

## Summary of the 13 Quality Wine-Producing Regions

*Ahr.* The majority of the vineyards (65 to 70 percent) in the Ahr region are planted with red grapes, especially Spätburgunder and Portugieser; most of the region's wine is consumed locally. Ahr, which contains 1070 acres/428 hectares of vineyard, has one Bereich: Walporzheim/Ahrtal. Red wines span several styles, from fiery to velvet smooth. Whites are crisp and fresh, with good acidity. The region contains one Grosslagen, and 43 Einzellagen.

*Mittelrhein.* Mittelrhein's northerly climate produces white wines of high acidity; most of the region's wine is consumed locally. With close to 75 percent of the Mittelrhein planted in Riesling, its 1877 acres/751 hectares under vine include two Bereiche: Loreley and Siebengbirge, subdivided into 11 Grosslagen and 111 Einzellagen. The wines are robust, but with pronounced acidity.

*Mosel-Saar-Ruwer.* This highly regarded region (see Map 10.3), with a large percentage of Riesling (60 percent) in the vineyards, produces very elegant wines; slate soil is said to provide the wines with their delicate character. With 32,150 acres/12,860 hectares of vineyard, the five Bereiche of the Mosel are Zell, Bernkastel, Obermosel, Saar-Ruwer, and Moseltor. They are subdivided into 18 Grosslagen and 506 Einzellagen. See the section below on Major Regions for further information.

*Rheingau.* Rheingau, relatively small at 7250 acres/2900 hectares, is an enormously important region that produces world-class white wines. The name of the region's major town (and only Bereich), Johannisberg, has been adopted by other wine-producing countries to define the "true" Riesling grape variety in those countries. Indeed, 80 percent of the ten Grosslagen and 119 Einzellagen are planted with Riesling. The wines produced from

## TABLE 10.5 INFORMATION INCLUDED ON BOTTLE LABELS\* BY QUALITY LEVELS

| Label item | Tafelwein | Landwein | QbA | QmP |
|---|---|---|---|---|
| † Bottler/shipper Name, Address | mandatory | mandatory | mandatory | mandatory |
| Contents in liters (l.), Centiliters (cl.), Milliliters (ml.) | mandatory | mandatory | mandatory | mandatory |
| Geographic origin | mandatory; one of 4 Tafelwein regions | mandatory; one of 19 Landwein regions | mandatory; one of 13 Quality wine Anbaugebiete plus smaller district *or* town + vineyard designation (vineyard name may be Grosslage or Einzellage) | mandatory; one of 13 Quality wine Anbaugebiete plus smaller district *or* town + vineyard designation (vineyard name may be Grosslage or Einzellage) |
| Grape variety name | optional; if shown, must be *at least* 85 percent of named variety | optional; if shown, must be *at least* 85 percent of named variety | optional, almost always; if shown, must be *at least* 85 percent of named variety | optional, almost always; if shown, must be *at least* 85 percent of named variety |
| Vintage year | optional | optional | optional, almost always | optional, almost always |
| Sweetness descriptor (e.g., trocken) | optional | optional | optional | optional |
| A.P. No. | never | never | mandatory | mandatory |

\*See Figures 10.6 and 10.7.

† Note: If the same person or corporation grew the grapes, picked them, made the wine, and bottled it, the label may carry the term **Erzeugerabfullung,** which translates loosely as, "Estate Bottled."

**Figure 10.6** A QbA Label.

**Figure 10.7** A QmP Label.

grapes grown on the hillsides are elegant and full of racy acidity, while the valley produces full-bodied and rich wines. See the section below on Major Regions for further information.

*Pfalz.* Pfalz, formerly called Rheinpfalz, is Germany's second-largest region (56,562 acres/22,625 hectares under vine), but it produces more wine than any other region. With 22 percent of plantings in Müller-Thurgau grapes, and 17 percent in Riesling, the Pfalz is almost completely a white wine-producing region, with the northern half recognized as producing higher-quality wines than the south. The Bereiche are Mittelhardt/Deutsche Weinstrasse and Südliche Weinstrasse. These comprise 25 Grosslagen and 328 Einzellagen. See the section on Major Regions below for further information.

***Rheinhessen.*** Rheinhessen is Germany's largest region (62,175 acres/24,870 hectares), but only the second-largest producer in volume of wine. A wide variety of grape types is planted, including some red. The Bereiche are Bingen, Nierstein, and Wonnegau, subdivided into 24 Grosslagen and 448 Einzellagen. See the section on Major Regions below for further information.

***Nahe.*** A wide variety of soil types throughout the Nahe region allows for many different grape types, mostly white, with about 25 percent each of Müller-Thurgau and Riesling planted on 11,350 acres/4540 hectares. The wines are said to resemble those from the surrounding regions of Mosel, Rheingau, and Rheinhessen. An important Anbaugebiet for trade within Europe, its two Bereiche are Kreuznach and Schloss Böckelheim. They include seven Grosslagen and 320 Einzellagen.

***Baden.*** Baden, Germany's third-largest (37,500 acres/15,000 hectares) and most southerly region, is located in the Upper Rhine Valley along the Black Forest. It is very diverse in its vine plantings, with almost one-quarter of its acreage given over to red varieties, especially Spätburgunder (Pinot Noir). Possibly the large production and variety of wines account for the fact that the average Baden citizen drinks more than 50 percent more wine per year than the average German. The eight Bereiche are Badische Bergstrasse Kraichgau, Tauberfranken, Bodensee, Markgräflerland, Kaiserstuhl, Tuniberg, Breisgau, and Ortenau; there are 15 Grosslagen and 312 Einzellagen.

***Franken.*** Franken is planted mostly to white grape varieties. Many of the new crossings, planted on 13,750 acres/5500 hectares east of Frankfurt, make wines with fuller, earthier characteristics than those of other regions. Top-quality wines are often bottled in the region's traditional short, flagon-shaped bottle, the **"Bocksbeutel."** Franken's three Bereiche are Mainviereck, Maindrieck, and Steigerwald, and the region contains 19 Grosslagen and 211 Einzellagen.

***Württemburg.*** This valley-based region, with its relatively warmer southern climate, is Germany's largest producer of red wines, and its white wines are generally full and hearty. Most of the region's wines, very few of which are grown on plots larger than 12.5 acres/five hectares, are consumed locally. The six Bereiche are Remstal-Stuttgart, Württembergisches Unterland, Kocher-Jagst-Tauber, Bayrischer-Bodensee, Württembergischer Bodensee, and Oberer Neckar; there are 17 Grosslagen and 210 Einzellagen.

***Hessische-Bergstrasse.*** This region produces mostly full-bodied and lower-acid white wines. Most of the region's wines are consumed locally. There are two Bereiche: Starkenburg and Umstadt, and only 972 acres/389 hectares under vine, comprising three Grosslagen and 24 Einzellagen.

***Saale-Unstrut.*** Formerly in East Germany, this region is now Germany's most northerly, growing mostly white grapes which produce some very good QbA and QmP Kabinett-level wines.

***Sachsen.*** Sachsen, also referred to as Elbtal, was also formerly in East Germany. This region is now Germany's most easterly wine region, producing mostly dry, medium-bodied white wines. Most are consumed locally.

## Major Regions

***Mosel-Saar-Ruwer.*** Visitors to the Mosel-Saar-Ruwer (often referred to simply as "the Mosel") usually come away with two lasting impressions, vines and rivers, for they are the heart and soul of the region (see Map 10.3). The two small tributaries of the Saar and the Ruwer flow in a generally northerly direction into the Mosel River as it winds its tortuously meandering way from France to Koblenz, where it empties into the Rhine.

The rivers play a vital part in making grape growing and wine making possible in an otherwise inhospitable climate. Everywhere the visitor looks, every available riverbank hillside, including the smallest, seemingly inaccessible ledges, are planted with vines. And the reason is simple: nothing else will grow in the slate soil, and no other crop warrants the care and devotion expended on the vines. The product of all this care is wines that are always acceptable and occasionally superb.

The climate of this northerly growing region generally produces good to excellent growing conditions in only three years out of ten, making some familiarity with "good vintages" almost a necessity for Mosel wines. Because of the likelihood of only average growing conditions in most years, the top-quality producers have been quick to realize that access to grapes from prime vineyard sites is absolutely essential. In other words, to make up for the disadvantages of climate, wine makers use the vineyard site, and in particular its exposure to sunlight and heat, as a guarantee of reasonably ripe grapes.

Again, it is the rivers which make this possible. The riverbanks are very steep, sometimes impossibly so, but they provide an elevated and angled piece of land and, in effect, lift the vineyards up into more direct sunlight, providing the essential elements of light and heat. In addition, the mirror surface of the rivers provides reflected light, and the massive bodies of water act as temperature-moderating influences, maintaining warmer air temperatures in September and October as the grapes reach the end of their growing season. This reliance on large bodies of water is common in all grape-growing areas of the world, but it is especially important here, where the rivers provide enough extra heat to allow the mercurial Riesling grape to

**Map 10.3** Mosel-Saar-Ruwer.

ripen fully and develop all of its delicious varietal characteristics. Grape growers also know that the rivers are slower to warm up in springtime, and this holds back the air temperatures on the hillsides, maintaining colder temperatures in the vineyards and delaying budding until most of the dangers of frost are past.

Of all the steep vineyard terraces, it is, understandably, the south-facing hillsides of the Mosel which are most prized. Such vineyards would fetch

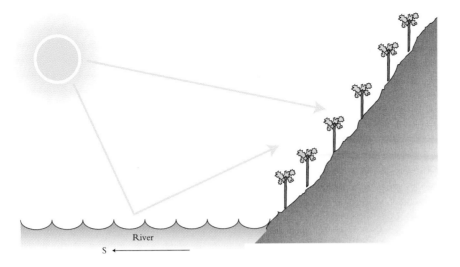

**Figure 10.8** Fluvial Influences.

The rivers play an important role in holding heat during the autumn months and in reflecting light and heat during the growing season.

enormous amounts of money if any grape grower was foolish enough to want to sell such a parcel of land. Figure 10.8 shows how the rivers influence the ability of some parcels to produce grapes of outstanding quality.

Despite the region's notoriously difficult climate, it is still the Riesling grape that is preferred by most growers and wine makers, accounting for about 60 percent of total acreage. The next most common grape in this region is Müller-Thurgau, with very small percentages of Elbling, Bacchus, Optima, and Kerner. The great advantage of new biological crossings like Bacchus and Optima is that they can ripen enough so that decent wine can be made even in years when the weather is not too cooperative. These wines can either be sold under their own varietal name or blended with Riesling to provide the extra ripeness that Riesling wines lack in poor years.

For all these reasons, the Mosel is not the most consistent region in terms of producing fine wines. There are some years when the grapes never reach sufficient maturity, and many producers will not even offer the wines for sale under their name. Plenty of Sekt producers are happy to buy the immature, high-acid grapes, or the finished wines, for their sparkling wine production.

But, when all of the planets are aligned, and all of the omens are right, Mosel wines can be some of the finest on earth. As QbA and QmP wines, they always show an astounding elegance, finesse, and balance of fruit and acidity. Even experienced tasters can be stopped in their tracks by the seemingly impossible high-wire balancing act that the wines represent, treading a very fine line between the fresh, but mouth-filling, Riesling fruit flavors and latent sweetness. At the same time, the lively, crisp citric qualities cleanse the palate and allow the delicate flavors to linger for an impossibly long time in the mouth. These characteristics are visually apparent in the lively tinge of green color of all Mosel wines. By comparison, the wines of the Rhein regions are most often deeper in color, fuller on the palate, and more assertive in aroma and flavor.

Famous villages in this district are:

Wiltingen, with the famous Einzellagen Braune Kupp, Rosenberg, Schlossberg, Kupp, Hölle, and Klosterberg. The most-renowned Einzellage is Scharzhofberger, whose name appears on labels without the town name of Wiltingen.

Ockfen, whose three best-known Einzellagen are Kupp, Herrenberg, and Bockstein.

Ayl, with the famous Einzellagen of Kupp and Herrenberger.

Oberemmel, where Karlsberg, Rosenberg, and Altenberg are the three most significant Einzellagen.

Zell, where the world-famous everyday wine Zeller-Schwarzekatz is made, primarily from Müller-Thurgau grapes.

Even in those rare years when Auslese or Beerenauslese wines are produced, the wines still maintain that alluring freshness and lightness that make them so appealing. Whatever style the wines are made in, they rarely exceed 10 percent alcohol by volume and more often contain 7.5 to 8 percent.

As with all fine wine-producing regions where the wines are named for their place of origin, the name of the producer is an equally important consideration. In the boxes on these pages, we have listed a selection of some of the most important villages, with some of the well-known Grosslagen and Einzellagen in those villages, plus some of the major producer names.

*Rheingau.*  There are a few rare places where it seems that every possible advantage for grape growing and wine making have come together in one glorious spot. The Rheingau (see Map 10.4) is one of those places, and its wine makers rightly boast that they produce some of the finest and most-respected wines in the world.

For most of its journey to the sea, the Rhine River heads in a northerly and northwesterly direction. But at Mainz it turns "left" in a west-south-westerly direction for about 18 miles/30 kilometers until it reaches Rudesheim, where it heads north again. This provides an uninterrupted strip of steep hillside running up from the river with an almost-perfect exposure to the summer sun during the daytime. In addition, the top of the hillside is heavily forested, providing a useful barrier to colder air from the north. Of course, the Rhine itself helps to maintain advantageous temperatures in the spring and autumn.

Kasel, Metersdorf, Waldrach, and Maximin Grünhaus are all famous villages in the Grosslage, Romerlay. Herrenberg and Nieschen are the best Einzellagen in the villages of Kasel and Maximin Grünhaus.

Bernkastel, which produces wines with Bereich labeling, but also contains the great Einzellagen Doktor, and Graben.

Piesport, where the large Grosslage Michelsberg and the Einzellage Goldtröpfchen are the most famous.

Graach, whose perfect location on the river makes it famous for the Einzellage Himmelreich.

Wehlen, which is world famous for the Einzellage Sonnenuhr.

Zeltingen, which is best known for its largest Einzellage, Schlossberg.

Brauneberg, where the finest Einzellage is Juffer.

Even more than the Mosel, the Rheingau is heavily planted with Riesling vines, to the tune of some 80 percent of all plantings. Where other grapes are planted, they are there mostly as a safety valve, to provide ripe juice to enhance the Riesling in those years when it may not ripen fully. The small size of the Rheingau (a little over 1000 acres/400 hectares), makes this region a useful model to explain more fully the systematic way in which all of Germany's quality wine regions are broken into smaller and smaller units (see Table 10.4).

- The name of the Anbaugebiet in this case is the *Rheingau*.

- Each Anbaugebiet can be subdivided into districts, or Bereiche (singu-

**(a)**

RHEINGAU
Village Locations

Lorchausen

Lorch

Rauenthal

Kiedrich

Hallgarten

Erbach

Johannisberg

Aulhausen

Oestrich

Mittelheim

Winkel

Aßmannshausen

Geisenheim

Rüdesheim

Hattenheim

Eltville

Dotzheim

Frauenstein

Martinsthal

Oberwalluf

Schierstein

Niederwalluf

Wiesbaden

Wicker

Hochheim

Flörsheim

Kostheim

Rhein

**(b)**

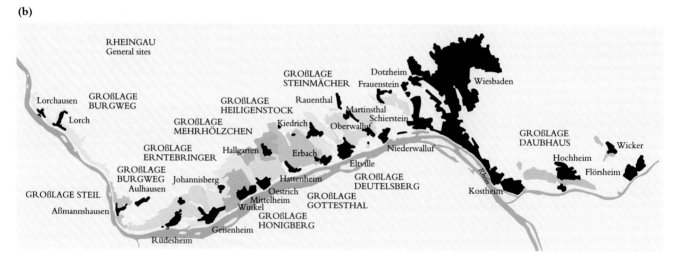

RHEINGAU
General sites

Lorchausen

GROßLAGE
BURGWEG

Lorch

GROßLAGE
STEINMÄCHER

Dotzheim

Frauenstein

Wiesbaden

GROßLAGE
HEILIGENSTOCK

Rauenthal

Martinsthal

Schierstein

GROßLAGE
MEHRHÖLZCHEN

Kiedrich

Oberwalluf

GROßLAGE
ERNTEBRINGER

Hallgarten

Erbach

Niederwalluf

GROßLAGE
DAUBHAUS

Wicker

Hochheim

Flörsheim

GROßLAGE
BURGWEG

Johannisberg

Eltville

GROßLAGE STEIL

Aulhausen

Hattenheim

GROßLAGE
DEUTELSBERG

Aßmannshausen

Oestrich

Mittelheim

Winkel

GROßLAGE
GOTTESTHAL

Kostheim

Geisenheim

GROßLAGE
HONIGBERG

Rüdesheim

Rhein

**(c)**

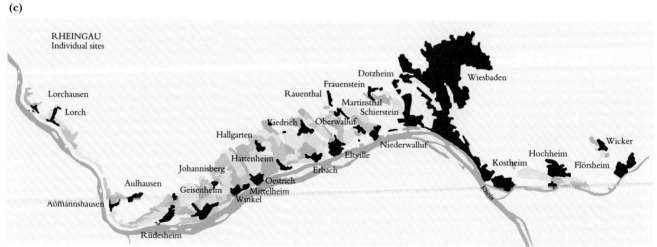

RHEINGAU
Individual sites

Lorchausen

Lorch

Dotzheim

Frauenstein

Wiesbaden

Rauenthal

Martinsthal

Schierstein

Kiedrich

Oberwalluf

Hallgarten

Niederwalluf

Wicker

Hochheim

Johannisberg

Hattenheim

Eltville

Flörsheim

Kostheim

Erbach

Aulhausen

Oestrich

Geisenheim

Mittelheim

Winkel

Aßmannshausen

Rüdesheim

Rhein

**Map 10.4**   Rheingau: a.) the General Area; b.) General Vineyard Sites; c.) Individual Vineyard Sites.

lar, Bereich). The Mosel-Saar-Ruwer region has five Bereiche. The Rheingau has only one such district, called Bereich Johannisberg. In other words, the Anbaugebiet Rheingau is the same unit of land called the Bereich Johannisberg.

- Within each Bereich there are several Grosslagen, or collective vineyards. The Mosel-Saar-Ruwer region has 18 Grosslagen. The Rheingau has only ten.

- Finally, within its Grosslagen the Rheingau boasts the relatively small number of 119 Einzellagen (single vineyard sites), compared to the Mosel-Saar-Ruwer's 506.

As a group, the wines of the Rheingau are considerably fuller in body and flavor than the Mosels. The best of them maintain the elegance and distinction of the Riesling grape grown in a cool climate, but they are generally firmer, riper, richer wines in color, aroma, and taste. As with the other wine regions with "Rhein" as part of their name, Rheingau wines are usually bottled in a tall, slim, brown bottle.

*Pfalz.* The recent history of the Pfalz is a very good example of how rapidly a region can change its identity, and how that rapid change mirrors many of the slower changes in grape growing and wine making that have been taking place in Germany and the rest of Europe over the last two decades. Not too long ago, it was easy to make generalizations: the best Pfalz wines came from the Riesling vineyards in the northern half of the region, with a very large quantity of lesser, ordinary wines produced from Silvaner in the southern half of the region (see Map 10.5). In fact, so much ordinary wine was produced in this region that it had a reputation as the region that produced the largest quantity of wine, even though it is the second largest in acreage.

While it is still true that the most elegant and the finest wines continue to be Rieslings from the northern section, southern grape growers have rev-

## MAJOR RHEINGAU VILLAGES AND VINEYARDS

Eltville contains the Grosslage Steinmacher and the Einzellage Sonnenberg.

Erbach is famous for the Grosslage Deutelsberg and the Einzellage Marcobrunn.

In Hattenheim, the Einzellagen Mannberg, Wisselbrunnen, and Nussbrunnen are best.

In Winkel, the Einzellage Schloss Vollrads is most famous, producing several wines of different quality levels, all noted by colored capsules only! ("Schloss" in German is equivalent to "Château" in French.)

Johannisberg's Einzellage Schloss Johannisberg is the best quality. Many U.S. "White" Rieslings are labeled Johannisberg in deference to this great wine.

Rudesheim contains the Einzellagen Roseneck, and Rosengarten.

## MAJOR PRODUCERS IN THE RHEINGAU REGION

| | |
|---|---|
| Balthasar Ress | Wegeler-Deinhard |
| Riedel | Dr. R. Weil |
| Langwerth von Simmern | Königin Victoria Berg |
| Schloss Vollrads | Schloss Schönborn |
| Schloss Reinhartshausen | Schloss Johannisberg |
| Schloss Groenesteyn | Domdechant Werner'sches Weingut |
| Verwaltung der Staatsweingüter Eltville | |

**Map 10.5**  The Pfalz Region.

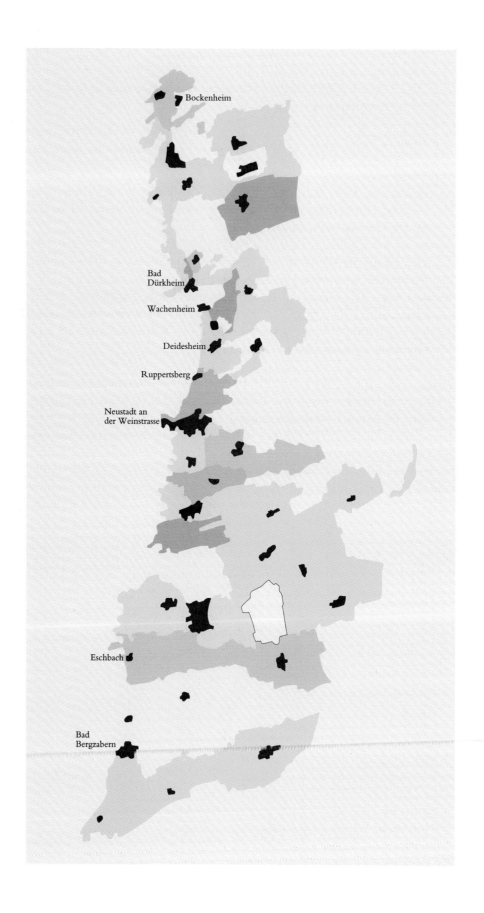

Bockenheim

Bad
Dürkheim

Wachenheim

Deidesheim

Ruppertsberg

Neustadt an
der Weinstrasse

Eschbach

Bad
Bergzabern

## BETTINA BÜRKLIN-WOLF

In 1875, the two families of Bürklin and Wolf were joined by marriage, forming what remains today as the largest privately owned wine-producing estate in Germany. Currently, the company is headed by Bettina Bürklin-Wolf whose father died in 1979 after guiding the company to prominence from 1924. On his death, Dr. Bürklin-Wolf's widow continued his work with the able assistance and skills of the much-respected wine maker Georg Raquet.

Now that Bettina heads the company, she controls a veritable wealth of famous vineyard plots, all located within the most prized section of the Pfalz, in and around the villages of Wachenheim, Forst, Ruppertsberg, and Deidesheim.

Like Dr. Raquet before her, Bettina Bürklin-Wolf trained at the Wine Academy at Geisenheim, and continues the philosophy of maintaining the traditions that make Bürklin-Wolf wines outstanding, while adopting innovations that can only improve the wines. Temperature-controlled stainless steel tanks and computer technology are found right alongside large oak fermenters, providing fresh, crisp fruit characteristics as a counterpoint to the depth and firmness obtained from optimum quality fruit from some of the most highly prized vineyard land in the region. The respect for tradition and the courage to try new things is also alive and well in the cellars at Bürklin-Wolf where Fritz Knorr, a sixth generation cellar-master, vigilantly watches over the wines until they are ready for bottling.

## PFALZ VILLAGES AND VINEYARDS

Ruppertsberg includes the Einzellagen Linsenbusch and Hoheburg.

Deidesheim boasts the Grosslage Hofstuck and the Einzellage Herrgottsacker.

In Forst are the Grosslage Mariengarten and the Einzellage Ungeheuer.

Wachenheim has the Grosslage Schenkenböhl and the Einzellage Mandelgarten.

---

olutionized their vineyard practices and planted newer grape varieties, such as Müller-Thurgau, Scheurebe, and Morio-Muskat. The result is that some fine wines from southern vineyards now compete for attention with the northern Rieslings.

Overall, Pfalz wines are recognized as being sturdier, higher in alcohol, rounder styles of German wine, with slightly lower acidity levels because of the warmer climate. The wines often show a light "earthiness" or spiciness. These characteristics make these some of Germany's most food-compatible wines, since they have the structure and authority to match even the strong flavors of game fish and meats.

***Rheinhessen.*** Rheinhessen has the largest vineyard area in all of Germany, though its production is second to that of the Pfalz. A fertile, flat plain located within the broad sweep of the Rhein where it changes direction at Mainz (see Map 10.2.), the region previously had large plantings of Silvaner. It now boasts high percentages of the newer crossings of Scheurebe, Kerner, and Bacchus. Each of these varieties can produce more than the average Riesling vine (which account for only five percent of all vine plantings in Rheinhessen). Additionally, the region is famous as the home of the original

## MAJOR PRODUCERS IN THE PFALZ REGION

Balbach Erben
Basserman Jordan
Dr. Bürklin-Wolf
Deinhard
Furst von Metternich
Sichel Söhne
Graf Matuschka-Greiffenclau'sche Guterverwaltung

# PETER M.F. SICHEL

It is curious, but extremely touching, to hear Peter Maximilien Ferdinand Sichel tell the story of how, as a captain in the United States army, he led the troops into his hometown in Germany in 1945 to find that the Nazis had not discovered the huge quantities of wine that his wine-making family had hidden away before fleeing the Nazi threat.

Since that time, Peter Sichel has led the company of H. Sichel Söhne Inc. back to prominence as a major producer and as a *negotiant* and exporter of German estate wines to numerous countries around the world. To many wine consumers, Peter Sichel will always be remembered as the man who continued the incredible success story of "Blue Nun," the Liebfraumilch wine that took many wine-importing countries by storm in the 1970s and made that style of German wine a household commodity for many people. In fact, the wine had been marketed by the Sichel company since the 1920s, and became known as Blue Nun from a label designed in 1925 which depicted nuns in blue habit harvesting grapes. Originally the words "Blue Nun" were not on the label. They were added later when consumers started asking for "the Blue Nun wine."

For all the success of Blue Nun, Peter would perhaps prefer to be known as the *negotiant* who has made available the fine wines of small growers for the enjoyment of wine lovers everywhere. Working with reputable but small estates that do not have the capital and equipment to produce and bottle their own wines, Sichel buys the wine from these small growers, bottles and labels it with the grower's estate name, and distributes the wines. By this process, fine wines, which otherwise might be destined for blending by a large cooperative, can be enjoyed as the singular product of an individual vineyard.

With this firmly established philosophy for the future, Peter has secured the continued success of the Sichel name by handing over the reins to his highly capable daughter, Bettina. There are certainly no indications of doubt when he quips "Oh I don't work any more!" After 50 years of doggedly promoting German wines to all wine consumers, Peter Sichel undoubtedly deserves to be able to sit back and enjoy his reputation as dedicated ambassador of German wine.

# LIEBFRAUMILCH

Most people have at least heard of, if not drunk, one of the wines called Goldener Oktober, or Blue Nun, or Hans Christof, or Black Tower. What many people do not realize is that each of these brand-name wines, and many, many more, are examples of an official category of German wine called Liebfraumilch.

The name means "the milk of our Dear Lady," or "the Virgin Mary," and it was originally applied to wines produced from a single vineyard surrounding a church called the *Liebfrauenkirche* in the town of Worms. Slowly but surely, the name was usurped by other producers inside and outside the region of Rheinhessen, with the result that any original style and character was lost in a veritable sea of Liebfraumilch.

In 1971, in an attempt to limit any fraudulent use of the name Liebfraumilch, laws were enacted to ensure that any wine labeled as such had to be produced at Qualitätswein level as a single regional wine, or a blend from any of the regions of Nahe, Rheingau, Pfalz, and Rheinhessen. Subsequent legislation decreed that Liebfraumilch cannot be blended from different regions, but must originate from within one of the listed regions. In addition, it is now required that at least 70 percent of the wine (previously 50 percent) must come from Riesling, Silvaner, Müller-Thurgau, or Kerner, as a single varietal or as a blend.

The label (see Figure 10.9) will show the following information: (1) the word *Liebfraumilch;* (2) the name of the region; (3) the name of the brand, if any; and (4) the name of the producer. The label *cannot* show any vineyard name, any *Bereich* name, or any grape variety names.

Liebfraumilch, which still makes up at least half of the total quantity of German wine in the export market.

The wines of the Rheinhessen are most appreciated for their soft, mild, flowery aromas and flavors, which show many of the newer grape crossings in their best light. They are straightforward, unpretentious wines, enjoyable as a chilled drink on their own or with simple food.

The best-known area for quality wine production in Rheinhessen is around the village of Nierstein, with its well-known Grosslage Niersteiner Gutes Domtal, and its fine Einzellage Findling.

# New Types of German Wine

Through the activities of the German government, the regional A.P. boards, associations of growers and producers, or a combination of some or all of these entities, several new types of wines have been introduced in Germany. The purpose of creating these wine types is to raise quality levels, to draw attention to regional and local grape varieties and wine styles, and to improve marketing of regional wines. The following sections describe some of these new German regional wines.

***Charta Wines.*** Charta Wine Estates was formed by an association of estate wine producers in the Rheingau. The goal of Charta is to enhance the reputation of the producers' wines, which are considered to be the finest Riesling wines of the region. Charta wines must be 100 percent Riesling (see Figure 10.10), with higher minimum sugar levels than the national laws set for QbA, Kabinett and Spätlese wines. With a minimum acidity of 7.5 percent, and allowable residual sugar of between 9 and 18 grams per liter (.9 to 1.8 percent residual sugar), Charta wines are semidry. They are bottled with labels illustrating twin Roman arches (see Figure 10.11), and the wines cannot be released before October of the year following the harvest. Most Charta wines are expensive and achieve astonishing quality levels.

***Rheinhessen Silvaner.*** The category of Rheinhessen Silvaner wines was created by the Rheinhessen Promotion Board. These QbA and Sekt "RS" wines (the letters appear on the requisite black and yellow label) demonstrate the quality possible in dry wines made totally from the ancient Silvaner grape. RS wines must be estate bottled and cannot exceed four grams of sugar per liter (.4 percent of residual sugar) making them truly trocken. The wines must contain at least five grams per liter (.5 percent) of total acidity and, in addition to passing the A.P. board examination, must be tasted by a special panel before they are released (no sooner than March of the year following harvest).

***Der Neue Wines.*** Like most wine-producing nations, Germany wants to produce a *nouveau* or *primeur*-style wine. "The New" *(Der Neue)* wines are Landwein (with QbA a possibility in the future) sold from November 10

The *Liebfrauenkirche* Church in the Town of Worms.

**Figure 10.9** A Liebfraumilch Label.

**Figure 10.10** A Charta Label.

**Figure 10.11** The Twin Roman Arches of a Charta Label.

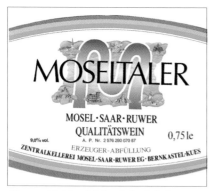

**Figure 10.12** A Moseltaler Label.

through January 15 following the harvest. Obviously, the idea is to produce a vintage wine that is young, fresh, and appealing—in a word, *Neue* wine.

*Moseltaler.*    Moseltaler was introduced in 1986 to create a typical Mosel-style wine from a blend of regional grapes, and with easy-to-read labels, including a blue M (see Figure 10.12).

*Der Rheinhess.*    Der Rheinhess takes a similar approach, but using the blended QbA halbtrocken wines of the Rheinhessen; it is sold only in one-liter bottles.

*Nahesteiner.*    Nahesteiner use the same approach again for the QbA-blended wines of the Nahe region. Using Müller-Thurgau, Silvaner, and Riesling varieties only, Nahesteiner wines are all halbtrocken in style.

*Pfalzer Löwe.*    Pfalzer Löwe mimics the other regions in intent but focuses on an easy-to-drink Pfalz halbtrocken wine made from Müller-Thurgau, Weissburgunder (Pinot Blanc), and Kerner grapes.

## Summary

For two millennia now, despite the inconsistent weather patterns, the lands which make up Germany have been used to grow grapes for wine production. Given the relatively cool climate, Germany's wine producers concentrate on white wines with high acidity and crisp, fresh fruit character. With extreme diligence and devotion, extraordinary wines are sometimes produced in what appear to be unfavorable conditions. It is unfortunate that current wine fashion does not sing the praises of German wines as loudly as they deserve, but fashions come and go. For the true wine lover, the wines of Germany hold a long-lasting attraction.

With the wine laws and organizational systems of other European countries already understood, we have attempted to show here that the language of the label need not be a barrier. With a little application, anyone can decipher even the most intimidating German wine label to discover the secrets locked within. And we feel that the rewards will merit the effort.

# Central and Eastern Europe

## Introduction

In this chapter we will discuss the major wine-producing countries of Central Europe (Switzerland and Austria), Eastern Europe (Hungary, Romania), and the Confederation of Independent States (Moldavia, Ukraine, Russia, and Bulgaria). We will discuss the history, wine laws, and regions of each country.

The wines from these countries have a small or negligible presence in the international and export markets and some, like Austria, suffer from an identity crisis.

Unlike Eastern Europe, whose constituent countries are neither members of the European Community (EC), nor economically stable, Switzerland and Austria have been unified countries for hundreds of years. While Austria's people, politics, and economy were devastated by World War II, today it is a modern, postindustrial European nation, much like its neighbor and former ruler, Germany. Ever-neutral Switzerland has maintained a healthy economy and stable political base for hundreds of years.

Swiss wines, made from native vinifera grapes as well as French varietals, are not well known in the North American export market, and tend to be quite expensive. Austrian wines have a minimal presence in the United States and Canada, where they, like the French wines of Alsace, are often mistaken for German wines. Eastern Europe is going through a turbulent period of political change, and while wine production may not seem like an important issue when people are fighting for basic survival, wine is a major agricultural and industrial sector of commerce in this part of the world. The next decade will be difficult for the wines of Eastern Europe. In order to compete internationally, standards of quality tolerated under the previous Communist government must be supplanted by a commitment to making consistent, high-quality wines.

Where do Eastern European wines fit in the wine world? Many of the indigenous grapes of these nations have been abandoned in order to produce a more "international" style of wine from French and German vinifera. This is a direction that will definitely continue in order to ensure survival in the marketplace, but it is an unfortunate historical and cultural trend. In their quest for international presence, these countries are losing their historical and cultural heritage. Most likely, the Eastern European nations will do global battle at the "fighting varietal" level, with wines made largely from Chardonnay, Merlot, and Cabernet Sauvignon. The wines will be priced aggressively and feature varietal labels, in order to compete against wines from the New World—the Americas, Australia, New Zealand, and South Africa—and inexpensive wines from the South of France.

# Central Europe

## *Switzerland*

### SWITZERLAND'S WINE PRODUCERS AND NÉGOCIANTS

Some of Switzerland's best-known wine producers and négociants are Domaine de Mont d'Or, Testuz, Indermuhle, Château de Vinzel, Cantine Valsangiacomo, Château d'Auvernier, Robert Gilliard, Henri Badoux, Jean Bernard Rouvinez, Tenuta Montalbano, and Château de Thun.

The small nation of Switzerland is nestled between the mountains of the Jura and the Alps. Most of the 38,000 acres/14,000 hectares under vine are located in the French-speaking "Romande" area of Switzerland, 26,400 acres/11,000 hectares, producing 11 million cases of wine per year), although the famous Neuchatel *canton* (province) in the northwest has a largely German-speaking population, and the red-wine region of Ticino is an Italian-speaking canton. Switzerland's total wine production is 22 million gallons/55 million liter, of which 75 percent is white wine. While Switzerland is hardly a major producer of wine, its citizens consume a healthy 20 gallons/50 liters of wine per capita, and the Swiss have shown a particular affinity for the wines of Italy and France, as well as for the local product. It is no secret that the Swiss save their best wines for the domestic market, but they also support an active import market for foreign wines.

***Wine Laws.*** The first modern Swiss agricultural laws were passed in 1936, and in 1953 the first wine statutes were proposed. In 1988, Appellation d'Origine Côntrolée (AOC) laws, similar to the French wine laws,

Lake Geneva, Switzerland.

were passed by Switzerland's Fédération des Caves Genevoises. Because Switzerland is a recent member of the EC, the wines must adhere to the wine laws of the federation, but currently there are no national percentage requirements for either viticultural areas or varietal types for any Swiss wines. While the term "Premier Cru" may appear on a Swiss wine label, it is not a guarantee of quality. Some sweet wines from Switzerland are labeled *"avec sucre résiduel"* ("with residual sugar").

*Wine Regions.* Since grape vines are planted everywhere from the valley floors to the foothills of the Alps, the vineyards of Switzerland (see Map 11.1) enjoy a wide range of microclimates. The coolest vineyard sites seek southern exposure to ensure as much sunshine as possible. The cost of labor in Switzerland is high, but both irrigation and chaptalization are legal in Switzerland, so harvest yields tend to be high as well. Switzerland's vineyards produce more than 40 varieties of wine grapes.

The most important wine regions of Switzerland are all named after their home cantons. They include Valais, Vaud, Geneva, Neuchâtel, and Ticino.

*Valais.* Located in the south of Switzerland, with many of its vineyards planted on the right bank of the Rhône River, Valais is quite a dry area, so the vignerons here depend on irrigation. Fully one-third of the nation's vineyards are planted in this canton, and holdings can be tiny. There are 20,000 growers in Valais, but only 12,355 acres/5000 hectares, with vines planted at altitudes as high as 3700 feet/1100 meters.

The most widely planted white grape in Valais is the Chasselas, which produces the light, crisp, fruity wine, Fendant (see Figure 11.1). Best drunk young, Fendant's label often includes the name of the town in which it was

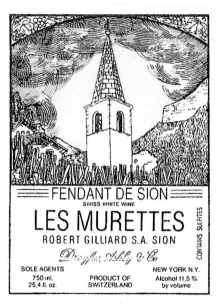

**Figure 11.1** A Wine from the Valais Region, Fendant de Sion is Made from the Chasselas Grape.

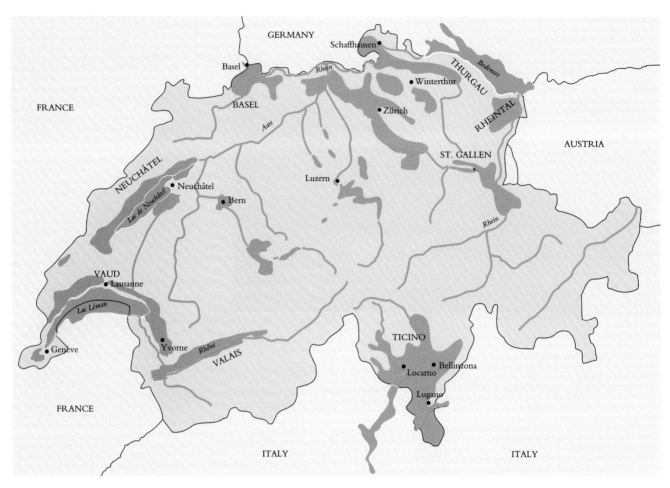

**Map 11.1** The Wine Regions of Switzerland.

Aging Blauburgunder (Pinot Noir) in Bottles at the Nussbaumer Winery Outside of Basel, Switzerland.

produced (*e.g.,* Fendant de Sion). Another important white wine from Valais is Johannisberg. Produced from Sylvaner grapes, Johannisberg often attains higher alcohol levels than the lighter, fresher Fendant.

Switzerland's most famous red wine, Dôle, also originates in the Valais region. It is a blend of at least 51 percent Pinot Noir, Switzerland's preeminent red varietal, with the balance being Gamay grapes. Dôle Blanche and Rosé du Valais are also made from the same grape varieties. While Dôle, Fendant, and Johannisberg account for most of the wine produced in Valais, other white wines include the high-alcohol Malvoisie, made from the Pinot Gris varietal, and Ermitage, made from the Marsanne grape. The native Armigne and Petite Arvine grapes produce white wines that are dry and spicy. The best of these wines can age gracefully, and the wines made from Petite Arvigne can resemble Viognier-based white wines from the Rhône Valley. Local specialty wines are also made.

*Vaud.*  Located in the southwest, close by Lakes Leman and Morat, fully 80 percent of plantings in Vaud are Chasselas, and the wines produced here may bear the name of the canton, district (*e.g.,* Lavaux), or smaller cru appellation (*e.g.,* Dézaley). The major wine districts of the Vaud region are La Cote, Lavaux, Le Chablais, Le Vully, Côte de L'Orbes, and Bonvillars. Dézaley and Calamin are crus that produce red wines made from Pinot Noir and Gamay and white wines made from Chasselas. (See Figures 11.2, 11.3, and 11.4.)

*Geneva.*  There are only 2400 acres/1000 hectares under vine in and around the Geneva canton, but it was the first to apply for Swiss appellation côntrolée status. The Chasselas, here called Perlan, accounts for 50 percent of

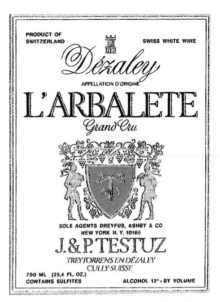

**Figure 11.2**  A Wine from the Vaud Region, Dézaley is a *Cru* Label. Dézaley's White Wines are Made from Chasselas Grapes, Its Reds from Pinot Noir and Gamay.

**Figure 11.3**  A White Wine from the Henri Badoux, a Major Wine Producer in the Vaud Canton.

**Figure 11.4**  Aigle is an Important Wine Village Situated on the Vaudois River.

The Nussbaumer Vineyards in the Neuchâtel Wine Region.

**Figure 11.5** An Unusual Label from the Nussbaumer Winery in the Neuchâtel Region.

**Figure 11.6** A Neuchâtel Wine Made from Riesling and Sylvaner Grapes.

vines planted. Red grapes are dominated by Gamay, with 30 percent of the vineyards in Geneva planted to this varietal.

*Neuchâtel.* There are 5280 acres/2200 hectares under vine in this northwestern canton on the banks of the lake of the same name. German-speaking Neuchâtel produces mostly Blauburgunder (Pinot Noir)-based wines (see Figures 11.5 and 11.6), which benefit from the warm *foehn* winds from the southeast and shelter from the Jura Mountains to the west.

*Ticino.* If you take the train to Ticino from almost any other town in Switzerland, it must travel into Italy before returning into Switzerland. The Italian culture and language dominate here. Most of the 2880 acres/1200 hectares under vine in this eastern canton bordering bucolic Lake Lugano are planted in Merlot, and most of the wine is made in the lighter Italian style. A sign of quality on a Ticino label is the word *"Viti,"* which means that the wine has passed a tasting analysis and is 100 percent Merlot. As in Neuchâtel, white-wine production is minimal in Ticino.

## Austria

**History.** Almost 3,000 years ago the Celts controlled the land that is now Austria, and these ancient inhabitants made wine. By 800 A.D., Charlemagne, Holy Roman Emperor, promulgated guidelines for viticulture and classified the vines of this area into *Frankish,* which represented the best varietals, and *Heunisch,* the minor Eastern European varietals. Charlemagne also established *Buschschenken,* the taverns or inns where vineyard owners sold their wines directly to the public.

In the Middle Ages, wine was produced largely at Austria's monasteries. Perhaps the most significant of these was the Cistercian Brotherhood, who brought the Pinot Noir grape (renamed Grauer Monch, which translates as "Gray Monk") from their native Burgundy. Benedictine monasteries were also responsible for the development of many vineyards, and some of modern Austria's most famous vineyards (Pfaffenberg and Sandgrube) were already well known as early as the thirteenth century. The Riesling grape, originally cultivated in Germany, was introduced to Austria around this time, and by the early 1500s Trockenbeerenauslese wines (see Chapter 10 on Germany) were being produced in some of present-day Austria's vineyards.

Austria is home to the world's oldest oenology school at Klosterneuburg, founded in 1860, about the same time Chardonnay (here called Morillon) grapes were introduced. In the nineteenth century, serious production of Sekt wines (see Chapter 10 on Germany) began. In 1866 a killing frost destroyed many of Austria's best vineyards and, as in the rest of Europe, Austria's vineyards fell victim to *phylloxera* shortly before the turn of the century. A painful process of rebuilding began, including the adoption of American rootstock and the development of new, more frost-resistant grape

types, such as Grüner Veltliner, Neuberger, and Zierfandler. These and other new varietals were developed in the laboratories of the Klosterneuberg wine academy, starting in the early twentieth century. Another important development in Austrian wine technology was the Lenz-Moser system *Hochkultur*— a method of trellising vines vertically, in order to allow for mechanical harvesting. To this day, fully 75 percent of Austria's vineyards employ this trellising system.

The Austrian wine scandal of 1985, involving the addition of diethylene glycol (a sweetening agent that renders wine more luscious and viscous) to export wines, may have been a blessing in disguise for the Austrian wine industry. Condemnation of the industry was swift and devastating, especially due to the fact that the *diethylene* glycol, which is less toxic than alcohol, was misunderstood to be *ethylene* glycol or, in common parlance, antifreeze. The actions of a few unscrupulous wine makers ruined the export market for 40,000 Austrian producers. Driven by the need to survive, the wine industry adopted the philosophy of "quality before quantity" and the Austrian wine laws of 1972 (see below) were revamped and toughened in 1985. In 1989, the letter "Q" was adopted as a quality designation for all Austrian wines that meet government standards.

*Wine Laws.*    Austrian wines are classified chiefly by grape variety and geographic origin, method of harvesting the grapes and, perhaps most important, amount of sugar in the grape must, Austria's wine producers use the *Klosterneuburger Mostwaage* (KMW) scale. Developed in 1869 at Austria's heralded enology school by A.v. Babo, the director of Klosterneuburger, this scale is expressed in degrees, such that 1° KMW is roughly equivalent to one percent sugar in the grape must.

Whenever a grape type is indicated on a bottle of Austrian wine, no matter the quality level, the wine must contain at least 85 percent of that varietal. The same percentage applies to the label's vintage year. If a growing area is indicated on the label, 100 percent of the grapes must come from that area. If the wine is labeled simply as Austrian wine, all grapes must have been grown in the country.

Much like Germany, Austria categorizes its lesser wines as Tafelwein and Landwein, which must measure minimum must weights of 13° and 14° KMW respectively. Austria's Qualitätswein (minimum 15° KMW) may be lightly chaptalized, but at the higher Kabinett level (17° KMW minimum, and its own quality classification in Austria), and the highest classification level, Prädikatswein, chaptalization is forbidden.

In order to attain Prädikatswein status, the wine must:

• be made with grapes from one growing area

• be certified by Austria's must weighing panel, the *Mostwaager*

• show an official examination number and vintage on the label

• not be chaptalized nor use *süssreserve* in the production of the wine.

All Prädikatswein must also fall into one of the following quality categories:

- Spätlese: the grapes must be completely ripe at harvest, with a minimum KMW of 19°.

- Auslese: ripe grapes only, with any unripe grapes removed from the bunch, with a minimum KMW of 21°.

- Strohwein: grapes must be a minimum of 25°KMW, overripe, and stored on straw mats for at least three months.

- Eiswein: produced from grapes that must be frozen when picked and pressed at a minimum KMW of 25°.

- Beerenauslese: grapes must be overripe or *botrytis*-affected, minimum KMW of 25°.

- Ausbruch: grapes must exhibit noble rot and reach a minimum of 27° KMW.

- Trockenbeerenauslese: the great majority of the grapes must show botrytis, with a minimum of 32° KMW.

The wines of Austria range from quite dry to very sweet, and legal guidelines describe the style of the wines. Trocken (dry) wines must contain less than .12 ounces (four grams) of sugar per .26 gallons (one liter), and halbtrocken must contain at least .18 ounces (five grams) but less than .32 ounces (nine grams) per .26 gallons (one liter). *Halbsuss* (half sweet) wines must contain a minimum of .35 ounces (ten grams) but less than .63 ounces (18 grams) per .26 gallons (one liter), while *Süss* (sweet wines) must contain over .63 ounces (18 grams) per .26 gallons (one liter).

***Major Grape Varieties.*** The 45,600 acres/19,000 hectares of Grüner-Veltliner planted in Austria account for more than a third of the nation's vines (see Figure 11.7). This grape ripens late and usually gives a wine with a pale color and a green tint. Muskiness, smokiness, or white pepper may be found in the nose, while the taste is tart. The wine may be prickly with a light to medium body, and most of it is made without aging in oak. Wine made from this varietal is best consumed within a couple of years.

Planted in eight percent of Austria's vineyards, the Welschriesling grape is another late-ripening grape that produces light-bodied tart wines with a spicy nose. Burgenland produces *botrytis* examples that are fuller in body and richness.

With nine percent of Austria's vineyards, the Müller-Thurgau grape produces wines with a floral nose and more body than the Grüner-Veltliner.

Rotgipfler and Zierfandler are the two white grapes that are blended to produce the famous Gumpoldskirchener wine. This dry wine has a spicy, perfumed nose and is full bodied. These grapes conspire to make lovely sweet wines, as well.

**Figure 11.7** Grüner Veltliner is an Important White Grape in Austria. Note This Label Designation, *Trocken,* Indicating a dry wine.

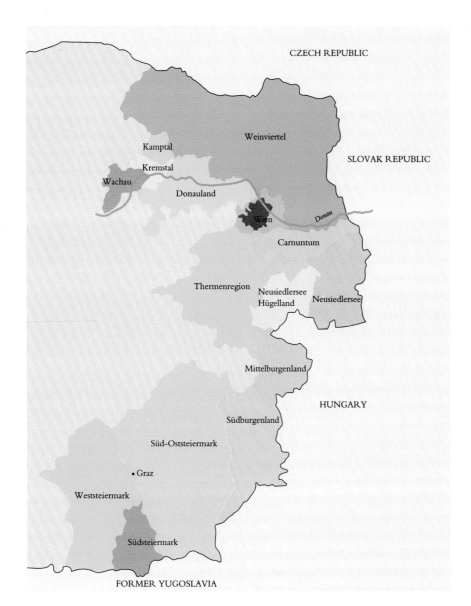

**Map 11.2**   The Wine Regions of Austria.

Blauer Portugieser is Austria's dominant red grape, with about 8000 acres/3200 hectares under vine, followed by the Blau Zweigelt varietal with 7000 acres/2800 hectares. Together these red grapes account for 11 percent of the nation's wines, producing light-bodied, fruity, dry reds.

*Regions.*   Austria has just over 144,000 acres/60,000 hectares under vine (see Map 11.2), mostly in the eastern half of the country.

*Niederösterreich.*   About 60 percent of the vineyards are located in the five growing districts of Austria's largest wine region Niederösterreich (Lower Austria). The five growing districts, all situated along Austria's legendary Danube river, are Weinviertel, Kamptal-Donauland, Donauland-Carnuntum, Thermenregion, and Wachau. Fine dry wines, mostly at the Kabinett

**Figure 11.8** A Sweet Wine made from the Rotgipfler Grape, from the Thermenregion Appellation, Located on the Banks of the Danube. This Wine is High in Residual Sugar and Alcohol (14 percent).

**Figure 11.9** A Red Wine from the Burgenland Region of Austria. The Blaufränkisch Grape is also Found in Eastern Europe.

level, are made here, as well as Sekt. The Thermenregion, south of Vienna, encompasses the famous wine village of Gumpoldskirchen (see Figure 11.8).

*Burgenland.* Burgenland is Austria's second-largest region, with about 48,000 acres/20,000 hectares under vine. Bordering Hungary, Burgenland's four wine districts are Neusiedlersee, Neusiedlersee-Hügelland, Mittelburgenland, and Südburgenland. Burgenland, a relatively warm growing area, is known for its light-bodied red wines and sweet white wines, now being made in a modern style, based on cool fermentation with less oak aging (see Figure 11.9).

*Steiermark (Styria).* Steiermark (Styria), nestled in the Southern Alps, with vineyards at high elevations, accounts for only about five percent of Austria's total vineyards. Styria's three wine regions are the South, best known for rich, aromatic white wines, the Southeast, with its volcanic soil in the Klöcherberg vineyard, and West Styria, which produces the fruity, acidic, and low-alcohol rosé called Schilcher. Together, these three regions make up a total of about 6480 acres/2700 hectares.

*Vienna.* There are about 1680 acres/700 hectares of vineyards within Vienna's city limits and environs. Both white and red wines are made here, and more than a third of the vines are cultivated in vineyards of mixed white and red grapes. The grapes are picked, pressed, and vinified together, a time-honored approach to growing grapes and making wine called "Gemischter Satz" (literally, "mixed batch").

> Major Austrian wine producers include Lenz Moser, Pichler, Freie Weingartner, Hirtzberger, Stiegelmar, Brundlmayer, Jurtschitsch, Holler, Schandl, Mantlerhof, Knoll, Salomon, Tement, and Polz. Two large wine cooperatives are Burgenlandischer Winzverband and Winzergegenossenschaft St. Martinus.

# Eastern Europe

Historically, wine's place in Eastern Europe (see Map 11.3) has gone through periods of expansion and contraction. During the sixteenth and seventeenth centuries many nations were under the rule of the Moslem Ottomans, whose faith forbids wine consumption. The devastation wrought by *phylloxera* in the late nineteenth century was followed by the World Wars, by Communist control, and the present period of violence and uncertainty, as different groups seek to establish their political autonomy. After World War II many small farms were reorganized into large cooperatives where quantity was stressed over quality production. The majority of wines were meant

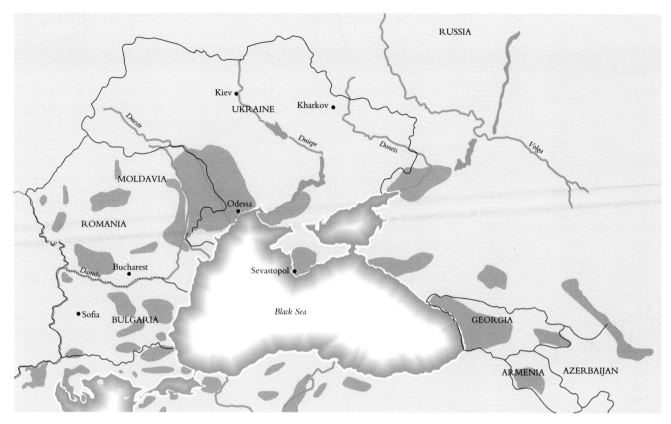

**Map 11.3**    The Wine Regions of Eastern Europe.

for consumption within the Communist bloc, and prices had to be low. The Russian penchant for some residual sugar in both still and sparkling wines was not shared by most of the international market, which preferred drier wines.

During the 1980s Russian President Gorbachev attempted to reduce alcoholism by limiting the amount of alcohol available. As a result, many vineyards were uprooted and replaced with other crops. Another problem was, and continues to be, less-than-total cleanliness of wine-making facilities and storage containers, such as vats, corks, and bottles. Neglect in these areas leads to inconsistent or flawed wines, some with unpleasant smells and tastes. Today these problems are being addressed, as international funds and wine advisors are working to map out a new direction for these wines. Wine laws are being updated, and so are vineyards and wineries.

## Hungary

Hungary, the world's eleventh-largest wine-producing nation, with a per-capita consumption of 12 gallons/30 liters per year, exports more than half of its annual 115 million gallons/4.6 million hectoliter production. The Federation of Hungarian Growers is involved with wine production, and

Eastern European wines are in a state of flux, due to a change from state-operated monopolies to private enterprise, but some of the brand labels to look for are Duna (from Hungary), Trakia (from Bulgaria), Premiat (from Romania), and Avia (from the former Yugoslavia). These brands, developed for the New World market, feature varietal labels, and deliver good value, usually less than $5 per bottle. The moderately priced "Bull's Blood" and the expensive, regional Tokaji Aszu, both from Hungary (see sidebars in this chapter) can be found easily.

the Association of Wine Merchants has replaced the federal monopoly, Monimpex, to lead export efforts. The term "Minesogi Bor" is the current designation for higher-quality or reserve-style wines found in the export market.

As with other Eastern European nations, the 1990s is a period of change for Hungary, as it strives to attract international investment to upgrade and expand production. A consortium of Western investors, led by Piero Antinori of Tuscany, is working with the Voolyseg Nepe Cooperative in the southern region of Szeksárd to make dry wines from international (Chardonnay) and local (Kéfrankos) grapes. Northeast of Budapest, the Gyongös winery makes dry whites, such as Chardonnay and Sauvignon Blanc under the direction of Hugh Ryman of Britain. Ryman is also involved with the Australian firm Penfolds, in Moldavia. Kym Milne, an Australian wine maker, is helping the Balaton Boglár company produce wines with international appeal.

During the Communist era, Hungarovin, the state-controlled trust, produced its own wines and controlled the production of others within the country. Hungarovin has been purchased by Henkell, a German firm famous for its sparkling wines. St. Stephan's Crown, named after Hungary's first king, will be the brand name for their varietal-based wines in the United States.

*Grape Types.* Two-thirds of Hungary's production is white wine. Furmint, the principal grape for Tokaji, an internationally acclaimed sweet wine, is also used throughout the nation for dry wines. Another grape used in Tokaji is Hárslevelü, or "lime leaf," which may be less acidic and not reach the sugar levels of Furmint, but contributes powerful, spicy aromatics. A third grape found in the Tokaji region and elsewhere is the Muskotályos, or Muscat Blancs à Petits Grains, used for semisweet and sweet wines. The Ezerjó is widely planted and can make light-bodied crisp whites, such as those from the Mór area. Mezesfehér is used to make dessert-style whites. Other eastern varieties include the white Feteasca of Romania, called Léanyka, and Austria's Grüner Veltliner, known as Zöldveltelini. The Austrian red grape Blaufränkisch, which may be labeled as "Nagyburgundi" or "Kéfrankos," is known for its high acidity. Szürkebarát is a Pinot Gris and Tamini is the Gewürtraminer grape.

Kadarka is the most-planted varietal, perhaps because of its ability to make full-bodied spicy reds with the power to match heavy dishes, such as gulyas and charcuterie, especially the peppery salamis of Szeged. Kadarka is quite resistant to disease and can give high yields. Sometimes it is also harvested late, to produce a wine with some sweetness, such as Nemes Kadar, which has about one ounce/28 grams of residual sugar per liter.

As in Australia, Rhein Riesling is sometimes used for the true white riesling varietal, while Olaszriesling is the same as the lesser Welschriesling found throughout eastern Europe. A wine labeled Cabernet may be from either the Sauvignon or Franc types and "Médoc Noir" may be used for Merlot.

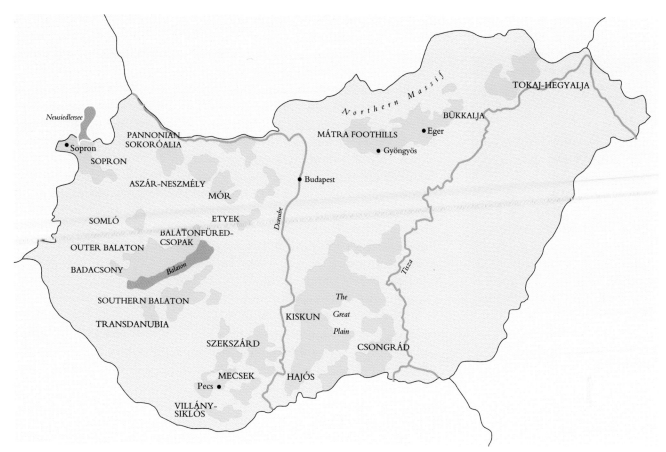

**Map 11.4** The Wine Regions of Hungary.

***Regions.*** The nation (see Map 11.4) is dissected by the Danube river, which is known as Duna in Hungary. Lake Balaton, Europe's largest lake, provides a moderating influence to the wines of the Transdubia region surrounding it. Traditional grape types are planted in the volcanic based soils of Badascony to the north of the lake, while international varieties such as Chardonnay and Cabernet Sauvignon are found on the fertile southern shores. South of the lake are the warmer Szeksard and Villany Siklos areas, producing mostly reds from the local Kadarka and international varieties. The Siklos subregion of Villany Siklos specializes in whites, while the nation's warmest region, the Meksek Hills, produces both white and red wines from local and international types.

*Great Plain.* East of the Danube is the Great Plain region where over half of all Hugary's wines are produced. The area was heavily planted after the late-nineteenth century *phylloxera* epidemic, when research showed that its sandier soils would be inhospitable to the deadly pest. Here, flat lands make mechanized harvesting easy, but the area suffers from dry, hot summers and possible frost damage in colder seasons.

**Figure 11.10** An Export Label for the Legendary Hungarian Red Wine, Egri Bikavér, or "Bull's Blood."

## "BULL'S BLOOD"

Hungary produces the famous Egri Bikavér, or "Bull's Blood," wine in the area around the town of Eger (see Figure 11.10). The name dates back to a battle with the Ottomans in 1540, when the largely outnumbered Hungarians were able to defend the castle due to the powers of the wine. According to one legend, the enemy was frightened by the beards of the soldiers, which were stained red from the wine; another states that the swords of the enemy could not cut through the Magyar (Hungarian) blood thickened by the wine. The wine is still produced in a full-bodied, rich-fruit style, and its popularity on the domestic and international market continues. Formerly based on Kadarka, today the blend is 40 percent Kéfrankos and 30 percent Oporto local grapes with the balance equally divided between Merlot and Cabernet Sauvignon. These are grown on the black-clay-and-lime foothills of the Bükk Mountains.

*Mátra.* The foothills of the Mátra Mountains are another wine-growing region specializing in whites, such as the local Debrói Hárslevelü with an average sugar level of ½ ounce/14.5 grams per liter. The Gyöngös winery concentrates on making dry wines from such popular varieties as Sauvignon Blanc and Chardonnay.

*Tokaji-Hegyalia.* Farthest east of the Massif mountainside areas is Tokaji-Hegyalia, the eponymous region of Hungary's most famous wine, Tokaji. Here, the principal grape is the Furmint, supported by the Hárslelú and Muskotály. The Carpathian Mountains provide protection from winds and cold. The Bodrog and Tisza Rivers, along with the warmth of the area, combine to facilitate the appearance of *Botrytis cinerea,* here known as *aszu.* The world's first *botrytis* wine is claimed to have been made here in 1650. That year, the harvest was delayed so the Ottoman Turks would not steal the juice. The late-harvested *botrytis* grapes were then added to the regular must, and the resulting wine was greatly appreciated.

When *botrytis* is not present but sugar levels attain .7 ounces per .26 gallons (20 grams per liter), wines from the Tokaji-Hegyalia region may still be labeled as aszu (see Figure 11.11). In this case, late-harvested *botrytis*-affected grapes are made into a paste. Unaffected juice is added to the paste in controlled quantities. A *puttony* is a small barrel of the paste that is blended into the larger cask, called a *gonci.* Wine labels read three, four, five, or six *puttonyos,* indicating increasing portions of paste to wine and therefore higher sugar levels. A three-puttonyos wine must be aged five years before release and have two to three ounces/60–90 grams of sugar per .26 gallons (one liter); four puttonyos, aged six years, must have three to four ounces/90–120 grams of sugar; five puttonyos must have four to five ounces/120–150 grams; and six puttonyos would have five to six ounces/150–180 grams and be aged for eight years.

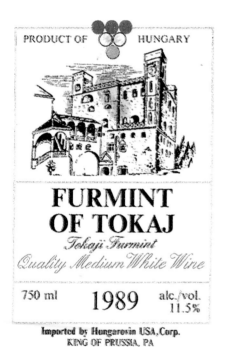

**Figure 11.11** A Label from a Dry Tokaji Wine Made, Like All Tokaji Styles, from the Furmint Grape.

An "essence" is made from the free-run juice before the paste process, and is fermented and aged for a few years to be used for future blending (see Figure 11.12). Essence was bottled in the past and is described by Michael Broadbent in his *Great Vintage Wine Book* as "the world's longest-living wine." He suggests storing it straight up, rather than on its side, to allow the wine to settle. The wines have high acidity to balance the rich sweetness. Essencia is the rarest, most complex, and most expensive of all Eastern European wines still produced. It is sweeter than six puttonyos, and may still be delicious after a century.

The Tokaji wines, that range from three puttonyos to Essencia, display the color, nose, and taste of apricots, as well as a rich sweetness. They are bottled in 500-ml bottles (see Figure 11.13), rather than the standard 750-ml size which is used for the "Tokay"- Furmint wines in the dry style. This dry wine results from a separate batch of grapes: lower-sugar berries are separated from the sweet *aszu* berries during picking. A *szamarodni* style is semidry to semisweet; less than half the grapes used are affected by *botrytis*. A szamorodni may be labeled "sweet" if the juice or must is at least 25 percent sugar, resulting in a wine of about two ounces/56 grams of sugar per .26 gallons (one liter). Szamorodni means "as it grows," and it is a useful method of harvesting *aszu* and regular grapes together when there is not enough aszu available to make separate pickings. The dry wines are served well chilled, and the sweet wines may be served between 50 to 60°F/10 to 16°C.

**Figure 11.12** Essencia is the Rarest and Most Expensive Wine Made in Eastern Europe. Aged at Least Eight Years Before Release, Its Character Can Develop for Decades.

**Figure 11.13** The Famous Tokaji Aszu, Sweet Wine from Hungary.

## TOKAJI

In the Tokaji region, millions of dollars will be spent to return the wine to its preeminent position among the dessert wines of the world (see Figure 11.14). Historically a dry-wine region, Tokaji began to produce sweet wines in the seventeenth century. These became the most-sought-after wines in Europe, served to nobility in courts and palaces. The laws regulating production of Tokaji were written in 1641, making Tokaji, along with Porto of Portugal, among the first demarcated and controlled wines of the world. During Communist rule the wines slipped in quality. Famous plots of Tokaji vineyard that have recently changed hands include the Oremus plot sold to Vega Sicilia of Spain and the Hétslózó and Disnókó sites sold to French insurance groups. The respected wine author Hugh Johnson and wine maker Peter Vinding-Diers have invested, with over 60 farmers of the region, to work together under the Royal Tokaji Wine Company name. The millions of dollars invested and the viticultural and vinicultural guidance should enhance the region's production and quality.

**Figure 11.14** Tokaji Szamorodni Can be Semi dry, Semisweet, or Sweet. For the Label to Read "Sweet" or "Doux," as Above, the Juice of the Furmint Grape Must be at Least 25 Percent Sugar.

**Figure 11.15** Premiat is an Export Label for Romanian Wines, Once Owned by PepsiCo (who traded Pepsi Syrup for Wine), and Now Owned by Sazerac of New Orleans.

# Romania

Romania is the ninth-largest wine-producing nation in the world, with 494,000 acres/200,000 hectares producing an average of 340 million gallons (850 million liters) annually. The bulk of production is consumed within the country, and per capita consumption is about eight gallons/20 liters. Historically, vineyard practices and wine making were based more on quantity than quality production but today, with a desire to increase exports, different trellising systems and more stainless steel vats for controlled fermentation are used.

The popular Cabernet Sauvignon is planted over 2880 acres/7200 hectares, along with other international varieties, such as Merlot, Chardonnay, Riesling, and Sauvignon Blanc (see Figure 11.15). However, the most-planted grapes are still the native Fetească Albă (white) and Fetească Regală (red).

## Regions

*Transylvania.* It is a cool growing region in the center of the country where whites do best and have refreshing acidity. Production is from the Fetească, Pinot Gris, Sauvignon Blanc, Muscat, Riesling, and Welschriesling. The Tirnave is the most famous subregion.

*Moldavia.* Moldavia is a region blessed with lots of sunshine and little rainfall, ideal conditions for making sweet wines from such local grapes as the Grasă. Cotnari is a sweet white wine made from Grasă, Tămîiaosă, Românesca, Fetească, and Frîncuşa. Perhaps foreign investment, such as in Tokaji, will resurrect the popularity of this luscious wine, which has a minimum of two ounces/60 grams of sugar per liter. The best vintages are achieved with the aid of noble rot. The wine must be bottled after a year of aging and, unlike the best Tokaji, is not exposed to air. A wide range of wines are found in the historic Odobeşti subregion.

*Muntenia.* Muntenia contains the Dealu Mare ("large hill") region and has been making good reds from Cabernet Sauvignon, Merlot, and a large clone of Pinot Noir ("Burgund Mare"), as well as local red grape varieties. Dry and sweet whites are also found. Banat, Crisana, Dobrudja, Oltenia, and the terraces of the Danube are the other main regions of Romania.

VSO and VSOC, the highest-quality wines in Romania, must be made from specific grape types grown in defined areas. VSO is the equivalent of *Appellation Côntrolée*, while VSOC is equivalent to QmP in Germany. VSOC wines also have categories based on sugar levels for the sweeter wines. These are CMD (late harvest), CMI (*botrytis*-affected late harvest), and CIB (selected *botrytis*-affected late harvest).

# Confederation of Independent States (CIS)

Since the end of the Communist era, the former Soviet Union has evolved into the Confederation of Independent States, or CIS. Each of the republics in the Confederation sets its own course for its wine industry. The former Soviet Union is still the world's fourth-largest wine producer, but production dropped from 8600 million gallons/34.4 million hectoliters per year in the early 1980s to 3250 million gallons/13 million hectoliters in 1991.

Selling in the international market will be a huge challenge for these newly independent states as many vineyards and wine-making facilities have not kept up with international standards. With investment in the vineyards and in sterile modern wine-making equipment, as well as guidance from international consultants, these states will have a chance to compete.

# Moldavia

This independent republic, created in 1991 between the Ukraine and Romania, has the potential to become a prime player in the export market because most of its vineyards are situated in a more temperate zone (heat summation region 2, similar to Bordeaux) than many other Eastern European countries. Rainfall is moderate and much of the 432,000 acres/180,000 hectares of vineyards are already planted with the popular international varieties. Exports increased from eight million to 30 million bottles between 1993 and 1995. A formal system of wine laws is being developed.

Foreign investments by such firms as the Australian Penfolds will mean not only a financial contribution but technical assistance in the vineyards and wineries. Sparkling, fortified, and dessert wines are available, but exports will probably concentrate on varietal-labeled, moderately priced dry table wines from such internationally popular grapes as Cabernet Sauvignon and Chardonnay.

# Ukraine

Ukraine contains over 372,000 acres/155,000 hectares of vines in Crimea and the Odessa region. Imperial Russia founded Magaratch, its top viticultural and vinicultural research institute, in Crimea in 1828. Over 3000 grape types are planted in Magaratch's vineyards, and one example of their laboratory work is the Magarath Ruby, a cross of two vinifera: Saperavi and Cabernet Sauvignon. The grape was created to have the high yields and resistance to disease of the regional grape, with some of the sensory characteristics of the more noble Cabernet.

High yields from mechanized vineyards has been the recent practice in Ukraine, resulting in about 70 million gallons/175 million liters of wine annually.

# Russia

During the 1950s, Russia's vineyards expanded, largely due to higher yields and the advent of mechanical harvesting. By the 1970s, 480,000 acres/200,000 hectares were under vine, but President Gorbachev ordered them reduced by about one-third. Now vineyards are being replanted with winter-hardy, disease-resistant, and prolific grapes, such as the Cabernet Saperavi, Saperavi Severny, and Stepniak. Resistance to the typically cold winters is important to farmers, who protect less hardy vines by covering them with soil. About 100 different grape types are permitted in Russia's vineyards, but leading all plantings is Rkatsiteli, which can make a floral-scented crisp white but is used to make other styles as well. The Saperavi, the principal red grape, has a pink-colored juice even before skin contact. The black Tsimlyansky, Narma, and Sibirkovy are some of the other quality grapes. As in most other nations, Cabernet Sauvignon, Riesling, Merlot, Pinot Gris, and other "international" varieties are found in Russia, along with indigenous grapes and hybrids, such as Isabella.

The vast majority of vineyards are in the northern Caucasus. Dagestan and Krasnodar are the largest and best-quality subregions.

## Bulgaria

As a nation, Bulgaria has existed since 1908, but wine making here dates back to the time of ancient Greece, when this area was known as Thrace. Today, the wines are mostly labeled by variety. Whites bearing the term "Reserve" or "Special Reserve" must be from a single variety and aged for two years; reds require three years aging. *Controliran,* defined quality geographic areas similar to French appellations, may also be included on a label.

Plantings have been shifting from the indigenous varieties planted for centuries to the internationals, such as Merlot, Cabernet Sauvignon, Chardonnay, Riesling, and Sauvignon Blanc.

# Summary

There are some fine wines to be had from Central Europe, but there is no great interest in wines from Switzerland and Austria in the North American market. Neither country is a major wine producer, but both are focused on making high-quality wines for the domestic and specialty export market. The world wine market is volume and value-driven, and this creates a problem for wines from Central Europe. They are both hard to find and undeniably expensive, when compared to wines of comparable quality from France, Germany, and the Southern Hemisphere.

The wines of Eastern Europe must improve dramatically to attract and sustain an international audience today and in the future. There will always be a market for inexpensive Eastern European wines, but perhaps the more important question is who, if anybody, in this politically and economically unstable region will elevate the image of these wines? Our guess is that it will be a syndicate of foreign investors, and a new generation of more optimistic, more individualistic native wine makers and entrepreneurs. Raising the quality of Eastern European wines will assure growth and prosperity in what is now, with a few exceptions that prove the rule, an industry focused on the lowest prices in the world.

### Chapter Twelve

# The Eastern Mediterranean

## Introduction

While few wine drinkers think of the countries of the Levant (the Eastern Mediterranean countries of Europe, "Asia Minor," and North Africa) as important wine regions (see Map 12.1), this part of the world is the cradle of ancient wine history, commerce, and culture. The ancient Turks, Greeks, Syrians, and Egyptians were among the first peoples to recognize the economic value of wine as an agricultural product and commodity.

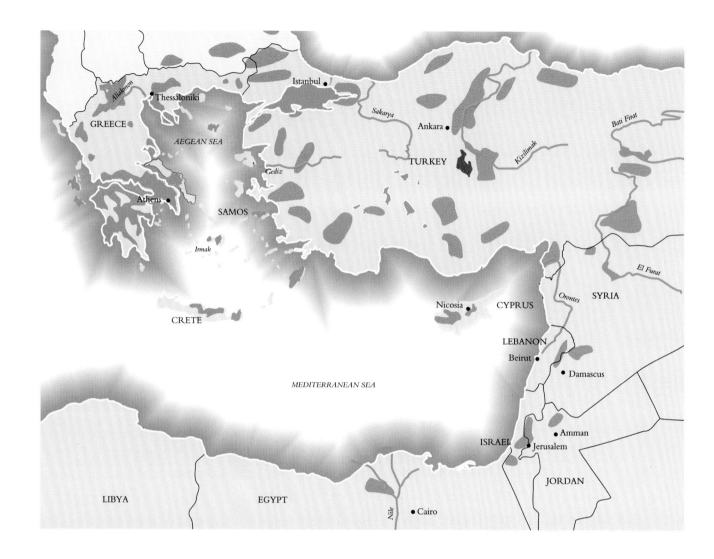

**Map 12.1** The Wine Regions of the Eastern Mediterranean.

# The Levant

Greece in particular was able to spread its dominion throughout the Mediterranean and the Black Sea, exporting wine in exchange for grains from Egypt and precious metals from Spain. The power of the god of wine, Dionysus (the Romans called him Bacchus) was celebrated, revered, and feared by the ancient cultivators of the vine. The epic poet Homer, as well as Aristotle, Plato, and the entire pantheon of classical Greek philosophers, all had something good to say about wine.

We know from the artifacts of antiquity that vines were grown and wine was made in Greece and Turkey at least 4,000 years ago, and the Talmud and Old Testament imply that one of the first things Noah did after the Great Flood was to plant a vineyard to celebrate life and fertility. So, there is no doubt that the Eastern Mediterranean is where the story of wine began.

The same area is also the historical home of the Ottoman Empire and the spread of the Moslem faith. Although the Ottomans in Greece and Turkey, and other Moslem rulers throughout the region, realized the financial importance of growing grapes and exporting wine, wine drinking was proscribed by Mohammed. Therefore, pious Moslems ripped out vineyards and instead planted grains, or raised sheep and goats.

While the Ottoman Empire flourished, the Levant lost its identity as a wine culture, only to regain it briefly when countries like Algeria and Morocco became colonies of France. French Algeria was, until 1960, the fourth-largest producer of wine in the world, much of it anonymously blended into wines of Burgundy and the Rhône. Independence came to Algeria in 1961, and the country is now only the twenty-third-largest producer of wine in the world. With independence in the 1950s and 1960s, other former colonies (Ethiopia, Tunisia, and Morocco, for example) quickly returned to their Moslem heritage. They no longer produce much wine.

We will briefly discuss the contemporary wines of Lebanon, Egypt, Algeria, Tunisia, and Morocco, but today the most prominent wine-producing countries in the Levant are Greece, Cyprus, parts of Turkey, and, coming on strong for quality, Israel.

## Greece

The world's fifteenth-largest producer of wine, modern Greece has about 225,000 acres/90,000 hectares under vine. Early in the twentieth century, during Europe's *phylloxera* epidemic, Greek wines were much in demand, as the infestation came late to Greece and spread very slowly there. For example, *phylloxera* did not reach Macedonia in the north until 1926; it only reached the Peloponnisos peninsula in the south in 1964. A small amount of *phylloxera,* genotype "A," from the turn-of-the-century epidemic, was discovered in Crete as late as 1972. Although there was strong demand for Greek wines at the turn of the century and beyond, Greece could not service the market, as most of its vineyards were in shambles due to the Moslem occupation of the country by the Turks. Only recently has Greece managed to become a quality-wine producer. Before Greece's entry into the European Community (EC) in the 1980s, wine technology in Greece was almost universally primitive, producing sweet wines—the product of warm weather and warm fermentation—and the traditional *retsina.*

In recent years, in order to compete with the other members of the European Community and to adhere to the wine laws of the EC, Greece has begun to develop modern wine-making methods and wine laws based on controlled appellations of origin and quality. Tremendous investment has been made in the Greek wine industry in the last decade, both in cooperatives and private companies. The best-known producers of classic Greek wines are Achaia-Clauss, Boutari, Cambas, Patras, and Tsantali, while the leader in quality is Château Carras, producing fine wines from both native and French vinifera grapes. About 12 percent of Greek wines qualify for appellation status from 26 wine regions. The most important regions are described here.

***Peloponnisos.*** Home to the famous city of Sparta, the Peloponnisos is by far Greece's largest wine region, with about 165,000 acres/66,000 hectares under vine. The Peloponnisos peninsula produces 34 million gallons/1.3

## RETSINA

Retsina has its roots in ancient Greece, when the ceramic amphorae that stored the wine were sealed with pine resin. Unavoidably, the resin would leech into the wine from the lip of the vessel and flavor the wine. Over the years, resinated white wines became so commonplace in the Greek wine world that the pine resin became a traditional additive during fermentation. Definitely a unique wine and an acquired taste—it really does have overtones of turpentine in its flavor and finish—retsina complements many of the simpler dishes of Greece. It has been said that during the Ottoman occupation of Greece, retsina producers would add double or triple the dose of pine resin to the must, if they knew the finished wine was destined for the Turkish armies. The enemy soldiers, who were Moslems, were not supposed to be drinking, so they were reluctant to report illness and death due to poisoned retsina. Retsina should be drunk very cold to deemphasize its turpentine flavor, and served with fish or vegetable dishes.

million hectoliters of wine, equivalent to 25 percent of total national production. Important native varietals grown here are Phileri, Aghiorghitico, Muscat (which makes a sweet white wine), and the famous Mavrodaphne. This red grape produces a heavy, sweet dessert wine of close to 15 percent alcohol, which at its best can mimic a good Tawny Port.

*Attica.*   The ancient cities of Athens and Thebes border Attica, the second-largest wine district in Greece. Producing about 15 percent of Greece's total wine output, Attica has a warm climate that results in quite a bit of undistinguished domestic table wine. Attica also produces Greece's best retsina, made from the white Savatiano grape, as well as palatable rosé made from the Rhoditis varietal. Red wines are made from a grape named Mandilaria.

*Macedonia.*   In the far north of the country, Macedonia is best known for its red wines, especially in the Naoussa appellation, where the Xynomavro grape is prized. The Carras family owns a vineyard and tourist resort in this region, where they produce Porto Carras. This wine was originally supervised by the famous Bordelais oenologist, Émile Peynaud. Some newer plantings in the eastern Chalkidiki appellation show some promise.

*Samos.*   An Aegean island physically closer to Turkey than to Greece, Samos is best known for its Muscat wines, made in sweet, dry, and fortified styles. Samos has special status among the appellations of Greece: no blended wine may be made on the island, and no wine from other parts of Greece may enter Samos. Aside from the Muscat wine made here from 5750 acres/2300 hectares of vine, fine Mavrodaphne is also produced on the island, which enjoys a rather mild climate.

*Santorini.*   This tiny island in the southern Aegean, situated north of Crete, is known for its volcanic soil, and its wide variety of grapes producing mostly dry and sweet red wines. The dry wine is labeled with the name of the appellation, while the sweet wine is more likely to be named Vino Santo. A dry white wine named Thira is also produced.

*Crete.*   A large island far to the south of the Greek mainland, Crete is the third-largest wine appellation, with more than 112,500 acres/45,000 hectares under vine. Crete is hilly and hot, and vineyard yields are quite high. The wines tend to be one dimensional: high in alcohol and big in body. The Greek government is making strong attempts to improve the quality of wines from Crete, which has four subappellations: Sitia, Dafnès, Peza, and Archanes.

# Cyprus

The third-largest and most-easterly island in the Mediterranean, Cyprus lies about 60 miles (96 kilometers) from the coasts of Lebanon and Syria. Despite its proximity to the Moslem world, the wine traditions in Cyprus are distinctly Greek and European. While its wine is little known in the United States, Cyprus exports about 75 percent of its 25 million gallons/950,000 hectoliters of wine, mostly to Britain, Russia, and the Balkan countries. The island has never been attacked by *phylloxera* and so, until recently, has depended on three native vinifera grapes: the red Mavron, which accounts for 80 percent of plantings, and the whites, Xynisteri (ten percent), and Muscat (three percent). In the late 1960s new plantings of the noble varietals began to be undertaken, but very carefully. To avoid the potential for *phylloxera* infestations, these new varieties were originally isolated in experimental stations and have only slowly been integrated into Cypriot viticulture. With ten percent of its arable land under vine, wine is an important part of the economy of Cyprus, accounting for close to ten percent of its exports. Cyprus has been quite aggressive in seeking advice and counsel from European wine technologists in order to modernize and expand its wine industry.

# Turkey

Although modern Turkey ranks fifth in the world for acres under vine (1.5 million acres/600,000 hectares), only five percent of its grapes are made into wine. This was not always true in Turkey. It is almost universally acknowledged that Turkey was the first country to produce wine, since vines grew wild in the mountains of its Anatolia province at least 4000 years ago, and archaeologists have discovered barrels of that era in central Anatolia. Until World War I, Turkish wines were well known and appreciated in Europe, but the war and the armed conflict between the Greeks and the Turks almost completely decimated the Turkish wine industry.

The best land in Turkey for growing wine grapes is, and always has been, in Thrace and Marmara, areas that are evenly divided between Europe and Asia. After the conflict with the Greeks in the 1920s, the vines of this area were ceded to table-grape growers. Of course, the strong Moslem tradition of the country was an important element in the weakness of the postwar wine industry. However, since 1928, when the government decreed that the Moslem faith was no longer the official religion of the country, Turkey has slowly regained some lost ground in the wine world. While the great majority of growers still do not make wine from their grapes, some sell their grapes to the government-controlled wine monopoly and to a few private concerns.

The Turkish government has invested heavily in modern wine-making equipment and has created a compulsory program to teach vignerons the most up-to-date approaches to viniculture and viticulture. However, Turkey still grows too many grapes, and not all of them make good wines. The current trend in the Turkish wine industry is to focus on the classic French varietals for both red and white wines. The red wines produced in Thrace, Anatolia, and the Aegean provinces are uniformly well made, and the white Izmir, made from Sémillon grapes, has developed a following among European tourists in Turkey. The country's best wine is a dry full-bodied red with the catchy name Buzbag.

## Israel

The Bible mentions wine often and with enthusiasm. The wine traditions of Israel, however, are really only about a century old, starting with the creation of Zionist settlements in Palestine. Some of these settlements were sponsored by Baron Edmond de Rothschild, who founded wineries near Tel Aviv and Haifa in 1882, and donated them to the Jewish state. The initial goal of these wineries was to make traditional kosher wines for religious observance. The original wines, best known by the brand Carmel, were similar to the kosher wines of the United States—sweet, alcoholic, and one dimensional.

Over the years, the focus of the Israeli wine industry has shifted, and now Israel, with much help from graduates of the University of California at Davis, is making very fine wines. Merlot, Cabernet Sauvignon, and Sauvignon Blanc do especially well in the relatively cool Golan Heights. Although some of this wine region was recently ceded to Israel's Arab population, early reports indicate that the new government will, for practical reasons, continue the progress made in Israel's wine industry. While quality wines produced by Yarden, Galil, and Gamla are imported to the United

The Bekaa Valley, just northeast of Beirut, is the center of Lebanon's tiny wine-making industry. In 1857, the Jesuits of Lebanon founded Ksara, a wine estate in Bekaa. Ksara still has 47,000 acres/19,000 hectares under vine, an amazing accomplishment, considering that Lebanon has been in a constant state of war for at least 30 years.

The wine world would pay scant attention to Lebanon were it not for one incredible red wine, Château Musar, produced just 15 miles from Beirut. Gaston Hochar, a Christian, started Château Musar in the mid-1930s, and in 1959, his son, Serge, who was trained in Bordeaux, became the wine maker. Although there have been a few missed harvests, due to civil war, and occasionally the grapes have been harvested under gunfire, there is no doubt that Château Musar, made from Cabernet Sauvignon, Carignan, and Cinsault grapes, is world class. Hochar, who has conducted vertical tastings of Musar going back to the 1940s, also makes a good white wine at the estate, and a lighter red wine, called Tradition, which is 75 percent Cinsault and 25 percent Cabernet Sauvignon.

States, Israel still has less than 9000 acres/3600 hectares of wine grapes planted.

# Egypt

Considering that Cleopatra proudly served Caesar Egyptian wine made from grapes grown on the banks of the Nile, Egyptian wine has taken a meteoric nosedive. Were it not for the patience and fortitude of Nestor Gianaclis, who at the beginning of this century began a 30-year quest for proper soil and grape types for Egyptian wine, there would probably be no Egyptian wine industry. Egypt, with 72,000 acres/29,000 hectares of wine grapes, exports most of its wine to Eastern Europe, and sells the rest to unsuspecting tourists. While its whites are more attractive than its red wines, its best-known wine, "Omar Khayyam," a red, needs work.

# Northwest Africa: Algeria, Morocco, and Tunisia

Under French rule (1830–1962) Algeria had 860,000 acres/344,000 hectares of wine grapes, was the fourth largest wine-producing nation in the world, and made wine that was blended into the wines of the French Midi and other vins ordinaires (see Chapter 6 on France). Independent Algeria, a Moslem country, now has less than 200,000 acres/80,000 hectares under vine. Despite religious prohibition, in 1970 the Algerian government began to establish seven *vins d'appellations d'origine garantie*—controlled wine appellations throughout the Oran and Alger regions.

Much of the best wine of Algeria is made by wine makers trained in France, using modern equipment. Medium- to full-bodied red wines account for close to 70 percent of production, and classic Rhône varietals are emphasized.

Morocco, with less than 35,000 acres/14,000 hectares of wine grapes, makes the finest red and rosé wines—*vins gris*—in North Africa. The best wine-growing regions in Morocco are those along the Atlantic coastline, plus the easterly areas of Fez and Meknès. The wines range from light to full bodied, and are strictly governed by Morocco's *appellation d'origine garantie* (AOG). As with Algeria, the French influence in the wine making of Morocco is palpable. Morocco does have a problem with *phylloxera,* as many of its vines are still planted on native roots, and wine technology has spread faster to viniculture than to viticulture. A central co-op, SODEVI, makes virtually all of Morocco's wine. The wine is bottled and distributed by the Moroccan-owned Comptoir des Vins du Maroc, located in Brussels.

Tunisia, independent since 1956 and located not far from Sicily, has picked up both French and Italian influences in its wines. With less than 22,000 acres/8800 hectares under vine, Tunisia's small wine output is best known for its Vin Muscat de Tunisie, a sweet dessert wine. Dry Muscat wines, some tasty rosés, and some passable red wines are made in Tunisia as well. Vineyards are located around the capital city of Tunis and the ancient city of Carthage on the country's north coast.

# Summary

For American wine consumers, the wines of the Eastern Mediterranean are a distinctly mixed bag. The arrival of modern wine-making methods and the influx of large investments made in some of the vineyards and wineries of Greece suggests that Greek wines are undergoing something of a renaissance. Israel, with its California wine makers, makes good varietal wines, especially Merlot and Cabernet Sauvignon. The finest versions of the ancient fortified wine from Cyprus, Commandaria, can be most enjoyable following a good meal. Lebanon's Château Musar is a singular wine of finesse and elegance, and will always find its audience.

Not much wine from Turkey, Egypt, Algeria, Tunisia, and Morocco is imported into the United States; no great loss to American wine lovers. The overwhelming majority of these wines are, at best, curiosities. The state of wine making in these countries is perhaps best summed up by Said Abraham, an Egyptian wine maker who was interviewed in the September 25, 1994 *New York Times*. When asked if he preferred to drink his own wines at home, he replied, "I don't let it in my house. I have to taste it here. That's enough."

# Wine, Food, and Health

Part 4 of Exploring Wine is divided into two chapters. Chapter 13, Wine and Food, discusses the theoretical and practical issues surrounding the successful pairing of foods with wines, while Chapter 14, Wine and Health, surveys some of the most current thinking about the role of wine in a healthy diet and lifestyle.

*Wine and Food* is a multilayered look at just how we approach the ideas of taste, texture, and flavor intensity, as well as understanding complementary and contrasting flavors, all in an effort to attain a happy marriage between food and wine. We have tried to make this chapter as free of dogma and jargon as possible, so that you, the reader, can think about some of our basic wine and food guidelines and apply them successfully in a social or professional environment.

We have worked and continue to work with literally thousands of students at the Culinary Institute of America, almost all of them aspiring chefs. Obviously, these future professionals want to know how to match their appealing culinary creations with wines and how wines can enhance the entire meal. We teach them using the same guidelines we have written about in this chapter, and assign each student to create a multicourse food and wine menu. Some of their ideas are original and provocative, not to mention very appetizing.

We urge our readers to create their own imaginative menus pairing food and wine, and to encourage you we have included some of our own menus. Reflecting a "global village" approach to the subject of food and wine pairing, our menus range from Classical French to Mediterranean, from regional African to regional American.

Chapter 14, *Wine and Health,* makes the point that wine, when consumed in moderation, plays a significant role in a healthy diet for adults. We have scanned some of the latest research and articles, conducted our own interviews, and attended symposia on the place of wine in the daily diet. The inescapable conclusion is that a small to moderate amount of wine consumed with meals provides an overall health benefit.

While physicians and other health professionals are in general agreement that moderate wine consumption can help lead to better health indices among the general population, they are not quite so sanguine about the public policy issues surrounding wine and alcohol in general. Should a doctor prescribe a glass of wine with dinner for a heart patient? Should the doctor withhold this prescription out of fear of alcohol abuse by even one patient? What about wine, women, and pregnancy, and the danger of fetal alcohol syndrome? We deal with these and other issues surrounding wine and health in Chapter 14, adding our voices to what is becoming an increasingly important and controversial discussion in American society.

### Chapter Thirteen

# Wine and Food

## Introduction

Matching food and wine to each other to enhance the quality of a meal is, at once, extremely simple and incredibly difficult. The simple part is this: if you remember a few basic guidelines, and enjoy a moderate degree of gastronomic exploration and experimentation, you cannot go too far wrong. The difficult part is this: there is no "perfect" food-and-wine combination that is right for everybody, but we are often called upon to come up with this elusive, even impossible combination. Somewhere between the two extremes—the casual, spontaneous approach and the rigorous, classical approach—most people find their own comfort zone.

In this chapter we will discuss how and why food and wine choices either marry well or should be divorced from each other. It is especially important to begin this discussion without a lot of preconceptions, prejudices, and pretenses. After all, what the convoluted, but certainly flawed, practice of food-and-wine matching boils down to are the twin issues of personal taste and experience. However, too many of us have had to suffer through dinners, lectures, or books by so-called wine experts in which some boorish, affected snob has laid down the law about what wine to drink with what food. We will try to avoid this approach, because we believe that pairing wine and food should not be intimidating; it should be educational, and as free of indecipherable "winespeak" as humanly possible. Above all, it should be fun, and serve as a useful tool to enhance the enjoyment of virtually any meal.

In writing this book we have been fortunate to find excellent research materials—books, databases, videotapes, and articles—to help us write a reasonably comprehensive text. The one area where we reached a research impasse was the subject of wine and food matching. Our problem was not that wine writers and lecturers have ignored the subject; quite the contrary. There is a great deal of material available about pairing wine and food, and some of it is quite good. No, the problem is not the quantity of information, but the fact that the various sources disagree with each other, both in theory and in practice (with the exception of certain agreed-upon "classic" combinations). In addition, it would be an understatement to say that the authors of this book are not in perfect harmony when it comes to this subject; each has his own likes and dislikes, his own personal theories, his own wine and food experiences, and, of course, his own tastes. The information and observations in this chapter, however, are the result of much discussion and tasting, leading to consensus on the subject by the authors.

# The Principles of Food and Wine Pairing

We consider the following topics to be most important in developing a fundamental understanding of the principles of food and wine pairing:

*   Basic Tastes and Sensations

*   Food and Wine Matching: A Learned Response

*   Texture

*   Cooking Methods

*   Matching Power with Power

*   Intensity in Food and Wine: Sauces and Garnishes

*   Complementing and Contrasting Flavors

*   The Dominant Flavor

We will list these topics, describe their importance, and then demonstrate how they work together as basic principles. Coupled with these principles will be some flexible guidelines to help guide you through a virtual maze of possible food and wine matches to help you as you start out on an exciting journey. This journey can be local or regional—matching the foods and wines of the bioregion in which you live—or it can be national—sampling the cuisine of a particular country—or it can be truly international—crossing borders, time zones, and datelines to pair foods and wines of many parts of the world, joined together by a culinary *détente* of ideas, memories, and taste buds.

## Basic Tastes and Sensations

In Chapter 3, How to Taste Wine, we mentioned that the human olfactory apparatus can experience innumerable smells, but that our palates can only distinguish four tastes: sweet, sour, bitter, and salt. Wines are not really salty, so we are left with sweet, sour, and bitter as our three basic tastes in wine. Food, of course, allows us to experience all four tastes, and perhaps just as importantly, the sensations of cold and heat. Heat is experienced as a temperature sensation and a taste sensation. The sensation of cold can also be experienced as a cooling contrast to heat (cold white wine with fried chicken, with its heat escaping from under the crispy batter), or as a cooling contrast to something spicy hot (sour cream served with spicy chili). The four basic tastes and the sensations of hot and cold are important when considering what wine to match with what food. Remember, that wine, like food, is composed of various flavors and textures and should be matched with the other elements of a meal based on those flavors and textures; it's as simple—and complex—as that.

## Food and Wine Matching: A Learned Response

It would be a highly unusual person who, upon first tasting a harsh, tannic, red wine, thinks, "Gee, this would be great with a triple-crème cheese." He or she would be more likely to dismiss the wine as undrinkable. Equally unusual would be a scenario where a taster experiences foie gras for the first time, and says, "If only I had some Sauternes," never having tasted, or at least read about, the luscious sweet wine from Bordeaux. Pairing food and wine just does not work this way. Rather, people make their judgments based on experience and personal preference.

We have noticed among the great majority of our students that the appreciation of wine, especially of dry, complex, challenging red wines, is a gradual process. It is not uncommon for Americans who enjoy wine to start tasting wines that are quite fruity, even sweet, and slowly, over time, develop an appreciation for drier whites and reds. Some people find brut Champagne bitter because they prefer the sweeter Asti, but little by little they acquire a taste for the drier wine. There is no law that people have to love dry wines, and some people are perfectly happy drinking sweet wines. On the other hand, some people never acquire a taste for the balance of razor-sharp acidity and fruitiness that Riesling wines from Germany deliver, thinking them too sweet. Again, personal taste rules.

Some people enjoy vegetables, fruits, and grains, while others eschew that "rabbit food" for a juicy steak. Obviously, most vegetarian dishes (with the possible exception of seitan or some mushrooms, which can be quite "beefy") will call for a different wine than Tournedos Rossini (filet mignon and sautéed foie gras with black truffles in Béarnaise sauce). In the United States, most of us grew up as true omnivores—we ate everything. As our personal tastes developed in adulthood, and our food and culture experiences broadened, many of us have refined our preferences: No meat. Meat at every meal. No dairy products. Pasta at home, steak in a restaurant. Always have a salad. I'll skip the salad, so I have room for dessert. I'll have the chicken. When we were kids we ate canned tuna fish, but now we love a grilled fresh tuna steak, served rare.

The same maturation process that happens with food happens with wine. At age 21, he liked beer. At 26, she drank only oaky Chardonnay from Napa Valley. At 30, he tasted a classic Margaux for the first time, and was hooked. At 35, she discovered the fruit and richness of red wines from the Rhône Valley. At 38, he traveled to Spain for the first time, and now searches for the perfect red Rioja. At 40, she attended her first serious wine tasting, and discovered she loved Riesling, and all the Chardonnays tasted alike. At 50, they each have a glass of Champagne every night before dinner. At 58, they taste wine with their adult children, teaching them all they know, all they have learned. Tastes change, our palates are conditioned by our life experience.

## Texture

Foods and wines both have texture, which we can loosely define as how they feel—on their own and together—in the mouth. This "mouth feel" is highly subjective, and is largely based on cultural and culinary experience, but we can all agree that certain foods and wines seem rich or fatty in the mouth, while others feel far more austere, or lean. Foie gras—the fatty liver of ducks or geese—has a rich texture, while lightly dressed salad greens have a lean texture. Tournedos Rossini is richly textured, while Dover sole poached in white wine, served with a mesclun salad, is quite a lightly textured dish. The mouth feel, or texture, of these dishes will be distinct, and this creates another consideration for matching wine and food.

Wine, too, has texture. A dry Chenin Blanc from California, fermented in stainless steel, will be refreshingly tart and light in texture, evaporating on the tongue rather quickly. An oak-aged Chardonnay wine from the Côte de Beaune in Burgundy will coat the palate and create a feeling of richness in the mouth due, in large part, to malolactic fermentation. Likewise, a Beaujolais-Villages, made from the Gamay grape, is a fruity, young, and simple red wine, suggesting a simple, light texture. However, a young Barbaresco, made in Piemonte, Italy, from Nebbiolo grapes, will exhibit a rich, complex balance of tannin and fruit and leave a rich, indelible taste in the mouth. So, just as we must consider the texture of the food we want to marry to the wine, we must also consider the texture of the wine in the matchmaking process. In fact, one of the simplest, but most important guidelines for matching food and wine is to match "power with power." Light-tasting and light-textured dishes go with lighter wines, heavier dishes go with fuller-bodied wines.

## Cooking Methods

While we all have our taste preferences, not many of us insist on eating foods that are prepared only one way. Most of us can enjoy poached salmon at lunch on Tuesday and grilled salmon over the weekend. We eat roast chicken, but we also enjoy braised coq au vin. Sometimes zucchini is steamed, sometimes it is marinated in olive oil and then grilled. Baked potatoes are great, but other times only French fries will do.

When matching food and wine, cooking method is of paramount importance. Obviously, a dish that is delicately poached in white wine will call for a far different wine than a perfectly seared New York strip steak served in a rich brown sauce. Just as important, however, the same product (a grouper fillet, for example) might call for a crisp, light white wine when poached but could support a full-bodied white, or even a light- to medium-bodied red wine, when grilled. Why? When you taste these dishes, it is obvious that the flavor intensity changes radically, at least partially due to the chosen cooking method.

## Matching Power with Power

As food flavor intensifies, so should the flavors in the accompanying wine. To put it another way, one important guideline in pairing food and wine is to match roughly the same levels of flavor intensity in both the food and the wine. Food that is (in rough order of flavor intensity) poached, steamed, sautéed, panfried, stir-fried, deep-fried, roasted, braised, broiled, grilled, or blackened, might respectively be matched to wines based in (again, in rough order of intensity) Chenin Blanc, Riesling, Sauvignon Blanc, Chardonnay, Gamay, Pinot Noir, Sangiovese, Merlot, Zinfandel, Cabernet Sauvignon, and Syrah, among a host of other varietals. The idea here is to match the flavor intensity of the dominant ingredient of a dish with the flavor intensity—the power—of the wine (see Tables 13.1 and 13.2). We are not looking to overpower either the wine or the food.

# Intensity in Food and Wine: Sauces and Garnishes

In many cases, we match wines to the flavor of the main ingredient of a dish. Another approach might be to match a wine to the sauce in the dish, or even to a garnish. London broil, a fairly lean cut of beef, served in its own juices, with matchstick potatoes and morels, would work well with a

## TABLE 13.1 WHITE WINE/COOKING METHODS

| White Wines | Poaching | Steaming | Sautéing | Pan-Frying | Stir-Frying |
|---|---|---|---|---|---|
| **Light- to Medium-Bodied Dry White Wines** | | | | | |
| Vinho Verde | ✦ | ✦ | ✦ | ✦ | ✦ |
| Galestro | ✦ | ✦ | ✦ | ✦ | ✦ |
| Muscadet | ✦ | ✦ | ✦ | ✦ | ✦ |
| Aligoté | ✦ | ✦ | ✦ | ✦ | ✦ |
| (French Colombard) | ✦ | ✦ | ✦ | ✦ | ✦ |
| Sancerre | ✦ | ✦ | ✦ | ✦ | ✦ |
| Pouilly Fumé | ✦ | ✦ | ✦ | ✦ | ✦ |
| Chablis | ✦ | ✦ | ✦ | ✦ | ✦ |
| Entre-Deux-Mers | ✦ | ✦ | ✦ | ✦ | ✦ |
| Graves | ✦ | ✦ | ✦ | ✦ | ✦ |
| Sauvignon Blanc | ✦ | ✦ | ✦ | ✦ | ✦ |
| Fumé Blanc | ✦ | ✦ | ✦ | ✦ | ✦ |
| Soave | ✦ | ✦ | ✦ | ✦ | ✦ |
| **Light- to Medium-Bodied Off-Dry to Lightly Sweet Wines** | | | | | |
| Riesling, Johannisberg Riesling, Rhine Riesling | | | ✦ | ✦ | ✦ |
| Sylvaner/Silvaner | | | ✦ | ✦ | ✦ |
| Chenin Blanc | ✦ | ✦ | ✦ | ✦ | ✦ |
| Liebfraumilch | | | ✦ | ✦ | ✦ |
| Gewürztraminer | | | ✦ | ✦ | ✦ |
| Muscat/Moscato di Canelli | | | ✦ | ✦ | ✦ |
| Saumur, Vouvray | | | ✦ | ✦ | ✦ |
| **Medium- to Full-Bodied Dry White Wines** | | | | | |
| Est! Est! Est! | | | ✦ | ✦ | ✦ |
| Verdicchio | | | ✦ | ✦ | ✦ |
| Orvieto | | | ✦ | ✦ | ✦ |
| Frascati | | | ✦ | ✦ | ✦ |
| Tocai Friulano | | | ✦ | ✦ | ✦ |
| Lacrima Christi Bianco | | | ✦ | ✦ | ✦ |
| Savennières | | | ✦ | ✦ | ✦ |
| Pinot Gris | | | ✦ | ✦ | ✦ |
| Pinot Blanc | | | ✦ | ✦ | ✦ |
| Sémillon | | | ✦ | ✦ | ✦ |
| Albariño | | | ✦ | ✦ | ✦ |
| Mâcon-Villages, Saint-Veran, Pouilly-Fuissé | | | ✦ | ✦ | ✦ |
| Chardonnay from U.S.A., Australia, others | | | | | |
| Viognier, Condrieu | | | | | |
| Côte-du-Rhône, Hermitage | | | | | |
| Meursault, Puligny-Montrachet, Chassagne-Montrachet, Corton-Charlemagne | | | | | |
| Montrachet | | | | | |
| **Medium- to Full-Bodied Sweet White Wines** | | | | | |
| Auslese, Beerenauslese, Trockenbeerenauslese | | | | | |
| Barsac, Sauternes | | | | | |
| Tokay Aszu | | | | | |

*(Table 13.1 continued on facing page)*

TABLE 13.1 WHITE WINE/COOKING METHODS *(CONTINUED)*

| White Wines | Deep-Frying | Roasting | Braising | Broiling | Grilling | Baking/ Pastry Making |
|---|---|---|---|---|---|---|
| **Light- to Medium-Bodied Dry White Wines** | | | | | | |
| Vinho Verde | ✿ | | | | | |
| Galestro | ✿ | | | | | |
| Muscadet | ✿ | | | | | |
| Aligoté | ✿ | | | | | |
| (French Colombard) | ✿ | | | | | |
| Sancerre | ✿ | | | | | |
| Pouilly Fumé | ✿ | | | | | |
| Chablis | ✿ | | | | | |
| Entre-Deux-Mers | ✿ | | | | | |
| Graves | ✿ | | | | | |
| Sauvignon Blanc | ✿ | | | | | |
| Fumé Blanc | ✿ | | | | | |
| Soave | ✿ | | | | | |
| **Light- to Medium-Bodied Off-Dry to Lightly Sweet Wines** | | | | | | |
| Riesling, Johannisberg Riesling, Rhine Riesling | ✿ | ✿ | | | | |
| Sylvaner/Silvaner | ✿ | ✿ | | | | |
| Chenin Blanc | ✿ | ✿ | | | | |
| Liebfraumilch | ✿ | ✿ | | | | |
| Gewürztraminer | ✿ | ✿ | | | | |
| Muscat/Moscato di Canelli | ✿ | ✿ | | | | |
| Saumur, Vouvray | ✿ | ✿ | | | | |
| **Medium- to Full-Bodied Dry White Wines** | | | | | | |
| Est! Est! Est! | ✿ | ✿ | | | | |
| Verdicchio | ✿ | ✿ | | | | |
| Orvieto | ✿ | ✿ | | | | |
| Frascati | ✿ | ✿ | | | | |
| Tocai Friulano | ✿ | ✿ | | | | |
| Lacrima Christi Bianco | ✿ | ✿ | | | | |
| Savennières | ✿ | ✿ | | | | |
| Pinot Gris | ✿ | ✿ | | | | |
| Pinot Blanc | ✿ | ✿ | | | | |
| Sémillon | ✿ | ✿ | | | | |
| Albariño | ✿ | ✿ | | | | |
| Mâcon-Villages, Saint-Veran, Pouilly-Fuissé | ✿ | ✿ | | | | |
| Chardonnay from U.S.A., Australia, others | | | ✿ | ✿ | ✿ | |
| Viognier, Condrieu | | | ✿ | ✿ | ✿ | |
| Côte-du-Rhône, Hermitage | | | ✿ | ✿ | ✿ | |
| Meursault, Puligny-Montrachet, Chassagne-Montrachet, | | | ✿ | ✿ | ✿ | |
| Corton-Charlemagne, Le Montrachet | | | ✿ | ✿ | ✿ | |
| **Medium- to Full-Bodied Sweet White Wines** | | | | | | |
| Auslese, Beerenauslese, Trockenbeerenauslese | | | | | | ✿ |
| Barsac, Sauternes | | | | | | ✿ |
| Tokay Aszu | | | | | | ✿ |

# TABLE 13.2  RED WINES/COOKING METHODS

| Red Wines | Poaching | Steaming | Sautéing | Pan-Frying | Stir-Frying |
|---|---|---|---|---|---|
| **Light- to Medium-Bodied Dry Red Wines** | | | | | |
| Bardolino, Valpolicella | | | ✿ | ✿ | ✿ |
| Gamay-Beaujolais | | | ✿ | ✿ | ✿ |
| Beaujolais-Villages | | | ✿ | ✿ | ✿ |
| Regnie, Chiroubles, Côte de Brouilly, Brouilly, Saint Amour | | | ✿ | ✿ | ✿ |
| Fleurie, Julienas, Chenas, Moulin-a-Vent, Morgon | | | ✿ | ✿ | ✿ |
| Grignolino | | | ✿ | ✿ | ✿ |
| Bourgeueil, Chinon, Saumur-Champigny | | | ✿ | ✿ | |
| Chianti | | | ✿ | ✿ | |
| Dolcetto | | | ✿ | ✿ | |
| Côtes-du-Rhône | | | ✿ | ✿ | |
| Corbières | | | ✿ | ✿ | |
| Rioja | | | ✿ | ✿ | |
| **Medium- to Full-Bodied Dry Red Wines** | | | | | |
| Barbera | | | ✿ | ✿ | |
| Chianti Classico | | | ✿ | ✿ | |
| Pinot Noir | | | ✿ | ✿ | |
| Merlot from U.S.A., Chile, others | | | | | |
| Rioja Reserva | | | | | |
| Côte de Beaune Villages, Beaune, Chambolle-Musigny, Pommard | | | | | |
| Nuits-Saint Georges, Vosne-Romanée, Gevrey-Chambertin | | | | | |
| Médoc, Margaux, St.-Julien, Pauillac, St.-Estephe | | | | | |
| Graves, St.-Émilion, Pomerol | | | | | |
| Zinfandel | | | | | |
| Châteauneuf-du-Pape | | | | | |
| Cabernet Sauvignon from U.S.A., Australia, others | | | | | |
| Nebbiolo | | | | | |
| Gattinara, Barbaresco, Barolo | | | | | |
| Brunello di Montalcino | | | | | |
| Côte Rotie, Hermitage | | | | | |
| Amarone | | | | | |

*(Table 13.2 continued on facing page)*

# TABLE 13.2  RED WINES/COOKING METHODS (CONTINUED)

| Red Wines | Deep-Frying | Roasting | Braising | Broiling | Grilling |
|---|---|---|---|---|---|
| **Light- to Medium-Bodied Dry Red Wines** | | | | | |
| Bardolino, Valpolicella | ✿ | | | | |
| Gamay-Beaujolais | ✿ | | | | |
| Beaujolais-Villages | ✿ | | | | |
| Regnie, Chiroubles, Côte de Brouilly, Brouilly, Saint Amour | ✿ | | | | |
| Fleurie, Julienas, Chenas, Moulin-a-Vent, Morgon | ✿ | | | | |
| Grignolino | ✿ | | | | |
| Bourgeueil, Chinon, Saumur-Champigny | ✿ | | | | |
| Chianti | ✿ | | | | |
| Dolcetto | ✿ | | | | |
| Côtes-du-Rhône | ✿ | | | | |
| Corbières | ✿ | | | | |
| Rioja | ✿ | | | | |
| **Medium- to Full-Bodied Dry Red Wines** | | | | | |
| Barbera | | ✿ | ✿ | ✿ | ✿ |
| Chianti Classico | | ✿ | ✿ | ✿ | ✿ |
| Pinot Noir | | ✿ | ✿ | ✿ | ✿ |
| Merlot from U.S.A., Chile, others | | ✿ | ✿ | ✿ | ✿ |
| Rioja Reserva | | ✿ | ✿ | ✿ | ✿ |
| Côte de Beaune Villages, Beaune, Chambolle-Musigny, Pommard | | ✿ | ✿ | ✿ | ✿ |
| Nuits-Saint Georges, Vosne-Romanée, Gevrey-Chambertin | | ✿ | ✿ | ✿ | ✿ |
| Médoc, Margaux, St.-Julien, Pauillac, St.-Estephe | | ✿ | ✿ | ✿ | ✿ |
| Graves, St.-Émilion, Pomerol | | ✿ | ✿ | ✿ | ✿ |
| Zinfandel | | ✿ | ✿ | ✿ | ✿ |
| Châteauneuf-du-Pape | | ✿ | ✿ | ✿ | ✿ |
| Cabernet Sauvignon from U.S.A., Australia, others | | ✿ | ✿ | ✿ | ✿ |
| Nebbiolo | | ✿ | ✿ | ✿ | ✿ |
| Gattinara, Barbaresco, Barolo | | ✿ | ✿ | ✿ | ✿ |
| Brunello di Montalcino | | ✿ | ✿ | ✿ | ✿ |
| Côte Rotie, Hermitage | | ✿ | ✿ | ✿ | ✿ |
| Amarone | | ✿ | ✿ | ✿ | ✿ |

medium-bodied red wine, such as Pinot Noir or a lighter Merlot. However, if the same cut of beef, cooked the same way, is encrusted in peppercorns and served with a soy-ginger glaze and creamy whipped potatoes, a Cabernet Sauvignon, Syrah, or Zinfandel might better match the spicy intensity in the dish.

In the first case—the simpler London broil preparation—the Pinot Noir or lighter Merlot will be a good choice because the flavors and textures of the dish are reasonably gentle. Both wines are medium bodied, with moderate tannins and good levels of fruit and acid. This dish is softer and lighter in texture and less intensely flavored than the same cut of meat served with a crust of peppercorns, the soy-ginger glaze, and the creamy potatoes. With this preparation, the flavors of the peppercorns (a garnish) and the soy-ginger glaze (a sauce) dominate. At the same time, the potatoes create a rich and creamy counterpoint to the intense spiciness and meaty flavors. Naturally, the wine that we will choose for this dish—Cabernet Sauvignon, Syrah, or Zinfandel amongst a myriad of possible choices—will exhibit more intensity of flavor to match the intensity of the pepper and sauce and, to create a contrasting texture with the smooth, rich potatoes, the wine will also contain high levels of tannin. The richness of the potatoes will cut the tannin, and the flavors and textures of both the dish and the wine will harmonize.

# Complementing and Contrasting Flavors

Depending on what flavors and textures you wish to highlight in the marriage of food to wine, there are two approaches to playing gustatory matchmaker. First, you can choose to *complement* the flavors and textures of the food and the wine, matching intensity with intensity, richness with richness, power with power. Second, you can *contrast* the flavors and the textures of the food with the wine, playing off tannin against fat, fruit against spice, complex against simple, but still maintaining approximate equality in intensity of flavor in the wine and the food. See Tables 13.3, 13.4, and 13.5 for wine and food pairing recommendations.

Say, for example, you are preparing boiled lobster, served cold and sliced thin, accompanied by an aïoli sauce, and you want to choose one white wine to match this dish. Ask yourself a few questions before making a choice. Do you want to emphasize the clean, medium-bodied flavor and texture of the lobster, or to celebrate the richness of the garlicky mayonnaise that coats the lobster (and our palates)? In choosing a wine for this dish, first decide if you want to cleanse the palate of the fat, thereby invigorating the appetite, or to emphasize the richness of both food and wine, so that the dish becomes a meditation from one bite to the next.

If you choose to cleanse the palate of the mayonnaise, so that you can enjoy the lingering clean flavors of the shellfish, you might choose a wine that is light in body and high in acid, like a Muscadet from the Loire Valley of France. This wine, with its fruity, tart flavors, will help to bring out the neutral flavor and the pleasing, but not overwhelming, texture of the lobster, while almost erasing the rich aïoli from the palate. Muscadet, a still, light white—sometimes called the perfect shellfish wine—will leave you wanting to taste another bite of the lobster. If you really want to de-emphasize the fat in this dish, you could also try a sparkling wine—a brut Champagne, for example—which would cleanse the palate with its dance of bubbles and bracing acidity. The choice of either the Muscadet or the Champagne would be a classic example of contrasting the food with the wine: light, fruity, wine with a good level of acidity versus the opulent richness of the lobster dipped in the sauce.

The Muscadet is light, fruity, and tart, as is the Champagne, and so contrasts with the full flavors of the dish, but if you want to complement this dish with a wine of similar taste and texture, how shall you proceed? You might think of the components of the dish (just lobster and aïoli) and seek a wine analog for flavor and texture. Look for a wine that demonstrates a richness similar to the tastes and textures of the dish. A rich, oak-aged Chardonnay, from California, Australia, or the Côte de Beaune in Burgundy, full of vanilla and cedar flavors that bear down on the palate, may be just the ticket. The net effect of this food and wine pairing will be a feeling of "weight," of "fullness" on the palate, honoring the sumptuous combination of shellfish and mayonnaise. For some people this combination might be too rich, especially if there are several other courses to come. However, if this classic dish is the main course for a three course summer lunch, then pairing it with a full-bodied, classic wine will provide a sensual, luxurious highlight to the meal.

## The Dominant Flavor

In the preceding example of lobster and aïoli we had to choose between a complementary or contrasting flavor in the accompanying wine. Just as important a choice in making this match is what flavor dominates the dish. The lobster? The sauce? Probably in this case, a lot will depend on how much mayonnaise you eat with the lobster; if you choose just a drop or two on each piece of lobster, then the fleshy, neutral, briny flavors of the lobster will dominate, but if we slather the lobster in the sauce, the lobster and the palate become encased in rich fat. In terms of marrying food and wine, this example is diner (or chef) dependent, because there are only two major elements in the dish, and it is up to the diner or chef to decide which element to emphasize.

Sauces are often intensely flavored and rich in texture, and so become an important consideration in matching food and wine. Traditional sauces, which can be high in fat, are frequently the main taste element in a complex dish. If poached fish is served with a meunière or hollandaise sauce, the richest part of the dish is the sauce. If a filet mignon is covered with a béarnaise sauce, the richness of the sauce de-emphasizes the flavor of a cut of meat that

# TABLE 13.3    WHITE WINES AND FOOD CHART

| White Wines | Mild Cheeses | Strong Cheeses | Light Appetizers | Patés/ Dips | Oysters | Shrimp | Crab/ Lobster | Clams/ Mussels | Seafood w/Light Sauce |
|---|---|---|---|---|---|---|---|---|---|
| **Light- to Medium-Bodied Dry White Wines** | | | | | | | | | |
| Vinho Verde | | | ✿ | ✿ | ✿ | ✿ | ✿ | ✿ | |
| Galestro | | | ✿ | ✿ | ✿ | ✿ | ✿ | | |
| Muscadet | | | ✿ | ✿ | ✿ | ✿ | ✿ | ✿ | |
| Aligoté | ✿ | | ✿ | ✿ | ✿ | ✿ | ✿ | ✿ | |
| (French) Colombard | ✿ | | ✿ | ✿ | | | | ✿ | |
| Sancerre | ✿ | | ✿ | ✿ | ✿ | ✿ | ✿ | ✿ | ✿ |
| Pouilly Fumé | ✿ | | | ✿ | | ✿ | ✿ | ✿ | ✿ |
| Chablis | ✿ | | ✿ | ✿ | ✿ | ✿ | ✿ | ✿ | ✿ |
| Entre-Deux Mers | ✿ | | ✿ | ✿ | ✿ | ✿ | ✿ | ✿ | ✿ |
| Graves | ✿ | | ✿ | ✿ | ✿ | ✿ | ✿ | ✿ | ✿ |
| Sauvignon Blanc | ✿ | | ✿ | ✿ | ✿ | ✿ | ✿ | ✿ | ✿ |
| Fumé Blanc | ✿ | | | | | ✿ | ✿ | ✿ | ✿ |
| Soave | | | ✿ | ✿ | | ✿ | ✿ | ✿ | ✿ |
| **Light- to Medium-Bodied Off-Dry to Lightly Sweet Wines** | | | | | | | | | |
| Riesling, Johannisberg Riesling, Rhine Riesling | | | ✿ | ✿ | | | ✿ | | ✿ |
| Sylvaner/Silvaner | ✿ | | ✿ | ✿ | | | ✿ | | |
| Chenin Blanc from U.S.A., others | ✿ | | ✿ | ✿ | ✿ | ✿ | ✿ | | ✿ |
| Liebfraumilch | ✿ | | ✿ | ✿ | | | | | |
| Gewürztraminer | ✿ | | | ✿ | | | | | |
| Muscat/Moscato di Canelli | ✿ | | | ✿ | | | | | |
| Saumur, Vouvray | ✿ | | | | | | ✿ | ✿ | ✿ |
| **Medium- to Full-Bodied Dry White Wines** | | | | | | | | | |
| Est! Est! Est! | | | ✿ | | | ✿ | ✿ | | ✿ |
| Verdicchio | | | ✿ | | | ✿ | ✿ | | ✿ |
| Orvieto | | | ✿ | | | ✿ | ✿ | | ✿ |
| Frascati | | | ✿ | | | ✿ | ✿ | | ✿ |
| Tocai Friulano | | | | | | | ✿ | ✿ | |
| Lacrima Christi Bianco | | | | | | | ✿ | ✿ | |
| Savennières | ✿ | | | | | | | | ✿ |
| Pinot Gris | ✿ | | | | | | | | |
| Pinot Blanc | ✿ | | | | | | | | |
| Sémillon | | | | | | ✿ | ✿ | ✿ | |
| Albariño | | | | | | ✿ | ✿ | ✿ | |
| Mâcon-Villages, Saint-Veran, Pouilly-Fuissé | ✿ | | | | | | ✿ | ✿ | ✿ |
| Chardonnay from U.S.A., Australia, others | ✿ | ✿ | | | | | ✿ | ✿ | ✿ |
| Viognier, Condrieu | | ✿ | | | | | ✿ | ✿ | ✿ |
| Côte-du-Rhône, Hermitage | | ✿ | | | | | | | |
| Meursault, Puligny-Montrachet, Chassagne-Montrachet, | | ✿ | | | | | | ✿ | ✿ |
| Corton-Charlemagne, Le Montrachet | | ✿ | | | | | | ✿ | |
| **Medium- to Full-Bodied Sweet White Wines** | | | | | | | | | |
| Auslese, Beerenauslese, Trockenbeerenauslese | | ✿ | | | | | | | |
| Barsac, Sauternes | | ✿ | | ✿ (foie gras) | | | | | |
| Tokay Aszu | | | | | | | | | |

*(Table 13.3 continued on facing p*

# TABLE 13.3 WHITE WINES AND FOOD CHART *(CONTINUED)*

| White Wines | Seafood w/Heavier Sauces | Salmon/Tuna | Poultry | Game Birds | Light Pasta | Hearty Pasta | Beef/Barbeques | Duck/Goose |
|---|---|---|---|---|---|---|---|---|
| **Light- to Medium-Bodied Dry White Wines** | | | | | | | | |
| Vinho Verde | | ✽ | ✽ | | | | | |
| Galestro | | | ✽ | | | | | |
| Muscadet | | ✽ | | | | | | |
| Aligoté | | ✽ | ✽ | | ✽ | | | |
| (French) Colombard | | | ✽ | | ✽ | | | |
| Sancerre | | ✽ | ✽ | | ✽ | | | |
| Pouilly Fumé | | ✽ | ✽ | | ✽ | | | |
| Chablis | | ✽ | ✽ | | ✽ | | | |
| Entre-Deux Mers | | ✽ | ✽ | | ✽ | | | |
| Graves | | ✽ | ✽ | | ✽ | | | |
| Sauvignon Blanc | | ✽ | ✽ | | ✽ | | | |
| Fumé Blanc | | ✽ | ✽ | | ✽ | | | |
| Soave | | | | | ✽ | | | |
| **Light- to Medium-Bodied Off-Dry to Lightly Sweet Wines** | | | | | | | | |
| Riesling, Johannisberg Riesling, Rhine Riesling | | ✽ | ✽ | | | | ✽ | |
| Sylvaner/Silvaner | | | ✽ | ✽ | | | | ✽ |
| Chenin Blanc from U.S.A., others | | | ✽ | | ✽ | | | |
| Liebfraumilch | | | ✽ | | | | | |
| Gewürztraminer | | ✽ | ✽ | | | | ✽ | |
| Muscat/Moscato di Canelli | | | | | | | ✽ | |
| Saumur, Vouvray | | ✽ | | ✽ | | | | |
| **Medium- to Full-Bodied Dry White Wines** | | | | | | | | |
| Est! Est! Est! | | | | | | | | |
| Verdicchio | | | | | | | | |
| Orvieto | | | | | | | | |
| Frascati | | | | | | | | |
| Tocai Friulano | ✽ | | ✽ | | ✽ | | | |
| Lacrima Christi Bianco | ✽ | | ✽ | | ✽ | | | |
| Savennières | ✽ | | ✽ | ✽ | ✽ | | | ✽ |
| Pinot Gris | ✽ | | ✽ | | ✽ | | | |
| Pinot Blanc | ✽ | ✽ | ✽ | ✽ | | ✽ | | ✽ |
| Sémillon | | | ✽ | ✽ | | ✽ | | ✽ |
| Albariño | | | ✽ | | | ✽ | | |
| Mâcon-Villages, Saint-Veran, Pouilly-Fuissé | | ✽ | ✽ | ✽ | ✽ | | | |
| Chardonnay from U.S.A., Australia, others | ✽ | ✽ | ✽ | ✽ | | ✽ | | ✽ |
| Viognier, Condrieu | ✽ | ✽ | ✽ | ✽ | | ✽ | | ✽ |
| Côte-du-Rhône, Hermitage | ✽ | ✽ | ✽ | ✽ | | ✽ | ✽ | ✽ |
| Meursault, Puligny-Montrachet, Chassagne-Montrachet, | ✽ | ✽ | ✽ | ✽ | | | ✽ | ✽ |
| Corton-Charlemagne, Le Montrachet | ✽ | ✽ | ✽ | ✽ | | | ✽ | ✽ |
| **Medium- to Full-Bodied Sweet White Wines** | | | | | | | | |
| Auslese, Beerenauslese, Trockenbeerenauslese | | | | | | | | |
| Barsac, Sauternes | | | | | | | | |
| Tokay Aszu | | ✽ | | | | | | |

*(Table 13.3 continued on next page)*

TABLE 13.3 WHITE WINES AND FOOD CHART (Continued)

| White Wines | Asian Foods | Pork/ Veal | Lamb | Ham | Game | Picnics/ Cold Cuts | Fruits/ Desserts |
|---|---|---|---|---|---|---|---|
| **Light- to Medium-Bodied Dry White Wines** | | | | | | | |
| Vinho Verde | ✽ | | | ✽ | | | |
| Galestro | | | | ✽ | | | |
| Muscadet | | | | | | | |
| Aligoté | | | | ✽ | | | |
| (French) Colombard | | ✽ | | ✽ | | | |
| Sancerre | | ✽ | | | | | |
| Pouilly Fumé | | ✽ | | | | | |
| Chablis | | ✽ | | | | | |
| Entre-Deux-Mers | | | | | | | |
| Graves | | ✽ | | ✽ | | | |
| Sauvignon Blanc | ✽ | ✽ | | ✽ | | | |
| Fumé Blanc | ✽ | ✽ | | | | | |
| Soave | | | | | | | |
| **Light- to Medium-Bodied Off-Dry to Lightly Sweet Wines** | | | | | | | |
| Riesling, Johannisberg Riesling, Rhine Riesling | ✽ | ✽ | | ✽ | ✽ | ✽ | ✽ |
| Sylvaner/Silvaner | ✽ | ✽ | | ✽ | ✽ | ✽ | ✽ |
| Chenin Blanc from U.S.A. | ✽ | ✽ | | ✽ | | | |
| Liebfraumilch | ✽ | ✽ | | ✽ | | | |
| Gewürztraminer | ✽ | ✽ | | ✽ | ✽ | | |
| Muscat/Moscato di Canelli | ✽ | ✽ | | ✽ | | ✽ | ✽ |
| Saumur, Vouvray | | ✽ | | ✽ | | | |
| **Medium- to Full-Bodied Dry White Wines** | | | | | | | |
| Est! Est! Est! | | | | | | | |
| Verdicchio | | | | | | | |
| Orvieto | | | | | | | |
| Frascati | | | | | | | |
| Tocai Friulano | ✽ | | | | | | |
| Lacrima Christi Bianco | | | | | | | |
| Savennières | | ✽ | | ✽ | | | |
| Pinot Gris | ✽ | ✽ | | ✽ | | ✽ | |
| Pinot Blanc | | ✽ | | ✽ | | ✽ | |
| Sémillon | | ✽ | | ✽ | | ✽ | |
| Albariño | | | | ✽ | | | |
| Mâcon-Villages, Saint-Veran, Pouilly-Fuissé | ✽ | ✽ | | ✽ | | ✽ | |
| Chardonnay from U.S.A. Australia, others | | ✽ | ✽ | | | ✽ | |
| Viognier, Condrieu | | ✽ | ✽ | | ✽ | ✽ | |
| Côte-du-Rhône, Hermitage | | ✽ | ✽ | | ✽ | ✽ | |
| Meursault, Puligny-Montrachet, Chassagne-Montrachet, | | ✽ | ✽ | | ✽ | | |
| Corton-Charlemagne, Le Montrachet | | ✽ | ✽ | | ✽ | | |
| **Medium- to Full-Bodied Sweet White Wines** | | | | | | | |
| Auslese, Beerenauslese, Trockenbeerenauslese | | | | | | | ✽ |
| Barsac, Sauternes | | | | | | | ✽ |
| Tokay Aszu | | | | | | | ✽ |

TABLE 13.4 RED WINES AND FOOD CHART

| Red Wines | Mild Cheeses | Strong Cheeses | Light Appetizers | Patés/Dips | Oysters | Shrimp | Crab/Lobster |
|---|---|---|---|---|---|---|---|
| **Light- to Medium-Bodied Dry Red Wines** | | | | | | | |
| Bardolino, Valpolicella | ✿ | | ✿ | ✿ | | | |
| Gamay-Beaujolais | ✿ | | ✿ | ✿ | | | |
| Beaujolais-Villages | ✿ | | ✿ | ✿ | | | |
| Régnié, Chiroubles, Côte de Brouilly, Brouilly, Saint Amour | ✿ | | ✿ | ✿ | | | |
| Fleurie, Julienas, Chenas, Moulin-à-Vent, Morgon | ✿ | | ✿ | ✿ | | | |
| Grignolino | ✿ | | ✿ | | | | |
| Bourgueil, Chinon, Saumur-Champigny | ✿ | | | | | | |
| Chianti | ✿ | | ✿ | | | | |
| Dolcetto | ✿ | | ✿ | | | | |
| Côtes-du-Rhône | ✿ | | ✿ | | | | |
| Corbières | ✿ | | | | | | |
| Rioja | ✿ | | | | | | |
| **Medium- to Full-Bodied Dry Red Wines** | | | | | | | |
| Barbera | ✿ | | | | | | |
| Chianti Classico | ✿ | | | | | | |
| Pinot Noir | ✿ | | | | | | |
| Merlot from U.S.A., Chile, others | ✿ | ✿ | | | | | |
| Rioja Reserva | | ✿ | | | | | |
| Côte de Beaune Villages, Beaune, Chambolle-Musigny, Pommard | | ✿ | | | | | |
| Nuits-Saint Georges, Vosne-Romanée, Gevrey-Chambertin | | | | | | | |
| Médoc, Margaux, St.-Julien, Pauillac, St.-Estephe | | ✿ | | | | | |
| Graves, St.-Émilion, Pomerol | | | | | | | |
| Zinfandel | | ✿ | | | | | |
| Châteauneuf-du-Pape | | ✿ | | | | | |
| Cabernet Sauvignon from U.S.A., Australia, others | | ✿ | | | | | |
| Nebbiolo | | ✿ | | | | | |
| Gattinara, Barbaresco, Barolo | | ✿ | | | | | |
| Brunello di Montalcino | | ✿ | | | | | |
| Côte Rotie, Hermitage | | ✿ | | | | | |
| Amarone | | ✿ | | | | | |

*(Table 13.4 continued on next page)*

TABLE 13.4 RED WINES AND FOOD CHART (continued)

| Red Wines | Clams/ Mussels | Seafood w/Light Sauces | Seafood w/Heavier Sauces | Salmon/ Tuna | Poultry | Game Birds | Light Pasta | Hearty Pasta | Beef/ Barbeques |
|---|---|---|---|---|---|---|---|---|---|
| **Light- to Medium-Bodied Dry Red Wines** | | | | | | | | | |
| Bardolino, Valpolicella | | ✿ | ✿ | ✿ | ✿ | ✿ | ✿ | ✿ | ✿ |
| Gamay–Beaujolais | | ✿ | ✿ | ✿ | ✿ | ✿ | ✿ | | ✿ |
| Beaujolais-Villages | | ✿ | ✿ | ✿ | ✿ | ✿ | ✿ | | ✿ |
| Régnié, Chiroubles, Côte de Brouilly, Brouilly, Saint Amour | | ✿ | ✿ | ✿ | ✿ | ✿ | ✿ | | ✿ |
| Fleurie, Juliénas, Chenas, Moulin-à-Vent, Morgon | | | ✿ | ✿ | ✿ | ✿ | ✿ | ✿ | |
| Grignolino | | | ✿ | ✿ | ✿ | ✿ | ✿ | ✿ | ✿ |
| Bourgueil, Chinon, Saumur-Champigny | | | ✿ | ✿ | ✿ | ✿ | ✿ | | ✿ |
| Chianti | | | ✿ | ✿ | ✿ | ✿ | ✿ | ✿ | ✿ |
| Dolcetto | | | ✿ | ✿ | ✿ | ✿ | | ✿ | |
| Côtes-du-Rhône | | | | ✿ | ✿ | ✿ | | ✿ | ✿ |
| Corbières | | | | ✿ | ✿ | ✿ | | ✿ | ✿ |
| Rioja | | | | ✿ | ✿ | ✿ | | ✿ | ✿ |
| **Medium- to Full-Bodied Dry Red Wines** | | | | | | | | | |
| Barbera | | | ✿ | ✿ | ✿ | ✿ | | ✿ | ✿ |
| Chianti Classico | | | ✿ | ✿ | ✿ | ✿ | | ✿ | ✿ |
| Pinot Noir | | | ✿ | ✿ | ✿ | ✿ | | ✿ | ✿ |
| Merlot from U.S.A., Chile, others | | | | | ✿ | ✿ | | ✿ | ✿ |
| Rioja Reserva | | | | | ✿ | ✿ | | ✿ | ✿ |
| Côte de Beaune Villages, Beaune, Chambolle-Musigny, Pommard | | | | | ✿ | ✿ | | | ✿ |
| Nuits-Saint Georges, Vosne-Romanée, Gevrey-Chambertin | | | | | ✿ | ✿ | | | ✿ |
| Médoc, Margaux, St.-Julien, Pauillac, St.-Estephe | | | | | ✿ | | | | ✿ |
| Graves, St.-Émilion, Pomerol | | | | | | | | | |
| Zinfandel | | | | | ✿ | ✿ | | ✿ | ✿ |
| Châteauneuf-du-Pape | | | | | | ✿ | | ✿ | ✿ |
| Cabernet Sauvignon from U.S.A., Australia, others | | | | | | | | | ✿ |
| Nebbiolo | | | | | | | | ✿ | ✿ |
| Gattinara, Barbaresco, Barolo | | | | | | | | ✿ | ✿ |
| Brunello di Montalcino | | | | | | | | ✿ | ✿ |
| Côte Rotie, Hermitage | | | | | | | | | ✿ |
| Amarone | | | | | | | | | ✿ |

*(Table 13.4 continued on facing page)*

## Table 13.4 RED WINES AND FOOD CHART (continued)

| Red Wines | Duck/Goose | Asian Foods | Pork/Veal | Lamb | Ham | Game | Picnics/Cold Cuts | Fruits Desserts |
|---|---|---|---|---|---|---|---|---|
| **Light- to Medium-Bodied Dry Red Wines** | | | | | | | | |
| Bardolino, Valpolicella | ✿ | | ✿ | | | | ✿ | |
| Gamay-Beaujolais | | ✿ | ✿ | | ✿ | | ✿ | ✿ |
| Beaujolais-Villages | | ✿ | ✿ | | ✿ | | ✿ | ✿ |
| Régnié, Chiroubles, Côte de Brouilly, Brouilly, Saint Amour | | | ✿ | | ✿ | | ✿ | |
| Fleurie, Julienas, Chenas, Moulin-à-Vent, Morgon | | | ✿ | | ✿ | | ✿ | |
| Grignolino | | | ✿ | | ✿ | | ✿ | |
| Bourgeueil, Chinon, Saumur-Champigny | | | ✿ | | ✿ | | ✿ | |
| Chianti | | | ✿ | | ✿ | | ✿ | |
| Dolcetto | | | ✿ | | ✿ | | ✿ | |
| Côtes-du-Rhône | ✿ | | ✿ | ✿ | ✿ | ✿ | ✿ | |
| Corbières | ✿ | | ✿ | ✿ | ✿ | ✿ | ✿ | |
| Rioja | ✿ | | ✿ | ✿ | ✿ | ✿ | ✿ | |
| **Medium- to Full-Bodied Dry Red Wines** | | | | | | | | |
| Barbera | ✿ | | ✿ | | ✿ | ✿ | ✿ | |
| Chianti Classico | ✿ | | ✿ | ✿ | ✿ | ✿ | ✿ | |
| Pinot Noir | ✿ | | ✿ | ✿ | ✿ | ✿ | ✿ | |
| Merlot from U.S.A., Chile, others | ✿ | | | ✿ | | ✿ | | |
| Rioja Reserva | ✿ | | | ✿ | | ✿ | | |
| Côte de Beaune Villages, Beaune, Chambolle-Musigny, Pommard | ✿ | | ✿ | ✿ | | ✿ | | |
| Nuits-Saint Georges, Vosne-Romanée, Gevrey-Chambertin | ✿ | | | | | | | |
| Médoc, Margaux, St.-Julien, Pauillac, St.-Estephe | | | | ✿ | | ✿ | | |
| Graves, St.-Émilion, Pomerol | | | | | | | | |
| Zinfandel | ✿ | ✿ | ✿ | ✿ | | ✿ | ✿ | |
| Châteauneuf-du-Pape | ✿ | | ✿ | ✿ | | ✿ | | |
| Cabernet Sauvignon from U.S.A., Australia, others | | | | | | ✿ | | |
| Nebbiolo | ✿ | | | | | ✿ | | |
| Gattinara, Barbaresco, Barolo | ✿ | | | | | ✿ | | |
| Brunello di Montalcino | ✿ | | | | | ✿ | | |
| Côte Rotie, Hermitage | ✿ | | | | | ✿ | | |
| Amarone | ✿ | | | | | ✿ | | |

TABLE 13.5 ROSÉ WINES, SPARKLING WINES, CHAMPAGNE, AND FOOD CHART

| Rosé Wines | Mild Cheeses | Strong Cheeses | Light Appetizers | Patés/ Dips | Oysters | Shrimp | Crab/ Lobster | Clams/ Mussels |
|---|---|---|---|---|---|---|---|---|
| **Light- to Medium-Bodied Rosé Wines (Dry to Off-Dry)** | | | | | | | | |
| Rosé de Marsannay | ● | | ● | ● | | ● | ● | ● |
| White Zinfandel and other "blush" wines, such as Grenache Rosé, Rosé of Cabernet | ● | | ● | ● | | ● | ● | |
| Grignolino Rosé | | | ● | | | ● | ● | ● |
| Rosé d'Anjou | ● | | ● | | | | | |
| Lirac, Tavel | ● | | ● | ● | | ● | ● | |
| Rosé Bandol | ● | | | | | | | |
| **Styles of Sparkling Wine and Champagne** | | | | | | | | |
| Blanc de Blancs | | | ● | ● | ● | ● | ● | ● |
| Blanc de Noirs | ● | | ● | ● | ● | ● | ● | ● |
| Extra Dry | ● | | ● | ● | ● | ● | ● | ● |
| Brut | | | ● | ● | ● | ● | ● | ● |
| Extra Brut, Natural | | | ● | ● | | ● | ● | |
| Rosé | ● | | ● | ● | | ● | ● | |
| Demi-Sec | ● | | | | | | | |
| Sec | | | | | | | | |
| Doux | | | | | | | | |

*(Table 13.5 continued on facing page)*

is not high in marbled (internal) fat. Sauces based in butter, cream, and other dairy fats tend to dominate the flavors of many protein-based dishes. In choosing a wine to marry with a richly sauced dish, you might choose the flavors in the sauce as dominant and match the wine with those flavors.

Increasingly, restaurant patrons are electing to enjoy sauces and other rich accompaniments "on the side," in order to consume fewer calories from fat, and also to taste the food relatively unadorned and unmasked. In addition, the nature of sauces is changing. A grilled salmon that in the past might have been served with a butter sauce now may be served with a spicy fruit or vegetable salsa. A poached salmon might be served in its poaching liquid of wine and herbs. Meats may be served with sauces based in vegetable juices and purées, or with a lentil ragout, instead of a full-flavored brown sauce. Grilled or steamed vegetables, and rice and pasta, once thought to be side dishes, now occupy the center of the plate and the center of the palate. Clearly, the wines chosen to match such contemporary cuisine will be quite different from those chosen to marry with rich sauces.

We use sauces and their changing nature to emphasize that choosing wines for certain dishes is most often dependent on the dominant flavors of those dishes. Sauces can be dominant, but so can meat, fish, poultry, vegetables, or grains. Even a garnish, fresh horseradish, for example, can be the dominant flavor in a light, delicate dish. It follows that if you are picking wines to accompany food you must know what the food tastes like, and unless you are trying to show off the wines at the expense of the food, you will

## Table 13.5 Rosé Wines, Sparkling Wines, Champagne, and Food Chart (Continued)

| Rosé Wines | Seafood w/Light Sauces | Seafood w/Heavier Sauces | Salmon/Tuna | Poultry | Game Birds | Light Pasta | Hearty Pasta | Beef/Barbeques | Duck/Goose |
|---|---|---|---|---|---|---|---|---|---|
| **Light- to Medium-Bodied Rosé Wines (Dry to Off-Dry)** | | | | | | | | | |
| Rosé de Marsannay | ✽ | | | | | ✽ | | | |
| White Zinfandel and other "blush" wines, such as Grenache Rosé, Rosé of Cabernet | ✽ | ✽ | ✽ | ✽ | | ✽ | | | |
| Grignolino Rosé | ✽ | ✽ | ✽ | ✽ | | ✽ | | | |
| Rosé d'Anjou | | | | | | | | | |
| Lirac, Tavel | ✽ | ✽ | ✽ | ✽ | ✽ | ✽ | ✽ | ✽ | |
| Rosé Bandol | | ✽ | ✽ | ✽ | ✽ | | ✽ | ✽ | ✽ |
| **Styles of Sparkling Wine and Champagne** | | | | | | | | | |
| Blanc de Blancs | ✽ | | | ✽ | | ✽ | | | |
| Blanc de Noirs | ✽ | | | ✽ | ✽ | ✽ | | | |
| Extra Dry | ✽ | ✽ | | ✽ | ✽ | ✽ | | | |
| Brut | ✽ | ✽ | ✽ | ✽ | | ✽ | | | |
| Extra Brut, Natural | ✽ | ✽ | ✽ | ✽ | ✽ | | | | |
| Rosé | | ✽ | ✽ | ✽ | ✽ | | | ✽ | ✽ |
| Demi-Sec | | | | | | | | | ✽ |
| Sec | | | | | | | | | |
| Doux | | | | | | | | | |

*(Table 13.5 continued below)*

## Table 13.5 Rosé Wines, Sparkling Wines, Champagne, and Food Chart (Continued)

| Rosé Wines | Asian Foods | Pork/Veal | Lamb | Ham | Game | Picnics/Cold Cuts | Fruits/Desserts |
|---|---|---|---|---|---|---|---|
| **Light- to Medium-Bodied Rosé Wines (Dry to Off-Dry)** | | | | | | | |
| Rosé de Marsannay | ✽ | ✽ | | ✽ | | ✽ | ✽ |
| White Zinfandel and other "blush" wines, such as Grenache Rosé of Cabernet, Grignolino Rosé | ✽ | ✽ | | ✽ | | ✽ | ✽ |
| Rosé d'Anjou | | | | | | | |
| Lirac, Tavel | ✽ | ✽ | | ✽ | | ✽ | |
| Rosé Bandol | | ✽ | | ✽ | ✽ | ✽ | |
| **Styles of Sparkling Wine and Champagne** | | | | | | | |
| Blanc de Blancs | ✽ | | | ✽ | | ✽ | |
| Blanc de Noirs | | ✽ | | ✽ | | ✽ | ✽ |
| Extra Dry | ✽ | ✽ | | ✽ | | ✽ | |
| Brut | ✽ | ✽ | | ✽ | | ✽ | |
| Extra Brut, Natural | | ✽ | | | | ✽ | |
| Rosé | | ✽ | | | ✽ | ✽ | |
| Demi-Sec | | | | ✽ | | | ✽ |
| Sec | | | | | | | ✽ |
| Doux | | | | | | | ✽ |

most often match the wine to the food, not the food to the wine. Certainly entire dinners can and do revolve around particular wines and their food affinities, but in most cases, wine should be seen as part of a harmonious whole, another flavor element in a successful meal.

# A Power Chart

One of the easiest ways to match food and wine is to remember that certain wines are light bodied, some are medium bodied, and some full bodied. The relative power of a wine is based not only on the grape types that comprise the wine but also on vineyard practices, especially grape yield levels, and on how the wine is made. For example, Chardonnay wine fermented in stainless steel and aged in the bottle will taste entirely different from an oak-fermented, oak-aged Chardonnay. The first wine may have been made from grapes in a high-yield vineyard; the more grapes per acre, the less concentration of flavor. The oaky Chardonnay has undergone malolactic fermentation and may have come from a low-yielding vineyard, with fewer grapes per acre but more flavor concentration per grape. So, the same grape can make wines that are light, medium, or full bodied. The same is true of certain red grapes, such as Sangiovese, which can make a medium- or quite full-bodied wine, depending on where the wine is made, how the grapes are grown, and how the wine maker treats the wine.

While the Power Charts (see Tables 13.6 and 13.7) are not foolproof (since tasting is always the final arbiter of the power of a wine), they do illuminate how certain wines express their intensity of flavor, texture, and body. Where the wines are not called by their varietal names in the left-hand column (Chardonnay or Barbera, for example), the varietal name is provided in the right-hand column. Likewise, if a wine is best known as native to a particular region or regions, those are listed in the middle column (in parentheses). Since some varietals or styles of wine are found in different regions of the same country, the country name is given first, followed by the most-prominent wine region. The Power Charts are presented in *approximate* order of power, from lightest to fullest body.

# Horizontal and Vertical Choices

Sometimes you will want to match a particular dish with one wine, rather than planning a multicourse, multiwine meal. This is called a *horizontal* wine choice, and in it you may choose to complement or contrast the wine to the food, as previously discussed. Often, however, you will match several food courses with several wines in a multicourse, progressive dinner. These marriages, by contrast or by complement, represent a series of *vertical* wine choices; one wine choice builds on another, and the next choice builds on

## TABLE 13.6 POWER CHART: WHITE WINES

| Light- to Medium-Bodied Dry White Wines | | |
|---|---|---|
| *Label* | *Place of Origin* | *Varietals* |
| Vinho Verde | Portugal (Minho) | Loureiro, Trajadura |
| Galestro | Italy (Tuscany) | Trebbiano, others |
| Muscadet | France (Loire) | Melon de Bourgogne |
| Aligoté | France (Burgundy) | varietal |
| (French) Colombard | France/California | varietal |
| Sancerre | France (Loire) | Sauvignon Blanc |
| Pouilly Fumé | France (Loire) | Sauvignon Blanc |
| Chablis | France (Burgundy) | Chardonnay |
| Entre-Deux-Mers | France (Bordeaux) | Sauvignon Blanc/ Sémillon |
| Graves | France (Bordeaux) | Sauvignon Blanc/ Sémillon |
| Sauvignon Blanc | various countries | varietal |
| Soave | Italy (Veneto) | Garganega, Trebbiano |

| Light- to Medium-Bodied Off-Dry to Lightly Sweet White Wines | | |
|---|---|---|
| *Label* | *Place of Origin* | *Varietals* |
| Riesling | France (Alsace) | varietal |
| Riesling | Germany (Rhine/Mosel) | varietal |
| Johannisberg Riesling | U.S.A. (California) | varietal |
| Rhine Riesling | Australia | varietal |
| Sylvaner | France (Alsace) | varietal |
| Silvaner | Germany (Rhine) | varietal |
| Chenin Blanc | U.S.A. (California) | varietal |
| Liebfraumilch | Germany (Rhine) | Müller-Thurgau, others |
| Gewürztraminer | France (Alsace) | varietal |
| Muscat | France (Alsace) | varietal |
| Moscato di Canelli | Italy (Piemonte) | varietal |
| Saumur | France (Loire) | Chenin Blanc |
| Vouvray | France (Loire) | Chenin Blanc |

*(Table 13.6 continued on next page)*

TABLE 13.6   POWER CHART: WHITE WINES *(continued)*

## Medium- to Full-Bodied Dry White Wines

| Label | Place of Origin | Varietals |
|---|---|---|
| Est! Est! Est! | Italy (Lazio) | Trebbiano, Malvasia |
| Verdicchio | Italy (Marche) | varietal |
| Orvieto | Italy (Umbria) | Trebbiano, Verdicchio |
| Frascati | Italy (Lazio) | Malvasia, Trebbiano |
| Tocai Friulano | Italy (Friuli Venezia-Giulia) | varietal |
| Lacryma Christi Bianco | Italy (Campania) | various grape types |
| Savennières | France (Loire) | Chenin Blanc |
| Pinot Gris | France (Alsace), U.S.A (Oregon) | varietal |
| Pinot Blanc | France (Alsace) | varietal |
| Sémillon | Australia, U.S.A | varietal |
| Albariño | Spain (Galicia) | varietal |
| Mâcon-Villages, Saint-Véran, Pouilly-Fuissé | France (Mâcon, Burgundy) | Chardonnay |
| Chardonnay | USA, Australia, others | varietal |
| Viognier | France, U.S.A. (California) | varietal |
| Condrieu | France (Northern Rhône) | Viognier |
| Côtes-du-Rhone, Hermitage | France (Rhône) | Marsanne, Rousanne, others |
| Meursault, Puligny-Montrachet, Chassagne-Montrachet, Corton-Charlemagne, Le Montrachet | France (Côte de Beaune, Burgundy) | Chardonnay |

## Medium- to Full-Bodied Sweet White Wines

| Label | Place of Origin | Varietals |
|---|---|---|
| Auslese, Beerenauslese, Trockenbeerenauslese | Germany (Mosel/Rhine) | Riesling and others |
| Barsac, Sauternes | France (Bordeaux) | Sémillon |
| Tokay Aszu | Hungary | Furmint |

## POWER CHART: ROSÉ WINES

### Light- to Medium-Bodied Rosé Wines (Dry to Off-Dry)

| Label | Place of Origin | Varietals |
|---|---|---|
| Rosé de Marsannay | France (Burgundy) | Pinot Noir |
| White Zinfandel, and other "blush" wine, Grenache Rosé, Rosé of Cabernet, Grignolino Rosé | U.S.A. (California) | varietals |
| Rosé d'Anjou | France (Loire) | Grolleau, Cabernet Franc |
| Tavel, Lirac | France (Southern Rhône) | Grenache, Cinsault |
| Rosé Bandol | France (Provence) | Mourvèdre, Grenache, Cinsault |

### TABLE 13.7 POWER CHART: RED WINES

### Light- to Medium-Bodied Dry Red Wines

| Label | Place of Origin | Varietals |
|---|---|---|
| Bardolino, Valpolicella | Italy (Veneto) | Corvina, Rondinella, others |
| Gamay Beaujolais | U.S.A. (California) | varietal |
| Beaujolais-Villages, Régnié, Chiroubles, Côte de Brouilly, Brouilly, Saint Amour, Fleurie, Julienas, Chenas, Moulin-à-Vent, Morgon | France (Southern Burgundy) | Gamay |
| Grignolino | Italy (Piemonte) | varietal |
| Bourgeueil, Chinon, Saumur-Champigny | France (Loire) | Cabernet Franc |
| Chianti | Italy (Tuscany) | Sangiovese |
| Dolcetto | Italy (Piemonte) | varietal |
| Côtes-du-Rhône | France (Rhône) | Grenache, Syrah |
| Corbières | France (Languedoc) | Carignan, Grenache |
| Rioja | Spain (Navarra) | Tempranillo, Garnacha |

*(Table 13.7 continued on next page)*

TABLE 13.7  **POWER CHART: RED WINES** (*continued*)

| Medium- to Full-Bodied Dry Red Wines | | |
|---|---|---|
| *Label* | *Place of Origin* | *Varietals* |
| Barbera | Italy (Piemonte) | varietal |
| Chianti Classico | Italy (Tuscany) | Sangiovese, Canaiolo, others |
| Pinot Noir | U.S.A. (California, Oregon), others | varietal |
| Rioja Reserva | Spain (Navarra) | Tempranillo, Garnacha |
| Côte-de-Beaune-Villages, Beaune, Chambolle-Musigny, Pommard, Nuits-Saint Georges, Vosne-Romanée, Gevrey-Chambertin, Le Chambertin | France, (Côte d'Or, Burgundy) | Pinot Noir |
| Médoc, Margaux St.-Julien, Pauillac, St.-Estephe | France (Médoc, Bordeaux) | Cabernet Sauvignon, Merlot |
| Graves | France (Graves, Bordeaux) | Cabernet Sauvignon, Merlot |
| St.-Émilion | France (St.-Émilion, Bordeaux) | Merlot, Cabernet Franc |
| Pomerol | France (Pomerol, Bordeaux) | Merlot, Cabernet Franc |
| Zinfandel | U.S.A. (California) | varietal |
| Châteuneuf-du-Pape | France (Southern Rhône) | Grenache, Syrah |
| Cabernet Sauvignon | U.S.A, Australia, others | varietal |
| Nebbiolo | Italy (Piemonte) | varietal |
| Gattinara, Barbaresco, Barolo | Italy (Piemonte) | Nebbiolo |
| Brunello di Montalcino | Italy (Tuscany) | Sangiovese |
| Côte Rotie, Hermitage | France (Northern Rhône) | Syrah, Grenache |
| Amarone | Italy (Veneto) | Corvina, Rondinella, others |

the previous choice. Throughout the meal, each wine and each succeeding food course should reflect an increase in flavor intensity.

A horizontal choice might simply involve matching one wine to an entrée, such as roast chicken studded with garlic under the skin, served in its own juices, accompanied by mushroom risotto and sautéed snap peas. The dominant flavor of the dish is the garlic-infused chicken, which is medium- to high-flavor intensity. You might choose a Sauvignon Blanc wine aged in oak that has undergone malolactic fermentation to complement the moderately rich flavors of the chicken's crispy skin and the creaminess of the risotto. If, on the other hand, you choose an unoaked Sauvignon Blanc, full of racy acidity (but still the same level of intensity of flavor as the chicken dish), the wine becomes a compelling counterpoint to the richer elements of the dish. The wine will become a fruity and refreshing accompaniment, charming in its simplicity.

For the same chicken dish, you could also choose a spicy red Zinfandel, with a good fruit-and-tannin balance to complement the subtly sweet garlic flavors and, secondarily, the earthiness of the mushrooms in the risotto. Many other choices are available, but the important issue here is that you are choosing one wine to match one dish.

Making vertical choices is somewhat more complex. The guidelines that will help you to make logical choices are linked closely to the idea of matching the intensity of the food and wine, and they apply whether you choose to complement or contrast food flavors in your wine choices. Again, remember that these guidelines are not rules but hints helpful in successfully marrying an array of foods, their textures and flavors, with an array of wines.

## Dry Wine Before Sweet Wine

Dry wines do not leave a lingering or cloying sweetness on the palate, which can interfere with the enjoyment of food, especially early in the meal. Although dry wines may be fruity, their lack of residual sugar allows the palate to be ready to taste more food. Sweet wines, on the other hand, especially those high in alcohol and low in acidity (sweet fortified wines are the best example) tend to deaden the palate, and so are more appropriate at the end of a meal.

Of course, there are exceptions to this guideline: Sauternes with terrine of foie gras is an obvious one. If the foie gras is served as an appetizer, it could be followed by a salad or sorbet to cleanse the palate of the fat. (A Champagne toast will also serve the same purpose.) Once the palate is cleansed, the multicourse dinner can resume with the service of dry wines.

## Lower Alcohol Before Higher Alcohol

While most table wines contain between 11 to 13 percent alcohol, this small difference is significant when they are served. If you serve a low-alcohol

# DESSERT WINES

Dessert wines are perhaps the most controversial wines served during a multicourse, multiwine meal. Not very popular in the United States, these sweet wines can be still, sparkling, or fortified. These wines engender controversy because sugar, even in relatively small amounts, tends to deaden the palate, masking other flavors. Also, these wines, especially the fortified versions, can be high in alcohol, and may be seen as the definition of "just too much" wine. Finally, perhaps the most controversial question arises, "Do these wines really complement dessert?"

Connoisseurs of *sweet* wines, many of whom prefer to call them by this name, rather than *dessert* wines, often opt to drink a small glass of Sauternes from Bordeaux, Trockenbeerenauslese from the Mosel-Saar-Ruwer, Vendange Tardive from Alsace, or P.X. Sherry on its own, in place of, rather than with, dessert. This makes a lot of sense, especially if you are tasting a very special, perhaps old or rare wine of great subtlety. If you pair a sweet wine with a sweet dessert, one or both of them will be lost in a swirl of sweetness. You will then lose the nuances of the wine if it is paired with a sweet dessert.

Should you decide to serve a sweet wine with dessert, a good rule of thumb is to make sure that the wine is sweeter than the dessert. Simple desserts without a pronounced sweet taste, cookies, apple tarts, or dried fruit compotes) will highlight the wine nicely. Perhaps the classic example of a sweet wine paired with a simple dessert comes from Italy: Vin Santo from Tuscany, Passito from Veneto or Sicily, and Picolit from Friuli-Venezia Giulia, are paired with *biscotti*, plain nut cookies that are often dipped in the wine. Elaborate desserts, full of cream or other rich flavors, even if they are not overly sweet, will still interfere with the enjoyment of the wine.

Sweet wines vary widely in character. A fine Sauternes will be luscious, redolent of honey and tropical fruits. For this reason Sauternes is often paired with a terrine of foie gras, leaving the diner to wonder how much silky luxury he or she can take. Sauternes is also high in acid and can be combined harmoniously with a plate of fresh berries or a berry tart (emphasizing the taste of the fruit in both the dessert and the wine). On the other hand, the finest sweet wines from Germany (Auslese, Beerenauslese, Eiswein, and Trockenbeerenauslese) and the Vendange Tardive and Sélection de Grains Nobles from Alsace, can be light and delicate, almost austere when compared to Sauternes. The sweetness of the German and Alsace wines is moderated by bracing and refreshing acidity and so, like Sauternes, makes a brilliant complement to simple fruit-based desserts. Of course, sparkling dessert wines like Asti (and the lesser-known red sparkler, Brachetto d'Acqui, also from Piemonte), refresh the palate with good levels of acidity and cleanse the palate with their bubbles. Finally, fortified wines, like Ports and sweet Sherries, are high in alcohol and rich in flavor, and are probably best served *after* dessert, and in cool weather.

wine after a high-alcohol wine, the low-alcohol wine could very well taste thin and watery, with unappealing flavor qualities. If all the wines served are about the same level of alcohol, say 12 percent, then other taste factors—acid, tannin, relative youth, production method (stainless steel or oak-barrel maturation, for example)—come into play. High levels of glycerin (the "legs" or "fingers" that coat the glass) in the wine will increase the feeling of softness and fatness in the mouth. Glycerin, a by-product of fermentation, is most pronounced in high-alcohol wines.

## Sparkling Wines Before Still Wines

Champagne and other fine sparkling wines can invigorate and cleanse the palate at the beginning of a meal. They can also serve as an intermezzo or toast after the main course of a meal to reinvigorate the taste buds. Although sparklers are often overlooked as dinner wines, an entire menu can be planned around them, starting with the lightest blanc de blancs, and working up to the fullest rosé brut Champagne. Sparkling wines work well with hors d'oeuvres at the beginning of a meal, especially salty and briny items like smoked salmon and shrimp, as well as food that, although served in small portions, is intensely flavored and rich, like foie gras. The bubbles in the wine wipe away the salt and the fat and stimulate the appetite.

## Younger Wine Before Older Wine

Younger wines usually lack the complexity and nuance of older wines and so should be served first. If you serve two wines with a single course—one younger, one older—the wines should somehow be differentiated, perhaps with a more-elegant glass for the older wine. Usually the oldest wines are more-elegant for the main course, or sometimes the cheese course, as complex, rich, somewhat tannic red wines served with creamy, rich, soft cheeses are the ultimate expression of the contrast between food and wine.

A corollary to this guideline is that as the meal progresses, the chosen wines might build in quality from one wine to the next, so that by the time the main course is served, a dramatic wine or wines is served with it. Of course, the best wine (and sometimes the most-powerful; red wine and cheese is the classic example of contrasting flavors) can be served with the cheese course, or even the dessert, but if a very fine, perhaps rare red wine is served with the main course, there is no need to top it with the final courses.

## Wine in the Sauce/Wine in the Glass

Food prepared with wine should be served with wine of the same type, style, or grape variety, because the wine in the glass will reemphasize and highlight the wine in the food. It is normally not a good idea to taste two dramatically different wines at once, as the flavors can fight each other. Matching the wine in the food with the wine in the glass makes for a basic complementary match. While it is a good rule of thumb never to cook with a wine you are unwilling to drink, you probably will want to serve a higher quality wine than you used to make the sauce or marinade.

## Light Wines Before Full-Bodied Wines

The normal progression of wine and food calls for the white wines to be served in order of intensity—light, medium-bodied, full—and then the red wines in the same order. The underlying idea is that even a light red wine has more intense flavors than a full-bodied white wine, but this is not always the case. For example, you might choose to serve a light red, such as Beaujolais-Villages, with a sautéed fish course, and in the next course serve an oaky Chardonnay with grilled quail. So, although the color of the wine is important, another critical issue is the level of tannin in each of the wines. The menu might also feature the oaky Chardonnay with the same fish course along with the young, fruity Beaujolais, but not accompanied by a full-bodied red, whose tannins will clash with both the fish and the white wine. The flavors of white wines are very different from those of red wines, and the levels of intensity are also quite different.

## Crossover Wines

If tannins are prominent in the flavor of any given wine, the accompanying food should be at least somewhat creamy textured, which usually translates as fat. The creaminess of fat cuts tannin, so that the fruit, and perhaps spice, of a full-bodied wine will be emphasized, and the tannin will be moderated. On the opposite end of the spectrum, if you try to pair a light-bodied, simple wine with a complex steak dish, the flavors and textures of the wine will be lost. Even a somewhat full-bodied white wine would be unlikely to stand up to the richness of the dish, and it will taste lean and, at best, inoffensive.

The uncoagulated proteins, the juices that flow in meats and fatty fishes cooked rare, often referred to as "blood," are important in the matching of wine and food. Fish, however, even at its fattiest, is usually far lower in fat than meat, so a grilled tuna fillet served on a ragout of lentils cannot support an intensely flavored, high-tannin wine, while a roasted leg of lamb in a pan gravy certainly can. In fact, if a high-tannin wine is served with a fish dish, even one that is grilled and full flavored, both the wine and the food will taste metallic and unpleasant.

We are not saying that red wines cannot be served with fish—far from it. A red wine that is low to moderate in tannins, and not overtly alcoholic in flavor, is a wonderful accompaniment to fatty fishes that are broiled, grilled, blackened, or cooked in a way that gives the fish a "meaty" flavor and texture. As we mentioned before, a poached fish cooked in white wine and herbs calls for a light, simple white wine, while the same fish grilled will call for a full-bodied white wine or a crossover red wine, such as young wines based in Gamay, Pinot Noir, Grignolino, or Dolcetto, among a whole host of fruity, easy-to-drink red wines. Without a preponderance of tannin and its attendant bitterness, these crossover wines work well with lighter meats and poultry dishes, as well as with meatier fish dishes.

# Mixing and Matching

If you have been reading this chapter closely, it is clear by now that the old dictum of "white wine with fish, red wine with meat," while serviceable in a pinch, is not the only way to go. As our palates have become more adventurous, and our interest in the foods of indigenous, ethnic, and foreign cultures has grown, we have experimented with new food-and-wine combinations. Today the formal notions of an earlier time, though based in logic and experience, just might not provide the excitement that our palates crave.

Geographical, cultural, and historical relationships among wine and food have often been taken as a given when matching regional food to regional wine (for example, in Tuscany pasta in a hare sauce with Chianti). In a world where authentic foods from Europe, Africa, Asia, or South America can be served in Chicago, New York, or San Francisco, one of the old saws now being exploded is nationalism or regionalism in food-and-wine pairing. Although you will not go too far wrong by matching food from a particular region with an appropriate wine from that region, there is nothing wrong with matching a wine from Oregon with a dish native to Burgundy. The classic Beef Bourguignon may have been born to marry with a regional or communal red wine from the Côte de Nuits, but a Pinot Noir from the Willamette Valley will also do the job nicely. Arcachón oysters on the half shell, from France's Bordeaux region, served with a mignonette of vinegar and shallots, make an incomparable match with the local young Entre Deux Mers, but a crisp Sauvignon Blanc from Sonoma may also be just the ticket, because of the high acidity, light body, and assertive fruit flavors.

The food and wine world is vast, and there is no doubt that when you visit the classic wine-growing regions of that world, it is always a special treat to taste the local food and wine together. That gastronomic world is also changing; instead of, or in addition to our traveling to Burgundy and Bordeaux, their wines travel to us, and Oregon and Sonoma wines travel to France. Intermarriage is sure to become the order of the day at the table, as we continue our quest for knowledge of, and experience with, both the classic cuisine and innovative dishes of so many cultures.

## The Vinegar Issue: Acid Plus Acid

Notice that in the example of the oysters served with Sauvignon Blanc (be it from Bordeaux or Sonoma), there is vinegar in the sauce. In fact, the sauce is nothing but vinegar and shallots. There is no doubt that vinegar, because of its overwhelming acidity, can be the enemy of wine. However, vinegar can provide an appealing, piquant character to a dish, when it is used with a restrained hand. It was not too long ago that wine was never served with a salad course if there was vinegar (or citrus) in the dressing. That is no longer the case, because fruity vinaigrette dressings, and naturally sweet elements in a dish, like the shallots in a mignonette, help to create a friendly environment for high-acid wines, especially those with assertive fruit. When acid in the dish is matched with acid in the wine, the result on the palate is less acid, not more. It is a case of $2 + 2 = 1$; acid matched with acid de-emphasizes the acidity of the wine and food match and highlights the other flavors in the food and the wine.

In most cases, acid and acid marry well, but is important to match the dominant flavors of the dish with the dominant flavors of the wine. You must also take into account the body of both the food and the wine. A thin, fruity wine that is high in acidity—Muscadet and Chenin Blanc are two examples that come to mind—work well with an appetizer of tuna ceviche (thin strips of fish "cooked" in the acid of lemon juice or vinegar) served with tomato and jalapeño garnish. The same wines, however, would get lost if paired with a pasta in a sauce of olive oil, garlic, mushrooms, and sun-dried tomatoes. For this dish, which features the medium-bodied but intensely acidic and fruity taste of tomatoes and the mellow sweetness of garlic, you might welcome a young Chianti or Barbera, thus matching intensity with intensity. These two red wines are reasonably high in acid and fruit and will strike an attractive balance with the garlic and tomatoes, the dominant flavors in the pasta dish.

A good rule of thumb for matching high-acid, refreshing wines with food that features acid in the overall taste is to strike a balance of flavors. To do so, try to match the wine and food at a fairly even level, not highlighting either one. Experience shows that acid in food does not come from protein or fat, but mostly from fruits, vegetables, and their derivative products (lemon juice, vinegar). Just as these foods and products are most often used to "awaken" the taste buds and to highlight flavor and texture, so too does an acidic wine—another fruit product— highlight the same aspects of a dish.

## Does Acid Cut Fat Successfully?

Just as fat cuts the bitter overtones of tannic wines, so too does acid—the refreshing, pleasantly citric-sour palate cleanser that makes the mouth water— also cuts through fat. So can you always match a moderate- to high-acid white or red wine with a fatty dish? The answer is an unequivocal . . . maybe.

We are not trying to be coy; whether the marriage of a high-acid wine with a high-fat food will be successful is a difficult question. The success of the pairing appears to depend primarily on the kind and amount of fat in the food. Is it plant-based (vegetable oil), animal based (meat, fish, poultry, offal), or dairy based (raw milk products, cultured milk products)?

Plant-based fats, such as olive or peanut oil tend to impart a lighter taste than animal-based fats, such as cream or butter; these vegetable oils do not normally coat the palate as much as rich dairy fats. Because these fats taste less rich, they can work nicely with the tastes of lemon and vinegar and therefore will also work well with high-acid wines. Animal fats are another story. Raw milk products, such as cream, butter, and whole milk, tend to be heavier on the palate than cultured and fermented milk products, such as yogurt and cheeses. In general, the heavier raw milk products do not react well with moderate-to-high acid wines; the combination creates an almost rancid taste in the mouth. Of course, there are exceptions to this sweeping generality, especially if the acidic wine is also full bodied, but in most cases these wines do not complement, for example, butter- or cream-based sauces.

On the other hand, cultured dairy products seem to be more flexible partners with high-acid wines. Yogurt can make a fine crust for broiled chicken, and some cheeses, like young, crumbly goat cheese, can be quite tart. Both the broiled chicken with yogurt crust and the tangy cheese will complement a light, fruity white wine, such as Vinho Verde from Portugal or an un-oaked Sauvignon Blanc, such as Sancerre from the Loire Valley; or a fruity, fairly acidic red wine, such as Veneto's Valpolicella or Beaujolais-Villages.

## Food and Wine Antagonists

Some foods need a little "finessing" to marry happily with wine. Vinegar is not the only problem one encounters when matching flavors of food and wine. Very spicy foods, such as those made with fiery hot chilies, easily overwhelm many wines. Often, beer is paired with these spicy dishes, but there are wines that work well with spicy food. With spicy Asian dishes—kung pao chicken, Szechuan pork, lamb vindaloo, fiery vegetarian curries—white wines that are spicy, like Gewürztraminer ("Gewürz" means "spicy") or off-dry Riesling, with assertive fruit and acidity; or low-alcohol, low-tannin, fruity red wines, like lightly chilled Côtes-du-Rhône, can cool down the heat and emphasize the savory aspects of the food. It helps to serve the wine somewhat colder than usual, to enhance the spice or acid in the wine.

Depending on their intensity, beef, poultry, or game dishes with spicy sauces, crusts, or accompaniments can support rosé wines and lighter-bodied to fuller-bodied red wines, all with forward fruit and reasonably high acid levels.

One problem common to highly spiced foods is that salt is a major seasoning. Highly salted foods, especially those with intense flavors—a grilled veal steak in a chipotle chile sauce, for example—emphasize the taste of alcohol in the wine. Red and white wines that are 11 to 12 percent alcohol will taste unbalanced and overly alcoholic with food that is intensely flavored and salty. Champagne or other, less-expensive sparkling wines, with their cooling, refreshing acidity, do well with salty food. Good examples are Champagne and caviar, or sparkling wines with smoked foods, marinated in a salt brine. Smoked salmon accompanied by Champagne is almost a given at formal brunches.

## THE ARTICHOKE QUESTION

Why are wines and artichokes a problem? Artichokes contain an acid, cynarin, that (for about 80 percent of the population) will make accompanying beverages, even water, taste sweet. If you are serving artichokes as a side dish or in a salad, choose a wine that is light and fruity, either white or red. Most likely the fruit in the wine will be emphasized at the expense of the other flavors, and usually this is an appealing reaction. If, however, you serve a dry white or tannic red wine with the artichokes, you might get an unpleasant, unctuously sweet taste in the wine, throwing the food and wine out of balance. One way to alleviate this problem is to deep-fry the artichokes (carciofa alla giudia), which seems to de-emphasize the cynarin reaction.

Speaking of brunches, another "problem food" is eggs. Most wines do not really enhance the flavors of most egg dishes, but light-bodied fruity whites and reds do well with omelets, as do sparkling wines. The choice of wine should be adjusted depending on the ingredients in the omelet, but try to avoid wines high in tannins. Classic egg dishes like Quiche Lorraine bring us back to the idea of geographical matching; Riesling or Sylvaner from Alsace (full name, Alsace-Lorraine) enhances this rich egg tart.

## *Seasonality*

Just as serving foods that are appropriate to the season has become an increasingly important part of dining in the United States, so too has serving seasonal wines. On a hot summer day, or in South Florida in January, we may want nothing heavier than some ice-cold oysters and a salad of local greens and garden-fresh tomatoes, or a simple roast beef sandwich on good bread, accompanied by potato salad. We certainly would not be looking for a heavy, complex, tannic red wine with the latter dish, and we definitely would not be interested in an oaky, full-bodied white wine with the oysters and salad. However, a crisp, light, low-alcohol Galestro from Tuscany, exhibiting simple, fruity flavors and mouth-watering acidity, would be a refreshing summer wine, matching the briny flavor and shimmering textures of the oysters, as well as the fresh crunch of the greens and the sweetness and acidity of the tomatoes. Likewise, the roast beef sandwich and potato salad would happily marry with a light fruity red wine, perhaps a Beaujolais or Valpolicella. These low-tannin "crossover" red wines work well because the cold roast beef and the potato salad are not overwhelmingly rich or fatty on the palate, and so could not support a very powerful, tannic red. In the intense heat we might want to chill the red wine in the refrigerator for about an hour before service, in order to emphasize its refreshing acidity and simplicity, in balance with fruit, very light tannins, and moderate alcohol.

In the dead of winter a menu as described above would hardly satisfy an appetite brought on by skiing, skating, or shoveling snow. In cold weather, we tend to gravitate to heartier fare, say a venison stew, served with winter root vegetables, all braised in a liquid of half veal stock/half Merlot red wine. Naturally, we will want to serve a Merlot-based wine with the dish, to make for a satisfying and warming meal. Similarly, the traditional roast goose could be served on Christmas day with an older Amarone, a "huge" red wine that, with its warming intensity of tannin, dried-fruit flavors, and especially its high alcohol (approaching 15 percent), is a cold-weather knockout punch.

To everything there is a season, and this includes wines. In the heat of the summer or in a year-round warm climate, a high-alcohol wine will make you sweat and make your head swim. In a bitter cold climate that same wine will make you feel warm and cozy. To serve a light, crisp wine with a complex cold weather meal is to dilute the effect of the heartiness that is so welcome in winter's chill.

## Summary

Exploring wine and food is a journey that can take a lifetime. The pleasures of the table are many, but few are more satisfying than the happy union of food and wine. The ideas, guidelines, and tools presented in this chapter will help you to make judgments about what wines to match with what foods. Every time you make a decision, you will be advancing your own wine and food knowledge. Whether you are planning a banquet in a hotel, giving wine advice to a party of two in an intimate restaurant setting, or just entertaining friends at home, pairing food and wine is a valuable skill.

# Menus

Following are a series of theoretical regional food and wine menus from different countries of the world. Notice that we are using the guidelines we have outlined in this chapter to match the foods and wines. First courses marry with the lightest wines, and the intensity of the wines increases as the intensity of the food increases. In some cases the flavors in the wine complement the flavors of the food, and in some cases they provide a contrast, creating a compelling counterpoint for the dish.

Notice also that for each course the first wine choice is native to the region, country, or continent, and the second choice comes from different wine-growing regions of the world. Sometimes these nonnative wines contain the same grapes as the native wine, sometimes not, but the style and intensity of flavor is a good theoretical match for each dish. Often, both wine choices will complement or contrast the flavors in the food, but sometimes one of the wines will complement the flavors, while the other will contrast. What we are emphasizing is that while native food and wine marriages are desirable, so are the intermarriages of food and wine from different parts of the world.

Please note that we have decided not to include vintages on any of the wines, as this is an exercise not in picking the wine from the best year but in picking the right style of wine for each dish. Where a wine is, by definition, nonvintage, like many Champagnes, we have included the letters NV.

# France

## Alsace

Tarte á l'Oignon/Onion Tart

*Pinot Blanc, Hugel. Alsace*
*or*
*Arneis dei Roeri, Ceretto, Piemonte, Italy*

..............................

Escargots en Raviole aux Graines de Pavot
Ravioli of Snails with Poppy Seeds

*Sylvaner, Trimbach, Alsace*
*or*
*Sauvignon Blanc, Cloudy Bay, Marlborough, New Zealand*

..............................

Salade de Betteraves/Beetroot Salad

..............................

Choucroute Garnie á l'Alsacienne/Alsatian Choucroute

*Reisling, Dopff, Alsace*
*or*
*Reisling Kabinett, Deinhard, Rheingau, Germany*

..............................

Tarte aux Myrtilles á l'Alsacienne/Alsatian Huckleberry Tart

*Gewürztraminer, Vendange Tardive, Domaine Weinbach, Alsace*
*or*
*Vidal, Icewine, Inniskillin, Ontario, Canada*

# France

## Provence/Côtes du Rhone

Tapenade/Pounded Capers, Anchovies, and Black Olives

*Blanc de Blancs, Moulin des Costes, Bandol*
*or*
*Galestro, Antinori, Toscana, Italy*

..............................

Rougets au Fenouil Sous la Cendre/Mullet with Fennel Baked in Ashes

*Bandol Rosé, Cuvée Marine, Domaines Ott, Côtes de Provence*
*or*
*Grenache Rosé "Mistral," Joseph Phelps, Napa, California*

..............................

Salade Aixoise/Artichoke and Bean Salad

..............................

Gigot d'Agneau Sauce à l'Ail/Leg of Lamb with Garlic Sauce

*Châteauneuf-du-Pape, Beaucastel, Rhône*
*or*
*Mourvèdre, Cline, Sonoma, California*

..............................

Melon de Cavaillon au Muscat de Beaumes-de-Venise et la Menthe
Cavaillon Melon with Muscat de Beaumes-de-Venise and Mint

*Muscat de Beaumes-de-Venise, Paul Jaboulet Ainé, Rhône*
*or*
*Essencia, Quady, San Joaquin, California*

# France

## Burgundy/Beaujolais

Ragout d'Asperges et Prèmieres Morilles Printanières
Ragout of Asparagus with Morel Mushrooms

*Chablis, Vocoret, Chablis, Burgundy*
*or*
*Chardonnay, "Calla-lees," Callaway, South Central Coast, California*

......................

Pauchose/River Fish Stew

*Meursault "Perrières" 1er Cru, Perrin-Ponsot, Côte de Beaune, Burgundy*
*or*
*Monopole, CVNE, Rioja, Spain*

......................

Pigeon de Bresse Poêle au Vin Rouge/Bresse Pigeon Fried in Red Wine

*Morgon, Jean Descombes, Duboeuf, Beaujolais, Burgundy*
*or*
*Pinot Noir, Millbrook, Hudson Valley, New York*

......................

Les Fromages/Cheeses
Charolais, Grand Vatel, Aisy Cendré, L'Ami du Chambertin

*Charmes-Chambertin Grand Cru, Joseph Roty, Côte de Nuits, Burgundy*
*or*
*Vega Sicilia, "Unico," Ribera del Duero, Spain*

# France
## Paris Bistro Menu with Loire Wines

(The wines of the Loire are much appreciated in the bistros of Paris)

Huitres Chaudes Sur Endives/Poached Oysters on a Bed of Endive

*Muscadet de Sevre et Maine Sur Lie, Marquis de Goulaine, Loire*
*or*
*Fumé Blanc, Fetzer, California*

..........................

Salade Maraîchère aux Truffes Frâiches
Warm Green Salad with Fresh Truffles

*Vouvray Sec, Marc Brédif, Loire*
*or*
*Chenin Blanc, Chalone, Monterey, California*

..........................

Turbot Grillé avec Beurre Blanc
Grilled Turbot with a White Butter Sauce

*Savennières, Coulée de Serrant, Loire*
*or*
*Chardonnay, Jean Léon, Penedés, Spain*

..........................

Rouelle de Veau Braisée aux Cèpes et Galette de Pommes de Terre
Braised Veal Shank with Cèpe Mushrooms and Sautéed Potato Pancake

*Chinon, Pierre Jacques Druet, Loire*
*or*
*Garrafeira, Grão Vasco, Dão, Portugal*

..........................

Tarte Tatin/Upside Down Apple Tart

*Vouvray, Gaston Huet, Loire*
*or*
*Château Coutet, Barsac, Bordeaux, France*

# France

## Bordeaux/Southwest

Les Moules à l'Oseille/Mussels with Sorrel

*Domaine de Chevalier, Graves, Bordeaux*
*or*
*Sémillon, Cousiño Maucul, Maipo, Chile*

...............................

L'Omelette aux Truffes/Truffle Omelette

*Château de Belingrad, Bergerac*
*or*
*Barbera, "Bricco dell'Uccelone," Giacomo Bologna, Piemonte, Italy*

...............................

Le Cassoulet/White Bean Stew
with Sausages, Tomatoes, Garlic, and Meats

*Château Clos Fourtet, St.-Émilion, Bordeaux*
*or*
*Cabernet Franc, Niebaum-Coppola, Napa, California*

...............................

Les Fromages/Cheeses
Camembert, Pont l'Eveque, Livarot, Tomme de Cantal

*Château Palmer, Margaux, Bordeaux*
*or*
*Marlstone, Clos du Bois, Sonoma, California*

...............................

Les Jacques/Apple Pancakes

*Château Lafaurie-Peyraguey, Sauternes, Bordeaux*
*or*
*Picolit, Jermann, Friuli-Venezia Giulia, Italy*

# France

## Champagne

Truite à l'Estragon/Trout in a Court-Bouillon with Tarragon

*Blanc de Blancs, Charbaut Certificate, Champagne, Vintage*
*or*
*Blanc de Blancs, Schramsberg, Napa, California, Vintage*

...........................

Agneau Roti/Roast Lamb

*Rosé, Taittinger, Comtes de Champagne, Vintage*
*or*
*Rosé, Ferrari, Trentino Alto-Adige, Italy NV*

...........................

Salade au Lard/Green Salad with Bacon Lardons

*Extra Dry White Star, Moët et Chandon, Champagne, NV*
*or*
*Sparkling Seyval, Clinton Vineyards, Hudson River, New York*

...........................

Les Fromages/Cheeses
Cendré, Brie, Coulommiers, Langres

*Brut, Bollinger R.D., Champagne, Vintage*
*or*
*Brut, Late-Disgorged, Iron Horse, Sonoma Green Valley, California*

...........................

Poires a la Champenoise
Pears Poached in Champagne, Biscuits, and Apricots

*Demi-Sec, Cordon Vert, Mumm, Champagne, NV*
*or*
*Vinho Espumante, Luis Pato, Bairrada, Portugal NV*

# Italy
## Roma/Lazio

Carciofi alla Giudia/Fried Artichokes Jewish-Style

*Frascati, Fontina Candida, Lazio*
*or*
*Vinho Verde, Casaliero, Minho, Portugal*

..........................

Rigatoni all'Ammiraglia/Rigatoni with Squid, Clams and Mussels

*Marino Superiore Secco, "Oro," Paola Di Mauro, Lazio*
*or*
*Sauvignon Blanc, Klein Constantia, Stellenbosch, South Africa*

..........................

Abbacchio alla Cacciatora e la Fava Romana
Baby Lamb Cooked with Rosemary, Garlic, Anchovies,
Vinegar, and Fava Beans

*Fiorano Rosso, Boncompagni Ludovisi, Lazio*
*or*
*Gran Reserva, Montecillo, Rioja, Spain*

..........................

Crema Caramella/Caramel-Glazed Custard

*Vellitri Bianco Amabile, Consorzio Produttori Vini Velletri, Lazio*
*or*
*Riesling Auslese, Bernakasteler Doktor, Kerpen, Mosel-Saar-Ruwer,*
*Germany*

# *Italy*
## *Toscana*

Insalata di funghi e tartufi/Salad of Wild Mushrooms and Truffles

*Vernaccia di San Gimignano, San Quirico, Toscana*
*or*
*Pinot Blanc, Buehler, Napa, California*

.............................

Tonnoaccio al Pesto e Vinaigrette
Grilled Tuna with a Pesto/Vinaigrette Marinade

*Chianti Colline Pisane, Tenuta di Ghizzano, Toscana*
*or*
*Sangiovese, Atlas Peak, Napa, California*

.............................

Pappardelle alla Lepre/Egg Noodles with Hare Sauce

*Carmignano, Fattoria Il Poggiolo, Toscana*
*or*
*Pinot Noir, Panther Creek, Willamette, Oregon*

.............................

Ossobuco al Vino e Tarragone/Veal Shank in Wine and Tarragon Sauce

*Brunello di Montalcino, Biondi-Santi, Toscana*
*or*
*Château Bon Pasteur, Pomerol, Bordeaux, France*

.............................

Biscotti di Prato/Almond and Hazlenut Cookies from Prato

*Vin Santo, Frescobaldi, Pomino, Toscana*
*or*
*Muscat Nectar, Tsantali, Samos, Greece*

# Italy

## Veneto

Broeto/Venetian Fish Soup

*Soave Classico, "Capitel Foscarino," Anselmi, Veneto*
*or*
*Albariño, Morgadio Rías-Baixas, Spain*

...............................

Insalata di Funghi Crudo/Salad of Raw Mushrooms

*Bardolino, Bolla, Veneto*
*or*
*Fleurie, Paul Sapin, Beaujolais, Burgundy, France*

...............................

Torresani alla Perverada
Spit-Roasted Pigeons with a Sausage-Liver Herb Sauce
Served on Polenta

*Recioto della Amarone, Valpolicella, Masi, Veneto*
*or*
*Côte-Rotie, Côte Blonde et Brune, Guigal, Rhône, France*

...............................

Strucolo/Cheese Pastry

*Prosecco di Conegliano-Valdobbiadene Amabile,*
*Santa Margherita, Veneto*
*or*
*Demi-Sec, H. Piper, Mendoza, Argentina*

# *Italy*

## *Emilia-Romagna*

Frizon con Salsiccia/Vegetable Sauté

*Albama di Romagna, Celli, Emilia-Romagna*
*or*
*Viña Sol, Torres, Penedés, Spain*

..............................

Ali di Pollo Parmigiana/Chicken Wings Parmesan

*Lambrusco di Sorbara, Fini, Emilia-Romagna*
*or*
*Periquita, Fonseca, Alentejo, Portugal*

..............................

Fegato di Vitello all'Aceto Balsamico
Calf's Liver with Balsamic Vinegar

*Sangiovese di Romagna Riserva Superiore, Cesari, Emilia-Romagna*
*or*
*Merlot, Yarden, Golan, Israel*

..............................

Bonissima/Emilian Nut Tart

*Malvasia Amabile, Terre Rosse, Emilia-Romagna*
*or*
*Moscato d'Oro, Robert Mondavi, Napa, California*

# *Italy*

## *Piemonte*

Bagna Cauda
A "Hot Bath" Dip of Oil, Garlic, and Anchovies Served with Crudités

*Gavi dei Gavi, Villa Sparina, Piemonte*
*or*
*Sauvignon Blanc, Byron, Santa Barbara, California*

..............................

Rane Verdi/Green Frog's Legs

*Grignolino, Aldo Conterno, Piemonte*
*or*
*Pinot Noir Rosé, Oeil de Perdrix, Neuchatel, Switzerland*

..............................

Tajarin al Tartufo/Egg Noodles with Butter, Parmesan and White Truffles

*Barbaresco, "Sori San Lorenzo," Gaja, Piemonte*
*or*
*Vacqueyras, Jaboulet, Rhône, France*

..............................

Cinghiale Brasato al Barolo/Wild Boar Braised in Barolo

*Barolo, "Marcenasco," Renato Ratti, Piemonte*
*or*
*Opus One, Mondavi/Rothschild, Napa, California*

..............................

Tome/Mild Sheep's Milk Cheese from the Langhe

*Dolcetto d'Alba, Sandrone, Piemonte*
*or*
*Pinot Noir, Pindar, North Fork, Long Island, New York*

..............................

Torta Gianduia/Hazelnut Torte

*Asti, Fontanafredda, Piemonte*
*or*
*Demi-Sec, Cordon Vert, Mumm, Champagne, France, NV*

# *Italy*

## *Sicilia*

Polipo Siciliano/Octopus in Garlic and Oil

*Corvo Bianco, Duca di Salaparuta, Sicily*
*or*
*Sauvignon Blanc, Cakebread, Napa, California*

.............................

Dentice alla Griglia/Grilled Red Snapper

*Cerasuolo di Vittoria, Nino Rallo, Sicily*
*or*
*Valpolicella Classico Superiore "da Marano," Boscaini, Veneto, Italy*

.............................

Insalata di Arancie, Finocchio, e Olive Nere
Orange, Fennel, and Black Olive Salad

.............................

Spezzato di Montone alla Menta/Lamb Stew with Fresh Mint

*Duca Enrico, Duca di Salaparuta, Sicily*
*or*
*Reserva, Contino, Rioja, Spain*

.............................

Cassata/Chocolate and Candied Fruit on Sponge Cake

*Malvasia della Lipari, "Capo Salina," Carlo Hauner, Sicily*
*or*
*Blanc de Noirs, "Wedding Cuvée," Iron Horse,*
*Sonoma Green Valley, California*

# Spain
## and Basque Regions

**Tapas: Tortillitas de Camarones, Gambas al Ajillo, Buñuelos de Bacalaos**
**Appetizers: Shrimp Pancakes, Prawns in Garlic, Salt Cod Puffs**

*Fino, Osborne, Jerez*
*or*
*Corvo Bianco, Duca di Salaparuta, Sicily, Italy*

..................................

Gazpacho Andaluz/Cold Tomato and Vegetable Soup

*Txacoli, Txomin Etxaniz, Guetaria (Basque Country)*
*or*
*Château Bouscaut Blanc, Graves, Bordeaux, France*

..................................

Zarzuela/Shellfish Medley

*Albariño, Valdamor, Rías Baixas*
*or*
*Tocai, Marco Felluga, Friuli-Venezia Giulia, Italy*

..................................

Conejo al Salmonejo y Habas con Jamón
Rabbit Cooked in Wine and Vinegar with Herbs
and Sautéed Lima Beans with Ham

*Reserva, Remelluri, Rioja Alavesa (Basque Country)*
*Pesquera, Alejandro Fernandez, Ribero del Duero*
*or*
*Savigny-Les Beaunes, Leroy, Côtes-de-Beaune, Burgundy, France*
*Le Pergole Torte, Monte Vertine, Toscana, Italy*

..................................

Churros/Fried Pastries

*Cava, Paul Cheneau, Cava/Penedés*
*or*
*Demi-Sec, Pol Roger, Champagne, France*

# *Portugal*

Açorda de Mariscos/Bread-Thickened "Dry" Shrimp Soup
with Eggs and Coriander

*Vinho Verde, Quinta da Aveleda, Minho*
*or*
*Saumer, Bouvet-Ladubay, Loire, France*

............................

Sardinas Grelhadas/Grilled Sardines

*Branco, Duque de Viseu, Dão*
*or*
*Sancerre, Comte LaFond, Loire, France*

............................

Arroz de Pato com Choriço e Feijão Verde com Coentro e Alho
Braised Duck and Rice with Sausages,
and Green Beans with Coriander and Garlic

*Vinho Tinto, Luis Pato, Bairrada*
*or*
*Syrah-Sirah, Preston, Sonoma, California*

............................

Totya de Laranja/Flourless Orange Torte

*Malmsey, Henriques & Henriques, Madeira*
*or*
*Pineau des Charantes, Noble, France*

# Germany

Heringsalat/Herring Salad

*Riesling QbA, Sichel, Rheingau*
*or*
*Aragosta, Sella & Mosca, Sardinia, Italy*

..................

Nudelsoupe mit Hühner/Noodle Soup with Chicken

..................

Schweinebraten mit Pflaumen, mit Rotkohl und Kastanien
Roast Pork with Prune Stuffing, served with Red Cabbage and Chestnuts

*Riesling Spätlese, Bernkasteler Doktor, Egon Müller, Mosel-Saar-Ruwer*
*or*
*Puligny-Montrachet, "Les Pucelles," Jadot, Côte de Beaune,*
*Burgundy, France*

..................

Verweltker Kopfsalat mit Specksosse/Wilted Lettuce
with Bacon Dressing

*Silvaner QbA, L. Guntrum, Rheinhessen*
*or*
*Chenin Blanc, Fleur du Cap, Stellenbosch, South Africa*

..................

Apfelalflauf/Apple Soufflé

*Riesling Auslese, Wehlener Sonnenuhr, J.J. Prüm, Mosel-Saar-Ruwer*
*or*
*Muscat de Beaumes-de-Venise, Domaine Coyeaux, Rhône, France*

# Austria

Erdbeersupe/Cold Strawberry Soup

Grüner Veltliner, Schlumberger, Wien
*or*
Muscat, Léon Beyer, Alsace, France

...................

Seezungenschnitten in Weisswein/Fillet of Sole in White Wine

Riesling, De Vite, Weinviertel, Niederösterreich
*or*
Chablis, Dauvissat, Chablis, Burgundy, France

...................

Hasenbraten mit Rahmsoss und Semmelknödel
Roast Hare with Sour Cream Sauce and Bread Dumplings

Blaufränkirsch, Feiler-Artinger, Neusiedlersee-Hügelland, Burgenland
*or*
Pinot Noir, Coldstream Hills, Yarra, Australia

...................

Haselnussmakronen/Hazelnut Macaroons

Spätrot-Rotgipgler Auslese, Franz Kurz,
Gumpoldskirchen, Thermenregion
*or*
Vin Santo, Il Poggione, Toscana, Italy

# Greece

Spararangia Latholémono/Asparagus Marinated in Olive Oil and Lemon

*Robola, Calliga, Kephalonia*
*or*
*Bianco di Custoza, Tommasi, Veneto, Italy*

..........................

Maritas Tighanités/Tiny Fried Fish

*Demestica Áspra, Achaia-Clauss, Patras*
*or*
*Sauvignon Blanc, Shaw & Smith, Southern Vales, South Australia*

..........................

Gouronunópoulo tis Soúvla/Spit-Roasted Suckling Pig

*Castello, Minos, Crete*
*or*
*Barbaresco, "Moccagatta," Produttori del Barbaresco, Piemonte, Italy*

..........................

Panzária Kritiká/Beet Salad with Allspice

..........................

Sika Piperáta/Peppered Dried Figs

*Mavrodaphne, Boutari, Peloponnisos*
*or*
*Elysium Black Muscat, Quady, San Joaquin, California*

# A Middle East / Mediterranean Feast

Ajlouke de Carrotes/Tunisian Carrot and Potato Appetizer

*Thrace, Tekel, Tunisia*
*or*
*Pinot Bianco, Collavini, Friuli-Venezia Giulia, Italy*

..........................

Shorbat Ads/Egyptian Lentil Soup

..........................

Samak Mahshi Bi Roz/Syrian Sweet and Sour Fish Stuffed with Rice

*Emerald Riesling, Carmel, Israel*
*or*
*Gewürztraminer, Lenz, North Fork, Long Island, New York*

..........................

Djej M'qualli/Moroccan Chicken with preserved Lemons and Olives

*Tarik, Chaudsoleil, Rabat, Morocco*
*or*
*Chardonnay, Han Krum, Provadya, Bulgaria*

..........................

Kibbeh/Lebanese Ground Lamb with Onion, Burghul, and Spices

*Château Musar, Bekaa Valley, Lebanon*
*or*
*Gigondas, Domaine les Gouberts, Rhône, France*

..........................

Slat Avocado Vepri Hada/Israeli Avocado and Citrus Salad

*Sauvignon Blanc, Yarden, Golan Heights, Israel*
*or*
*Riesling, Hogue Cellars, Yakima, Washington*

..........................

Ayva Tatlisi/Turkish Baked Quince

*Commandaria, SODAP, Limassol, Cyprus*
*or*
*Vignoles, Baldwin, Hudson River, New York*

# Hungary

Szerb Bableves/Serbian Bean Soup

...........................

Halkolblasz/Fish Sausage

*Szurkebarat, Mátraalja, Hungary*
*or*
*Silvaner, Dopff & Iron, Alsace, France*

...........................

Párolt Vadilha Gombóccal/Braised Wild Goose with Dumplings

*Bikáver, Eger, Hungary*
*or*
*Zinfandel, "Dickerson Vineyard," Ravenswood, Napa, California*

...........................

Alma-Kelkáposztasalata/Apple and Savoy Cabbage Salad

*Kéknyelü, Badacsony, Hungary*
*or*
*Gran Fuedo, Chivite, Navarra, Spain*

...........................

Csokoládes Máktorája/Poppyseed Torte

*Tokaji Asjú/4 Puttonyos, Hungary*
*or*
*Portblanc, Yarden, Israel*

## *South Africa*

Kaltschale/Curried Fish Stew

*Blanc Fumé, La Motte, Franschhoek*
*or*
*Sauvignon Blanc, Silverado, Napa, California*

.........................

Bobotie Geelrys
Baked Ground Lamb Casserole with Yellow Rice and Raisins

*Pinotage, Fleur du Cap, Bergkelder, Stellenbosch*
*Rubicon, Meerlust, Stellenryck Collection, Stellenbosch*
*or*
*Pinot Noir Reserve, Robert Mondavi, Carneros, California*
*Rubicon, Neibaum-Copolla, Napa, California*

.........................

Caramongscraps/Cardamom and Coconut Cookies

*Rhine Riesling, Noble Late Harvest, Nederburg, Paarl*
*or*
*Moscato Passito, Maccotta, Sicily, Italy*

# South America

Cebiche de Atún/Tuna Ceviche

*Sauvignon Blanc/Sémillon, Los Vascos, Maipo, Chile*
*Gran Vino Blanco, Viña Tacama, Ica, Peru*
*or*
*Seyval, Boordy Vineyards, Maryland*
*Fumé Blanc, Fritz, Sonoma, California*

..............................

Pavo Asado y Purée de Batata y Jengibre/
Roasted Wild Turkey with Bread and Nut Stuffing
with Sweet Potato and Ginger Purée

*Malbec, Trapiche, Mendoza, Argentina*
*Cabernet Sauvignon, "Don Melchior," Concha y Toro, Maipo, Chile*
*or*
*Merlot, "Three Palms Vineyard," Duckhorn, Napa, California*
*Dominus, Moueix, Napa, California*

..............................

Budin de Santa Rosa
Farina and Almond Pudding with Blackberry Sauce

*Sparkling Wine, Proviar/Chandon, Mendoza, Argentina*
*or*
*Doux, Moët et Chandon, Champagne, France*

# THE UNITED STATES
## NEW ENGLAND/NORTHEAST

Haddock Stew with Saffron, Tomatoes, and Mussels

*Riesling, Hermann Wiemer, Finger Lakes, New York*
*Chardonnay, West Park, Hudson River, New York*
*or*
*Pouilly-Fumé, deLadoucette, Loire, France*
*Chablis, "Vaudesir," Louis Michel, Chablis, Burgundy, France*

.....................

Roast Breast of Duck Wrapped in Smoked Bacon,
with Cider Vinegar Sauce
served with Wild Rice Pancakes and Glazed Onions

*Pinot Noir, Sakonnet, Little Compton, Rhode Island*
*Mythology, Pindar, North Fork, Long Island, New York*
*or*
*Mercurey, Faiveley, Côte Chalonnaise, Burgundy, France*
*Château Pavie, St. Émilion, Bordeaux, France*

.....................

Mixed Greens with Red Onions, Chiogga Beets, Blue Cheese, and Olives

*Gewürztraminer, Lenz, North Fork, Long Island, New York*
*or*
*Gewürztraminer, Trimbach, Alsace, France*

.....................

Pumpkin Pie

*Muscat Ottonel, Konstantin Frank, Finger Lakes, New York*
*or*
*Muscat de Frontignan, Domaines Gavoty, Provence, France*

# THE UNITED STATES
## TEXAS/SOUTHWEST

Ancho Navy Bean Soup

......................

Southwest Caesar Salad with Pan-Fried Crab Cakes

*Sauvignon Blanc, Fall Creek, Bell Mountain, Texas*
*or*
*Entre-Deux-Mers, Cordier, Bordeaux, France*

......................

Texas Hunter's Quail Dinner

*Chardonnay, Llano Estacado, Texas*
*Cabernet Sauvignon, Pheasant Ridge, Bell Mountain, Texas*
*or*
*Condrieu, Delas Frères, Rhône, France*
*Gran Coronas Reserva, Black Label, Torres, Penedés, Spain*

......................

Banana Soft Tacos with Papaya and Strawberry Salsas

*Sparkling Rosé, Cap Rock, Texas*
*or*
*Brut Rosé, Crozer, Claire Valley, South Australia*

# THE UNITED STATES
## CAJUN/CREOLE

Crawfish Pie

*Chenin Blanc, Chappellet, Napa, California*
*or*
*Pinot Grigio, Lageder, Trentino Alto-Adige, Italy*

.........................

Chicken and Andouille Smoked Sausage Gumbo

*Cuvée des Philosophes, Bonny Doon, Santa Cruz, California*
*Pinot Noir, Wild Horse, San Luis Obispo, California*
*or*
*Châteauneuf-du-Pape Blanc, Chapoutier, Rhône, France*
*Pernand-Vergelesses, Bonneau du Martray, Côte de Beaune,*
*Burgundy, France*

.........................

Greens in Hard-Boiled Egg and Hot Pepper Vinegar Dressing

*Gamay, Fetzer, California*
*or*
*Beaujolais-Villages, Sylvain Fessy, Beaujolais, Burgundy, France*

.........................

Spiced Pecan Cake with Pecan Frosting

*Port, Ficklin, San Joaquin, California*
*or*
*Port, LBV, Sandeman, Douro, Portugal, Vintage*

# THE UNITED STATES
## PACIFIC RIM/NORTHWEST

Thai Chicken Soup with Coconut

..................

Tempura with Cabbage Salad and Cinnamon Oil

*Fumé Blanc, Iron Horse, Sonoma Green Valley, California*
*or*
*Sauvignon Blanc, Echeverria, Maipo, Chile*

..................

Lobster Poached in Lemon Grass Broth

*Chardonnay, Dutton Ranch, Kistler, Sonoma, California*
*or*
*Meursault, "Les Charmes," Matrot, Côte de Beaune,*
*Burgundy, France*

..................

Litchis with Bitter Almond Pancakes

*Blanc de Noirs, Domaine Chandon, Napa, California NV*
*or*
*Rosé, Veuve Clicquot, Champagne, France, Vintage*

# THE UNITED STATES
## SPA STYLE

Grilled Shrimp and Sea Scallops with Eggplant and Peppers

*Chardonnay, Inniskillin, Ontario, Canada*
*or*
*Cabreo La Pietra, Ruffino, Toscana, Italy*

...........................

Cornish Hens with Wild Rice Stuffing and Port Sauce

*Merlot, Shafer, Napa, California*
*or*
*Clos René, Pomerol, Bordeaux, France*

...........................

Wilted Spinach and Mushroom Salad

...........................

Pineapple Madagascar

*Electra, Quady, San Joaquin, California*
*or*
*Moscato d'Asti, Braida, Piemonte, Italy*

## VEGETARIAN

Pepper and Corn Soup with Basil

...........................

Ravioli Filled with Eggplant, Roasted Garlic, and Romano Cheese

*Pinot Noir, Knudsen-Erath, Willamette, Oregon*
*or*
*Pinot Nero, Zonin, Veneto, Italy*

...........................

Lettuces, Watercress, and Escarole with Goat Cheese and Sun-Dried Tomatoes

...........................

Apple-Rhubarb Crisp

*Riesling, Château Ste. Chapelle, Snake River, Idaho*
*or*
*Muscat, Keo, Limassol, Cyprus*

# Wine and Health

## Introduction

In the New Testament, Timothy, on the advice of his mentor, St. Paul, said to "drink no longer water, but use a little wine for thy stomach's sake and thine often infirmities." The Bible, like far more ancient civil and religious texts, is replete with references to the healing properties of wine and its positive place in spiritual life and practice. The ancients knew that drinking wine in moderation was an aid to health. They therefore encouraged, even celebrated, its use as a daily beverage.

More than 200 years ago, Thomas Jefferson, the third president of the United States, and an ardent lover of wines, spoke in support of wine as a national beverage of moderation. Jefferson said. "No nation is drunken where wine is cheap; and none sober, where the dearness of wine substitutes ardent spirits as the common beverage. It is, in truth, the only antidote to the bane of whiskey . . . Who will not prefer it? Its extended use will carry health and comfort to a much enlarged circle."

In February of 1993, President Bill Clinton, a light-to-moderate drinker, echoed Jefferson's sentiments when he said that he had "reached the age that when all this health data comes out, I want to take another glass of wine." To the applause of members of the Wine Institute, Clinton beat his chest, thumping away to emphasize his healthy heart. The week after this statement, Clinton, in an interview with MTV, stated that "there's some evidence that wine . . . is good for your heart if you use it in moderation."

In the modern world, Timothy's dictum, Tom's declaration, and Bill's disclosure have been accepted as gospel by many, but questioned or rejected by many more. The entire Moslem world officially eschews the consumption of alcohol, including wine (*alcool* is Arabic for "like a monster," certainly not a linguistic incentive to imbibe). Other religions wail against the evils of drink, and even in those societies where alcohol is not banned, the secular consumption of alcohol, including wine, is often viewed as a negative trait.

Although much of the Mediterranean world is peopled by Moslems, the European sector of the Mediterranean countries—Italy, Spain, southern France, and Greece in particular—have, for centuries, embraced wine as a part of a healthy daily diet. These countries have rich wine histories and wine cultures and produce more wine than any other area of the world, some of it very fine. Drinking wine with meals is part of daily life in the European Mediterranean, and few doubt the overall health benefits of a glass of wine or two each day, coupled with the world's highest per-capita consumption of fruits, grains, and vegetables. In this diet, most fat comes from a virtually unrestricted intake of olive oil, a largely monounsaturated fat.

In the United States, at least until recently, wine and other alcoholic beverages have been regarded with caution, with heavy emphasis placed on the dangers of overindulgence. It was not so long ago that all alcoholic beverages were illegal in the United States. From 1919 to 1933 Prohibition was the law of the land, and the production and consumption of alcoholic beverages, save for religious observance, was banned. Today, there are still "dry" towns and counties, and the nation as a whole continues to cast a wary eye on drinking, even if that drinking is largely confined to a glass or two of wine with a meal. This picture, however is beginning to change.

As Americans travel more, and as the culinary culture of a nation of immigrants is celebrated in restaurants and homes, there is new interest in wine as part of the meal. Similarly, as Americans have become interested in healthy patterns of eating and drinking, they have looked to the Mediterranean diet as a model to follow. We know the benefits of fruits, vegetables, and grains. The consumption of olive oil is at an all-time high in the United States. Vegetarian pastas and pizzas are the new comfort foods, along with risotto and other rice dishes. Because wine is part of the classic Mediterranean diet, it is beginning to be seen as what it always has been, when consumed in moderation: a healthy beverage.

## The French Paradox

France is often thought to be the land of artery-clogging, heart-stopping foie gras, rich cheeses, buttery croissants, and Gauloise cigarettes, and in truth, it is. Why, then, does France, along with the other Mediterranean nations, have some of the lowest rates of coronary heart disease—America's number one killer—in the industrialized world? The answer may lie in a glass of wine.

Scientists and researchers in Europe and the United States have for a long time linked the protective elements of alcohol with lowered risk of heart disease and some cancers. It is a scientific certainty that for most people, one to three drinks per day are associated with improved health indices, on both the personal and national levels.[1] But more recently, research has begun to focus on the specific benefits of wine, especially red wine, as opposed to other alcoholic beverages.

Dr. Serge Renaud, director of the nutrition and cardiology department of the French National Institute of Health Research, has been studying the relationships between alcohol, especially wine, and health for the last 30 years. Renaud has posited that the moderate consumption of wine is an important element in overall health. He points out that the French consume the same amount or more dairy fat (a definite link to heart disease) than the British and the Americans do, yet the French are 66 percent less likely to suffer fatal heart attacks or develop coronary heart disease. Of course, neither the British nor Americans consume a great deal of wine; citizens of both countries prefer beer and spirits. Renaud claims that moderate consumption of wine with meals coupled with an absolute prohibition against binge drinking is a prescription for a healthy heart, lower rates of cancer and stroke, and even accidents.

How much is moderate? Renaud has a surprising answer. "For every 18 milliliters [about ½ ounce] of red wine you drink in a week, you decrease your risk of heart disease by one percent. It's only a drop of wine, just a taste, almost an empty glass. You don't have to drink it, just sniffing it is enough."[2]

Arthur Klatsky, M.D., is the Chief of the Division of Cardiology at Kaiser Permanente Medical Center in Oakland, California, and is a pioneer in American research on the relationship between alcohol and heart disease. With data collected from more than 100,000 patients since 1974, Klatsky confirms, by citing more than a dozen studies performed in several countries, that light to moderate drinkers (less than three drinks per day, with a drink defined as 12 ounces [360 ml] of beer, five ounces [150 ml] of wine, or one and half ounces [45 ml] of spirits) have lower levels of heart disease and fatal heart attacks than nondrinkers or heavy drinkers. Moderate to heavy drinkers also have fewer occurrences of hospitalization than do nondrinkers or very light drinkers.

Klatsky points out that his research indicates that alcohol is protective, and that wine drinkers fare slightly better than beer drinkers, who fare slightly better than spirit drinkers, when it comes to heart disease. Klatsky states, "We can't conclude that the wine itself gives greater protection, it may be caused by the lifestyle of wine drinkers," citing studies that found 75

Dr. Serge Renaud, Director of the Nutrition and Cardiology Department of the French National Institute of Health Research, and father of the "French Paradox."

Arthur Klatsky, M.D. (left) is the Chief of the Division of Cardiology at Kaiser Permanente Medical Center in Oakland, California. Michael Criqui, M.D., M.P.H. (right) is Chairman of the Department of Community and Family Medicine at the University of California at La Jolla.

[1] Thomas Matthews, "Wine: Prescription for Good Health," *Wine Spectator*, March 15, 1994, 37.
[2] Edward Dolnick, "Beyond the French Paradox," *Health*, October, 1992, 40.

percent of all wine is consumed at home, and 80 percent of that consumption is with meals, about a glass and a half with each meal. Basically, he believes that "if you drink any alcohol two or more days per week, you are at lower risk for a fatal heart attack."[3]

While the world's scientists explored the possibility that wine has unique health effects, it was not a scientist who captured the attention of the health-conscious, wine-drinking American public. Instead, the French Paradox was explored by Morley Safer, a wine-loving coanchor of the television news magazine *60 Minutes*. In November 1991, in an interview with Serge Renaud, Safer posed this question to Americans:

> Why is it that the French, who eat 30 percent more fat than we do, suffer fewer heart attacks, even though they smoke more and exercise less? All you have to do is look at the numbers. If you're a middle-aged American man, your chances of dying of a heart attack are three times greater than a Frenchman of the same age.[4]

Safer seemed almost messianic in his answer. While he did mention that the French diet included more fruits, vegetables, and bread than the American diet, he reserved his greatest enthusiasm for red wine, when he reported that:

> There has been for years the belief by doctors in many countries that alcohol, in particular red wine, reduces the risk of heart disease. Now it's been all but confirmed.[5]

The effect of the "French Paradox" report on the American wine-buying public was dramatic and measurable. The day after the broadcast, sales of red wine began to skyrocket, and for the month following the report, sales were up 44 percent (about 2.5 million bottles) over the same month of the previous year. When the report was rebroadcast in July 1992, sales of red wine went up 49 percent for that month. Sales of red wine for the entire year following the initial broadcast were up by about 39 percent.[6] It seemed like a portion of the American public embraced red wine as the newest health food—the oat bran of the 1990s.

According to R. Curtis Ellison, M.D., Chief of Preventive Medicine and Epidemiology, and Professor of Medicine and Public Health at Boston University School of Medicine, although wine consumption is falling in France and other European countries overall, countries that consume the most wine (France, Italy, Spain, and Switzerland) have the lowest rates of

R. Curtis Ellison, M.D. (right), Chief of Preventive Medicine and Epidemiology, and Professor of Medicine and Public Health at Boston University School of Medicine.

[3] Dr. Klatsky moderated a panel on "Wine, Health and Culture: What Can We Learn from the Mediterranean?," as part of the international symposium, Changing American Appetites: Mediterranean Inspirations/American Interpretations, on June 24, 1994 in San Francisco (author's symposium notes).

[4] Morley Safer, *60 Minutes,* CBS-TV, November 18, 1991.

[5] Safer, *op. cit.*

[6] Ben Sherwood, "Wine and Poses," *Washington Monthly,* May, 1993, 22.

**Figure 14.1** Wine and Mortality.

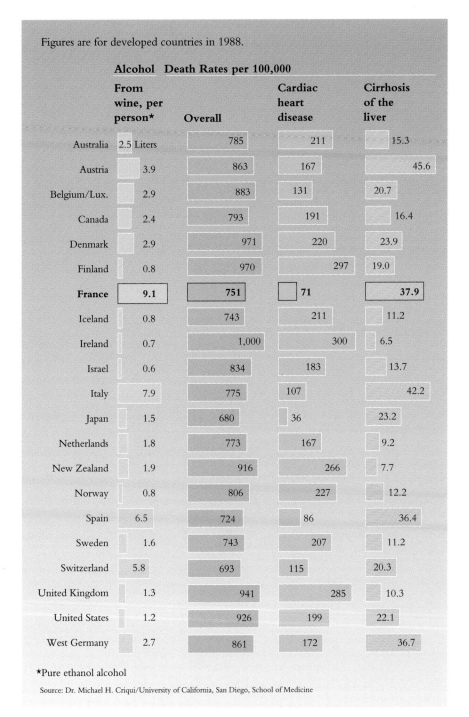

Figures are for developed countries in 1988.

**Alcohol Death Rates per 100,000**

| | From wine, per person* | Overall | Cardiac heart disease | Cirrhosis of the liver |
|---|---|---|---|---|
| Australia | 2.5 Liters | 785 | 211 | 15.3 |
| Austria | 3.9 | 863 | 167 | 45.6 |
| Belgium/Lux. | 2.9 | 883 | 131 | 20.7 |
| Canada | 2.4 | 793 | 191 | 16.4 |
| Denmark | 2.9 | 971 | 220 | 23.9 |
| Finland | 0.8 | 970 | 297 | 19.0 |
| **France** | **9.1** | **751** | **71** | **37.9** |
| Iceland | 0.8 | 743 | 211 | 11.2 |
| Ireland | 0.7 | 1,000 | 300 | 6.5 |
| Israel | 0.6 | 834 | 183 | 13.7 |
| Italy | 7.9 | 775 | 107 | 42.2 |
| Japan | 1.5 | 680 | 36 | 23.2 |
| Netherlands | 1.8 | 773 | 167 | 9.2 |
| New Zealand | 1.9 | 916 | 266 | 7.7 |
| Norway | 0.8 | 806 | 227 | 12.2 |
| Spain | 6.5 | 724 | 86 | 36.4 |
| Sweden | 1.6 | 743 | 207 | 11.2 |
| Switzerland | 5.8 | 693 | 115 | 20.3 |
| United Kingdom | 1.3 | 941 | 285 | 10.3 |
| United States | 1.2 | 926 | 199 | 22.1 |
| West Germany | 2.7 | 861 | 172 | 36.7 |

*Pure ethanol alcohol

Source: Dr. Michael H. Criqui/University of California, San Diego, School of Medicine

heart disease, and those countries that consume the least wine (Ireland, Finland, New Zealand, the United Kingdom, the United States) have the highest rates (see Figure 14.1).

Ellison, who has conducted his own research and worked with Renaud, also points out an important fact about patterns of consumption in Europe.

**Figure 14.2** The Total Mortality Rate Compared to Alcohol Consumption.

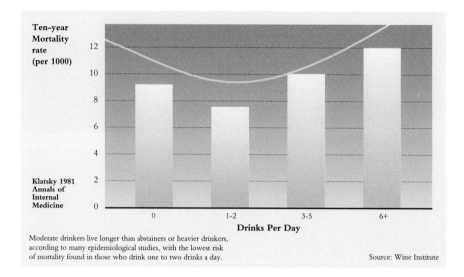

Moderate drinkers live longer than abstainers or heavier drinkers, according to many epidemiological studies, with the lowest risk of mortality found in those who drink one to two drinks a day.

Source: Wine Institute

Although overall per capita consumption of wine is falling in France and Italy, "death rates from heart disease in both of these countries are less than half the rate of the United States and falling."

Ellison adds, "If you look at people who are in the heart disease-risk group, over age 45 or so, about 80 percent of them are regular consumers of wine. All the reports I've seen indicate that it's young people who have stopped drinking, or never started. And that's not the group that has heart attacks."[7]

Michael Criqui, M.D., M.P.H., and Chairman of the Department of Community and Family Medicine at the University of California at La Jolla, expands on the less-pleasant notions of the French Paradox. Criqui points out that "countries with less coronary heart disease have higher levels of cirrhosis." (See Figure 14.2) France, however, has recognized this public health problem connected to alcoholism and abuse. "In 1965, per capita consumption of alcohol in France was 14.3 liters [5.7 gallons], while in 1991 personal consumption dropped to 9.1 liters [3.64 gallons]," according to Criqui. "During this time, cirrhosis deaths were cut in half, and heart disease rates remained just as low or lower."

Criqui also has a stricter definition of "moderation" than do some of his colleagues. Criqui notes that "at more than two drinks per day, there is an increase in stroke, violence, accidents, and cancer. Keep it under two."[8]

## Protective Qualities of Red Wine

Although all alcoholic beverages, when consumed in moderation, protect the heart, red wine contains a number of nonalcoholic elements that have been identified by the scientific community as particularly protective to the

[7] Dolnick, op. cit.
[8] Dr. Criqui was a participant in the Klatsky panel (author's symposium notes).

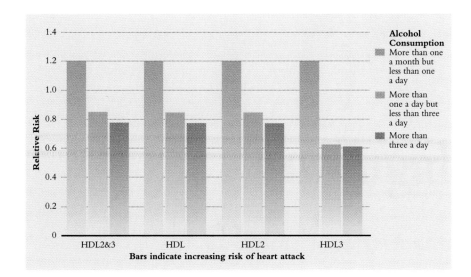

**Figure 14.3** The Links Between HDL and Heart Attack Risk.

body as a whole. These **phenolic** compounds, which have to do with the color and tannins in grapes, are all **antioxidants.** When LDL (low-density liproprotein, aka, "bad" cholesterol) is oxidized in the blood, plaque can form on the arteries, which can lead to atherosclerosis (hardening and clogging of the arteries) and heart disease. Antioxidants, such as beta-carotene and Vitamin E, along with the phenols in red wine, inhibit the oxidation of LDL and increase HDL (high-density liproprotein, aka, "good" cholesterol) levels. These antioxidants can also prevent platelet aggregation, blood clots that can lead to stroke and heart disease (see Figure 14.3). A 1990 French study indicated that only red wine, unique among other alcoholic beverages, *both* decreased platelet aggregation *and* increased HDL (olive oil has also been shown to perform the same function).

Resveratrol is a natural fungicide found on the skin of red wine grapes (almost none is found on white wine grapes or white or red table grapes). The concentration of resveratrol in red wine is directly proportionate to the amount of fungus and disease exposure of the grapes during the growing season. Quercetin (which is also found in tea, onions, and apples), and catechin are naturally occurring constituents of red wine grapes, and both are far more abundant than resveratrol. Catechin, quercetin, and resveratrol are all phenolic antioxidants.

Dr. Andrew Waterhouse, assistant professor of viticulture and enology at the University of California at Davis, believes that the phenolic antioxidants in wine can prevent atherosclerosis and inhibit LDL oxidation. Waterhouse notes that the phenols are related to astringency and bitterness in wine: the tastes of tannin. He notes that "your tongue is a good indicator of their level."[9]

[9] Matthews, op. cit.

In the last 100 years the industrialized world has seen a dramatic shift in the way we get sick. A century ago, most people who did not die of old age died from infectious diseases. Today, people are far more likely to die of chronic diseases—heart disease, stroke, cancers.

Diet can be a major culprit in the development of chronic diseases, and it can also be a path to better health. Fortunately, several cultural models allow us to eat a healthy diet and still enjoy the pleasures of the table. One of these is the Mediterranean Diet, which calls for daily consumption of bread, pasta, and grains, as well as fruits, vegetables, beans, legumes, and nuts (see Figure 14.4). The primary source of dietary fat is monounsaturated olive oil, plus cheese and yogurt. Fish is consumed three or four times per week; poultry, eggs, and sweets only a few times per week. Little red meat is consumed in the Mediterranean, only a few times per month. Integral parts of this regimen are regular exercise and the consumption of wine in moderation.

The Traditional Healthy Mediterranean Diet Pyramid presents a cultural model for Americans to follow. It emphasizes grains, fruits, vegetables, legumes, olive oil, and fermented dairy products while deemphasizing foods high in processed sugars, animal proteins, and fats. Notice that the pyramid includes daily exercise and a glass of wine with meals. This pyramid was jointly developed by the World Health Organization (WHO) European Regional Office, the WHO/FAO Collaborating Center for Nutritional Epidemiology at the Harvard School of Public Health, and Oldways Preservation & Exchange Trust in Boston (Oldways sponsors seminars and conferences about the issues surrounding food, traditional diets, and sustainable agriculture.) The pyramid has been endorsed by The Culinary Institute of America.

Dr. Terrence Leighton, professor in the division of biochemistry and molecular biology at University of California at Berkeley, has also done extensive research to the effect of quercetin on the body. He notes that this phenolic antioxidant inhibits LDL oxidation, lowers cigarette-smoke toxicity, and exhibits certain anticarcinogenic effects by inhibiting the malignant transformation of normal cells. Quercetin enhances the activity of anticancer agents in the body and has been shown to inhibit mammary cancer in rats and skin cancer in mice.[10]

Both Waterhouse and Leighton cite a study by Dutch epidemiologist Dr. Michael Hertog of 800 men over a five-year period. Those men who consumed 16–30 milligrams [less than 1/1000th of an ounce] of quercetin a day, mostly from tea, onions, and apples, were found to be only half as likely to get heart disease than those who consumed small daily amounts of quercetin. Two glasses of red wine per day provide more than 30 milligrams of quercetin per day, as does the basic "Mediterranean Diet," which includes wine.

[10] Dr. Leighton was also a participant in the Klatsky panel (author's symposium notes).

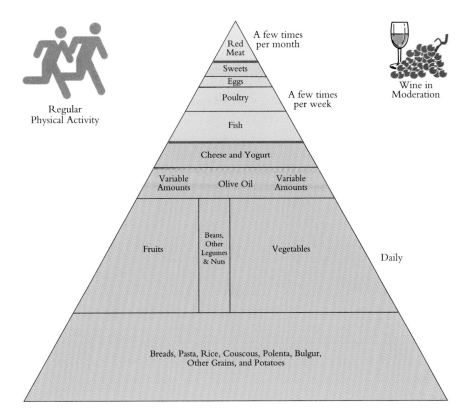

Regular
Physical Activity

Red Meat — A few times per month

Sweets

Eggs

Poultry — A few times per week

Fish

Cheese and Yogurt

Variable Amounts · Olive Oil · Variable Amounts

Fruits · Beans, Other Legumes & Nuts · Vegetables — Daily

Breads, Pasta, Rice, Couscous, Polenta, Bulgur, Other Grains, and Potatoes

Wine in Moderation

**Figure 14.4** The Traditional Healthy Mediterranean Diet Pyramid. (Copyright held by The Oldways Preservation & Exchange Trust.)

## Public Policy Issues

Many physicians agree with a 1990 editorial in the *American Journal of Public Health,* which stated that after 40 years of research into diet and heart disease, there are only two findings that consistently appear in the experimental and clinical literature: exercise and moderate drinking are good for human beings. This being the case, will doctors prescribe a glass or two of wine for their patients, much as they prescribe regular physical activity as part of a healthy lifestyle?

Arthur Klatsky believes that because of the potential for abuse and possible hereditary tendencies toward alcoholism, "indiscriminate advice to nondrinkers to take up alcohol for health reasons is inappropriate." He has said that if a patient already drinks in moderation, it is appropriate to mention that a glass of wine with a meal will do no harm. Klatsky recognizes the truth of the old German proverb: "There are more old wine drinkers than old doctors." However, he also believes that public policy surrounding wine and health is a complex and thorny issue and illustrates the quandary with another anonymous quote: "For every complex problem there is a solution that is short, neat, and wrong."[11]

Other physicians are far more cautious, and for a variety of medical, ethical, and legal reasons will not prescribe a glass or two of wine or a drink be-

---

[11] Klatsky, op. cit.

fore dinner to their patients. Dr. R. Curtis Ellison claims that "we've known for quite some time that alcohol tends to decrease the risk of heart disease," and can think of no other drug that is more effective than alcohol in protecting the heart. He admits that until recently the medical community, for reasons of self-protection and concern for the potential of abuse by patients, has not been trumpeting the consistent results of alcohol and health studies. Ellison states that "we hadn't been suppressing it, but we hadn't been making it widely known either." In an interview, Ellison suggested that "if alcohol could be dispensed in a pill"—the medical model we're most comfortable with—"it would be the most-prescribed drug for avoiding fatal heart disease."[12] In the spirit of moderation, Ellison wrote an editorial in a 1990 issue of the medical journal *Epidemiology,* advising normally healthy middle-aged American men to "consider the advantages of washing down their aspirin with a glass of cabernet"[13] to reduce their risk of heart disease.

Most doctors agree that their concern for even the remote possibility of alcohol abuse outweighs the scientific evidence that light to moderate drinking is good for the vast majority of their patients. However, there are some physicians who, given the right circumstances, will mention that a glass or two of wine *for people who already drink in moderation,* is perfectly acceptable. In the March 15, 1994 *Wine Spectator,* as part of an issue dedicated to wine and health, Jane Shufer quotes 15 doctors with different ideas of specialization about their attitudes towards wine. Most of the doctors, who all enjoy wine themselves, generally see little problem with recommending moderate consumption of wine to patients who are moderate drinkers.[14]

A lot of what we know about heart disease and diet is this: men are far more likely to die of heart disease at younger ages than pre-menopausal women, moderate alcohol is good for the heart, and so is exercise. These facts may have prompted Dr. Norman Kaplan to joke, "To live the longest, be a woman who jogs to the liquor store everyday."[15]

# Alcohol and Women

Women, too, are candidates for heart disease, though in somewhat smaller percentages, and later in life then men. Dr. Elizabeth M. Whelan, president of the American Council on Science and Health notes that about two and a half ounces of 80 proof (40 percent) alcohol (the rough equivalent of two glasses of wine) each day can decrease a woman's chances of dying from heart disease by 50 percent. Whelan recommended aerobic exercise as well, and echoing Dr. Kaplan, states that "The best way to prevent a heart attack may be to run from bar to bar."[16]

Research on women's health and alcohol consumption is not nearly as exhaustive as studies done on men. Women metabolize alcohol somewhat

[12] Interview with the author at a conference on the Mediterranean Diet held on the Island of Hawaii in July, 1993.
[13] *Ibid.*
[14] Jane Shufer, *Wine Spectator,* March 15, 1994.
[15] Dr. Norman Kaplan, quoted by Klatsky, op. cit. (author's symposium notes).
[16] Quote given to *Mademoiselle* by Dr. Whelan, cited by Sherwood, op. cit.

differently than men, and the effect of alcohol on younger women (under 40, child bearing years) seems far less beneficial than the effect on older women (over 50). A famous study undertaken in 1988 by Meir Stampfler, M.D., Dr.P.H., of Harvard University, surveyed more than 87,000 nurses aged 34 to 59. Dr. Stampfler found that women who had one or two drinks per day had a 50 percent lower risk of heart disease, heart attack, and stroke, than nondrinkers. The protective effect was highest in women over the age of 50, who are at higher risk for these chronic diseases and attacks than younger women.[17]

And women are more at risk than men for certain cancers, especially breast cancer. In October of 1992, a University of Wisconsin Comprehensive Cancer Study revealed that women who consume three or more glasses of wine weekly decrease their cancer risk by 60 percent. Conversely, the study found that women who consume more than ten cans of beer per week more than double their risk of cancer.[18]

Another study, however, undertaken by Harvard University in 1987, surveyed more than 3000 women, and found a correlation between alcohol consumption and breast cancer. Even light to moderate drinkers, who consumed one to two drinks per day were found to have a 50 percent greater risk of developing breast cancer. This study is quite controversial, and has been widely disputed by scientists and researchers. The key problem in the study is actually twofold. First, scientists are at a loss to understand what in alcohol could have such a pernicious effect on breast tissue. Second, doctors know so little about how breast cancer develops that this finding has made that picture less clear.[19]

Other studies, especially a survey of 1500 women with breast cancer undertaken by the American Health Foundation in Valhalla, New York, has shown no causal link between alcohol and breast cancer. Dr. Stampfler of Harvard is undertaking a follow-up study, and so far her preliminary findings are that when it comes to alcohol and breast cancer, "the higher the dose, the greater the chance for trouble." Stampfler also advises that women under 30 must "drink in moderation, always."[20]

## Alcohol and Pregnancy

Perhaps the most controversial issue surrounding women and alcohol is the relative safety of moderate alcohol consumption during pregnancy. The fear surrounding this issue has to do with Fetal Alcohol Syndrome (FES) and Fetal Alcohol Effects (FAE), a host of problems that includes birth defects, low birth weight, problems in mental and emotional development and motor skills, and even alcohol addiction by the newborn (see Figure 14.5).

[17] Trisha Thompson, "Wine, Women . . . and Questions," *Redbook,* June, 1992, 74.
[18] "Women and Liquor—A Dangerous Mix," *USA Today,* October, 1992, 3.
[19] Thompson, op. cit.
[20] Thompson, op. cit.

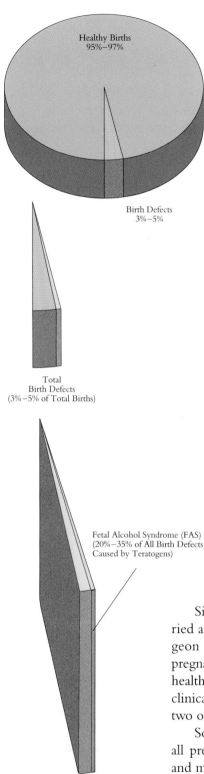

Healthy Births
95%–97%

Birth Defects
3%–5%

Total
Birth Defects
(3%–5% of Total Births)

Fetal Alcohol Syndrome (FAS)
(20%–35% of All Birth Defects
Caused by Teratogens)

Birth Defects Caused by Teratogens
(1%–3% of Total Births)

Healthy Births
95%–97%

Birth Defects
Caused by Teratogens
(1%–3% of Total Births)

Birth Defects
3%–5%

Birth Defects Caused by Teratogens
(Substances such as Alcohol and Drugs)
(1%–3% of Total Birth Defects)

Fetal Alcohol Syndrome (FAS)
(20%–35% of All Birth Defects
Caused by Teratogens)

**Figure 14.5**  How Common is Fetal Alcohol Syndrome (FAS)?

Since 1990, every alcoholic beverage sold in the United States has carried a warning label advising pregnant women that "According to the Surgeon General, women should not drink alcoholic beverages during pregnancy because of the risk of birth defects." While most physicians and health providers adhere to this warning in the interest of safety, there is no clinical or anecdotal evidence that light consumption of alcohol—a glass or two of wine per week—leads to birth defects or an unhealthy fetus.

Society makes choices based on many criteria. In the case of warning all pregnant women against drinking during pregnancy, our government and medical establishment have chosen to protect all fetuses from a minuscule percentage of mothers who drink to excess before and during pregnancy.

According to Lyn Weiner, who, with Barbara Morse, is codirector of the Fetal Alcohol Education Project in Brookline, Massachusetts, "In a review of

## ALCOHOLISM AND ALCOHOL ABUSE

Underlying the controversies engendered by public policies surrounding alcohol is the undeniable fact that the United States, like many other countries, has a serious problem with alcohol abuse and clinical alcoholism. People who have histories of alcohol and drug abuse must abstain from all alcohol, including wine. People who are genetically predisposed to the disease of alcoholism are better off not drinking at all.

According to the National Council on Alcoholism and Drug Dependence, 10.5 million Americans are alcoholics or alcohol dependent, and more than 7.2 million more drink to the point of impaired health and dysfunctional social patterns. More than 100,000 people in the United States die each year because of alcohol abuse, and 35 percent of all hospital admissions are alcohol related. One out of four American families suffers with alcohol-related problems and crimes, including domestic violence and drunken driving (nationally, in 1992, only three percent of all arrests for drunken driving involved wine; 75 percent involved beer, and 22 percent involved spirits). It is scary to think that two out of five people in the United States will be in an alcohol-related "accident" sometime during their lifetime.

Alcohol is causally linked to the leading causes of accidental death (perhaps this should be termed "avoidable death" instead): half of all car crashes and 38 percent of all drownings, as well as incalculable numbers of falls, fires, and burns.[21]

With frightening statistics such as these, it is no wonder that physicians are cautious to recommend light to moderate drinking for their patients. On the other hand, it is clear that the American people need to be educated about both the dangers and benefits of alcohol, if citizens are to make well-informed, socially positive choices for themselves, their families, and their communities.

245 cases of FAS, 75 percent of the mothers were dead or missing from alcohol-related problems within five years of the births of their babies." Weiner and Morse work closely with alcohol-addicted mothers-to-be who are likely to give birth to unhealthy children.

Barbara Morse claims that "People have misinterpreted the Surgeon General's warning to mean that any drinking at all causes birth defects. I don't believe that if a woman has a glass of wine with dinner once or twice a week, she's putting her fetus at risk." Despite this belief, neither Morse nor Weiner will endorse drinking of any kind during pregnancy, because they also believe the potential for abuse by some women is all too real.[22]

[21] Sherwood, op. cit.
[22] Thomas Matthews, "The Difficult Choice: New Information About Drinking and Pregnancy," *Wine Spectator,* August 31, 1994, 60.

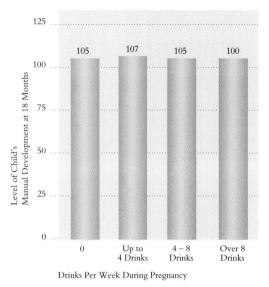

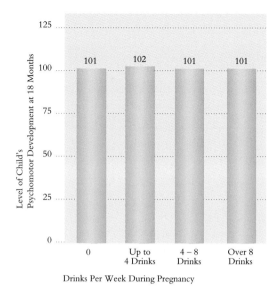

Source: Forrest, F. et al British Medical Journal 1991

**Figure 14.6**   Prenatal Drinking and Child Development.

Paul Dolan, President of Fetzer Vineyards in Mendocino County, California, Looking at a Bunch of Fetzer's Organically Grown Chardonnay Grapes.

Paul Scholten, M.D., is an associate clinical professor of obstetrics, gynecology, and reproductive sciences at the University of California at San Francisco. He is a past president of the Society of Medical Friends of Wine, a California group that includes many physicians, some of whom are also wine makers or winery owners. He states that there is no evidence to suggest that pregnant women who drink one or two glasses of wine per day are at increased risk for FAS. "Wine is a healthy food, an accompaniment to good living," according to Dr. Scholten.[23]

In a study conducted in seven European countries in 1992, researchers examined 8500 mothers and infants to see what effect light to moderate drinking had on babies up to 18 months after birth (see Figure 14.6). The researchers found that:

• If women drank more than two to three drinks per day during pregnancy, their babies showed a decrease in birth weight and height.

• Light drinkers have the best chance of giving birth to a baby of optimal weight.

• Children of moderate drinkers scored highest on development tests given at 18 months of age.

• One drink a day in early pregnancy does no damage to the fetus, and children of these mothers were not impaired mentally or physically by 18 months of age.[24]

[23] Claudia Morain, "Grape Grower's Wrath," *American Medical News,* June 22, 1992, 45.
[24] Matthews, "The Difficult Choice."

# The Health of the Planet

The health of the wine drinker is not the only health issue where wine is concerned. Just as important is the health of the planet, its water, and its soils. Over the last ten years, there has been a subtle shift in the way grapes are grown and wine is made, and these changes are gaining momentum. Increasingly, wine producers are harvesting organically grown grapes, and some are making totally organic wine.

"Our goal is that by the year 2000, all wine grapes grown in California will be organically grown, using sustainable agriculture practices," says Paul Dolan, president of Fetzer Vineyards, a major wine producer in California's Mendocino County that has had major success with wines made from certified organic vineyards. While Dolan's goal may be overly optimistic, the thrust of California viniculture is heading his way. Well-known producers, such as Gallo, Sutter Home, Buena Vista, Robert Mondavi, and Fetzer are producing more and more wines from organically grown grapes: grapes that do not rely on inorganic pesticides and fungicides for their health, but traditional, tried-and-true agricultural techniques that produce fine grapes without polluting and poisoning the precious natural resources of water and land.

Currently, only about ten percent of California's 600 wineries, large and small, have had some or all of their vineyards certified organic by California Certified Organic Farmers (CCOF). There is definitely a trend towards sus-

A Varietal Chardonnay and Cabernet Sauvignon are Part of Fetzer's *Bonterra* Line of Wines from Organically-grown Grapes.

Cover Crops, Like Alfalfa and Clover, are Grown between Rows of Grapevines in Order to Enrich the Soil, Cut Down on Weeding, and to Encourage Beneficial Insects, Like Ladybugs.

Fetzer's Compost Pile is the Largest on the North Coast of California. Composting the Soil is an Important Part of Organic Agriculture.

tainable, organic farming of vineyards, however. Since wine grapes do not have to have the same pristine appearance as table grapes, spraying has always been moderate in the vineyards. Now, many producers recognize that spraying with synthetic chemicals may not be necessary at all.

Major producers who have embraced organic viticulture now use cover crops (like alfalfa and clover) to diminish weeds in the vineyard, increase soil nutrients, and provide a home for beneficial insects, such as ladybugs, that thrive on unwelcome pests. To control fungi and plant diseases, growers are using elemental sulfur, which is allowed in organic vineyards, instead of spraying dangerous chemicals that, in some cases, can cause cancer and birth defects among grape pickers.

Some producers do not only grow organic grapes but also make certified organic wine. Unlike the fairly easy transition to organics in the vineyard, organic wine making is tough going. Wine makers traditionally use chemical stabilizers, and making wines without them can be difficult. It is particularly difficult to make organic white wines, as white grapes do not contain the natural antioxidants, such as resveratrol and quercetin, found in red wine grapes.

Perhaps the most ambitious organic wine maker in California is Jonathan Frey, who owns Frey Vineyards. He has won several awards and medals for his organic red and white wines, and his Zinfandel has merited special attention from consumers and the wine press.

Speaking of the difficulties in producing fragile organic white wines, Frey mentions that "we use steam heat to sterilize the wines, and we're moving away from oak barrels with white wines to keep them from oxygen." Oxidized wines will develop an "off" color, bouquet, and taste.

While organic wine making is controversial, organic viticulture is not. Long practiced without fanfare in many vineyards in France, it seems to have taken hold in California, and is part of a nationwide movement toward sustainable agriculture and healthier food and wine choices.

# Summary

The idea of linking wine and health is as old as humankind and as new as the latest clinical studies. There is no longer any scientific doubt that wine consumed in moderation, with food, as part of an overall healthy diet and lifestyle, is beneficial to health. At the same time, there is no doubt that alcohol abuse is an immense medical and social problem. While the scientific issues surrounding moderate wine consumption and alcohol abuse may be clear, our social policies are not.

There is great debate within the medical community as to whether or not wine should be recommended in small amounts for middle-aged patients. Dr. Michael Criqui frames the debate when he states "if everybody could drink a glass of wine a day, period, that would be fine. But everybody can't drink a glass of wine a day. It would be OK for physicians to recommend a drink a day to patients they know won't abuse alcohol, but I think a general recommendation is dangerous."[25]

Dr. R. Curtis Ellison disagrees with Criqui when he says that "the best recommendation should be: if you choose to drink alcohol, it will reduce your risk of heart disease. I think it would be irresponsible not to let patients know that."[26]

It is a curious situation when the model for enjoying wine in moderation is a medical one, with wine drinkers as patients. Wine is not a medical panacea, nor is it the latest health food. Public policy as it applies to alcohol—a message of abstinence—is unlikely to change anytime soon. In the meantime, it might be helpful to remember that enjoying a glass of wine with our meal should be a pleasure, not a dose of medicine. However, it is comforting to know that something pleasing to the senses is also good for the heart.

---

[25] Jane E. Brody, "Wine for the Heart: Over All, Risks May Outweigh Benefits," *New York Times,* December 28, 1994.
[26] Brody, ibid.

## Part Five

# Wine Service and Storage

*W*ine service, purchasing, and storage are the topics of Part 5 of Exploring Wine. In this section we explore some of the appropriate methods and procedures to provide professional wine service, set up purchasing and storage systems, and create several different kinds of wine lists.

Chapter 15, *Wine Service,* explains the art of professional service, and includes the basics of approaching the table, suggesting wines to guests, taking the order, issuing the wine, presenting the wine to the customer, mastering the tools necessary for proper wine service, opening the bottle at the table, and pouring the wine for the guests. In this chapter the authors detail important information on how to market and "hand-sell" wines in the dining room, and they share the subtleties of service etiquette. *Wine Service* is a valuable chapter not only for the wine professional, but also for the customer, as we outline what a restaurant guest should look for in professional wine service.

Chapter 16, *Purchasing and Storage,* addresses the back-of-the-house issues of how to buy wine, how to store it properly, and how to keep track of the wine. Purchasing strategies for the consumer and the professional are recommended, as are some basic designs of wine cellars, and control systems for proper wine inventory. The authors mention the value of tastings, software, vintage cards, and wine books and periodicals as helpful references in finding the right wines to fit the reader's needs and budget.

Chapter 17, *Wine Lists,* deals with the role of the wine list in the professional dining room. The authors stress that the wine list plays a pivotal role in not only marketing wines, but selling the overall concept of food, wine, and service in the restaurant. Several different approaches to the wine list are presented, from the simplest, short bistro wine list to the list of an elegant "wine destination" restaurant. Actual wine lists are reproduced, all of them chosen to illustrate a particular approach to the wine list as a marketing tool for the menu and ambiance of a restaurant. This chapter is also a clinic for wine list problems, offering common-sense solutions to these problems, making the repaired wine list a useful tool for both the restaurant and the guest.

# Wine Service

## Introduction

While a restaurant may have terrific food, an engaging menu and wine list, beautiful decor, and lovely ambiance, an otherwise enjoyable meal can be marred or even ruined by poor service. Restaurant guests deserve the best in professional service, and servers should endeavor to provide the highest possible level of attention to the guest's needs. Proper wine service is a customer's right and a service professional's duty and pleasure.

While we are familiar with the jokes about an incompetent, uninformed, ostentatious, or condescending waiter, waitress, captain, maître d', or wine steward, some of these jokes are not far off the mark. Unfortunately in real life these jokes are not so funny. The days when a server could dictate what wines a guest should or should not drink should be over, and so should the days of incompetent wine service be a thing of the past.

**Figure 15.1** Madeline Triffon is the Only Female American Master Sommelier.

**Figure 15.2** Roger Dagorn is President of the American Sommelier Society and is also a Master Sommelier.

## SOMMELIERS

There are fewer sommeliers or wine stewards in the contemporary American dining room. A **sommelier** is a wine steward whose role in a dining room is assisting guests with choosing wines and then opening and pouring them (see Figures 15.1 and 15.2). A complete knowledge of the menu items and collaboration with the chef is essential. A trial tasting of the food-and-wine pairings is often organized for staff or with a potential banquet customer to ensure successful pairings. Duties of a sommelier may also include selecting and ordering wines for the list as well as organizing the wine cellar. The title **cellar master** is sometimes used for sommeliers whose responsibilities include the layout and maintenance of the cellar and the systems of controls to track sales and inventory. A sommelier will also train fellow workers to make them more familiar with the products the establishment carries as well as proper service techniques. Sommeliers in the past had the responsibility of tasting a wine in front of the guests to ensure it was palatable and not poisonous. The tastevin is the tasting cup (see Figure 15.3) and is most often worn on a chain around the neck of the sommelier. Today at some formal restaurants the practice continues of tasting a small portion at the table before the guest is poured a sample. This is done to ensure the guest does not have to suffer through tasting a wine that is bad, and also to allow the sommelier to judge at what stage the wine is and share comments with the guests on the wine's character. Some sommeliers will only use the tastevin if there is a complaint on a wine and others shun use of tastevins completely, believing they are antiquated tools. Sommeliers have the task of studying the wine regions of the world and keeping current on how the wines are being shaped by the producers and the effects of climate from vintage to vintage.

Sommeliers today realize they have to offer the highest possible level of service and professional counsel to the dining public. As with any true professional, the best sommeliers are in demand by large hotels and restaurants, especially those serving a corporate clientele. However, with a growing trend toward more informal dining, and the customer's interest in the perception of value as part of the successful dining experience, the role of the sommelier is often filled by an energetic, friendly, helpful, and informed waitstaff. Be they the owners, hostesses, waiters, captains, maître d's, or managers, the role of wine service professional is being filled by folks who are eager to give the pleasure of good service and, just as important, learn as much as they can about wine, the wine list, and its relation to food.

The American restaurant customer, whether dining for business or pleasure, is more informed about wine than at any time in gustatory history, and knows the difference between contemporary service, which is friendly, fluid, and communicative, and old-fashioned service, which was dictatorial, snobbish, and overbearing. While the bad news is that some wine professionals continue to disserve the public, the good news is that, for those who

**Figure 15.3** Wine Service Tools; (clockwise from top left) Basket or Cradle (Used to Transport Old Red Wines to the Table); Candle (Used for Decanting Old Red Wines); Wine Chiller (Maintains Temperature without Ice); Decanting Funnel; Thermometer; Sparkling Wine Pliers; Cork Retriever; Sparkling Wine Cap or Preserver; Cork Retriever; Tastevin; Thermometer.

want to enjoy the rewards of a job well done, all it takes is common sense and an interest in some basic service guidelines.

In this chapter the tools required for service and their uses will be discussed. Taking the order, opening, and pouring wines will be covered as well as etiquette at the table.

## Setting the Table/Glassware

The table may be preset with an all-purpose wine glass, or with both white wine and red wine glasses (see Figure 15.4). Wine glasses must be clear, colorless, and unadorned, so that the true color of the wine may be appreciated. Glasses with a tapered top are best, because they allow the diner to appreciate the wine's aroma and bouquet (see Chapter 3 on How to Taste Wine). The glasses should be rinsed and hand polished with a lint-free cloth (a clean cotton napkin is ideal) so there is no soapy residue. The advantage of presetting the table is that it allows time for better service, especially when the restaurant and its staff are busy, and it sends a message to the guest that wine is a part of the meal.

**Figure 15.4** Preset Table with Wine Glasses.

The type of glass used affects the taster's perception of the wine. A proper glass should be large enough to hold three to four ounces of wine, and still have enough empty space at top to allow swirling the glass to release the nose. The glass should have a stem long enough so it can be held, so that the bowl of the glass is not warmed by the hands, and no fingerprints are left on the glass, marring the appreciation of the wine's color. The lip should not be too thick, and the glass should be widest at the bowl, narrowing to a smaller diameter at the rim. Restaurants have the option of using one sparkling and one all-purpose glass for still wines or may opt to have a range of glassware for the different types of wine (see Chapter 3 on How to Taste Wine). A savvy restaurateur may endear their establishment to wine lovers by placing more-specific or finer-quality glasses on the table.

## Presenting and Discussing the Wine List

The wine list is not only a listing of the wines available but also a marketing tool for the restaurant and a statement of its image. Obviously, the list should be free from stains and should not appear dog-eared, old, or overused. All of the wines listed should be available. The best way to make sure that the list is current and clean is to print the list on a computer. Using a laser printer or ink-jet printer allows the restaurateur to select a type style that reflects the appropriate image. Computerizing the wine list also allows the restaurateur to coordinate the printed list with cellar inventory, sales records, and wine ordering. While large restaurants and hotels print the lists daily or every few days, this may not be appropriate for smaller operations. However the list is produced, whether by hand or by computer, it must be accurate and up-to-date (see Chapter 17 on Wine Lists).

The wine list may be presented at the same time as the menus, which again emphasizes that wine is an integral part of the dining experience. Unless one guest asks for the list, it should be placed toward the center of the table opened to the first page or presented to the host. The first page often presents sparkling wines, champagnes, or premium wines by the glass, or a table of contents for extensive lists. If the server presents the list with the menu the customer is more likely to begin considering wine either as an apéritif or as an accompaniment to the first course of the meal. In general, wine contains less alcohol than spirit-based drinks and is more effective as an appetite stimulant.

When the server approaches the table to take the order he or she should not interrupt a conversation. Speaking in a clear and friendly voice, the server might ask, "May I help you with a wine selection?" or "Will you be having wine this evening?" A more assertive statement, such as "Which wine have you chosen to enjoy with your meal?" may be in order. The service professional establishes a rapport with the host at the table and, whenever possible, addresses the host by name. The server should *not* assume that the host is male. While it is important to acknowledge all the guests at the table, it is the guest who orders the wine whom the server should approach to carry out the meal's wine service (bringing a second bottle, or switching to a different wine).

The service staff must understand what is happening at the table and suggest wines that fit the situation. People dine out for many reasons. The guests may be celebrating a special occasion or, at the other extreme, conducting business during the meal. While an anniversary or birthday dinner may call for a festive bottle of champagne, a working lunch may be alcohol-free. On the other hand, some business dinners involve entertaining a special client, so a special bottle of wine may be appropriate.

If the guest asks for assistance in choosing a wine to accompany the meal, the wine server should ask what styles of wine the host enjoys: Dry whites? Fruity, semidry wines? Medium-bodied Italian reds? The host may ask his or her guests what wines they prefer, and a conversation about matching the wine with the food may ensue. In that case the server should remember to listen as well as talk. The server's tact and enthusiasm can be a strong selling point. If servers have tasted a wine with particular dishes, then they can gain the confidence of the guests. Servers should always describe wine in simple-to-understand terms, and never show off presumed wine knowledge or make guests feel intimidated. A server must develop a sense of

**Figure 15.5** Presenting, Opening, and Serving White Wine.

*Present the bottle with the label facing the taster.*

*Cut the foil or capsule at the lower lip of the bottle neck.*

*Use the edge of the corkscrew knife to remove the cap.*

*Insert the worm of the corkscrew near the center of the cork.*

*Twist the corkscrew in a clockwise motion until just one spiral of the worm is showing.*

*Tilt the corkscrew back so the lever or foot may be placed on the lip of the bottle.*

*Place the foot on the lip of the bottle. Ensure the foot is flush with the lip, if not, lift the foot and twist the corkscrew in reverse a half turn and try again.*

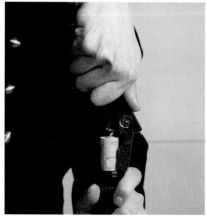

*Bracing the foot with a finger or thumb, pull straight up with the corkscrew. Age-worthy wines may require a second series of turning and lifting.*

*Once most of the cork is visible, grip the cork at the end near the bottle and jiggle it out.*

how each table's needs are different. While one table may be fascinated by additional information about a wine, another table's needs may be just the selection of an appropriate bottle and attentive service.

During conversation, it will often become clear whether the guest wants a good, basic dinner wine, or something very special. Service professionals should never push the consumer to buy an expensive bottle. In fact, the best wine marketing at the table often includes the perception of good value, making the guest more comfortable with wine. Suggesting a bottle of wine to accompany a meal demands thorough knowledge of the wine list. If, for example, the host wants to order a bottle of Cabernet Sauvignon from Napa Valley, it is a good idea for the server to suggest three choices, each at a different price point. When conferring with the host, or any guest, staff should not discuss price directly; instead, list suggestions, and direct the guest's attention to where they are on the wine list.

The server must determine the style of wine and price range the customers prefer and also be sensitive to how the wine will perform with the menu items the guests have chosen.

## Serving the Wine

***Proper Temperature.*** When the server brings the wine to the table, she or he holds the bottle with the label facing out. Whites, rosés, and sparkling wines may be accompanied by an ice bucket, filled with ice and enough water to slide the bottle in easily. See Figure 15.5 for the proper steps to serve white wine. There should also be a clean, neatly folded napkin draped over the bucket or around a handle. The use of the ice bucket, once a commonplace in restaurant service, has now become something of a controversy. Many Americans like their wines served very cool, while some do not. Tabletop chillers made of clay, marble, or plastic, which maintain the temperature of a refrigerated wine without the danger of numbing it, are gaining in popularity. Some guests (and almost all wine makers) prefer their complex white wines served at, or close to, cellar temperature, while simple, fruity white wines can do with some chilling (see the sidebar on Serving Temperature Ranges in this chapter).

In the past, red wines were served at room temperature, but now there is widespread agreement that "cellar temperature"—slightly cooler than the dining room—is more appropriate. If there is a point of differentiation in the service of reds it is that lighter, fruitier red wines may be served with a slight chill; full-bodied, tannic reds are served at about

The server should hold the lower half of the bottle to pour. The bottle is positioned just above the glass with the label facing the guest.

- Sparkling wines: 41°–47°F = 5°–8°C

- Dry whites and rosés: 44°–54°F = 6.6°–12°C

- Light-bodied reds: 50°–55°F = 10°–12.75°C

- Medium-bodied to full-bodied reds: 55°–65°F = 12.75°–18°C

- Sweet wines: 41°–47°F = 5°–8°C, but sweet, fortified wines, such as vintage-style Ports, should be room temperature.

room or cellar temperature. Also, the same wine consumed at a summer barbecue might be refreshing served cool, but during the winter at a formal dinner it will taste better served at room temperature. Room temperature during January a century ago in a French château in Bordeaux was closer to the 55–60°F (12.75–15.5°C) common in cellars today, whereas room temperature today infers 65–70°F (18–21°C). The server should always ask the guest what temperature the guest prefers, if there is a question of chilling the wine.

The sidebar lists general guides only; some experts argue that all these temperatures are slightly too low. Opinion is divided about serving dessert wines as cold as listed here. A good rule of thumb is that both fuller-bodied wines and older wines are served warmer than lighter or younger counterparts, in order to better appreciate the nose and taste. The volatile elements are released as odors at higher temperatures, so when the wine is too cold the aromas and bouquet are faint. Warmer temperature also translates as both increased perception of sugars and the "hot" feeling of acids and alcohol together (see Chapter 3 on How to Taste Wine).

A wine served between 44° and 59°F (6.6 and 15° C) warms up a degree about every seven minutes in the glass; a wine served between 39° and 44°F (4° and 6.6°C) gains about a degree every four minutes. The palm of the hand can also warm the bowl of the glass. Serving wine quite cold will accentuate the bitter and astringent flavors in the wine. A barrel-fermented Chardonnay is a tannic white wine and would not be served too cold, as the temperature would exacerbate the harsh tannins. A simple, stainless steel-fermented white wine of high acidity, such as a dry Chenin Blanc, would not produce the same reaction and could be more refreshing served quite cool. For either white or red wines it is the tannin level that is the most important factor to determine service temperature. Lower-tannin wines are served cooler than higher-tannin wines.

Long-term refrigeration of wine can eventually rob the cork of moisture, so it is important for restaurants that use refrigerators to rotate the stock (see Chapter 16 on Purchasing and Storage). All glassware should be room temperature. A very warm glass is the wrong choice for a chilled white and a cool glass is wrong for a full-bodied tannic red or Port, which are served at higher temperatures because of their high tannins. Never re-frigerate a Champagne glass, as the moisture that forms on the glass will di-lute the wine and break the delicate bubbles.

***Presenting the Wine.*** Proper wine service dictates that the wine server ap-proach the table, show the label on the wine bottle to the person who or-dered the wine, and quietly announce the product name, producer, and vintage. This allows the guest to verify the selection or to make a change. Sometimes, especially when ordering varietal-labeled wines, some confu-sion can occur in ordering. For example, a guest may order a Zinfandel, a red wine, but really mean to order a White Zinfandel (a "blush" or rosé wine). Presenting the wine to the guest allows the server to clarify the order before the wine is opened.

The bottle should be opened in view of the table, and the bottle should never leave the sight of the host during the meal, unless requested. Before opening the bottle, the server should have ready a corkscrew, preferably the classic "waiter's tool" (see Figure 15.5), and a napkin that is damp at one end. The dining room staff must work as a team, and the wine waiter or captain should always check the table first to see if empty glasses should be removed, if ashtrays should be changed, or bread crumbs cleaned off the tablecloth.

The best place to open wine is on a side stand or cart. Red wines may be opened on the table, while whites and rosés are opened in the ice bucket or cooler, if one or the other is being utilized. Sparkling wines may be opened either in or out of the ice bucket. Common sense and house poli-cies will usually win over steadfast rules, but opening still wines in the air, without surface support, is the least-desirable choice, especially for older red wines, whose sediment can be jostled. A crowded table in a corner may leave the server no alternative but to open a wine in the air; again, let com-mon sense prevail.

The server should check older red wines for **ullage** (see Figure 15.6), which means that the bottle fill is lower than normal in the neck of the bot-tle, and oxygen may have deteriorated the wine. This is rare and only occurs with reds after more than a decade in the bottle. Not all wines with ullage are spoiled, but the server should be prepared for that possibility and may advise the maitre d' or manager before presenting the wine to the guest.

Because sediment in older red wines could be shaken and dispersed, some restaurants may employ cradles, or baskets, for transporting the wine to the table. Decanting is another consideration for red wines (see the side-bar on Decanting in this chapter).

***Continuing Service.*** The server should serve the guests in a clockwise fashion. In a mixed group, women are to be served first, then men, and fi-nally the person who ordered the wine. A full bottle of dinner wine is con-sidered to be sufficient for a table of six, providing portions of about four ounces each. A sweet dessert wine for which a two-ounce pour is adequate, is usually poured for six from a half-bottle.

The server should pour the wine in a firm and steady motion with the bottle mouth placed just over the glass, but not touching it. After pouring, the

**Figure 15.6** Ullage in a Bottle of Maya-camas Cabernet Sauvignon from Napa, California.

# UNCORKING THE WINE

To open the wine the server uses the broad part of the knife blade on the corkscrew to cut the foil or plastic at the lower lip of the bottle neck, to ensure a clean, more uniform cut. The foil or cap is sometimes removed by pulling an extended, perforated metal strip, or plastic "zipper" provided on the bottle. The cap should be placed in the server's pocket, not in the ice bucket or in any other receptacle. The bottle lip should be wiped with the moist end of the napkin, if necessary, to remove any encrusted dirt. This step is almost always essential when opening an older wine.

Next, the server closes the blade and opens the spiral, or "worm," of the corkscrew. A good corkscrew should have a spiral with at least four or five coils. Holding the corkscrew at an angle, the server firmly twists and inserts the worm in the cork, just slightly off-center. The cork should remain stable. If it plunges into the bottle, it is a sign that the closure was not airtight and the wine may be spoiled.

The server next twists the corkscrew until only one spiral notch is visible above the cork. (Generally rosés, light whites, and younger red wines have shorter corks than age-worthy wines, whose corks can be quite long.) Push the back part of the corkscrew down, and place the lever, or "foot," of the corkscrew onto the lip of the bottle. Make sure that the lever is flush to the lip; if not, twist the corkscrew in reverse a half turn and try again. Be careful not to place the lever at anything other than a right angle to the bottle, because if you exert pressure at the wrong angle the bottle lip may chip or splinter. With expensive, older bottles, or as a measure of extra caution and better leverage, an end of the napkin may be placed between the glass lip and the lever.

The server positions the bottle with the label facing the guest. The server's thumb should be extended on the corkscrew for leverage. The server should use the other hand to hold the bottle and as a brace where the foot of the corkscrew meets the lip of the bottle. The server lifts the cork straight up, in one motion by raising the back of the corkscrew handle while keeping the foot on the bottle lip. Some older wines, or wines that are meant to age, will require turning the corkscrew about two more turns, then lifting up a second time. The server may jiggle the cork out of the bottle with a rocking motion, using the index finger and thumb.

The cork should be presented to the person who ordered the wine. Some establishments use a very small plate for cork presentation. Quite a few misconceptions surround this service ritual, but there are really only two things a guest can tell by examining the cork. The guest can verify the name of the producer, which usually

Tartrate Crystals on a Shafer Cabernet Sauvignon from Napa, California.

appears on the cork, and make sure that the cork is moist at one end only, ensuring that the wine has been stored properly. Corks may have crystals on their moist end. These **tartrate** crystals do not indicate a faulty wine, and do not affect the wine's flavor (see Figure 15.11). While the guest examines the cork, the server wipes the mouth of the bottle with the moist end of the napkin.

Beverage service is performed to the right side of a guest, whenever practical. When removing a bottle from an ice bucket the server should wipe it dry enough so that no water drips on the table. The server should hold the bottle by its bottom half, allowing the label to be mostly visible. A tasting portion of about one ounce should be poured for the person who ordered the wine. The server then waits for approval before serving the rest of the table. Occasionally a guest may refuse a bottle (see the sidebar on Refused Bottles in this chapter).

# DECANTING

Red wines are fermented with their skins which contribute both color and tannins. Over time the pigments and tannins form sediment. The process of decanting is done to separate the sediment from the wine before serving it to the guests (see Figures 15.7, 15.8, and 15.9). A server would ask the guest if they would prefer to have the wine decanted. Older bottles of fine red wine are decanted as an extra touch of service but some customers do not want to draw attention to their table and just ask for the bottle to be poured slowly so the sediment is not agitated too much. The tools used to decant a wine are illustrated in Figures 15.3, 15.7, 15.8, 15.9, and 15.10.

The bottle is brought to the table in a basket unless it has been ordered in advance and has been standing up to allow the sediment to settle to the bottom. The cork is removed. A light source such as a candle is positioned just under the neck or shoulder area of the bottle. The server pours in a steady, continuous motion into a glass decanter. The server watches the neck and stops transferring the wine if sediment or haze appears in the neck (see Figure 15.11). It is important for the server not to stop in the middle of transferring the wine, for the rocking motion will cause the sediment to be stirred up throughout the wine. If the server only gets through one-half or two-thirds of the bottle before the haze or sediment appear, the wine should be left for a half hour or more if possible before attempting to decant again. The server would respectfully ask the guests not to pick up the wine as sediment would be disturbed, while assuring the guests that the sediment is not poisonous and is a natural part of the wine.

Many guests do not want their wines decanted. Some experts say French Burgundy wines are best not decanted but Bordeaux which are made with thicker-skinned grapes should be decanted. It is best to allow the guest the option. The other reason a wine may be decanted is to aerate it. Young tannic red wines are less harsh after **breathing.** The bottle opening is small and it only takes a few seconds to pour a young red into a decanter, thereby exposing all the wine to oxygen. The merits of allowing young reds to aerate is another subject without one correct answer (see Figure 15.10). Franco Biondi Santi of Brunello di Montalcino in Italy insists his Riserva needs 24 hours to open up and show at its best, while many other wines have been proven to taste best when freshly opened.

**Figure 15.7** The First Step in Decanting an Older Wine Is Opening It in a Cradle.

**Figure 15.8** The Next Step Is to Pour the Wine Using a Candle as a Light Source.

**Figure 15.9** The Wine Is Poured Until Some Sediment Is Viewed.

**Figure 15.10** Opening, Decanting, and Serving a Young California Cabernet Sauvignon.

*Presenting the wine list.*

*Presenting the bottle.*

*Opening the bottle.*

*The taster inspects the cork.*

*The wine is poured into a glass decanter to aerate, rather than to remove sediment.*

*A tasting portion is offered.*

*The aeration from decanting and the larger glasses make a young Cabernet Sauvignon enjoyable.*

When serving wine, the person who ordered the bottle is offered a chance to inspect the cork. If the cork is dry on both ends, the wine probably was not stored on its side, which is not a problem for a young, simple wine. However, if the cork feels very dry and crumbles a bit, air may have invaded the wine through the cork, and the wine could be bad. A cork that is wet on both ends suggests a similar problem. Both cases warrant suspicion, but the guest should still smell the wine. If the smell is very unpleasant (the smell of rotten eggs or of a moldy cork) the guest may ask the server to taste it or may refuse the bottle outright.

A guest has the right to refuse a bottle of bad wine. Although it is not proper for a guest to return a bottle simply because he or she does not like the style of the wine, the old adage "the customer is always right" may hold true. A hospitality business can ill afford to alienate its guests, whether they are technically right or wrong about the wine. As always, house policies apply, but a server facing an unpleasant situation should try to be as diplomatic and gracious as possible. Of course, it is proper procedure for the server to involve the restaurant manager in any decision concerning a refused bottle. While restaurant guests do occasionally refuse wines, modern wine making has resulted in the majority of the world's wines being clean, sound, and enthusiastically welcomed at the table.

A restaurant that carries very expensive older wines, which sell for $200 to $2000 per bottle or even more, may print a disclaimer on its wine list stating, "Not responsible for the condition of wines over $200." Of course, an occasional guest may test the staff by ordering and refusing a very expensive wine as a gaffe, but it is more likely that a valued patron may, with the best of intentions, order a fine, older wine, yet be unhappy with its condition. Each situation requires a decision call by the manager or owner that she or he believes to be fair to both the guest and the establishment.

bottle neck should be lifted, twisted a half turn, and then dabbed clean with the napkin, ensuring that no wine drips on the table or customers' clothes.

The server should ask the person who tasted the wine if corks and finished bottles may be removed, and if new glasses are preferred for another bottle of the same wine. The server may also inquire after a bottle is finished if the guests are enjoying the wine and would like to continue with more of the same, or try something different. A new wine is offered through the wine list or by verbal suggestion, but it is usually best to bring the list to the table and point out the price of the new wine to the host, so there is no confusion surrounding this issue. In some situations the host may allow the server to pick appropriate wines within a certain price range and does not want to be bothered with seeing each wine and price on the list. The server or sommelier must accept that each table and occasion is a distinct situation that requires more or less interaction with the host. Of course, a new wine calls for new glasses. The server should ask the guest's permission when removing a glass from the previous bottle even if there is only a small amount left.

A service professional will be sensitive to the ambiance of the restaurant and to the particular guests he or she is serving. When walking the fine line between familiarity and formality, it is always best to maintain a professional, but friendly, attitude. Service professionals not only respond to their guests' requests, they also *anticipate* their guests' needs.

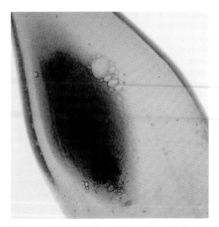

**Figure 15.11** When Decanting Old Red Wines, the Server Watches for Sediment and Avoids Transferring it to the Decanter.

**Figure 15.12** Presenting, Opening, and Serving Champagne.

*Presenting the bottle with the label facing the taster.*

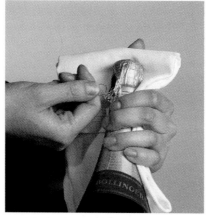

*Find the pull or hasp to remove the foil.*

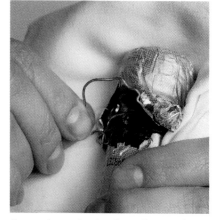

*Loosen the cage keeping the napkin over the top.*

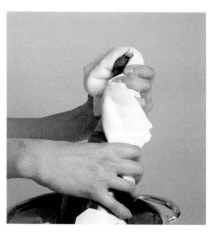

*Hold the cork with a thumb over the top, then twist the bottle in one direction.*

*Catch the cork in the napkin.*

*Pour a one ounce taste for the taster.*

*Hold the bottle just over the glass and pour.*

*Prime each glass with an ounce or two.*

*Wait for the foam to subside from the primed pour before the second pouring.*

***Serving Sparkling Wine.***   A standard bottle of sparkling wine served at 45°F (7.2°C) has six to eight atmospheres of pressure (one atmosphere equals 14 pounds of pressure per square inch), and so must be treated with caution and respect. Warm sparkling wines are liable to foam over the lip of the bottle when opened and go flat quickly, so sparkling wines should always be served well chilled (see sidebar on Serving Temperature Ranges in this chapter). Many restaurants keep sparkling wines refrigerated and ready to serve.

The bottle should be handled carefully during transit from the cellar to the table. A bottle that has been swung about or bumped is more likely to explode when the cage is removed or to foam over when the cork is removed.

As with all wines, the bottle is presented to the person who ordered it (see Figure 15.12). Sparkling wines may be opened either in or out of the ice bucket. After removing the foil, the server may remove the cage with caution, using a napkin. The thumb must be placed on top of the cage, to avoid a flying cork. Many sparkling wines have a pull strip which can be used to remove the foil. If there is no pull strip, the server should first pull the hasp of the metal cage out and down, then twist the hasp about five times to unwind it, and finally, pull the cage outward and upward to remove both the cage and the foil that surrounds it. Never use the blade of the corkscrew to cut the foil before the cork is removed. Later, when the bottle has been safely opened, the server may use the blade to neatly trim any foil bits that might fall into the glass. The bottle should be held at about a 45° angle. The server should cover the top of the bottle with the napkin, while the thumb exerts subtle downward pressure on the cork.

Some people believe it is best to loosen the entire cage and remove it, while others simply loosen it, a safe alternative. Once the cage is loosened or removed, the bottle is ready to be opened. Hold the bottom of the bottle with one hand and, with the other, hold the napkin on top of the cork with downward pressure. Twist the bottle in one direction while holding the cork steady. Do not twist the cork, because the "mushroom"—the top half of the cork—can break off from the bottom half, and because it is easier to apply force to the larger bottle than to the smaller cork. Continue to hold the bottle at a 45° angle.

The formal way to open a bottle of sparkling wine is to avoid making a loud "pop." The desired sound is the slightest hiss or "sigh," which allows surface carbon dioxide to escape in a regular pattern, and helps to maintain the **perlage,** the small bead of bubbles. On certain occasions, like New Year's Eve, loud pops may be encouraged to add to the festivities, and with a very inexpensive product, that's fine. When opening a fine sparkler or true champagne, however, stay away from popping.

The mouth of the bottle should be wiped off with the napkin and the cork presented. The server should dry off the bottle if it was opened in the bucket. The bottle should be held in a similar manner as a still wine with the label exposed. Some servers place their thumb in the punt under the bottle. Not all sparkling wines have the punt indentation, and it is also a very unwieldy practice for larger size bottles. The server should pour about one ounce into a clean dry tulip- or flute-shaped glass for the host or the person they designate to be in charge of the wine ordering. The saucer-shaped sorbet glasses, so popular at catered events, allow too many bubbles to escape. Sparkling wines' first sensory appeal is the hissing sound of the wine being poured into the glass, then the color of the wine and movement of the bubbles in the glass. When sparkling wine is poured, a foam, or mousse, rises toward the top of the glass.

Once the host approves the wine the guests at the table are served. Sparkling wine should be poured in two motions. The first ounce or so provides a base, and when the mousse settles after the first pour, the wine is poured again, filling the glass about two-thirds full. After all the guests are served the wine bottle is then placed back in the ice bucket or cooler with a draped napkin, so the server can dry off the bottle next time the sparkling wine is poured.

### Serving Fortified Wines

*Port.* Vintage Port and some Late-Bottled Vintage Ports must be decanted as they may contain sediment. Tawny, ruby, or white ports do not require decanting, as they have spent more time in barrels and have been racked and fined more often to obtain clarity (see Chapter 1 on How Wine Is Made).

Wines usually have a metal or plastic cap over the cork, but a true Vintage Porto from Portugal often has sealing wax covering its cork. The blade of the corkscrew must be used to scrape the wax off the top so that the cork is exposed. A damp napkin is used to clean off any bits of hardened wax. Vintage Porto is intended to age for a long time in the bottle, so corks are quite long. A good tool to have for opening Vintage Porto is a corkscrew with two "feet." Proceed with the opening of the Port as you would any other still wine.

Traditionally, the British would drink Port in a room with a fireplace. Port tongs were heated in the fire and then placed around the neck of the bottle just below the cork bottom. A wet string was used to stroke the neck, and the bottle would crack neatly, but tongs have fallen into disuse for obvious reasons. Aside from Vintage, most Ports are easily opened by removing the foil with the blade of the corkscrew, and then twisting a plastic cap which has a cork stopper.

Vintage and Late-Bottled Vintage Ports are served at the same temperature as full-bodied reds, while Tawny Ports may be served slightly cooler. Ruby and white Ports may be served slightly chilled. A 2 to 2.5-ounce/6 to 7.5-centiliter portion in a Port glass or small tasting glass is standard.

### Sherry, Madeira, and Marsala.
Sherry, Madeira, and Marsala often have plastic-capped cork stoppers, and so can be opened without any special tools. The exception would be the finest vintage Madeira, which would be handled in the same manner as vintage Porto. As an apéritif or with food, the dry and semi dry versions are served well-chilled. The sweet versions are

served at room temperature. A 2 to 2.5 ounce (6 to 7.5 centiliter) portion is poured using small tasting glasses and, when available, a copita glass is ideal for Sherry. (See the photo of glassware in Chapter 3 on How to Taste Wine.)

When Sherry, Madeira, or Marsala are served with consommé or other soups, the wines are not chilled, in order to compliment the temperature of the hot soup.

## Summary

Customers pay a premium when ordering wine in restaurants and should be provided with courteous, knowledgeable servers and sound wines. The most important issues in serving wine so that it can be enjoyed are having it brought to its correct temperature, uncorking the bottle, and pouring the wine into the glass.

A restaurant must meet its customer's expectations. A formal establishment with expensive wines will most likely have the types of wines and tools to offer decanting. A casual spot may have less exacting standards, but it must still have a training program to ensure servers know the style of wines available and the basics of service.

The next chapter deals with purchasing wines and taking the steps to ensure they are maintained properly so they arrive at the table in good condition.

# Purchasing and Storage

## Introduction

There are many resources for increasing proficiency in the purchase and storage of wine. Enhanced knowledge can add to both the enjoyment and success of the decision-making and purchasing process.

Proper storage is a vital element in protecting your investment. Strategies for selecting and storing wines, for both the consumer and the professional, are described in this chapter. Vigilant attention to these guidelines increases the likelihood of a pleasurable experience each time you or the consumer enjoy the fruits of your labor.

The Wine Cellar at The Culinary Institute of America.

## Why a Cellar?

A consumer may get started by purchasing a case of assorted wine to avoid repeated trips to the store. A favorite wine may be purchased by the case to save money or as a way to chart its evolution by trying bottles over a period of time. The first cache for a collector may be a cool dark corner of a basement or closet. As the amount of bottles increases so does the need for space and a system for recording what the wine cost and how it tasted.

## Types of Cellars

There are two types of wine cellars: the home/wine shop/restaurant cellar and the investor/collector cellar. The main differences are purpose and scope of inventory.

***Home/Wine Shop/Restaurant.*** A home/wine shop/restaurant cellar usually has three types of wine: A good deal of wines at inexpensive prices as a casual beverage or for a simple meal; moderately priced wines for more elaborate lunches or dinners; and a small amount of expensive wines for special occasions. A wealth of inexpensive well-made wines under $10 are available and the moderate price range goes from there up to the $30 retail level, while premium wines and the rarities of the world command prices even higher. The rare wines are for special occasions while the everyday drinking wine category is the mainstay for a restaurant and the most-used section

Wine Storage at The Culinary Institute of America's American Bounty Restaurant.

of a private cellar. Therefore, the cellar's focus may switch with the seasons. The warmer months require a cellar to have more light whites, rosés, and sparklers which can be refreshing indoors or outside. The approach of winter signifies a time to stock up on hearty reds for their warmth and ability to match the heavier fare consumed during those months.

*Investor/Collector.* The investor's/collector's cellar requires a different strategy. The majority of wines are not purchased for casual use, but are specific styles of wines whose worth most likely will escalate over time. The investor/collector buys wines for their ability to increase in value, for the enjoyment of collecting exclusive items, and for the pleasure of drinking a great wine. Powerful wines achieve more harmony over time and as others consume them prematurely the remaining stocks increase in value. A wine's price can be attributed to consumer awareness and acceptance, the amount produced, and its predicted longevity. For example, Chardonnay is the most popular white grape, and when produced in ideal vintages and locations, has the ability to age over two decades. The Chardonnay-based Grand Cru "Montrachet" in France can only come from 20 acres/eight hectares and the limited supply increases its value. The Côte D'or of France is not the sole area making superlative Chardonnays today, and age-worthy fine examples are produced in limited amounts in the United States and other nations. The other white wine areas for investment are those which produce luscious dessert wines—some can improve over a century. Vintage Porto from Portugal and genuine champagne from France are the most sought after in their respective categories of fortified and sparkling wines. Some collectors specialize in a particular grape or an area which produces complex wines. An investor may focus on Zinfandels from California, Shiraz from Australia, Ribera del Duero from Spain, or Barolo from Italy. There are wines from those areas that can be inspiring in taste and fine investments. However, the leading wines for financial speculation continue to be the highest quality Pinot Noirs from Burgundy, France and Cabernet Sauvignon/Merlot-based wines from the New or Old World. The classified Châteaux of Bordeaux still generate the most interest and speculation at auctions.

Some collectors devote a portion of their cellar budget to long-term aging and investment while non-drinkers treat wine purely as a financial speculation. Just as the racetrack and stock market are perilous, so is wine speculation a gamble. It is just as impossible to predict a wine's character 20 years from its birth as it is to predict a person's development. Educated guesses for both are based on ancestry, place and time of birth, and upbringing. Were the grape types used vitis vinifera and planted in soils well suited for those varieties? Was there a low yield of grapes during a warm and dry harvest or was it a rainy year? These would be some of the questions raised about events in the vineyard. Skin maceration time for a red, and the temperature and vessel used for fermentation could be some of the winery decisions affecting life span (see Chapter 1 on How Wine Is Made).

# Decisions and Directions on Buying Wine

How does a person get specialized information before buying an expensive bottle or case of wine? Which wines are decent, inexpensive products worth a try? Some may choose a bottle because of an attractive label or name and take their chances, but there are methods that can help the wine buyer.

## Shop Around Before Buying

Price is important when purchasing anything but it is not the sole consideration when buying wine. Finding a store with a knowledgeable salesperson, where the customer feels at ease, is the key to building a relationship of trust. Just as snooty attitudes and intimidation by servers should not be tolerated in a restaurant, they are also an indication to find the exit sign in a wine shop or wine section of a supermarket. As a sommelier would take the time to determine each guest's personal preferences in wine styles and price level, so should a store's staff be sensitive to shoppers. Many stores keep a profile on customers' purchase preferences and will send out newsletters alerting them about sales and tastings focusing on specific wines.

## Try Before You Buy

Prospective buyers can usually listen to tunes before buying compact discs or test drive a car. Similarly, many stores selling wines offer a small taste of featured inexpensive or moderately priced wines. Instead of buying a bottle of wine, a tasting or glass portion can be purchased at wine bars or restaurants known for their variety of selections by the glass.

# Get Expert Advice

Advice from a salesperson is helpful, as is shopping with a knowledgeable acquaintance or friend. The wine festivals and wine maker nights at restaurants are yet another avenue for gaining confidence to purchase wine. A collector or business ready to invest a large amount of money may save time and money by paying a consultant fee to a professional whose priority will be to objectively purchase wines on behalf of the client.

The same magazines, newspapers, and journals that offer schedules for seminars have sections devoted to reviewing wines. Books with tasting notes on specific wines and assessment of regions by vintage are available. When purchasing books rating wines, it is best to buy the most current editions. Tasting notes on the character of a wine tasted a decade ago cannot describe the present state of the wine, yet they do offer an educated opinion of when the wine should be at its prime. Vintage charts can relieve the burden for consumers who have absolutely no intention of memorizing the weather patterns of the major wine-growing regions for the past few decades (see the sidebar in this chapter on Vintage Cards).

As mentioned in the section on tasting we all taste differently and one person's favorite selection may be a barely tolerable wine for the next. A group of knowledgeable writers at the same tasting often disagree among themselves as to which wines are best and why they are so deserving of

## CONSUMER AND TRADE NEWSLETTERS AND JOURNALS WITH WINE FEATURES

There are two ways that businesses may purchase wine in the United States. Control State Alcohol Boards in states such as Pennsylvania act as exclusive agents selling all wines whether wholesale or retail. Other states will sell wholesale licenses to companies which then sell to restaurants, wine shops, or other retail outlets. In the license states, a Beverage Media Journal or Guide is available. It contains the names and telephone numbers of the wholesalers, the prices of the products they sell, and other information such as special discounts and industry updates on local events. Each wholesaler will also have sales representatives who visit clients and provide catalogues of their company's products. The catalogue or salesperson may provide background information on a product the client is considering purchasing. Wholesalers and consumers may also purchase wine at wine auctions.

Material available to consumers and professionals includes *The Wine Advocate* (Parkton, MD), *American Wine Society Journal* (Rochester, NY), *Beverage Dynamics* (Braintree, MA), *Bordeaux International* (New York, NY), *Wine Business* (Sonoma, CA), *Wine Enthusiast* (Pleasantville, NY), *American Wine Review* (Stroudsburg, PA), *Decanter* (British, but domestic office in Denville, NJ), *Food Arts* (New York, NY), *Food and Wine* (New York, NY) *Gourmet* (New York, NY), *Gourmetour* (Madrid, Spain), *International Wine Review* (Ithaca, NY), *Wines of Spain* (New York, NY), *Italian Wine and Spirits* (New York, NY), *Market Watch* (New York, NY), *Wine News* (Miami, FL), *The Wine Spectator*—the largest circulation wine magazine in America—(New York, NY), *Wine and Spirits Magazine* (Princeton, NJ), and *Wine Trader* (Carson City, NV).

In addition to features on wine some of these also list schedules of wine events and advertisements to purchase through auctions, stores that ship wines, and wine-of-the-month clubs.

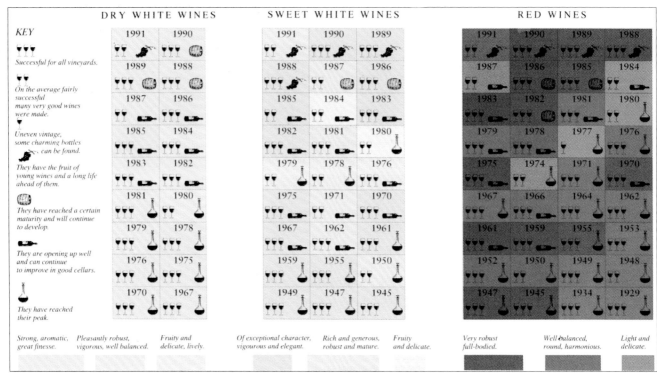

**Figure 16.1**  A Vintage Chart for Bordeaux Wines.

---

**Figure 16.2**  A Vintage Chart of Selected Italian Red DOC and DOCG Wines.

**KEY TO VINTAGES:**  1—FAIR   2—GOOD   3—VERY GOOD   4—EXCEPTIONAL

- To drink young
- Suitable for moderate aging
- Suitable for long aging
- May also be drunk young
- Sometimes suitable for moderate aging
- Sometimes suitable for long aging

---

## CLASSIFICAÇÃO DE COLHEITAS

| ANOS | DÃO | BAIRRADA | COLARES | DOURO | BUCELAS | ALENTEJO |
|------|-----|----------|---------|-------|---------|----------|
| 1981 | 1 | 1 | 3 | 3 | 1 | 1 |
| 1982 | 1 | 2 | 3 | 2 | 2 | 2 |
| 1983 | 4 | 4 | 4 | 2 | 3 | 2 |
| 1984 | 1 | 1 | 4 | 3 | 2 | 2 |
| 1985 | 4 | 3 | 3 | 2 | 3 | 2 |
| 1986 | 2 | — | 2 | 1 | 2 | 2 |
| 1987 | 3 | 2 | 3 | 2 | 3 | 3 |
| 1988 | — | — | — | — | — | — |
| 1989 | 2 | 2 | 2 | 2 | 2 | 3 |
| 1990 | 2 | 2 | 2 | 2 | 1 | 4 |
| 1991 | 2 | 2 | 2 | 1 | 1 | 3 |
| 1992 | 2 | 2 | 1 | 2 | 2 | 2 |

4 - EXCELENTE   3 - MUITO BOM
2 - BOM   1 - MÉDIO

FONTE: INSTITUTO DA VINHA E DO VINHO
– CÂMARA DE PROVADORES

**ICEP**
*Investimentos, Comércio e Turismo de Portugal*

**Figure 16.3**  A Vintage Chart of Selected Wines of Portugal.

praise. One of the pleasures of wine for beginner or seasoned tasters alike is supporting claims for individual preferences. Samples of tasting terminology are in Chapter 3 on How to Taste Wine and abound in professional tasting reviews, but may boil down to "I just think that wine is delicious." Reviews and opinions are just that but they can be helpful in selecting wines for a cellar. A bottle of highly touted wine can be purchased and, if it lives up to expectations, a consumer can buy more based on personal judgment.

## Visit a Winery

Many wineries are open to the public for tours and have a tasting room where a small tasting portion of their wines are either poured for free or for a small charge. The wineries may sell bottles of their own wines at reduced rates and some will even send the wines to the customer's home or business when permitted by law. Each state and country has its own laws to control the import of wines.

Wineries that do not have regular business hours for tours and tasting may be available to visit by writing or phoning in advance. Some wineries maintain a mailing list to send free newsletters to their customers, with such information as current wines available, the growing season, or promotional events.

Other venues for trying wines are tastings organized by local wine and food societies, government trade commissions, and wine festivals. Listings for these events are generally found in local or national newsletters and magazines that specialize in wine and food (see sidebar on periodicals with wine features).

## Keeping a Cellar Book

Having a record of which wines are in the cellar and how much they cost is a starting point for organizing your cellar. A scrapbook which includes tast-

# Under $10 a Bottle

*Please Note:* Due to space restrictions not all of the world's good-value wines are listed and many are waiting to be discovered. Also, varietals suggested, such as Chardonnay and Cabernet Sauvignon, may be found in both price ranges as they are available at different price points. Suggested varietals listed for both New World and Old may be identified by checking the appropriate chapter. An example would be Chapter 6 on France, which identifies Merlot as used in Pomerol at the regional and Château level.

*Category: **Sparkling Wine.*** Brut Cava from Spain, Prosecco di Conegliano from Italy; Crémant from France; Brut from the New World (i.e., South Africa, New Zealand, Australia, and the Americas).

*Category: **Dry White Wine, Light Body.*** Vinho Verde from Portugal; Soave, Galestro from Italy; Muscadet, Aligoté, Entre-Deux-Mers from France.

*Category: **Semidry White Wine, Light Body.*** Chenin Blanc, Riesling, or Gewürztraminer from the United States or France; Riesling QA level from Germany.

*Category: **Dry White Wine, Medium to Full Body.*** Sauvignon Blanc, Sémillon or Chardonnay from the New World; Dão from Portugal; Vernaccia di San Gimignano, Verdicchio Orvieto from Italy; Pinot Blanc from France; Grüner Veltiner from Austria; Furmint from Hungary.

*Category: **Dry Reds, Light Body.*** Gamay, Dolcetto from the United States; Beaujolais from France; Grignolino, Dolcetto, Valpolicella from Italy; Pinotage from South Africa.

*Category: **Dry Red, Medium to Full Body.*** Merlot, Cabernet Sauvignon, Pinot Noir, Syrah, Shiraz, or Petite Sirah from the New World, Eastern Europe, or Israel; Egri Bikavér from Hungary; Rioja, Ribera del Duero at Crianza level from Spain; Dão, Douro, Periquita Bairrada from Portugal; Côtes du Rhône, Minervois, Faugères, Madiran from France; Barbera, Sangiovese from Italy or from the United States; Sassella, Inferno, Spanna, Chianti, Tereldego Rotliano, Salice Salentino from Italy.

*Category: **Dry Rosé.*** "Rhône Rangers" from the United States; Navarra from Spain.

ing notes of how a wine tasted and which friends or business clients enjoyed it is also useful information. Comments on the wine may be a few simple words such as "dry, green-apple smell, tastes tart and not too heavy in the mouth." A more rigorous system using tasting sheets such as the ones in Chapter 3 on How to Taste Wine could also be warranted for the more serious collector or for business needs.

Charting a wine's character over time is important. Perhaps a specific white wine is starting to brown on the rim, indicating full maturity (see Chapter 3 on How to Taste Wine). An owner of a couple of cases of the wine would not have to panic but would likely plan an event to use the wine in the near future. On the other hand, if a red was opened and it was

*Category: Sweet Wine.*   Muscat for white and Mavrodaphne for red from Greece; Muscat from the New World; Ports from the New World.

## Explorer Cellar $10 and Up

*Category: Sparkling Wines.*   Champagne from France; Brut, Blanc de Blanc, Blanc de Noirs, rosé from New World or Old.

*Category: Dry Apéritif.*   Fino, Manzanilla Sherry from Spain.

*Category: Dry White Wines, Medium to Full Body.*   Sauvignon, Fumé Blanc, Viognier, Sémillon from the New World; Sancerre, Pouilly-Fumé, Savennières, Condrieu, Hermitage, Châteauneuf-du-Pape, Pinot Gris from France; Chardonnay from the New World or Old, Fendant from Switzerland; Tocai Friulano, Gavi, Arneis, Greco di Tufo, Fiano di Avellino from Italy; Albariño from Spain, Alvarinho from Portugal.

*Category: Sweet White Wines.*   Late Harvest or *Botrytis* Riesling, Chenin Blanc and Gewürztraminer from New World or Old; Pedro Ximénes Sherry from Spain; Moscatel de Sétubal from Portugal; Tokaji 5 Puttonyos or Essencia from Hungary; Malvasia delle Lipari, Recioto di Soave, Vin Santo from Italy.

*Category: Dry Rosé.*   Tavel, Bandol from France; Lacryma Rosa from Italy.

*Category: Dry Red Wines, Medium to Full Body.*   Zinfandel from the United States; Pinot Noir, Merlot, Cabernet Franc, Cabernet Sauvignon, Syrah from New World or Old, Proprietary Reds from the New World or Old: Rioja, Ribera del Duero at Reserva or Gran Reserva levels from Spain, Barca Velha, Morgado de Requengo, and Tapada do Chaves from Portugal, Château Musar from Lebanon; Barolo, Barbaresco, Brunello di Montalcino, Amarone, "Super Tuscans" such as Solaia, Sagrantino de Montefalco, Taurasi, and Riserva wines of Sicily from Italy.

*Category: Sweet Red Wines.*   Porto from Portugal, Banyuls from France.

opaque, black cherry in color, and very astringent on the palate, the owner would not use the wine in the near future as it would only improve in balance with age. Another consideration is that many fine wines go through a *"dumb stage."* The dumb stage is the time when a wine seems to close up and not offer much complexity in aromatics or flavor. The owner of a case of awkward (dumb or overly tannic) red wine has the luxury of trying another bottle a year or two later and then waiting for the optimum time to serve it.

The cellar book, whether an actual log book or a computer software program maintaining a wine inventory, functions as a business tool. Wine shared is also a source of pleasure to be remembered. Labels of a wine may be soaked and peeled off the bottle to be pasted in a book. Another memento could be photographs of the foods served and people attending when the wine was enjoyed. If a menu was printed up which included the wines served it could also be placed in a cellar book. There are no steadfast rules of how much can be in a cellar log book.

## Future Market

The term refers to a purchasing strategy that involves buying cases of a wine after the harvest but before it is bottled. A certificate of purchase is the buyer's proof of ownership. The wine is shipped to the broker or middleman who closes the deal between winery and customer. Speculators gamble that the wine will increase in price during the aging period. French Bordeaux is the most common commodity sold this way but other rarities, such as fine California Cabernet Sauvignons, are also available through this system. Sometimes, portions of the futures may be resold a half dozen times in the couple of years before the wine leaves the winery.

# Storing Wines

Wine is a product that is sensitive to change in temperature, humidity, light, and vibration. Taken to the extreme, these conditions can ruin a wine. Terms such as "bottle shock," "cooked," or "light struck" are some of the words used to describe why a wine tastes bad or is ruined. Some wines suffer from being shipped and stored at temperatures too high and are ruined in transit. If saved and returned to the source of purchase as soon as possible, moderately priced wines are usually accepted for credit or exchange. There are indicators that a wine may be bad without smelling or tasting it. *Ullage* is the term used for the space between the top of the wine and the cork (see Figure 15.6 in Chapter 15). A lot of ullage could be the result of a low bottle fill or some other problem. It is not certain that the wine with more ullage is bad but it is enough to raise concern over the wine's quality, and rare wines with more ullage sell for less than those with a higher fill. If a sealed case of wine contains bottles of different ullage levels it is advisable to drink the wines with the most ullage first as they mature quicker. A cork that is pushing the capsule over the bottle lip line is another sign of trouble as is a bottle with evidence of liquid that seeped from the top capsule. Another problem occurs with faulty corks (see the sidebar on Corks in this chapter).

Wine storage systems are available through specialty shops and catalogues. Some are built to offer temperature control as well as meeting organizational or structural needs. There are also professional storage facilities available for rent and they are listed in the yellow pages phone directory and wine publications.

# CORK—THE CONTROVERSIAL STOPPER

Cork is the most popular stopper used for quality wine. Portugal is the world's leading grower and producer with 1.65 million acres/670,000 hectares of the *quercus suber* type of oak. Spain has 1.18 million acres/480,000 hectares and Algeria, Tunisia, and Morocco are also major growers that export cork to be processed in Portugal.

A cork tree is first stripped of its outer bark after 25 years. Cork trees usually live for over a century and a half and are stripped once every nine years. After drying outdoors, the long strips are boiled then dried again and shaped. The corks were traditionally bleached for appearance and sanitary reasons. Unfortunately the compound *trichloranisole* can result from the bleaching process and molds in the cork, causing an unpleasant moldy smell referred to as *"corked."* Research is underway to offer alternative methods to preserve the cork's natural flexibility and avert problems related to bacteria or molds.

To facilitate their insertion and extraction into bottles, corks are usually coated with wax or other lubricants. Corks are often stamped with the name of the wine producer and may have a symbol or name of the cork producer as well. The cheapest-quality corks are made from dust or small bits of cork called *agglomerate*. Sparkling wine corks have to be wider to withstand the carbon dioxide pressure and are often made from agglomerate with disks of whole cork at the bottom. Simple wines for early consumption may have corks as short as an inch (2.54 centimeters). The finest wines that are intended for long aging use whole cork with less markings with lengths up to 2.3 inches (six centimeters). A wine maker purchasing corks in advance would do best storing them at temperatures of 59–68°F (12–15°C). Humidity should be under 70 percent as there is much less chance of molds forming under 80 percent humidity. A cork's elasticity has made it the preferred protector of liquids inside a bottle from the dangers of excessive exposure to the the smells, molds, bacteria, and oxygen outside the bottle.

Although cork cells are tightly packed, even when stored correctly, the cork may harbor some molds and allow some air to enter. Warmer temperatures in a cellar cause an expansion of both the wine and the air in a bottle. The cork resists some of the pressure of slight variations in temperature but usually succumbs to large swings in temperature. Air expands 32 times more than water and much more than the glass bottle. A wine laid on its side in a cellar could have liquid leak out of the cork. When the temperature in the cellar gets cooler the wine contracts and may draw air into the bottle. Oxygen is the agent that accelerates the maturation of the wine. Another reason oxygen enters through a cork is that the air outside the bottle has 20 percent oxygen and there is none within, putting pressure on the cork. The longer the cork the more resistant it is. However, once oxygen enters the bottle it is absorbed by the wine. If too much air gets into the ullage space there is also the danger that the alcohol could be converted to *acetic acid* by the acetobacter bacteria, turning the wine into vinegar.

Older corks (over 20 years) may begin to deteriorate and are sometimes replaced. The leading Châteaux in Bordeaux will advertise advance dates they will be in major American cities to recork their wines. Other wineries may have an annual date when they recork, and will have an official certificate drawn up to verify the wine's authenticity and recorking date. There are also companies not connected with a winery that specialize in recorking.

Even young wines may suffer from problems with corks. Debate continues over the use of other stoppers, and some wineries have begun to use synthetic cork. Both consumers and wineries want reliable stoppers, but there is a feeling among consumers that wines with real corks are more authentic and always of higher quality than those with a metal cap or screw-off top.

Bottles in a wine cellar are laid on their side so the cork is in contact with the wine. If bottles were left straight up the cork could dry out and deteriorate, allowing excess air to enter.

Bottles of Sparkling Wine Stored on Their Side.

The private consumer should not be too concerned about a wine's stability if it is just a few bottles intended for drinking in the immediate future. It is for the wines that are meant to be left to mature over years that the most caution should be taken.

Assuming a sound wine is purchased the ideal conditions are:

## Temperature

55°F (13°C) is considered the best temperature. Having an area which heats up to 75°F (24°C) in the day and chills down to 35°F (2°C) at night will not average out to be a good location. It is better to have a more-constant temperature slightly lower or higher than severe fluctuations. Cellars that are too cold retard a wine's maturation whereas hot temperatures such as over 75°F (24°C) can cause a wine to taste hot as well. The wine is described as "cooked" and there is no way for it to recover. Thermometers are common equipment in wine cellars as are air conditioners. A business may opt to have a power generator to protect their investment in case of an outage. A couple of degrees higher or lower than 55°F (13°C), or of vacillation would not warrant the expense or energy depletion of air conditioning.

## Humidity

The best level of humidity is around 75 percent for storing bottles of wines. As mentioned in the sidebar on corks in this chapter, mold is less likely to form under 80 percent. Higher humidity causes less evaporation and many wineries store barrels or bottles closer to 90 percent to avoid loss. The higher humidity can deteriorate labels so many European companies age the wines on their sides in cellars and put on the label and top capsule just before shipping. In contrast, most New World wineries will put the capsule and label on the bottle and put the wine in cases on pallets for storage. This may explain why, when removing the capsules of some Old World wines, a slight amount of mold is on top of the cork. When visiting European wine cellars, guests are advised not to kill spiders as they eat molds. New World producers often invert the bottles in a cardboard case so they will be stored and shipped with the corks remaining moist from contact with the wine.

A way to increase humidity in a very dry cellar is to spread a bed of stones or gravel on the floor and intermittently sprinkle the floor with water. Wines stored in low-humidity conditions will cause evaporation of wine which will later be replaced by oxygen. A cork that is wet on both sides and increased ullage are warning signs of this condition. The wine will also age faster. An electric ultrasonic dehumidifier could be used for overly damp conditions. A *hygrometer* is the device used to measure relative humidity and they can be found at hardware stores or wine shops.

If there is mildew on the cellar walls a solution of half water and half laundry bleach is one means of removing it.

## Light

Extreme vacillations between light and darkness can harm a wine. If wines are stored exposed to direct sunlight then the temperature is also a factor because the wine gets hotter in the day and cools at night. Temperature is not the only problem, as the ultraviolet light can give a wine unpleasant aromas and ruin it. Sparkling wines seem to be the most sensitive to the problem. Most sparkling wine producers are moving away from clear glass to green except for their rosés and Blanc de Noirs, where they want to show off the attractive colors. The clear glass bottle of Louis Roederer Cristal Champagne comes individually wrapped in yellow plastic for protection and many other products in lighter glass have similar paper protectors that should be left on until service. Technological advances in the 1990s have allowed for the production of green-colored Champagne bottles that are 90 percent effective in blocking ultraviolet rays. A brown-colored bottle has 100 percent filtration but is not seen as something consumers would find attractive.

Fluorescent lights are said to be more harmful to wine than mercury vapor, sodium, or incandescent lights and some retailers are switching to those alternatives. Consumers shopping in a wine store with fluorescent lights may choose to buy the bottle that is stored below, behind, or under the one on display which receives the most light, or to buy a sealed case of wine.

## Vibration

Excessive vibration may disturb a red wine's sediment and possibly the wine itself. Some jostling of a bottle will not destroy a wine, but Californians, wary of earthquakes, should take extra precautions. Wine bottles may be surrounded by plastic bubble wrap or some other protective material in case they fall out of their storage spot or are jarred against each other.

## Oxygen

As discussed earlier in this section, oxygen can accelerate the maturing of a wine or ruin it completely. Traditionally, all wines were stored on their sides but there is research underway that suggests sparkling wines may be best stored upright. Although tests have not been concluded, a number of sparkling-wine companies are experimenting with storing sparkling wines straight up. Because the ullage space is carbon dioxide, the wine is not negatively affected by oxygen, and the corks are less likely to shrink because they are not in direct contact with the wine.

## Water

This is another potential hazard. It is best not to set bottles or cases of wine directly on the floor. Wood palettes can be used to raise cases of wine off the floor. The wine itself may not be harmed by the water but the deterioration of the label will make the wine look less attractive for home consumption or business sales.

# Establishing Initial Inventory

Although a private consumer may keep records only for his or her personal pleasure and information, the business operator has a large investment in wine that demands a more stringent system of organization and planning.

A wine shop or restaurant stocks wines to supply to customers. An explanation for wine list strategy is described in Chapter 17 on Wine Lists. A wine shop develops its catalogue of wines based on information gleaned through periodicals and tastings, the personal preferences of the managers and owners, and a strategy that targets a certain clientele. The demographics of the area close to the business may point the way to including more wines from specific areas or at lower-, or higher-end price level. Tourism from certain nations may also be a determinant to carry those nations' wines. A store must decide how much space to devote to low-end, medium-range, and high-priced wines just as a restaurant does. The business must decide whether to offer a wide range of products or be known more as a specialist in a particular country's wines.

What percentage of a business' investment should be toward expensive wines that require cellar time before they are best? Is a business better off foregoing the expensive wines and taking advantage of the discounts available when purchasing multiple cases of inexpensive and moderately priced wines?

There are costs assigned to maintaining inventory and 30 percent annually is a number used by many businesses. The four possible contributors to cost are:

1. Cost of the facility. A wine cellar takes up space that could be used by a restaurant for seating customers at tables and bringing in more revenue. In high-rent areas, restaurants may opt to devote a minimum of space to wine's on-premise storage and keep the majority of stock off-premise at a less-expensive warehouse.

2. Cost of labor. The more extensive the cellar the higher the labor cost to maintain the facility.

3. Inability to use money in inventory. Funds tied up in inventory are not available for speculative investments that could be more lucrative, or for other needs such as promotion of the business.

4. Some states in the United States, such as Florida, charge a tax on alcohol inventory which increases the cost of maintaining a cellar.

Most wines do not increase very much in value and the small amount saved on multi-case purchases of inexpensive wine may not be the best financial return. The most expensive and rare wines are those that lead to the highest possible gain and risk. Wine is a perishable commodity and just as when playing the stock market, the investor has to know the background information on the wine and its potential to determine when to buy or sell. When dealing with imported wines, the fluctuations of the American dollar against the French franc or other currencies is another indicator that affects the timing of purchases and sales.

Just as restaurant tracks its sales of food products so must a business check wines sales and inventory to be able to replenish stock and assess a product's popularity. A number of software programs are available to computer users to be able to update wine lists, figure out sales and percentage costs on items, and schedule reordering wines (see the following section on maintaining inventory).

Before scheduling the reordering of wines, it is important to establish a *par stock*. The par stock is defined as the amount of each wine, or the maximum amount of each wine that should be in stock. The par stock for a popular item such as an inexpensive Chardonnay will be much higher than that of a more expensive, lesser-known wine. New businesses make an educated guess when setting the first par stock for each item, then maintain data on sales, so they may adjust the par. A par stock should be set at a high enough level that the establishment has enough product to meet anticipated sales.

A business also creates a *minimum reorder point*. This is the point where sales bring stock down to the *minimum* amount of wine in-house before reordering. The quantity ordered should bring the wine back up to par. For example, if the par stock for Iron Horse Brut was 60 bottles and inventory decreased to 12 bottles the reorder amount would be 48 bottles, or four cases. A business that orders and receives deliveries only once a week would have to calculate the expected depletion of bottles during the time before the next delivery and would increase the order by that amount.

An owner may decide to allocate a portion of inventory for fine expensive wines bought as a long-term investment. Those wines are not intended to sell and be replaced as quickly as the regular inventory. The formula used to measure inventory turnover is:

$$\text{Inventory Turnover} = \frac{\text{Cost of Sales of Beverages Used}}{\text{Average Dollar Inventory of Beverages}}$$

Purchasing efficiency involves turning inventory over often without disappointing customers by frequently running out of a number of wines.

## Maintaining Inventory

The people in charge of receiving wine orders should always check to make sure that the product received is identical to the one ordered. A vintage discrepancy on a very popular inexpensive bottle of wine, such as a white Zinfandel, may not amount to much difference in price or quality. However, with fine wines, vintage plays a pertinent role in character and price. Foreign terms for specific vineyards should be spelled out clearly for the receiver to distinguish when important. Finally, the boxes should be checked to ensure there are no broken bottles or bottles missing. With businesses in warm climates, it may be prudent to pick up a bottle of fine wine and feel it to ensure it was not overheated in the back of a nonrefrigerated truck. Any discrepancies can be noted on the receiving sheet and a company has the right to send back an incorrect delivery of goods.

A computer program can be used for maintaining inventory of wines. Cash-register systems may also be programmed to break down sales by server and bin numbers. Records of wine sales help to determine when and how much more to order. Separating dining room sales from banquet sales is advisable, as a wine may appear to be a stronger performer simply because it was ordered at one large banquet. Another wine may not achieve as high a volume but be consistent and have its steady customers who would be disappointed if the wine was replaced.

Along with the computer inventory many establishments have a double check system with bin cards. The bin card lists some vital facts concerning the wine and is initialed by the person responsible as wines are brought in and distributed out. The information includes:

* description of product, including vintage, and any special attributes, such as "reserva" or "late harvest" or a single vineyard designation

- name of wholesaler purchased from

- bottle size and number of bottles per case (most cases are 2.376 gallons/nine liters but there are exceptions)

- par stock and minimum reorder level

- date and amount of wine received

- date and amount of wine issued, and location issued if multiple locations exist (as in a hotel, resort, or club)

- initials of the person making the entry

The person making the entry for issuing wines would immediately note on paper or in a computer any wine that fell below its minimum reorder point to alert the purchasing agent to order the wine. A *perpetual inventory* is established when using this system of maintaining minimum and maximum amounts of each wine.

The bin card system may take some extra time to use but it is a control device that is as important as taking the physical inventory of bottles each month.

Restaurants that sell very expensive wines may store them in a separate cellar, with a separate key and better conditions. The wine destination restaurant may also set up a table in the cellar for patrons who wish to have a private wine and food experience in a unique setting.

Once the wines are accepted they are transferred to their designated areas in the wine cellar. The bin containing the bottles for a business will usually hold a case or more. It is imperative to rotate stock so that an establishment and their potential customers do not wind up with the remaining bottles of a wine having a different vintage. A sticker may be affixed to the ends of the necks of the last wines of a vintage that is being phased out. When establishing a system of control for wine inventory a first step is to develop a numbering system for each product. The "bin" or "inventory identification number" not only makes it easier to share information with fellow workers but also takes a lot of the worry or intimidation out of wine for staff and for customers. Not being able to pronounce a foreign word is not an issue when wine lists and inventory sheets indicate bin numbers. The system may be based solely on numbers or may incorporate letter prefixes to indicate categories. For example, a dozen different American sparkling wines could be labeled AS–1 through AS–12, or simply 001 through 012. When establishing these numbers, ensure that no two different wines have the same number and that space is left for types for future acquisitions. For example, if as above, sparkling wines are numbered 001 through 012, still red wines might be 101 through 119, white wines 201 through 217, and so forth. The idea is to keep similar items in one location for inventory and easy access in a cellar.

Wines are issued from a cellar when appropriate requisition forms are received. The forms are usually in triplicate to avoid collusion between two employees. Copies are retained by the issuer, the person receiving the goods, and the accounting office or manager.

## BOTTLE SIZES

For the sake of consistency, the bottle sizes are listed in ounces and gallons first, but in the trade the metric system is used. The standard bottle size is 25.4 ounces/750 milliliters and comes 12 to a case for a total of 2.376 gallons/nine liters. Other sizes: A split is a quarter bottle or 6.35 ounces/187.5 ml, a half is 12.7 ounces/375 ml, a Magnum is two bottles or 50.8 ounces/1.5 liters, a Jeroboam is four bottles or 101.6 ounces/three liters, a Rehoboam is six bottles or 152.4 ounces/4.5 liters, a Methusaleh is eight bottles or 203.2 ounces/six liters, Salmanazar is 12 bottles or 304.8 ounces/nine liters, Balthazar is 16 bottles or 406.4 ounces/12 liters, and a Nebuchadnezzar is 20 bottles or 508 ounces/15 liters.

These terms are generally used for Champagne bottles: In Bordeaux the term Double Magnum is for four bottles, Jeroboam for six bottles, and Imperial for the eight-bottle size.

# Summary

In this chapter we have covered the basic methods for acquiring and storing wine. A rare painting or sculpture can be admired for decades but wine may take a quirky turn in its development. The joy of sharing a fine bottle at a peak stage of its life can excite even the most jaded gourmet. Storing enough bottles of a wine to be able to discuss its potential for the future is a way to engage other tasters in controversy. The perfect time to open a bottle for one taster may be judged as too soon and with too forward and aggressive character for another. Sometimes it's just dumb luck that results in a wine being opened that all guests enjoy.

The cellar is a treasure chest a consumer or restaurateur works to establish and maintain. It is a reflection of the personality of the owner or of the restaurant that creates it. As wines are depleted and replaced with other wines the cellar changes and shifts just as a person's preferences and a restaurant menu evolve over time.

# Wine Lists

## Introduction

Despite important advances in the last two decades in the understanding of wine and wine service, and despite the greater profile which wine now enjoys in many restaurants, wine lists continue to be a source of justifiable concern and criticism. In this chapter we will lay out the concerns and criticisms and then discuss the considerations that go into a successful wine list. We will also discuss the growing popularity of wines served by the glass and present a variety of wine lists, both real and hypothetical.

# Concerns

Of all the problems that are associated with wine lists, one of the most common is that the list is not available or is not presented to the diner. This means that the restaurant guest who is a wine-drinking consumer has to ask (and wait) for the list. In the most extreme case, the hesitant customer will never have the opportunity to order wine. In both cases, the restaurant will lose out. The guest has formed a negative image of the restaurant, especially of its service, and the restaurant has lost a wine sale. By not presenting the wine list, the total revenue for the restaurant is reduced, and the tip-earning potential of the service staff is diminished drastically.

Assuming that the wine list is available to the customer, the most-frequently voiced concerns about restaurant wine lists revolve around three main issues: organization, content, and pricing. We will first consider organization.

## Wine List Organization

A major problem in organizing wine lists arises when there are too many wines to choose from. This may not be a problem for the consumer who is familiar with wine, but it certainly is a deterrent to the unfamiliar, uninitiated, or intimidated restaurant guest. The frustration experienced by a confused customer trying to wade through an overly long wine list is likely to result in no wine order.

A second problem arises when the wine list is disorganized or inconsistently organized. Even knowledgeable wine consumers can become frustrated by a wine list that presents wines in no particular order, or that jumps from category to category. The end result is that customers may not find the kind of wine they are looking for, and may develop an uneasy or even antagonistic attitude toward the restaurant and its staff. If such frustration is the result for a knowledgeable wine consumer, then the unfamiliar consumer stands no chance at all.

Third, the list may be out-of-date, either because items are no longer available or vintages have changed. For the wine-savvy customer, as well as for the less knowledgeable, it is frustrating to choose from a list, only to be advised that the item is not available, or that the details of the particular wine listed (vintage or specific growing area, for example) have changed. Such inconsistencies antagonize customers and may convince them to stick with the glass of iced water that is already on the table.

Finally, servers may be unfamiliar with the list and its contents. For the "expert" wine customer, this obviously does not present a problem. But for the hesitant customer who wants to order wine but needs help, the likely result is, again, lost revenue and an unhappy guest. What else could be the result when somebody who knows nothing about a product tries to purchase something from somebody who is equally ignorant?

## Wine List Content

Problems just as serious arise when the list's content is at fault. For example, if the list contains no information about the wines, novice wine consumers are unlikely to discover wines that they like. For educated consumers, the lack of information on any listed wine will probably not deter them from ordering the wine they want. For the customer who is just getting to know wines, small snippets of useful information and general descriptive phrases can easily result in the sale of a glass or bottle of wine from a higher price bracket than might otherwise be the case.

A similar problem may occur if the list offers no food-and-wine matching suggestions. Such suggestions are a great way to help the hesitant or unknowledgeable consumer make a choice. If there are hints about which wines go well with simple seafood appetizers, or which wines are more suited to braised meats, even a totally wine-ignorant customer can make a comfortable choice about wines to complement the meal. Comfortable customers are repeat customers, and such customers are likely to leave bigger tips.

A third content problem is that there are no wines available by the glass, or the selection of by-the-glass wines is very limited. Those restaurants that have been selling wines by the glass for many years could probably write volumes about the advantages and benefits of such a program—increased sales and revenue, higher numbers of repeat customers, and so forth. At a time when most customers are wary about their total alcohol consumption, offering wines by the glass has obvious benefits. But there are also the less obvious advantages; the perception that a greater selection is being offered, providing the customer with the opportunity to enjoy more than one type of wine with a meal, and of making it possible for two, three, or four diners to enjoy wines of their choice with their meal, rather than all sharing the same bottle of wine. When no wines are available by the glass, or the selection is limited to the same old choices, many customers may not order wine at all. For more information on this topic, see the section on wines by the glass in this chapter.

A final criticism pertaining to the list's content may be there are no local wines offered. For obvious reasons, most of us like to stick with the known, the comfortable, and the socially acceptable. For wines, this generally means that we will readily order and drink wines from Europe, California, and the Northwest, but we are not so accepting of wines from the less well-known or "local" areas. However, restaurants that do feature local wines often find that it pays off. Locals and tourists alike enjoy sampling the local product, and local wines fit very well into the current food trend of using as much local produce as possible.

## Pricing

There is only one criticism of wine list prices: Prices are too high. In too many cases, fine restaurants have closed because of their refusal to accept that customers will not pay the high prices demanded for the restaurant's food and wine. The last decade has seen a steady acceptance of the need to bring menu prices down, and customers are grateful for it. All too often though, the wine list is an afterthought, and wine prices remain unjustifiably, even ridiculously, high. The obvious results are fewer bottles or glasses of wine sold, increased inventory costs, and reduced revenue. In other words, a restaurant headed for extinction.

Not all of the above concerns apply to all restaurants. Similarly, not all restaurants should even try to respond to them. A successful restaurant wine list is a reflection of the restaurant itself, meaning, of course, that there are as many types of good wine lists as there are types of good restaurants. In the mid-1970s, Kevin Zraly became famous when he organized and implemented an 800-item wine list at Windows on the World restaurant in New York City. Zraly now admits that "anybody could do that today; there's no genius in doing that. Today the genius is in putting together a 30-to-50 item wine list *which has something for everybody* within the stylistic parameters of the restaurant."

# Preparing the Wine List

The functions of a wine list are to inform and sell, but the mere existence of a wine list does not achieve that. The list needs to be one piece in an overall management concept and part of a staff-training program that emphasizes wine as an important, natural element in the total dining experience. If a wine list, by its use or misuse, projects a notion that wine is for special occasion dining only, then wine sales will suffer. The list must reflect the fact that the restaurant, its managers, and its staff expect the customer to order wine. This cannot occur if the list is not available, is too highly priced, or makes choosing wine a chore or a pseudoacademic exercise.

Two major considerations drive the design, content, organization, and price structure of the wine list:

- The theme and style of the restaurant

- The customers and their expectations

## *Theme and Style*

A formal, elegant dining experience in an upscale restaurant requires a formal wine list (see Figure 17.1). This probably means that the wine list is printed, possibly bound, and is formally presented with verbal information and suggestions from the staff.

A more casual dining environment allows for a more relaxed presentation of wine information, including these possibilities:

- Wines listed on the menu, possibly the back side

- Wines listed on a chalkboard or on table tents

- Handwritten wine lists

If there are any major culinary emphases in the restaurant, then these should provide some direction for the wine list. This is not to suggest that a

# Bordeaux Rouges

## Médoc

| | | | Mag. | 1/1 | 1/2 |
|---|---|---|---|---|---|
| 1986 | Château Loudenne | Cru Bourgeois | | 165 | |
| | Château La Tour de By | Cru Bourgeois | 300 | 155 | 85 |
| 1985 | Château La Tour de By | Cru Bourgeois | 330 | 170 | 95 |

## Haut-Médoc

| | | | Mag. | 1/1 | 1/2 |
|---|---|---|---|---|---|
| 1986 | Château Beaumont | Cru Bourgeois | | 250 | 130 |
| 1985 | Château Beaumont | Cru Bourgeois | | 150 | |
| | Château Hanteillan | Cru Bourgeois | 240 | 120 | 75 |
| | Château Cissac | Cru Bourgeois | 460 | 230 | 120 |
| 1983 | Château Hanteillan | Cru Bourgeois | | 175 | |
| | Château Beaumont | Cru Bourgeois | | 185 | |
| 1970 | Château Cissac | Cru Bourgeois | 880 | | |

## Saint-Estèphe

| | | | Mag. | 1/1 | 1/2 |
|---|---|---|---|---|---|
| 1986 | Château Calon Ségur | 3e Grand Cru Classé | | 380 | |
| | Château Cos Labory | 5e Grand Cru Classé | | 180 | 90 |
| 1985 | Château Cos Labory | 5e Grand Cru Classé | 400 | 200 | 120 |
| | Château Calon Ségur | 3e Grand Cru Classé | 990 | | |
| 1983 | Château Calon Ségur | 3e Grand Cru Classé | | 450 | |
| | Château Andron Blanquet | Cru Bourgeois | 260 | 130 | 75 |
| 1982 | Château Calon Ségur | 3e Grand Cru Classé | | 475 | |
| | Château Capbern Gasqueton | Cru Bourgeois | | 170 | |
| 1981 | Château Calon Ségur | 3e Grand Cru Classé | | 450 | |
| 1966 | Château Calon Ségur | 3e Grand Cru Classé | | 1700 | |
| | Château Phélan Ségur | Cru Bourgeois | | 1150 | |
| 1964 | Château Phélan Ségur | Cru Bourgeois | | 1350 | |
| 1948 | Château Cos d'Estournel | | | 1410 | |

## Pauillac

| | | | Mag. | 1/1 | 1/2 |
|---|---|---|---|---|---|
| 1987 | Château Batailley | 5e Grand Cru Classé | | 195 | |
| 1985 | Château Haut Batailley | 5e Grand Cru Classé | | 275 | 150 |
| 1983 | Château Pontet Canet | 5e Grand Cru Classé | 750 | 380 | 195 |
| | Château Grand Puy Lacoste | 5e Grand Cru Classé | | 350 | 185 |
| | Château Batailley | 5e Grand Cru Classé | 590 | 295 | 160 |
| 1982 | Château Grand Puy Lacoste | 5e Grand Cru Classé | | 470 | |
| | Château Pichon Longueville Baron L. | 2e Grand Cru Classé | | 620 | |
| 1981 | Château Grand Puy Lacoste | 5e Grand Cru Classé | | 410 | |
| | Château Lafite Rothschild | 1er Grand Cru Classé | | 1750 | |
| 1980 | Château Lafite Rothschild | 1er Grand Cru Classé | | 1150 | |
| | Château Grand Puy Lacoste | 5e Grand Cru Classé | | 350 | |
| 1979 | Château Les Forts de Latour | | | 510 | |
| 1977 | Château Mouton Rothschild | 1er Grand Cru Classé | | 1130 | |
| 1976 | Château Lafite Rothschild | 1er Grand Cru Classé | | 2250 | |
| | Château Les Forts de Latour | | | 1190 | |
| 1966 | Château Fonbadet | | | 720 | |
| 1965 | Château Latour | 1er Grand Cru Classé | | 1840 | |
| 1962 | Château Latour | 1er Grand Cru Classé | | 2500 | |
| 1961 | Château Grand Puy Lacoste | 5e Grand Cru Classé | | 1950 | |
| 1959 | Château Lynch Bages | 5e Grand Cru Classé | | 2250 | |

## Saint-Julien

| | | | Mag. | 1/1 | 1/2 |
|---|---|---|---|---|---|
| 1983 | Château Gloria | Cru Bourgeois | 500 | 250 | 140 |
| 1982 | Château Ducru Beaucaillou | 2e Grand Cru Classé | 1600 | 760 | 400 |
| | Château Gloria | Cru Bourgeois | | 330 | |
| 1981 | Château Ducru Beaucaillou | 2e Grand Cru Classé | | 700 | |
| | Château Lalande Borie | Cru Bourgeois | | 280 | |
| | Château Gruaud Larose | 2e Grand Cru Classé | 1320 | 660 | |
| | Château Léoville Las Cases | 2e Grand Cru Classé | | 540 | |
| 1980 | Château Léoville Las Cases | 2e Grand Cru Classé | | 510 | |
| 1978 | Château Ducru Beaucaillou | 2e Grand Cru Classé | | 860 | |
| 1975 | Château Ducru Beaucaillou | 2e Grand Cru Classé | | 1400 | |
| | Château Lagrange | 3e Grand Cru Classé | | 440 | |
| 1970 | Château Ducru Beaucaillou | 2e Grand Cru Classé | | 1900 | |

| | **CHAMPAGNE and SPARKLING WINES** | | |
|---|---|---|---|
| **Bin** | | | |
| 01 | Domaine Ste. Michelle Brut | N.V. | 22.00 |
| 02 | Domaine Chandon Blanc de Noir | N.V. | 35.00 |
| 03 | Schramsberg Blanc de Blanc, half bottle | 1990 | 24.00 |
| 05 | Jordan "J" | 1990 | 38.00 |
| 25 | Iron Horse Brut | 1990 | 40.00 |
| 06 | Moet et Chandon White Star | N.V. | 48.00 |
| 07 | Dom Perignon | 1985 | 110.00 |
| | **AMERICAN WHITE WINES** | | |
| **Hudson Valley and New York State** | | | |
| 08 | Clinton Vineyards Seyval Blanc | 1993 | 16.00 |
| 09 | John Given Dry Riesling | 1993 | 17.00 |
| 10 | Beekman 1766 Tavern<br>Private Reserve Chardonnay<br>"Millbrook Vineyards" | 1992 | 20.00 |
| **California** | | | |
| 12 | Domaine St. George White Zinfandel | 1993 | 15.00 |
| 13 | Au Bon Climat Pinot Blanc | 1993 | 27.00 |
| 14 | Groth Sauvignon Blanc | 1993 | 20.00 |
| 15 | Steltzner Sauvignon Blanc | 1992 | 22.00 |
| 16 | Robert Mondavi Fume Blanc | 1992 | 28.00 |
| 17 | Larry Forgione's An American Place<br>Napa Valley Chardonnay<br>"Joseph Phelps Vineyards" | 1991 | 22.00 |
| 19 | Zaca Mesa Chardonnay | 1993 | 24.00 |
| 20 | William Hill Chardonnay | 1992 | 25.00 |
| 22 | Neyers Chardonnay | 1989 | 28.00 |
| 23 | Kendall Jackson Vintners Reserve Chardonnay | 1993 | 28.00 |
| 24 | Sonoma-Cutrer Chardonnay | 1992 | 30.00 |
| 26 | Logan Chardonnay | 1992 | 32.00 |
| 27 | Domaine Michel Chardonnay | 1991 | 36.00 |
| 28 | Joseph Phelps Los Carneros Chardonnay | 1992 | 40.00 |
| 29 | Franciscan Chardonnay Cuvee Sauvage | 1992 | 52.00 |
| 18 | Kistler Chardonnay "Dutton Ranch" | 1992 | 60.00 |
| **Washington** | | | |
| 30 | Chateau Ste. Michelle Johannisberg Riesling | 1993 | 18.00 |

**Figure 17.2**   Excerpt from an American Wine List, with States and Grape Types Listed.

"French" restaurant should offer only French wines. However, it would be reasonable to expect to find a good representation of French wines on the wine list of a restaurant which is considered by its customers or its management to offer "French" food. It would not be unreasonable, though, to find wines from other countries as well. If regional American cuisine is emphasized in the restaurant, or if local foods and produce are stressed, the wine list should reflect these regional and local themes as well (see Figure 17.2).

# Customers' Expectations

On rare occasions, some lucky people have the opportunity to open a brand new restaurant, designing the restaurant (and, of course, the menu and wine list) with a specific type of customer in mind. More often, though, restaurateurs and their staff inherit a set clientele in an existing establishment or location. In either case, if the restaurant is to serve its customers properly, today and in the future, it will help to know something about those customers:

- Who they are in a demographic sense (sex, age, ethnic background, employment status, family/single status, income level)

- When and what they like to eat and drink, and how much time and money they spend on this activity

As part of a larger set of data, demographic information and culinary profiles of restaurant guests can help the restaurant understand what the customers want to eat and drink, how they want it presented and served, and how much they are willing to pay for it. This information is readily available from organizations such as the National Restaurant Association, and pertinent information is often published in trade journals such as *Wine Spectator* and *Restaurant Business*. The local chamber of commerce may also have relevant demographic information.

# Quantity and Content

Given that the wine list should be an integral part of the restaurant's theme and style, it follows that the number and selection of wines on the list is also driven by the style of the restaurant, the type, number, and variety of food items offered on the menu, and the customers' expectations. There is no direct relationship between the number of seats in a restaurant and the number of wines on the wine list. Some large restaurants have short lists, sometimes contained on small, laminated table "tents." The most intimate restaurant, with fewer than 50 seats, may be a "wine-destination" restaurant (diners go there as much for the wine selection as for the good food) and have an extensive wine list and a sommelier to assist in wine service.

Many casual restaurants, with customers who are interested in but not preoccupied with wine, will offer short, focused wine lists. These types of lists are "user friendly"; the customer can "handle" the list, and will not be intimidated (see Figure 17.3). This is especially common and effective in restaurants where the range of menu items is narrow and concentrated. Restaurants that offer a more complete dining experience, with a wider range of food and culinary styles, will usually offer more diverse wine lists, with consideration of both breadth and depth on the list (see the sidebar in this chapter).

## BREADTH AND DEPTH

A wine list that has *breadth* is a list which offers an extensive, even inclusive, range of wines from the regions of the countries represented (see Figure 17.4). In other words, the list has a wide array of wines. An example would be a list that represents all of the major wine regions of France, as well as some of its less-known regions.

A wine list that has *depth* is a list that offers several different vintages of many of the individual wines on the list (see Figure 17.5). An example would be a list that offers Robert Mondavi's Cabernet Sauvignon Reserve wines in 1978, 1982, 1985, and 1987 vintages.

## BEVERAGES

| SPARKLING WINE | 3 oz | 5 oz | Bottle |
|---|---|---|---|
| Kriter, Brut de Brut, Blanc de Blancs, Côte d'Or, France | – | $4.25 | $18.00 |
| Domaine Ste. Michelle, Brut, Columbia Valley, WA | – | – | $24.00 |
| Glenora, Brut, New York State – 1989 | – | – | $24.00 |
| Iron Horse, Brut, Sonoma County, CA – 1990 | – | – | $38.00 |
| **WHITE WINE** | | | |
| Sichel, Riesling, Mosel-Saar-Ruwer, Germany – 1993 | – | – | $18.00 |
| Tâmega, Vinho Verde, Portugal – 1993 | $2.00 | $3.00 | $12.00 |
| Millbrook Chardonnay, "Reserve," Hudson River Region – 1993 | – | – | $27.00 |
| Clos du Bois, Gewürztraminer, Sonoma, CA – 1993 | $2.25 | $3.75 | $16.00 |
| Fetzer, Chardonnay, "Bonterra," Mendocino County, CA – 1992 | $2.75 | $4.50 | $19.00 |
| Hidden Cellars, Sauvignon Blanc, Mendocino, CA – 1993 | $2.75 | $4.50 | $19.00 |
| Rosemount, Chardonnay, Hunter Valley, Australia – 1993 | $3.00 | $4.75 | $21.00 |
| **RED WINE** | | | |
| Vichon, Cabernet Sauvignon, CA – 1991 | – | – | $21.00 |
| Preston, Syrah, Dry Creek Valley, CA - 1992 | $3.75 | $6.25 | $28.00 |
| Dr. Konstantin Frank, Pinot Noir, Finger Lakes, NY - 1991 | $4.00 | $6.50 | $29.00 |
| Markham, Merlot, Napa Valley, CA – 1992 | – | – | $28.00 |
| Don Melchor, Cabernet Sauvignon, Maipo, Chile – 1988 | – | – | $25.00 |
| Hidden Cellars, Zinfandel, Mendocino, CA – 1992 | – | – | $24.00 |
| Badia a Coltibuono, Chianti, "Cetamura," Italy – 1991 | – | – | $18.00 |
| **BLUSH WINE** | | | |
| Beringer, White Zinfandel, CA – 1993 | $2.25 | $3.75 | $16.00 |
| **DESSERT WINE** | | | |
| Quady, Electra, Orange Muscat, "4% Alcohol," – 1992 | $2.75 | – | $20.00 |
| Quady, Elysium, Black Muscat, CA – 1993 | $3.50 | – | $26.00 |

**BEERS**

| | | | |
|---|---|---|---|
| Rolling Rock | $2.25 | Amstel Light | $2.75 |
| Celis White (Wheat) | $3.25 | Samuel Adams Lightship | $2.75 |
| Heineken | $2.75 | Samuel Adams (Amber) | $2.75 |
| Haake Beck (0.5 % Alcohol) | $2.75 | Dos Equis (Mexico) | $2.75 |

**JUICES and MINERAL WATERS**

| | | | |
|---|---|---|---|
| Fresh Orange Juice | $2.25 | Fresh Grapefruit Juice | $2.25 |
| Cranberry Juice | $1.75 | White Grape Juice | $1.50 |
| Saratoga (Carbonated) | $1.75 | Evian (Non Carbonated) | $1.75 |

**CAFE COCKTAILS and COOLERS**

| | |
|---|---|
| Tio Pepe, Dry Sherry, Jerez, Spain | $3.50 |
| Berry Sparkler (Sparkling Wine with a Splash of Cranberry Juice) | $3.75 |
| Madras (Alcohol Free) | $2.25 |
| Sea Breeze (Alcohol Free) | $2.25 |
| Crodo Bitters (Alcohol Free) and Saratoga Water | $2.75 |
| Crodo Bitters (Alcohol Free) and Orange Juice | $2.75 |

*AMERICA'S CENTER FOR CULINARY EDUCATION SINCE 1946*

**Figure 17.3** A Short, User-Friendly Wine List (St. Andrew's Café at The Culinary Institute of America, Hyde Park, New York).

| Bin No. | UNITED STATES | |
|---|---|---|
| | **CALIFORNIA - Red** | |
| 5411 | Pinot Noir, Robert Mondavi 1985 / 20.00 | |
| 5408 | Pinot Noir, Acacia 1985 / 24.00 | |
| 5456 | Pinot Noir, Jensen, Calera 1985 / 32.00 | |
| 5463 | Zinfandel, York Creek, Ridge 1985 / 19.00 | |
| 5508 | Merlot, Rutherford Hill 1983 / 17.00 | |
| 5514 | Merlot, Clos du Val 1979 / 27.00 | |
| 5515 | Merlot, Belvedere, Robert Young Vineyards 1984 / 22.00 | |
| 5659 | Cabernet Sauvignon, Louis Martini 1984 / 17.00 | |
| 5611 | Cabernet Sauvignon, Beaulieu Vineyards 1985 / 20.00 / 10.00 half | |
| 5614 | Cabernet Sauvignon, Beringer Knight's Valley 1985 / 22.00 | |
| 5701 | Cabernet Sauvignon, Simi 1984 / 24.00 | |
| 5653 | Cabernet Sauvignon, Inglenook Reserve 1981 / 24.00 | |
| 5750 | Cabernet Sauvignon, Robert Mondavi 1984 / 27.00 | |
| 5729 | Cabernet Sauvignon, Freemark Abbey 1975 / 38.00 | |
| 5658 | Cabernet Sauvignon, Jordan Vineyards 1984 / 36.00 | |
| 5656 | Cabernet Sauvignon, Stags Leap 1985 / 30.00 | |
| 5737 | Cabernet Sauvignon, Heitz 1982 / 28.00 | |
| 5663 | Cabernet Sauvignon, Joseph Phelps 1979 / 38.00 | |
| 5657 | Cabernet Sauvignon, Silver Oak 1983 / 35.00 | |
| | **CALIFORNIA - White** | |
| 5200 | Fumé Blanc, Beringer 1987 / 16.00 | |
| 5202 | Fumé Blanc, Robert Mondavi 1986 / 20.00 | |
| 5211 | Sauvignon Blanc, Cakebread 1986 / 22.00 | |
| 5204 | Sauvignon Blanc, Carmenet 1985 / 18.00 | |
| 5051 | Chardonnay, Hawks Crest 1987 / 17.00 | |
| 5008 | Chardonnay, Beringer 1986 / 22.00 | |
| 5023 | Chardonnay, Dry Creek 1986 / 24.00 | |
| 5002 | Chardonnay, Alexander Valley 1985 / 23.00 | |
| 5055 | Chardonnay, Chimney Rock 1985 / 22.00 | |
| 5020 | Chardonnay, Chateau St. Jean 1986 / 25.00 | |
| 5110 | Chardonnay, Freemark Abbey 1985 / 26.00 | |
| 5015 | Chardonnay, Rutherford Hill 1981 / 30.00 | |
| 5050 | Chardonnay, Robert Mondavi 1986 / 30.00 / 15.00 half | |
| 5058 | Chardonnay, Russian River, Sonoma-Cutrer 1986 / 28.00 | |
| 5093 | Chardonnay, Acacia 1987 / 32.00 | |
| 5017 | Chardonnay, Chateau Montelena 1986 / 36.00 | |
| 5029 | Chardonnay, Edna Valley 1986 / 25.00 | |
| 5091 | Chardonnay, Far Niente 1986 / 40.00 | |
| 5263 | White Riesling, Trefethen 1986 / 15.00 | |
| 5268 | Johannisberg Riesling, Chateau St. Jean 1986 / 18.00 | |
| 5258 | Johannisberg Riesling, Joseph Phelps 1986 / 16.00 | |
| | **CALIFORNIA - Rosé** | |
| 5801 | White Zinfandel, Napa Ridge 1987 / 16.00 | |
| 5802 | Rosé of Cabernet Sauvignon, Simi 1986 / 16.00 | |
| | **WASHINGTON STATE - Red** | |
| 5313 | Cabernet Sauvignon, Château St. Michelle 1983 / 17.00 | |
| | **OREGON - Red** | |
| 5851 | Pinot Noir, Knudsen Erath 1986 / 24.00 | |
| | **NEW YORK STATE - Red** | |
| 5305 | Merlot, Lenz Vineyard (Long Island) 1985 / 16.00 | |
| | **NEW YORK STATE - White** | |
| 5306 | Johannisberg Riesling, Hermann Wiemer (Finger Lakes) 1986 / 14.00 | |
| 5311 | Chardonnay, Wagner (Finger Lakes) 1986 / 18.00 | |
| 5304 | Chardonnay, Hargrave (Long Island) 1986 / 20.00 | |
| | **SPARKLING WINES** | |
| 5955 | Schramsberg Blanc de Blancs 1985 / 30.00 | |
| 5950 | Domaine Chandon Brut / 27.00 | |
| 5954 | Korbel Brut / 25.00 | |
| 5958 | Gloria Ferrer Brut / 24.00 | |

White and Red Wine - by Carafe 10.00

**Figure 17.4** Excerpt from a Wine List with Breadth, Offering Examples of Different Wines from Different Producers (Windows on the World, World Trade Center, New York, New York).

STEAK HOUSE

123 WEST 52ND STREET, NEW YORK, N.Y. 10019 / 581-8888

| | |
|---|---|
| FAR NIENTE,"Estate Bottled", 1985, Napa Valley.............................. | 100 |
| SILVER OAK, "Bonny's Vineyard", 1988, Napa Valley......................... | 105 |
| HEITZ CELLARS,"Martha's Vineyard",1989 , Napa Valley................. | 115 |
| STAGS LEAP WINE CELLARS,"Cask 23",1990, Napa Valley............... | 135 |
| **VERTICAL SELECTIONS** | |
| CLOS PEGASE, "Hommage",1989, California................................... | 40 |
| CLOS PEGASE, "Hommage",1990, Napa Valley | 37 |
| CLOS PEGASE, "Hommage" 1991 | 10 |
| DALLA VALLE, 1987, Napa.................................................. | 47 |
| DALLA VALLE,1989 | 42 |
| DALLA VALLE,1990 | 47 |
| VIADER, 1989,Napa ....................................................... | 44 |
| VIADER, 1990 | 45 |
| VIADER, 1991 | 46 |
| ANDERSON'S CONN VALLEY,1989,Napa Valley................................ | 44 |
| ANDERSON'S CONN VALLEY, 1990 | 47 |
| CLOS DU VAL,"Reserve", 1982, Napa Valley............................ | 62 |
| CLOS DU VAL, 1984 | 48 |
| CLOS DU VAL 1985 | 55 |
| CLOS DU VAL,1986 | 40 |
| PETER MICHAEL"Les Pavot",1988, Knights Valley....................... | 50 |
| PETER MICHAEL "Les Pavot", 1990 | 44 |
| CAIN CELLARS FIVE,1986, Napa......................................... | 56 |
| CAIN CELLARS FIVE,1987 | 45 |
| SIGNORELLO, "Founder's Reserve", 1990, Napa Valley.................... | 59 |
| SIGNORELLO, "Founder's Reserve", 1991 | 59 |
| GIRARD RESERVE,1986,Napa............................................. | 60 |
| GIRARD RESERVE, 1987 | 55 |
| CHAPPELLET,1979, Napa................................................. | 45 |
| CHAPPELLET,1980 | 40 |
| CHAPPELLET,1981 | 40 |
| CHAPPELLET,1982 | 45 |
| CHAPPELLET,1983 | 35 |
| CHAPPELLET,"Signature Reserve",1984................................... | 50 |
| CHAPPELLET,"Signature Reserve", 1985 | 52 |
| CHAPPELLET,"Signature Reserve",1987 | 60 |
| LAUREL GLEN,1989,Sonoma Mountain..................................... | 55 |
| LAUREL GLEN, 1991 | 60 |
| JORDAN, "Estate Bottled",1986, Alexander Valley...................... | 70 |
| JORDAN,"Estate Bottled",1988 | 48 |
| JORDAN,"Estate Bottled", 1990 | 45 |
| SHAFER,"Hillside Select" Stag's Leap District,1986,Napa............... | 100 |
| SHAFER, "Hillside Select" Stag's Leap District,1987 | 75 |
| SHAFER, "Hillside Select" Stag's Leap District,1988 | 64 |
| SHAFER, "Hillside Select" Stag's Leap District,1989 | 50 |
| SPOTTSWOODE, 1989, Napa Valley....................................... | 75 |
| SPOTTSWOODE, 1990 | 79 |

**Figure 17.5** Excerpt from a Wine List with Depth, Offering Several Vintages of Cabernet Sauvignon Wines from the Same Producer (Ben Benson's Steak House, New York, New York).

**Figure 17.6** A Wine List with Good French Representation (Windows on the World, World Trade Center, New York, New York).

| Bin No. | FRANCE |
|---|---|

**ALSACE - White**

6122 Riesling, Trimbach 1985 / 16.00
6123 Gewürztraminer, Hugel 1985 / 19.00

**BORDEAUX - Red**
*Médoc*

6404 Château Larose Trintaudon (Haut-Médoc) 1983 / 17.00
6308 Château Meyney (St. Estèphe) 1979 / 19.00
6278 Château Gruaud Larose (St. Julien) 1979 / 33.00
6300 Château Grand-Puy-Lacoste (Pauillac) 1979 / 36.00
6405 Château Rauzan-Gassies 1976 / 44.00
6377 Château Beychevelle (St. Julien) 1979 / 42.00
6513 Château Lynch Bages 1979 / 48.00
*St. Émilion*
6509 Château Monbousquet 1981 / 22.00
*Graves*
6609 Château Smith Haut Lafitte 1976 / 25.00
*Pomerol*
6557 Château de Sales 1983 / 22.00

**BORDEAUX - White**
*Graves*
6013 Château Carbonnieux 1986 / 23.00
*Sauternes*
6043 Château Sigalas Rabaud 1981 / 16.00 half

**BURGUNDY - Red**
6866 Beaujolais-Villages, Jadot 1987 / 16.00
6863 Beaujolais, Fleurie, Mommessin 1987 / 18.00
6852 Mercurey, Clos Voyen, Suremain 1985 / 24.00
6757 Ladoix Côte de Beaune, Prince de Mérode 1985 / 35.00
6711 Corton, Mommessin 1985 / 44.00
6775 Chambolle-Musigny, Premier Cru, Mugnier 1985 / 48.00
6776 Chambertin-Clos de Bèze, Laboure Roi 1976 / 58.00

**BURGUNDY - White**
6080 Macon-Vire, Le Grand Cheneau 1987 / 16.00
6079 Rully, Clos St. Jacques, Domaine de la Folie 1986 / 24.00
6073 Chablis, Vaillons, Moreau 1986 / 30.00
6078 Pouilly Fuissé, Bouchard Pére et Fils 1986 / 32.00
6064 Meursault, Latour 1986 / 38.00
6072 Puligny-Montrachet, Chavy 1986 / 36.00
6071 Puligny-Montrachet, Les Chalumeaux, O. Leflaive 1986 / 50.00
6074 Bienvenue-Bâtard-Montrachet, Ponnelle 1984 / 58.00

**LOIRE - White**
6100 Muscadet, Marquis de Goulaine 1986 / 16.00
6105 Sancerre, Château de Maimbray, Roblin 1987 / 18.00
6102 Pouilly Fumé, Ladoucette 1986 / 30.00

**RHONE - Rosé**
6920 Château d'Aqueria Tavel Rosé, Estate Bottled 1987 / 16.00 / 8.00 half

**RHONE - Red**
6902 Châteauneuf-du-Pape, Domaine de Beaucastel 1984 / 26.00
6911 Hermitage, La Chapelle, Jaboulet 1984 / 32.00

**CHAMPAGNE**
6977 Veuve Clicquot Brut n.v. (Windows 10th Anniversary Cuvée) / 32.00
6965 Perrier-Jouët Brut n.v. / 38.00
6951 Bollinger Brut n.v. / 42.00
6962 Moët et Chandon Brut Imperial n.v. / 44.00 / 22.00 half
6964 Mumm Cordon Rouge, Brut n.v. / 40.00
6975 Taittinger Brut, La Française n.v. / 44.00
6950 Billecart-Salmon Brut Rosé n.v. / 58.00

It is generally agreed that the best wine lists, whether long or short, offer a good representation, and perhaps a cross section of:

- Regions that are relevant to the restaurant's theme

- Grape types that are typical of those regions

- Prices

The restaurant's management and wine service staff need to decide which countries or regions to represent on the list. This is best done through a consideration of the menu items, as well as a consideration of the ethnic roots, life experiences, and food and wine expectations of the majority of the customers. Special consideration should be given to the decision to list or not list wines from France. If French wines are to be on the list you should consider all of the major French regions (see Figure 17.6):

- Whites from Burgundy, Bordeaux, Alsace, and the Loire Valley

- Reds from Burgundy, Bordeaux, and the Rhône Valley

- Rosés from the Loire and Rhône Valleys

- Sparklers from Champagne, and perhaps from Burgundy, Alsace, and the Loire Valley

## Organization

The options of which organizational structure to adopt for the wine list are almost endless, and there is no right answer. The format selected will depend on the restaurant style, the range of foods, and the customer base. The following are the most important considerations.

*Information content.* The pieces of information needed in the wine list are:

*Headings.* The most common headings used are color, grape type, regions, wine style; other possibilities are price brackets, course (appetizer wines, entrée wines, dessert wines), food type (fish wines, poultry wines, meat-and-potatoes wines).

*Bin numbers.* Bin numbers are useful for customers and for service staff to order wines without fears or foul-ups.

*Wine name.* For example, Chardonnay, Chianti, Beaujolais-Villages, Rubicon.

*Special information and attributes of the wine.* For example, Barrel Fermented, Riserva, Hillside Select.

**Figure 17.7** Excerpt from a Wine List with Geographic Main Headings (Windows on the World, World Trade Center, New York, New York).

| Bin No. | |
|---|---|
| | **ARGENTINA** |
| | White |
| 7510 | Chardonnay, Andean / 10.00 |
| | **AUSTRALIA** |
| | Red |
| 7452 | Cabernet Sauvignon, Petaluma 1982 / 22.00 |
| 7451 | Cabernet/Shiraz Bin 389, Penfolds 1984 / 18.00 |
| | White |
| 7400 | Chardonnay, Petaluma 1985 / 22.00 |
| 7401 | Chardonnay, Rosemount, Show Reserve 1986 / 26.00 |
| | **CHILE** |
| | Red |
| 7511 | Concha y Toro, Cabernet Sauvignon 1984 / 10.00 |
| | **GERMANY** |
| | White |
| | *Mosel* |
| 7149 | Piesporter Goldtröpfchen Kabinett, Kesselstatt 1986 / 18.00 |
| 7150 | Bernkasteler Lay Spätlese, Dr. Thanisch 1985 / 16.00 |
| | *Rhein* |
| 7107 | Schloss Johannisberger Kabinett, Von Metternich 1985 / 19.00 |
| | **GREECE** |
| | White |
| 7520 | Santa Helena, Achaia-Clauss / 10.00 |
| | **HUNGARY** |
| | Red |
| 7530 | Egri Bikavér 1982 / 10.00 |
| | **ISRAEL** |
| | Red |
| 7540 | Cabernet Sauvignon, Carmel / 12.00 |
| | **ITALY** |
| | Red |
| 7073 | Valpolicella, Bolla / 12.00 |
| 7065 | Chianti Classico, Riserva Ducale Ruffino 1983 / 18.00 / 9.00 half |
| 7075 | Dolcetto, Pio Cesare 1983 / 16.00 |
| 7077 | Barolo, Giacomo Conterno 1980 / 32.00 |
| 7076 | Brunello di Montalcino, Barbi 1982 / 30.00 |
| 7051 | Amarone, Tommasi 1977 / 26.00 |
| | White |
| 7002 | Soave, Bolla / 14.00 / 7.00 half |
| 7004 | Corvo, Duca di Salaparuta / 17.00 |
| 7003 | Pinot Grigio, Barone Fini 1986 / 16.00 |
| 7001 | Lacryma Christi, Mastroberardino 1986 / 16.00 |
| 7008 | Gavi, La Scolca, White Label 1986 / 21.00 |
| | **PORTUGAL** |
| | Red |
| 7351 | Dao Grao Vasco / 12.00 |
| | **SPAIN** |
| | Red |
| 7250 | Rioja, Marqués de Cáceres 1985 / 15.00 |
| 7255 | Torres Gran Coronas Black Label 1976 / 36.00 |
| | **SWITZERLAND** |
| | Red |
| 7500 | Dôle Valais, Provins 1985 / 18.00 |
| | White |
| 7501 | Chasse D'Or, Chevalley 1986 / 19.00 |

*Producer name.* For example, Robert Mondavi, Joseph Drouhin, Penfolds.

*Vintage date or nonvintage notation.*

*Region.* Include region names if they are not used as headings. For example, Côte de Nuits, Russian River Valley, Coonawarra.

**Consistency.** Regardless of the number of wines, the amount of information included, and the organizational structure, wine lists always work much better when the information is presented consistently. For example, if the restaurant has elected to have the major headings of Red Wines and White Wines, with the selections coming from France and North America, the order of the regions must be the same in each section. In addition, if France and North America are further subdivided into the regions of Burgundy, Bordeaux, the Loire Valley, and Alsace (for France), and California, Oregon, and Washington (for North America), the sequence of regions must be the same in the Red and White sections.

**Groupings.** It is wise to group the wines on the list into categories, not only to break up the print but also to make it easier to find specific items. The grouping system chosen will be driven by what you believe the customers know about wine, by the number of wines on the list and their origin, and sometimes by the culinary emphasis of the menu. Most commonly, the items on the list are grouped by grape variety, by region, by wine style, or by price range.

Grape variety groupings have the advantage of being immediately recognizable by consumers, especially since many of today's wines in the global market are labeled by grape type (also referred to as varietal, such as Chardonnay). However, this system has two specific drawbacks:

1. The list becomes cluttered if, for example, there is only one Pinot Gris wine and one Sémillon, and there is a heading for each of those wines.

2. Using grape types accurately is impossible for wines from France, Italy, Spain, and Portugal, since many of the wines are made as blends from several grape types; this is also becoming an issue with North American wines which fit the Meritage mold or the Rhône style.

If the wine list is short enough, and the selection of wines makes it possible, using grape variety groupings is acceptable. However, an American regional restaurant may choose to use only American wines, grouped by region and/or state, rather than by grape variety (see Figure 17.2). A wine list which incorporates wines from many countries is probably better off grouping by geographic unit than by grape type. Even then, the restaurant must decide whether to cluster all of the whites together, subdivided by region or grape, and then all of the reds, also subdivided. In some cases it is preferable to group by region (see Figure 17.7) and list the whites and the reds separately under the geographic heading.

Most restaurants have to try several different organizational styles before they finally choose the format which is the cleanest, least-cluttered, easiest to follow, most visually attractive, and fits best onto the page space available.

For customers who know they like wine but are unfamiliar with wine jargon, a successful approach has been to use wine-style headings, such as:

- Light, dry whites

- Fruity, slightly sweet whites

- Medium-bodied, dry whites

- Full-bodied, flavorful, dry whites

As a more radical departure, some restaurants have successfully increased wine sales by grouping the wines according to price ranges. Still others use headings such as:

- Appetizer wines

- Entrée wines

- Dessert wines

or

- Fish wines

- Chicken wines

- Beef wines

- Pasta wines

An example of a price category wine list might be as follows:

### $15–$20 California White Wines

| | |
|---|---|
| Dunnewood Chardonnay, North Coast | $15 |
| Callaway Chardonnay, Temecula | $18 |
| Hidden Cellars Sauvignon Blanc, Mendocino | $18 |
| Z Moore Gewürztraminer, Sonoma | $19 |

### $21–$30 California White Wines

| | |
|---|---|
| Lolonis Chardonnay, Mendocino | $23 |
| Silverado Sauvignon Blanc, Napa | $23 |
| Hagafen Chardonnay, Napa | $25 |
| Duckhorn Sauvignon Blanc, Napa | $27 |
| Sonoma-Cutrer Chardonnay, Sonoma | $28 |

The following is an example of how wines might be grouped according to course type:

## APPETIZER WINES

### Whites

Morgadio Albariño, Spain

Antinori Galestro, Italy

Alois Lageder Pinot Grigio, Italy

Bürklin-Wolf Wachenheimer Gerumpel Kabinett, Germany

Marquis de Goulaine Muscadet de Sèvre et Maine, France

### Reds

Jadot Beaujolais-Villages, France

Boscaini Valpolicella, Italy

A grouping of wines by food type might be as follows:

### Beef Wines

Banfi Brunello di Montalcino, Italy

Trefethen Cabernet Sauvignon, Napa

Penfolds Shiraz, Australia

Alejandro Fernandez Pesquera, Spain

Chateau La Lagune, France

The desire to make the ordering of wine as painless as possible has resulted in many experiments, some more successful than others. For example, some restaurants have tried:

- Specific wine suggestions printed on the menu
- Specific food suggestions printed in the wine list
- Generalized comments under the heading on the wine list (see Figure 17.8)
- Stylized symbols on the menu or the wine list
- Printing the rating of a wine awarded by *The Wine Spectator* (see Figure 17.8

One of the most obvious, but commonly overlooked, possibilities which makes ordering wines easier is the adoption of different lists in the same restaurant. For example, a restaurant might prepare two or more of the following wine lists to suit the different customers' needs.

## Zoë

| Bin | | Year | $ | Score |
|---|---|---|---|---|
| 225 | Kent Rasmussen Winery, Carneros- Napa | 1992 | 37. | 87 |
| 222 | Etude Wines by Tony Soter, Carneros-Napa | 1993 | 50. | - |
| 223 | Cosentino Winery, Carneros-Napa | 1993 | 45. | 84 |
| 226 | Saintsbury Winery, Carneros Cuvee, Napa | 1993 | 34. | - |
| 227 | Robert Mondavi Winery, Reserve, Napa | 1992 | 49. | - |
| 231 | Mahoney Estates, Las Piedras Vineyards, Carneros-Napa | 1991 | 35. | - |
| 210 | Wild Horse Winery, Central Coast, Templeton | 1992 | 32. | 86 |
| 214 | Chalone Vineyards, Estate Cuvee, Gavilan-Mountains-Monterey | 1990 | 46. | - |
| 229 | Santa Cruz Vineyards, Estate Vineyard, Santa Cruz | 1990 | 39. | - |
| 211 | Sanford Winery, Barrel Select Reserve, Santa Barbara | 1992 | 54. | 88 |
| 218 | Fiddlehead Vineyard, Santa Maria Valley, Arroyo Grande | 1992 | 52. | 88 |
| 221 | Cambria Winery, Julia's Vineyard, Santa Maria Valley | 1993 | 28. | 87 |
| 217 | Calera Wine Co., Central Coast Cuvee, Hollister | 1992 | 26. | - |

## Merlot

-Merlot as an independent grape varietal came unto its own in America. Merlot had been widely used for blending in Bordeaux and as a primary grape in the region of Pomerol within Bordeaux. In general, Merlot is softer, round, fleshy and elegant. Merlot is also quick maturing, although some specific producers design their Merlots to age. They have good fruit and herbal tea-like qualities.

| Bin | | Year | $ | Score |
|---|---|---|---|---|
| 254 | Matanzas Creek Winery, Sonoma | 1992 | 60. | 89 |
| 239 | Stonestreet Winery, Alexander Valley-Sonoma | 1992 | 35. | 90 |
| 250 | Mill Creek Winery, Dry Creek Valley-Sonoma | 1992 | 28. | - |
| 240 | Silverado Vineyards, Napa | 1992 | 39. | 85 |
| 241 | St. Francis Winery, Sonoma | 1992 | 29. | - |
| 242 | Chateau St. Jean Winery, Sonoma | 1992 | 26. | 86 |
| 243 | Shafer Vineyards, Napa | 1992 | 41. | - |
| 244 | Clos Du Val Vineyards, Napa | 1992 | 38. | - |
| 245 | Frog's Leap, Napa | 1992 | 36. | - |
| 246 | Freemark Abbey Winery, Napa | 1992 | 29. | - |
| 247 | Robert Pecota Vineyard, Steven André Vineyard, Napa | 1992 | 32. | 89 |
| 248 | Swanson Vineyards, Napa | 1992 | 34. | - |
| 249 | Newton Winery, Unfiltered, Napa | 1992 | 45. | - |
| 251 | Pride Mountain Vineyards, Spring Mountain-Napa | 1992 | 41. | - |
| 253 | Merryvale Vineyards, Napa | 1992 | 44. | |
| 256 | Pahlmeyer, Unfiltered, Napa | 1991 | 52. | 85 |
| 262 | Hogue Cellars, Reserve, Prosser-Washington | 1992 | 36. | 88 |

## Zinfandel

-Zinfandel is arguably America's most unique and what many consider truly an original varietal. Its roots can be traced to Southern Italy. In general, Zinfandel is described as being hearty and robust, yet they can be filled with jammy fruit and complexity.

| Bin | | Year | $ | Score |
|---|---|---|---|---|
| 270 | Mara Wines, Reserve (Unfined-Unfiltered), Alexander Valley-Sonoma | 1993 | 29. | - |
| 271 | Green & Red Cellars, (Unfiltered), Chiles Mill Vineyard-Napa | 1992 | 32 | - |
| 272 | Martinelli Vineyards, Jackass Vineyard, Russian River Valley-Sonoma | 1992 | 35. | - |
| 273 | Teldeschi Wine Cellars, Sonoma | 1990 | 31. | - |
| 274 | Nalle Winery, Dry Creek Valley-Sonoma | 1993 | 34. | - |
| 277 | Ridge Vineyards, Geyserville Vineyard-Sonoma, Santa Cruz | 1992 | 38. | 86 |
| 269 | Ridge Vineyards, Geyserville Vineyard-Sonoma, Santa Cruz | 1987 | 75. | 90 |
| 278 | The Terraces, by Hogue Vintners, Napa | 1990 | 35. | 84 |
| 280 | "Edizione Pennino", By Niebaum-Coppola Estate Winery, Napa | 1992 | 29. | - |
| 281 | Chateau Potelle,"VGS" Reserve, Mt. Veeder-Napa | 1992 | 51. | 92 |
| 284 | Saucelito Canyon Vineyard, Arroyo Grande-San Luis Obispo | 1993 | 28. | - |

## Other Reds

| Bin | | Year | $ | Score |
|---|---|---|---|---|
| 290 | Syrah, Bonny Doon Vineyard, Santa Cruz | 1992 | 60. | - |
| 291 | Le Cigar Volant, Bonny Doon Vineyards, Santa Cruz | 1992 | 36. | - |
| 292 | "Vin Du Mistral", Syrah, Joseph Phelps Vineyards, Napa | 1990 | 35. | 81 |
| 293 | Pleiades, By Sean H. Thackery, Bolinas | 1992 | 39. | - |
| 294 | Carignane, Rosenblum Cellars, TLK Ranch-Napa | 1992 | 19. | - |
| 295 | Cabernet Franc, La Jota Vineyards, Howell Mt.-Napa | 1991 | 55. | 84 |
| 296 | Vendimia, by Murrieta's Well, Livermore Valley | 1990 | 47. | 86 |
| 297 | Mourvedre, Contra Costa County, Stonestreet Winery, Sonoma | 1990 | 34. | - |
| 299 | Nebbiolo Vecchio, Martin Brothers Wine Co., Paso Robles | 1990 | 35. | - |
| 304 | "Pietre Rosse" by Dalle Valle Vineyards, Napa | nv | 65. | - |
| 301 | Sangiovese, Coturri & Sons, Sonoma | 1993 | 38. | - |
| 302 | Barbera, Preston Vineyards, Dry Creek Valley-Sonoma (Estate Bottled) | 1992 | 25. | 82 |
| 303 | Pinot Meunier, Eyrie Vineyards, Dundee-Oregon | 1989 | 38. | - |
| 305 | Petite Syrah, Turley Cellars, Hayne Vineyard-Napa | 1993 | 40. | - |

- A regular, fairly short, well-rounded list

- A special or captain's list, with far more breadth and depth (see Figure 17.9)

- An appetizer list

- A dessert list (see Figure 17.10)

| CALIFORNIA - RED | page 9 |
| --- | --- |
| **PINOT NOIR** | |
| ACACIA, CARNEROS 1984 | 24.00 |
| ACACIA, CARNEROS 1985 | 24.00 |
| BEAULIEU VINEYARDS, LOS CARNEROS 1976 | 30.00 |
| CALERA, JENSEN 1985 | 32.00 |
| CARNEROS CREEK 1978 | 24.00 |
| CARNEROS CREEK 1979 | 20.00 |
| CARNEROS CREEK 1983 | 20.00 |
| CHALONE 1980 | 40.00 |
| CHALONE 1981 | 38.00 |
| CHALONE, RESERVE 1982 | 52.00 |
| EDNA VALLEY 1984 | 19.00 |
| HANZELL 1981 | 30.00 |
| ROBERT MONDAVI 1985 | 20.00 |
| ROBERT MONDAVI, RESERVE 1979 | 22.00 |
| ROBERT MONDAVI, RESERVE 1981 | 23.00 |
| SAINTSBURY 1986 | 25.00 |
| TREFETHEN 1984 | 18.00 |

| **ZINFANDEL** | |
| --- | --- |
| CHATEAU MONTELENA 1976 | 25.00 |
| CLOS DU VAL 1977 | 20.00 |
| CLOS DU VAL 1978 | 26.00 |
| CLOS DU VAL 1982 | 20.00 |
| CLOS DU VAL 1985 | 24.00 |
| GRGICH HILLS 1983 | 22.00 |
| JOSEPH PHELPS 1987 | 15.00 |
| RIDGE, GEYSERVILLE 1985 | 19.00 |
| RIDGE, PASO ROBLES 1982 | 20.00 |
| RIDGE, YORK CREEK 1985 | 19.00 |
| RIDGE, SHENANDOAH 1979 | 20.00 |
| WILLIAMS SELYEM 1986 | 22.00 |

| **RED TABLE WINE** | |
| --- | --- |
| LE CIGARE VOLANT, BONNY DOON 1986 | 30.00 |

| **MERLOT** | page 10 |
| --- | --- |
| BELVEDERE, ROBERT YOUNG VINEYARDS 1984 | 22.00 |
| CLOS DU BOIS 1985 | 21.00 |
| CLOS DU BOIS 1986 | 21.00 |
| CLOS DU VAL 1983 | 20.00 |
| DUCKHORN VINEYARDS 1983 | 25.00 |
| DUCKHORN VINEYARDS, THREE PALMS VINEYARD 1981 | 45.00 |
| DUCKHORN VINEYARDS, THREE PALMS VINEYARD 1983 | 40.00 |
| RUTHERFORD HILL 1979 | 20.00 |
| RUTHERFORD HILL 1981 | 19.00 |
| RUTHERFORD HILL 1983 | 17.00 |
| STAGS LEAP VINEYARD 1978 | 38.00 |
| STAGS LEAP VINEYARD 1985 | 25.00 |

| **CABERNET SAUVIGNON** | |
| --- | --- |
| BEAULIEU VINEYARDS PRIVATE RESERVE 1973 | 65.00 |
| BEAULIEU VINEYARDS PRIVATE RESERVE 1974 | 110.00 |
| BEAULIEU VINEYARDS PRIVATE RESERVE 1975 | 60.00 |
| BEAULIEU VINEYARDS PRIVATE RESERVE 1976 | 55.00 |
| BEAULIEU VINEYARDS PRIVATE RESERVE 1979 | 36.00 |
| BEAULIEU VINEYARDS PRIVATE RESERVE 1982 | 38.00 |
| BEAULIEU VINEYARDS NAPA 1974 | 42.00 |
| BEAULIEU VINEYARDS RUTHERFORD 1980 | 24.00 |
| BEAULIEU VINEYARDS RUTHERFORD 1982 | 20.00 |
| BEAULIEU VINEYARDS RUTHERFORD 1985 | 20.00 |
| BERINGER PRIVATE RESERVE 1978 | 30.00 |
| BERINGER PRIVATE RESERVE 1981 | 26.00 |
| BERINGER PRIVATE RESERVE 1982 | 28.00 |
| BERINGER KNIGHTS VALLEY ESTATE 1979 | 25.00 |
| BERINGER KNIGHTS VALLEY ESTATE 1982 | 24.00 |
| BERINGER KNIGHTS VALLEY ESTATE 1985 | 22.00 |
| BUENA VISTA SPECIAL SELECTION 1980 | 32.00 |
| CAKEBREAD 1985 | 30.00 |
| CARNEROS CREEK, FAY VINEYARDS 1978 | 27.00 |
| CAYMUS 1977 | 25.00 |
| CAYMUS, SPECIAL SELECTION 1983 | 45.00 |
| CHAPPELLET 1975 | 35.00 |

**Figure 17.9** A Special, or Captain's, Wine List with Far More Breadth and Depth (Windows on the World, World Trade Center, New York, New York).

# Pricing

The price structure of the wine list should reflect the price structure of the menu and should not be exorbitant. This is best achieved by careful planning of the wine list, and by calculating a **hot zone** for the wine prices on the list.

The hot zone is a predetermined range of prices within which most of the wines on the list will fall. It is important to emphasize that not all of the

## Dessert Wines
### Half Bottles

Veuve Clicquot, Demi Sec N.V. 29.00
Blackwood Canyon, "Pinnacle" Columbia 1986 37.00
Phelps, Scheurebe SSLH Napa 1982 42.00
St. Martinshof, Siefersheimer Hoelberg, Scheurebe
 Eiswein, Rhine 1983 42.00

## Ports, etc.
### by the Glass

Smith-Woodhouse L.B. 1981 9.00
Croft's Distinction Port 5.00
Taylor Fladgate, Quinto Vargellas 1974 12.00
Offley Tawny Port 1951 15.00
Ferreira, Vintage 1975 15.00
Blandy's Malmsey 10 yr 7.00

## Brandies, etc.

Courvoisier VSOP 8.00
Hine VSOP 8.00
Hine Antique 15.00
Remy VSOP 8.00
Martel Cordon Bleu 14.00
Moyet Fine Champagne 8.00
Hennessey XO 15.00
Remy Martin XO 15.00
Martell XO 15.00
German - Robin Reserve 15.00
A.E. Dor, #7, 45 yrs. 37.00
Henessey Paradis 45.00
Hine Founder's Reserve 50.00
Remy Louis XIII 75.00
Larressingle XO Armagnac 12.00
Sempe Armagnac 1965 25.00
Laberdolive, Dom. de Jaurrey, Bas Armagnac
 1946 60.00
Calvados Hors d'Age, Chort-Mutel 10.00
Framboise, St. George 6.00
Mirabelle, Massenez 6.00
Poire William, F. Meyer 8.00
Grappa Martinega 6.00
Pear William, Clear Creek 5.00
Grand Marnier, Centcinquantenaire 25.00

**Figure 17.10** A Dessert Wine List (Biba, Boston, Massachusetts).

wines should fit neatly into the hot zone. The restaurant needs to be able to offer wine at several price levels to please as many customers as possible. Some diners simply will not or cannot spend much on wine, but the restaurant should still try to accommodate them. Just as important is the customer who wants to spend a lot, and all restaurants want to encourage that kind of behavior! The hot zone can be established in a number of different ways, but whatever method is used, it must relate to the menu prices.

## Calculating the Hot Zone

There are two main methods of calculating the hot zone. Both are based on menu prices. The first works from the average check per person, the second from the average entrée price. The first is used in restuarants where the average check is in the moderate $25–$35 per person. The second can be applied to a wider span of restaurant prices.

*Method #1*

• Calculate the average check per person for the restaurant.

• Divide the average check by two.

• Add a standard, predetermined dollar amount (we suggest $15).

• The hot zone begins at the average check total, and ends at half the average check amount plus the dollar amount.

For example: Average check = $28
$28 divided by 2 = $14
Add $15 ($14 plus $15 = $29)
*The hot zone begins at $14 and ends at $29.*

The clear disadvantage to this method occurs in high-end restaurants where the average check is much higher than the example given, say $60 per person. In this case, $30 is too high for the low end of the wine list, and $45 is not high enough for the high end of the list. The second method, useful for these cases, assumes that most diners are willing to spend as much on a bottle of wine as they do on one entrée.

*Method #2*

• Calculate the average entrée price from the menu.

• Subtract approximately one-third from the average entrée price to get the bottom end of the hot zone.

• Add approximately two-thirds of the average entrée price to the average entrée price to get the top end of the hot zone.

For example: Average price of entrée from menu = $18
One-third of $18 = $6
$18 − $6 = $12 as bottom end of the hot zone
Two-thirds of $18 = $12
$18 + $12 = $30 as top end of the hot zone
*The hot zone is from $12 to $30.*

These methods are only guidelines. The point to stress is that *somehow* you establish a viable range of prices within which most of the wines on the list will be placed. There is certainly room for subjectivity, and in the second example, we would probably agree that $12 is *not* a good starting point for the hot zone. It is just too cheap! But in that example, $15–$30 would make an excellent hot zone.

It is also important to realize that all good wine lists may have one or two wines under the hot zone, and should have three or four wines above the hot zone (see Figure 17.11). The wines above the hot zone are very often referred to as **kickers.** They are there for several reasons:

**Figure 17.11** Excerpt from a Wine List That Has a Good Hot Zone (Approximately $18 to $45) (Biba, Boston, Massachusetts).

# WINE LIST

## Reds

Trimbach, Pinot Noir, Alsace 1988 23.00
Leclerc, Bourgogne, "Les Bons Batons" 1988 27.00
Sakonnet, Pinot Noir, Little Compton 1987 28.00
Faiveley, Mercurey, Dom de la Croix Jacquelet 1988 36.00
Volpato, Bourgogne Passetoutgrain 1987 28.00
Saintsbury, Pinot Noir, Carneros 1989 29.00
Hudelot, Hautes-Cotes de Nuits, "Les Genevrieres" 1988 38.00
Rochioli, Pinot Noir, Sonoma 1989 30.00
Pelle, Menetou Salon, "Moroques" 1990 31.00
Rex Hill, Pinot Noir, Willamette 1988 35.00
Mondavi, Pinot Noir Reserve, Napa 1988 50.00
Rion, Nuits St. George, "Haut Pruliers" 1986 68.00
Latour Giraud, Volnay "Clos des Chenes" 1987 52.00

Steltzner, Cabernet Sauvignon, Napa 1987 30.00
Sequoia Grove, Cabernet Sauvignon Napa 1987 32.00
Shafer, Cabernet Sauvignon, Napa 1987 37.00
Johnson Turnbull, Cabernet Sauvignon, Napa 1987 37.00
Arrowwood, Cabernet Sauvignon, Sonoma 1987 45.00
Livingston, Cabernet Sauvignon, Napa 1986 48.00
Cain, "5," Napa 1986 49.00
Courison, Cabernet Sauvignon, Napa 1987 42.00

Chat. Les Annereaux, Lalande de Pomerol 1986 25.00
Newton, Merlot, Napa 1988 36.00
St. Francis, Merlot, Sonoma 1987 38.00

Sky, Zinfandel, Napa 1987 25.00
Sierra Vista, Zinfandel, El Dorado 1988 20.00

Cape Mentelle, Shiraz, Margaret River 1988 27.00
Ch. Rayas, "La Pialade" Cotes du Rhone 1988 19.00
Qupe, Syrah, Central Coast 1989 23.00
Chapoutier, Chateauneuf du Pape 1988 33.00
Dom. Raspail-Ay, Gigondas 1988 32.00
Penfolds, Grange Hermitage, Bin 95 1981 95.00
Dom. Clusel-Roch, Cote Rotie 1987 50.00

Avignonesi, Rosso di Montepulciano 1989 22.00
Travignoli, Chianti Rufina 1987 20.00
Pepi, Colline di Sassi, Napa 1988 42.00
Dal Forno Romano, Valpolicella Superiore 1986 33.00

Vega Sicilia, Valbuena 3 Ano, Ribera del Duero 1985 52.00
Vina Berceo, Rioja Crianza 1986 15.00
Palacios Remundo, Herencia, Rioja Res. 1982 22.00
Bodegas Fernandez, "Tinto Pesquera" Ribera del Duero 1986 60.00

Chateau de Gourgazaud, Minervois 1988 17.00

Dom. de Trevallon, "Les Baux", Coteaux D'Aix 1987 28.00

Duboeuf, Morgon, "Jean Descombes" 1990 25.00

## Whites

Knapp Chardonnay, Cayuga 1989 21.00
Ferrari-Carano, Chardonnay, Alexander Valley 1989 34.00
Au bon Climat, Chardonnay, St. Barbara Res. 1989 37.00
Guillemot-Michel, Macon Clesse, "Quintaine" 1988 26.00
Silver Canyon, Chardonnay, Paso Robles 1989 37.00
Sonoma-Cutrer, Chardonnay, "Cutrer" 1988 30.00
Sterling, Chardonnay, "Winery Lake" Carneros 1988 37.00
Laurier, Chardonnay, Sonoma 1989 26.00
Swanson, Chardonnay, Napa 1988 27.00
Moreau, Chablis Premiere Cru, "Vaillons" 1989 42.00
Cain Cellars, Chardonnay, Carneros 1988 26.00
Stag's Leap Wine Cellars, Chardonnay, Napa 1989 39.00
Rosemount, Chardonnay "Roxburgh" 1988 55.00
Sauzet, Puligny Montrachet 1988 75.00

Columbia Winery, Semillon, Columbia 1989 16.00
Peterson, Semillon, Hunter Valley 1987 29.00
Chat. Vieux Gaubert, Graves 1989 29.00

Groth, Sauvignon Blanc, Napa 1989 17.00
Cloudy Bay, Sauvignon Blanc, Marlborough 1989 25.00
Chat. Pannisseau, Bergerac Sec 1990 18.00
Quivira, Sauvignon Blanc, Sonoma 1989 20.00
Cain Cellars, "Musque", Napa 1989 25.00
Chat. Reynon, Vielle Vignes, Bordeaux 1988 27.00
Chateau LaLouviere, Graves 1988 33.00
La Doucette, Pouilly Fume, Loire 1989 36.00
Babcock, Sauvignon Blanc "11 Oaks Ranch", Lompoc 35.00
Bourgeois, Sancerre "Bonnes Bouches" 1989 30.00

Lorentz, Riesling "Domaine Lorentz", Alsace 1989 27.00
Burklin-Wolf, Wachenheimer Rechbachel Kabinett, Rheinpfalz 1989 21.00

Bonny Doon, Grahm Crew Vin Blanc, Santa Cruz 1990 15.00

Guigal Cotes du Rhone Blanc 1989 17.00
Dom Pradelle, Crozes Hermitage Blanc 1989 20.00
Dom. St. Anne, "Le Viognier de Domaine" 1989 45.00
Chat. Tahbilk, Marsanne, Goulburn 1989 19.00

White Oak, Chenin Blanc, Sonoma 1989 16.00
Soulez, Savennieres, "Dom. de la Bizoliere" 1988 24.00
Huet, Vouvray Sec, Clos du Bourg 1987 31.00

Lopez de Heredia, Rioja White 1986 23.00
Martin Codax, Albarino, Rias Baixas 1990 28.00

Rolly Gassman, Pinot Blanc, Alsace 1988 23.00

Sauvion, Muscadet "Chateau du Cleray" 1990 19.00

Hallcrest, Gewurztraminer, "Talmadge" Santa Cruz 1989 18.00
Zind-Humbrecht, Gewurztraminer Grand Cru, "Goldert", Alsace 1988 39.00

- They may be seen as adding an extra dimension of quality or prestige to the list.

- At some point in time, somebody will want to buy a wine of that type at that high price.

- They have the psychological effect of making the one or two wines priced below them look like a good buy.

## Pricing Individual Wines

There are several different approaches to pricing the wines on the list. The most common are:

- Standard percent markup

- Standard dollar markup

- Sliding-scale markup, % or dollar

- Fixed-amount markup

The most important aspect of pricing is that the more expensive wines should have a relatively smaller markup ratio than the less expensive wines. No matter what the cost of the wine to you as the restaurateur, it costs the restaurant a certain amount of money to open a bottle of wine: money for labor, equipment, glasses, and direct and indirect overhead. It follows that on the sale of any bottle of wine, there is a predetermined markup which needs to be added, whether the bottle of wine cost you $5 wholesale or $50. Once that has been achieved, whatever else is added is profit.

Using a straight-percentage markup effectively means that you are reaping an inordinate and unjustifiable amount of profit from a bottle of wine which cost you $50 wholesale. If, for example, a markup of 300 percent is used to price the wine which cost you $5 and the wine which cost you $50, you would end up with:

$5 wholesale cost x 300% = $15 selling price on the wine list
$50 wholesale cost x 300% = $150 selling price on the wine list

Not only would it be fairer to the customer to offer the expensive bottle at a reduced percentage markup, but it most likely will result in greater sales, ultimately making that item more profitable at a lower price.

Some restaurants have been able to determine exactly how much money they need to generate from the sale of one bottle to cover all of their costs and leave some profit. They then use that dollar figure as the markup on every bottle of wine. If, for example, your restaurant, through its accounting system, has found that a $10 "profit" on any bottle sold is enough to cover all costs and leave some over for actual profit, then our wine prices would be:

$5 wholesale cost + $10 markup = $15 selling price on the wine list

$50 wholesale cost + $10 markup = $60 selling price on the wine list

The sliding-scale method of markup applies the same principle of a reduced markup on higher-cost items. Thus, lower-cost items might be marked up at a rate of 350 percent, or by a standard dollar markup of, for example, $13, whereas higher-cost items might be marked up at a rate of only 150 percent, or by a standard dollar markup of $20. For example:

$5 wholesale cost x 350% = $17.50 selling price on a wine list

*or* $5 wholesale cost + $13 markup = $18 selling price on a wine list

*and* $50 wholesale cost x 150% = $75 selling price on a wine list

*or* $50 wholesale cost + $20 markup = $70 selling price on a wine list.

Just as many restaurants now offer a *prix fixe* menu, a few restaurants have been bold enough to offer a fixed-price wine list, where all the wines on the list are the same price (see Figure 17.12). This obviously requires careful buying, continuous monitoring of wholesale costs, and the willingness and flexibility to change the list fairly frequently and at short notice.

# Wines by the Glass

Many successful restaurants would attest to the fact that at least part of their success lies in the strength of their wine program, and that part of their wine program success lies in their by-the-glass program. That is not to say that a by-the-glass program automatically ensures success. Any wine program needs strong management direction and an integrated training program which can maintain the enthusiasm and interest of the service staff on a continuous basis.

The advent of the automated dispensing/preservation systems have revolutionized the selling of wines in restaurants because they allow the wines to be sold by the glass, but still keep the wines in good condition over a period of three to four weeks. As wine is dispensed from the bottle, the empty space is filled with an inert gas such as nitrogen to prevent air from mixing with the wine and causing oxidation and the loss of flavor and character. In fact, some restaurants argue that their dispensing machines are a major promotional asset, since the machine itself can be a focal point in the restaurant (see Figure 17.13).

## *Dispensing Systems*

Dispensing systems are particularly useful when many of the wines are expensive, since they allow the restaurant to offer such wines without fear of the wine spoiling after only one glass has been poured. Very few restaurants,

**Figure 17.12** A Fixed-Price Wine List (Becco, New York, New York).

## WINE LIST

## ALL SELECTIONS $15.00

### ITALIAN REDS
AGLIANICO 1990, D'angelo
AVELLANIO 1991, Mastroberardino
BARBERA D'ALBA 1993,Marchese di Barolo
BARBERA D'ALBA "FIULOT" 1992, Prunotto
BARCO REALE (70% Sangiovese, 30% Cabernet Sauvignon) 1989, Il Poggiolo
BRUSCO DEI BARBI 1991, Fattoria dei Barbi
CANNONAU DI SARDEGNA "RISERVA" 1989, Sella & Mosca
CABERNET DI SAN LEONARDO 1989, Marchese Carlo Guerrieri Gonzaga
CABERNET SAUVIGNON 1991, Lison Pramaggiore
CENTINE ROSSO DI MONTALCINO 1992, Banfi
CHIANTI CLASSICO "AZIANO" 1992, Ruffino
CHIANTI CLASSICO 1990, LaPratola
CHIANTI CLASSICO 1991, Rocca della Macie
CHIANTI CLASSICO 1991, San Felice
DOLCETTO D'ALBA 1993, Renato Ratti
DOLCETTO DIANO D,ALBA 1992, Colue
ETNA ROSSO 1992, Murgo
MERLOT (Colli Orientali del Friuli) 1993, Midolini
MONTEPULCIANO D'ABRUZZO 1988, Caroso
ROSSO 1991, Regaleali
ROSSO DI MONTEPULCIANO 1992, Avignonesi
SALICE SALENTINO 1987, Ca'ntele
SANGIOVESE DI ROMAGNA 1993, Villa del Borgo
VILLA GIUSTINIAN (Cabernet, Merlot blend)1988, Castello di Roncade
VINO NOBILE DI MONTEPULCIANO 1991, Cecchi
VALPOLICELLA 1990, Bertani

### AMERICAN REDS
CABERNET SAUVIGNON 1992, Estancia
CABERNET SAUVIGNON 1991, Sebastiani
MERLOT 1991, Monterra
PETIT SIRAH 1991, Foppiano
PINOT NOIR 1992, Seghesio
ZINFANDEL 1992, Seghesio
ZINFANDEL 1992, Cline

### OTHER REDS
CABERNET 80%, MERLOT 20% 1992, Tyrrell's
CABERNET SAUVIGNON ANTIGUAS RISERVAS 1990, Causino Macul

### ITALIAN WHITES
BIANCO (60% Chardonnay, 40% Sauvignon Blanc) 1992, Avignonese
BIANCO 1992, Regaleali
CHARDONNAY 1992, Francesco Pecorari
CHARDONNAY 1993, Villa del Borgo
CHARDONNAY "TUFETO" 1993, Banfi
GAVI 1993, Sigillo dell'Abate
LA CALA, VERMENTINO DI SARDEGNA 1993, Sella & Mosca
LIBAIO (CHARDONNAY) 1993, Ruffino
ORVIETO 1993, Antinori
PINOT GRIGIO 1992, Francesco Pecorari
PINOT GRIGIO 1993, Villa del Borgo
SAUVIGNON (COLLI ORIENTALI DEL FRIULI) 1992, Midolini
SYLVANER 1992, Abbazia di Novacella
TOCAI FRIULIANO 1991, Borgo Magredo
TORRE DI GIANO 1991, Lungarotti
TRAPPOLINE 1993, Coltibuono
VERNACCIA DI SAN GIMINGNANO 1993, Giannina

### AMERICAN WHITES
CHARDONNAY 1992, Clos du Val
CHARDONNAY 1993, Estancia

### SPARKLING WINES
BRUT, Castello Gancia
MOSCATO D'ASTI 1992, Saracco
PROSECCO, Contessa Giulia

✱ ✱ ✱

MOET & CHANDON WHITE STAR...$30.00
BRUT 1988, Banfi...$30.00

**Figure 17.13** A System for Dispensing Wine by the Glass.

for example, can regularly sell full bottles of wine priced at $200 or $300. But in the right restaurant, it is possible that a number of customers will pay $20 or $25 for a two-ounce portion of a great wine.

Dispensing systems have also made possible a relatively new concept in resturants—the wine bar, where customers can sample several different wines. They have also allowed restaurants to offer every customer the opportunity to conduct a minitasting during a meal, sampling several different wines with the different courses.

For those restaurants that rely more on volume sales of $3–$6 glasses of wine, the dispensing machines may not be necessary. These restaurants rely on the skill and knowledge of the service staff to ensure that by-the-glass sales are so high that few bottles of wine are discarded due to oxidation in an opened bottle.

## Benefits of a By-the-Glass Program

Restaurants that do have successful by-the-glass programs (see Figure 17.14) contend that it helps to increase overall sales of wine on a regular basis because:

• By-the-glass programs meet the needs of customers who are concerned about total alcohol consumption

## Wines by the Glass

Veuve Clicquot, Brut N.V. 11.50
Scharffenberger, Brut, Mendocino N.V. 6.00

Laurier, Chardonnay, Sonoma 1989 5.25
Quivira, Sauvignon Blanc, Sonoma 1989 4.25
Lopez de Hereida, Rioja white 1986 4.50
Hallcrest, Gewurztraminer, "Talmadge"
　　　Santa Cruz 1989 3.50

Trimbach, Pinot Noir, Alsace 1988 4.75
Volpato, Bourgogne Passetoutgrain 1987 5.50
Chateau de Gourgazaud, Minervois 1988 3.75

Flavio Accornero, Muscato d'Asti N.V.
　　　with biscotti 4.00

## Sherries
## by the Glass

Light Fino, Jarana 3.50
Dos Cortados, Rosario Farfante 4.50
Amontillado de Jerez, Giron 5.25
Very Rare Oloroso, Emperatriz Eugenia 8.00
East India, Rare Solera 7.00
Pedro Ximenez Cream, Argueso 5.00

**Figure 17.14** A By-the-Glass Wine List (Biba, Boston, Massachusetts).

- The restaurant can offer customers the opportunity of enjoying more than one type of wine with a meal

- Each person in a large group can order their own preferred wine

- The restaurant can offer special food and wine menus, matching each dish to a particular wine

In addition, by-the-glass programs allow the restaurant to try new things, and to bring new items to their customers. For example, some restaurants will use by-the-glass programs to:

- Offer specials on bin ends or items going out of stock

- Try new wines on an experimental basis to see how well they are received

- Promote specialty items

- Promote local wines

## Sparkling Wines

One of the most exciting applications of by-the-glass wine sales has been in the area of sparkling wines. For many years, restaurants argued that sparkling wine could not be sold by the glass because the wine would lose its effervescence. And, of course, it is not possible to put bottles of sparkling wine which contain carbon dioxide gas into a dispensing system which is designed to fill the empty space in the bottle with nitrogen gas. However, any high-quality sparkling wine will maintain its effervescence for several hours. It must be a high-quality wine to begin with, it must be chilled and opened properly (without a loud pop), and it must be kept cold after opening, preferably with a clamped stopper in the bottle. If these guidelines are followed, good service staff can sell a case of sparkling wine per night in a restaurant which previously was lucky to sell a case per month by the bottle.

## Organization on the List

Wines offered by the glass must be easily identifiable as such by the customer, and easily located in a list. This may mean listing all by-the-glass offerings on a separate list, or placing them in a very prominent position, such as on the first page or at the top of the list. These strategies make it possible to promote the by-the-glass selections, and to point them out to customers. Again, this makes the by-the-glass listings an excellent place to promote local wines or specialty items.

The choice of how many wines to offer by the glass will depend on the type of restaurant and the desires of the customers. There are famous examples of restaurants with extensive lists which boldly offer to open any wine on the list if a customer wants a glass. For most restaurants that is excessive, and a small range of white, red, rosé, and sparkling is probably sufficient in most cases. For a wine list of only 20 wines, a by-the glass selection of three white, two red, one rosé, and one sparkling wine would be considered enough.

## Pricing Wines by the Glass

As with all sales in the restaurant, the major consideration is that by-the-glass sales be profitable. In addition, the selling price of a wine by the glass must bear some relation to the selling price of a bottle of the same wine.

A few restaurants maintain that there is no need to make more profit on a glass of wine than on a bottle, and they keep their by-the-glass prices exactly relative to the bottle price. For example, if a bottle sells for $25 on the list, and the restaurant offers that wine by the glass in a five-ounce portion, the glass of wine will sell for $5 (approximately five five-ounce portions in a 750ml bottle).

Most restaurants insist that selling wines by the glass requires more labor and therefore charge more by the glass than by the bottle. Exactly how much more per glass is largely subjective, and the final decision may simply be an assessment of how much more any customer would be willing to pay. Using the same wine as in the example above, some restaurants will charge $5.25 for the glass, others will charge $6.

## Summary

What most restaurateurs will readily admit is that there is no magic formula to create the perfect wine list. But with careful planning, it is possible to get pretty close on the first try. So, it is best to view all wine lists as temporary. As soon as one list is put into place, you will realize that there are mistakes and that, for some reason, some wines are not selling. You must therefore be willing to try different strategies to get those wines to sell. It may well be that a one-dollar increase or decrease in the selling price will create a dramatic change in sales volume. And, of course, there will always be new wines that become available, and which you will want to add to the list.

The willingness and flexibility to change the list and update it on a constant basis are therefore very important. The computerized technology available now means that all restaurants can control their wine lists in ways which were previously unimaginable. There are many examples today of restaurants that change the wine list (along with the menu) on a regular basis—perhaps seasonally, perhaps monthly. Utilizing current technology, wine lists could even be printed daily, as the "perfect" match to the daily menu.

It is important to accept that a wine list does not have to be a work of art. In fact, as important as the visual aspect may be, it is worthless if the core content does not provide the selection that the diner is looking for. By concentrating on content and organization, the visual aspect will usually take care of itself.

Finally, a good wine list is a valuable tool in helping any restaurant sell more wine, but even the best wine list in the world will not sell wine if it is not used by a competent and interested service staff.

# Conversion Tables

## Volume

Standard wine bottle = .75 liter/750 ml/75 cl
1 liquid pint = .473 liter     1 liter = 2.114 liquid pints
1 quart = .946 liters     1 liter = 1.057 quarts
1 gallon = 3.785 liters     1 liter = 0.264 gallons
1 hl = 100 liters = 26.4 gallons
1 barrique = 60 gallons = 300 bottles
1 tonneau = 4 barriques = 900 liters = 1200 bottles

## Capacities (liquid measure)

10 hectoliters is nearly 265 U.S. gallons (1 hl = 1000 l = 26.4 U.S. gallons = 22 Imperial gallons)
1 liter is just over two pints, or one quart (quarter of a gallon)
1 hectoliter fills 133 standard 75 cl bottles
10 gallons (80 pints) is nearly 38 l or just over 50 x 75 cl bottles

# Bottles (sizes and equivalents)

Half-bottle = 37.5 cl = 12.7 fluid ounces = 0.79 pint
Bottle = .75 cl = 25.4 fluid ounces = 1.58 pint
Magnum = 1.5 l = 50 fluid ounces = 3.16 pints
Double-magnum = 3 l (4 bottles) = 100 fluid ounces = 6.32 pints
Jeroboam = 4.5 l (6 bottles) = 150 fluid ounces = 1.19 gallon
Imperial = 6 l (8 bottles) = 200 fluid ounces = 1.58 gallon

# Area

1 acre = .404 hectare        1 hectare = 2.47 acres
10 hectares is nearly 25 acres (1 hectare = 10,000 sq. meters = 2.47 acres)
10 acres is just over 4 hectares (1 acre = 4840 sq. yards = 0.405 hectare)
5000 vines per hectare is approximately 2000 per acre.

# Yield (production per acre)

1 hectoliter per hectare equals 10.7 gallons/acre
45 hectoliters/hectare (average standard yield) is equivalent to 6000 bottles per
  hectare, or per 2430 bottles per acre

# Temperature

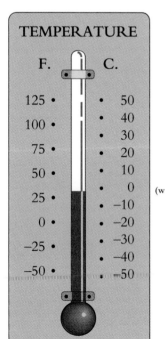

|  | *Degrees* *Centigrade* | *Degrees* *Fahrenheit* |
|---|---|---|
| To convert | × 9/5 and add 32 | Subtract 32 and × 5/9 |

# How to Read a Wine Label

**Figure B.1**   An American Generic Wine Label.

**Figure B.2**   An American Varietal Wine Label (Estate Bottled).

# American Generic Wine Label

1.  Name of producer.

2.  Name of wine. "Mountain Chablis" is a generic white wine label, as Chablis is a famous white wine region in Burgundy, France. Other generic labels include: Champagne, Burgundy, Sherry, and Chianti, all of them famous wine regions, but none of them located anywhere in the United States. Generic labels are legal in the United States, except for the state of Oregon, which forbids that state's wines to be labeled generically.

3.  Approved Viticultural Area (AVA). When the name of a state appears as the appellation, the grapes can come from vineyards anywhere in that State.

4.  **"Vinted and Bottled by"** could mean that the producer made wine from its own grapes or purchased grapes, or blended wine from finished wines delivered to its facilities. We only know for sure that the producer bottled the wine.

5.  Address of producer and legally required alcohol percentage.

# American Varietal Label/Estate-Bottled

1.  Name of producer.

2.  **"Estate Bottled"** means that the same company (in this case, Trefethen Vineyards) grew the grapes, made the wine, and bottled the wine. According to law, it also means that Trefethen owns the land on which the grapes were grown, and that all of its facilities—the vineyards, the winery, and its bottling plant—are located in the appellation of origin (in this case, Napa Valley).

3.  The Approved Viticultural Area (AVA). According to United States wine laws, 85 percent of the grapes in this wine had to come from the Napa Valley.

4.  The vintage. According to United States wine laws, 95 percent of the grapes in this wine had to come from the 1990 vintage.

5.  The varietal. According to United States wine laws, 75 percent of the grapes in this wine must be White Riesling (also known as Johannisberg Riesling in the United States).

6.  An optional descriptor of the style of the wine.

7.  **"Estate Grown, Produced & Bottled by"** reiterates that the wine is estate-bottled.

8.  Name and address of producer.

9.  Alcohol percentage is legally required.

1987 ③

*Napa Valley* ④

FUMÉ BLANC ⑤

*Dry Sauvignon Blanc* ⑥

ALCOHOL 13.5% BY VOLUME ⑦

PRODUCED AND BOTTLED BY ⑧

ROBERT MONDAVI WINERY ⑨

OAKVILLE, CALIFORNIA ⑩

**Figure B.3** An American Varietal Wine Label with Special Attributes.

# American Varietal Label with Special Attributes

1. The term, Reserve★, although a special attribute, has no legal meaning under United States wine laws. For some producers, the term is used strictly for marketing the wine. For other producers, such as Robert Mondavi, the term has ethical meaning, at least; the best wine made that vintage.

2. Name of a single vineyard of high quality; another special attribute.

3. The vintage. According to United States wine laws, 95 percent of the grapes in this wine had to come from the 1987 vintage.

4. The Approved Viticultural Area (AVA). According to United States wine laws, 85 percent of the grapes in this wine had to come from the Napa Valley.

5. The name of the varietal grape. Fumé Blanc, however, is not a true varietal, but a recognized style of its varietal, Sauvignon Blanc. According to United States wine laws, 75 percent of the grapes in this wine must be Sauvignon Blanc/Fumé Blanc.

6. An optional descriptor of Fumé Blanc.

7. Alcohol percentage is legally required.

8. **"Produced and Bottled by"** means that the Robert Mondavi winery made the wine and bottled it, but may have purchased grapes from other growers to make the wine, or the grapes were grown by the producer on leased land. It is not **estate-bottled.**

9. Name of producer.

10. Address of producer.

★As of 1995, the term "Reserve" can only be used on any vintage-dated varietal wine, but still without specific meaning.

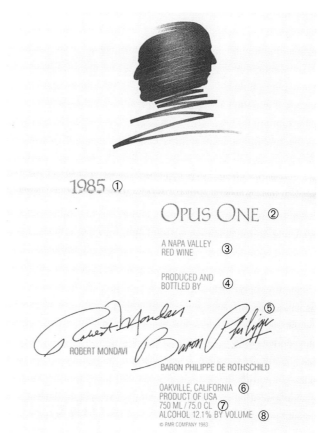

1985 ①

OPUS ONE ②

A NAPA VALLEY
RED WINE ③

PRODUCED AND
BOTTLED BY ④

⑤

ROBERT MONDAVI

BARON PHILIPPE DE ROTHSCHILD

OAKVILLE, CALIFORNIA ⑥
PRODUCT OF USA
750 ML / 75.0 CL ⑦
ALCOHOL 12.1% BY VOLUME ⑧
© RMR COMPANY 1983

**Figure B.4** An American Proprietary Wine Label.

# American Proprietary Label

1. The vintage. According to United States wine laws, 95 percent of the grapes in this wine had to come from the 1985 vintage.

2. The name of the wine, in this case a **proprietary** name. This allows the producer the freedom to not adhere to the "75 percent law" governing American varietal labels.

3. The Approved Viticultural Area (AVA). According to United States wine laws, 85 percent of the grapes in this wine had to come from the Napa Valley. Also, an optional descriptor of the wine is provided.

4. **"Produced and Bottled by"** means that the Opus One winery made the wine and bottled it, but may have purchased grapes from other growers to make the wine, or the grapes were grown by the producer on leased land. It is not **estate-bottled.**

5. The (optional) signatures of the producers. Opus One is a joint venture by Robert Mondavi and the estate of the late Baron Philippe de Rothschild.

6. Address of winery.

7. Bottle size is legally required.

8. Alcohol percentage is legally required.

**Figure B.5** An American Botrytis Varietal Wine Label.

**Figure B.6** An American Late Harvest Varietal Wine Label.

# American Botrytis Varietal Label

1. **"Botrytis"** indicates that the grapes in this wine were attacked by *Botrytis cinerea,* often called "noble rot." *Botrytis* is a mold that pierces the skin of the grape, drinks the water in the grape, and thereby concentrates the sugars in the semidried grapes.

2. The vintage. According to United States wine laws, 95 percent of the grapes in this wine had to come from the 1981 vintage.

3. The Approved Viticultural Area (AVA). According to United States wine laws, 85 percent of the grapes in this wine had to come from the Napa Valley.

4. The varietal. According to United States wine laws, 75 percent of the grapes in this wine must be Sauvignon Blanc.

5. Alcohol percentage is legally required. It is not uncommon for *botrytis* wines to be both sweet and high in alcohol, because of the high level of sugar in the grapes.

6. **"Produced and Bottled by"** means that the Robert Mondavi Winery made the wine and bottled it, but may have purchased grapes from other growers to make the wine, or the grapes were grown by the producer on leased land. It is not **estate–bottled.**

7. Name of producer.

8. Address of producer.

# American Late Harvest Varietal Label with Mandatory Government Warning Label

1. According to United States wine laws, under the aegis of the Bureau of Alcohol, Tobacco, and Firearms (BATF), this Government Warning must appear on all alcoholic beverages sold in the United States.

2. Name of producer.

3. The vintage. According to United States wine laws, 95 percent of the grapes in this wine had to come from the 1993 vintage.

4. **"Late Harvest"** indicates that the grapes were left on the vine longer than normal to develop a higher concentration of sugar in the grapes. Normally, late harvest wines are much sweeter than wines produced from a normal harvest.

5. The varietal. According to United States wine laws, 75 percent of the grapes in this wine must be Vignoles, a hybrid grape.

6. The Approved Viticultural Area (AVA). According to United States wine laws, 85 percent of the grapes

*(continued on facing page)*

in this wine had to come from Cayuga Lake, an AVA located in the New York State.

7. Optional harvesting information, including the fact that the grapes were picked by hand, and the °Brix, or sugar concentration in the grapes. If the wine is **"9.6% Residual Sugar by Weight,"** it is quite sweet. Since the grapes were picked at 29.6° Brix, the wine is about 10 percent alcohol.

8. Name and address of producer.

9. By law, all wines sold in the United States must have the words **"Contains Sulfites"** on the label.

**Figure B.8** An American Nonvintage Sparkling Wine Label.

# American Nonvintage Sparkling Wine

1. **"Fermented in this Bottle"** indicates that the sparkling wine was made by the *méthode champenoise,* the classic Champagne method.

2. Name of the producer.

3. The approved Viticultural Area (AVA). According to United States wine laws, 85 percent of the grapes in this wine had to come from the Sonoma Valley.

4. **"Produced and Bottled by"** means that the Gloria Ferrer Winery made the wine and bottled it, but may have purchased grapes from other growers to make the wine, or the grapes were grown by the producer on leased land. It is not **estate-bottled.**

5. Style of sparkling wine; in this case, **"Brut,"** a relatively dry style.

6. Indicates that the wine is made by the *méthode champenoise,* the classic Champagne method. An outward sign of quality.

**Figure B.9** An American Vintage-Dated Sparkling Wine Label.

# American Vintage-Dated Sparkling Wine

1. The vintage. According to United States wine laws, 95 percent of the grapes in this wine had to come from the 1986 vintage.

2. The style of the wine. **"Blanc de Noirs"** means a white sparkling wine made from red grapes. In a quality wine such as Iron Horse, this usually means the wine is made from Pinot Noir. Legally, however, any red grapes will do.

3. **"Sonoma County Green Valley"** is the Approved Viticultural Area (AVA). According to United States wine laws, 85 percent of the grapes in this wine had to come from this appellation.

4. Name of the producer.

5. **"Grown, Produced & Bottled by"** indicates that the producer grew the grapes, made, and bottled the wine. Very close in meaning to **estate-bottled**. However, the phrase "estate-bottled" can only be used when the producer owns all of the vineyard land, and when the wine is bottled in the stated appellation. Iron Horse probably leases at least some of their vineyard land.

6. Alcohol percentage is legally required.

7. Bottle size is legally required.

8. Legally, all wine sold in the United States must have the phrase, **"Contains Sulfites"** printed on the wine label.

9. Indicates that the wine is a sparkling wine.

**Figure B.7** An Australian Blended Varietal Wine Label.

# Australian Blended Varietal Label

1. The name of the producer.

2. South Eastern Australia is the appellation of this wine.

3. The blend of grapes. Legally, the percentage need not appear, but the dominant grape must be listed first.

4. The year in which the grapes were harvested.

5. Country identification.

6. The bottle size, legally mandated.

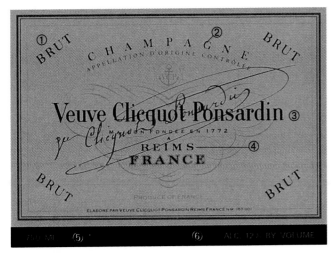

**Figure B.10** A Nonvintage Champagne Label.

**Figure B.11** A Vintage Champagne Label.

# Nonvintage Champagne Label

1. Style of the Champagne; in this case **"Brut,"** a relatively dry style.

2. The appellation of origin is the Champagne region. The phrase "Appellation d'Origine Contrôlée" on a Champagne label is optional.

3. Name of producer.

4. Return address of producer. Reims, along with Epernay and Ay, is a major center for Champagne production.

5. Bottle size must appear on label.

6. Alcohol percentage must appear on label.

# Vintage "Cuvée De Prestige" Champagne Label

1. The vintage—the year in which the grapes were picked.

2. Name of producer.

3. Proprietary name of the Champagne, usually reserved for the best and most expensive wine produced by the Champagne house.

4. Appellation of origin. Champagne is the only approved appellation that does not legally require the phrase "Appellation d'Origine Côntrolée" on the label.

5. Style of the Champagne; in this case, **"Brut,"** a relatively dry style.

6. Reims, along with Epernay and Ay, is a major center for Champagne production.

7. Bottle size must appear on label.

8. Alcohol percentage must appear on label.

**Figure B.12** An Appellation d'Origine Contrôlée French Wine Label.

**Figure B.13** A Burgundy, France Regional Wine Label.

# Typical Appellation d'Origine Contrôlée French Wine Label

1. Bottle size is legally required on the label.

2. Percentage of alcohol is legally required on the label.

3. The name of the wine, in this case it is named for the Tavel district in the southern Rhône Valley. This is typical of many of the Appellation d'Origine Contrôlée (AOC) wines of France.

4. Appellation of origin, indicating that Tavel is an AOC wine, the highest quality level in France.

5. The vintage—the year in which the grapes were harvested.

6. Indicates that the wine is bottled by the producer or in this case, *négociant* (wine broker), Delas, whose headquarters are in the town of Tournon in the southern Rhône Valley.

7. Legally, all wine sold in the United States must have the phrase, **"Contains Sulfites"** printed on the wine label.

8. Name of the importer.

# Burgundy, France: Regional Label

1. Name of producer or *négociant* (wine broker).

2. Percentage of alcohol is legally required on the label.

3. Legally, all wine sold in the United States must have the phrase, **"Contains Sulfites"** printed on the wine label.

4. Proprietary name for the wine ("The Forest").

5. **"Bourgogne"** means "Burgundy" in French. This is a regional wine, meaning that all the grapes in the wine were harvested anywhere in Burgundy.

6. Optional varietal label, obviously for export to the United States (a white wine from Burgundy is, most often, Chardonnay, unless another grape name appears on the label). If a varietal appears on a French wine label, the wine must contain 100 percent of that varietal.

7. Appellation of origin (all of Burgundy).

8. Indicates that the wine is bottled by the producer or in this case, *négociant* (wine broker), Joseph Drouhin, whose headquarters are in the town of Beaune in the Côte de Beaune, Burgundy.

9. Name of importer.

**Figure B.14**  A Burgundy, France Communal Wine Label.

**Figure B.15**  A Burgundy, France Premier Cru Wine Label.

# Burgundy, France: Communal Label

1. Name of the commune. Pouilly-Fuissé is a town in the Mâcon region of Burgundy.

2. Indicates that Pouilly-Fuissé is the appellation of origin. The phrase could read, "Appellation Pouilly-Fuissé Contrôlée" as well.

3. Indicates that the wine is bottled by the producer or in this case, *négociant* (wine broker), Louis Jadot, whose headquarters are in the town of Beaune in the Côte de Beaune, Burgundy.

4. Percentage of alcohol is legally required on the label.

5. Name of importer.

6. Bottle size is legally required on the label.

# Burgundy, France: Premier Cru Label

1. Name of the commune. Beaune is an important town for the wine trade in the Côte de Beaune in Burgundy.

2. Name of the Premier Cru vineyard, in this case "Clos des Couchereaux." Premier Cru loosely translates as "first growth," indicating a vineyard of very good quality.

3. Appellation of origin.

4. Indicates that the wine is bottled by the producer or in this case, *négociant* (wine broker), Louis Jadot, whose headquarters are in the town of Beaune in the Côte de Beaune, Burgundy.

5. Indicates that the wine comes from vineyards owned or controlled by the *négociant*.

6. Percentage of alcohol is legally required on the label.

7. Name of importer.

8. Bottle size is legally required on the label.

**Figure B.16** A Burgundy, France Grand Cru Wine Label.

**Figure B.17** An Alsace, France Wine Label.

# Burgundy, France: Grand Cru Label

1. Name of the Grand Cru vineyard (note that it appears *without* the name of the town in which it is located, Gevrey-Chambertin).

2. Indicates that **"Le Chambertin"** is a **"Grand Cru"** vineyard, meaning a vineyard of the highest possible quality. Ironically, this phrase is optional.

3. Since it is preceded by "Le Chambertin Grand Cru" all that is needed is this simple phrase. If the optional phrase "Grand Cru" did not follow Le Chambertin, this line would read, "Appellation Le Chambertin Grand Cru Contrôlée," or simply, "Appellation Grand Cru Contrôlée."

4. Indicates that the wine is bottled by the producer or in this case, *négociant* (wine broker), Louis Jadot, whose headquarters are in the town of Beaune in the Côte de Beaune, Burgundy.

5. Percentage of alcohol is legally required on the label.

6. Name of importer.

7. Bottle size is legally required on the label.

# Alsace, France Wine Label

1. Appellation of Origin (AOC). The only approved appellation for all of Alsace is "Appellation Alsace Contrôlée."

2. A special attribute; is this case a special blend (optional).

3. Name of producer/*négociant* (wine broker).

4. Varietal name. Alsace is the only AOC region in France to label the wine with the name of the grape. If a varietal appears on a French wine label the wine must contain 100 percent of that varietal.

5. Percentage of alcohol is legally required on the label.

6. Bottle size is legally required on the label.

7. **"e"** indicates that this wine is labeled for sale in the European Community (EC).

8. Indicates that the wine is bottled by the producer or in this case, *négociant* (wine broker), Hugel and Sons, whose headquarters are in the town of Riquewihr in Alsace.

Figure B.18 A Château-Bottled Bordeaux Wine Label.

# Typical Château-Bottled Bordeaux Wine Label

1. The name of the product *and* the producer. There is only one Château Belair, only one Château Margaux, etc. So, in Bordeaux the named château is both product and producer.

2. The Appellation of origin, in this case the Saint-Emilion district of Bordeaux.

3. Status granted by the 1955 Classification of Saint-Emilion. **"1er Grand Cru Classé"** is the highest level of quality, and loosely translated as "first great growth."

4. Official notice of appellation of origin and classification status, as controlled by the Appellation Contrôlée of France.

5. The vintage—year in which the grapes were harvested.

6. Proprietor of the château and its estate vineyards.

7. **"Mis en Bouteilles au Château"** indicates that the wine is estate-bottled. The grapes were grown, and the wine was made and bottled at the estate. True of all of Bordeaux's Château-bottled wines.

8. Percentage of alcohol is legally required on the label.

9. Bottle size is legally required on the label.

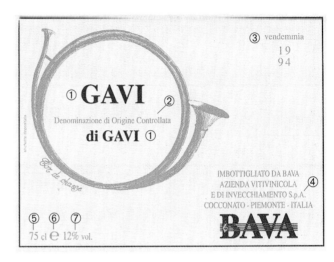

Figure B.19 An Italian DOC Wine Label.

# Italian Wine Label: Denominazione di Origine Controllata (DOC)

1. Name of the wine, which is also the name of the appellation of origin. In this case, **"Gavi di Gavi."**

2. Indicating that the wine is from the DOC zone, Gavi di Gavi.

3. **"Vendemmia"** means "vintage"—the year in which the grapes were harvested.

4. Bottled by the wine company, Bava. Not estate-bottled.

5. Bottle size is legally required on the label.

6. **"e"** indicates that this wine is labeled for sale in the European Community (EC).

7. Percentage of alcohol is legally required on the label.

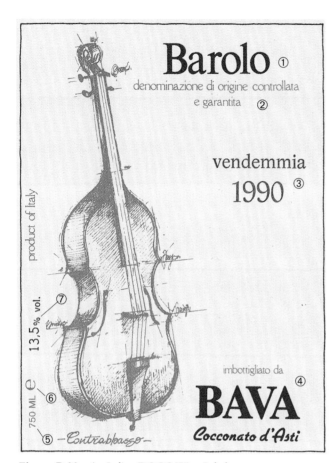

**Figure B.20**  An Italian DOCG Wine Label.

# Italian Wine Label: Denominazione di Origine Controllata e Garantita (DOCG)

1.  Name of the wine, which is also the name of the appellation of origin. In this case, **"Barolo."**

2.  Indicating that the wine is from the DOCG zone, Barolo.

3.  **"Vendemmia"** means "vintage"—the year in which the grapes were harvested.

4.  Bottled by the wine company, Bava. Not estate-bottled.

5.  Bottle size legally required on the label.

6.  **"e"** indicates that this wine is labeled for sale in the European Community (EC).

7.  Percentage of alcohol is legally required on the label.

**Figure B.21**  An Italian Proprietary Wine Label.

# Italian Wine Label: "Super Tuscan" Vino da Tavola

1.  Proprietary name of the wine, named for the estate on the Tuscan coast where the grapes for this wine grow.

2.  The vintage—year in which the grapes were harvested.

3.  Name and address of the producer and the Ornellaia estate.

4.  The wine is estate-bottled.

5.  Indicating that the wine is not DOC or DOCG, but a "vino da tavola," a table wine, albeit a very expensive one.

6.  Percentage of alcohol is legally required on the label.

7.  Bottle size is legally required on the label.

**Figure B.22** A German Wine Avalitätswein Label.

# German Wine Label: Qualitätswein Level

1. Name of producer or wine broker. In this case, **"Madrigal"** is a name created for the export market.

2. The vintage—year in which the grapes were harvested.

3. The *prüfüngsnummer*—a number assigned to quality German wines by each of 13 regional bureaus of the federal Amtliche Prüfstelle (the State Institute for Quality Control). This **"APN"** indicates that the Mosel-Saar-Ruwer bureau (hence the first number, **"1"**) has passed this wine as being free of chemical and sensory defects. The wine was tasted in 1987 (last two digits of the label number: **"87"**).

4. **"Zeller"** means "from Zell." Zell is a *bereich* (commune or town) in the Mosel-Saar-Ruwer *anbaugebiet* (wine region).

5. **"Schwarze Katz"** is the name of the vineyard, in this case a *grosslage* (collective vineyard). The names of the town and the vineyard are also a play on words. "Zeller Schwarze Katz" means "cellar of the black cat."

6. Name of the varietal (optional).

7. **"Qualitätswein"** is shorthand for *Qualitätswein Besstimter Anbaugebiete* (QbA), meaning "quality wine from a specific wine-producing region," in this case Mosel-Saar-Ruwer. Wines at this level can be chaptalized.

8. Name of the *anbaugebiet or* wine region, Mosel-Saar-Ruwer.

9. Bottle size is legally required on the label.

10. Percentage of alcohol is legally required on the label.

11. Name of importer.

Figure B.23  A Proprietary QbA German Wine Label.

wine from a specific wine-producing region," in this case Rheinhessen. Wines at this level can be chaptalized.

6.  Name and address of the wine broker and shipper.

7.  Bottle size is legally required on the label.

8.  Percentage of alcohol is legally required on the label.

9.  The ***prüfüngsnummer***—a number assigned to quality German wines of each of 13 regional bureaus of the federal Amtliche Prüfstelle (the State Institute for Quality Control). This **"APN"** indicates that the Rheinhessen bureau (hence the first number, **"4"**) has passed this wine as being free of chemical and sensory defects. The wine was tasted in 1989 (last two digits of the label number: **"89"**).

# Proprietary German Wine Label: Qualitätswein Besstimter Anbaugebiete (QbA) Level

1.  Proprietary label. A name like Blue Nun simplifies the German wine label, especially for the American and English-speaking export market.

2.  The vintage—year in which the grapes were harvested.

3.  Style of wine. **"*Liebfraumilch*"** translates as "milk of the blessed mother," and indicates an off-dry, light-bodied white wine from the Rheinhessen *anbaugebiet* (wine region).

4.  Name of the *anbaugebiet* or wine region, Rheinhessen.

5.  **"Qualitätswein"** is shorthand for *Qualitatswein Besstimter Anbaugebiete* (QbA), meaning "quality

Figure B.24  A QmP German Wine Label.

# Proprietary German Wine Label: Qualitätswein Mit Prädikat (QmP) Level

1.  Name and address of the wine broker and shipper.

2.  Name of the *anbaugebiet* or wine region, Mosel-Saar-Ruwer.

3.  **"Piesporter"** means "from Piesport." Piesport is a

*(continued on facing page)*

*bereich* (commune or town) in the Mosel-Saar-Ruwer *anbaugebiet* (wine region).

4. **"Goldtröpfchen"** is the name of the vineyard, in this case an *einzellage* (single vineyard).

5. Name of the varietal (optional).

6. Special attribute. All QmP wines **must** list the *prädikat*, the special attribute of the wine. **"Kabinett"** means grapes from a normal harvest. Other special attributes that could appear on this label. *Spätlese, Auslese, Beerenauslese, Eiswein, Trockenbeerenauslese.* QmP wines may **not** be chaptalized.

7. Quality statement, legally required.

8. The *prüfüngsnummer.* A number assigned to quality German wines by each of 13 regional bureaus of the federal Amtliche Prüfstelle (the State Institute for Quality Control). This **"APN"** indicates that the Mosel-Saar-Ruwer bureau (hence the first number, **"1"**) has passed this wine as being free of chemical and sensory defects. The wine was tasted in 1984 (last two digits of the label number: **"84"**).

9. Bottle size is legally required on the label.

10. Percentage of alcohol is legally required on the label.

**Figure B.25** A Spanish Wine Label.

# Spanish Wine Label: Rioja Reserva

1. The name of the producer.

2. The seal of the Rioja *consejo regulador*—the regional control bureaucracy of the federal *Denominación de Origen* (appellation of origin) control board.

3. **"Reserva"** indicates a red wine from Rioja that has been aged in a 225-liter/60-gallon oak barrel for a minimum of a year, and a minimum of two more years in a bottle. The wine cannot be released until the fourth year following the harvest.

4. The vintage—the year the grapes were harvested.

5. Bottle size is legally required on the label.

6. Percentage of alcohol is legally required on the label.

7. The appellation of origin; in this case, Rioja.

8. Indicating that the wine is an approved *denominación* or appellation. Rioja is currently the only *Denominación de Origen Calificada* (DOCa) among the 33 demarcated regions *(denominaciónes)*.

9. The wine is estate-bottled.

10. Address of the producer in Rioja Alavesa.

**Figure B.26** A Sherry Label.

**Figure B.27** A Portuguese Wine Label.

## Sherry

1. **"Pedro Ximenez"** is the name of the grape and style of the Sherry. Other popular Sherry styles include *fino, manzanilla, amontillado,* and *oloroso.*

2. **"San Emilio"** is the proprietary name for this Sherry. The producer makes several Pedro Ximenez Sherries, each with its own proprietary name.

3. A description of the Sherry. Obviously this is an export label, as the description is written in English.

4. The name of the producer.

5. **"Jerez"** is the region of Spain that produces Sherry.

6. The alcohol percentage must appear on the label.

7. The bottle size, also legally mandated.

## Portuguese Wine Label: Denominação de Origem Controlada

1. Proprietary name of the wine; the equivalent of a "Château" in Bordeaux, France.

2. Appellation of origin; in this case, **"Dão."**

3. Indicating that the wine is from the demarcated wine region, Dão.

4. Name of the actual wine maker or *vigneron.*

5. Name and address of the producer.

6. Botte size is legally required on the label.

7. Percentage of alcohol is legally required on the label.

**Figure B.28**  A Tawny Age Port Label.

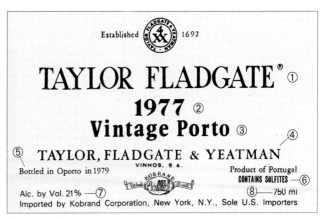

**Figure B.29**  A Vintage Port Label.

# Indicated Age Tawny Port Label

1.  Name and location of producer.

2.  Indicating a 30-year-old Tawny Port, ideally meaning that the youngest wine in this blend of Tawny Port had to age in wood for 30 years. A very smooth and mellow wine.

3.  Name of product is Tawny Porto. "Rich" is an optional descriptor.

4.  Bottling date in Oporto, the center of the Port trade in the Douro Valley.

5.  Name of United States importer.

6.  Bottle size is legally required.

7.  Legally required alcohol percentage. Since Porto is a fortified wine, it will always be high in alcohol.

# Vintage Port Label

1.  Name of producer.

2.  The vintage—all of the grapes in the wine must have been harvested in 1977.

3.  Name and style of product.

4.  Official name of producer.

5.  Vintage Port must be bottled between the second and third year from the harvest of the grapes. Oporto is the famous port from which the wine is shipped.

6.  Obviously bound for the United States, because the label reads **"Contains Sulfites."** Legally, all wine sold in the United States must have this phrase printed on the wine label.

7.  Legally required alcohol percentage. Since Porto is a fortified wine, it will always be high in alcohol.

8.  Bottle size is legally required.

# American Appellations

# AMERICAN APPELLATIONS OF ORIGIN: FEDERAL REQUIREMENTS FOR APPELLATION USE ON WINE LABELS

| *Appellation* | *BATF Requirements For Use* |
| --- | --- |
| State | Must meet the following conditions: (1) At least 75 percent of the grapes used to produce the wine must be grown in the state indicated on the label; (2) wine must be fully finished (except for cellar treatment pursuant to §4.22(c), and blending which does not result in an alteration of class or type under §4.22(b)) within the labeled State or an adjacent State (T.D. ATF-53; 27 CFR §425(a)). |
| More than One State (two or no more than three contiguous states) | Must meet the following three conditions: (1) all of the grapes must be grown in the States indicated, and the percentage of the wine derived from grapes grown in each State must be shown on the label, with a tolerance of plus or minus 2 percent; (2) it must be fully finished (except for cellar treatment pursuant to §4.22(c), and blending which does not result in an alteration of class or type under §4.22(b)) in one of the labeled appellation States, and; (3) it must conform to the laws and regulations governing the composition, method of manufacture, and designation of wines in all the States listed in the appellation (T.D. ATF-53; 27 CFR §4.25(d)). |
| County | Must meet the following conditions: (1) At least 75 percent of the grapes used to produce the wine must be from the labeled county; (2) it must be fully finished (except for cellar treatment pursuant to §4.22(c), and blending which does not result in an alteration of class or type under §4.22(b)) within the State in which the labeled county is located; (3) it must conform to the laws and regulations of the named appellation area governing the composition, method of manufacture, and designation of wines made in such place (T.D. ATF-53; 27 CFR §4.25(b)). The label must be identified with the word "county," in the same size and type, and in letters as conspicuous as the name of the county (T.D. ATF-53; 27 CFR §4.25(a)). |
| More than One County (two or no more than three counties in the same state) | Must meet the following conditions: (1) All of the grapes must be grown in the counties indicated; (2) the percentage of the wine derived from grapes grown in each county must be shown on the label, with a tolerance of plus or minus 2 percent. (T.D. ATF-53; 27 CFR §425(c)) |
| Viticultural Area | At least 85 percent of the grapes used to produce the wine must be from within the confines of the viticultural area stated on the label (T.D. ATF-53; 27 CFR §4.25(e)(3)(ii)). |
| More than One Viticultural Area | Must meet the following conditions: (1) A label may state the names of more than one viticultural area only when the stated viticultural areas *overlap;* (2) no less than 85 percent of the volume of the wine must be derived from grapes grown in the overlapping area, (3) and it has been fully finished within the State, or the States, within which the labeled viticultural area is located (T.D. ATF-53; 27 CFR §4.25(e)(4)). |
| Imported Wine Non-U.S. Non-viticultural area appellations | The U.S. recognizes foreign appellations as (i) a country, (ii) a state, province, territory, or similar political subdivision of a country equivalent to a state or county; or (iii) a viticultural area (27 CFR §4.25a(a)(2). Imported wines may be labeled with an appellation of origin other than a viticultural area if (1) at least 75 percent of the wine is derived from fruit grown in the area indicated by the appellation; and (2) the wine conforms to the requirements of the foreign laws and regulations governing the composition, method of production, and designation of wines available for consumption within the country of origin. |
| Imported Wine Non-U.S. Viticultural Areas | A viticultural area for imported wines is defined as a delimited place or region the boundaries of which have been recognized and defined by the country of origin for use on labels of wine available for consumption within the country of origin (T.D. ATF-53; 27 CFR §4.25(d)(2)). Imported wines may use a non-U.S. viticultural area if (1) the appellation has been approved by the appropriate foreign government; (2) not less than 85 percent of the wine is derived from grapes grown within the boundaries of the viticultural area; and (3) it conforms to the requirements of the foreign laws and regulations governing the composition, method of production, and designation of wines within the country of origin (T.D. ATF-53; 27 CFR §4.25(d)(3). |
| Vineyard Designations | Not considered an appellation, the name of a vineyard, orchard, farm or ranch shall not be used on a wine label unless 95 percent of the wine in the container was produced from primary winemaking materials grown on the named vineyard, orchard, farm or ranch. 27 CFR 4.39(m). |

*Source.* The Wine Institute

# AMERICAN STATES WITH VITICULTURAL AREAS†

### Arkansas
Altus
Arkansas Mountain
Ozark Mountain★

### Arizona
Sonoita

### California
Alexander Valley
Anderson Valley
Arroyo Grand Valley
Arroyo Seco
Atlas Peak
Ben Lomond Mountain
Benmore Valley
California Shenandoah Valley
Carmel Valley
Central Coast
Chalk Hill
Chalone
Cienega Valley
Clarksburg
Clear Lake
Cole Ranch
Dry Creek Valley
Dunnigan Hills
Edna Valley
El Dorado
Fiddletown
Guenoc Valley
Hames Valley
Howell Mountain
Knights Valley
Lime Kiln Valley
Livermore Valley
Lodi
Los Carneros
Madera
McDowell Valley
Mendocino
Merritt Island
Monterey
Mount Harlan
Mount Veeder
Napa Valley
North Coast
North Yuba
Northern Sonoma
Oakville
Pacheco Pass
Paicines
Paso Robles
Potter Valley
Russian River Valley
Rutherford
San Benito
San Lucas
San Pasqual Valley
San Ysidro District
Santa Clara Valley
Santa Cruz Mountains

Santa Lucia Highlands
Santa Maria Valley
Santa Ynez Valley
Sierra Foothills
Solano County Green Valley
Sonoma Coast
Sonoma County Green Valley
Sonoma Mountain
Sonoma Valley
South Coast
Spring Mountain District
Stags Leap District
Suisun Valley
Temecula
Wild Horse Valley
Willow Creek
York Mountain

### Colorado
Grand Valley

### Connecticut
Southeastern New England★
Western Connecticut Highlands

### Indiana
Ohio River Valley★

### Kentucky
Ohio River Valley★

### Louisiana
Mississippi Delta★

### Massachusetts
Martha's Vineyard
Southeastern New England★

### Maryland
Catoctin
Cumberland Valley★
Linganore

### Michigan
Fennville
Lake Michigan Shore
Leelanau Peninsula
Old Mission Peninsula

### Missouri
Augusta
Hermann
Ozark Highlands
Ozark Mountain★

### Mississippi
Mississippi Delta★

### New Jersey
Central Delaware Valley★
Warren Hills

### New Mexico
Mesilla Valley★
Middle Rio Grande Valley
Mimbres Valley

### New York
Cayuga Lake
Finger Lakes
Hamptons, Long Island
Hudson River Region
Lake Erie
North Fork of Long Island

### Oklahoma
Ozark Mountain★

### Ohio
Grand River Valley
Isle St. George
Kanawha River★
Lake Erie★
Loramie Creek
Ohio River Valley★

### Oregon
Columbia Valley★
Rogue Valley
Umpqua Valley
Walla Walla Valley★
Williamette Valley

### Pennsylvania
Central Delaware Valley★
Cumberland Valley★
Lake Erie★
Lancaster Valley

### Rhode Island
Southeastern New England★

### Tennessee
Mississippi Delta★

### Texas
Bell Mountain
Escondido Valley
Fredericksburg in the Texas Hill Country
Mesilla Valley★
Texas High Plains
Texas Hill Country

### Virginia
Monticello
North Fork of Roanoke
Northern Neck George
Washington Birthplace
Rocky Knob
Shenandoah Valley★
Virginia's Eastern Shore

### Washington
Columbia Valley★
Walla Walla Valley★
Yakima Valley

### West Virginia
Kanawha River★
Ohio River Valley★
Shenandoah Valley★

### Wisconsin
Lake Wisconsin

There are 27 states where viticultural areas are located. This table lists the states and the viticultural areas located, in whole or in part, in those states.

71 of the 125 approved American Viticultural Areas are located in California. California has the most viticultural areas of all the states.

The Ohio River Valley is the only approved American Viticultural Area that is located across four U.S. states. The viticultural area spans across parts of Indiana, Kentucky, West Virginia, and Ohio.

There are 12 multi-state viticultural areas. These are Central Delaware Valley (NJ, PA); Columbia Valley (OR, WA); Cumberland Valley (MD, PA); Kanawha River (OH, WV); Lake Erie (NY, OH, PA); Mesilla Valley (NM, TX); Mississippi Delta (LA, MS, TN); Ohio River (IN, KY, OH, WV); Ozark Mountain (AR, MO); Shenandoah Valley (VA, WV); Southeastern New England (CT, MA, RI); and Walla Walla Valley (OR, WA).

Augusta, MO, was the first recognized American Viticultural Area (T.D. ATF-72 published 45 FR 41632, effective date June 20, 1980).

Napa Valley soon followed and was the first California Viticultural Area established. (TD. ATF-201; published 49 FR 9061, effective date January 1, 1983).

† As of May 1, 1994
★ multi-state viticultural area

# CALIFORNIA VITICULTURAL AREAS BY COUNTY†

Of the 125 American Viticultural Areas already established, 71 of them are entirely contained within the state of California.

Sonoma leads the California counties with 12 viticultural areas located at least in part in the county.

Napa has 11 viticultural areas wholly or partially within its boundaries.

Solano County Green Valley and Sonoma County Green Valley are two separate and distinct viticultural areas.

Shenandoah Valley is a viticultural area both in Virginia as well as in El Dorado County, California. Technically, El Dorado's area is called "California Shenandoah Valley."

**Alameda**
Central Coast★
Livermore Valley

**Amador**
California Shenandoah Valley★
Fiddletown
Sierra Foothills★

**Calaveras**
Sierra Foothills★

**El Dorado**
California Shenandoah Valley★
El Dorado
Sierra Foothills★

**Fresno**
Madera★

**Humboldt**
Willow Creek★

**Lake**
Benmore Valley
Clear Lake
Guenoc Valley
North Coast★

**Los Angeles**
South Coast

**Madera**
Madera★

**Marin**
North Coast★

**Mariposa**
Sierra Foothills★

**Mendocino**
Anderson Valley
Cole Ranch
McDowell Valley
Mendocino
North Coast★
Potter Valley

**Monterey**
Arroyo Seco
Carmel Valley
Central Coast★
Chalone★
Monterey
San Lucas

Santa Lucia Highalnds
Hames Valley

**Napa**
Atlas Peak
Howell Mountain
Los Carneros★
Mount Veeder
Napa Valley
North Coast★
Oakville
Rutherford
Spring Mountain District
Stag's Leap District
Wild Horse Valley★

**Nevada**
Sierra Foothills★

**Placer**
Sierra Foothills★

**Riverside**
Temecula

**Sacramento**
Lodi★

**San Benito**
Central Coast★
Chalone★
Cienega Valley
Lime Kiln Valley
Mount Harlan
Pacheco Pass
Paicines
San Benito

**San Diego**
San Pasqual Valley

**San Joaquin**
Lodi★

**San Luis Obispo**
Arroyo Grand Valley
Central Coast★
Edna Valley
Paso Robles
Santa Maria Valley
York Mountain

**San Mateo**
Santa Cruz Mountains★

**Santa Barbara**
Central Coast★
Santa Maria Valley★
Santa Ynez Valley

**Santa Clara**
Central Coast★
San Ysidro District
Santa Clara Valley
Santa Cruz Mountains★

**Santa Cruz**
Ben Lomond Mountain
Central Coast★
Santa Cruz Mountains★

**Siskiyou County**
Seiad Valley

**Solano**
North Coast★
Solano County Green Valley
Suisun Valley
Wild Horse Valley★

**Sonoma**
Alexander Valley
Chalk Hill
Dry Creek Valley
Knights Valley
Los Carneros★
North Coast★
Northern Sonoma
Russian River Valley
Sonoma Coast
Sonoma County Green Valley
Sonoma Mountain
Sonoma Valley

**Trinity**
Willow Creek★

**Tuolumne**
Sierra Foothills★

**Yolo**
Clarksburg
Dunnigan Hills
Merritt Island

**Yuba**
North Yuba
Sierra Foothills★

† As of May 1, 1994
★ multi-county California viticultural area

# Official Classifications
# of Bordeaux

# BORDEAUX WINE: THE OFFICIAL CLASSIFICATION OF 1855

| First Growths (Premiers Crus) | Commune |
|---|---|
| Château Lafite-Rothschild | Pauillac |
| Château Margaux | Margaux |
| Château Latour | Pauillac |
| Château Haut-Brion★ | Pessac (Graves) |
| Château Mouton Rothschild★★ | Pauillac |

| Second Growths (Deuxièmes Crus) | Commune |
|---|---|
| Château Rausan-Ségla | Margaux |
| Château Rauzan-Gassies | Margaux |
| Château Léoville-Las Cases | Saint-Julien |
| Château Léoville-Poyferré | Saint-Julien |
| Château Léoville-Barton | Saint-Julien |
| Château Durfort-Vivens | Margaux |
| Chateau Gruaud-Larose | Saint-Julien |
| Château Lascombes | Margaux |
| Château Brane-Cantenac | Cantenac |
| Château Pichon-Longueville-Baron | Pauillac |
| Château Pichon-Longueville, Comtesse De Lalande | Pauillac |
| Château Ducru-Beaucaillou | Saint-Julien |
| Château Cos d'Estournel | Saint-Estèphe |
| Château Montrose | Saint-Estèphe |

| Third Growths (Troisièmes Crus) | Commune |
|---|---|
| Château Kirwan | Cantenac |
| Château d'Issan | Cantenac |
| Château Lagrange | Saint-Julien |
| Château Langoa-Barton | Saint-Julien |
| Château Giscours | Labarde |
| Château Malescot Saint-Exupéry | Margaux |
| Château Boyd-Cantenac | Cantenac |
| Château Cantenac-Brown | Cantenac |
| Château Palmer | Cantenac |
| Château La Lagune | Ludon |
| Château Desmirail | Margaux |
| Château Calon-Ségur | Saint-Estèphe |
| Château Ferrière | Margaux |
| Château Marquis d'Alesme-Becker | Margaux |

| Fourth Growths (Quatrièmes Crus) | Commune |
|---|---|
| Château Saint-Pierre | Saint-Julien |
| Château Talbot | Saint-Julien |
| Château Branaire-Ducru | Saint-Julien |
| Château Duhart-Milon-Rothschild | Pauillac |
| Château Pouget | Cantenac |
| Château La Tour-Carnet | Saint-Laurent |
| Château Lafon-Rochet | Saint-Estèphe |
| Château Beychevelle | Saint-Julien |
| Château Prieuré-Lichine | Cantenac |
| Château Marquis-de-Terme | Margaux |

| Fifth Growths (Cinquièmes Crus) | Commune |
|---|---|
| Château Pontet-Canet | Pauillac |
| Château Batailley | Pauillac |
| Château Haut-Batailley | Pauillac |
| Château Grand-Puy-Lacoste | Pauillac |
| Château Grand-Puy-Ducasse | Pauillac |
| Château Lynch-Bages | Pauillac |
| Château Lynch-Moussas | Pauillac |
| Château Dauzac | Labarde |
| Château Mouton-Baronne-Philippe | Pauillac |
| Château du Tertre | Arsac |
| Château Haut-Bages-Libéral | Pauillac |
| Château Pédesclaux | Pauillac |
| Château Belgrave | Saint-Laurent |
| Château de Camensac | Saint-Laurent |
| Château Cos-Labory | Saint-Estèphe |
| Château Clerc-Milon | Pauillac |
| Château Croizet-Bages | Pauillac |
| Château Cantemerle | Macau |

★ This wine, although a Graves, was universally recognized and classified as one of the four first-growths.
★★ This wine was decreed a first-growth in 1973.

## SAUTERNES-BARSAC: THE OFFICIAL CLASSIFICATION OF 1855

| *First Great Growth (Premier Crus Supérieur)* | *Commune* | *Second Growths (Deuxiemes Crus)* | *Commune* |
|---|---|---|---|
| Château d'Yquem | Sauternes | Château de Myrat | Barsac |
| | | Château Doisy-Daëne | Barsac |
| *First Growths (Premiers Crus)* | *Commune* | Château Doisy-Dubroca | Barsac |
| Château La Tour-Blanche | Bommes | Château Doisy-Védrines | Barsac |
| Château Lafaurie-Peyraguey | Bommes | Château d'Arche | Sauternes |
| Château Clos Haut-Peyraguey | Bommes | Château Filhot | Sauternes |
| Château de Rayne-Vigneau | Bommes | Château Broustet | Barsac |
| Château Suduiraut | Preignac | Château Nairac | Barsac |
| Château Coutet | Barsac | Château Caillou | Barsac |
| Château Climens | Barsac | Château Suau | Barsac |
| Château Guiraud | Sauternes | Château de Malle | Preignac |
| Château Rieussec | Fargues | Château Romer-du-Hayot | Fargues |
| Château Rabaud-Promis | Bommes | Château Lamothe-Despujols | Sauternes |
| Sigalas-Rabaud | Bommes | Château Lamothe-Guignard | Sauternes |

## GRAVES: 1959 OFFICIAL CLASSIFICATION

| *Classified Red Wines of Graves* | *Commune* | *Classified White Wines of Graves* | *Commune* |
|---|---|---|---|
| Château Bouscaut | Cadaujac | Château Bouscaut | Cadaujac |
| Château Haut-Bailly | Léognan | Château Carbonnieux | Léognan |
| Château Carbonnieux | Léognan | Château Domaine de Chevalier | Léognan |
| Domaine de Chevalier | Léognan | Château d'Olivier | Léognan |
| Château de Fieuzal | Léognan | Château Malartic Lagravière | Léognan |
| Château d'Olivier | Léognan | Château La Tour-Martillac | Martillac |
| Château Malartic-Lagravière | Léognan | Château Laville-Haut-Brion | Talence |
| Château La Tour-Martillac | Martillac | Château Couhins-Lurton | Villenave d'Ornon |
| Château Smith-Haut-Lafitte | Martillac | Château Couhins | Villenave d'Ornon |
| Château Haut-Brion | Pessac | Château Haut-Brion | Pessac★ |
| Château La Mission-Haut-Brion | Talence | | |
| Château Pape-Clément | Pessac | | |
| Château Latour-Haut-Brion | Talence | | |

★ Added to the list in 1960.

# ST. EMILION: 1955 OFFICIAL CLASSIFICATION (OFFICIALLY RECLASSIFIED 1985)

## Premiers Grands Crus Classes

### (A)
Château Ausone
Château Cheval Blanc

### (B)
Château Beausejour-Duffau la Garrosse
Château Belair
Château Canon
Clos Fourtet
Château Figeac
Château La Gaffelière
Château Magdelaine
Château Pavie
Château Trottevieille

## Grands Crus Classes

*Grands Crus Classes*
Château L'Angelus
Château L'Arrosée
Château Balestard la Tonnelle
Château Beau Sejour-Becot
Château Bellevue
Château Bergat
Château Berliquet
Château Cadet Piola
Château Canon-la-Gaffelière
Château Cap de Mourlin
Château Le Chatelet
Château Chauvin
Château Clos des Jacobins
Château Clos La Madeleine
Château Clos de l'Oratoire
Château Clos Saint-Martin
Château La Clotte
Château La Clusière
Château Corbin
Château Corbin Michotte
Château Couvent des Jacobins
Château Croque-Michotte
Château Curé-Bon-la-Madeleine
Château Dassault
Château La Dominque
Château Faurie de Souchard
Château Fonplégade
Château Fonroque
Château Franc-Mayne
Château Grand-Barrail-Lamarzelle-Figeac
Château Grand-Corbin
Château Grand-Corbin Despagne

Château Grand-Mayne
Château Grand-Pontet
Château Guadet-Saint-Julien
Château Haut-Corbin
Château Haut-Sarpe
Château Laniote
Château Larcis-Ducasse
Château Lamarzelle
Château Larmande
Château Laroze
Château Matras
Château Mauvezin
Château Moulin-du-Cadet
Château l'Oratoire
Château Pavie-Decesse
Château Pavie-Macquin
Château Pavillon-Cadet
Château Petit-Faurie-de-Soutard
Château le Prieuré
Château Ripeau
Château Saint-Georges-Côte-Pavie
Château Sansonnet
Château la Serre
Château Soutard
Château Tertre-Daugay
Château La Tour-Du-Pin-Figeac (Giraud-Belivier)
Château La Tour-Du-Pin-Figeac (Moueix)
Château La Tour-Figeac
Château Trimoulet
Château Troplong-Mondot
Château Villemaurine
Château Yon-Figeac

# Glossary

**Abboccato** Italian. Semidry; also AMABILE.

**Abocado** Spanish. Semidry.

**Acacia** Chemical used for clarifying and stabilizing wine.

**Acerbic** A bitter, unpleasant taste from unripe grapes.

**Acescence** Vinegar-like smell and taste due to bacterial spoilage.

**Acetaldehyde** Formed when carboxylase, an enzyme, forms acetaldehyde and carbon dioxide from pyruvic acid. Colorless, soluble, volatile liquid. During final stage of fermentation it is reduced to ethyl alcohol, but a small quantity remains, adding flavor to the wine. Vinegar-like odor in large amounts.

**Acetic** Wine that has gone sour due to prolonged exposure to oxygen. Acetic acid combines with ethyl acetate to give the vinegary smell and taste that a spoiled wine emits.

**Acetic Acid** Colorless, volatile acid found in all wines. Normally present in small quantities and if there is excessive development of it, the wine turns to vinegar. Key ingredient of vinegar.

**Acetobactor** Airborne, aerobic microorganism that causes the oxidation of alcohol primarily to acetaldehyde by pro-

longed exposure of oxygen. Oxygen is essential for its formation: Barrels should be kept full and air spaces in bottles kept to a minimum to inhibit its formation.

**Acidification** The addition of acid to wine, during or after fermentation, to adjust or improve balance and flavor.

**Acidity** Quality of tartness or sharpness to the taste due to the presence of pleasant fruit acids. Contributes flavor and freshness to wine when it is in proper balance, and contributes to its controlled aging. The principal acids found in wine are tartaric, citric, malic, and lactic.

**Acidulous** Wine that displays an unpleasant, sour taste due to high acidity, often more than one percent of total acid.

**Activated Charcoal** Assists precipitation of solids during fermentation. Clarifies and purifies wine. Removes excess color in white wine.

**Additives** Collective name for a group of materials added to wine to improve or preserve it. Some additives are colors, flavors, acids, vitamins, minerals, yeast, and bacterial inhibitors.

**Adulteration** Treating wine with unauthorized or prohibitive ingredients, or excessive levels of a permitted substance.

**Aeration** Allowing a wine to breathe in the open air. Swirling wine already present in a glass.

**Aerobic Fermentation** Fermentation conducted in the presence of oxygen.

**Aftertaste** Flavor that lingers or remains in the throat or on the tongue after wine is swallowed.

**Aging** Period of storage in oak barrels or bottles to develop character and palatability.

**Albariza** Spanish. White chalky soil in vineyards between Jerez de la Frontera and Sanlucar de Barrameda.

**Albumen** Egg whites used as a fining agent, mostly in wine making.

**Alcohol** Colorless, volatile, flammable liquid that is the intoxicating agent in all beverages that are fermented or distilled. Ethyl alcohol is a preservative and the intoxicating constituent of wine.

**Alcoholic** Term used to describe a wine that has too much alcohol for its body and weight, making it unbalanced.

**Aldehyde** Colorless, volatile fluid with a distinct odor that is a natural by-product of fermentation and increases in concentration as a wine ages. One of the organic chemical ingredients of wine formed by the partial oxidation of alcohol.

**Allier** Small forest centered around the city of Moulins, noted for its production of wooden barrels. Has a medium-tight grain, with moderate oak flavor and tannin extractions, displaying an intense, earthy component, and a floral perfumed character.

**Alluvial** Type of soil made of mostly sand and clay, formed by gradual deposits in the bottomlands along a river by the currents of moving water, as along a riverbed or a lakeshore.

**Almacenista** Spanish. Shopkeepers and hobbyists who produce or purchase Sherry wine, then carefully mature it in their cellars.

**Amber** Golden tints reminiscent of the color amber. Color change results from oxidation of the anthocyanins. Color often describing Sherries.

**American Oak** Often considered higher than European oak in the aromas of vanillin and related compounds. As barrels, used for fermenting and aging wines.

**American Viticultural Area (AVA)** Delimited, geographical grape-growing area that has officially been given appellation status by the BATF. Sometimes called Approved Viticultural Area.

**Amontillado** Style of Sherry that has more color and body than finos, with a medium dry taste and nutty flavor.

**Ampelography** Descriptive study and identification of grapevines; grape vine botany.

**Amphora** Ancient vessel often made of ceramic or earthenware, usually with two handles, which was used as a container for wine.

**Amtliche Prüfungsnummer** German. A.P. Number that appears on some wine labels. It certifies that the wine has met all legal requirements and has passed a series of laboratory and sensory tests.

**Amylase** Enzyme that converts starch to sugar.

**Añada** Spanish. Year of harvest. Youngest wine in a Sherry solera.

**Anaerobic Fermentation** Fermentation without oxygen.

**Anbaugebiete** German. Wine-producing regions.

**Angular** Wines without much delicacy, often referred to as being stiff or hard, with bitter or tart flavors.

**Anthocyans** Phenolic compound of wine that gives it its red color. The purple-red color of a young wine is caused by unstable anthocyanin molecules that, during aging, combine with tannins to give the wine its ruby-red color.

**Antioxidants** Phenolic compounds present in grape color and tannin that provide protection to the human body, inhibiting LDL (low-density liproprotein) cholesterol, and stimulating HDL (high-density liproprotein) cholesterol.

**Aperitif** Alcoholic beverage taken before meals to stimulate the appetite.

**Appearance** Refers to clarity of a wine. Wines should usually be free of cloudy and suspended particles when evaluated in a glass.

**Appellation Contrôlée** French. Wine laws specific to each of the wine-producing regions of France. Laws govern each of the defined areas, the varietals that can be used to produce each wine, minimum alcohol for each wine, and maximum yields per hectare.

**Appellation d'origine** Created by the French authorities in 1935 to establish areas of production, and wine laws for each area.

**Apple** Odor detected in certain wines, like Chardonnay and Riesling. Also a taste detected in some wines due to high levels of malic acid.

**Approved Viticultural Area (AVA)** Delimited, geographical grape-growing area that has officially been given appellation status by the BATF. Sometimes called American Viticultural Area.

**Apricots** Odor present in wines affected by *Botrytis cinerea (noble rot)* that totally masks the varietal character and substitutes an odor reminiscent of apricots.

**Aqueous** Watery. Detected in appearance and in taste of some lighter wines.

**Arenas** Spanish. Type of soil found in approximately 17 percent of the Sherry region of Spain. It consists of about 80 percent sand, red-yellow in color with alumina, silica, and clay. Produces more coarse wines than either albariza or barros soils.

**Aroma** A particular smell, odor, or fragrance of a specific grape used to produce the wine.

**Aromatic** Describes wines that have intense aromas—fruits, herbs, or other odors either directly from the grape or developed by the wine-making process.

**Aromatized Wine** Fortified wine with a wide variety of related aromatic plants or bitter herbs, roots, bark, or other plant parts infused into its bouquet. An example of an aromatized wine is vermouth.

**Assemblage** French. Blending of various cuvées in the making of Champagne.

**Astringency** Tactile, bitter sensation that makes the mouth pucker. Wines with high levels of astringency may be described as coarse, harsh, and rough. Also describes wines with too much tannin.

**Atmosphere** In physics, a unit of pressure equal to 14.69 psi (pounds per square inch). Champagne is bottled under five to seven atmospheres.

**Auslese** German. A prädikat wine made from very ripe, selected, late-harvested bunches of grapes. These wines are full, rich, and sweet.

**Autolysis** Self-destruction of yeast cells. Sometimes gives wine a toasty aroma and flavor.

**Awkward** Describes a wine that has poor structure or is out of balance.

**Azienda Agricola** Italian wines produced by companies whose wines have been made solely from grapes gathered in their own vineyards, and vinified in their own cellars.

**Bac a Glâce** French. Shallow brine bath used to freeze the necks of champagne bottles prior to degorgement.

**Bacchus** Roman God of wine.

**Backbone** Wines that are often full bodied, well structured, and balanced by a desirable level of acidity.

**Bacterial Spoilage** Bacteria that attacks must or wine during and after fermentation. Often due to formation of mold from improperly cleaned equipment, lack of sterile conditions, and faulty sanitation procedures.

**Bag in Box** Wine packaged in plastic membranes, closed by an air lock, and then placed in a cardboard box, which acts as a label for the wine, and a holder for the plastic bladder.

**Baked** A negative smell or flavor in wine—warm, cooked, or roasted—often resulting from extremely ripe grapes grown in hot climates.

**Balance** Pleasant harmony of the elements and components of a wine. A balanced wine is one whose components of sugar, fruit, tannin, acid, alcohol, wood, and extract are evident, but do not mask or dominate each other.

**Balloon Glass** Oversized wine glass whose bowl has a capacity of between ten and 26 fluid ounces/300 and 760 ml.

**Balthazar** Oversized Champagne bottle, equal to 16 750-ml bottles, or 12.7 quarts/12 liters.

**Barrel Aging** Process of mellowing wine through extraction, as the alcohol dissolves flavor-affecting chemicals present in the wooden barrels. The wine extracts certain aroma and flavor elements present in the wood.

**Barrel Fermentation** The must is fermented in wooden barrels rather than temperature-controlled stainless steel containers. During this time, extractables of tannin, color, and various odors and flavors are leached into the wine, creating more complexity and depth.

**Barrica** Spanish. Small oak barrel.

**Barrique** French. Small oak barrel.

**Barros** Spanish. Heavy, dark soil with some chalk, but mostly made of clay and sand. Often found in valleys between hills of albariza.

**Basket Press** Grapes are put in a wooden tub with slotted sides and pressure is applied by means of a large screw, which presses the grapes and allows the juice to run out through the slots.

**BATF** Bureau of Alcohol, Tobacco, and Firearms.

**Baumé** French. Term used to measure the level of unfermented sugar present in the grapes or must. If degrees Baumé are multiplied by 1.8, the result is degrees Brix.

**Beads** Describes the chain of tiny bubbles found in sparkling wines, formed by the presence of carbon dioxide.

**Beerenauslese** German. Wines made from overripe grapes affected by *Botrytis cinerea,* picked individually and produced in very small quantities.

**Bell Pepper** Odor characteristic of bell peppers sometimes detected in Cabernet Sauvignon, Sauvignon Blanc, and certain other grape varieties.

**Bench Grafts** Grafted grape vines of a desired fruiting species on rootstocks resistant to *phylloxera* or nematodes.

**Bentonite** Fining agent. Clay originating from the state of Wyoming and containing montmorillonite, produced from the decomposition under water of volcanic glass.

**Bereich** German. Wine subregion. (Plural: Bereiche)

**Berries** Fruity characteristic often linked with young red wines, such as Beaujolais.

**Berry Set** Successful pollination of grape flowers. The pollinated grape blossoms start to develop, with each flower in the floral cluster transformed into a miniature grape berry about the size of a small BB pellet.

**Big** Rich, powerful, full-bodied, and intensely flavored wine. Big wines are generally high in alcohol, tannin, and extract.

**Bin** Where bottles of wine are stored, usually by number ("Bin Number").

**Bitter** A wine that is quite high in tannin may be negatively described as "bitter" by a taster with a low tannin threshold.

**Blanc de Blancs** French. White wine made only from white grapes.

**Blanc de Noirs** French. White wine made only from black or red grapes.

**Blending** Marrying wines to obtain uniform quality and style from year to year.

**Blind Tasting** System of evaluating wine without knowledge of the grape, the producer, the country or origin, the vintage year, and so on.

**Bloom** When young flowers open and caps fall from the flowers.

**Blush** White wine made by limited skin contact with red grapes, extracting a hint of color.

**Bocksbeutel** German. Short, flat-sided, flask-shaped bottle used in parts of Germany, Chile, and Portugal.

**Body** Tactile sensation of weight or fullness on the palate, usually from a combination of alcohol, extracts, glycerin, tannin, and other physical components in wine.

**Bordeaux Bottle** Bottle shape originating in Bordeaux, France. Easily recognized by its regular, cylindrical form. Characterized by a short neck and high shoulders.

**Bota** Spanish. Portuguese. Bag made of goatskin from which wine is squirted into the mouth.

**Botrytis Cinerea** Mold which develops on grapes. Depending on the grape variety, the time of year, and climatic conditions it can greatly enhance or severely damage the grapes in a vineyard. *See* Noble Rot and Edelfäule.

**Bottle** Glass container that typically holds 25.4 ounces/ 750 ml.

**Bottle Aging** Aging process which takes place in the bottle at the winery or in private cellars.

**Bottle Fermentation** Refers to Champagne and Sparkling wine. Means that the secondary fermentation took place in the bottle or that the transfer method was used.

**Bottle Sickness** Stage that can affect a wine just after bottling. During bottling, the aroma, flavor, and/or balance of a wine may be temporarily diminished. Also known as bottle shock.

**Bottle Variation** Differences detected, bottle by bottle, in the appearance, nose, and taste of the same wine.

**Bouchon d'Expédition** French. Final cork used in a finished bottle of sparkling wine.

**Bouchon de Tirage** French. Temporary cork sometimes used to close the bottle during secondary fermentations of sparkling wines.

**Bouquet** Various fragrances noted by smell, created by a wine's development and imparted to the wine from the fermentation and aging process, whether in barrel or bottle.

**Brandy** Spirit made by distilling wines or the fermented mash of fruit, which may be aged in oak barrels.

**Breathing** Practice of allowing air to reach wine by uncorking and pouring it. Sheds unpleasant odors and brings out aroma and bouquet.

**Brick** Shade of red-brown often found in well-aged, mature red wines or slightly old red wines.

**Bright** When a wine begins to naturally clarify shortly after fermentation has ceased.

**Brilliant** Quality of a wine when it is free from any visible suspended solids or haziness.

**Brix** Measurement of the sugar content of the grape. *See* Baumé.

**Browning** Oxidation's effect on the color, odor, and taste of a wine which is past its prime, or has been carelessly exposed to a prolonged period of aeration.

**Brut** Champagne, France. Very dry.

**Bud** Compressed shoot located at the node of a cane.

**Bud Break** Forcing open of the bud by the increasing pressure of sap in a grapevine.

**Bung** Plug that fits into the opening at the top of a barrel for a tight seal. Can be cork, wood, or silicon.

**Burgundy Bottle** Bottle of conical shape, not regular in form, with a fat belly. Bottle is used to house both red and white wines of Burgundy, France.

**Burnt** Wine having cooked or baked characteristics.

**Butt** Barrel used to store or ship ale, Sherry wine, or other wines.

**Buttery** Descriptor of odor and/or taste; creamy.

**Calcaire/Calcerous** French. Limestone soil.

**Calcium Carbonate** Reduces the excess natural acids in high-acid wines.

**Candling** Helps to determine clarity in wine. Bottle held horizontally in front of light source to see how the light penetrates the glass.

**Cane Pruning** At pruning time extra growth is cleared away, leaving only the strongest. The remaining vines are trellised in the shape of a T, which allows for maximum sun exposure.

**Cap** Grapeskins, stems, and seeds which rise to the top of the tank or barrel during fermentation and harden. For maximum flavor extraction and the release of carbon dioxide gases, the cap must be disturbed several times a day.

**Capitolare** Italian. New style of wine, originally ranked vino da tavola, but has applied for DOC status. Formerly "Predicato."

**Capsule** Cover placed over the cork to protect the wine and improve the appearance of the bottle. Can be made of plastic, lead, or aluminum.

**Carafe** French. Decanter or glass bottle for serving wines.

**Carbon Dioxide** Odorless, colorless gas. By-product of wine fermentation. Creates effervescence.

**Carbonic Maceration** Intracellular fermentation. Whole uncrushed clusters of grapes are placed into a stainless steel fermenter, the tank is filled with carbon dioxide, and sealed. Process causes the malic acid to break down, the lack of oxygen causes skin cells to die, and the pigments are transfered to the pulp. Process produces a light-bodied, less-alcoholic, young and fruity wine meant for early consumption. Grape ferments from the inside out. Also called whole-berry fermentation.

**Case** Container that holds bottles of wine. Usually 12 25.4-oz/750-ml bottles.

**Cava** Spanish sparkling wine made through the *méthode champenoise*. Must remain in cellar for a minimum of nine months.

**Cellar** Storage or aging facility for alcoholic beverages, generally underground.

**Cellared & Bottled by** Individual bottler or packer must have aged the wine without changing the classification and type of the wine.

**Cellar Master** Key individual with sole authority over the vineyard and winery.

**Centrifuge** Machine using centrifugal force to separate particles and sediment from the wine.

**Cépage** French. Grape variety.

**Chai** French. Aboveground area for storing and aging wines.

**Chalk** Type of soil high in calcium carbonate.

**Champagne Bottle** Specific bottle type used by the Champagne region for sparkling wines. Similar in shape to a Burgundy bottle with a thicker body and an indentation on the bottom, called a punt.

**Chaptalization** French. A small amount of sugar added to the must, which results in a higher-alcohol level for the wine.

**Charmat Method** French. Tank method of producing sparkling wines. Least-expensive method for producing reasonable-quality wines.

**Charring** Burning the inside of the wooden barrel to be used for aging wine, whiskey or other distilled spirits. Adds color to the product and helps to mellow it.

**Château Bottled** French. Wine bottled at an estate.

**Cherry** Term used to describe the aroma or taste of cherries found in some light-bodied red wines such as Gamay-Beaujolais and Pinot Noir.

**Chewy** Rich texture on the palate. Full-bodied, very tannic.

**Citric Acid** Generally found in citrus fruits, but grapes also contain a small amount. Too much can cause the wine to become cloudy.

**CIVC** French. Comité Interprofessionnel du Vin de Champagne. The regulatory agency in the Champagne region.

**Claret** British name for Bordeaux red wines, derived from an old French adjective meaning a wine that was clear, light, and bright.

**Clarifying** Process of making a wine clear by fining or filtering.

**Classification of 1855** Applies to the wines of the Médoc, Sauternes, and Barsac, and Château Haut-Brion in Graves. Divides vineyards into five categories based on their quality in 1855.

**Clay** Type of soil that retains too much moisture due to poor drainage. Density of soil hampers good root penetration.

**Climat** French. Designation for single vineyard or plot in Burgundy.

**Clonal Selection** Choice for intravarietal genetic variability in grapes.

**Clone** Particular variety of grape that developed either by natural adaptation or asexually from an original "mother" grapevine.

**Closed in** Condition present in some young wines which have not yet harmonized and are still displaying young characteristics. Indicated primarily in the nose of the wine.

**Cloudy** Wines containing excess colloidal material or sediment in suspension.

**CM/CV** Classic Methods/Classic Varietals, a term that describes some *méthode champenoise* wines in the United States. The CM/CV group of wines are mostly European owned, and produce their wines on the North Coast of California.

**Cold Fermentation** Method generally used for white wines. The juice is fermented at temperatures colder than traditional, which retains much of the fruit, aroma, and varietal character of the grape.

**Cold Stabilization** Clarification technique that involves lowering the temperature to 25 to 30°F (-4 to -1°C) for one to three weeks.

**Color** Distinct hue specific to each wine type.

**Commune** French. Town or village.

**Complex** Wine that is multidimensional. Contains many elements that are in harmony with each other.

**Consejo Regulador** Spanish. Regulatory board of a specific region governing the production and quality-control regulations of all wine produced within that region.

**Consorzio** Italian. A nongovernmental consortium of wine producers from a particular wine-growing region.

**Cooked** Odor and flavor found in wines made from grapes which have been exposed to heat.

**Cooperage** Containers used for fermenting, holding, or aging wine while in the cellar and prior to bottling. A workshop to make oak barrels.

**Cooperative** Winery or cellar owned and operated by many small producers or growers.

**Copita** Spanish. Tulip-shaped stem glass that contains six fluid ounces/175 ml and is traditionally used for the service of Sherry.

**Copper Sulfate** Clarifies and stabilizes wine.

**Cordon Training** Training the grapevine into the shape of a T.

**Cork** Spongy natural material used as a stopper for bottles.

**Corked/Corky** Musty smell or flavor infused into the wine by a defective cork.

**Corkscrew** Device for removing a cork.

**Cosecha** Spanish. Vintage.

**Covercrop** Crops planted between rows of vineyards to absorb excess moisture and prevent runoff.

**Cramant** Champagne generally produced from Chardonnay grapes.

**Criadera** Spanish. The term for each level of aging butts utilized in the solera system for aging Sherry, placed vertically. There are as few as two, as many as 13 criaderas in a solera.

**Crianza** Spanish. Refers to the aging process in a Sherry bodega or winery.

**Cross/Crossing** New grape variety created by combining one variety with another.

**Crown Cap** Metal stopper whose edges are crimped over the mouth of the bottle.

**Cru** French. Growth. Synonymous with a special vineyard or a vineyard of high quality.

**Crush** Harvest.

**Crusher/Destemmer** Mechanical device utilized for breaking or cracking of the grape skins.

**Cultivation** Turning soil to aerate and control weeds.

**Cuvaison** French. Time spent by the wine in fermenting vats in contact with the skins.

**Cuvée** French. Blend of wines bottled as one product.

**Dealcoholized Wine** Wine with virtually all of the alcohol removed, made by one of several processes.

**Decanter** Carafe or bottle into which wines are poured prior to service.

**Decanting** Aerates the wine and removes sediment by pouring wine from one container to another.

**Dégorgement** French. Process of freezing the neck of the bottle that contains champagne and a small amount of riddled sediment. The ice plug of sediment is forced out by pressure in the bottle.

**Degree Days** Unit of measure in heat summation calculation. System devised by University of California at Davis to measure an area during the grape-growing season. Enables wine maker to grow the ideal grapes for a particular area.

**Delicate** Wines that are soft, pleasing, and light in style.

**Demijohn** Large glass container that usually holds five gallons/19 liters of liquid and is often used for the transportation or storage of wine.

**Denominaçao de Origem** Portuguese equivalent of France's AOC and Italy's DOC wine laws.

**Denominación de Origen** Spanish equivalent of France's AOC and Italy's DOC wine laws.

**Denominazione de Origine Controllata** Italy's wine laws. Comprehensive laws that govern every aspect of grape cultivation and wine production.

**Denominazione de Origine Controllata Garantita** Italian. Designation given to wines that are considered to be of a higher quality than DOC wines and made under even stricter guidelines.

**Density** Compactness of a substance, referred to as its specific gravity.

**Depth** Wine with intense, complex flavors that seem to fill the mouth from front to back. Subtle layers of flavor that are long lasting.

**Diatomaceous Earth** Filtering agent used in the production of some alcoholic beverages. Pure silica mined from the sea.

**Dolce** Italian. Sweet.

**Domaine** French. Wine estate.

**Dosage** French. Addition of a mixture of sugar syrup, grape concentrate and/or brandy to Champagne or sparkling wines before recorking. Corrects the sweetness in the final product.

**Doux** French. Very sweet.

**Drainage** After the primary fermentaion of red wines the juice is drained off and the skins, which are still heavily laden with juice, are sent to a press for further juice extraction.

**Drip Irrigation** Slow, frequent, precise application of water directly to the plant through devices known as emitters. The emitters are placed on the soil or just below the surface of the row crop soil.

**Dry** Wine with little or no noticeable residual sugar.

**Dulce** Spanish. Sweet.

**Dull** Wine that lacks brilliance in its appearance.

**Dumb** Wine with potential, but not developed enough to offer its full character.

**DWI** Driving While Intoxicated.

**Earthy** Describes scents or odors reminiscent of soil or the earth in which grapes are grown.

**EC/EEC/EU** European Community/European Economic Community/European Union. The political and economic federation of European countries.

**Edelfäule** German. *Noble mold* responsible for Eiswein, Beerenauslese, and Trockenbeerenauslese wines.

**Edelzwicker** German. An Alsace wine that is a blend of *noble* grape varieties.

**Égrappage** French. Separation of the grapes from the stalks before pressing and fermenting.

**Einzellage** German. Single vineyard. (Plural: Einzellangen.)

**Eiswein** German. Specific classification of wine made from grapes that are picked and harvested frozen. Produces a sweeter and more-concentrated wine.

**Elegant** Wine with dignified richness, grace, and refinement.

**Enologist** Technician of the grapevine and of wine.

**Enology** Science or study of wine and wine making.

**Enophile** One who loves wine and wine lore.

**Enrichment** *See* Chaptalization.

**En Tirage** French. Refers to second fermentation of sparkling wines and translates as "on the yeast."

**Erzeugerabfüllung** German. Estate bottled.

**Espumante** Portuguese and Brazilian term for sparkling wine.

**Estate Bottled** May be used by a bottling winery on a wine label only if the wine is labeled with a viticultural area appellation of origin and the bottling winery: (1) is located in the labeled viticultural area; (2) grew all of the grapes used to make the wine on land owned or controlled by the winery with the boundaries of the labeled viticultural area; and (3) crushed the grapes, fermented the resulting must, and finished, aged, and bottled the wine in a continuous process.

**Esters** Organic, volatile compounds that contribute fruity aromas to wines and distilled spirits.

**Estufa** Portuguese. Large heating chambers or ovens used to make Madeira.

**Ethanol/Ethyl Alcohol** Principal alcohol found in all alcoholic beverages.

**Eucalyptus** Odor of an evergreen species occasionally found in some California Cabernet Sauvignon or Pinot Noir wines.

**Extract** Nonvolatile, soluble solids present in a wine.

**Extra Dry** Term used for a Champagne that is not as dry as brut, but drier than sec.

**Faded** Wine that has lost its bouquet, character, and definition, generally through age.

**Fat** Heavy, intense wine that has a higher-than-average glycerin level.

**Fattoria** Italian. Farm or estate.

**Fermentation** Conversion of sugar in the grapes into ethyl alcohol or ethanol. Yeast is needed to begin the process. Fermentation stops when the sugars are depleted or when the alcohol level reaches about 14 percent and kills the yeast.

**Fermentation Lock** Low-pressure valve made of glass or plastic that seals a barrel or other container of fermenting wine from the outside air while permitting carbon dioxide gas given off during fermentation to escape through sulfited water.

**Fermentation Tank** Barrel, stainless steel tank, concrete vat, or other type structure utilized for the primary fermentation of grapes and grape juice into wine.

**Fermented in the Bottle** Terminology used in producing sparkling wines using the transfer method.

**Fermented in this Bottle** Terminology used in producing sparkling wines using the *méthode champenoise*.

**Fiasco** Italian. Wine lacking body and structure. Also name for wicker basket that was popular for shipping poor-quality Chianti.

**Field Blend** Practice of growing several varieties of grapes in the same vineyard and combining them to make one wine.

**Fill Level** The point in the bottle neck to which the wine is filled.

**Filtering** Mechanical process by which wine is forced through a porous filtering medium.

**Fining** Process of clarifying a cloudy or hazy wine to brilliance by removing suspended particles.

**Finish** Tactile and flavor impressions left in the mouth after the wine is swallowed.

**Fino** Spanish. The driest Sherry.

**Flavonoids** Flavoring compounds/phenols, found in the skins of grapes.

**Flinty** Taste of wine whose bouquet is similar to two flints being rubbed together or struck with steel.

**Flor** Spanish. Yeast-like substance that forms a white film on the surface of certain Sherries.

**Flûte** Elongated wine bottle used in Alsace, France, and in Germany. Also used for wines from other countries made in German or Alsace style.

**Flute** Elongated V-shaped glass used for serving Champagne and sparkling wine. *See* Tulip Glass.

**Foil Cutter** Semicylindrical instrument used to cut the foil or plastic cover on the bottle so the cork can be removed.

**Fortification/Fortified Wine** Addition of distilled spirits to a wine to arrest fermentation and leave some residual sugar or to give better keeping properties.

**Foxy** Grapy aroma and flavor of native American grapes Vitis Labrusca.

**Free-run Juice** Initial juice released by the grapes by the sheer weight or pressure of the mass, before the press is used.

**Fresh** Describes younger white or lighter red wines displaying a youthful, lively fruity aroma and clean, acidic taste.

**Frizzante** Italian. Spritz.

**Fructose** Simple sugar. Generally found in fruits.

**Fruity** Describes wines that have a definite pleasant aroma and flavor of grapes or other fresh fruits.

**Fuder** German. Large barrel with a capacity of 264 gallons/1000 liters. Mostly used in the Mosel region.

**Full-Bodied** Describes mouth-filling capacity of a beverage. Usually refers to beverages with high extracts and levels of glycerin.

**Fungicide** Chemical substance used to control the growth, infection, and spread of fungi on plants.

**Garrafeira** Portuguese. Specially aged wine, similar to Reserve.

**Gay-Lussac** Famous French chemist who correctly devised the overall equation for fermentaion in 1810.

**Generic** Designation of a particular class or type of wine of limited quality. Wine can be named or labeled after wine-producing region—Burgundy, Chablis, Champagne, etc.

**Glycerin** By-product of the fermentation of grapes into wine. Increases the feeling of fatness in the mouth, giving the wine a soft, almost oily tinge on the tongue and palate.

**Goblet** Bowl-shaped glass containing a stem and a base.

**Goût de Terroir** French. Earthy smell or taste imparted to a wine by the soil in which the grapevine is grown.

**Governo** Italian. Process occasionally used to produce Chianti wine. During secondary fermentation five to ten percent must is added to produce a roundness and liveliness to the wine.

**Grafting** Viticulture technique that joins a bud or other part of one grape vine to a portion of another so that their tissues unite.

**Grand Cru** French. A vineyard designated as a "Great Growth"; the best vineyards in Burgundy, also Alsace and Loire. Champagne vineyard rated at 100 percent, assuring highest price for the grapes.

**Grand Cru Classé** French. A great growth that is a legal grade of quality in areas of Bordeaux. The Médoc, for example, established five levels of Grand Cru Classé in 1855.

**Gran Reserva** Spanish. Red wines that have been aged in oak barrels for a minimum of two years, followed by three years in the bottle and may not leave the bodega until the sixth year after the vintage. Produced only in the best years.

**Grape** Juicy, round, smooth-skinned, edible fruit, generally green or red-purple, sometimes black, grown in clusters on a woody vine.

**Grappa** Italian. Distillate made from the stems, pulp, skins, and seeds of grapes. A pomace brandy.

**Green** Immature, underdeveloped wine that usually displays an austere, somewhat sour taste. Also, term for unripe grapes.

**Grosslage** German. Composite, collective vineyard made up of numbers of individual vineyards within subregions. (Plural: Grosslagen.)

**Gypsum** Calcium Sulfate.

**Halbtrocken** German. Semidry ("half dry") German wine. Maximum of one ounce per quart/18 grams per liter of residal sugar.

**Heat Summation** Geographic classification of regions in terms of heat degree days during the seven-month growing season. Used to determine vineyard sites for appropriate grapes.

**Hectare** Metric measure equal to 10,000 square meters of land or 2.471 acres.

**Hectoliter** Metric measurement equal to 100 liters or 26.418 gallons. Wine production is often referred to in hectoliters per hectare.

**Herbaceous** Describes the odor or taste of herbs. Grassy or vegetal smell may be contributed by hops or the varietal character of certain grapes.

**Herbicide** Chemical substance used to destroy plants or weeds or to check their growth.

**Hogshead** Barrel used in many wine-producing countries where its capacity varies from region to region.

**Hot** Highly alcoholic wines with heady odors. Burning qualities noticed in the smell and back of the throat when swallowing.

**Hot Zone** The price range in which the overwhelming majority of wines on a restaurant wine list are priced, such as $20 to $40 or $35 to $55.

**Hybrids** Cross between two grape species, *Vitis labrusca* and *Vitis vinifera*.

**Hydrometer** Cylindrical glass instrument of various lengths with a scale running along its length and a bulbous weighted end used to measure sugar concentration.

**Ice Bucket** Metal vessel that contains ice and water for the chilling of bottles of white and sparkling wine.

**IGT** Italy. Under law, Indicazione Geografica Tipica (IGT) is one quality level above vino da tavola. Wine typical of a region.

**Impériale** Oversized bottle equivalent in capacity to eight 750-ml bottles or 202.8 fluid ounces.

**Integrated Pest Management** A progressive agricultural practice that encourages the growth and maintenance of certain beneficial pests to control diseases and dangerous pests.

**Intoxicated** Under the influence of excessive alcohol consumption and being incapable of complete control of one's actions. Drunk.

**Irrigation** Controlled system that applies the right amount of water at the right time to the grapevines.

**Isinglass** Protein fining agent derived from dried sturgeon air bladder.

**Jacketed Tank** Mechanized system that circulates hot and cold water, enabling the temperature of the grape must to be controlled.

**Jeroboam** Oversized bottle with a capacity of four standard 750-ml bottles or 101.4 fluid ounces.

**Jug Wine** Inexpensive wine of no particular breed or quality that is usually sold in quantity.

**Kabinett** German. Most-basic grade of QmP wines. Indicates quality.

**Kicker** Term for an expensive wine outside the hot zone of a wine list. By definition, many true Champagnes are kickers.

**Kosher Wine** Wine made under strict rabbinical supervision and is suitable for Jewish religious practice.

**KWV** South African wine cooperative to which all the nation's wine producers belong.

**Lactic Acid** Organic acid that appears during the malolactic fermentation of the wine when malic acid changes into this smooth acid and carbon dioxide.

**Landwein** German. Category of wines defined according to the 1982 wine laws as a step above Tafelwein in quality. Landwein may be chaptalized.

**Late Harvest** Denotes wines made from very ripe grapes that have been picked or harvested later than usual. They are often shriveled, resembling raisins, and often make sweeter wines, due to their increased sugar levels. Dry late harvest wines are usually high in alcohol.

**Leakage** Bottle of wine that is leaking through the cork due to improper storage or a faulty cork.

**Leathery** Odor occasionally found in red wines rich in tannin; similar to rawhide.

**Lees** Dead yeast cells, pulp, skins, seeds, and other solids that settle to the bottom of a barrel or tank during and after fermentation.

**Legs** Trails or streaks of a transparent liquid apparent on the inner walls of a wine or brandy glass that run downward after it has been swirled. Substantial legs indicate high levels of glycerin, and relatively high alcohol.

**Liebfraumilch** German. Name applied to some QbA wines from Rheinhessen, Germany.

**Light** Pleasant, refreshing wine, lacking in body, color, or alcohol.

**Limousin Oak** Soft oak with loose grain used to make barrels for wine. Made from wood grown in the Limousin forest near Limoges, France.

**Liqueur d'Expedition** French. Shipping dosage in Champagne that determines its relative dryness.

**Liqueur de Tirage** French. Sugar or sweetener added to still wine to induce yeast cells to begin secondary fermentation to produce a sparkling wine.

**Liter** Metric unit of capacity equal to 1000 cubic centimeters at 20°C or 33.814 fluid ounces at 68°F.

**Lively** Describes white wines that are young and fresh with plenty of zestiness, acidity and fruit with a small amount of spritz.

**Luscious** Soft, sweet, fat, and fruity.

**Madeirized** Wine that is past its prime. Excessive heat and poor storage cause the wine to oxidize and turn a brownish tinge.

**Magnum** Bottle of wine equivalent in capacity to 50.8 fluid ounces or two 750-ml bottles.

**Maître de Chais** French. Employee in charge of the cellar. Responsible for the vinification and aging of all wines.

**Malic Acid** Principal acid of apples and second major acid in grapes. Tart, astringent taste. Decreases in grapes as they become fully ripe.

**Malolactic Fermentation** Bacterial fermentation, converting malic acid to lactic acid while releasing carbon dioxide. Has four major effects on wine: (1) changes a harsh acid to a smooth acid, making the wine softer and more pleasant to drink; (2) lowers overall acidity; (3) increases biological stability in the wine by assuring that a malolactic fermentation will not take place in the bottle; and (4) increases the sensory quality, complexity, and flavor of the wine.

**Manzanilla** Spanish. Palest and driest fino Sherry produced in Sanlucar de Barrameda.

**Marc** French. Distillate made from the stems, pulp, skins, and seeds of grapes. Pomace brandy.

**Mature** Stage in the aging of wines when they have developed all of their characteristic qualities in harmony.

**Mechanical Harvester** Large machine that mechanically removes grapes from clusters by gently shaking the vines. Once picked, the machine helps to sort leaves from grapes and stems.

**Meniscus** Curved upper surface of a column of liquid. The "rim" of the wine in a wine glass.

**Mercaptans** Chemical compounds in wine which cause the wine to smell "skunky." Mercaptans are formed when, after fermentation, yeast reacts with sulphur. Mercaptans and their foul odors can be easily removed by racking the wine promptly and completely.

**Meritage** Wines made in the United States predominately from a blend of two or more of the traditional Bordeaux grape varieties. Cabernet Sauvignon, Merlot, Cabernet Franc, Petit Verdot, and Malbec, for red wine; Sauvignon Blanc and Sémillon for white.

**Méthode Champenoise** French. Fermented wine is bottled with yeast cells and sugar to induce a secondary fermentation. When fermentation is complete, the wine is aged, and the yeast sediment is removed.

**Methuselah/Methusalem** Oversized bottle. Equivalent to eight 750-ml bottles or 6.3 quarts/six liters.

**Metodo Classico/Metodo Tradizionale** Italian. Terms for sparkling wine made by the *méthode champenoise*.

**Microclimate** Climate of a small distinct area that has either slightly or greatly varying degrees of difference from the general climate of the larger area.

**Mildew** Fungal disease that attacks grapevines in rainy or damp seasons. Must be treated or it will cause crippling damage to tissue and the fruit.

**Millésimé** French. Dated or vintage wine. Term is mostly used to indicate a vintage Champagne.

**Mint** Describes odor or taste of fresh green mint.

**Mise en Bouteilles au Château** Bordeaux, France. Estate bottled.

**Mise en Bouteilles au Domaine** Burgundy, France. Estate bottled.

**Mouldy** The indication, usually by smell, of bacterial spoilage in a wine.

**Mousse** French. Froth or foam on the surface of a glass of Champagne.

**Must** Unfermented juice or any mixture of juice, pulp, skins, and seeds from fruit, berries, or grapes. The must is fermented to make wine.

**Must Weight** The difference, in grams, between about one quart/one liter of grape juice—the must—and a liter of distilled water. Sugar has a higher specific gravity than water, so the must weight indicates the amount of sugar present in the must.

**Musty** Describes odor or flavor in wine similar to a moldy smell.

**Mutage** French. Process of retarding fermentation of grape juice and adding brandy or other distilled spirits.

**Natural** North American designation for bone-dry sparkling wines.

**Nebuchadnessar** Large bottle with a capacity of about 16 quarts/20 750-ml bottles. Used almost exclusively for charity events and festivals.

**Négociant** France. Middleman who operates between grower and shipper. The négociant is at the center of the wine trade in both Alsace and Burgundy.

**Nevers Oak** French. Named after the French city. Hardwood with fine, medium grain from which barrels are made.

**Nitrogen** Needed by yeast cells to multiply.

**Noble Rot** *Botrytis cinerea*. Gray, hairy mold present in most vineyards. Affected berries look like cracked raisins, but do not resemble them in taste. Needs humid climate to grow. Affected grapes are handpicked to produce a very sweet, expensive wine.

**Nonvintage** Term applied to sparkling wines whose cuvées contain wine from previous vintages. Also applies to blended, still jug wines.

**Nose** Aroma and bouquet.

**Nouveau/Novello** French/Italian. New wine.

**Nutty** Describes odor and flavor of Madeira, Marsala, Sherry, or other fortified wines.

**Oak** Species of hardwood trees used for aging wine.

**Oak Chips** Pieces of oak often used when aging inexpensive wines in stainless steel vats, to provide the essence that oak barrels impart to the wine.

**Oaky** Odor or taste of wines aged in oak.

**Öechsle** German. Specific gravity of must. Method to determine level of sugar present in the must. Named after chemist who invented method, Christian Ferdinand Öechsle.

**Oenology** Science or study of wine and wine making.

**Off** Wines that display undesirable attributes.

**Oidium** European name for powdery mildew.

**Organic Wines** Wines made from organically grown grapes, vinified naturally with absolutely minimum addition of sulfites.

**Organically Grown** Wines made from grapes grown without potentially harmful chemical sprays, but traditionally vinified with the judicious addition of sulfites.

**Organoleptic** Analytical evaluation (of wine) using all of the senses.

**Overcropping** Growing more grape clusters than a grapevine can bring to maturity at normal harvest time, leading to diluted levels of sugar and nutrients.

**Oxidation** Chemical change in wine due to exposure to oxygen during any phase of production, aging, or storage.

**Palate** Sense of taste in the mouth.

**Palo Cortado** Spanish. Lightest of the oloroso Sherries. True palo cortado is considered very rare.

**Passe-Tout-Grains** French. Red Burgundy wine made from a blend of Pinot Noir with Gamay or other lesser grapes.

**Passito** Italian. Sweet wine made from overripe grapes that have been allowed to dry in the sun, increasing sugar levels.

**Peppery** Describes smell or taste, usually in full-bodied red wines, reminiscent of black pepper, herbs, or spices.

**Perfume** Refers to floral smells encountered in the aroma and bouquet of some white wines.

**Perlage** French. The small bubbles in Champagne or sparkling wine that emerge in the glass from a single point of departure and in a straight line; these qualities are referred to as "good" perlage.

**Pesticides** Chemical compounds used to kill insects.

**Petillant** French. Spritzy.

**pH** A measure of the relative acidity of grape musts and finished wines.

**Phenols** Antioxidant compounds that occur naturally in wine grapes. Often referred to in wine terms as tannins. (Phenolic, adj.)

**Phylloxera Vastatrix** Aphid-like insect; a plant louse. Lives on grapevines and burrows through the plant, eating its roots.

**Pierce's Disease** Virus found in coastal California vineyards. Leaves yellow along the veins, edges burn, the vine puts out dwarf shoots, fruit wilts, and vines die in one to five years.

**Pinot** Name of grape family—Blanc, Gris, Noir.

**Pipe** 110-gallon/416-liter barrel used to store and ship Sherry, Madeira, Marsala, Port, and other fortified wines.

**Polishing Filter** Ultra-fine filtering medium used to clarify wine just prior to bottling.

**Pomace** Skins, stems, and seeds remaining after the grapes have been pressed. A very compact mass often referred to as "cake."

**Pourriture Noble** French for *Botrytis cinerea*.

**Powdery Mildew** Fungal disease that retards grapevine growth and interferes with winter hardiness.

**Prädikat** German. Designation reserved for highest quality of wines; those with special attributes. Equivalent to Appellation Contrôlée wines. See Qualitätswein mit Prädikat (QmP).

**Premières Taille** French. Second pressing of grapes used to produce some nonvintage Champagnes.

**Press Wine** Portion of wine that is pressed from the skins and pulp under pressure, after the free run wine is produced. Concentration of color, flavor, and harshness is found in this wine which, if used at all, is most often used for blending.

**Primary Fermentation** First stage of fermentation in which the yeast begins to metabolize the sugar, converting it into alcohol and carbon dioxide.

**Prise de Mousse** French. Secondary fermentation of wine into a sparkling wine.

**Produced and Bottled by** Used by U.S. producers and bottlers if they have made at least 75 percent of the wine by fermenting the must and clarifying the wine.

**Prohibition** Eighteenth Amendment to the U.S. Constitution that repealed the right to manufacture, sell, transport, import, and export alcoholic beverages in, to, or from the United States. Passed in 1919, repealed in 1933.

**Pruning** Removal of excess vines from the plant. Produces a finer grape, lower yields, and increases the strength of the crop.

**Pumping Over** During fermentation the cap of skins must be redistributed with the juice, in order to release carbon dioxide. The wine is pumped from the bottom of the tank over the cap several times a day.

**Punt** Dome-shaped indentation found on the bottom of sparkling wine bottles. Serves to strengthen the bottle and, prior to dégorgement, collect the sediment.

**Pupitre** French. Hand-riddling rack in the shape of an A-frame, used for sparkling wines. The sparkling wine bottles are placed at an angle in the racks, and the solids in the wine are collected in the neck of the bottle, for later freezing and removal.

**Puttonyos** Hungarian buckets used for measuring quantity of selected grapes used in sweet Tokaji wine. Labels read 3 Puttonyos, 4 Puttonyos, etc.

**Qualitätswein besstimter Anbaugebiete (QbA)** German. Classification for quality table wines. Label indicates that certain requirements have been met.

**Qualitätswein mit Prädikat (QmP)** German. Designation reserved for highest-quality wines. Chaptalization is prohibited at the QmP level. Every QmP label must include the class of the wine, based on the ripeness of the grapes at harvest (e.g., Auslese).

**Quinta** Portuguese. Wine estate.

**Quintal** Metric measurement of weight. Equivalent to 220.46 pounds.

**Racking** Moving wine from one barrel or tank to another in order to remove solids and to aerate the wine.

**Rainwater** Type of Portuguese Madeira made for the British market.

**Rancio** Spanish. Describes odor and taste of wine as Sherry-like.

**Recently Disgorged** After extra aging on its lees, a bottle of sparkling wine or Champagne undergoes disgorging (see Dégorgement) shortly before release, often resulting in richer, fuller flavors.

**Recioto** Italian. Semidry or sweet wine made from the ripest grapes, most often in the Veneto province.

**Refractometer** Measures sugar/acid ratio in grapes by refracting light.

**Regiao Demarcada** Spanish. One of 33 appellations or wine regions of Spain.

**Rehoboam** Large bottle with a capacity of about 5 quarts/six 750-ml bottles.

**Rémuage** Process of eliminating sediment in sparkling wines by working them into the neck of the bottle by methodically tilting them upside down and shaking and turning them as necessary.

**Remueur** The person (or sometimes machine) that lifts, shakes, and turns sparkling wine bottles to move the solids in the wine into the neck of the bottle.

**Reserva** Spanish. Portuguese. Wines from an exceptional harvest that are aged longer in order to develop fuller character and more delicacy of the bouquet.

**Reserve** Often found on U.S. wine labels, this term has no specific legal or ethical meaning.

**Residual Sugar (RS)** Natural grape sugar intentionally left in the wine after fermentation to make a sweeter wine.

**Resin** Added to Greek table wine, in powder form, to create Retsina.

**Rich** Describes wine mouth feel, bouquet, and flavors.

**Riddler** *See* Remueur.

**Rim** The outer edge of wine in a glass. Color of rim helps determine age of wine. Sometimes called the meniscus.

**Ripe** Describes wines that have reached their full term of aging or have achieved desired bouquet and flavor.

**Riserva** Italian. DOC wine with extra aging before release.

**Robe** French. Term that refers to color and other visual aspects of a wine.

**Robust** Describes flavor and mouth feel of wine. Full bodied.

**Rootstock** Special roots that vines can be grafted to. Specific types are chosen for their resistance to disease and weather.

**Rosé** Wine made from red grapes that have limited contact with the skin. Wine made from a combination of both red and white wines.

**Rot** Decomposistion of wine due to bacteria.

**Rough** Describes young, immature wines that are unbalanced and very astringent, often due to high levels of tannin.

**Saccharomyces Ellipsodium** The dominant yeast strain used in making wine.

**Sack** Antiquated English term for Sherry.

**Sacramental Wine** Wines used during religious ceremonies.

**Salmanazar** Large bottle with the capacity of 9.5 quarts/12 750-ml bottles, generally used for Champagne.

**Schaumwein** German. Low-quality sparkling wine.

**Scion** Shoot or bud to be grafted onto rootstock.

**Sec** French. Dry.

**Secondary Fermentation** Addition of sugar and yeast to already-fermented wine. Technique used to create sparkling wine.

**Sediment** Precipitation of fruit acids, tannins, tartrates, and pigments as the wine ages in the bottle. Red wines high in tannins will create sediment in the form of brownish solids.

**Seeds** Pit in the grape berry.

**Sekt** German. Sparkling wine.

**Sélection des Grains Nobles** French. Designation for wines from Alsace that are classified as the vendanges tardives. The grapes are *botrytis*-affected and produce a very concentrated sweet wine. Similar to Germany's Beerenauslese.

**Sercial** Portuguese. Driest fortified wine from the island of Madeira.

**Serving Temperature** Best temperature for serving wine.

**Sherry** Spanish. Fortified wine produced in Jerez, Spain. Produced using the solera system. Traditionally contain 17-22 percent alcohol.

**Shoot** Living growth from a grapevine. Bears leaves and tendrils and possibly fruit.

**Single Vineyard** Special designated area within a specific vineyard site or commune, where the grapes produce wines with more unique characteristics.

**Site Selection** Specific area chosen for planning a vineyard, based on weather patterns, heat summation, soil types, etc.

**Skin** Outer covering of grape. Grape color and yeasts are found on the skins.

**Skin Contact** Refers to grape skin contact with the fermenting grape juice. Lends color, flavor, complexity, and longevity to the wine. Most often an important part of red wine production.

**Smoky** Describes odor present in bouquet of wines fermented in charred oak barrels.

**Snifter** Balloon-shaped, wide-rimmed brandy glass.

**Soft** Describes the mouth feel of wine. Smooth, without harshness.

**Soil** Different types of grapes need different types of soil. All grape varieties need ample amounts of water and nutrients in the earth to produce quality fruit.

**Solera** Spanish. System used to produce Sherries. Series of old white American oak barrels set up in tiers, up to 13 layers high (youngest on the top tier, oldest on the bottom). The wine in the bottom barrel is then replaced by the tier above and so on, so that the older wines are refreshed, and the younger wines gain complexity. Wine sold is from the bottom, but no more than 33 percent of the bottom barrel is removed.

**Sommelier** French. Individual in charge of the wine, wine service, the wine list, and the wine cellar in the restaurant.

**Soutirage** French. The process of moving wine from one barrel to another in order to separate it from the accumulated sediment or lees. *See* Racking.

**Spätlese** German. Means late picking or late harvesting as determined by the degree of ripeness of the fruit.

**Spicy** Describes odor and/or taste which resembles spices and herbs.

**Spirit** A high-alcohol beverage (often 40 percent or more) made by the distillation of recognized fermentable products, such as fruits or grains. For this reason, by the widest possible definition, spirits can be classified as distilled "wine" or "beer."

**Spraying** The application of liquid fungicides and insecticides to combat pests and diseases.

**Spritz** Light, pleasant effervescence created by carbon dioxide in the wine.

**Spumante** Italian. Sparkling wine.

**Stabilizers** Various additives used to retard deterioration of the wine.

**Steely** Describes taste found in white wines that resemble minerals.

**Stem** Part of the glass found between the bowl and the base.

**Structure** Describes interaction of components of wine and the level of complexity they create on the palate.

**Stuck Fermentation** When fermentation stops before all the sugar has been converted to alcohol. Caused by death of yeast cells.

**Style** Combination of flavor, aroma and balance of a wine which depends on grape quality and wine maker's expertise, as well as the use of techniques and equipment. Can be the wine maker's or producer's "signature."

**Sulfur Dioxide** Used by wine makers as an antioxidizing agent. Excessive amounts will create an unpleasant odor in the wine.

**Superiore/Supérieur** Italian/French. Superior. Higher level of alcohol in the wine, lower yield in the vineyard.

**Supple** Describes mouth feel of wine as soft, full, and easy to drink.

**Sur Lie** French. Wine fermented and aged on its lees. See Autolysis.

**Süssreserve** German. Unfermented grape juice that is added after fermentation to sweeten the wine.

**Sustainable Agriculture/Viticulture** Utilizing a number of progressive, though often traditional, agricultural practices in the vineyard in order to keep the land and plants healthy for the long term. Organic farming practices and minimizing the use of chemicals in the vineyard are important components of the overall approach to agriculture.

**Sweet** Describes a wine that retains some natural sugars after fermentation has ceased.

**Table Wine** Still reds, whites, and rosés containing between seven and 14 percent alcohol.

**Tafelwein** German. Table wine. German wine law allows this category of wine to be chaptalized.

**Tannic Acid** Acid that can be added to wine or must to retard the aging process.

**Tannins** Phenolic polymers that lend density and richness to wine. Organic compound found in the seeds, stems, and skins of grapes. Creates astringent character in wine, and is an important preservative for the proper aging of selected red wines.

**Tart** Astringent, citric flavor of fruit acid that refreshes the mouth.

**Tartaric Acid** Natural acid found in grapes. When the wine is chilled, or cool-fermented, it can crystallize out as cream of tartar.

**Tartrates** Crystals formed from the combination of tartaric acid and potassium in wine.

**Taste** Overall flavor impression left on the palate by wine.

**Tastevin** French. Small, saucer-like silver cup used by a sommelier to examine and taste wine before serving. Ornamented with dimples to refract light in young wines.

**Tawny Port** Portuguese. Tawny color in this fortified wine is derived from long aging—a minimum of seven years—in barrels.

**Tenuta** Italian. Estate.

**Terroir** French. Taste of the earth in wine.

**Tête de Cuvée** Antiquated term used in Burgundy for an outstanding growth. *See* Grand Cru.

**Texture** Describes mouth feel of wine on the palate.

**Thin** Describes lack of body in wine.

**Three-Tier System** Traditional system for distributing wine: producers, wholesalers, and retailers.

**Tirage** French. Phase of producing sparkling wines where the bottles are placed on their sides in large stacks during the second fermentation.

**Toasty** Describes odor and taste similar to that of something baked or grilled. Can be created from wine being aged in wood barrels, autolysis, or oxidation in whites.

**Topping Up** Adding wine to wood barrels to replenish what has been lost through evaporation.

**Total Acidity** Measurement, by volume, of acid in must or wine.

**Training Systems** System of training grapevines on the trellis so that vines will receive the most beneficial exposure to light.

**Transfer Method** Method of producing sparkling wine. After second fermentation in the bottle, wine is emptied into a pressurized tank and filtered. The wine is then transferred to new bottles, and the final dosage is added.

**Trellising System** Support structures for grapevines in a given training system, such as *guyot, gobelet,* or *pergola* systems.

**Trocken** German. Dry.

**Trockenbeerenauslese** German. Wine made from late, *botrytis*-affected, individually picked grapes. The grapes dry and shrivel on the vine before being picked. They are high in sugar, producing a very sweet, rich wine, usually low in alcohol.

**Tronçais Oak** French. Very hard wood, grown in the Allier region of France. Known for the spicy component it imparts to the wine.

**Tulip Glass** Proper glassware for Champagne and sparkling wines. Shaped like a tulip with an eight- to 10-ounce/237–295 ml capacity. *See* Flute.

**Ullage** Air space in the bottle between the bottom of the cork and the top of the wine.

**Unbalanced** Wine with components that are unharmonious.

**Unctuous** Describes taste in wine that is rich, sweet, and almost oily.

**Vanilla** Scent of vanilla bean detected in wines that have been aged in new oak barrels.

**Varietal** Wine made completely or predominately from a single grape. Most New World wines feature varietal labels—the name of the wine is the name of the grape (*e.g.,* Chardonnay).

**Varietal Character** Unique combination of odor, taste, and mouth feel in a wine, generally attributed to a particular variety of grape.

**Vatting** Process where skins are left in contact with the fermenting wine for an extended period of time.

**VDP** German. Verband Deutscher Prädikatsweinguter, an association of single-estate wine producers, committed to producing high-quality wines with strong regional and varietal character, mostly made from Riesling grapes.

**VDQS** French. Vins Délimités de Qualité Supérieur. Classification of wine just below the Appellation Contrôlée designation in quality.

**Vegetal** Odor or taste of wine as one that resembles grass and herbs.

**Vendange** French. Year that grapes were harvested. Vintage.

**Vendange Tardive** French. In Alsace, sweet, late-harvest wines.

**Vendemmia** Italian. Year that grapes were harvested. Vintage.

**Vendimia** Spanish. Year that grapes were harvested. Vintage.

**Veraison** French. Point in growing season when grapes begin turning to true color.

**Vermouth** A fortified wine flavored with herbs and spices (aromatized), much of it made in Italy and France.

**Vigneron** French. One who tends the grapevines. The grower or wine maker.

**Vin de Pays** French. Just above vin de table in quality levels of AOC wine laws. "Country Wine."

**Vin de Table** French. Table wine under AOC wine laws.

**Vin Doux Naturel** French. Sweet wines made by arresting fermentation (thereby capturing residual sugar), followed by the addition of alcohol, making a fortified sweet wine that is almost always at least 14 percent alcohol. An example is Muscat de Beaumes-de-Venise from the Rhône Valley.

**Vine** Plant with long stems that grow above the ground and climbs on walls or supports. *See* Trellising System.

**Vinegar** Wine product high in acetic acid. Not for drinking purposes.

**Vineyard** Land used to grow grapevines.

**Viniculture** Theory, art, and science of making wine.

**Vinifera** European grape variety. Premium grapes for making wine.

**Vinification** Process of converting grapes into wine.

**Vino da Tavola** Italian. Table wine under DOC wine laws.

**Vino de Calidad** Spanish. Quality wine under DO wine laws.

**Vin Ordinaire** French. Everyday wines.

**Vinosity** Refers to wine-like aroma and flavor of wine due to its alcohol level.

**Vintage** The year the grapes were harvested.

**Vintage Port** Portuguese. Ports produced in years determined by shippers to be the best quality.

**Vintner** Grower, blender, and seller of grapes and wines.

**Viscous** Describes full-bodied, "fat"-tasting wines, usually full bodied reds or sweet dessert wines.

**Viticulture** Theory, science, and study of the production of grapes.

**Vitis Labrusca** Eastern North American species of grapevines, such as Concord and Niagara.

**Vitis Riparia** North American species of grapevines.

**Vitis Rotundifola** North American species of grapevine, found predominately in the southern Atlantic states, such as Muscadine and Scuppernong.

**Vitis Vinifera** European species of grapevine. Translates as "grapes to make wine."

**Volatile Acidity** Describes odor and taste found in wines with high level of acetic, butyric, formic and propionic acids.

**Vosges Oak** French. Forest located in the Vosges mountains near Alsace. Tight grain with neutral oak flavor and medium tannin extraction.

**Weingut** German. Wine estate.

**Well Balanced** *See* Balance.

**Wild Yeast** Yeasts indigenous to certain vineyards.

**Wine** Alcoholic beverage produced from fermenting fruit juice (generally grapes).

**Wine Cradle** Basket designed to hold a bottle of mature wine that contains sediment. Keeps the bottle in a semihorizontal position to minimize disruption of the sediment.

**Wine Maker** Individual in charge of producing wine in a winery.

**Winery** Building where grape juice is fermented into wine.

**Woody** Describes odor and taste of some wines aged in wood barrels for an extended period of time.

**Yeast** Brings about fermentation of grape juice to wine by secreting the enzyme, zymase, which converts sugar to ethyl alcohol and carbon dioxide.

**Yeasty** Describes odor in wine as that of freshly made bread.

**Yield** Refers to the production from an area (in acres or hectares) of land.

# Bibliography

Adams, Leon. *The Wines of America*. New York: McGraw-Hill, Inc., 1990.

Allegra, Antonia. *Napa: The Ultimate Winery Guide*. San Francisco: Chronicle Books, 1993.

Amerine, Maynard, and M.A. Joslyn. *Table Wines: The Technology of Their Production*. 2d ed. Berkeley: University of California Press, 1970.

————. and Edward B. Roessler. *Wines: Their Sensory Evaluation*. 2d ed. W.H. Freeman, 1983

————. and C.S. Ough. *Wine and Must Analysis*. New York: John Wiley & Sons, 1974.

————. *Table Wines: the Technology of their Production in California*. Berkeley: University of California Press, 1951.

————. *The Technology of Wine Making*. Westport, Conn: Avi Publishing, 1980.

Anderson, Burton. *The Simon & Schuster Pocket Guide to the Wines of Italy*. New York: Simon and Schuster, 1993.

————. *The Wine Atlas of Italy*. New York: Simon and Schuster, 1992.

————. *Treasures of the Italian Table*. New York: Morrow, 1994.

————. *Vino: the Wines and Winemakers of Italy*. Boston: Little, Brown and Company, 1980.

Anderson, Stanley and Raymond Hull. *The Art of Making Wine*. New York: NAL-Dutton, 1991.

Asher, Gerald. *On Wine*. New York: Random House, 1982.

Ashley, Maureen. *The Encyclopedia of Italian Wines*. New York: Simon and Schuster, 1992.

Barr, Andrew. *Pinot Noir*. London: Viking Penguin, 1983.

Benson, Jeffrey and Alastair Mackenzie. *The Wines of Saint-Emilion and Pomerol*. Sothebys Publications.

Bespaloff, Alexis. *The New Frank Schoonmaker's Encyclopedia of Wine*. New York: Morrow, 1988.

————. *The New Signet Book of Wine*. New York: NAL-Dutton, 1980.

Blue, Anthony Dias. *American Wine*. New York: Doubleday, 1985.

Broadbent, Michael. *The Great Vintage Book*. New York: Alfred A. Knopf, 1981.

————. *Michael Broadbent's Guide to Wine Vintages*. New York: Simon and Schuster, 1993.

————. *The New Great Vintage Wine Book*. New York: Alfred A. Knopf, 1991.

————. *The Simon & Schuster Pocket Guide to Wine Tasting*. New York: Simon and Schuster, 1988.

Brook, Stephen. *Liquid Gold*. New York: William Morrow, 1987.

———. *Sauvignon Blanc & Sémillon*. London: Viking Penguin, 1993.

Brunet, Paul, ed. *Les Vins et les Vins Étrangers*. Paris: Éditions B.P.I., 1991.

Buller, Michael. *The Winemaker's Year in Beaujolais*. New York: Thames and Hudson, 1993.

———. *The Winemaker's Year: Four Seasons in Bordeaux*. New York: Thames and Hudson, 1991.

Cammara, Caroline and Cammara Paireault. *The World of Wine*. New York: Mallard Press, 1990.

Casas, Penelope. *Foods and Wines of Spain*. New York: Alfred A. Knopf, 1982.

Clark, Corbet. *American Wines of the Northwest*. New York: Morrow, 1990.

Clarke, Oz. *The Essential Wine Book: An Indispensable Guide to the Wines of the World*. New York: Simon and Schuster, 1989.

———. *Oz Clarke's Encyclopedia of Wine*. New York: Simon and Schuster, 1994.

———. *Oz Clarke's Wine Advisor*. New York: Simon and Schuster, 1993.

———. *Oz Clarke's Wine Handbook*. New York: Simon and Schuster, 1993.

Conaway, James. *Napa*. New York: Avon, 1992.

Cossart, Noël. *Madeira, The Island Vineyard*. London: Christies Wine Publications, 1984.

The Culinary Institute of America. *The New Professional Chef*. 5th ed. New York: Van Nostrand Reinhold, 1991.

———. *Techniques of Healthy Cooking*. New York: Van Nostrand Reinhold, 1993.

Dallas, Philip. *Italian Wines*. London: Faber and Faber, 1989.

Darlington, David. *Angels' Visits: An Inquiry into the Mystery of Zinfandel*. New York: H.Holt, 1992.

De Blij, Harm Van. *Wine Regions of the Southern Hemisphere*. Totowa, N.J.: Rowman and Allanheld, 1985.

De Groot, Roy. *The Wines of California, the Pacific Northwest, and New York*. New York: Summit Books, 1982.

De Villiers, Marq. *The Heartbreak Grape: A California Winemaker's Search for the Perfect Pinot Noir*. New York: HarperCollins, 1993.

Debuigne, Gérard. *Larousse Dictionary of Wines of the World*. New York: Larousse, 1976.

Dittmer, Paul R. and Gerald G. Griffin. *Principles of Food, Beverage, and Labor Cost Control*. New York: Van Nostrand Reinhold, 1994.

Duijker, Hubert. *The Great Wines of Burgundy*. New York: Crescent Books, 1982.

———. *The Wine Atlas of Spain*. New York: Simon and Schuster, 1992.

———. *The Wines of Loire, Alsace and Champagne*. New York: Crescent Books/Crown Publishers, 1987.

———. *The Wines of Rioja*. London: Mitchell Beazley, 1985.

Edwards, Michael. *The Champagne Companion*. Philadelphia: Quintet Publishing/Running Press, 1994.

Ensrud, Barbara. *American Vineyards*. New York: Random House, 1990.

———. *Wine with Food: a Guide to Entertaining through the Seasons*. New York: Congdon and Weed, 1984.

Evans, Len. *Australia and New Zealand: Complete Book of Wine*. London: Paul Hamlyn, 1973.

Fadiman, Clifton and Sam Aaron. *The New Joys of Wine*. New York: Abrams, 1990.

Faith, Nicholas. *The Story of Champagne*. New York: Facts on File, 1989.

Farkas, J. *The Technology & Biochemistry of Wine*. New York: Gordon & Breach, 1988.

Fisher, Mary Frances Kennedy. *The Story of Wine in California*. Berkeley: University of California Press, 1962.

Flower, Raymond. *Chianti*. New York: Universe Books, 1979.

Ford, Gene. *The French Paradox: Drinking for Your Health*. San Francisco: Wine Appreciation Guild, 1993.

Foulkes, Christopher, ed. *Larousse Encyclopedia of Wine*. Paris: Larousse, 1994.

Galhano, Amandândio. *A Demarcated Region, a Denomination of Origin: Vinho Verde*. Portugal: Commisão de Viticultura da Região dos Vinhos Verdes, 1986.

Garner, Michael and Paul Merritt. *Barolo: Tar and Roses*. London: Century, 1990.

George, Rosemary. *Chianti and the Wines of Tuscany*. London: Sothebys Publications 1990.

———. *Lateral Wine-Tasting*. London: Trafalgar, 1993.

———. *The Simon & Schuster Pocket Wine Label Decoder*. New York: Simon and Schuster, 1989.

*German Wine Atlas and Vineyard Register*. New York: Hastings House, 1977.

Ginestet, Bernard. *Margaux*. New York: Holt, Rinehart, and Winston, 1985.

———. *Saint-Julien*. New York: Holt, Rinehart, and Winston, 1985.

Gold, Richard M. *How and Why to Build a Wine Cellar*. Amherst: Sandhill Publishing, 1983.

Goldstein Joyce. *The Mediterranean Kitchen*. New York: Morrow, 1989.

Hallgarten, S. F. *German Wines*. London: Faber and Faber, 1976.

Halliday, James. *Pocket Guide to the Wines of Australia and New Zealand*. New York: HarperCollins, 1994.

———. *Wine Atlas of Australia and New Zealand*. New York: HarperCollins, 1992.

———. *The Wine Atlas of California*. London: Viking Penguin, 1993.

Hazan, Victor. *Italian Wine*. New York: Alfred A. Knopf, 1982.

*Impact Databank Report: The International Wine Market*. New York: M. Shanken, 1992.

Jakisch, Philip. *Modern Winemaking*. Ithaca: Cornell University Press, 1985.

Jamieson, Ian. *The Simon & Schuster Pocket Guide to the Wines of Germany*. New York: Simon and Schuster, 1993.

Jobe, Joseph. *The Great Book of Wine*. New York: Galahad, 1988.

Johnson, Frank. *The Professional Wine Reference*. New York: Harper & Row, 1983.

Johnson, Hugh and Hubrecht Duijker. *The Wine Atlas of France*. New York: Simon and Schuster, 1987.

———. and James Halliday. *The Vintner's Art: How Great Wines are Made*. New York: Simon and Schuster, 1992.

———. and Ian Jamieson. *The Atlas of German Wine*. New York: Simon and Schuster, 1986.

———. *How to Enjoy Wine*. New York: Simon and Schuster, 1990.

———. *Hugh Johnson's Modern Encyclopedia of Wine*. New York: Simon and Schuster, 1991.

———. *Hugh Johnson's Pocket Encyclopedia of Wine*. New York: Simon and Schuster, 1995.

———. *Vintage: The Story of Wine*. New York: Simon and Schuster, 1989.

———. *Wine*. New York: Simon and Schuster, 1987.

———. *The World Atlas of Wine*, 4th ed. New York: Simon and Schuster, 1994.

Johnson, Robert. *The Consumer's Guide to Organic Wine*. Lanham, Md.: Rowman & Littlefield, 1993.

Joseph, Robert. *The Wines of the Americas*. Los Angeles: HP Books, 1990.

Kochilas, Diane. *Food & Wine of Greece*. New York: St. Martin's Press, 1990.

Kramer, Matt. *Making Sense of Burgundy*. New York: William Morrow, 1990.

Lambert-Gocs, Miles. *The Wines of Greece*. London: Faber and Faber, 1990.

Lang, George. *The Cuisine of Hungary*. New York: Atheneum, 1971.

Laube, James. *California's Great Cabernets: The Wine Spectator's Ultimate Guide for Consumers, Collectors, and Investors*. San Francisco: Wine Spectator Press, 1990.

Lembeck, Harriet. *Grossman's Guide to Wines, Beers, and Spirits*, 7th ed. New York: Scribner's, 1983.

Lichine, Alexis. *Alexis Lichine's Guide to the Wines and Vineyards of France*. 4th ed. New York: Knopf, 1989.

———. *Alexis Lichine's New Encyclopedia of Wine and Spirits*. New York: Knopf, 1987.

———. *Guide to the Wines of France*. New York: Alfred A. Knopf, 1982.

Liddell, Alex. *Port and the Quintas of the Douro*. London: Sothebys Publications, 1992.

Lipp, Martin R. and David N. Whitten. *To Your Health: Two Physicians Explore the Health Benefits of Wine*. San Francisco: Harper, 1994.

Loubère, Leo. *The Wine Revolution in France*. Princeton: Princeton University Press, 1990.

Lynch, Kermit. *Adventures on the Wine Route*. New York: Farrar, Straus & Giroux, 1990.

Mac Donogh, Giles. *Syrah, Grenache and Mourvèdre* London: Viking Penguin, 1993

———. *The Wine and Food of Austria*. London: Mitchell Beazley, 1992.

MacQuitty, Jane. *Pocket Guide to The Wines of Australia and New Zealand*. New York: Simon and Schuster, 1990.

———. *Pocket Guide to Champagne and Sparkling Wines*. New York: Simon and Schuster, 1986.

Maresca, Tom. *Mastering Wine: A Learner's Manual*. New York: Grove-Atlantic, 1992.

———. *The Right Wine*. New York: Grove-Atlantic, 1992.

Markham, Dewey, Jr. *Wine Basics: A Quick & Easy Guide*. New York: John Wiley & Sons, 1993.

Matthews, Thomas. *A Village in the Vineyards*. New York: Farrar, Straus & Giroux, 1993.

Mayo, Oliver. *The Wines of Australia*. London: Faber and Faber, 1991.

Mayson, Richard. *Portugal's Wines and Winemakers*. San Francisco: Wine Appreciation Guild, 1992.

McCoy, Elin and John F. Walker, *Thinking About Wine*. New York: Simon and Schuster, 1989.

McGee, Harold. *On Food and Cooking*. New York: Scribner's, 1984.

McWhitter, Kathryn and Charles Metcalfe. *Encyclopedia of Spanish and Portuguese Wines*. New York: Simon and Schuster, 1991.

Novitski, Joseph. *A Vineyard Year*. San Francisco: Chronicle Books, 1983.

Olney, Richard. *Ten Vineyard Lunches*. New York: Interlink Books, 1988.

———. *Yquem*. London: Dorling Kindersley, 1985.

Ordish, George. *Vineyards in England and Wales*. London: Faber and Faber, 1977.

Parker, Robert. *Wines of Burgundy*. New York: Simon and Schuster, 1990.

———. *Bordeaux*. New York: Simon and Schuster, 1985.

———. *Wine Buyers Guide*. New York: Simon and Schuster, 1993.

———. *Wines of Provence and Rhône*. New York: Simon and Schuster, 1987.

Penning-Roswell, Edmund. *Wines of Bordeaux*. San Francisco: Wine Appreciation Guild, 1983.

Peppercorn, David. *Bordeaux*. London: Faber and Faber, 1991.

Perdue, Lewis. *The French Paradox & Beyond: Live Longer with Wine and the Mediterranean Lifestyle*. San Francisco: Renais, 1992

Peynaud, Emile. *Knowing and Making Wine*. New York: John Wiley & Sons, 1984.

————. *The Taste of Wine*. San Francisco: Wine Appreciation Guild, 1987.

Philpott, Don. *The Wine and Food of Bulgaria*. London: Mitchell Beazley, 1989.

Pigott, Stuart. *Riesling*. London: Viking Penguin, 1993.

Prial, Frank. ed. *The Companion to Wine*. New York: Prentice Hall, 1992.

Price, Pamela and Christopher Felden. *Alsace Wines and Spirits*. London: Sothebys Publications, 1984.

Price, Pamela. *The Wines of the Graves*. London: Sothebys Publications, 1988.

Read, Jan. *Chilean Wine*. London: Sothebys Publications, 1988.

————. *The Simon & Schuster Guide to the Wines of Spain*. New York: Simon and Schuster, 1993.

————. *Wines of the Rioja*. London: Sothebys Publications, 1984

————. *The Wines of Portugal*. London: Faber and Faber, 1982.

————. *Wines of Spain*. London: Faber and Faber, 1986.

Ribérau-Gayon, Pascal. ed. *The Wines and Vineyards of France*. New York: Viking Penguin, 1990.

Robertson, George. *Port*. London: Faber and Faber, 1978.

Robinson, Jancis. *The Great Wine Book*. New York: Morrow, 1982.

————. *Jancis Robinson's Food and Wine Adventures*. London: Headline, 1987.

————. *Masterglass*. London: Pan, 1987.

————. *Oxford Companion to Wine*. Oxford: Oxford University Press, 1994.

————. *Vines, Grapes, and Wines*. New York: Alfred A. Knopf, 1986.

————. *Vintage Timecharts: The Pedigree and Performance of Fine Wine to the Year 2000*. New York: Weidenfeld & Nicolson, 1989.

Roby, Norman and Charles Olken. *The New Connoisseur's Handbook of California Wines*. New York: Alfred A. Knopf, 1993.

Root, Waverly. *The Food of France*. New York: Random House, 1992.

Rosengarten, David and Joshua Wesson. *Red Wine with Fish: The New Art of Matching Wine with Food*. New York: Simon and Schuster, 1989.

Roux, Michel P. *A Guide to the Vineyards and Châteaux of Bordeaux*. Dallas: Publivin, 1972.

Schreiner, John. *The World of Canadian Wine*. Vancouver: Douglas & McIntyre, 1984.

Sichel, Peter M.F. *Which Wine?* New York: Harper & Row, 1975.

————. *The Wines of Germany: Frank Schoonmaker's Classic. rev. ed.* New York: Hastings House, 1980.

Simon, André. *The History of Champagne*. New York: Octopus Books, 1971.

————. *The Wines, Vineyards and Vignerons of Australia*. London: Paul Hamlyn, 1966.

————. *Wines of the World*. New York: McGraw-Hill, 1972.

Simon, Joanna. *Discovering Wine*. New York: Simon and Schuster, 1995.

*Slow Food Guide to Wines of the World*. Cuneo, Italy: Slow Food Editore, 1993.

Spurrier, Steven, and Michael Dovaz. *L'Académie du Vin Complete Wine Course*. New York: Macmillan, 1991.

Spurrier, Steven. *The Académie du Vin Concise Guide to French Country Wines*. New York, Perigree Books, 1983.

————. *The Académie du Vin Guide to French Wines*. Topsfield, Mass.: Salem House, 1986.

Steinberg, Edward. *The Vines of San Lorenzo*. Hopewell, N.J.: Ecco Press, 1992.

Sterling, Joy. *A Cultivated Life: A Year in a California Vineyard*. New York: Random House, 1993.

Stevenson, Robert Louis. *Napa Wine*. San Francisco: Westwind Books, 1974.

Stevenson, Tom. *Sothebys World Wine Encyclopedia*. Boston: Little, Brown and Company, 1988.

Suckling, James. *Vintage Port: The Wine Spectator's Ultimate Guide for Consumers, Collectors, and Investors*. New York: M. Shanken, 1990.

Sutcliffe, Serena. ed. *Great Vineyards and Winemakers*. New York: Rutledge, 1981.

Thompson, Bob. *Simon & Schuster Pocket Guide to California Wines*. New York: Simon and Schuster, 1990.

————. *The Wine Atlas of California, with Oregon and Washington*. New York: Simon and Schuster, 1993.

Unwin, Timothy. *Wine & the Vine*. London: Routledge, 1991.

*Vins et Vignobles de France*. Paris: Librairie Larousse/Le Savour Club, 1987.

Voss, Roger. *The Simon & Schuster Pocket Guide to French Regional Wines*. New York: Simon and Schuster, 1987.

Wagner, Philip. *Grapes Into Wine: The Art of Winemaking in America*. New York: Alfred A. Knopf, 1976.

Wasserman, Sheldon. *White Wines of the World*. New York: Stein and Day, 1978.

————. and Pauline Wasserman. *Italy's Noble Red Wines*. New York: Macmillan, 1992.

Waugh, Alec. *Wines and Spirits*. New York: Time-Life, 1968.

White, Jasper. *Jasper White's Cooking from New England*. New York: Harper and Row, 1989.

Willinger, Faith. *Eating in Italy*. New York: Hearst Books, 1989.

Wine Spectator Press Staff. *The Wine Spectator's Annual Wine Buying Guide*. New York: M. Shanken, 1995.

Wolfert, Paula. *The Cooking of the Eastern Mediterranean*. New York: HarperCollins, 1994.

————. *Mediterranean Cooking*. New York: Quadrangle, 1977.

Youell, Tessa and George Kimball. *The Pocket Guide to French Food and Wine*. New York: Simon and Schuster, 1985.

Zraly, Kevin. *Windows on the World Complete Wine Course*. New York: Sterling, 1995.

# Figure and Photography Credits

## PART III
pp. 204-5, Tony Stone Images/Paul Dunn.

### Chapter 6
p. 209, Tony Stone Images/Earth Imaging; p. 218, Michael J. Belardo; pp. 232-35, Michael J. Belardo; p. 238, Michael Weiss; p. 239, Michael J. Belardo; p. 241, Michael Weiss; p. 245, Michael J. Belardo; p. 250, Steven Kolpan; p. 256, Michael J. Belardo; p. 268, p. 272, Seagram Chateau & Estates Wine Company; Michael J. Belardo; p. 275, Michael J. Belardo; p. 276, Seagram Chateau & Estates Wine Company; p. 277, Michael J. Belardo; p. 282, Michael J. Belardo; p. 299, The Culinary Institute of America.

### Chapter 7
p. 301, Tony Stone Images/Earth Imaging, pp. 302, 304-6, 314-15, 318-20, 323-27, 329-30, Michael J. Belardo; p. 331, Steven Kolpan; pp. 333-34, 336-37 Michael J. Belardo (top), Steven Kolpan (bottom); pp. 340-42, Michael J. Belardo, pp. 344-46, Steven Kolpan; p. 349, Michael J. Belardo (top, bottom, left) Steven Kolpan, (bottom, right); p. 350, Michael J. Belardo; p. 351, Michael J. Belardo (top), Steven Kolpan (bottom); pp. 353-55, Michael J. Belardo.

### Chapter 8
p. 359, Tony Stone Images/Earth Imaging; pp. 360-63, Steven Kolpan; pp. 367-71, Steven Kolpan; p. 382, Figure 8.27, Jose MaQuiross Carrasco; pp. 383-87, Steven Kolpan.

### Chapter 9
p. 389, Tony Stone Images/Earth Imaging; p. 390, Michael A. Weiss; pp. 396-97, Michael A. Weiss; pp. 401-3, Michael A. Weiss; p. 406, Michael A. Weiss; pp. 408-12, Michael A. Weiss; p. 413, Michael A. Weiss (left), Steven Kolpan (right); pp. 415-16, Steven Kolpan.

### Chapter 10
p. 421, Tony Stone Images/Earth Imaging; p. 423, Steven Kolpan; p. 445, Dr. Peter Pauly; p. 451, German Wine Bureau.

### Chapter 11
p. 453, Tony Stone Images/Earth Imaging; pp. 455-57, Steven Kolpan.

### Chapter 12
p. 472, Tony Stone Images/Earth Imaging.

## PART IV
pp. 480-81, The Image Bank/Eliane Sulle.

### Chapter 13
p. 483, The Image Bank/John W. Banagan.

### Chapter 14
p. 543, Tony Stone Images/Chris Craymer; p. 551, Figure 14.4, The Oldways Preservation & Exchange Trust; Figure 14.5, data from *The Well Pregnancy Book* and studies by Abel and Sokol., pp. 556-57, George Rose, Fetzer Vineyards.

## PART V
pp. 560-61, Tony Stone Images/Graeme Norways.

### Chapter 15
p. 563, The Culinary Institute of America, all photographs from The Culinary Institute of America.

### Chapter 16
p. 581, The Culinary Institute of America; pp. 581-83, The Culinary Institute of America; p. 586, Academie du Vin de Bordeaux (top), Italian Trade Commission (bottom left), Investimentos, Comercio e Turismo de Portugal (bottom right); p. 592, The Culinary Institute of America.

### Chapter 17
p. 599, The Image Bank/Schmid-Langsfeld; p. 614, Figure 17.8, Stephen Loffredo, Sommelier/Wine Director; Figures 17.10, 17.11, 17.14, Lydia Shire, owner/chef, Craig R. Gandolf, Wine Manager.

**NOTE**: *The Wine Aroma Wheel* shown on p. 99 is a plastic, laminated color wheel which is avaiable for purchase from A.C. Noble at the Department of Viticulture and Enology, University of California, Davis, California 95616. Phone: 916-752-0387 or fax: 916-752-0382. The WWW address is:

http://pubweb.ucdavis.edu/documents/wine/ven1.HTML

*Every effort has been made to trace the owners of copyright photographs and illustrations. Anyone who may have been inadvertently omitted from this list is invited to write to the publishers who will be pleased to make any necessary amendment to future printings of this publication.*

# Index

Great Plain wine region, Hungary, 465
Great Western wine region, Australia, 190
Greece, 55, 472-474
  wine producers, 473
Greengrape, 201
*Gremios dos Exportadores do Vinho do Porto,* 392
Grenache grape, 62-63
Grey Monk Winery, 174
Grignolino wine region, 346-347
Gristina winery, 159
Groot Constantia winery, 202
*grosslage,* 433
Grüner-Veltliner grape, 459, 460, 464
Grux, Frank, 238
Guedes, Antonio, 408
Guenoc Valley, CA, AVA, 133
Guenoc Winery, 133
Guimarens, Bruce, 402
Gumpoldskirchener wine, 460, 462
Gyöngös winery, 464, 466
gyro-palettes, 218

# H

Haight Vineyard, 160
halbsus wines, 460
halbtrocken, 436, 460
Halliday, James, 190
Hamilton Russell Vineyards, 202
Hamptons, Long Island, NY, AVA, 159
handpicking the grapes, 12
hand-riddling, 37
Haraszthy, Agoston, 145
Hardy winery, 194
Hargrave, Alex and Louisa, 158
Hargrave winery, 159
Harslevelu grape, 464, 466
harvesting, 9-13
  date, 69-70
  deciding when to, 10
  scene, 9
Hauner, Carlo, 316
Haut Marne region, 216
Haut-Médoc wine region, 168
Hawke's Bay wine region, New Zealand, 197
head-spur pruning, 68
health, and wine, 543-559
  applications, 2
  of the planet, 557-558
health warnings on U.S. wine bottles, 112, 113
heart disease and alcohol consumption, 544-550
heat summation theory, 121-125, 210
Heemserk winery, 191
Heitz, George, 174
Heitz, Joe, 117
Heitz winery, 142
Henkell winery, 464
Henri Badoux winery, 457

Henschke winery, 194
Hermann Wiemer winery, 156
Hermitage commune, 283-284
Hermitage grape, 62, 186, 200
Hess Collection Winery, 137
Hessische-Bergstrasse wine region, Germany, 441
Heublein do Brazil winery, 184
Heunisch vines, 458
Hidden Cellars, 132
high-alcohol wine, 18
high-quality wine, characteristics of, 6
  production of, 113-114
Hillcrest Vineyards, 165
Hill-Smith, Michael, 186
history of grape growing, 44-48
Hobart wine region, Australia, 191
Hochar, Gaston and Serge, 477
Hochkultur trellising system, 459
Hogue, Gary, 161, 163
Hogue, Mike, 161, 163
Hogue Cellars, 161
home wine cellar, 582-583
horizontal wine tasting, 75
Hospices de Beaune, 246
hot on the tongue wine taste, 98
Howell Mountain subappellation, 136, 137
how to:
  taste wine, 73-109
  read a wine label, 627-643
  smell wine, 94-98
how wine is made, 5-41
Hudson River, NY, wine region, 156-157
Humboldt Currents, 176
humidity, in wine storage area, 592
Hungarovin, 464
Hungary, grape types, 464
  wine regions, 463-467
Hunter Valley wine region, Australia, 56, 62, 189
hybrid grapevines, 47-48
hydrogen sulphide smell, 103
hydrometer, 10-11

# I

ice wine, 173, 435
Idaho, US, wine regions, 166-166
IGT. *See* Indicazione Geografica Tipica
Ihumatao wine region, New Zealand, 197
*imbottigliato dalla cantine sociale,* 311
*imbottigliato dal produttore all'origine,* 311
*imbottigliato dal produttori riuniti,* 311
*imbottigliato nella zona di produzione,* 311
INAO. *See* Institut National des Appellations d'Origine
INCAVI. *See* Instituto Catalan de Vino
*Indicação de Proveniência Regulamentada* (IPR), 207, 393
indicated-age Tawny Port, 402
*Indicazione Geografica Tipica* (IGT), 207, 309
INDO quality designations, 364-365

Northwest Italy wine regions, 335-347
nosing a wine, 94-96
nouveau wines, 246
Nuits-St. Georges commune, 236
Nussbaumer Winery, 456, 457

# O

oak, used in barrels, 25; taste in wine, 101
Oakencroft Vineyard, 169
Oakville, CA, subappellation, 139, 142
O'Callaghan, Robert, 193
Oceania, 184-202
*Öeschle* scale, 11
Oeste region, Portugal, 414
off flavors in wine, 102
official classifications of wine:
  Bordeaux, 650
  Graves, 651
  Sauternes-Barsac, 651
*Office International du Vin* (OIV), 364
oidium, 229, 264
  in Italy, 306
  in Portugal, 418
Okanagan Valley, CAN, DVA, 173
Olaszriesling grape, 464
*oloroso* Sherry, 384, 386
Ontario, Canada, wine region, 173
opening the wine bottle, 568
Oporto grape, 466
Optima grape, 173, 428, 443
Opus One wine, 117
Oregon, US, AVAs, 54, 60, 120, 163-166
  climate, 163
  wine regions, 165-166
  wine styles, 163, 165
organoleptic response to wine, 73
*Origem Controlada*, 184
origins of grape growing, 44
Orlando winery, 194
Osborne winery, 170
Overberg wine region, South Africa, 200, 202
Overgaauw winery, 201
Owens, Robert, 193
oxidation process, 13, 15-16
oxidized wines, 90, 97
oxygen, contact with grapes during wine making, 13
  in wine storage area, 594

# P

Paarl wine region, South Africa, 201
Pacherenc du Vic Bihl wine, 298
Padthaway Estate winery, 194
Padthaway/Keppoch wine region, Australia, 192, 194
Paicines, CA, AVA, 151
Pais grape, 180
*palacio*, 394
palate, 94, 96

Palette appellation, 290
Palmer, David and Diana, 194
Palmer winery, 159
*palo cortado* Sherry, 386
Palomas Santa Rosa winery, 184
Palomino grape, 201, 380, 381, 383
pappillae, 98
Parducci Wine Cellars, 132
Parellada grape, 57, 373
Paso Robles, CA, AVA, 132, 151
passerillage, 297
Pasteur, Louis, 212
Pato, Luis, 409
Patras winery, 473
Patrimonio appellation, 299
Pauillac commune, 270-271
Paul Masson wines, 128
Pauly, Peter, 445
Pays d'Oc, 216
Pecharmant appellation, 297
Pedernão grape, 407
Pedroncelli vineyards, 145
Pedro Ximenéz grape, 182, 373, 381, 383
Pedro Ximenéz/P.X. wine, 388
Pelée Island, CAN, DVA, 173
Peloponnisos wine region, Greece, 473-474
Penedès wine region, Spain, 59, 373, 375
Penfolds winery, 190, 192, 194
Pennsylvania, US, AVAs, 159
Periquita grape, 413-414, 415
perlage, 94, 577
Perlan grape, 457
Pernand-Vergelesses commune, 237
peronospera, 212
Peru Currents, 176
Pessac commune, 272
Petaluma Vineyards, 165, 192, 194
Peter Lehmann winery, 194
Petit Arvine grape, 457
Petit Chablis wines, 242
Petite Syrah grape, 62
Petit Verdot grape, 66
Peynaud, Emile, 212, 474
Pfalzer Löwe wine, 452
Pfalz villages and vineyards, 449
Pfalz wine region, Germany, 51, 439-440, 447-449
  major producers, 449
Pheasant Ridge winery, 167
phenolic compounds, 549
phenylethyl acetate, 96
phenylpropionic aldehyde, 96
Phileri grape, 474
pH level, 10
*Phylloxera vastatrix* louse, 45-48
  in Australia, 187
  in Austria, 458
  in California, 130-131
  in Cyprus, 475
  in Eastern Europe, 462